# AGRICULTURE AND THE WTO

## CREATING A TRADING SYSTEM FOR DEVELOPMENT

# AGRICULTURE AND THE WTO

## CREATING A TRADING SYSTEM FOR DEVELOPMENT

Merlinda D. Ingco and John D. Nash
Editors

1818 H Street, NW
Washington, DC 20433
Telephone 202-473-1000
Internet www.worldbank.org
E-mail feedback@worldbank.org

First printing 2004
**First Indian Reprint 2005**

ISBN 81-269-0465-8

Published for **The World Bank** by

**ATLANTIC®**

PUBLISHERS & DISTRIBUTORS
B-2, Vishal Enclave, Opp. Rajouri Garden,
New Delhi-110027
Phones : 25413460, 25429987, 25466842

Sales Office
7/22, Ansari Road, Darya Ganj,
New Delhi-110002
Phones : 23273880, 23275880, 23280451
Fax : 91-11-23285873
web : www.atlanticbooks.com
e-mail : info@atlanticbooks.com

The findings, interpretations, and conclusions expressed herein are those of the author(s) and do not necessarily reflect the views of the Board of Executive Directors of the World Bank or the governments they represent.
The World Bank does not guarantee the accuracy of the data included in this work. The boundaries, colors, denominations, and other information shown on any map in this work do not imply any judgment on the part of the World Bank concerning the legal status of any territory or the endorsement or acceptance of such boundaries.



Photo credits: Ship/Grain image—© Paul A. Souders/Corbis; Tomator/conveyor belt image—Willard R. Culver/NATIONAL GEOGRAPHIC IMAGE COLLECTION/Getty Images.

***This edition is for sale in India, Sri Lanka, Pakistan, Maldives, Bhutan, Nepal and Bangladesh only.***

Printed in India at Nice Printing Press, Delhi

# CONTENTS

# LIST OF BOXES

# LIST OF TABLES

# LIST OF FIGURES

# FOREWORD

There are misconceptions that trade liberalization is a done deal. In fact, we are a long way away from free world trade, particularly in areas of interest to developing countries. The Doha negotiations mark the first time that developing country interests have been placed at the center of a multilateral round of trade negotiations. Those interests include agriculture, implementation of textile agreements, the use of antidumping, and the nature of special and differential treatment for developing countries, including the extent to which these countries should undertake more substantive commitments to liberalize their own trade regimes. But these are some of the hardest areas for countries to address and, unfortunately, from the very beginning key negotiating deadlines on most of these issues were missed. As a result, substantial gaps remain between the developing and the industrial countries, and in none of the areas is this more true than in agriculture. If any further proof of this were needed, it became painfully clear at the Cancún Ministerial meetings.

The World Bank has been actively advocating the reduction of trade-distorting payments and subsidies to farmers and exporters in industrialized countries, as well as the reduction of non-tariff barriers to trade and tariffs by both developed and developing countries, which act as a tax on development. We have also been supporting developing countries in analyzing the outcomes of the Uruguay Round and preparing for the Doha negotiations, through a program of research, technical assistance, and capacity building in order to help ensure a pro-development outcome of the negotiations.

We have stressed the importance of trade integration as an instrument for achieving the Millennium Development Goals (MDGs); though increased aid is essential to meeting the MDGS, the gains from trade integration are estimated to be far larger than any contemplated increase in aid flows. In our view a pro-development outcome is, above all, one that crafts the world trading system in such a way that developing countries are given both strong incentives and better opportunities to use trade integration more actively as a growth lever. To help these countries to take full advantage of global market opportunities, the World Bank has also stepped up efforts to make trade a more central part of the policy dialogue in its operations. As one example, comprehensive trade diagnostic studies have been launched in 20 low-income countries in the last two years, and about 40 countries—both low and middle income—have been targeted for stepping up the Bank's trade-related operational activity. The Bank took advantage of the opportunity of the Cancun Ministerial meeting to announce a special Trade Assistance Program designed to support progress on the Doha Development Agenda and to increase assistance to countries that take on development-promoting trade reforms. This will make needed resources available for countries implementing new trade reform programs associated with commitments they may make in the Doha Agenda. These resources could be used to expand activities that up-grade competitiveness over the long term, such as training of workers and reforms of trade-related institutions. Such loans can be accelerated and, depending on country circumstances, could be additional to existing country lending levels.

This volume is an integral part of the Bank's advocacy, research, and capacity-building program, with messages aimed at audiences in both developing and industrialized countries. Its messages build on those of two previous publications of the World Bank: *The Uruguay Round and the Developing Countries* (1996), and more recently, *Development, Trade, and the WTO: a Handbook* (2002). The latter publication covers most areas of interest to developing countries in the Doha negotiations, with the exception of agriculture. The current volume is thus its complement. Other forthcoming publications will focus on topics in the agricultural trade negotiations that are of interest to specific regions of the developing world.

Funding for the research that is the basis for this publication, regional copublications, and workshops was provided primarily through the United Kingdom's Department for Foreign and International Development (DFID). Additional resources were contributed by the World Bank–Netherlands Partnership Program (BNPP). We gratefully acknowledge their support.

Although the outcome of the Cancún Ministerial was not what we had hoped, it seems likely (indeed essential) that the Doha process will continue to move forward and contribute to the achievement of long-term poverty reduction objectives. Given the central role of agriculture in the Doha process, we hope this book will contribute to its ultimate success.

Kevin M. Cleaver
Director
Agriculture and Rural Development

Uri B. Dadush
Director
International Trade Department

# ACRONYMS AND ABBREVIATIONS

| | |
|---|---|
| AACP | African ACP countries |
| ABARE | Australian Bureau of Agricultural and Resource Economics |
| ABS | Access and benefit sharing |
| ACP | African, Caribbean and Pacific Group of States |
| AFTA | ASEAN Free Trade Area |
| AGOA | African Growth and Opportunity Act |
| AGST | Agriculture Supporting Tables |
| AIA | Advance Informed Agreement |
| AMS | Aggregate Measurement of Support |
| APEC | Asia Pacific Economic Co-operation Forum |
| ASERCA | Support Services for Agricultural Marketing (Mexico) |
| ATPA | Andean Trade Preference Act and Drug Eradication Act |
| BSE | Bovine Spongiform Encephalopathy |
| CAAS | Chinese Academy of Agriculture Sciences |
| CAC | Codex Alimentarius Commission |
| CAP | Common Agricultural Policy |
| CARICOM | Caribbean Community |
| CBD | Convention on Biological Diversity |
| CBERA | Caribbean Basin Economic Recovery Act |
| CBTPA | Caribbean Basin Trade Partnership Act of 2000 |
| CCFICS | Codex Committee on Food Import and Export Inspection and Certification Systems |
| CCGD | Canadian Council of Grocery Distributors |
| CER | Closer Economic Relations (Agreement) |
| CES | Constant elasticity of substitution |
| CFF | Compensatory Financing Facility (IMF) |
| CGE | General equilibrium model |
| CGIAR | Consultative Group on International Agricultural Research |
| CGSB | Canadian General Standards Board |
| CIF | Cost, insurance, and freight |
| CMOB | Common Market Organization for Bananas |
| CNL | Competitive Need-Limitation |
| CONASUPO | National Company of Popular Subsistence (Mexico) |
| COP | Conference of the Parties |
| CRP | Conservaton Reserve Program |
| CSE | Consumer Subsidy Equivalent |
| CTA | Committee on Trade in Agriculture (GATT) |
| CTD | Committee on Trade and Development (WTO) |
| DS | Domestic Support |
| EBA | Everything But Arms Trade Agreement |
| EC | European Community or European Commission |
| EMS | Equivalent Measurement of Support |
| EPA | Economic Partnership Agreement |
| ES | Export subsidies |
| ESE | Export subsidy equivalent |
| FAC | Food Aid Convention |
| FAO | Food and Agriculture Organization of the United Nations |
| FAOSTAT | Food and Agriculture Organization Statistical Database |
| FDI | Foreign direct investment |
| FOB | Freign on board |
| FCFS | First-come, first-served |
| FSC | Foreign Sales Corporation |
| FTA | Free trade area |
| FTAA | Free Trade Areas of the Americas |
| GATS | General Agreement on Trade in Services |
| GATT | General Agreement on Tariffs and Trade |
| GDP | Gross Domestic Product |
| GEF | Global Environment Facility |
| GI | Geographical indication |
| GM | Genetically modified |

| | |
|---|---|
| GMO | Genetically modified organism |
| GSP | Generalized System of Preferences |
| GTAP | Global Trade Analysis Project |
| IARC | International Agricultural Research Centre |
| IATRC | International Agricultural Trade Research Consortium |
| ICPM | Interim Commission on Phytosanitary Measures |
| IFPRI | International Food Policy Research Institute |
| IGC | Intergovernmental Committee on Intellectual Property and Genetic Resources, Traditional Knowledge and Folklore |
| ILA | Agreement on Import Licensing Procedures |
| IMF | International Monetary Fund |
| IPGRI | International Plant Genetic Resources Institute |
| IPPC | International Plant Protection Convention |
| IPS | Input price subsidies |
| ISAAA | International Service for the Acquisition of Agri-biotech Applications |
| ISPM | International standard for phytosanitary measures |
| ITF | International Task Force on Commodity Price Risk Management |
| ITO | International Trade Organization |
| ITPGRFA | International Treaty on Plant Genetic Resources for Food and Agriculture |
| IU | International Undertaking on Plant Genetic Resources for Food and Agriculture |
| LDC | Least-developed country |
| LDBDC | Least Developed Beneficiary Developing Country |
| LES | Linear Expenditure System |
| LMO | Living modified organism |
| MAT | Mutually agreed terms |
| MERCOSUR | Southern Common Market (Mercado Comune del Sur) |
| MFN | Most favored nation |
| MPS | Market price support |
| MTA | Material transfer agreement |
| NAFTA | North American Free Trade Agreement |
| NFIDC | Net-food-importing developing country |
| NGO | Nongovernmental organization |
| NTM | Nontariff measure |
| NTB | Nontrade barrier |
| OECD | Organisation for Economic Co-operation and Development |
| OIE | International Office of Epizooties |
| OPS | Output price support |
| PBRs | Plant Breeder's Rights |
| PEM | Policy Evaluation Matrix |
| PIC | Prior informed consent |
| PNT | Plants with novel trait |
| PPM | Processing and production method |
| PROCAMPO | Farmers Direct Support Program (Mexico) |
| PRSP | Poverty Reduction Strategy Papers |
| PSE | Producer Support Estimate |
| PVP | Plant variety protection |
| QR | Quantitative restriction |
| R&D | Research and development |
| ROO | Rules of origin |
| RTA | Regional trade agreement |
| RUNS | Rural-Urban North-South |
| S&D | Special and Differential (treatment) |
| SP | Sugar Protocol (EU) |
| SPS | Sanitary and Phytosanitary Agreement |
| SSA | Sub-Saharan Africa |
| SSG | Special safeguard |
| STE | State trading enterprise |
| SW | Swiss formula |
| TAED | Transatlantic Environmental Dialogue |
| TBT | Technical Barriers to Trade |
| TNC | Trade Negotiations Committee |
| TRIPS | Trade-Related Intellectual Property |
| TRQ | Tariff Rate Quota |
| TSE | Total support estimate |
| UNCTAD | United Nations Conference on Trade and Development |
| UNEP | United Nations Environment Programme |
| UPOV | International Union for the Protection of New Varieties of Plants (Union pour la Protection des Obtentions Végétales) |

| | |
|---|---|
| URAA | Uruguary Round Agreement on Agriculture |
| USITC | U.S. International Trade Commission |
| USTR | Office of the United States Trade Representative |
| WHO | World Health Organization |
| WIPO | World Intellectual Property Organization |

1

# WHAT'S AT STAKE? DEVELOPING-COUNTRY INTERESTS IN THE DOHA DEVELOPMENT ROUND

*Merlinda D. Ingco and John D. Nash*

## Introduction

Developing countries have a huge stake in the success of the Doha Development Round. First, there are the potential gains from the strengthening of a rules-based global trading system for agriculture and reducing distortions in global agricultural markets. Developing countries are the weaker players in the trading system, and thus will benefit the most when the dominant trading countries play by common rules that discipline government activities supporting agriculture in the three key areas of domestic support, market access, and export competition. Developing countries will benefit from further reforms in these three areas and will also benefit from reforms in antidumping rules, which are used in an increasing number of countries (including developing countries). Small economies and the least-developed countries will especially benefit from the expansion of beneficial provisions for developing-country exporters.

Second, multilateral agreements and trade negotiations should help developing countries undertake and lock-in their own trade and domestic policy reforms needed to advance their development objectives. Ideally, countries will implement trade and other policy reforms unilaterally because it is in their interest to do so. However, in practice, most governments have difficulty in overcoming the resistance of domestic lobbies for protection of agriculture without securing support from other sectors of the economy that would gain from trade reforms in other countries. In such cases, reciprocal trade agreements under the auspices of the World Trade Organization (WTO) may be easier to undertake and are thus an important part of the political economy of policy reform in developing countries. In addition, supply response to reform depends upon the credibility of the reform process. Experience in many countries shows that the private sector does not invest if the persistence of reforms is in doubt. Policy measures can be made more credible through a framework of a multilateral agreement that requires adherence to rules and is equipped with built-in instruments that prevent policy reversals and backsliding.

Third, the new round of trade negotiations should help advance global agricultural trade liberalization and thereby expand trade. In particular, the negotiations should achieve further cuts in domestic and export subsidies in the Organisation for Economic Co-operation and Development (OECD) countries and in reductions in high tariffs in OECD and developing countries. These reductions will be difficult to achieve outside the context of global trade talks. Most developing countries will benefit from increased market access to industrial country markets for products such as sugar, beef, and fruits and vegetables. Increasing trade will be useful in its own right to expand markets and will also reduce the volatility of world prices (which is high partially because of the thinness of markets when so many countries try to insulate their domestic production). Since both producers and consumers in poor countries are especially vulnerable to large unpredictable price fluctuations, these groups have a special interest in reducing world price volatility. Even though agricultural trade liberalization may raise world food prices slightly, the net benefit should be positive for most developing countries, not just for current agricultural exporters. Those countries close to food self-sufficiency may become net exporters following protection cuts in other countries. Other countries may remain net food importers only because they retain strong anti-agricultural domestic policies. Those countries, too, may benefit from global trade liberalization because that would discourage some of their resources from being employed in less socially productive activities outside agriculture. Even net importing countries, where many of the poor are in farm households, may benefit directly from a global increase in prices and increased prosperity in the rural sector.

### *The Plan of This Chapter*

This chapter elaborates on the basic theme that it is of critical interest for developing countries that the current Doha Round succeed in meeting its objectives, particularly in reducing barriers to trade in agricultural and agroindustrial products. It begins by demonstrating the importance of growth in the agricultural sector, and discussing the connection between growth on the one hand, and on the other, the increasing trade and integration of the sector into the world economy. It then shows how growth in agricultural trade has lagged behind that in manufactured products and examines why this is the case. It finds that trade reform in agriculture has made much less progress than that in manufactured goods, and that many barriers remain to both North–South and South–South trade in these products. Next, it quantifies the potential gains of a large-scale liberalization of trade that would presumably be an outcome of a successful round of negotiations. Finally, it discusses some of the complementary measures and preconditions for trade policy reforms to have their greatest positive impacts.

## A Vibrant Agricultural Sector Is Crucial

Agricultural sector growth is crucial for achievement of a number of development goals for developing countries. Among these goals are enhancing overall economic growth and poverty reduction, improving food security, and conserving natural resources.

### *Reducing Poverty through Economic Growth*

In low-income countries, owing to its relative size and its important growth linkages to the rest of the economy, the agricultural sector is the primary engine of overall economic growth (see box 1.1). Agriculture is by far the largest employer in these countries, employing 68 percent of the labor force and producing 24 percent of gross domestic product (GDP). In middle-income countries the share of GDP falls below 10 percent, but agriculture still accounts for one-quarter of total employment. Many of the world's poor depend directly on agriculture for their livelihoods (Fan, Hazell, and Thorat 1999). Increased agricultural productivity also provides cheaper food, which makes up a large share of expenditures of poor households (Fan 2000). In addition, a modernizing agriculture creates jobs in agricultural processing and marketing, input supply, and consumer products and services, and indirectly generates jobs for those leaving the farm. The agricultural sector thus contributes to growth both directly, through greater production and exports, and indirectly, by raising demand in farm and rural communities for industrial goods and services.[1]

Growth in agriculture has a disproportionately positive effect on poverty reduction, since poverty is predominantly a rural phenomenon.[2] Approximately 75 percent of the poor reside in rural areas, and the rural poor worldwide will outnumber their urban counterparts for at least another generation (Alderman 2001; Ravallion 2000). For example, the incidence of rural poverty reported in seven of the first Poverty Reduction Strategy Papers (PRSPs) was between 10 and 40 percentage points greater

## BOX 1.1 The Importance of Agriculture to Developing Countries

Historically, during the course of development the share of agriculture in both output and labor falls. This has led some development experts to view agriculture as only ancillary to development. However, the fall in agricultural output and labor can be a result of biased domestic policies and international trade policies. The agricultural sector must be an engine of economic growth, especially in the very poorest developing countries where agriculture still represents a significant percentage of GDP and where the rural population accounts for a large percentage of the poor.

A well-integrated agricultural sector should enhance food security; reduce real food prices (especially beneficial to the poor who spend a disproportionate share of their income on food), increase employment and income, create important economic linkages in production chains, and have a positive impact on the environment.

During the 1990s, international support for agricultural development was weakened, as evidenced by the declines in funds allocated to agricultural projects and research by governments and international development agencies. In light of the challenges currently being posed by industrialized country agricultural trade policies, the severity of rural poverty, and the central role of agriculture in developing countries' economic growth, there is an urgent need to refocus on this sector in order to take advantage of the comparative advantages most developing countries have in agricultural production.

Given the chronic incidence of rural poverty and the concomitant harmful environmental practices, a development framework for agriculture must now focus on, among other things, equity and sustainability. Such a framework should therefore include, at least:

- Economic policies in developing countries that are not biased against primary production and export
- Trade policies in rich economies that are not biased against developing countries
- Public and private investment in infrastructure, technical development, and credit, which are necessary for modernizing production and improving competitiveness.

**The Role of Agriculture in Developing Countries by Region**

| Region | *Agricultural Value Added (percent of total GDP)* | | *Agricultural Raw Materials Exports (percent of total merchandise export)* | | *Rural Population (percent of total)* | |
|---|---|---|---|---|---|---|
| | 1980 | 2000 | 1980 | 2000 | 1980 | 2000 |
| East Asia and Pacific | 24.4 | 12.6 | 12 | 2 | 78 | 65 |
| Europe and Central Asia | — | 10.5 | — | 9 | 41 | 35 |
| Latin America and the Caribbean | 10.3 | 7.1 | 4 | 3 | 35 | 25 |
| Middle East and North Africa | 10.3 | 14.3 | 1 | 0 | 52 | 41 |
| South Asia | 38.0 | 25.1 | 10 | 1 | 78 | 72 |
| Sub-Saharan Africa | 17.6 | 17.0 | 6 | 4 | 77 | 66 |

(Continued)

**Box 1.1 (Continued)**

**The Role of Agriculture to Developing Countries by Income Group**

| Income Group | *Agricultural Value Added (percent of total GDP)* 1980 | 2000 | *Agricultural Raw Materials Exports (percent of total merchandise exports)* 1980 | 2000 |
|---|---|---|---|---|
| Low income | 33.6 | 23.9 | 12 | 4 |
| Middle income | 15.8 | 9.3 | 7 | 2 |
| Lower middle income | 24.7 | 13.3 | — | 2 |
| Upper middle income | 11.2 | 6.6 | 7 | 2 |
| Low and middle income | 18.5 | 11.6 | 8 | 2 |
| High income | nd | nd | 4 | 2 |

— Not available.
*Source:* World Bank 2002b.

**TABLE 1.1 Rural–Urban Poverty Gap**

| Country | Percentage Points Difference between the Incidence of Rural and Urban Poverty (Rural Percent–Urban Percent) |
|---|---|
| Bolivia | 42 |
| Burkina- Faso | 35 |
| Honduras | 23 |
| Mauritania | 41 |
| Mozambique | 9 |
| Nicaragua | 38 |
| Tanzania | 16 |

*Source:* PRSP documents.

than in urban areas (table 1.1). Moreover, in most developing countries the severity of poverty is greater in rural areas than in urban areas. People living in rural areas score lower on average than urban residents by every quality of life indicator, and suffer more. A rural child has a much greater chance of dying before age five than an urban child; public services in the rural areas, as measured by per capita public expenditure, are approximately one-half that of urban areas; and more children and adults in rural areas die or get sick from lack of access to clean water than in urban areas.

Perhaps not as obvious is the fact that urban poverty reduction can be accelerated by the growth of the rural sector, especially in agriculture. For example, in India general poverty measures have responded more to rural economic growth than to urban economic growth (Datt and Ravallion 1996). Agricultural growth indirectly benefits urban and rural households by promoting higher wages, lowering food prices, increasing the demand for consumer and intermediate goods and services, encouraging the development of agribusiness, raising the returns to labor and capital, and improving the overall allocative efficiency of factor markets. A 1997 study of 35 representative countries showed that a 1 percent increase in agricultural GDP per capita created a 1.61 percent gain in the per capita incomes of the poorest 20 percent of the population (Timmer 1997).

### *Improved Food Security*

On a global scale, future food and feed needs are large and expanding, driven by population and income growth and by rapid demand for grain for livestock feed. Projections by the International Food Policy Research Institute (IFPRI) indicate that unless there is a renewed commitment to agriculture through increased public and private investment and conducive policies, the long-term trend toward lower food prices will not be maintained to 2020, and the international millennium targets for reducing poverty and malnutrition will not be met (IFPRI 2001). At the national level, agricultural growth makes important contributions to access to food—another dimension of food security—by increasing the incomes of the poor who depend on agricultural production for their livelihoods.

### *Conservation*

Agriculture is the greatest user of natural resources and has an important role in natural resource conservation. The deteriorating land and water base in many regions is a concern for many producers, and wider public awareness of environmental issues is bringing urgency to conservation issues, many global in nature. In some countries the overuse of chemicals and pesticides—often encouraged by input and output subsidies—contributes to environmental problems. Removing these subsidies while raising incomes of farmers through improved productivity are important components of a strategy in reducing resource degradation.

## Trade Liberalization Fuels Prosperity

Openness and integration with the world economy promotes growth and reduces poverty. There is a preponderance of evidence in many countries that economy-wide trade liberalization and openness to trade increases the growth rate of income and output.[3] In addition, numerous individual country studies performed from the 1970s through the 1990s have concluded that "trade does seem to create, even sustain higher growth" (Srinivasan and Bhagwati 1999). A country's trade policy is the key link in the transmission of price signals from the world market to the national economy. The undistorted price signals from world markets, in combination with the exchange rate, allow resource allocation consistent with comparative advantage, thereby increasing productivity. An open trade and investment regime encourages integration into the global trading environment and also encourages the import of diverse and modern technologies important for productivity improvements.[4]

More specifically, trade liberalization has been shown in a number of studies to be associated with enhanced growth in the agricultural sector. In comparing episodes of trade policy reform, Michaely, Choksi, and Papageorgiou (1991) found that if the liberalization efforts were sustained, then the agricultural sector would grow at an average rate of 5.7 percent in the four years following the reform, in comparison with 2.8 percent in the year previous to reforms. When the reform program was partially or fully reversed, the analogous figures were 2.3 percent and 2.8 percent. Schiff and Valdés (1992a, 1992b) in a detailed study of the effects on agriculture of trade, pricing, and macroeconomic policies of 18 developing countries found that the protectionist, anti-export policies pursued by many of these countries had the effect of reducing both agricultural and general economic growth. Similarly, when looking at a sample of 11 countries that had initiated trade liberalization, Valdés (1998) found that sustained reforms were associated with much higher growth rates of both overall and agricultural GDP (5.2 percent and 5.7 percent per annum) in the years following reforms than were reform episodes that collapsed (–1.5 percent and 1.1 percent). A World Bank (1994) study of 29 Sub-Saharan African countries found that when overall macroeconomic policies (including trade policy and related exchange rate policy) are considered, the group of countries that showed a "large improvement" had a weighted agricultural growth rate of 3.5 percent per year between 1986 and 1993 in contrast to 2.5 percent for those with a "small improvement" and 0.3 percent for those with a "deterioration" in macroeconomic policies.

Reducing barriers such as high tariffs to imports of agricultural and food products has another important poverty-reduction dimension. Reducing barriers helps keep food prices low, and low food prices benefit consumers. Since the poor spend a disproportionate part of their income on food, they will benefit disproportionately from low trade barriers.

To support agricultural growth and poverty reduction goals, developing economies need to be better integrated into the world economy by *reducing trade barriers—their own and, through multilateral agricultural trade negotiations,* those of developed countries. However, to compete globally, developing countries will have to increase their agricultural competitiveness and productivity through appropriate changes in cropping patterns, improvements in production techniques, the upgrading of marketing channels, and other complementary measures to realize any true benefits of trade liberalization. This means, of course, that in

**FIGURE 1.1 Trade has Propelled Growth, 1965–2000**

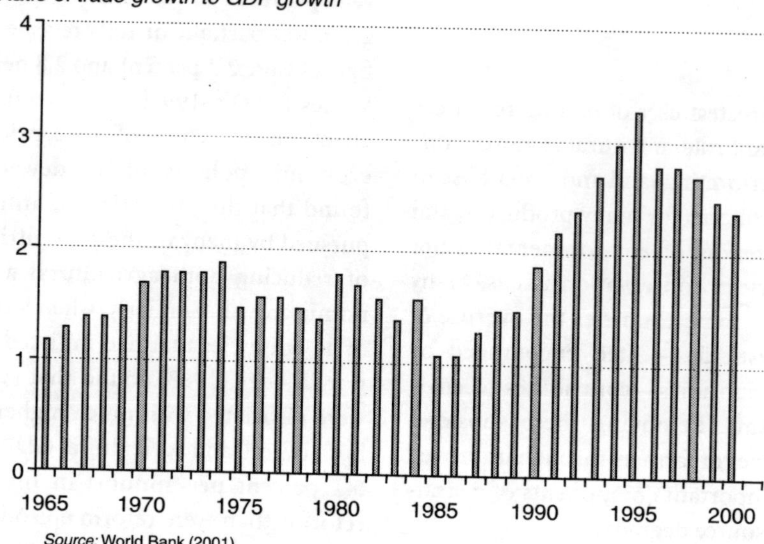


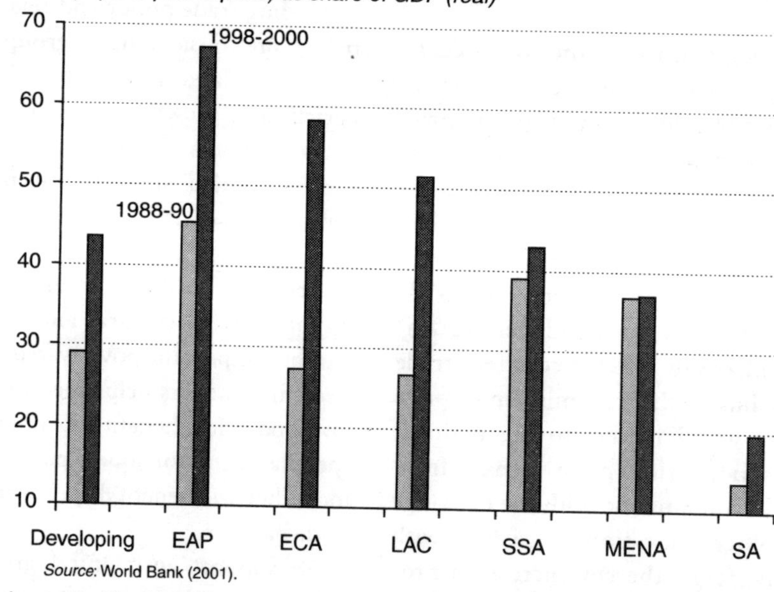


Note: EAP = East Asia and Pacific. ECA = Europe and Central Asia. LAC = Latin America and the Caribbean. SSA = Sub-Saharan Africa. MENA = Middle East and North Africa. SA = South Asia.

trade negotiations there may have to be special consideration for those countries (see chapter 14). It also emphasizes the importance of providing adequate safety nets to cushion adverse effects of adjustment on vulnerable population groups, such as the rural laborer (see chapter 10). But the long-term goal of lowering trade barriers should be fundamentally the same for developing and for more developed countries.

## Agricultural Trade Lags Industrial Goods Trade

For more than a generation trade has been a driver of global growth across all global regions (figure 1.1). In every year from the 1970s through the 1990s, export growth worldwide has outpaced the growth of total output by an average ratio of 1.5 to 1. Moreover, this trend has increased over time and, after a pause in the mid-1980s, jumped to nearly 2.5 to 1 in

**FIGURE 1.2 Tariffs and Trade Growth**

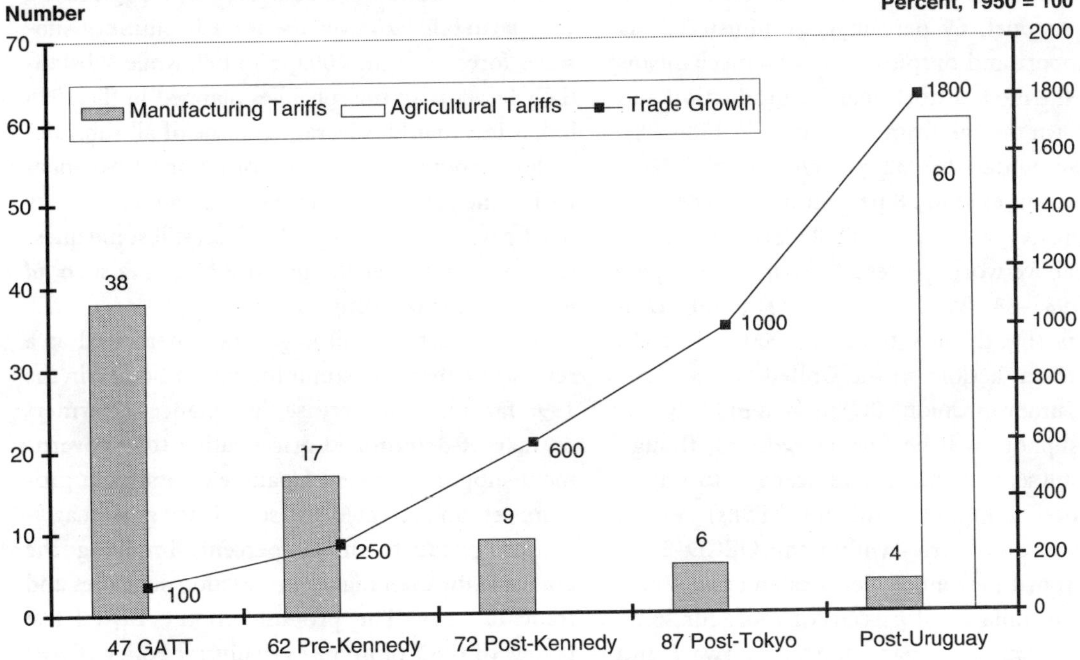


the 1990s. Consequently, in the space of just the 1990s, the average ratio of trade-to-GDP in developing countries has risen from 29 percent to 43 percent.

### *World Merchandise Trade*

The volume of total merchandise trade has increased 18-fold since the founding of the General Agreement on Tariffs and Trade (GATT) in 1947, with much of the credit due to trade liberalization. Figure 1.2 presents an overview of world merchandise trade against the backdrop of continually falling tariffs for manufactured products that have declined after each of the multilateral trade rounds, and the continuing high tariffs for agricultural products. In the 1990s, the value of world exports of agriculture products increased from US$274 billion in 1990–2001 to US$394 billion in 2000–01, more than 1.4 times its previous level. However, the increase in the manufacturing sector was much larger: worldwide exports of manufactures increased to more than 1.8 times its 1990 level.

By the end of the 1990s, global trade in food and agricultural products was about 10 percent of the value of total merchandise trade. Although agricultural trade is increasing in absolute terms, its share of total world trade has declined steadily throughout the last century. This trend shows no sign of abating: The share of food and agriculture in total merchandise trade fell from 17 percent to 10 percent between 1980 and 1997.

### *High Tariffs and Other Barriers to Trade*

Overall, there has been some progress in global agriculture and trade policy reform, but this remains fragile and fails to provide the liberalization and technical support that developing countries had expected from the Uruguay Round (UR) accords: the spirit is missing. A review of the experience to date on the implementation of the UR Agreement on Agriculture (URAA) indicates that domestic policy reform and trade liberalization have been difficult to achieve in both the OECD and developing countries for four main reasons.

First, domestic policy distortions and support remain high in many OECD countries. Rich country border measures and subsidies that artificially increase production and distort trade have been reduced during the implementation period of the URAA, but still remain extremely high. Total support amounted to US$311 billion in 2001 in the OECD countries. While this amount was 1.3 percent of their own GDP, it was roughly equal to the GDP of all countries in the Sub-Saharan Africa region. Of this support, 69 percent is administered via price support and output payments, mechanisms that are the most distortional for production and trade (down though from 82 percent in 1986–88), and it accounted for 32 percent of total farm receipts (compared to 38 percent in 1986–88). On average, prices received by OECD farmers were 31 percent above world prices (compared to 58 percent in 1986–88). While total support in OECD in 2001 was slightly less than in 2000 by US$10 billion, recent actions in the United States (U.S.) and the European Union (EU) make it unlikely that overall support will be further reduced, though there is still scope to make it less trade distorting.

Producer support estimates (PSEs) varied widely across countries within the OECD. PSEs ranged from 1 percent in New Zealand and 4 percent in Australia to 60 percent or more for some countries such as Japan, Korea, Norway, and Switzerland. For the U.S., the average PSE is about 20 percent and for the EU it is about 35 percent. Producer support levels also vary greatly among commodities: rice, 81 percent; sugar, 45 percent; milk, 45 percent; sheep meat, 55 percent; wheat, 36 percent; beef and veal, 36 percent; oilseeds, 28 percent; pig meat, 16 percent; poultry, 16 percent; wool, 6 percent; and eggs, 10 percent. The highest levels of support are directed at temperate products, and it is sometimes argued that these are not the products of greatest interest to developing countries in the trade negotiations. However, these products are significant in some developing countries at present, and the heavy subsidies prevent growers of tropical products from diversifying into these temperate crops in the current depressed market conditions (see box 1.2).

Thus, the current levels of agricultural support in OECD countries are still a major factor influencing world production, distorting trade and depressing world prices of agricultural products. More importantly, the structure of protection is such that support (protection) mainly benefits large farms. Meanwhile, the support is a significant burden to both developing country farmers and low-income consumers whose food consumption still constitutes a large share of total household expenditure.

The future plans of the major OECD countries are unclear to developing nations. The U.S. in 2002 passed legislation (a farm bill) that would sharply increase subsidies when compared with those in the 1996 farm bill. However, the annual volume of subsidies forecast in the 2002 farm bill, while substantially larger than the subsidies planned in the 1996 bill, is less than the average volume of all subsidies including both payments forecast in the 1996 bill as well as the government-provided *ad hoc* emergency relief payments. There is, of course, still some question about whether the practice of giving such *ad hoc* payments will continue.

The 2002 farm bill is generally perceived as a reversal of the U.S.'s commitment, embodied in the 1996 farm bill, to increase the reliance of farmers on market-determined prices rather than government support. A recent Japanese government program sets an increased self-sufficiency goal in agriculture products of 45 percent, implying the potential for even higher production subsidies and trade barriers. The proposal in the EU's latest review of the Common Agricultural Policy (CAP) would reduce intervention (support) prices and increase reliance on decoupled payments, which are less trade distorting than other forms of support. However, adoption of this proposal is far from assured. A recent decision fixed the total budget of the CAP through 2013 at a level close to its current level in real terms.[5]

Second, high tariff barriers and tariff escalation on agricultural and agroindustrial products remain in many countries. Reflecting current levels of support, agricultural tariffs remain extremely high, in spite of the reductions introduced with the URAA. Recent estimates indicate average agricultural tariffs are about six times as high as industrial tariffs (Gibson and others 2001; OECD 2001b). While new tariff rate quotas as a result of the URAA have replaced nontariff barriers, out-of-quota tariff rates remain high and sometimes prohibitive. Even in-quota tariff rates are often high, leading to the underutilization of quotas. Tariffs of more than 50 percent exist for 60 tariff lines in Canada, 71 in the EU, 14 in Japan, and 8 in the U.S. (McCulloch, Winters, and Cirera 2001). These harm nearly US$5 billion of developing countries' exports (despite the high tariff rates) and are almost exclusively focused on agriculture. Tariffs range from 129 percent for sugar in the U.S. to 162 percent for grains in the EU (Elbehri and others 1999). Protection also escalates with the level of processing, particularly in markets

## BOX 1.2 The Human Face of Policy Incoherence

Policy incoherence refers to the interference of government policy in one sphere of policy with the achievement of strategic objectives in another. Agricultural subsidies in OECD countries have often been cited as inconsistent with the goals of those countries to support economic development in poorer countries, and this point is made strongly in two investigative news reports in the U.S. paper, *The Wall Street Journal* (see Thurow and Kilman [2002] and Fritsch [2002]).

The story by Thurow and Kilman contrasts the situation of two families farming cotton. The U.S. family lives comfortably, since the average full-time American cotton-farming household has assets worth about $800,000, according to the U.S. Department of Agriculture. Owing to the approximately US$3.4 billion in subsidy checks, U.S. farmers last year harvested a record crop of 9.74 billion pounds of cotton, glutting the market and pushing prices far below the break-even price of most growers around the world. Under the 2002 U.S. farm bill, cotton farmers can expect to receive about US$0.70 per pound (in comparison with a world price of around US$0.40). Many U.S. cotton growers are expected to receive half of their income from the government in 2002. The article cites the recent study which estimates that the increased U.S. cotton production due to subsidies—and the consequent lower world prices—are responsible for a reduction in revenue to West and Central African countries of about US$250 million annually.

In contrast, in Mali the price offered to Mali's cotton farmers this year is 10 percent lower than in 2001, which was at the lowest level in three decades. After the last harvest, once the farming costs were paid, the Malian family was left with less than US$2,000 for the year to support two dozen family members and relatives. This year's lower prices, along with higher fertilizer and pesticide costs, probably mean that the family will be unable to replenish their cattle stock and may also have to stop supporting their youngest brother's high-school education. Given that the United States spends US$40 million a year on education, health, and other development programs in Mali, the article notes the obvious inconsistency and further notes that the subsidies are also inconsistent with the U.S. foreign policy goal of fighting terrorism. The people who are supposed to be soothed by this antipoverty offensive are becoming more alienated and angry with the United States. Mali, a predominantly Muslim country, has been largely peaceful since September 11, 2001 (the terrorist attacks in the United States), but frustrations are increasing nonetheless. "This is where America is heading: It wants to dominate the world, economically and militarily," says a leader of the farmer's union in the Malian regional center of Bougouni. According to the article, citizens of the cotton countries of West and Central Africa, where Islam is the major religion, are crowding into the cities of Europe, and those who remain are seeing more clerics from Pakistan and the Middle East visit their mosques and Quranic schools. In Mali, western diplomats hear reports of some Malians crossing the Algerian border for religious training abroad.

Finally, the article notes that these subsidies undermine the program of the World Bank and IMF to support a basic reform of Mali's state cotton marketing monopoly, which is being restructured to increase reliance on the private sector to provide more money for the farmers. But it is not clear that these reforms will show significant results without changes in cotton subsidy policies elsewhere in the world.

The story by Fritsch deals with the worldwide depression in the coffee market, examining in detail the situation of farmers and laborers in Nicaragua, and finding that many of those farmers and laborers are destitute and on the verge of malnutrition. While coffee is not a crop that is grown or subsidized by OECD countries on a large scale, the article makes the point that there are important interconnections among markets. For many years, foreign aid donors and governments have advocated and financially supported the objective of diversification out of traditional crops as a way of increasing value and reducing poor farmers' vulnerability to the dramatic price fluctuations in these markets. This goal has become even more pressing in the current severe depression in the coffee market. Yet, the article notes, farmers who consider switching out of coffee "are discouraged . . . by the experience of farmers who have grown peanuts and sesame. Those growers now find themselves on the verge of bankruptcy after trying to compete against U.S. farmers receiving generous subsidies from Washington."

for processed tropical products, preventing the development of value-added activities in developing countries. Specific tariffs are used widely in agriculture and are generally regarded as less transparent and more distortional than *ad valorem* tariffs. Since the weight of specific tariffs (as a percentage of the total price of the product) is lower with higher-price products, there is therefore an incentive to supply higher-value products within each dutiable category. Given these levels of industrialized countries' trade barriers, improved market access offers the potential for huge increases in income in developing countries that can supply these products.[6]

Third, high levels of export subsidies continue to distort world markets for key commodities. These high levels in OECD countries remain a major factor in world food markets and have a wide effect on world prices and market conditions. Between 1995 and 1998, global export subsidies amounted to more than US$27 billion cumulatively, of which more than 90 percent is from the EU (Elbehri and Leetma 2002). Export subsidies reduce prices and make it difficult for potential agricultural exporting countries to compete. For importers, export subsidies bring short-term benefits in terms of lower import prices. But for both groups of countries they can be detrimental to agricultural development in the longer run. The URAA placed limits on export subsidies for individual commodities, but allowed for some flexibility in their use as low usage levels early in the URAA implementation period (1995 was a period of high world prices) enabled some countries to bring forward unused subsidies and apply these when prices were low and the subsidy ceilings had been reached.[7]

Fourth, policies of many developing countries continue to create a bias against their own agricultural sectors and those of other developing countries. Schiff and Valdés (1992a, 1992b) found that in the past, developing countries have typically taxed their agricultural sectors to some extent directly (for example, by taxes on exports or by controlled food prices) but also indirectly (for example, through trade barriers and macroeconomic policies that overvalued the exchange rate). In so doing, these policies turned the internal terms of trade (manufactures prices vis-à-vis agricultural prices) against agriculture and kept the prices of agricultural inputs high. Since those findings were published in the 1980s, developing countries as a group have improved their macroeconomic and trade policies, raising the question of whether these findings are still valid. While the magnitude of the bias has clearly been reduced, it still remains significant in many countries owing to the continuing protection of manufactured goods, the operation of inefficient state-owned marketing enterprises for key agricultural exports in some countries, and in some cases direct taxation of exports. In addition to creating an overall bias against agriculture, the trade policies of developing countries create barriers to increased South–South trade in agricultural products. Tariffs for both processed foods and primary agricultural products are higher in developing countries than in industrialized countries, although tariffs on some temperate crops and products and nontariff barriers (NTBs) in general are higher in the industrialized countries. Both average tariffs and incidence of NTBs in developing countries are also slightly higher for agricultural imports than for manufactured goods (see tables 1.2, 1.3, 1.4, and 1.5). While both tariffs and NTBs were substantially reduced in the late 1980s and 1990s, the high levels continue to create very significant barriers to greater trade among the developing countries, though there is some reason to believe that barriers in OECD countries are even more effective in stifling trade. Further real reductions in trade barriers have the potential to improve productive efficiency based on true comparative advantage.

### *World Export Growth*

Table 1.6 shows export growth over each of the last two decades through 2001 for agricultural and manufacturing exports from developing and industrialized countries. Worldwide, both agricultural and manufacturing export growth in the 1990s continued at about the same pace as in the 1980s. Growth of developing countries' agricultural exports rose, as did manufacturing export growth, but this similarity masks an important difference. Within developing countries' agricultural exports, the growth rate of those to other developing countries more than doubled, while those to developed countries stagnated. As a result of these trends, the share of developing countries' agricultural exports

**TABLE 1.2 Agricultural Protection in Developing Countries, 1984-87 and 1994–98**

| Exports by Partner Countries in Region or Group | Food | | | | Primary Foods | | | |
|---|---|---|---|---|---|---|---|---|
| | *Applied Tariff* | | *NTB Frequency* | | *Applied Foods* | | *NTB Frequency* | |
| | 1984–87 | 1994–98 | 1984–87[a] | 1994–98[b] | 1984–87 | 1994–98 | 1984–87[a] | 1994–98[b] |
| Industrial Countries | — | 6.2 | — | 28.9 | — | 8.1 | — | 32.0 |
| Developing Countries | 30.7 | 25.0 | 47.8 | 12.1 | — | 23.9 | — | 13.9 |
| East Asia & Pacific (EAP) | 22.2 | 25.2 | 33.6 | 19.4 | — | 22.5 | — | 24.0 |
| Europe & Central Asia (ECA) | 8.3 | 13.9 | 42.9 | 2.1 | — | 14.4 | — | 1.8 |
| Latin America, Caribbean | 29.5 | 15.2 | 40.2 | 22.1 | — | 14.8 | — | 24.6 |
| Middle East & North Africa | 27.7 | 26.8 | 60.0 | 14.1 | — | 30.4 | — | 18.9 |
| South Asia (SA) | 65.5 | 41.8 | 54.4 | 12.0 | — | 36.2 | — | 11.0 |
| Sub-Saharan Africa (SSA) | 31.2 | 27.0 | 55.4 | 3.0 | — | 24.9 | — | 3.0 |
| Low-Income Ctys (LIC) | 40.0 | 27.2 | 53.6 | 5.3 | — | 24.7 | — | 5.5 |
| Lower Mid. Income (LMIC) | 33.9 | 20.3 | 71.3 | 12.6 | — | 21.1 | — | 13.9 |
| Upper Mid. Income (UMIC) | 20.1 | 17.9 | 13.3 | 21.8 | — | 16.7 | — | 26.3 |
| High Income Dev. (HIC) | 12.7 | 17.1 | 23.0 | 17.2 | — | 18.4 | — | 21.8 |
| **Exports by Partner Countries in Region or Group** | **Processed Foods** | | | | **Agricultural Raw Materials** | | | |
| | *Applied Tariff* | | *NTB Frequency* | | *Applied Tariff* | | *NTB Frequency* | |
| | 1984–87 | 1994–98 | 1984–87[a] | 1994–98[b] | 1984–87 | 1994–98 | 1984–87[a] | 1994–98[b] |
| Industrial Countries | — | 6.2 | — | 24.8 | — | 1.8 | — | 14.9 |
| Developing Countries | — | 26.4 | — | 9.8 | 18.8 | 14.3 | 35.2 | 8.4 |
| East Asia & Pacific (EAP) | — | 27.1 | — | 13.5 | 11.9 | 9.6 | 22.8 | 13.7 |
| Europe & Central Asia (ECA) | — | 14.4 | — | 2.3 | 5.9 | 8.2 | 48.8 | 0.0 |
| Latin America, Caribbean | — | 15.6 | — | 18.7 | 23.9 | 8.0 | 20.3 | 20.3 |
| Middle East & North Africa | — | 25.5 | — | 10.4 | 10.6 | 14.0 | 36.5 | 12.9 |
| South Asia (SA) | — | 47.1 | — | 12.2 | 39.4 | 30.9 | 43.4 | 2.8 |
| Sub-Saharan Africa (SSA) | — | 28.8 | — | | 21.2 | 15.0 | 39.6 | 0.5 |
| Low-Income Ctys (LIC) | — | 29.6 | — | 4.5 | 25.5 | 16.1 | 39.2 | 2.6 |
| Lower Mid. Income (LMIC) | — | 20.0 | — | 10.6 | 17.0 | 10.5 | 45.6 | 8.7 |
| Upper Mid. Income (UMIC) | — | 18.8 | — | 17.4 | 16.9 | 10.0 | 7.2 | 20.1 |
| High Income Dev. (HIC) | — | 19.4 | — | 8.2 | 9.7 | 4.3 | 7.7 | 14.0 |

— Not available.

a. "Core" nontariff barriers, including quantitative import restrictions, measures to directly control import prices, and restrictive trade finance measures.

b. Change may be biased by differences in data coverage of developing countries and nontariff barriers between time periods.

*Note:* Protection statistics are simple averages of tariff and NTB measures for countries and product categories.

*Source*: World Bank

**TABLE 1.3 Applied Tariff Rates in Developing and Industrial Countries, 1994–98 (Percent)**

| Product Category | | | EAP | ECA | LAC | MENA | SA | SSA | LIC | LMIC | UMIC | HIC | OECD |
|---|---|---|---|---|---|---|---|---|---|---|---|---|---|
| Primary Products | Primary Foods | Live Animals | 8.1 | 10.6 | 8.3 | 27.2 | 27.3 | 16.8 | 16.5 | 13.5 | 12.5 | 4.8 | 47.4 |
| | | Meat Products | 22.1 | 21.3 | 18.4 | 54.9 | 45.2 | 30.9 | 30.3 | 31.2 | 22.7 | 13.4 | 7.9 |
| | | Dairy Products | 21.1 | 22.5 | 18.5 | 32.4 | 33.4 | 25.8 | 25.8 | 23.1 | 21.8 | 22.2 | 45.5 |
| | | Cereal Grains | 37.0 | 8.9 | 11.1 | 12.4 | 14.7 | 13.7 | 14.0 | 11.7 | 10.9 | 54.1 | 2.7 |
| | | Vegetables | 31.9 | 15.6 | 14.7 | 17.9 | 34.3 | 26.4 | 25.5 | 20.4 | 15.3 | 29.4 | 3.5 |
| | | Fruits & Nuts | 27.3 | 11.1 | 17.2 | 30.6 | 44.8 | 30.5 | 30.7 | 21.8 | 17.0 | 20.0 | 2.5 |
| | | Sugar & Honey | 21.9 | 19.7 | 16.7 | 23.0 | 42.0 | 25.9 | 25.9 | 20.4 | 23.2 | 13.6 | 8.0 |
| | | Animal Feed Stuffs | 5.8 | 5.6 | 9.3 | 11.6 | 22.7 | 14.4 | 14.3 | 9.8 | 7.4 | 2.7 | 0.7 |
| | | Oil Seeds | 20.5 | 30.4 | 7.4 | 13.7 | 32.2 | 18.7 | 18.8 | 9.8 | 8.2 | 23.2 | 1.2 |
| | Processed Foods | Fats & Oils | 13.1 | 9.5 | 14.5 | 20.8 | 41.2 | 20.4 | 22.8 | 15.4 | 13.5 | 7.3 | 4.4 |
| | | Cereal Preparations | 36.6 | 16.9 | 14.8 | 24.5 | 33.7 | 26.5 | 25.8 | 20.2 | 16.9 | 49.3 | 8.5 |
| | | Prepared Vegetables | 22.8 | 15.6 | 15.1 | 24.2 | 41.2 | 30.4 | 29.3 | 20.5 | 16.8 | 16.4 | 5.8 |
| | | Prepared Fruits | 28.5 | 15.9 | 17.0 | 31.0 | 47.1 | 33.3 | 32.8 | 23.1 | 18.7 | 23.6 | 8.7 |
| | | Coffee, Tea & Spices | 21.1 | 9.1 | 15.3 | 21.7 | 42.9 | 30.5 | 29.6 | 17.3 | 15.6 | 14.3 | 3.2 |
| | | Beverages | 46.7 | 24.2 | 18.0 | 45.1 | 115.2 | 34.1 | 46.4 | 27.2 | 37.5 | 16.0 | 7.3 |
| | | Other Processed Foods | 20.2 | 17.6 | 16.3 | 24.7 | 46.9 | 30.3 | 30.6 | 20.2 | 19.9 | 12.2 | 13.0 |
| | Agricultural Raw Materials | Tobacco & Manufs. | 42.9 | 32.3 | 18.7 | 33.9 | 84.5 | 36.9 | 42.5 | 24.0 | 46.3 | 16.0 | 14.7 |
| | | Hides & Skins | 3.9 | 5.2 | 8.0 | 10.1 | 30.6 | 16.4 | 17.3 | 7.8 | 7.0 | 0.6 | 0.1 |
| | | Natural Rubber | 5.4 | 1.4 | 7.3 | 8.6 | 21.8 | 9.9 | 10.9 | 6.9 | 6.1 | 0.4 | 0.2 |
| | | Natural Fibers | 4.1 | 5.1 | 6.5 | 10.7 | 29.5 | 11.7 | 13.2 | 8.2 | 5.7 | 1.1 | 0.3 |
| | | Other Agr. Raw Mats. | 10.1 | 8.4 | 7.1 | 12.2 | 27.7 | 14.4 | 15.0 | 10.5 | 8.3 | 6.3 | 2.0 |
| | Miscellaneous | Mineral Ores | 3.4 | 3.4 | 6.2 | 9.4 | 25.0 | 11.4 | 11.9 | 6.8 | 6.1 | 0.7 | 0.2 |
| | | Mineral Fuels | 4.2 | 3.0 | 7.0 | 10.6 | 29.3 | 11.4 | 12.8 | 7.2 | 6.3 | 2.2 | 0.9 |
| | | Non-Ferrous Metals | 5.3 | 5.1 | 8.2 | 12.8 | 31.6 | 14.5 | 14.9 | 9.4 | 8.6 | 2.1 | 2.0 |

**TABLE 1.3 (Continued)**

| Product Category | | | EAP | ECA | LAC | MENA | SA | SSA | LIC | LMIC | UMIC | HIC | OECD |
|---|---|---|---|---|---|---|---|---|---|---|---|---|---|
| Manufactures | Chemical | Pharmaceuticals | 3.5 | 3.0 | 5.5 | 8.2 | 22.3 | 7.3 | 9.0 | 5.2 | 5.7 | 2.8 | 0.1 |
| | | Toiletry & Perfumes | 14.7 | 9.6 | 14.4 | 22.7 | 48.2 | 26.3 | 26.8 | 16.7 | 16.0 | 6.6 | 3.7 |
| | | Manuf. Fertilizers | 3.2 | 4.3 | 3.4 | 11.8 | 15.5 | 3.5 | 4.6 | 5.8 | 5.0 | 5.4 | 0.7 |
| | Iron & Steel | Iron & Steel | 6.2 | 5.9 | 8.8 | 11.1 | 37.1 | 13.2 | 14.7 | 8.7 | 11.2 | 3.4 | 2.9 |
| | Machinery | Non-Electric Mach. | 5.1 | 4.4 | 7.1 | 10.7 | 30.1 | 10.7 | 12.2 | 6.7 | 9.5 | 3.5 | 2.1 |
| | | Electric Machinery | 9.4 | 6.6 | 11.5 | 15.7 | 41.7 | 20.9 | 20.7 | 11.7 | 14.7 | 4.4 | 2.9 |
| | | Transport Equipment | 14.4 | 7.9 | 11.0 | 14.3 | 41.3 | 14.7 | 17.3 | 12.8 | 13.3 | 5.1 | 3.1 |
| | Other Manufactures | Leather & Travel Goods | 11.8 | 9.0 | 14.3 | 21.6 | 39.5 | 26.8 | 26.0 | 16.4 | 14.0 | 3.0 | 5.4 |
| | | Rubber Products | 13.0 | 6.2 | 11.6 | 19.4 | 45.7 | 20.8 | 21.3 | 13.5 | 15.5 | 4.9 | 3.9 |
| | | Wood Products | 16.5 | 8.5 | 12.8 | 22.7 | 43.3 | 24.6 | 24.2 | 17.6 | 14.4 | 5.1 | 3.4 |
| | | Paper Products | 12.4 | 7.1 | 11.7 | 19.8 | 47.1 | 20.6 | 22.0 | 14.3 | 13.5 | 4.5 | 3.3 |
| | | Textiles & Clothing | 17.9 | 11.9 | 17.1 | 28.9 | 50.7 | 29.2 | 30.2 | 20.8 | 17.1 | 8.0 | 10.0 |
| | | Non-Metallic Min. Prods. | 12.1 | 9.6 | 11.8 | 19.1 | 45.9 | 22.9 | 24.0 | 14.7 | 13.2 | 4.5 | 2.7 |
| | | Furniture | 20.2 | 13.7 | 17.8 | 27.8 | 52.1 | 34.0 | 32.4 | 22.3 | 20.6 | 7.6 | 3.2 |
| | | Footwear | 19.1 | 11.5 | 17.6 | 27.3 | 47.3 | 31.3 | 29.8 | 20.1 | 21.6 | 8.3 | 11.9 |
| | | Professional Equipment | 7.6 | 7.5 | 10.8 | 13.0 | 35.3 | 19.7 | 19.8 | 10.8 | 11.8 | 3.4 | 2.3 |

*Notes:* See Table 4B for description of product categories. Values are simple averages of rates of protection in each country group. EAP = East Asia and Pacific, ECA = Europe and Central Asia, LAC = Latin America and Caribbean, MENA = Middle East and North Africa, SA = South Asia, SSA = Sub-Saharan Africa, LIC = low income countries, LMIC = lower middle income countries, UMIC = upper middle income countries, HIC = high income countries, and OECD = major industrial countries. Darkly (lightly) shaded values indicate highest (intermediate) rates of protection in each country group.

*Sources:* UNCTAD 1999; author's calculations.

**TABLE 1.4 World Trade Simulation Model Product Categories**

| Product Category | Standard International Trade Classification (SITC), Rev. 2 | Product Category | Standard International Trade Classification (SITC), Rev. 2 |
|---|---|---|---|
| Primary Products | (0 to 4) + 68 | Manufactured Products | (5 to 8) −68 |
| Primary Foods | AGGR | Chemicals | 5 |
| Live animals | 0 | Pharmaceuticals | 54 |
| Meat products | 1 | Toiletry & perfumes | 55 |
| Dairy products | 02 − 025 | Manufactured fertilizers | 56 |
| Cereal grains | 041 to 045 | | |
| Vegetables | (0541 to 0545) + 05481 | Iron & Steel | 67 |
| Fruits & nuts | 57 | | |
| Sugar & honey | 6 | Machinery & Equipment | 7 |
| Animal feed stuffs | 08 − 08142 | Non-electric machinery | 71 to 75 |
| Oil seeds | 22 | Electric machinery | 76 + 77 |
| | | Transport equipment | 78 + 79 |
| Processed Foods | AGGR | | |
| Animal & vegetable oils & fats | (091 + 4) − 4111 | Other Manufactured Products | (6 + 8) - (67 + 68) |
| Cereal meals, flours, & preparations | 046 to 048 | Leather & travel goods | 61 + 83 |
| Prepared vegetables | (0546 to 056) − 05481 | Rubber products | 62 |
| Prepared fruits | 58 | Wood products | 63 |
| Coffee, tea, & spices | 7 | Paper products | 64 |
| Beverages | 11 | Textiles & clothing | 65 + 84 |
| Other processed agricultural products | 025 + 098 | Non-metallic mineral products | 66 |
| | | Furniture | 82 |
| Agricultural Raw Materials | AGGR | Footwear | 85 |
| Tobacco & tobacco manufactures | 12 | Professional equipment | 87 + 88 |
| Hides & skins | 21 | | |
| Natural rubber | 232 | All Product Categories | 0 to 9 |
| Natural fibers | (261 to 265) + 268 | | |
| Other agricultural raw materials | 29 | | |
| Crude Fertilizer & Mineral Ores | 27 + 28 | | |
| Mineral Fuels | 3 | | |
| Non-Ferrous Metals | 68 | | |

*Note:* AGGR = sum of SITC numbers in the given product category. Negative sign (–) = "less."

*Sources:* OECD 1998; UNCTAD 1994.

**Table 1.5 Frequency of NTBs in Developing and Industrial Countries, 1994–98 (Percent)**

| Product Category | | | EAP | ECA | LAC | MENA | SA | SSA | LIC | LMIC | UMIC | HIC | OECD |
|---|---|---|---|---|---|---|---|---|---|---|---|---|---|
| Primary Products | Primary Foods | Live Animals | 35.3 | 3.6 | 27.4 | 25.3 | 0.0 | 1.2 | 2.3 | 18.3 | 30.2 | 36.6 | 28.4 |
| | | Meat Products | 26.5 | 1.9 | 21.5 | 16.4 | 16.2 | 5.7 | 6.7 | 12.8 | 24.0 | 33.4 | 32.1 |
| | | Dairy Products | 28.7 | 3.2 | 23.0 | 30.3 | 16. 0 | 0.0 | 2.8 | 19.9 | 23.7 | 28.0 | 62.1 |
| | | Cereal Grains | 35.8 | 7.7 | 33.8 | 17.1 | 0.0 | 1.9 | 7.1 | 20.9 | 28.9 | 23.4 | 39.3 |
| | | Vegetables | 28.0 | 0.8 | 29.7 | 21.6 | 12.6 | 4.3 | 8.0 | 14.5 | 32.6 | 22.4 | 30.8 |
| | | Fruits & Nuts | 21.3 | 0.0 | 25.7 | 21.6 | 11.0 | 3.6 | 6.6 | 12.8 | 27.3 | 18.2 | 27.9 |
| | | Sugar & Honey | 10.3 | 6.5 | 15.5 | 8.5 | 9.2 | 0.1 | 3.5 | 9.0 | 16.4 | 3.6 | 34.3 |
| | | Animals Feed Stuffs | 11.7 | 0.2 | 20.8 | 14.1 | 4.2 | 0.9 | 2.1 | 9.2 | 25.3 | 1.6 | 21.6 |
| | | Oil Seeds | 20.5 | 0.4 | 30.8 | 15.0 | 11.6 | 0.0 | 4.8 | 16.0 | 27.5 | 4.8 | 23.0 |
| | Processed Foods | Fats & Oils | 21.5 | 1.5 | 12.0 | 9.8 | 6.4 | 1.3 | 3.3 | 10.3 | 9.7 | 18.8 | 27.6 |
| | | Cereal Preparations | 14.9 | 1.8 | 21.9 | 11.5 | 16.2 | 0.6 | 4.9 | 10.9 | 20.7 | 10.2 | 27.6 |
| | | Prepared Vegetables | 9.9 | 0.0 | 20.0 | 7.0 | 14.2 | 3.1 | 6.2 | 8.0 | 17.1 | 8.0 | 20.8 |
| | | Prepared Fruits | 9.9 | 4.3 | 20.7 | 1.6 | 14.2 | 2.9 | 5.2 | 9.7 | 17.6 | 7.8 | 22.8 |
| | | Coffee, Tea & Spices | 11.8 | 2.2 | 21.6 | 12.1 | 7.4 | 0.1 | 3.2 | 11.5 | 19.9 | 2.8 | 21.5 |
| | | Beverages | 18.6 | 9.2 | 18.3 | 31.6 | 26.4 | 2.9 | 7.3 | 17.7 | 27.4 | 0.2 | 33.3 |
| | | Oth. Processed Foods | 4.7 | 2.2 | 17.5 | 8.0 | 12.6 | 0.9 | 2.7 | 8.7 | 16.6 | 1.2 | 27.4 |
| | Agr. Raw Mat. | Tobacco & Manufs. | 9.5 | 0.0 | 14.8 | 29.1 | 13.2 | 1.4 | 5.2 | 7.8 | 23.6 | 0.0 | 16.9 |
| | | Hides & Skins | 7.8 | 0.0 | 18.5 | 6.8 | 0.0 | 0.0 | 1.1 | 3.9 | 21.9 | 10.0 | 25.4 |
| | | Natural Rubber | 7.3 | 0.0 | 1.0 | 0.0 | 14.0 | 0.0 | 4.7 | 0.7 | 0.0 | 0.0 | 0.0 |
| | | Natural Fibers | 15.0 | 0.0 | 15.7 | 3.6 | 2.0 | 0.0 | 1.2 | 6.5 | 14.5 | 17.8 | 12.1 |
| | | Oth. Agr. Raw Mats. | 16.0 | 0.0 | 2.0 | 19.4 | 2.2 | 0.9 | 3.5 | 12.2 | 24.1 | 16.2 | 14.4 |
| | Misc. | Mineral Ores | 5.0 | 0.6 | 8.0 | 0.6 | 0.6 | 0.1 | 0.6 | 5.1 | 4.6 | 1.0 | 0.6 |
| | | Mineral Fuels | 4.5 | 0.4 | 8.3 | 4.8 | 1.4 | 0.0 | 0.7 | 5.2 | 6.6 | 0.4 | 7.1 |
| | | Non-Ferrous Metals | 2.2 | 0.9 | 5.4 | 0.6 | 0.4 | 0.3 | 0.8 | 3.6 | 2.4 | 0.0 | 0.3 |

*Note:* Values are simple averages of rates of protection in each country group. EAP = East Asia and Pacific, ECA = Europe and Central Asia, LAC = Latin America and Caribbean, MENA = Middle East and North Africa, SA = South Asia, SSA = Sub-Saharan Africa, LIC = low income countries, LMIC = lower middle income countries, UMIC = upper middle income countries, HIC = high income countries, and OECD = major industrial countries. Darkly (lightly) shaded values indicate highest (intermediate) rates of protection in each country group.

*Sources:* UNCTAD 1999; author's calculations.

**TABLE 1.6. Export Growth Rates (Constant 1995 US$)**

| | World Export Growth Rates, percent | | Developing Countries' Export Growth Rates, percent | | | | | |
|---|---|---|---|---|---|---|---|---|
| | | | Total | | Developing to Developing | | Developing to Industrial | |
| | 1980/81–90/91 | 1990/91–00/01 | 1980/81–90/91 | 1990/91–00/01 | 1980/81–90/91 | 1990/91–2000/01 | 1980/81–90/91 | 1990/91–2000/01 |
| Agriculture | 4.5 | 3.6 | 3.5 | 4.8 | 3.8 | 7.9 | 3.4 | 3.4 |
| Manufacturing | 5.9 | 4.8 | 7.6 | 8.9 | 7.3 | 10.0 | 7.8 | 8.3 |

*Note*: Manufacturing exports are deflated by U.S. producer price increases for finished goods less food and energy. Agriculture exports are deflated by U.S. producer price indexes for farm products.
*Source*: COMTRADE, calculated for World Bank 2003.

**TABLE 1.7 Shares of Developing and Industrialized Countries in World Exports (Percent)**

| | Developing Countries | | | Industrial Countries | | |
|---|---|---|---|---|---|---|
| | 1980–81 | 1990–91 | 2000–01 | 1980–81 | 1990–91 | 2000–01 |
| *Agriculture* | | | | | | |
| Total | 35.4 | 32.2 | 36.3 | 64.6 | 67.8 | 63.7 |
| To Developing | 9.5 | 8.9 | 13.4 | 16.0 | 12.2 | 14.5 |
| To Industrialized | 25.8 | 23.3 | 22.9 | 48.6 | 55.6 | 49.3 |
| *Manufacturing* | | | | | | |
| Total | 19.3 | 22.7 | 33.4 | 80.7 | 72.3 | 66.6 |
| To Developing | 6.6 | 7.5 | 12.3 | 21.7 | 15.2 | 19.0 |
| To Industrialized | 12.7 | 15.2 | 21.1 | 59.0 | 62.1 | 49.6 |

*Source:* COMTRADE, calculated for World Bank 2003.

to other developing countries increased between 1980–81 and 2000–01 from 9.5 percent to 13.4 percent, while their share of agricultural exports to industrialized countries fell from 25.8 percent to 22.9 percent (see table 1.7). Meanwhile, developing countries' share in manufacturing exports to industrialized countries continued to boom, increasing from 12.7 percent in 1980–81 to 15.2 percent in 1990–91 and 21.1 percent in 2000–01.

Simple statistics such as these cannot by themselves prove or disprove any hypothesis. Nonetheless, combined with what is known about worldwide barriers to trade, the data are certainly consistent with the hypothesis that barriers have been more effective in stifling trade in agricultural products than in manufacturing. With respect to agricultural products specifically, barriers to trade in industrialized countries have been more effective than those in developing countries in reducing growth in exports.

## Potential Gains of a Successful Doha Round Are Substantial

According to the findings of a recent World Bank study (World Bank 2002a) on the economic welfare benefits from global agricultural trade reform, the potential to increase the aggregate welfare of the developing world would be some US$142 billion annually (table 1.8). This does not include any economic welfare gains from liberalization of trade in services, or investments, or reductions in imperfect competition. Most of these gains could be realized from trade policy reforms within the developing countries themselves (about US$114

**TABLE 1.8 Gains from Removing All Trade Barriers in Agriculture and Food Globally, Post-Uruguay Round, 2005 (in 1997 US$ Billions)**

| Liberalizing Region | Benefiting Region | With Fixed Productivity | With Endogenous Productivity |
|---|---|---|---|
| ***High Income*** | | | |
| | High Income | 73 | 144 |
| | Low Income | 31 | 99 |
| | Total | 104 | 243 |
| ***Low Income and Middle Income*** | | | |
| | High Income | 23 | 53 |
| | Low Income | 114 | 294 |
| | Total | 137 | 347 |
| ***All Countries*** | | | |
| | High Income | 106 | 196 |
| | Low Income | 142 | 390 |
| | Total | 248 | 586 |

*Source*: World Bank 2002a.

billion), while the impact of liberalization only in high-income countries upon developing countries would be about US$31 billion,[8] amounting to around 60 percent of the official development assistance for developing countries. When more dynamic effects of liberalization, including investment, are considered, the gains are potentially much larger.

### *All Gains from Liberalization*

Overall, the potential gains from liberalization of agricultural markets (US$248 billion) are estimated to be substantially higher than the potential benefits from manufacturing (US$111 billion, not reported in table 1.8), even though agriculture accounts for a much smaller share of total world merchandise trade. For the most part, this is due to the high level of agricultural protection in high-income countries. Considering that agricultural and processed food products in high-income countries contribute only around 4 percent of global GDP and only 6 percent of world trade, a disproportionately large share of the global welfare gains would come from abolishing protection and trade barriers in these countries.

The geographical distribution of the gains from full trade liberalization is also clear. As should be expected, most of the gains accrue to the liberalizing region. For example, 70 percent of the gains from high-income countries' removal of agricultural trade distortions accrues to those same high-income countries. Even so, agricultural trade reform contributes more than 40 percent (US$31 billion) of the total welfare gains to developing countries from industrialized countries' liberalization of all their merchandise trade (US$75 billion, not reported in table 1.7).

As for developing countries liberalizing their own agricultural trade policies, 83 percent of the benefits from their own reforms would stay with the developing countries themselves. And the gains from developing countries' liberalization contribute more than half of the gains from those countries' overall merchandise trade reform. These large gains reflect not only the significant distortions in those countries but also the fact that the food and agricultural sector is such a large part of the economy of developing countries.

There is of course a large literature on the gains from agricultural trade liberalization, of which the study discussed above is only one contribution.[9] Some other recent contributions to this literature have estimated relatively small static welfare gains to developing countries.[10] While these gains are not trivial when compared to official development assistance of around US$50 billion per year, the gains seem small when compared with trade volumes. There are, however, good reasons to believe that the gains underestimate the true value of liberalization in the context of a multilateral agreement. All of these simulation studies (with the exception of the one discussed above) only estimate static welfare gains and so miss the dynamic gains that increased trade flows can bring. But these studies also understate on another level the gains to a successful conclusion of the Doha negotiations in agriculture. It has become increasingly clear since the beginning of these negotiations that an agreement in agriculture is certainly a necessary—and some argue virtually a sufficient—condition for an overall agreement. In that sense, the potential gains attributable to an agreement in agriculture will have to include at least partial credit for the gains in other areas, which are considerable for developing countries. All of these simulations of course show large gains to the industrialized countries from liberalization, particularly from removing their own trade barriers in agriculture.

### *Reaping the Benefits of Liberalization*

For developing countries especially, capturing the full gains from trade liberalization will require complementary reforms and investments, including the establishment of safety net mechanisms to cushion any negative impacts (see chapter 10). "Decoupling" payments for agricultural support is one option for putting a safety net in place. Box 1.3 discusses the experiences of two developing countries that have carried out such reforms.

Changes are often needed in the rules governing factor markets to complement trade policy reforms, either those undertaken unilaterally or through international negotiations. To either create factor markets or make them more efficient, certain reforms are particularly important. Privatization of land and security of property rights are central to ensuring that private farming is the main component of the farming system. Land markets should facilitate entry to and exit from farming. Land markets have been especially rigid in some countries, which is a serious problem when changing incentives require fluid movement of this and other factors across different uses within agriculture, or between this and other sectors.

Reform of inefficient state-owned enterprises is another priority, particularly in the agricultural sector, since these still dominate food distribution, agroprocessing, and input supply in a number of countries. These markets need to be privatized and de-monopolized by allowing the emergence of new and restructured private firms in processing, input supply, and services. Finally, financial institutions that serve the agricultural sector must be developed.

Investment in infrastructure (both physical and human) is important in reducing barriers to and the high costs of marketing, especially for small producers. Some of the most critical investments for agricultural trade policy reform include those in trade-related infrastructure and institutions. Development of the entire agricultural production and marketing infrastructure is essential in capturing all the economic gains that trade liberalization offers developing countries (see box 1.4).

Agricultural imports into OECD and other major markets face an array of sanitary and phytosanitary measures and other technical requirements. These measures, though ostensibly designed to protect human, animal, and/or plant life, can potentially restrict trade and pose major market access problems for developing country suppliers. This is an issue to be taken up in the negotiations as a priority for developing countries (see chapter 11). Even when the standards are legitimate, developing countries may have serious difficulties proving that their exports actually meet these standards, owing to the high cost of some testing and certification procedures. Technical capacity constraints—both in the public and private sectors—may also seriously hinder developing country compliance with the emerging array of international standards and technical requirements. Investments are needed to build testing facilities and laboratories as well as to build up the necessary human capital.

Most developing countries also lack a strong trade support service infrastructure. Investments are needed to build networks of trade support institutions capable of providing key services to exporters: trade policy information and commercial intelligence; export promotion and marketing; product development and financial services; and training. The institutional building program also includes developing national institutional capacity for international negotiations, interministerial coordination, and public-private sector dialogue.

### BOX 1.3 Reforming Inefficient Support Systems: Recent Experience in Two Developing Countries

A number of countries in both the industrialized and developing world have begun to reform their agricultural support systems by removing or reducing traditional price or income supports and substituting payments that are decoupled from (and do not, in principle, affect) farmers' current decisions on input usage or output. This was the major principle motivating the changes in U.S. policy embodied in the 1996 farm bill (the "Freedom to Farm Act") and in the 1992 MacSharry reforms in the EU's Common Agricultural Policy, which reduced support prices and gave farmers area-based "compensatory payments." Neither of these reforms went far enough, and the U.S. measures have been partially reversed, but they were clearly steps in the direction of decoupling payments.

Among the experience of developing countries with decoupling, two countries stand out: Mexico and Turkey. In the mid-1980s, the government of Mexico embarked upon a reform program that included extensive changes in its agricultural support programs, which until then had been almost totally dominated by direct government interventions. It foresaw that as a result of the North American Free Trade Agreement (NAFTA) with the United States and Canada its agricultural sector would have to become highly competitive. As a result Mexico began to reduce support prices and make area-based payments to farmers instead under the "PROCAMPO" program (starting in 1994). There were some startup problems. One major problem was caused by the advanced announcement that the payments would be based on the area planted in specific "program crops," using as a baseline a 3-year period including the year following the announcement, rather than using the area from some past period as the baseline. Farmers responded by greatly expanding their plantings of these crops. Another shortcoming was that in the early years of the program the payments were contingent upon the farmer's planting crops on a rather limited eligible list. That is, payments were not really very decoupled (that is, delinked from production), so these did not leave farmers free to make their own planting decisions based on market prices. The list of eligible land use was subsequently greatly expanded, so there are now few constraints, other than that the land must be in agriculture. An additional problem was that the payments were not initially assignable as collateral for loans, and this also was eventually remedied.

These initial shortcomings notwithstanding, the program has on balance been quite successful. An ex post evaluation found that each peso in this form of direct payment generated 1.5–2.6 pesos in income for the recipient (Sadoulet, de Janvry, and Davis 2001). In addition, the program must be judged a success in the political sense, given that it has allowed the government to exceed its NAFTA commitments in opening the very sensitive maize market to import competition. Before NAFTA, there had been dire predictions that imports would impoverish smallholder maize growers, causing large-scale social unrest. The share of output and input-linked support in gross farm receipts has been reduced to less than half its previous level (see OECD 2002).

Turkey's program is more recent, so its impact cannot yet be definitively judged, but the experience is instructive from two perspectives. First, it demonstrates that with proper preparation and consensus, this kind of program can be implemented quite rapidly. After a pilot program of about 1 year, the large-scale roll-out of the program began in late 2001. By mid-2002, more than half of the farmers in the country (2.18 out of about 4 million total) had been registered and given their first payments. This far exceeded expectations, given the incomplete state of the land records (cadastre) and registration system. The payments are area-based and completely decoupled from production or input decisions, except that the land has to be used in agriculture. The second lesson is one of political economy. The program has allowed the government to sustain its phase out of the previous credit and fertilizer subsidies and support prices, which had become so large as to be macroeconomically unsustainable. While an ex post evaluation is yet to be carried out, it seems clear that the program will distribute benefits more evenly than did the previous system, since all farmers are eligible—even the small noncommercial farmers who benefited little if any from the previous input- and output-based subsidies—and there is a cap on payments to the largest farmers.

## BOX 1.4 Cambodia Rice: Challenges to Integration

Cambodia offers an interesting example of a low-income developing country that is integrating into the world marketplace for rice exports. Still recovering from the devastation of the Khmer Rouge years in the late 1970s, the country just recently transformed itself into a net-exporter of rice. Two of the world's largest rice exporters, Vietnam and Thailand, are also located in the lower Mekong River basin, and because of Cambodia's proximity to China's industrializing coast, its potential to become a successful agricultural exporter is evident.

Agriculture accounts for nearly half of Cambodia's GDP and rice represents about 90 percent of hectares under cultivation. At least 80 percent of the population spends 70 percent or more of household income on food, and rice is the largest single food item expenditure across all income levels.

Inconsistency in the quality of the grain has harmed Cambodia's ability to export product. Farmers source their seed from their own crops or from neighbors, causing seed varieties to mix and often resulting in several different varieties of rice in the same paddy. Recent efforts at contract farming where seed is provided to the farmer and financial incentives are given to ensure a quality crop have proven effective. In one effort involving corn, the rejection rate of product was reduced from 80 percent to 15 percent in four years. A similar effort for rice was begun in 2001 by a private investor who also made a substantial investment in a new mill. The government also distributes rice seed to farmers through the Cambodian Agricultural Research Institute and the Agriculture Quality Improvement Project.

Improvement of post harvest management is a critical area for increasing Cambodian farm income. Losses due to broken grains, moisture damage, and pests during storage seriously erode crops suitable for consumption, sale, and export. Inconsistent grain quality and older milling technology also cause losses. In September 2000, an International Finance Corporation (IFC)-sponsored program estimated that rice mills in Thailand produced 95 percent unbroken rice, but for farmers in Cambodia grain successfully milled for export was no more than 30 percent. The low literacy rate and weak communications infrastructure of Cambodia make educating farmers about better management techniques a challenge, but it is not insurmountable as demonstrated by the corn contract pricing experience.

The 2002 Cambodian rice crop is in peril owing to widespread drought followed by flooding. The government initially responded with charitable donations of rice and additional rice seed so that farmers could replant lost seedlings. Further hardship caused by the extreme conditions was mitigated by the government and the Cambodian Red Cross. The simultaneous goals of export expansion and food security present great challenges to Cambodia, but ones that trends show can benefit the country in the long term.

*Sources*: Cambodia PRSP; Ministry of Cambodia, IFC, *Phnom Penh Post,* www.foodmarketexchange.com

There are some differences in priority between the low-income and the middle-income countries in the area of related reforms and investments (Valdés 1998). It is in the middle-income countries that the bottlenecks in infrastructure and financial markets are felt most strongly. For the low-income and transitional countries, the more important question is how to facilitate the creation of factor markets. For the middle-income countries the issue is more about how to make these markets more efficient. Furthermore, in middle-income countries, where the agricultural sector represents a smaller share of the economy, there should be a more elastic factor supply than in lower-income countries.

## Notes

1. On the contribution of agriculture to growth and economic development, see, among others, Adelman (1984), Adelman and Robinson (1978), Johnston and Kilby (1975), Johnston and Mellor (1961), and Mellor (1966, 1995). On the issue of "consumption linkage" effects critical to the influence of agricultural growth on the overall growth performance of rural and national economies of developing countries, see, for instance, Mellor and Lele (1973) and Ranis, Stewart, and Reyes (1989).

2. For a fuller discussion of the linkages between agricultural growth and rural and urban poverty and growth see Johnson and Mellor (1961) and Timmer (1995, 1997).

3. See, among others, Ben-David (1993), Dollar (1992), Edwards (1993, 1998), Frankel and Romer (1999), and Sachs and Warner (1995). World Bank (2002a) has a good survey.

4. See Coe, Helpman, and Hoffmaister (1997) for evidence and (Romer 1994a, 1994b) for a further discussion.

5. Chapter 6 discusses domestic support policies and options for reform in more detail.

6. Chapters 4 and 5 discuss how to improve market access.

7. Chapter 3 discusses how to discipline and eventually eliminate export subsidies, a topic of critical importance to developing countries.

8. Note that the sum of gains from liberalization only by developed countries and only by developing countries (31 plus 114) are slightly greater than the gain from liberalization by both simultaneously (142).

9. For a discussion, see, for example, Anderson and others (2001) or Hertel and Martin (2000).

10. For example, ranging from US$14 billion per year (Rosegrant and Meijer 2002) to as low as US$7 billion per year for only selected commodities (Vanzetti and Sharma 2002).

## Select Bibliography

The word *processed* describes informally reproduced works that may not be commonly available through libraries.


Adelman, I. 1984. "Beyond Export-Led Growth." *World Development* 12: 937–49.

Adelman, I., and S. Robinson. 1978. *Income Distribution Policies in Developing Countries: A Case Study of Korea*. Stanford, Calif.: Stanford University Press.

Alderman, Harold. 2001. "What Has Changed Regarding Rural Poverty Since Vision to Action?" Rural Strategy Background Paper 5. World Bank, Washington, D.C.

Anderson K., B. Hoekman, and A. Strutt. 1999. "Agriculture and the WTO: Next Steps." CIES Discussion Paper 99/14, University of Adelaide, Australia.

Anderson K., Betina Dimaranan, Joseph Francois, Thomas Hertel, Bernard Hoekman, and Will Martin. 2001. "The Cost of Rich (and Poor) Country Protection to Developing Countries." *Journal of African Economies* 10(3): 227–57.

Ben-David, Dan. 1993. "Equalizing Exchange: Trade Liberalization and Income Convergence." *Quarterly Journal of Economics* 108(3).

Coe D., E. Helpman, and A. W. Hoffmaister. 1997. "North–South R&D Spillovers." *Economic Journal*, 107: 134–9.

Datt, Gaurav, and Martin Ravallion. 1996. "Why Have Some Indian States Done Better Than Others at Reducing Rural Poverty?" Poverty, Income Distribution, Safety Nets, Micro-Credit Working Papers, 1594, World Bank, Washington, D.C.

Dollar, David. 1992. "Outward-Oriented Developing Economies Really Do Grow More Rapidly: Evidence from 95 LDCs, 1976–85." *Economic Development and Cultural Change*, 40(3): 523–44.

Edwards, Sebastian. 1993. "Openness, Trade Liberalization, and Growth in Developing Countries." *Journal of Economic Literature* XXXI(3) (September): 1358–93.

———. Sebastian. 1998. "Openness, Productivity, and Growth: What Do We Really Know?" *Economic Journal* 108(March): 383–98.

Elbehri, A., and S. Leetma. 2002. "How Significant Are Export Subsidies to Agricultural Trade? Trade and Welfare Implications of Global Reforms." Paper presented at the 5th Annual Conference on Global Economic Analysis, June, Taipei.

Elbehri, A., M. D. Ingco, T. W. Hertel, and K. Pearson. 1999. "Agriculture and WTO 2000: Quantitative Assessment of Multilateral Liberalization of Agricultural Policy." Paper presented at the WTO/World Bank conference on Agriculture and the New Trade Agenda in the WTO 2000 Negotiations. October, Geneva.

Fan, S. 2000. "Technological Change, Technical, and Allocative Efficiency in Chinese Agriculture." *Journal of International Development* 12:1–7.

Fan, S., P. Hazell, and S. Thorat. 1999. "Linkages between Government Spending, Growth, and Poverty in Rural India." IFPRI Research Report 110, International Food Policy Research Institute, Washington, D.C.

Frankel, Jeffrey, and David Romer. 1998. "Does Trade Cause Growth?" Unpublished, University of California at Berkeley.

Frankel, J., and D. Romer. 1999. "Does Trade Cause Growth?" American Economic Review 89(3): 379–99.

Fritsch, Peter. 2002. "An Oversupply of Coffee Beans Deepens Latin America's Woes." *Wall Street Journal*, July 8.

Gibson, P., J. Wainio, D. Whitley, and M. Bohman. 2001. *Profiles of Tariffs in Global Agricultural Markets*. Agricultural Economic Report 796. U.S.D.A. Economic Research Service, Washington, D.C.

Hertel, Thomas, and Will Martin. 2000. "Liberalizing Agriculture and Manufactures in a Millennium Round: Implications for Developing Countries." *World Economy* 23: 455–70.

IFPRI (International Food Policy Research Institute). 2001. *2020 Global Food Outlook: Trends, Alternatives, and Choices*. IFPRI, Washington, D.C.

International Finance Corporation. 2000. "A Rice Industry Revives, The Millers' Tale." *IFC SME Facts* 1:9.

Johnston, Bruce F., and John W. Mellor. 1961. "The Role of Agriculture in Economic Development." *American Economic Review* 51(4): 566–93.

Johnston, B. F., and P. Kilby. 1975. *Agriculture and Structural Transformation*. New York: Oxford University Press.

McCulloch, N., A. Winters, and X. Cirera. 2001. *Trade Liberalization and Poverty: A Handbook*. London: Centre for Economic Policy Research.

Mellor, J. W. 1966. *The Economics of Agricultural Development*. Ithaca, N.Y.: Cornell University Press.

———. 1995. *Agriculture on the Road to Industrialization*. Baltimore: Johns Hopkins University Press.

Mellor, J. W., and U. Lele. 1973. "Growth Linkages of the New Foodgrain Technologies." *Indian Journal of Agricultural Economics* 28: 35–55.

Michaely, M., A. M. Choksi, and D. Papageorgiou. 1991. "The Design of Successful Trade Liberalization Policies." In A. Koves and P. Marer, eds., *Foreign Economic Liberalization: Transformation in Socialist and Market Economies*. Boulder, Colo.: Westview.

Ministries of Agriculture, Trade, and Industry, Cambodia. 2001. *Integration and Competitiveness Study Parts A, B, C, and D*. November.

Nara, Lon. 2002. "Rains Arrive But Situation 'Still Serious.'" *Phnom Penh Post* (Cambodia), Aug. 17.

OECD (Organisation for Economic Co-operation and Development). 1998. "Background on Tables/Graphs." Workshop on Emerging Trade Issues in Agriculture. October 26–27, Paris.

———. 2001a. *The Uruguay Round Agreement on Agriculture: The Policy Concerns of Emerging and Transition Economies*. Paris: OECD.

———. 2001b. *OECD Observer*. Policy Brief, November, Paris: OECD.

———. 2002. *Agricultural Policies in OECD Countries: Monitoring and Evaluation*. Paris: OECD.

Ranis, G., F. Stewart, and E. A. Reyes. 1989. "Linkages in Development: A Philippine Case Study." Working Paper Series No. 89-02. Manila: Philippine Institute for Development Studies.

Ravallion, Martin. 2000. Processed. "On the Urbanization of Poverty." World Bank, Washington, D.C.

Romer, Paul M. 1994a. "New Goods, Old Theory, and the Welfare Costs of Trade Distortions." *Journal of Development Economics.* 43: 5–38.

———. 1994b. "The Origins of Endogenous Growth." *Journal of Economic Perspectives* 8(1): 3–22.

Rosegrant, M., and S. Meijer. 2002. "Agricultural Trade Liberalization to 2020: Impacts on Trade, Prices, and Economic Benefits." Paper presented at the World Bank/International Agricultural Trade Research Consortium Conference, June 16–17, Whistler Valley, British Columbia, Canada.

Sachs, Jeffrey D., and Andrew M. Warner. 1995. "Economic Reform and the Process of Global Integration." *Brookings Papers on Economic Activity* (1): 1–118.

Sadoulet, Elisabeth, Alain de Janvry, and Benjamin Davis. 2001. "Cash Transfer Programs With Income Multipliers: PROCAMPO in Mexico." *World Development* 29(6): 1043–56.

Schiff, M., and A. Valdés. 1992a. *A Synthesis of the Economics in Developing Countries.* Vol. 4. *The Political Economy of Agricultural Pricing Policy.* Baltimore: The Johns Hopkins University Press.

———. 1992b. "Agriculture and the Macroeconomy." Policy Research Working Paper. 1967. World Bank, Washington, D.C.

Srinivasan, T. N., and Bhagwati, J. 1999. "Outward-Orientation and Development: Are Revisionists Right?" Economic Growth Center Discussion Paper 806. Yale University, New Haven, Conn.

Thurow, Roger, and Scott Kilman. 2002. "U.S. Subsidies Create Cotton Glut That Hurts Foreign Cotton Farms." *Wall Street Journal*, June 26.

Timmer, C. Peter. 1995. "Getting Agriculture Moving: Do Markets Provide the Right Signals?" *Food Policy* 20(5) (October): 455–72.

———. 1997. "How Well Do the Poor Connect to the Growth Process?" Consulting Assistance on Economic Reform Discussion Paper 178. Harvard Institute for International Development, Cambridge, Mass.

U.S. Department of Labor. 2003. *Global Economic Prospects.* Washington, D.C.

UNCTAD (United Nations Conference on Trade and Development). 1994. *Directory of Import Regimes.* Geneva.

———. 1999. *Trade Analysis and Information System.* Version 6.02, CD-ROM. Geneva.

Valdés, A. 1998. "Trade Policy Reform and Agriculture." In J. Nash and W. Takacs, eds., *Trade Policy Reform: Lessons and Implications.* Washington, D.C.: World Bank.

Vanzetti, D., and R. Sharma. 2002. "Impact of Trade Liberalization on Developing Countries: Results of the ATPSM Partial Equilibrium Model." Paper presented at the World Bank/International Agricultural Trade Research Consortium Conference, June 16–17, Whistler Valley, British Columbia, Canada.

World Bank. 1994. *Adjustment in Africa: Reforms, Results, and the Road Ahead.* New York: Oxford University Press.

———. 2001. *Global Economic Prospects. 2001.* Washington, D.C.: World Bank.

———. 2002a. "Reshaping Global Trade Architecture for Development." In *Global Economic Prospects.* Washington, D.C.: World Bank.

______. 2002b. *Rural Development Indicators Handbook.* Washington, D.C.: World Bank

———. 2003. *Global Economic Prospects 2003.* Washington, D.C.: World Bank.

2

# TRADE AGREEMENTS: ACHIEVEMENTS AND ISSUES AHEAD

*Merlinda D. Ingco and John Croome*

## Introduction

Arguments in favor of trade liberalization as a means of encouraging balanced economic development and reducing poverty do not depend on whether the liberalization is undertaken unilaterally, bilaterally, on a regional basis, or as part of a multilateral effort such as the current Doha Round. Virtually all economists agree that the largest share of the welfare gains from liberalization accrues to the country that undertakes it, thereby reducing distortions to its economy.

Each approach to liberalization has its advantages. A government that opts for unilateral liberalization escapes the pressures, complications, and delays involved in negotiating with other countries. Bilateral and regional liberalization agreements also have practical attractions, compared with broad multilateral negotiations (see box 2.1). With fewer participants, there are usually fewer competing aims to be reconciled, which helps speed up and simplify the negotiating process. Very possibly there may also be a closer identity of interests, and therefore scope for greater ambition, than is feasible when more countries are involved.

Multilateral negotiations, too, have real advantages—not least because the basic rule of most-favored-nation (MFN) treatment that applied under the General Agreement on Tariffs and Trade (GATT) and continues to apply under its successor, the World Trade Organization (WTO), means that whatever liberalization is achieved is extended to all, and thus does not discriminate against economic efficiencies. These advantages explain why the GATT engaged in successive liberalization "rounds"(formal trade negotiations) from 1948 to 1994, and why the WTO has now launched the Doha Round.

## The Plan of This Chapter

This chapter outlines the history of agricultural negotiations in the GATT/WTO, briefly describes the provisions of the Uruguay Round Agreement on Agriculture (URAA), and discusses some issues for developing countries in the WTO's current round of trade negotiations.

## How the Uruguay Round Agreement on Agriculture Came About

### *Legal Position in the GATT*

The importance of the URAA can be understood only by looking at the history of efforts to provide rules for trade in agricultural commodities. Planners for the post-Second World War reconstruction and

## BOX 2.1 The Price of Multilateral Negotiations

Though multilateral negotiations have their advantages, they also have their price. They are long, slow, and complex, and make great demands on governmental attention at both political and official levels. They are prone to recurrent delays and crises that may be triggered by events such as foreign elections that would normally be no concern of most participants. (Most of the major Uruguay Round crises, however, were directly linked to the agricultural negotiations.) A further problem arises from the linkages created among the disparate elements of a multilateral round that is—like the Doha Round—explicitly "a single undertaking." When "nothing is agreed until everything is agreed," the most powerful or reluctant participants are given additional bargaining power with which they can make demands on other participants that may be economically unjustified but politically unavoidable. This happened, for instance, in the final days of the Uruguay Round. The very terms on which multilateral WTO negotiations are conducted, with their focus on "reciprocity," "concessions," and so on, encourage a mercantilist approach to trade policy in which attention is focused on making other countries open their markets, while retention of one's own trade barriers and distortions becomes a mark of success. In these circumstances, it is all too easy to lose sight of the fundamental fact that trade liberalization is first and foremost to the economic advantage of the country that undertakes it.

### Reciprocity, Concessions, and All That

Reciprocity—the idea that each step a participant in negotiations takes toward liberalization is a concession, to be balanced or "paid for" by an equivalent concession from other participants whose trade will benefit—is a concept that is deep-rooted in the work of the WTO and the GATT. Its origins and clearest expression are in bilateral tariff negotiations, in which countries seek the reduction of import duties that hamper access of their export products to foreign markets, value the offers made by their negotiating partners in terms of present tariff levels, the percentage reduction in prospect, current trade flows, and the size of the potential market, and use this valuation in setting their own offers. All early GATT negotiations were explicitly conducted, and their outcome assessed, on this basis. More recent tariff negotiations have had as their starting point the assumption that most reductions will be made according to an agreed formula. However, the choice of formula is itself influenced by participants' calculations of its expected impact in terms of "equality of sacrifice," and reciprocity remains the basis for item-by-item bargaining on products excluded from the formula. Even with the formula approach, or in negotiations on matters other than tariffs, there is a persistent tendency for any participant to welcome or reject a negotiating proposal on the grounds that it appears to demand less or more movement on its part than is required of another participant.

Perhaps fortunately, the valuation of tariff offers is an inexact and subjective matter. Even in mercantilist terms, and even if the negotiators have access to the same detailed information about current trade flows and applied tariffs needed for product-by-product bargaining, all parties to a tariff deal can usually convince themselves that they have "won." Each participant will have its own goals and will make its own judgments, in light of advice from its own domestic producers, about how demand and supply will respond to the tariff reductions they and others have conceded. These differences are usually sufficient for everyone to feel that, in their terms, the outcome of a negotiation has been a success. Such a judgment may eventually be proved wrong. Changes in consumer tastes and government policies, technical developments, and many other factors can result in unanticipated and far-reaching shifts in the composition, volume, and value of trade flows. Nevertheless, what matters at the time, in political terms, is that every participating government can claim to have gained more than it gave away—and in the longer run, provided the outcome of the negotiations has been a shift in the overall direction of greater liberalization of trade, an economic judgment can probably be favorable, too.

economic cooperation set up the International Trade Organization (ITO) to oversee the operation of a multilateral code of trade conduct (Josling, Tangermann, and Warley 1996, p. 3). Trade issues then included tariffs, quantitative restrictions, state-trading entities, export subsidies and preferential arrangements, and the possibility of a special regime for trade in commodities (of concern to developing countries). Politics prevented the ITO's establishment, but its commercial policy provisions provided the framework for discussing global trade. The 1947 Geneva trade conference resulted in a trade accord—the GATT 1947—signed by 23 Contracting Parties (countries). The features of the agreement—its limited mandate, qualified legal obligations, rudimentary dispute settlement mechanism, improvised institutional arrangements in Geneva, and unsatisfactory arrangements for agricultural trade—were to stay with the GATT for the next 47 years.

Protectionism and discrimination are key features of international trade in agricultural products. Governments have always used various measures to assist or subsidize agriculture both in domestic production and in the trade of agricultural goods. Trade policy instruments such as domestic subsidies on products and inputs, export subsidies, import barriers, quantitative restrictions, and nontariff barriers have dealt with the disposal of surplus production associated with the cyclical nature of agricultural production, instability and inadequacy of agricultural prices and earnings, and access to domestic markets. In addition, agricultural trade policies have been shaped by major political and economic developments: the 1930s' Global Depression and the collapse in agricultural prices; the Second World War and regulation of the agrifood sector with price controls, production planning, and food rationing; the 1956 process of forming the European Economic Community (EEC) with the 1958 adoption of a protectionist and inward-looking Common Agricultural Policy; and the increase in the number of countries becoming Contracting Parties to the GATT.

The 38 Articles of the GATT have always applied to agriculture as well as to manufactures. However, two "agricultural exceptions" to the general rules were built into GATT: Article XI:2(c) on imports and Article XVI:3 on exports. Article XI:2(c) provided for nontariff border measures (quantitative restrictions), used to enforce domestic market management programs of the economically advanced countries. Article XVI:3 determined that agricultural export subsidies (illegal for industry) were legal, provided they were not used to gain "more than an equitable share of world trade." On domestic subsidies, the GATT had no special rules but a number of provisions that covered agriculture as well as manufactures: Article III:8(b) on like treatment of domestic and imported products, Article XVI:1 on notifications to the GATT, and Article XXIIII:1(b) on the nullification of benefits.

The Contracting Parties to the GATT engaged in formal trade negotiations in 1947, 1949, 1951, and 1956. These negotiations did little to improve the conditions of agricultural trade as they focused on border measures, such as tariffs. In a significant development in the thinking about international agricultural trade policy, the 1958 Haberler Committee Report and the work by subsequent committees linked national farm income support programs and conditions of world agricultural trade, attempted to measure the extent of agricultural protection (increased transparency of agricultural policies domestically and internationally uncovered the most trade-disruptive instruments), and determined the impact of developed-country policies (surplus disposal issues) on developing countries. This work enabled the United States (U.S.) and nonsubsidizing exporters to create the political momentum needed to make agricultural trade a major element of the Dillon and Kennedy Rounds. Both rounds aimed at removing distortions caused by protectionist national agricultural polices, providing improved and ensured access to import markets for efficient exporters, and dealing with the particular trade problems of developing countries (textiles and apparel). Little was achieved on agriculture in the Dillon Round. For agriculture, the Kennedy Round was, in practice, a negotiation between the U.S. and the EEC. The limited trade liberalization resulted in some tariff reductions on farm and food goods and the International Grains Arrangement. The Tokyo Round (1973–79) reached agreements affecting trade in temperate zone agricultural products for access, commodity arrangements (grains; dairy products; and beef, veal, and cattle), and the code on subsidies and standards, but agricultural subsidies continued, with no specific definition and no obligation to reduce their use. Bilateral access negotiations reduced tariffs, but the Swiss formula, applied to tariffs on manufactured products, was not used for agricultural tariffs.

In the 1970s, world market developments in agricultural goods suggested that the problem of agriculture was not oversubsidization and lack of market access but global food scarcity and unreliable supplies. In the 1980s, agricultural producers faced weak world markets (owing among others to the economic crises in Latin America), agricultural production stockpiles in the U.S. and the European Union (EU) and the increasing costs of supporting their agriculture, a collapse in prices, and an increasing number of disputes between the EU and the U.S.

With a farm policy crisis in most of the major industrialized countries, the 1982 Geneva Ministerial outlined a work program for the 1980s and established a GATT Committee on Trade in Agriculture (CTA) in preparations for a new GATT round. This examined all trade measures affecting market access and supplies, as well as the operation of subsidies affecting agriculture—especially export subsidies and other forms of export assistance. This process involved 41 countries and the European Community (EC) listing, by product, all measures affecting exports and imports, and the relevant GATT provisions on which the measures were based. The CTA's discussions on a rules approach or tariff approach to reform were the start of the negotiating process. At the same time in 1982, the Organisation for Economic Co-operation and Development (OECD) began an analytical study of agriculture policies and trade that used the concepts of Producer Subsidy Equivalent (PSE) and Consumer Subsidy Equivalent (CSE). The quantitative impact of policies was estimated using a multicommodity trade model developed by the OECD Agriculture Directorate. The study provided transparency in agricultural policies at the international level showing the value of agricultural production that resulted from government policies rather than from markets.

### *The Uruguay Round*

Initial attempts to launch a round of trade negotiations at a GATT Ministerial meeting in Geneva in 1982 failed. It took another four years of preparations to succeed in starting the Uruguay Round at Punta del Este, Uruguay, in 1986. For the next seven and a half years, negotiations continued. Both the mid-term review (1988, in Montreal) and the first attempt at concluding the Round (1990, in Brussels) resulted in failure and in walkouts by delegations of some agricultural exporting countries. It was only in December 1993 that an overall bargain was reached among the Contracting Parties in Geneva, allowing the round to be successfully concluded in Marrakesh in 1994. The WTO was established and when compared with the GATT, was much wider in scope, with a stronger institutional basis and with treaty status. The final outcome substantially changed the multilateral trading environment.[1] The achievements of earlier rounds were codified, new areas of trade were brought within the rules, a new system for settling disputes was established, and a separate agreement on agriculture was concluded. However, the URAA is a result of numerous compromises and—as in any product of negotiations—its basic principles have a number of exceptions, and in some cases its wording is somewhat ambiguous.[2]

## The Agreement on Agriculture

The URAA contains 21 articles and five annexes. It applies to all agricultural products as defined by Annex 1 of the agreement (essentially all agriculture and food products including raw fibers and hides, but excluding fish and forestry products). Other documents are important to understanding the process (see box 2.2).

Other WTO agreements also apply to trade in agricultural products. If a conflict arises between the URAA and any other WTO agreements, the URAA has priority. However, in many areas it is the general GATT/WTO rules that apply, because the URAA does not include detailed implementation provisions. For example, the administration of tariff quotas is governed by GATT Article XIII (Non-discriminatory Administration of Quantitative Restrictions) and by the Agreement on Import Licensing Procedures (ILA). Many WTO disputes involving agricultural products have involved the GATT itself or other agreements. For example, cases on alcohol against Japan, the Republic of Korea, and Chile involved the principle of national treatment (GATT Article III); the EC–Bananas case (see below for details) involved GATT Article XIII, the Agreement on Import Licensing Procedures, and the General Agreement on Trade in Services; and the

## BOX 2.2 Uruguay Round Agreement on Agriculture: Important Documents

### Schedules of Commitments

The 1994 WTO signatories' Schedules of Commitments, agreed to during the negotiations, detail how the URAA commitments are to be implemented. For tariffs, for example, each Members' Schedule sets out for each product the tariff rates (that is, the bound rate—the commitments not to increase the tariff above that stated level or ceiling) at the start and end of the implementation period. New members acceding to the WTO after the Uruguay Round have to submit their Schedule of Commitments following negotiations with WTO members.

### Agriculture Supporting Tables (AGST)

For commitments on export subsidies and domestic supports, the starting-point is the "Supporting Tables Relating to Commitments on Agriculture Products in Part IV of the Schedules" (GATT documents G/AG/AGST/Vols.1–3). These tables show the amount each member country spent on different products and support schemes during the base periods, and how the starting point for reductions was calculated. Some provisions that were negotiated after the AGST tables were submitted are not reflected in the tables. Countries acceding to the WTO after the Uruguay Round have had to prepare their own supporting tables, and for them the base period can be different from that used for the Uruguay Round negotiations. "Accession to the WTO—Information to be Provided on Domestic Support and Export Subsidies in Agriculture," WT/ACC/4; 18 March 1996.

### Modalities Document

For many of the commitments made, such as the specific percentage reductions relating to domestic support and export subsidies, the methods of calculation establishing these reductions were set out in the important Uruguay Round working document, "Modalities for the Establishment of Specific Binding Commitments under the Reform Programme" (MTN.GNG/MA/W/24). This has no legal force, but the reduction commitments, used to calculate Members' Schedules, are legally binding. However, as in the case of the AGST tables, the commitments sometimes changed following negotiations between members.

tariffs on milk powder case against the Republic of Korea involved the Agreement on Subsidies and Countervailing Measures. To ensure compliance with their obligations, members are required to notify the WTO of their commitments (see this chapter's Annex on Notification Requirements). Commencing in 1995, the implementation period for completing URAA commitments is defined in Article 1 as six years for developed countries, but for the purpose of Article 13 (Peace Clause), a nine-year period applies. Article 15 provides an implementation period of 10 years for developing countries. The following sections discuss selected articles.

### Article 4: Market Access

Before the Uruguay Round, trade liberalization negotiations covered border protection for all goods, except agricultural products for which there were often no bound tariffs or for which tariffs were supplemented by nontariff measures (NTMs), such as quantitative restrictions (quotas, import bans, embargoes, the monopoly purchase power of state-owned entities). Some countries used the simple border protection method of tariffs while other methods used were more complicated, such as the EU variable levy system. This system maintained a stable price within the EU by using the same post-customs duty price for all imports. The lower the border price of the product, the higher the tariff, resulting in a stable consumer price. With the stable price objective, other countries restricted the import volume, allowing imports when the domestic price increased and banning imports when it fell. These approaches stabilized prices within the importing country, but usually at a high level and have been blamed for amplifying international price fluctuations. If prices rose and imports were allowed, this meant that international demand increased, driving up the international price. If prices fell, imports were restricted, reducing demand on the international market and pushing international prices down.

With the intention of aligning agricultural trade rules with those applying to trade in other goods, negotiators agreed that all barriers to imports, other than those in place for health and safety reasons, should be subject to tariffs only—the only permitted form of domestic protection (Article 4.2). All forms of import restrictions had to be converted into tariffs—a process defined as "tariffication," with the method differing according to country status (that is, developed or developing). The country committed not to raise tariffs above a specific (bound) level (also referred to as ceiling binding) for all products covered by the agreement (see Appendix B). Countries were free to use lower rates (applied)—provided these were consistent with GATT Article I and used on an MFN basis, or used in cases in which the imports were subject to special arrangements such as trade agreements or beneficiaries of preferential schemes.

In general, tariffication involved converting NTMs into tariffs using the price-gap method, that is, the difference between domestic and world market prices. Thus, if the world price for a product was US$150 per ton, and the price inside the country was US$200 per ton, then a tariff of US$50 per ton could be the result from tariffication.

After establishing the tariff equivalent of an import restriction, reductions were required: developed countries by an average of 36 percent and a minimum of 15 percent over six years; and developing countries by an average of 20 percent and a minimum of 10 percent over 10 years. These were simple averages and were not weighted for the volume of trade. However, an even more serious problem was that the reduction commitments were based on "average cuts" rather than cuts in the average tariff. That is, if a tariff of 1 percent was cut to one-half percent, this counted as a 50 percent reduction. Thus, countries could achieve the target cuts by reducing already-low tariffs a lot, while making only the minimum reduction in sensitive products with high tariffs.

Having made the necessary calculations for all the different tariff lines, countries drew up their schedules of commitments for agricultural products, showing bound rates and reduction commitments. The draft schedules, after being checked by other countries during a final verification phase, were then included in each Member's Schedule of Concessions (Article 3 and legally enforceable through Article 4 of the URAA and Article II:1(b) of the GATT 1994).

Developing countries were not required to undertake tariffication in the same way as developed countries. They were not required to convert NTBs into tariffs giving the same protection, as estimated by taking the difference between domestic and border prices. Instead, they could opt to bind tariffs at arbitrary levels (often quite high) or through a combination of tariffication for some products and bindings on others.

On its own, a tariff-only situation improves transparency but does not necessarily result in better market access. For this reason, countries agreed that to preserve existing market access and to create greater access, current access opportunities had to be maintained. With the removal of NTMs and with some countries concerned about sudden surges in import volumes or a fall in prices of imports, negotiators agreed that a special agricultural safeguard (Special Safeguard Provisions (SSG) see Article 5) could be applied to certain products. The URAA's Annex 5 provided limited opportunities for countries to undertake minimum import commitments for certain products, rather than adopting tariffs for them. This option was taken by Japan, the Republic of Korea, and the Philippines for rice, and by Israel for certain sheep and dairy products. Japan has since tariffied all rice imports.

While *ad valorem* (that is, value-based) tariffs may be the simplest to establish and implement, some countries have relatively complicated tariff structures, using fixed charges or a combination of fixed and *ad valorem* tariffs.

### *Tariff Peaks and Tariff Escalation*

Post-URAA agricultural tariffs remain high compared to those on industrial products, with tariff peaks defined as rates exceeding 15 percent or three times the average nominal tariff, and tariff escalation defined as much higher tariffs on processed products compared to unprocessed commodities. For example, the EU-applied tariff is 18 percent for fresh grapes but 215 percent for grape juice.

### *Exceptions to Bound Tariffs*

Article XX (General Exceptions) of GATT 1994, which lists the general GATT exceptions to the tariff-only border measure rule, now applies to agricultural products in the same way as it does to industrial products:

- Article XX allows import restrictions for a number of reasons including the protection of human, animal, or plant life or health [Article XX(b), elaborated in the Uruguay Round Agreement on the Application of Sanitary and Phytosanitary Measures], reasons of public morals [XX(a)], and protection of national treasures [XX(f)].
- National security measures are exempt from the WTO Agreements (GATT 1994 Article XXI).
- Balance-of-payments difficulties may justify restrictions (GATT 1994 Articles XII and XVIII).
- General safeguard action is possible under GATT 1994 Article XIX and the Agreement on Safeguards.
- Antidumping action may be taken under GATT 1994 Article VI and under the Agreement on the Implementation of Article VI, and countervailing action may be taken under the Agreement on Subsidies and Countervailing Measures. However, action under the subsidy provisions may be restricted by the URAA "Peace Clause" (Article 13, Due Restraint), which restricts retaliation rights in cases where the provisions of the URAA itself on domestic support and export subsidies are being complied with during the period of implementation.

### *Tariff Rate Quotas*

As noted, tariffication did not necessarily result in liberalization or greater market access, although it did make the level of protection more transparent by establishing tariff bindings (ceilings). However, high tariffs can prevent realistic market access opportunities. Prior to the Uruguay Round, some member countries permitted limited imports at relatively low tariff rates, but charged higher tariffs on additional imports or did not allow imports over the quota limit. Members allowing import opportunities of more than 5 percent of the domestic market agreed to maintain these opportunities, while other members undertook to create opportunities equivalent to 3 percent of domestic demand, rising to 5 percent by the end of the implementation period. These current and minimum market access commitments are listed in each member's Schedule of Concessions. In most cases, market access commitments were implemented by tariff quotas, which allow imports at low tariff rates up to certain volumes. This arrangement, known as a tariff rate quota (TRQ), has not been without difficulties, with members' notifications often questioned in the Committee on Agriculture. Although the general principles are clear, many members believe that there is not enough clarity or detail in the rules on distribution of TRQs by countries and companies.

### *GATT Article XIII*

Each member's market access concessions set out in its Schedule of Concessions must comply with GATT 1994 Articles, most notably Article XIII (WTO 1997) and the Agreement on Import Licensing Procedures (ILA) (WTO 1997). As regards the distribution of TRQs among supplying countries, Article XIII requires that import restrictions be applied in a nondiscriminatory manner: each supplying country should have the same share of the import market as it would achieve in the absence of an import restriction. In other words, if country A supplies 10 percent of the import demand for a product in the absence of import quotas and then quotas are introduced, it should expect to supply 10 percent of the total import quota.

Article XIII:2 (d) gives some guidance—quotas allocated among new supplying countries can be allocated after consultations and agreement with countries that have a substantial interest. If this is not practical then allocations should be based on some representative period. The WTO's Appellate Body clarified this requirement to some extent in the dispute case, "European Communities—Regime for the Importation, Distribution, Sale, and Distribution of Bananas." Its report stated that in allocating quotas among supplying countries, the importing country should allocate first to substantial suppliers and then to smaller suppliers (WTO 1997)—that is, allocation to the largest suppliers first before it can allocate to the smaller suppliers.

For some TRQs, there may not be a representative period, and it may not be possible to negotiate satisfactorily with all supplying countries. In the EC–Bananas case, after the Appellate Body decision the EU tried to negotiate with supplying countries. When this failed, it allocated quotas to the principal suppliers on the basis of a historical period. However, under arbitration it was pointed out that to satisfy Article XIII the historical period must be representative (WTO 1999).

### *Agreement on Import Licensing Procedures*

Article 3 of the ILA on nonautomatic licensing requires that in operating TRQs, the administration system should not distort or restrict trade any further than the TRQ itself. It requires that information be provided to the WTO on the administration system. In the EC–Bananas case, the Appellate Body found that although the ILA applies to import licenses made under TRQs, it does not apply to the systems of licensing—only to the application of the system (WTO 1999). The systems themselves may not be fair and neutral, but they must be applied in a nondiscriminatory manner and should not increase any trade distortions arising from the quotas. Thus, a system that allocates licenses among countries may be considered unfair by the supplying countries, but it satisfies the ILA if no individual country is discriminated against in the administration of the license allocation system.

### *Administration of TRQs*

There are different methods of administering TRQs, ranging from the relatively straightforward method of first-come, first-served (first applications get allocations), to more complicated methods of auctioning quotas or allocating quotas on a historical basis. Although no single method seems to operate perfectly and questions have been asked about the different systems (especially the auctioning system), there have been no formal challenges made under WTO dispute settlement so far, apart from the EC–Bananas dispute.

## Article 5: Special Safeguard Provisions

The SSG is available only to the 39 WTO members that undertook tariffication, and reserved the right to have, subject to the relevant conditions being met, recourse to the SSG in respect to certain designated products. These provisions may be used only on imports outside the tariff quota, with additional tariffs imposed if import prices fall or if volumes rise. Article 5.9 stipulates that the SSG is to remain in force for the duration of the reform period "as defined by Article 20." This sets no time limit for reform, which is defined only as "an ongoing process" of "substantial progressive reductions in support and protection resulting in fundamental reform." The SSG provisions could thus remain in force for some time. However, Article 5.9 can be interpreted as meaning that the right to use the SSG depends on the continuation of the reform process, so that a failure of negotiations to continue this reform process would mean that the right to use the SSG would lapse.

In the period 1995–2001, 10 of these 39 WTO members notified the WTO of action under or, in the case of the European Communities, made operational by the SSG (WTO 2002b).

### *Price-Based SSG*

The method of calculating the SSG is set out in Article 5. For the price-based SSG, the trigger price is the average 1986–88 c.i.f. price with the additional rate of duty depending on the difference between the trigger price and the price of the imported product.

As the price of the imported commodity falls, the SSG tariff rises. This compensates for the fixed tariff and reduces or eliminates the effect of falling prices on the domestic market. The degree of total protection to the domestic market increases when international prices fall, and the SSG tariff blocks the transmission of sudden price drops to the home market.

### *Volume-Based SSG*

The volume-based SSG can be just as hard to calculate as the price-based SSG. Although the rate of additional duty is up to one-third of the applied tariff, the calculation of the trigger volume is either 125 percent of the average imports over the past three years or calculated by a formula set out in Article 5 on the level of market access opportunities and the change in domestic consumption.

## Article 6: Domestic Support Commitments

Not all subsidies distort trade to the same extent. In some countries the widespread use of production-related subsidies, such as price supports, led to increasing agricultural production above the market equilibrium level. This excess production had to be stockpiled or exported. With world market prices often much lower than domestic prices, exports required export subsidies. Thus one subsidy (domestic supports) led to another (export subsidies). Even without exports, domestic supports increase production and reduce demand for imports, thus affecting trade.

To apply reduction commitments to distorting agricultural subsidies, these were classified according to "boxes," using the traffic light approach, with red for prohibited subsidies, amber for subsidies that had to slow down, and green for nontrade-distorting subsidies. The negotiators decided to treat export subsidies separately, so the red box disappeared, while a new blue box covered direct payments to producers under production-limiting programs, considered to be less trade-distorting than market price supports. In this way an exception was made from the general rule that production-linked subsidies should be reduced.

### *Amber Box*

Article 6 sets out the reduction commitments for domestic supports. These are expressed in terms of the total Aggregate Measurement of Support (AMS), calculated according to provisions in Article 6, Annex 3 and Annex 4. To establish a basis for reductions, each country set out its financial supports by product and program during the base period (1986–88) and data are in the Agricultural Supporting Tables (G/AG/AGST/) series of documents. Each country agreed to reduce its supports on the basis of this data.

Countries with no amber box support agreed not to use supports over a *de minimis* level of 5 percent (10 percent for a developing country) of the total value of agricultural production.

Calculations of compliance start at the product level and if the value of support at the product level is less than the *de minimis* figure, it is treated as zero. For nonproduct-specific supports the same rule applies, except that its value is compared with the total value of agricultural production. Only product-specific supports greater than *de minimis* and nonproduct-specific support greater than *de minimis* are then added together, and only if that total is greater than the *de minimis* of total production is the Current Total AMS established for a country.

Reduction commitments apply only to the Current Total AMS and not to its components. A country could redistribute supports among different products, provided it has complied with its obligations to reduce the total figure. If no supports have been paid and no reduction commitments apply, that country may use production-distorting supports—provided the total value of such supports is not greater than the *de minimis* level of 5 percent for developed countries and 10 percent for developing countries.

The reduction commitments, using the 1986–88 base period, were 20 percent by 2000 for developed countries and 13.3 percent by 2004 for developing countries, with the following exemptions excluded from the AMS calculation for developing countries under Article 6.2:

- Investment subsidies generally available in developing countries
- Input subsidies generally available to low-income or resource poor producers
- Subsidies to encourage diversification away from illicit narcotics production.

### *Green Box General Requirements*

Annex 2 lists the types of subsidies exempt from reduction commitments. Exemption means that, subject to the provisions of Annex 2, countries may increase spending or introduce or amend these subsidies. To qualify as a green box measure, a subsidy must satisfy the overall requirements set out in paragraph 1 of Annex 2: it must have no, or at most a minimal, trade-distorting effect; and must be provided through publicly funded government programs and not have the effect of providing price support to producers. Despite these general requirements, the green box covers a wide range of programs as listed below.

### *Government Programs*

Government programs set out in paragraph 2 of Annex 2 are exempted from any reduction commitments. These cover many of the traditional government duties associated with various economic sectors, such as expenditures for research, training, and inspection services; and infrastructure services, including capital works programs for electricity, transport, irrigation, dams and drainage, and environmental programs. Food security, addressed to some extent in paragraphs 3 and 4, allows public stockholding for food security and domestic food aid programs.

### *Direct Payments*

Direct payments to farmers are covered in Annex 2, paragraphs 5 to 13. Paragraphs 5 and 6 require that, for a direct payment to qualify under the green box, it must comply with the general requirement of paragraph 1 and the specific criteria set out in paragraphs 7 to 13. Basically, direct payments must not be linked to current production and can be provided even if there is no production.

Payments can be made for income support, disaster relief, structural adjustment, and as part of environmental and regional assistance programs. Such programs are detailed below:

- Decoupled income support is provided as payment based on production at some fixed time prior to the base period (1986–88) and not based on current prices, current production, or other factors of production. No production is necessary to receive this support.
- Income insurance support is allowed when income loss is greater than 30 percent, based on the average for the previous three years. The protection must not exceed 70 percent of the income loss.
- Disaster relief support is possible when production has declined by at least 30 percent compared to the average for the previous three years, and the payments must be related to loss of income or of factors of production such as land or livestock. The value of the payments should cover only the loss suffered and, when made along with income insurance payments, must not exceed 100 percent of the lost income.
- Structural adjustment support is possible for retirement programs for producers (permanent retirement) and resource retirement programs (the land must not be used for agriculture for at least three years). Payments can also be made through investment aids aimed at overcoming structural disadvantages, or for land reprivatization. Although targeted at countries in transition from centrally planned economies to market-oriented economies, this provision has also been used by other countries with structural problems in agriculture. Countries trying to encourage younger farmers may have farmer retirement programs, while countries trying to increase average farm size may have land purchase grants or subsidized loans.
- Environmental programs support is provided to farmers to encourage compliance with environmental rules or enrollment in environmental programs. The value of payments should be limited to the extra costs or reduced income associated with the environmental program.
- Regional assistance support is given to overcome the difficulties faced by producers in disadvantaged areas. Although the payments should be based on some historic reference period, they cannot be related to current production and are limited to the extra costs or lower income associated with farming in such areas.

### *Blue Box*

A special exemption from AMS commitments included in Article 6.5 covers payments made under production-limiting programs, provided that such payments are based on fixed areas, crop yields, or livestock numbers, or, if the payments are variable, on 85 percent of the base level of production. These payments are used in some countries (such as those in the EU) where traditional market support payments have caused problems of overproduction, have become too expensive to maintain, or are too inefficient compared to the objective of maintaining farm incomes or rural employment.

Direct payments to producers are much more efficient than market supports in maintaining incomes, planted areas, or livestock numbers. However, basing support on animal numbers or on areas under crops can distort trade. It has been argued that this distortion is probably not as great as would be the case under market support-type payments.

### *Varying Domestic Support Levels among Members*

The level of domestic support provided by WTO members varies widely. Members with high support levels during their base periods, and with reduction commitments, have tended to continue giving high levels of support but have shifted support from amber box measures to blue and green box measures. Examining notifications of measures on domestic supports requires care, given different currencies (subject to varying fluctuations in exchange rates and inflation), the size of the agriculture sectors, and the structure of support that is provided (often not evenly across all sectors). Although the concept of the AMS calculation was based on the OECD's PSE, there are several important differences between the AMS and the PSE. The PSE includes supports that are excluded from the Current Total AMS because they fall within the blue box, the exemptions for developing countries, or the green box. For the past few years some OECD countries have increased their levels of domestic support, but as WTO members, these same OECD countries have been within their commitments because they reduced market and price supports in favor of direct payments decoupled from production.

## Article 8: Export Competition Commitments

Under Article XVI of GATT 1947, export subsidies were prohibited. However, Article XVI:3 gave an exemption for primary products provided they did not give the concerned GATT Contracting Party more than "an equitable share of world export trade." This provision's lack of clarity allowed some Contracting Parties to use export subsidies to increase or maintain their shares of world agricultural trade. The negative effects of export subsidies have been blamed for amplifying world market price variations because the level of subsidy tends to increase in times of low world prices and decrease when prices rise. This exaggerates the swings in world prices by reducing supply in times of high prices and increasing it in times of low prices. Because of the extent to which export subsidies distort competition, members agreed to introduce special rules for controlling their use. Export subsidy reduction commitments are based on use during the years 1986 to 1990, but members were given the flexibility of using 1992 levels if these were higher than in the base period. Members using export subsidies agreed to reduce them, while those not using them agreed not to start doing so. Twenty-five members have export subsidy commitments covering 428 product groups. Some members have used none of their commitments, and others are well below their commitment levels for most products. Export subsidies are concentrated on a few products such as bovine meat and dairy.

## Article 9: Export Subsidy Commitments

Export subsidies are subject to special treatment in the URAA under Articles 3, 8, 9, 10, and 11, with Members' Schedules of Commitments detailing reduction commitments. Articles 3 and 8 require members to abide by their commitments and act in conformity with the agreement. Article 9 lists the types of subsidies subject to reduction commitments, and Article 10 states that other measures cannot be used as a way to circumvent export subsidy commitments.

Only 25 countries listing reduction commitments are allowed to use such subsidies as detailed in their Schedules. No new subsidies can be introduced, nor can existing commitments be transferred to other agricultural products. The reduction commitments in Article 9.2(b)(iv) require that members reduce export subsidies by 21 percent in volume and 36 percent in value over the six-year period from 1995 to 2000. For developing countries, the reduction commitments are 14 percent in volume and 24 percent in value over the 10-year period from 1995 to 2004—a special provision in Article 9.4 exempts developing-country members from commitments on subsidies aimed at reducing the cost of marketing, including internal and external transport, handling, and processing costs. This exemption is available only during the implementation period as defined by the URAA.

### *Rollover of Commitments*

Article 9.2(b) allowed some flexibility in meeting export subsidy commitments. For the years 1996–99, countries could exceed their commitments or carry over unused commitments, provided that by the end of 2000 the total amount for 1995–2000 did not exceed the total in their Schedules. The annual commitment could not be exceeded by more than 3 percent in value, or 1.75 percent in volume. Although an implementation period described in Article 9.2(b) no longer applies, a number of notifications are still being made showing members' usage of the rollover relief provision.

## Article 10: Prevention of Circumvention of Export Subsidy Commitments

Article 10 reinforces the limitations on the use of export subsidies by trying to prevent circumvention of commitments, by stating that export subsidies not listed in Article 9.1 must not be used to circumvent members' obligations. To reinforce this, members undertake to work toward developing disciplines on export credits. OECD negotiations on disciplines on export credits covered by Article 10.2, although not finalized, cover export credits with the aim of reducing their ability to circumvent export subsidy commitments.

Under Article 10.3, an exporting country must show that any exports above its commitment levels receive no export subsidies. According to the dispute settlement panel in the EC request relating to the U.S. Foreign Sales Corporations Tax (FSC) (WTO 2002a), a country with export subsidy commitments must prove that any exports in excess of its commitments do not benefit from the FSC subsidies. If, however, a country has no export subsidy commitments, the country making the accusation needs to prove that subsidies were involved.

Article 10 also requires that food aid comply with the Food and Agriculture Organization's "Principles of Surplus Disposal and Consultative Obligations" and not be tied directly or indirectly to commercial exports of agricultural products to the recipient countries. The objective of this is to prevent members from dumping excess production under the disguise of food aid, while continuing to allow food aid donations.

## Article 12 and Article 13: Export Restraints and Due Restraint

Article 12 sets out the disciplines relating to export prohibitions or restrictions. Countries are required to take into account the effect on an importing country's food security. Before implementing any restraint, a country must notify the Committee on Agriculture and, if requested, enter into consultations with any member having a substantial interest in the products concerned. Article 12 does not apply to developing countries unless they are net exporters of the foodstuff subject to the export restraint. Some countries feel that such restrictions may help encourage the domestic food processing industry to develop, while others consider export restraints a threat to their food security.

### *Due Restraint*

Article 13, the "Peace Clause"—a temporary measure due to expire at the end of 2003—is intended to restrain members from taking action against others with respect to their commitments on market access, domestic support, and export subsidies. The Article does not prevent all challenges to subsidized agricultural production or exports, but it does restrict the right to challenge. Article 13 does not prevent a member from using other provisions that allow protection such as safeguards (Agreement on Safeguards) and balance-of-payments difficulties (Articles XII and XVIII:B of GATT 1994). The WTO Agreement on Subsidies and Countervailing Measures (SCM) is usually used to retaliate against subsidies, while the antidumping provisions of GATT 1994 (Article VI) are used for goods sold at prices below the domestic market. Article XXIII of GATT 1994 is used in cases in which another member takes action nullifying or impairing benefits from its tariff commitments.

**Green Box** Article 13(a) prevents any action against green box subsidies, which have no, or at most minimal, trade effect and therefore are unlikely to qualify for countervailing duties. If they have more than a minimal effect they are, by definition, not green box subsidies.

**Amber Box and Blue Box** Article 13(b) prevents retaliation under the SCM Agreement, including under the serious prejudice provisions of Article 6. This means that if a member loses market share because of subsidized production from another country, it cannot retaliate. It is also not possible to use the nullification and impairment provisions of Article XXIII of GATT 1994 for retaliation. Action under Article VI of GATT 1994 is possible if injury, or threat thereof, can be determined, although due restraint must be shown before initiating a countervailing duty investigation.

**Export Subsidies** A member's right to apply countervailing or antidumping duties on subsidized exports is restricted by Article 13(c), which requires a determination of injury or threat of injury and also requires that due restraint be shown in initiating any countervailing duty investigations. There is no prohibition on nullification and impairment action under Article XXIII of GATT 1994, although this would require "reasonable expectation" of a benefit and it could be argued that a member would be expected to use any flexibility allowed by its export subsidy commitments. It is not possible to take action under Article V or VI of the SCM Agreement for this purpose, which means that actions in response to serious prejudice (such as the loss of a third market) are not possible.

Article 13 therefore does not prevent action to counter damage caused by export subsidies or by domestic supports that have an effect on trade. Some members have successfully introduced antidumping measures against other members based on these provisions and, although some have been challenged and have withdrawn the measures, others have been able to maintain them. Obviously, in applying countervailing duties a member must comply with the relevant provisions of the Uruguay Round agreements concerned. The Article 13 prohibition from taking action in response to serious prejudice may restrict action from some countries. Concern about the exports of another WTO member is not always about the exports into the domestic market—it can also arise from competition for third-country markets. In these cases, a countervailing duty to protect the home market is pointless as market share may only be regained if the subsidy is withdrawn.

## Article 15: Special and Differential Treatment

Article 15 covers special and differential (S&D) treatment for developing countries. There are many references to such treatment throughout the agreement, including the Preamble, which notes that developed countries "would take fully into account" the particular needs and conditions of developing countries in the implementation of market access commitments and also recalls that S&D treatment such as longer implementation periods had been an integral element of the Uruguay Round negotiations. Developing-country Schedules reflect the use of special treatment. On market access, many did not tariffy all of their NTMs, instead opting for ceiling bindings for a range of agricultural products. Least-developed countries did not have to make any reduction commitments on tariffs, domestic support, or export competition.

It has been argued that, apart from market access, many of the provisions on S&D treatment are of little use to developing countries, given their inability to provide subsidies (10 percent *de minimis* rule for market supports), and for input subsidies (exempted from the Amber Box calculations). In addition, for some developing countries that are in transition from state control to more market-orientated economies, or that are dealing with the effects of natural or human-made disasters, their domestic reform, rather than WTO rules, will have a much greater impact on their agriculture.

## Article 16: The Marrakesh Decision

Trade liberalization is expected to improve global prosperity and food security, but negotiators recognized that there were some possible negative effects for least-developed and net-food-importing developing countries, arising from world market price increases.

The least-developed countries (LDCs) are defined as those recognized by the Economic and Social Council of the United Nations. Net-food-importing developing countries (NFIDCs) are Barbados, Botswana, Côte d'Ivoire, Cuba, Dominica, Dominican Republic, Egypt, Honduras, Jamaica, Jordan, Kenya, Mauritius, Morocco, Namibia, Pakistan, Peru, St. Kitts and Nevis, St. Lucia, St. Vincent and the Grenadines, Senegal, Sri Lanka, Trinidad and Tobago, Tunisia, and Venezuela.

To address the concerns of LDCs and NFIDCs, the Marrakesh Ministerial Conference of 1994 approved a decision on the possible negative effects of the reform program providing for the following:

- A review of the level of food aid and initiation of negotiations on food aid commitments sufficient to meet the needs of developing countries.
- Adoption of guidelines to ensure that food aid is given in grant form and/or on concessional terms in line with Article IV of the Food Aid Convention of 1986.
- Technical assistance by members, in the context of their aid programs, to LDCs and NFIDCs for improving agricultural productivity and infrastructure.

## Articles 17 and 18: Committee on Agriculture

The Committee on Agriculture, established under Article 17, has as its main role to oversee the implementation of the URAA and provide a forum for discussing matters related to agriculture trade. In practice, it currently functions almost as two separate bodies. In its regular sessions, it reviews and discusses matters arising out of members' present obligations under the URAA, reporting regularly to the WTO's Council for Trade in Goods. In separate special sessions, largely carried out on an informal basis (that is, without observers or formal records), it provides the forum in which the current round of multilateral negotiations on agriculture takes place.

In regular sessions, held about four times a year, a principal task of the committee is to examine notifications made under the URAA provisions outlined earlier in this chapter. The notifications are circulated to all members, who then put questions to the notifying countries for answer at the committee meetings. Under Article 18.6 other matters related to the reform program can be raised, and under Article 18.7 counter-notifications can be made when one member has information that suggests another should have notified the committee of a particular measure or action. The committee is also responsible for monitoring the implementation of the Decision of the Possible Negative Effects of the Reform Programme on LDCs and NFIDCs, and developments in trade in agricultural products.

## Article 20: Continuation of the Reform Process

Article 20 required that the reform process on agricultural trade continue and that negotiations start by 1 January 2000, one year before the end of the main implementation period for Uruguay Round commitments by developed countries. In its introductory paragraph, Article 20 states that the long-term objective should be "substantial progressive reductions" in agriculture protection and support. Factors to be taken into account in the negotiations are: (a) experience in putting the previous commitments into effect; (b) the effect of these commitments on world trade in agriculture; (c) nontrade concerns, S&D treatment for developing countries, the objective of a fair and market-oriented agricultural trading system, and other objectives set out in the URAA's Preamble; and (d) further commitments that are necessary to reach all of these long-term objectives.

## Implementation of the Agreement on Agriculture

A review of the experience of implementing the new rules on market access, export subsidies, and domestic support reveals that the results have been modest. The reasons include weaknesses in many specific aspects of the URAA, such as the modalities and the historically high support levels in developed countries in the base period (1986–88) from which reductions were made. In some countries such as the U.S., reforms undertaken prior to the negotiations were adequate to fulfill the new rules on reducing domestic support.

A comprehensive analysis of protection indicators (tariff protection in market access, nontariff barriers, trade-distorting domestic policies such as market price support, and export subsidies) in the OECD and developing countries provides several key conclusions, summarized below.

First, significant trade and domestic policy distortions remain in national, regional, and global trade in both OECD and developing countries. Tariffication—the conversion of nontariff barriers to tariffs—under the URAA was an important step forward, but in most OECD countries average agricultural tariffs are higher (some exceed 500 percent) than applied tariffs for nonagricultural products and continue to restrict trade. The global, unweighted average bound tariff rate for agricultural products is over 60 percent (Ingco 2000). For industrial countries, the unweighted average bound agricultural tariff rate is 45 percent. These figures compare with tariffs for nonagricultural products, which are below 5 percent for most OECD countries and about 20 percent on average for developing countries. Tariffs remain high in many countries with the level of tariff protection uneven, ranging from relatively open access for tropical raw materials to very high protection for products such as milk, sugar, cotton, and rice. Some countries have raised their applied tariffs for some commodities while others have made greater use of export subsidies, export credits, or other export-enhancing policies.

Second, the objective of tariffs providing greater transparency of protection levels through tariffication has not been fully realized. Tariff Rate Quotas and their administration have resulted in more complex tariff regimes, with different applied rates for the same product, specific and mixed tariffs with both *ad valorem* and specific elements, and high tariffs often applying only to imports above the quotas.

Third, in many cases, tariffication has resulted in higher actual or potential protection than before the Uruguay Round (Ingco 1995, 1997). The tariffication process allowed significant scope for flexibility, resulting in tariff bindings at rates much higher than actual protection rates applied during the base period and prior to 1995. Tariff dispersion and tariff peaks have increased in some countries. Tariffs escalated with the level of processing, particularly in markets for processed tropical products, thereby increasing the level of protection and obstructing the development of value-added activities in developing countries.

Fourth, domestic support remains highly concentrated in a few OECD countries with levels increasing in recent years. In 1994, the EU, U.S., and Japan accounted for about 90 percent of total domestic support by OECD countries. Levels declined during the first years of implementation, coinciding with a marked increase in world prices of grains. This allowed countries to reduce subsidies or in the case of the EU, to impose a tax on cereal exports. Some countries shifted part of their domestic support from amber box programs into less distorting green box programs (which are exempt from global trade disciplines, even though many measures are not totally production- or trade-neutral). In response to low world prices since 1998, domestic support has increased in some OECD countries.

And fifth, although use of export subsidies (illegal since 1955 on nonagricultural products) has been reduced, high levels of export subsidies remain and continue to distort world markets. During 1995–98, WTO members used 42 percent of the budgetary expenditure and 64 percent of the volume allowed for export subsidies, with the EU accounting for 90 percent of all OECD export subsidies. The URAA placed limits on export subsidies for individual commodities but allowed some flexibility. With low usage levels early in the implementation period, when world prices were high, several countries carried forward unused export subsidy credits to be used at a later date. Circumvention—possibly through the subsidy elements in export credits, export restrictions, and revenue-pooling arrangements in major products—is of concern.

## The Present Negotiations: The Doha Round

The current negotiations on agriculture were launched early in 2000, under the terms of Article 20, to carry forward the reform process as defined by the URAA. The November 2001 launch by the WTO Ministerial Conference in Doha of the broader Doha Round with its Doha Development Agenda was seen as a positive development with the mandate for agricultural negotiations being further described in the Doha Declaration, particularly paragraphs 13 and 14 (GATT Article XXXVI:8). The texts closed off few options for the negotiations, except to state that the overall aim remains "fundamental reform encompassing strengthened rules and specific commitments on support and protection in order to correct and prevent restrictions and distortions in world agricultural markets," so as to establish "a fair and market-oriented trading system"(WTO 2000). A direct gain from the Doha launch of broader negotiations will be tariff negotiations on industrial products (agricultural inputs) that are not within the scope of the URAA. Negotiations, in the context of the Agreement on Trade-Related Aspects of Intellectual Property Rights, could improve protection of geographical indicators for food products. The Doha Declaration also modified the terms of reference for the agricultural negotiations themselves, although the practical effects of these modifications remain to be seen. More substantially, the Doha Round opens up possibilities for tradeoffs between trade sectors; WTO members that are unwilling to provide new market openings for agricultural imports, or to limit subsidies to agriculture, may see an advantage in doing so now. The tradeoffs represent bargaining power to obtain commitments from agricultural exporters in other sectors, such as industrial products. Finally, agriculture can benefit from broader trade liberalization if this cuts farmers' costs for nonagricultural goods and services and, more generally, if it reduces an overall bias of national policy against agriculture. Additional benefits may be obtained if the liberalization is expressed in terms of binding WTO commitments, which can simultaneously provide bargaining power to obtain useful concessions from trading partners and add credibility, through the promise of permanence, to a country's own reforms.

Prior to the Doha Declaration, the negotiating process set out and discussed initial proposals ("Phase 1" of the negotiations, March 2000–March 2001) and examined these proposals in depth, issue by issue ("Phase 2," March 2001–February 2002). Altogether, 45 proposals were put forward in Phase 1, with 121 WTO members (some 85 percent of total WTO membership) sponsoring one or more proposals. During Phase 2, WTO members submitted over 100 further papers, almost all informal in character (and therefore not circulated publicly), most of which elaborated or commented on the proposals made during Phase 1. As a result of this two-stage process, a fairly complete view of the ideas, ambitions, and concerns of participants was available. No decisions were taken on any of these proposals, although some clearly enjoyed greater support than others. Nor was the door closed to new ideas.

The Doha Declaration (November 2001) came only toward the end of Phase 2 and it set three new deadlines for the agriculture negotiations:

- March 31, 2003—for the establishment of the modalities for future commitments (that is, the ground rules that will shape members' offers, exceptions, and so on), including provisions for special and differential treatment.
- September 10–14, 2003—the Fifth WTO Ministerial Conference (held in Cancun, Mexico) for members to submit their comprehensive offers based on these modalities.
- January 1, 2005—for concluding the whole negotiating round. In the third phase of the agriculture negotiations, the main focus was on developing the modalities for future commitments to meet the deadline of March 31, 2003. This stage, the first to involve real negotiation, required clarification of, and if possible decisions on, key points such as objectives in terms of overall percentage reductions in tariffs and support, the starting points (reference levels) for these reductions, exceptions, and treatment of past unilateral liberalization. Intensive bargaining—the real core of the negotiations, and almost certainly their most difficult stage—was expected only after the 2003 Mexico meeting, on the basis of each member's comprehensive initial offer. Because final offers demand politically difficult decisions that, in a broad round of negotiations, are never made until governments have a clear view of potential overall gains and losses, this bargaining can be expected to continue and intensify right up to the end of the Doha Round. In any event, the March 31 deadline was not met, thereby postponing decisions and underscoring the importance of the Fifth Ministerial.

### *WTO Committees and Pattern of Negotiations*

The Doha Round as a whole is supervised by an *ad hoc* Trade Negotiations Committee (TNC), chaired by the Director-General of the WTO, under the authority of the WTO's standing General Council, which itself is normally chaired by a national representative elected by the WTO membership. Provision for collective political-level guidance, when necessary, is made primarily through meetings of the WTO's Ministerial Conference. Ministerial Conferences occurred in Singapore (1996), Geneva (1998), Seattle (1999), Doha (2001), and Cancún (2003).

Direct responsibility for the negotiations on agriculture has been given to the Committee on Agriculture meeting for this purpose in special session. This committee has been responsible for the agriculture negotiations since they were launched in 2000, so the post-Doha decisions have not changed their institutional arrangements significantly. WTO members automatically have full membership in all of these bodies. If precedent is followed, the TNC will not, at least until the very end of the negotiations, intervene directly in sectoral negotiations: its task will be to review progress, ensure that the round as a whole continues to move forward, and prepare decisions for adoption by a future conference.

## Issues for Developing Countries in the Current Negotiations

The focus in WTO negotiations on considerations of reciprocity—the idea that each step a participant in negotiations takes toward liberalization is a concession, to be balanced or "paid for" by an equivalent concession from other participants whose trade will benefit—is particularly unhelpful to developing countries. It has been more than 45 years since developed countries pledged in GATT that they would "not expect reciprocity for commitments made by them in trade negotiations to reduce or remove tariffs and other barriers to the trade of less-developed contracting parties" (GATT Article XXXVI:8). However, as long as tariff commitments continue to be assessed by the traditional mercantilist measures, a lesser contribution by developing countries, in terms of tariff cuts or bindings, is likely to reduce their bargaining power.

A related difficulty concerns negotiating credit for unilateral liberalization. "Credit" in tariff negotiations remains based on the extent to which each country reduces its own import duties, or at least binds them (in other words, commits itself not to increase them above stated levels). If a country has, since the previous round of multilateral tariff negotiations, reduced some import duties unilaterally, it is unlikely to be given credit for having done so unless it can document the liberalizing effect and WTO-conformity of these changes, provide undertakings that they will be maintained, and show that trading partners will in fact benefit from them. This issue has frequently been raised by developing countries, but thus far developed countries have been unwilling to give negotiating credit for any liberalization that is not expressed as a binding GATT obligation, included in the scheduled commitments of the country giving it. In addition, there is a perception that although negotiations are in principle concerned with bound (ceiling) tariff rates, less credit is given in practice for binding a lower tariff rate that is already applied than for one that reduces the duty actually faced by imports. Unilateral liberalization is thus not always given the credit it deserves.

For many developing countries, a further problem in negotiations on tariffs and other obstacles to market access is that for most products they are generally among the smaller exporters, and as such may find it difficult to engage with participants with large markets. However, to the extent that larger suppliers can negotiate tariff cuts, smaller players also will benefit because the cuts must be applied either on an MFN basis to all WTO members, or on a basis that is nondiscriminatory among beneficiaries of preferential rates.

Negotiations on trade rules are also influenced by the habit of expecting reciprocity, but less so than those on market access, since rule changes lend themselves less readily to calculations in support of claims of victory or defeat than to the outcome of bargaining on specific trade barriers such as tariffs. Even so, such considerations will certainly arise also in the negotiations on domestic support and export subsidies for agriculture, since a key element in their outcome will be the choice of percentages and other figures that will define permitted subsidy levels, and that, in terms of consideration of reciprocity, will correspond to the tariff reduction formulae applied in market access negotiations.

The concept of reciprocity can help multilateral negotiations by providing bargaining leverage to persuade trading partners to reduce their trade barriers. It is also vague enough that each participant can claim, when the final bargain is struck, to have given less than it has won, thereby enlisting domestic support for the outcome. But it puts developing countries at some disadvantage, and it can be seriously damaging—most of all to the countries whose governments that invoke it—to the extent that it encourages mercantilism and diverts attention away from real economic interests.

A considerable problem for many developing countries is their own limited resources available to participate meaningfully in the negotiations. The core institution for the agriculture negotiations will probably remain the special sessions of the Committee on Agriculture, and its meetings—so far, held about four times a year in Geneva—will set the pattern of work in this sector. Typically, for agriculture as for other subjects dealt with in the WTO, the pattern of multilateral work is a cyclical one, each cycle being completed by a periodic meeting of the core institution. In parallel with all these multilateral activities directly tied to the periodic special sessions of the Committee on Agriculture, there are also many bilateral meetings, particularly in the later stages when bargaining is taking place on tariffs and other specific barriers to market access for particular products. The meetings make considerable demands on all participants but especially those from smaller developing countries where the representation in Geneva and back-up in the national capital is a significant drain on resources. And while many developing countries form coalitions of interests and can seek guidance from the WTO's Secretariat and other bodies, the final responsibility for the negotiations remains with each country as its Schedule of Commitments becomes part of the WTO treaty obligations.

## Chapter Annex: Notification Requirements

### *Market Access*

Market Access commitments require notifications as follows:

Market Access: 1 Administration of Tariff Quotas: A single notification is required of method of allocation, with *ad hoc* notifications made subsequently if there are changes.

Market Access: 2 Imports under Tariff Quotas: This shows the volume of imports made under tariff quotas, relative to the market access opportunities. Notification is required annually.

### *Special Safeguards*

For SSGs, notification requirements take the following forms:

Market Access: 3 Volume-Based SSG: The volume-based notification should as far as practicable be made before taking such action for the first time in any year for each product, and in any event within 10 days of the implementation of such action.

Market Access: 4 Price-Based SSG: The price-based notification can be used either to provide an up-front notification of trigger prices or, on a case-by-case basis, for the first use of the price-based SSG for any particular product. The notification should be to the extent possible in advance, but in any event within 10 days of the taking of such action.

Market Access: 5 Annual Notification: An annual notification should be made indicating the use of the special safeguard provisions in any year. The notification should be submitted no later than 30 days following the year in question. If the special safeguard provisions have not been invoked in any year, a statement to this effect should be made.

### *Domestic Support (DS)*

Notification requirements for domestic support take the following forms:

DS:1: Summary of Current Total AMS: All members with base and annual commitment levels shown in Section 1 of Part IV of their Schedule are required to make a notification 90 days after the end of their marketing or fiscal year. This table shows the result for the previous 12-month period. Supporting tables DS:1 to DS:9 contain the details of the calculation.

DS:1: Supporting Table DS:1: Lists the Green Box measures that are exempt from reduction commitments. Under each of the headings contained in Annex 2 the reporting member is required to give a brief description of each measure, its value, and the data source.

DS:1: Supporting Table DS:2: Developing-country members using the exceptions listed in Article 6.2 are required to list the measures under each of the three headings of Article 6.2 (investment subsidies, input subsidies, and diversification from illicit narcotic crops) along with a brief description of the measures, their value, and the data source.

DS:1: Supporting Table DS:3: Those members making use of the exception from AMS commitments under Article 6.5 for direct payments under production-limiting programs must list the programs, the monetary value of the measures, and the data source.

DS:1: Supporting Table DS:4: This summarizes the product-specific AMS. Details of the individual elements are in other tables.

DS:1: Supporting Table DS:5: This table includes data on market price support schemes for each product, and covers intervention schemes through which the state buys products at certain minimum prices. The data must include the description of the basic product, the applicable year, the name of the measure, the applied administrative price, the external reference price, the eligible production, any associated levies or fees, and the total market price support for each product.

DS:1: Supporting Table DS:6: Includes data on nonexempt direct payments. This would normally cover deficiency price schemes whereby farmers are paid the difference between the price they get on the market and the target price set by the government. Similar to Supporting Table DS:5, the data must include the basic product, the year, the name of the measure, the applied administrative price, the external reference price, the eligible production, the total price-related direct payments, other nonexempt direct payments, associated fees, and the total value of direct payments.

DS:1: Supporting Table DS:7: If there are any remaining product-specific supports, they are included in this supporting table. This could include subsidies per hectare planted or per animal that are not related to price but are aimed at increasing production. Also included in Supporting Table DS:7 are the results from Supporting Tables DS:5 and DS:6.

DS:1: Supporting Table DS:8: For market price support schemes under which the price gap method of calculating the AMS is not practicable, the Equivalent Measurement of Support is calculated as set out in Annex 4 of the Agreement on Agriculture and notified in Supporting Table DS:8. This could include an intervention scheme of limited application or the cost of disposing of surpluses. The budgetary outlay associated with the scheme is usually used in the calculation.

DS:1: Supporting Table DS:9: This shows general non-product-specific supports.

### *Green Box Measures*

Table DS:2: New Green Box Measures: New or modified domestic support measures exempt from reduction are notified to the Committee on Agriculture on an *ad hoc* basis.

### *Export Subsidies (ES)*

Export subsidy notifications take the following forms:

ES:1 Budgetary Outlay and Quantity Reduction Commitments: Members with base and annual commitments in Section II of Part IV of their Schedules must make an annual notification along with Supporting Table ES:1.

ES:1 Supporting Table ES:1: This shows the details of the export subsidies provided.

ES:2 Notification of Total Exports: Members with export subsidy commitments, along with those members that are significant exporters of the different product groups (that is, members accounting for over 5 percent of world exports) make an annual notification showing the total value of exports of the product group concerned.

Statement of Non-Use of Export Subsidies: Members with no export subsidy commitments must make an annual statement stating that no such subsidies have been used in the past year.

Statement of Non-Use: Supporting Table ES:2: Developing-country members using the exemption in Article 9:4 for marketing and internal transport are required to list these subsidies, along with the volume of goods benefiting from them.

ES:3 Food Aid: Food aid donors are required to make an annual notification showing the total volume of food aid given in the previous year. Donors with export subsidy commitments will have already provided this information in ES:1 notification and therefore do not need to make an ES:3 notification.

### *Marrakesh Declaration*

Notification takes the following form:

NF:1: Notification under Article 16.2: Annual notification sets out the quantity of food aid provided to LDCs and NFIDCs, the proportion in fully grant form, and technical assistance provided for developing productivity and infrastructure.

## Notes

1. All individual Uruguay Round agreements, decisions, understandings, and declarations are in "The Legal Texts: The Results of the Uruguay Round of Multilateral Trade Negotiations." Other documents pertaining to the WTO may be found online through the organization's website.

2. Material for this section is largely drawn from Josling, Tangermann, and Warley's (1996) excellent description of the history of agriculture in the GATT.

## Select Bibliography

Anderson, K., Erwidodo, and M. Ingco. 1999. "Integrating Agriculture into the WTO: The Next Phase." Paper prepared for the World Bank's Conference on Developing Countries and the Millennium Round, WTO, September 19–20, Geneva.

Croome, John. 1999. *Reshaping the World Trading System: A History of the Uruguay Round.* New York: Kluwer.

Ingco, M. D. 1995. "Agricultural Trade Liberalization in the Uruguay Round: One Step Forward, One Step Back?"

Supplementary paper prepared for a World Bank Conference on the Uruguay Round and the Developing Countries, January 26–27, Washington, D.C.

———. 1997. "Has Agricultural Trade Liberalization Improved Welfare in the Least-Developed Countries? Yes." Policy Research Working Paper No. 1748. International Trade Division, International Economics Department, The World Bank, Washington, D.C.

Ingco, M. D., and F. Ng. 1998. "Distortionary Effects of State Trading in Agriculture: Issues for the Next Round of Multilateral Trade Negotiations." Policy Research Working Paper 1915, Development Research Group, World Bank, Washington, D.C.

Josling, Timothy E., Stefan Tangermann, and T. K. Warley. 1996. *Agriculture in the GATT*. New York: Palgrave Macmillan.

Mitchell, D. O., M. D. Ingco, and R. C. Duncan. 1997. *The World Food Outlook*. Trade and Development Series. Cambridge, New York, and Melbourne: Cambridge University Press.

WTO (World Trade Organization). 1997. "Appellate Body Report, EC–Regime for the Importation, Sale, and Distribution of Bananas." 25 September, WT/DS27/AB/R. Office of the Secretary General, Geneva.

———. 1999. "Decision by the Arbitrators. Regime for the Importation, Sale, and Distribution of Bananas: Recourse to Arbitration by the European Communities under Article 22.6 of the DSU." 9 April, WT/DS27/ARB. Office of the Secretary General, Geneva.

———, ed. 2000. *The Legal Texts: The Results of the Uruguay Round of Multilateral Trade Negotiations*. Cambridge: Cambridge University Press.

———. 2001. "Doha Ministerial Declaration." 20 November, WT/MIN(01)/ DEC/1. Office of the Secretary General, Geneva.

———. 2002a. "Report of the Appellate Body: U.S.—Tax Treatment for 'Foreign Sales Corporations' Recourse to Article 21.5 of the DSU by The European Communities." 14 January, WT/DS108/AB/RW. Office of the Secretary General, Geneva.

———. 2002b. "Special Agricultural Safeguard." Background Paper by the Secretariat, Revision. 19 February, G/AG/NG/S/9/Rev.1. Office of the Secretary General, Geneva.

3

# EXPORT COMPETITION POLICIES

*Harry de Gorter, Lilian Ruiz, and Merlinda D. Ingco*

## Introduction

The Uruguay Round Agreement on Agriculture (URAA) instituted important commitments to reduce agricultural protection in the area of export competition. The purpose of this chapter is to review and evaluate the export subsidy commitments in the URAA in the implementation period. The effectiveness of the disciplines imposed on export subsidies are assessed. Options are presented for new multilateral rules to improve disciplines on export subsidies in the current World Trade Organization (WTO) trade negotiations on agriculture.

A total of 25 WTO members can subsidize exports, but only for products on which they have commitments in their schedules to reduce the subsidies. Those without commitments cannot subsidize agricultural exports at all. Some among the 25 have decided to greatly reduce their subsidies or drop them completely since the URAA was signed. The agreement includes certain temporary exemptions for developing countries, allowing them to subsidize marketing and transport (Article 9.4).[1]

Limits on and reductions in the volume and value of export subsidies are the key policy commitment on export competition in the URAA. Each country agreed to reduce the volume of subsidized exports by 21 percent over six years from a 1986–90 base period level (14 percent over a 10-year period for developing countries), and reduce the value of export subsidies by 36 percent (24 percent over 10 years for developing countries). The URAA provides flexibility by allowing countries to redistribute the value of subsidies or the volume of subsidized exports over years but the cumulative totals through the year 2000–01 are not to exceed those that would have resulted from full compliance. Countries were also permitted to aggregate products to a limited degree within a commodity group in their commitments. The reductions apply to each of 23 product categories (see table 3.1). The least-developed countries are not subject to reduction commitments (Article 15.2).

World Trade Organization notifications on export subsidies required by each country annually have the European Union (EU) spending the biggest share (over 80 percent) of total world export subsidies (table 3.2). The EU had a similar share of subsidies in the baseline period (figure 3.1). The United States (U.S.) export subsidy expenditures were less than those of several countries including South Africa (which eliminated export subsidies in 1997) and Switzerland. Canada eliminated transportation subsidies for exports and thereby reduced its support in this category dramatically (see table 3.3).

**TABLE 3.1 Percentage of Total Export Volume Receiving Export Subsidies**

| | 1995–96 | | 1996–97 | | 1997–98 | | 1998–99 | |
|---|---|---|---|---|---|---|---|---|
| Country | All | OECD | All | OECD | All | OECD | All | OECD |
| Wheat and Flour | 7.1 | 6.0 | 20.4 | 21.0 | 22.0 | 23.0 | 24.1 | 24.0 |
| Coarse Grains | 33.9 | 33.0 | 41.3 | 45.0 | 37.9 | 43.0 | 55.4 | 59.0 |
| Rice | 13.6 | 4.0 | 24.3 | 10.0 | 14.5 | 3.0 | 15.6 | 52.0 |
| Oilseeds | 0.1 | 0.0 | 0.1 | 0.0 | 0.0 | 0.0 | 0.0 | 0.0 |
| Vegetable Oil | 6.4 | 0.0 | 5.8 | 0.0 | 2.7 | 0.0 | 0.4 | 0.0 |
| Oilcakes | 0.0 | 0.0 | 0.0 | 0.0 | 0.0 | 0.0 | 0.0 | 0.0 |
| Sugar | 15.2 | 19.0 | 20.1 | 29.0 | 26.7 | 30.0 | 21.6 | 28.0 |
| Butter and Butter Oil | 39.0 | 99.0 | 54.5 | 103.0 | 35.6 | 109.0 | 93.9 | 104.0 |
| Milk Powder | 64.0 | 89.0 | 64.0 | 88.0 | 39.7 | 68.0 | 73.2 | 74.0 |
| Cheese | 11.9 | 78.0 | 43.6 | 76.0 | 9.9 | 76.0 | 7.6 | 61.0 |
| Other Milk Products | 92.9 | 81.0 | 57.2 | 79.0 | 54.6 | 78.0 | 53.7 | 74.0 |
| Beef | 44.8 | 58.0 | 43.8 | 70.0 | 31.5 | 61.0 | 30.3 | 40.0 |
| Pig Meat | 15.2 | 38.0 | 9.0 | 31.0 | 7.3 | 20.0 | 22.8 | 52.0 |
| Poultry Meat | 24.1 | 25.0 | 13.7 | 14.0 | 11.9 | 13.0 | 11.6 | 13.0 |
| Sheep Meat | 5.6 | 49.0 | 4.8 | 17.0 | 6.3 | 6.0 | 1.9 | 2.0 |
| Live Animals | 12.0 | 34.0 | 10.7 | 41.0 | 0.1 | 0.0 | 3.4 | 3.0 |
| Eggs | 9.4 | 52.0 | NA | 42.0 | 3.0 | 50.0 | 17.5 | 17.0 |
| Wine | 3.4 | 26.0 | 5.2 | 28.0 | 6.1 | 23.0 | 6.7 | 24.0 |
| Fruits and Vegetables | 12.0 | 28.0 | NA | 33.0 | 65.8 | 29.0 | NA | NA |
| Tobacco | 5.4 | 4.0 | 3.6 | 1.0 | 1.1 | 0.0 | 1.9 | 0.0 |
| Cotton | 0.4 | 0.0 | 0.0 | 0.0 | 0.0 | 0.0 | 0.0 | 0.0 |
| Incorporated Products | 31.0 | 0.0 | 20.6 | 0.0 | 22.7 | 0.0 | 15.3 | 16.0 |
| Other Agricultural Products | 8.7 | 23.0 | 1.9 | 72.0 | 2.4 | 56.0 | 2.1 | 0.0 |

*Source:* Ruiz (2000).

**TABLE 3.2 Total Export Subsidy Commitments**

| | Base | 1995/96 | 1996/97 | 1997/98 | 1998/99 | 1999/2000 | 2000 bound |
|---|---|---|---|---|---|---|---|
| European Union (million US$) | 14,800 | 6,292 | 6,684 | 4,915 | 5,835 | 5,588 | 9,400 |
| United States (million US$) | 930 | 26 | 122 | 113 | 150 | 80 | 600 |
| World Total (million US$) | 20,000 | 6,991 | 7,489 | 5,729 | 6,477 | 5,972 | 13,400 |

*Source:* World Trade Organization.

Most observers consider the rules on export subsidies to be the most important element of the URAA (for example, IATRC 2001a, 2001b). However, a closer examination of the evidence reveals that the reduction commitments are less effective than originally thought. The base period from which reductions were agreed was unrepresentative, since it was a time of low world prices and high levels of export subsidies. Both "front-loading" and "rollover" occurred. In the former, countries could designate a different base period while in the latter, subsidy commitments could be banked across years if unused, to be used later in the implementation period. Several countries converted export subsidy policies into domestic support, which was convenient because the restrictions on the aggregate measurement of support were weak (see chapter 6).

### *The Plan of This Chapter*

The following sections will address how effective the disciplines on export competition are by evaluating the ways in which countries have circumvented their commitments, the efficacy of value *versus* volume reduction commitments, consumer-financed export subsidies, and other issues such as how food aid, export credits, public stocks, and state trading enterprises (STEs) can subsidize exports.

## Circumvention of Export Subsidy Reduction Commitments

The baseline for the export subsidy reductions was calculated in both volume and value terms as an average level applied by the countries on export subsidies from 1986–90. However, reductions could be made from the 1991–92 levels if higher than the 1986–90 average. By taking advantage of this mechanism ("front-loading"), countries were able to increase their export subsidies expenditures from the 1986–90 levels and start the reductions from a higher level.

The schedule of reductions imposed equal annual reduction instalments on a commodity-specific basis. However, the agreement provided flexibility by allowing countries to redistribute the value of subsidies or the volume of subsidized exports from the second to the fifth year of the implementation period. Allowing countries to "bank" unused subsidies from previous periods was subject to conditions in Article 9.2(b):

- The cumulative amounts of budgetary outlays and quantities of subsidized exports, from the beginning of the implementation period through the year in question, could not exceed the cumulative amounts that would have resulted from full compliance with the relevant annual outlay and quantity commitment levels specified in the country's schedule by more than 3 percent and 1.75 percent, respectively, of the base period levels; and
- The total cumulative amounts of budgetary outlays for such export subsidies and the quantities benefiting from such export subsidies over the entire implementation period could be no greater than the totals that would have resulted from full compliance with the relevant annual commitment levels specified in the country's schedule.[2]

Export subsidies that are subject to reductions include direct export payments by governments to firms, industries, or producers of agricultural products contingent on export performance; subsidized stock exports; producer-financed export subsidies; export marketing cost subsidies; export-specific transportation subsidies; and subsidies on goods incorporated into exports. Export subsidies may not be extended to commodities that are not subsidized in the base period. Widely available export market promotion and advisory services, exempted from reduction commitments, were to be negotiated later. Countries were also permitted to aggregate products within a commodity group in their commitments. This flexibility allowed countries to switch subsidies among commodities within the same group.

An important indicator of the use of export subsidies is the proportion of total exports that are subsidized. This is a measure of the overall reliance on export subsidies for a given commodity. WTO notifications reveal that the figures for subsidized exports and total exports are different, with no explanation regarding the mechanism by which a certain volume is subsidized and the remaining is not. Table 3.1 shows the share of total exports that received export subsidies in each period. The two columns for each period compare the share of total exports receiving export subsidies for all 25 countries' exports with the share for Organisation for Economic Co-operation and Development (OECD) countries' exports only.

The disparity in the percentage use of export subsidies between the two columns for each period shows that, in general, OECD countries subsidize exports more. In addition, most countries did not make use of export subsidies for a significant share of their exports. However, most of the agricultural exports for OECD (industrial) countries rely on subsidization to some extent. For some commodities, the share of subsidized exports is even larger than 100 percent, because some countries report data from export certificates issued, which do not always result in actual exports. The products that rely most heavily on export subsidies are dairy and meat products with the least for oilseeds, sheepmeat, and live animals.

The use of the countries' respective export subsidy value commitment for each period is shown in table 3.3, ranging from 0 percent use in Uruguay to

**FIGURE 3.1 Baseline Allocation of the Value of Export Subsidies**

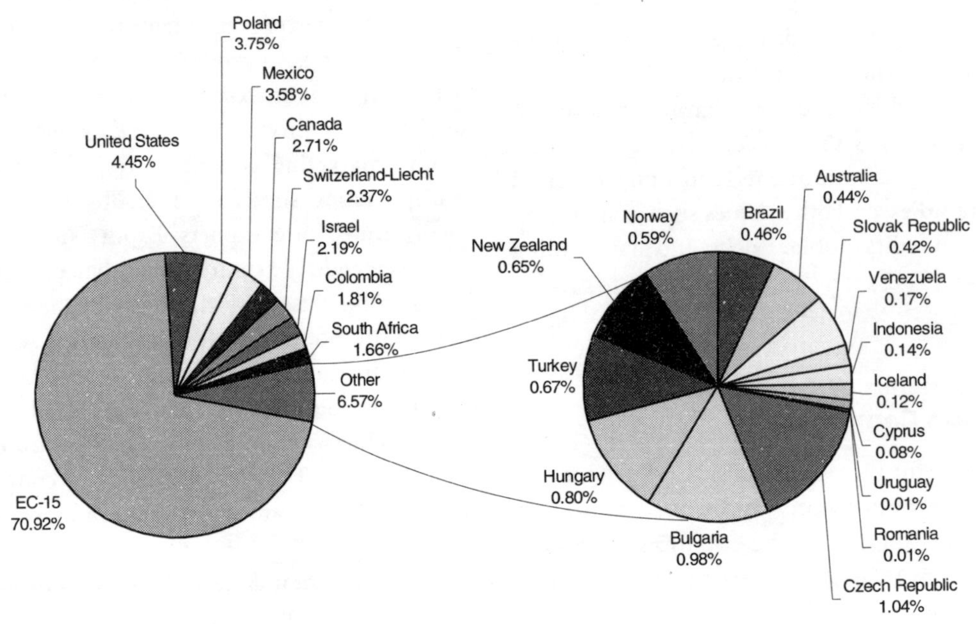


**TABLE 3.3 Percentage Use of Value Commitments by Country**

| Country | 1995–96 | 1996–97 | 1997–98 | 1998–99 |
|---|---|---|---|---|
| Australia | 0 | 0 | 0 | 0 |
| Brazil | 0 | 0 | 0 | 0 |
| Bulgaria | 0 | 0 | 0 | 0 |
| Canada | 7 | 1 | 0 | 0 |
| Colombia | 4 | 5 | 6 | 6 |
| Cyprus | 18 | 17 | 12 | 23 |
| Czech Republic | 29 | 33 | 34 | 42 |
| EC-15 | 42 | 51 | 44 | 58 |
| Hungary | 25 | 14 | 10 | 15 |
| Iceland | 21 | 3 | 1 | 0 |
| Indonesia | 0 | 0 | 0 | 0 |
| Israel | 34 | 24 | 11 | 2 |
| Latvia | 0 | 0 | 0 | 0 |
| Mexico | 0 | 0 | 0 | 0 |
| New Zealand | 0 | 0 | 0 | 0 |
| Norway | 57 | 59 | 94 | 86 |
| Poland | 0 | 36 | 21 | 30 |
| Romania | 0 | 0 | 0 | 0 |
| Slovak Republic | 15 | 22 | 34 | 31 |
| South Africa | 17 | 23 | 11 | 3 |
| Switzerland | 82 | 79 | 74 | 81 |
| Turkey | 53 | 91 | 76 | 66 |
| Uruguay | 0 | 0 | 0 | 0 |
| United States | 2 | 12 | 12 | 18 |
| Venezuela | 9 | 60 | 7 | 0 |

*Source:* Ruiz (2000).

**TABLE 3.4 Percentage Allocation of Total Value Commitments by Commodity**

| Period | Base | 1995–96 | 1996–97 | 1997–98 | 1998–99 |
|---|---|---|---|---|---|
| Wheat and Flour | 17.86 | 21.54 | 21.40 | 20.86 | 19.93 |
| Coarse Grains | 12.47 | 11.94 | 11.96 | 11.95 | 11.64 |
| Rice | 1.12 | 1.16 | 1.30 | 1.38 | 1.68 |
| Oilseeds | 0.58 | 0.52 | 0.54 | 0.53 | 0.30 |
| Vegetable Oil | 0.82 | 0.91 | 0.91 | 0.90 | 0.92 |
| Oilcakes | 0.03 | 0.03 | 0.03 | 0.03 | 0.00 |
| Sugar | 5.62 | 5.52 | 5.57 | 5.62 | 5.80 |
| Butter and Butter Oil | 10.03 | 9.98 | 10.03 | 10.08 | 10.14 |
| Milk Powder | 4.17 | 4.06 | 4.11 | 4.20 | 4.27 |
| Cheese | 4.07 | 4.66 | 4.60 | 4.45 | 4.32 |
| Other Milk Products | 9.39 | 9.59 | 9.54 | 9.54 | 9.91 |
| Beef | 13.21 | 13.60 | 13.58 | 13.65 | 13.69 |
| Pig Meat | 2.31 | 2.30 | 2.29 | 2.26 | 2.34 |
| Poultry Meat | 1.37 | 1.27 | 1.26 | 1.23 | 1.30 |
| Sheep Meat | 0.31 | 0.17 | 0.17 | 0.17 | 0.06 |
| Live Animals | 0.23 | 0.25 | 0.25 | 0.25 | 0.31 |
| Eggs | 0.49 | 0.48 | 0.49 | 0.49 | 0.51 |
| Wine | 0.51 | 0.47 | 0.47 | 0.47 | 0.48 |
| Fruits and Vegetables | 2.44 | 1.99 | 2.09 | 2.41 | 2.73 |
| Tobacco | 0.67 | 0.77 | 0.74 | 0.71 | 0.61 |
| Cotton | 0.43 | 0.45 | 0.53 | 0.57 | 0.74 |
| Incorporated Products | 6.32 | 6.45 | 6.17 | 6.23 | 6.28 |
| Other Agricultural Products | 0.67 | 0.43 | 0.39 | 0.47 | 0.47 |

*Source:* Ruiz (2000).

86 percent in Norway in the period 1998–99. Countries did not exceed their total expenditure commitments. The same aggregate analysis by country cannot be made with respect to volumes, owing to the differences in units of the various commodity groups. That is, it is problematic to aggregate metric tons of commodities that differ greatly—such as honey and whey powder. Table 3.3 shows that, on a country-by-country basis, value commitments are not binding.

However, on a commodity basis, the analysis of the use of value allowances generates different results. Table 3.4 shows the percentage allocation of total export subsidy expenditure commitments for each period to each commodity group. The largest percentage allocation of value commitments is for wheat, coarse grains, dairy products, and beef. The differences in the percentage allowances during the implementation period are due to front-loading (when reductions were made from a value larger than the 1986–90 average) and also due to exchange rate effects. In terms of the actual expenditures, meat, dairy, and related products used the largest proportions of the total expenditures in export subsidies, averaging more than 70 percent for the period 1995–99. (Meats accounted for 25 percent, dairy for 34 percent, and incorporated products for 12 percent.)

Table 3.5 shows the percentage use of the value allowances allocated to each commodity group.[3] Coarse grains and wheat used a smaller proportion of the allowances, owing to the high world prices in the beginning of the implementation period (1995–98). Sugar exceeded the commitments, as well as wine during 1996–97. Pig meat exceeded the commitments during 1998–99. The largest percentage use of the commitments is that of dairy, meats, and incorporated products.

Table 3.6 shows the percentage use of the volume allowances allocated to each commodity group.[4] Coarse grains and wheat used a small proportion of the allowances during 1995–96 owing to the high

**TABLE 3.5 Percentage Use of the Total Value Commitments Allocated to Each Commodity Group**

| Period | 1995–96 | 1996–97 | 1997–98 | 1998–99 |
|---|---|---|---|---|
| Wheat and Wheat Flour | 4 | 11 | 7 | 22 |
| Coarse Grains | 18 | 24 | 18 | 57 |
| Rice | 18 | 41 | 19 | 13 |
| Oilseeds | 0 | 0 | 0 | 0 |
| Vegetable Oil | 47 | 31 | 7 | 1 |
| Oilcakes | 0 | 0 | 0 | 0 |
| Sugar | 48 | 72 | 112 | 121 |
| Butter and Butter Oil | 19 | 42 | 25 | 25 |
| Milk Powder | 31 | 46 | 38 | 70 |
| Cheese | 72 | 52 | 42 | 43 |
| Other Milk Products | 70 | 74 | 81 | 88 |
| Beef | 76 | 83 | 49 | 41 |
| Pig Meat | 30 | 24 | 30 | 133 |
| Poultry Meat | 68 | 43 | 52 | 64 |
| Sheep Meat | 35 | 16 | 21 | 19 |
| Live Animals | 58 | 32 | 0 | 1 |
| Eggs | 22 | 14 | 25 | 33 |
| Wine | 89 | 109 | 72 | 58 |
| Fruits and Vegetables | 37 | 37 | 22 | 24 |
| Tobacco | 17 | 5 | 1 | 1 |
| Cotton | 0 | 0 | 0 | 0 |
| Incorporated Products | 67 | 83 | 86 | 98 |
| Other Agricultural Products | 5 | 24 | 3 | 4 |

*Source:* Ruiz (2000).

world prices. However, the use increased sharply after 1996, and it became close to binding for coarse grains during 1998–99. Sugar, milk powder, and other milk products have also increased the use of volume allowances to levels very close to the limits. Pig meat exceeded the commitments during 1998–99 because of a sharp increase of 350 percent in European subsidized exports. Dairy products, meat (beef and pork) products, and wine make the largest percentage use of the volume commitments.

The percentage use of value and volume allowances shows that the commitments are binding for some commodity groups, while for others they are far above the actual volumes and values used. By averaging the percentage use of commitments presented in tables 3.5 and 3.6, the data show that, on average, 36 percent of the value allowances have been used, while 45 percent of the volume allowances have been used. These figures suggest that the volume limits have been more binding than the value limits. This is a result of decrease in the domestic support price of several important commodities (the EU even taxed exports of cereals in the beginning of the implementation period), and increases in world market prices, which reduced the need for large per unit export subsidies.

Reduction commitments have been more binding for some specific commodities when analyzed in a more detailed breakdown of commodity sectors and countries than that presented so far. But as indicated in tables 3.1–3.6, commitments have not generally been binding in aggregate. The effectiveness of the limits imposed on value and volume on export subsidies depends on several factors, such as world prices and shifts in excess supply and demand, "banking" of unused subsidies, and "rollovers." Several other factors determine the effectiveness of the reduction commitments—such as the particular baseline that was used.

**TABLE 3.6 Percentage Use of the Total Volume Commitments Allocated to Each Commodity Group**

| Commodity | 1995–96 | 1996–97 | 1997–98 | 1998–99 |
|---|---|---|---|---|
| Wheat and Wheat Flour | 8.0 | 27.0 | 26.0 | 39.0 |
| Coarse Grains | 33.0 | 54.0 | 42.0 | 96.0 |
| Rice | 17.0 | 44.0 | 30.0 | 29.0 |
| Oilseeds | 0.2 | 0.2 | 0.0 | 0.0 |
| Vegetable Oil | 13.0 | 15.0 | 11.0 | 2.0 |
| Oilcakes | 0.0 | 0.0 | 0.0 | 0.0 |
| Sugar | 34.0 | 50.0 | 88.0 | 74.0 |
| Butter and Butter Oil | 28.0 | 55.0 | 37.0 | 35.0 |
| Milk Powder | 66.0 | 63.0 | 54.0 | 80.0 |
| Cheese | 95.0 | 95.0 | 83.0 | 65.0 |
| Other Milk Products | 91.0 | 93.0 | 95.0 | 88.0 |
| Beef | 79.0 | 97.0 | 79.0 | 65.0 |
| Pig Meat | 54.0 | 44.0 | 37.0 | 120.0 |
| Poultry Meat | 74.0 | 71.0 | 77.0 | 74.0 |
| Sheep Meat | 61.0 | 58.0 | 49.0 | 3.0 |
| Live Animals | 56.0 | 41.0 | 0.4 | 2.0 |
| Wine | 66.0 | 99.0 | 98.0 | 83.0 |
| Tobacco | 11.0 | 7.0 | 2.0 | 4.0 |
| Other Agricultural Products | 13.0 | 2.0 | 4.0 | 7.0 |

*Source:* Ruiz (2000).

### *Binding Commitments and the Rollover of Unused Export Subsidies*

Several countries exceeded the export subsidy value and volume allowances throughout the implementation period. The excess is justified by the countries as being "unused subsidies rolled over to subsequent years," in accordance to the flexibility offered in Article 9.2(b) of the URAA. This flexibility has also been called "banking." The "banking" practice weakens the effect of the reduction commitments, allowing strategic trade behavior in exploiting market share and allowing countries to circumvent export subsidy commitments. Several countries resorted to the "banking" practice, including the EU countries, U.S., Poland, and Norway.

The countries that are close to or above the export subsidy value limits are shown in table 3.7. The value commitments have been binding on various occasions, and it is clear that more countries exceeded the commitments as the end of the implementation period approached. Some commitments were exceeded by more than 300 percent. The EU countries' expenditures were above the 2000–01 bound rates for several commodities during the implementation period, and in some cases, including alcohol, pig meat, and sugar, exceeded the annual commitments.

The countries that reached or exceeded the export subsidy volume limits are shown in table 3.8. The products that are close to or above the volume commitment levels most often are dairy, meats, sugar, and rice. The limits on coarse grains became more binding during 1998–99, whereas in the former periods, wheat and coarse grains had been well below the commitment levels. The volume commitments again became more binding as the end of the implementation period approached. The same occurred with the value commitments.

### *The Baseline and the Front-Loading Flexibility*

The reduction commitments are based on 1986–90, a period of unusually high export subsidies worldwide. The base period, calculated as an average of the values and volumes applied during 1986–90, resulted in commitments that are, in general, higher than the actual levels applied during the implementation period. Moreover, countries were

**TABLE 3.7 Countries Using over 90 Percent of Value Commitments**

| Member | Commodity | 1995–96 | 1996–97 | 1997–98 | 1998–99 |
|---|---|---|---|---|---|
| Colombia | Sugar | — | 105 | — | 95 |
| Cyprus | Cheese | 406 | 100 | 100 | 100 |
| EC-15 | Alcohol | — | 90 | — | 106 |
| EC-15 | F & V | 92 | — | — | — |
| EC-15 | Other Milk Products | — | — | — | 92 |
| EC-15 | Pig Meat | — | — | — | 155 |
| EC-15 | Rice | — | 141 | — | — |
| EC-15 | Sugar | — | — | 122 | 134 |
| EC-15 | Wine | — | 111 | — | — |
| Hungary | Corn | 282 | — | — | 413 |
| Hungary | Red Pepper Meal | 147 | 141 | — | — |
| Norway | Bovine Meat | — | — | — | 106 |
| Norway | Cheese | — | — | 113 | 117 |
| Norway | Poultry Meat | 243 | — | — | — |
| Norway | Processed Products | 97 | — | 92 | — |
| Norway | Sheep Meat | — | — | 112 | — |
| South Africa | Cocoa and Prep. | 108 | 323 | 99 | — |
| South Africa | Tea | 112 | — | — | — |
| South Africa | Waters | — | 144 | — | — |
| South Africa | Wine Products | 94 | 179 | 107 | — |
| Switzerland | Cattle for Breeding | 94 | — | — | — |
| Switzerland | Fruits | — | — | — | 91 |
| Switzerland | Processed Prods. | — | — | — | 100 |
| Turkey | Creams | — | — | — | 98 |
| Turkey | Chocolate | 97 | — | — | — |
| Turkey | F & V | — | 99 | 99 | 100 |
| Turkey | Eggs/Dozen | — | — | 100 | — |
| Turkey | Poultry Meat | 99 | — | — | — |
| United States | Cheese | — | — | — | 96 |
| United States | Other Milk Products | — | — | 100 | 129 |
| United States | Skim Milk Powder | — | — | — | 136 |
| Venezuela | F & V | — | 96 | — | — |

F & V. Fruits and vegetables.
*Source:* Ruiz (2000).

given the flexibility to start the reductions from the 1991–92 levels, if higher than the baseline. This makes the commitments even less effective in reducing trade distortions. With this provision, the subsidies can be higher (during all but the last year of the implementation period) than they would have been if the 1986–90 baseline for reductions had been maintained. An examination of the pattern of use over the implementation period indicates that rather than a gradual reduction as intended by the URAA, subsidies in some cases remained high or even increased in some years.

Tables 3.9 and 3.10 show selected cases in which countries have a higher level of subsidies compared to the baseline, in terms of both value and volume. The column for 1986–90 shows the levels for value/volume in the baseline in table 3.9. The next column shows that the average levels for 1991–92 are higher than the 1986–90 average baseline levels. In these cases, the reductions started from the 1991–92 average. The first year of the implementation period is shown in column 1995–96. The reduction commitment levels in 1995–96 are higher than the 1986–90 baseline because they are

**TABLE 3.8 Countries Using over 90 Percent of Volume Commitments**

| Member | Commodity | 1995–96 | 1996–97 | 1997–98 | 1998–99 |
|---|---|---|---|---|---|
| Colombia | Fruits | — | — | 115 | 138 |
| Colombia | Processed Products | 129 | 91 | 19 | — |
| Colombia | Sugar Confection | 316 | 473 | 332 | 1033 |
| Cyprus | Cheese | 189 | 100 | 99 | 100 |
| EC-15 | Coarse Grains | — | 90 | — | 123 |
| EC-15 | Sugar | — | — | 118 | 112 |
| EC-15 | Rice | — | 144 | 103 | 99 |
| EC-15 | Other Milk Products | 98 | 100 | 102 | 91 |
| EC-15 | Cheese | 99 | 99 | — | — |
| EC-15 | Olive Oil | 96 | 104 | — | — |
| EC-15 | Beef Meat | 90 | 110 | 94 | — |
| EC-15 | Poultry Meat | 96 | 99 | 105 | 99 |
| EC-15 | Wine | | 111 | 115 | 98 |
| EC-15 | F & V, Fresh | 99 | 99 | 98 | 93 |
| EC-15 | Eggs | — | — | 90 | 104 |
| Norway | Sheep Meat | — | — | 142 | 106 |
| Norway | Pig Meat | — | — | 106 | — |
| Norway | Cheese | — | — | 102 | 122 |
| Norway | Eggs and Products | — | 99 | 117 | — |
| Norway | Poultry Meat | 214 | — | — | — |
| Poland | Sugar | — | 116 | 149 | 119 |
| Slovak Republic | Sugars | — | — | 100 | 100 |
| Slovak Republic | Other Dairy Products | — | 95 | 99 | 110 |
| South Africa | Beer | 106 | — | 105 | — |
| South Africa | Other Milk Products | 139 | — | — | — |
| South Africa | Wine Products | 103 | 619 | 227 | — |
| Switzerland | Cattle for Breeding | 111 | — | — | — |
| Turkey | F&V, Fresh or Proc. | 100 | 97 | 100 | 100 |
| Turkey | Poultry Meat | 100 | — | — | — |
| United States | Other Milk Products | — | — | 100 | 107 |
| United States | Skim Milk Powder | — | — | 104 | 154 |
| United States | Cheese | — | — | 100 | 93 |

*Note:* F & V = Fruits and vegetables.
*Source:* Ruiz 2000.

based on the 1991–92 average. The last column shows the percentage increase in the base value and volume when using the 1991–92 average instead of the 1986–90 average.

Although Canada only subsidized its butter exports in the first year of the implementation period (1995–96), the front-loading mechanism allowed the volume reductions to start at a volume that was 141 percent higher than the 1986–90 baseline. The 1995–96 commitment level was above the baseline level. In other cases, the increase in the baseline for reductions is still more dramatic. For example, the baseline value of export subsidies for milk products in the U.S. was increased by 426 percent, as shown in table 3.9.

The 1980s were characterized by a period of intensive use of export subsidies for cereals, coarse grains, dairy, and other products. The EU used higher subsidies in the baseline than at the beginning of the 1990s (except for wheat). Therefore, the export subsidy commitment allowances, including the 2000–01 bound levels, are higher than the actual levels in previous years (from 1990–95) for some commodities, which eliminated the need for dramatic changes in the domestic policies to accommodate the export subsidy reduction commitments.

**TABLE 3.9 Value Front-Loading**

| Member | Commodity | 1986–90 Outlays | 1991–92 Outlays | 1995–96 Outlay Commitment | Increase in Base Outlays |
|---|---|---|---|---|---|
| Canada | Butter | 17,227 | 44,444 | 38,874 | 158 |
| EC-15 | Beef Meat | 1,959 | 2,029 | 1, 923 | 4 |
| EC-15 | Cheese | 534 | 550 | 594 | 3 |
| EC-15 | Incorporated Products | 648 | 702 | 717 | 8 |
| EC-15 | Poultry Meat | 142 | 147 | 136 | 4 |
| EC-15 | Raw Tobacco | 63 | 106 | 97 | 69 |
| EC-15 | Wheat | 2,015 | 2,255 | 2,309 | 12 |
| Norway | Bovine Meat | 55 | 116 | 102 | 112 |
| Norway | Cheese | 384 | 596 | 538 | 55 |
| Norway | F & V | 1 | 1 | 1 | 56 |
| Norway | Whey Powder | 04 | 5 | 4 | 1, 225 |
| USA | Eggs (dozen) | 2,505 | 8, 784 | 7,587 | 251 |
| USA | Other Milk Products | 3,277 | 17,244 | 14,374 | 426 |
| USA | Rice | 3,701 | 18,373 | 15,705 | 396 |
| USA | Vegetable Oils | 22,004 | 60,734 | 52,959 | 176 |
| USA | Wheat | 568,460 | 845,836 | 765,499 | 49 |

*Source:* Ruiz (2000).

**TABLE 3.10 Volume Front-Loading**

| Member | Commodity | 1995–96 | 1996–97 | 1997–98 | 1998–99 |
|---|---|---|---|---|---|
| Canada | Butter | 4,431 | 10,657 | 9,464 | 141 |
| EC-15 | Beef Meat | 1,040,100 | 1,179,200 | 1,137,000 | 13 |
| EC-15 | Cheese | 406,700 | 427,000 | 426,500 | 5 |
| EC-15 | Poultry Meat | 362,000 | 470,000 | 434,500 | 30 |
| EC-15 | Raw Tobacco | 140,300 | 206,000 | 190,000 | 47 |
| EC-15 | Wheat | 18,276,000 | 20,255,000 | 20,408,100 | 11 |
| Norway | Bovine Meat | 1,895 | 3,610 | 3,258 | 90 |
| Norway | Cheese | 20,516 | 24,333 | 22,979 | 19 |
| Norway | F & V | 841 | 1,577 | 1,425 | 88 |
| Norway | Whey Powder | 30 | 143 | 123 | 377 |
| United States | Butter and Butter Oil | 36,705 | 47,368 | 42,989 | 77 |
| United States | Cheese | 3,836 | 3,989 | 3,829 | 4 |
| United States | Eggs (dozen) | 8,758,991 | 34,930,255 | 30,261,813 | 299 |
| United States | Other Milk Products | 4,300 | 14,940 | 12,456 | 247 |
| United States | Rice | 48,802 | 318,281 | 271,660 | 552 |
| United States | Vegetable Oils | 178,860 | 676,786 | 587,538 | 278 |
| United States | Wheat | 18,282,354 | 21,381,546 | 20,238,298 | 17 |

*Source:* Ruiz (2000).

The EU and the U.S. used only 42 percent and 2 percent, respectively, of the value allowances in the first year of the implementation period (table 3.3). This was due to the high international prices that caused the decrease in the per unit subsidy necessary, rather than to the commitments themselves. The EU increased the expenditures on sugar, other milk products, pig meat, poultry meat, and eggs during 1997–98 and the expenditures on almost all products during 1998–99 over the previous periods. It also increased the volumes subsidized of almost all products during 1996–97 compared to the 1995–96 levels, of sugar and eggs during 1997–98 and of wheat, coarse grains, skimmed milk, pig meat, and eggs during 1998–99. The U.S. increased the expenditures on all subsidized exports (except for poultry meat) during 1996–97 over 1995–96, and subsequent increases occurred in the dairy products, coarse grain, and poultry sectors. The aggregate expenditures during 1996–97 and 1998–99 were higher than in the previous period in each case. The volume subsidized increased for all subsidized products during 1997–98 with respect to the previous period (1996–97), for dairy products during 1996–97, and for poultry and skimmed milk powder during 1998–99.

### *The Per Unit Subsidy and Asymmetry of Protection*

In comparison with the discipline on tariffs, with bound per unit or *ad valorem* duties, only the total amount of the expenditures (or total volume exported) is regulated for export subsidies. This results in less transparent constraints on the distortion to trade caused by export subsidies, because the same value of export subsidy allocated to a commodity can have different effects on the volume exported and hence on the world price.

Instead of a per unit export subsidy on all exports, governments may be targeting all export subsidies to a few exports for the country in that year because of uncertainty as to how the market will evolve. The per unit subsidy would increase for those exports, enabling governments to maximize the export subsidy value (or to reach a spending target) by subsidizing fewer exports at higher subsidy rates, thereby circumventing quantity limits. The degree of trade distortion created by an export subsidy depends on the conditions of excess supply and demand, and on the amount of export subsidy expenditure. It is possible that a larger amount of export subsidy used by a given country will distort the world price minimally, while a smaller value applied by another country will have a larger impact in decreasing the world price.

In addition, the conditions of trade will influence the way in which a country will allocate its expenditure allowance. With no limit on the per unit subsidy applied, the trade distortion might not be decreased by the current rules, because value and volume constraints will rarely bind at the same time. For example, suppose that the volume limit only is binding. If a shock in the world demand causes the world price to decrease, the exporting country will be able to increase the per unit subsidy, and to continue to export the same quantity at a lower world price. In contrast, if limits were imposed on the amount of distortion in the world price that a subsidy can cause, the country in question would have to decrease the volume exported, causing less distortion in the world price.

Having no limits on per unit subsidies allows export subsidies to isolate the domestic market from changes in the world market. In the above example, when the world price decreases because of an excess demand shock, if the country can increase the per unit subsidy and hence export the same volume, the domestic price for this commodity will not change, despite the drop in price in world markets (Ruiz 2000).

The failure to discipline per unit subsidies creates another problem. As they are not directly linked to the world price or the quantities exported, the rate of subsidization across commodities differs significantly. Therefore, different incentives are created for the commodities involved, because the effective per unit subsidy changes the relative domestic prices with respect to the world markets (the nominal protection rates), adding to the distortions and efficiency losses caused by the export subsidies themselves.

The resource misallocation caused by the use of export subsidies can be represented through the measure of export subsidy equivalents (ESEs), which shows the relationship between the per unit subsidy awarded and the world price of the commodity. Table 3.11 shows ESEs for selected countries and commodities, based on the per unit subsidy calculated in the countries' notifications to the WTO, and free-on-board prices from the

**TABLE 3.11 Export Subsidy Equivalents (ESEs) (percent)**

| Member | Commodity | Base | 1995–96 | 1996–97 | 1997–98 | 1995–97 |
|---|---|---|---|---|---|---|
| European Union | Wheat and Wheat Flour | 104 | 36 | 15 | 10 | 15 |
| European Union | Coarse Grains (Barley) | 142 | 49 | 26 | 28 | 32 |
| European Union | Rice | 226 | 191 | 130 | 148 | 145 |
| European Union | Sugar | 195 | 146 | 151 | 164 | 154 |
| European Union | Butter and Butter Oil | 248 | 102 | 138 | 112 | 118 |
| European Union | Skim Milk Powder | 106 | 36 | 40 | 43 | 39 |
| European Union | Cheese | 86 | 60 | 38 | 29 | 43 |
| European Union | Beef | 102 | 63 | 57 | 49 | 57 |
| European Union | Pig Meat | 111 | 135 | 127 | 378 | 173 |
| European Union | Poultry Meat | 44 | 29 | 16 | 16 | 20 |
| European Union | Eggs | 54 | 20 | 11 | 14 | 15 |
| Hungary | Pig Meat | 105 | 25 | 16 | 6 | 13 |
| Hungary | Sheep Meat | 30 | 11 | 7 | 5 | 8 |
| Hungary | Poultry | 95 | 40 | 16 | 23 | 26 |
| Norway | Beef | 201 | 143 | 141 | 207 | 166 |
| Norway | Pig Meat | 336 | 169 | 125 | 160 | 163 |
| Norway | Sheep Meat | 300 | 89 | 128 | 98 | 116 |
| Norway | Eggs | 354 | 354 | 150 | 162 | 200 |
| Norway | Butter | 127 | 81 | 98 | 90 | 89 |
| Norway | Cheese | 184 | 149 | 151 | 155 | 152 |
| USA | Butter and Butter Oil | 136 | 0 | 117 | 30 | 58 |
| USA | Skim Milk Powder | 114 | 12 | 68 | 53 | 44 |
| USA | Cheese | 98 | 28 | 37 | 53 | 39 |

*Source:* Ruiz (2000).

OECD. The ESE is the ratio of per unit subsidy to world price, multiplied by 100.

Table 3.11 shows that in many cases the per unit export subsidies provided are very high with respect to the world price of the commodity. It is not unusual that the amount the producers or exporters receive from the export subsidy is two or three times larger than the price paid in the world market. The table also shows the asymmetry of the ESE across commodities for the same country. In the EU for example, the ESE for pig meat was 378 percent of the world price during 1997–98, while only 16 percent for poultry meat.

Such asymmetry of incentives will not only distort the domestic productive sector and affect domestic demand, but will also skew the relative incentives (prices) in world markets. During 1995–96, the ESE for skim milk powder in the EU was 36 percent, three times that of the U.S. This difference reflects the different levels of domestic price support, which absorbs differences in the competitive advantages of these two countries. For all these reasons, there is a strong case for regulating the *ad valorem* per unit export subsidy.

Finally, there is the issue of export taxes that are not adequately addressed in the URAA. During years in which world prices are high for traditionally subsidized export commodities, an export tax can be used to prevent an increase in domestic prices relative to world levels, isolating the domestic market from the world market. This protects the domestic processing industry, and also can improve the terms of trade for large exporting countries. This practice, although unregulated by the agreement, is also trade distorting to the extent that it keeps world prices at levels higher than they would otherwise be. This has consequences on food security for developing countries in times of relative shortage. Making supply less responsive to prices only aggravates the problem, contributing to more instability and uncertainty in the food supply. The EU used export taxes on wheat and coarse grains (barley) after the rise in prices that occurred at the beginning of the implementation period in 1995.

## Expenditure versus Quantity Limits

A key policy issue is whether the formula for further cuts in export subsidies should focus on volumes or expenditures or per unit subsidies. Ruiz and de Gorter (2001) analyze the conditions under which volume or value limits will be more binding.

Factors affecting the effectiveness of volume *versus* value limits include the level of world prices and internal price supports, elasticities of excess supply and demand, and the way the free trade equilibrium changes over time with shifts in excess supply and demand. (See the annex to this chapter.)

With regard to the current reduction commitments, value reduction commitments will not generally be binding in a static framework (that is, in a model in which demand and supply schedules do not shift). For value commitments to be binding in such a framework, the percentage reductions in volume *and* value would have to occur within specific ranges. For example, for identical percentage reductions in volume and value, the volume reduction is always more effective. This result is independent of the elasticities of excess supply and excess demand.

Ruiz and de Gorter (2001) determine that the ratio of value over volume reduction commitments is always smaller than the ratio of the initial over the reduced per unit export subsidy. This relationship allows us to predict the effects of bindings on the reduction of per unit subsidies for a given set of market parameters. Using this relationship, a country can predict the final per unit export subsidy resulting from the proposed volume and value reductions for each commodity sector.

Other relationships between value and volume reductions can also be established. For a larger initial per unit export subsidy, other factors being equal, volume reduction commitments are more effective, and for larger initial quantities exported, again other things being equal, value reductions are more likely to bind. This means that with more elastic trade curves, when other factors are constant, value reduction commitments tend to be more effective.

Volume reduction commitments are always more effective than expenditure reduction commitments in the following sense: a less-than-100-percent reduction in the volume of subsidized exports is needed to reach a "free trade" condition (in which the country exports only the same quantity as it would export if it did not offer any export subsidies), whereas a 100 percent reduction in subsidy expenditure is needed to reach this free trade condition if there are no binding volume reduction commitments.

Within a dynamic framework, conditions of trade change, and therefore the analysis needs to include cases where the free trade equilibrium shifts during the export subsidy reduction implementation period, or thereafter. This makes the results more complicated, but the conclusions of the analysis in the annex are, in short, that volume constraints are binding in the case of a positive shift (that is, a shift that moves the free trade equilibrium to the right, or alternatively stated, a shift that reduces the per unit subsidy necessary to achieve a given level of exports), and that expenditure constraints are always binding in the case of a negative shift.

## Consumer-Only Financed Export Subsidies

The agreement has placed limits on taxpayer- and producer-financed export subsidies, but has not recognized "consumer-only-financed" export subsidies.[5] A consumer-only-financed export subsidy exists when a government-sanctioned organization (for example, a marketing board) price-discriminates (that is, charges a higher price in the domestic market than in the export market for the same product) *and* pools revenues to producers (Sumner 1996; Schluep and de Gorter 2001). Such a scheme is similar to a taxpayer-financed export subsidy in that it increases supply and decreases domestic demand alike, but the consumer-financed export subsidy distorts trade more for a given domestic price (Schluep and de Gorter 2001). Both a taxpayer- and a consumer-only-financed export subsidy scheme require import tariffs or nontariff barriers in order to be effective, since both raise the domestic price above the world price of the product. To the extent that such import barriers are reduced under the market access part of the agreement, it may not be of paramount importance to recognize consumer-only-financed export subsidies as a separate issue. However, a number of taxpayer-financed export schemes are not covered in the URAA at all. Examples include the Canada–U.S. wheat agreement (according to which

### BOX 3.1 Two Examples of Consumer-Only-Financed Export Subsidy Schemes

The U.S. Federal Milk Marketing Order is an example of a consumer-financed export subsidy scheme because of higher domestic prices and price pooling (Sumner 1996). In addition, an implicit export subsidy prevails when one or more dairy products are sold in the domestic market at world prices. Supply increases to the export market for those products (sold in domestic markets at world prices as well) for two reasons: consumption of higher-priced products is reduced and pooling causes production to expand. Exports are subsidized even if export revenues for some products are not pooled to farmers (but domestic sales at the world price are). Schluep and de Gorter (2001) provide conditions when such a scheme is a full-fledged export subsidy and when it approaches a production subsidy.

The Federal Order system does not use explicit production controls, but regional price differentials for fluid milk have a similar effect. Because fluid milk prices are not allowed to equalize and consumer fluid prices are higher in high-production-cost regions (with lower weights for low class prices in the pool price), inefficiency in milk production does put somewhat of a brake on total U.S. milk production expansion arising from pooling.

By contrast, New Zealand dairy policy under the control of the producer-controlled dairy board has price discrimination among multiple markets for many products in the world market. Pooling these revenues has the effect of a production subsidy (Schluep and de Gorter 2001). Price discrimination in world markets leads to higher prices for consumers worldwide and therefore lowers consumption and trade. But prices in the more elastic demand markets—which are the markets in which New Zealand competes with other exporters—are lower than they otherwise would be. The producer board also pools downstream profits, domestic price premia, and import quota rents, resulting in an expansion in farm milk supply.

Canada "free-rides" on the U.S.-taxpayer-financed export subsidy—see Peterson, Minten, and de Gorter 1999) and fluid milk premia in several countries (see box 3.1).

Domestic price discrimination for milk used in different products in domestic markets alone acts as a consumer tax. Price discrimination between a nontraded product such as fluid milk and traded products such as butter, and the pooling of revenues (so that the producer is paid a price that is an average of the two) also constitutes an export subsidy. Price discrimination in world markets combined with revenue pooling in the domestic market (such as the New Zealand Dairy Board's practices) acts as a production subsidy. In the presence of an export subsidy, the degree of trade distortion from a production tax differs, depending on whether the subsidy is taxpayer financed, or consumer-only (with the latter always distorting trade). For this reason, or perhaps because of their effects, export subsidies have not been well understood, and consumer-funded export subsidies are inadequately dealt with in the URAA, the Agreement on Subsidies and Countervailing Measures, and Article XVI of the GATT 1994.

## Producer-Financed Export Subsidies

Mandatory or government-regulated producer-financed export subsidies are subject to reduction commitments. A producer-financed export subsidy cannot exist on its own, without a taxpayer- and/or consumer-only-financed export subsidy. Introducing a producer levy when a taxpayer-financed export subsidy is already in place decreases the price to both farmers and consumers. If the levy maintains net price (and producer welfare), the price to consumers increases, as do the tax costs of the program. A producer levy to finance part of the costs of a taxpayer-financed export subsidy program can reduce tax costs only if producer welfare declines.

The situation differs for a producer levy to partially or fully finance exports under a non-taxpayer-financed export subsidy scheme. Indeed, it turns out that a producer levy with a consumer-financed export subsidy scheme results in an identical outcome as a consumer-financed export subsidy in terms of market effects, holding producer welfare constant between the two scenarios (Schluep 1999;

Schluep and de Gorter 2001). A levy imposed on a consumer-only-financed export subsidy results in the same average revenue (pooled domestic and export sales) curve because export revenues are not pooled at the world price anymore, but at some higher price, which is used to justify the use of producer levies in the first place.

## Other Issues

### *Export Credit Programs*

Export credit programs totaled US$7.9 billion in 1998 in the form of credit guarantees, interest rate subsidies, public assumption of risk, and insurance subsidies (OECD 2000). These programs are designed to assist export sales by providing credit and reducing risk associated with purchase and subsequent default by the borrower. The export subsidy component is the taxpayer outlays for expected defaults, which can have major impacts on exports because of the risk reduction effects. Export credits can expand demand for exports, because they help to alleviate financial constraints in the importing country, and reduce the adverse effects of exchange rate fluctuations during the length of the contracts. Use of export credits has increased for agricultural products, but agricultural export credit programs are not covered by the international agreement that regulates export credits for manufactured goods.

The export subsidy component of export credit guarantees is very complex to measure. Subsidized risk premiums need to be converted into a present value of expected costs of defaults to be borne by taxpayers. It is possible that reducing the risk and enhancing purchasing power of importers may correct for a market failure that temporarily disrupts normal financial mechanisms. For example, export credit guarantees are useful for food security programs in importing countries suffering from financial crises or food supply disruptions.

The same reasoning is valid for export insurance. When the government or private agents offer export insurance at levels and rates that are not standard in the domestic markets of the countries involved, this creates an incentive for exports and may have the effect of decreasing the product's price to the buyer because it would reduce transportation costs and risk.

The subsidy rates for existing export credit schemes are estimated to be small. An OECD study shows that the average subsidy for export credits was 3.6 percent of export value in 1998, with the U.S. having the highest at 6.6 percent. These low subsidies notwithstanding, disciplines on the use of subsidized export credits and insurance need to be negotiated and enforced to ensure that they are not increased in the future.

### *Public Stock Disposal*

The Australian Bureau of Agricultural and Resource Economics (ABARE) shows the direct correlation of export subsidies and the rundown of public stocks. There is a large literature on government stock disposal procedures: some economists argue that such schemes can decrease domestic prices and hence not act as an export subsidy (Houck 1986; Chambers and Paarlberg 1991; Anania, Bohman, and Carter 1992). However, Peterson, Minten, and de Gorter (1999) show that these traditional models of export subsidy programs focus only on the effects of *disposing* public stocks on the world market. The conclusions regarding economic effects of these export subsidy programs are significantly different when costs of *acquiring* these stocks are included. Stock acquisition always causes the domestic price to rise. When stock acquisition costs are included in the analysis, an export subsidy scheme can be shown to be equivalent to cash export subsidies.

### *Food Aid*

Food aid can have market effects similar to those of an export subsidy. However, food aid is not included in reduction commitments on export subsidies. Food aid that displaces commercial exports (for example, it is resold on the domestic market of the recipient country) depresses world prices while emergency food aid that increases total world consumption (that is, given only to those who would not otherwise have purchased it) has the opposite effect. Food aid and export promotion programs have complex effects, which makes it difficult in a practical sense to determine whether they constitute an export subsidy. Therefore, it is important to determine when food aid is a result of commercial export diversion by the exporting country, as the resulting effect may be trade distorting but not categorized as an export subsidy.

On the other hand, when food aid is used to move surplus production (in other words, as a surplus disposal tool), it may be used to support prices in the exporting country, creating the prerequisite for an export subsidy: a price gap with reduced domestic demand and increased domestic supply. Therefore, it has the same effect as a cash export subsidy in depressing and destabilizing world prices, hurting farmers and thereby reducing food production. If the donated commodity is resold in the domestic market of the recipient country, its world price will only be affected if it displaces a significant volume of potential imports (which depends, among other things, on whether the country would otherwise have had the possibility to pay for the commodity in a commercial transaction). If the commodity is re-exported from the recipient country, the trade distortion is more evident (Gardner 1996).

Although food aid can alleviate hunger in emergencies, a large proportion of it is currently being provided to support farm prices and dispose of surpluses (ABARE 2001). Alternative methods of assistance can be adopted to help the poor countries, including cash aid.

### *Activities of State Trading Enterprises (STEs)*

The activities of state trading enterprises/agencies were not disciplined in the URAA except for an "understanding" on the interpretation of Article XVII of the GATT 1994. Progress on improving the efficiency of international trade may result if a country with such entities agrees or is required under proposed rules to open domestic markets for private trade, to create more competition for state entities and thereby reduce their ability to control exports. Otherwise the trading activity of state trading entities needs to be subject to disciplines or rules directly, because in many cases they have a monopoly when buying commodities for export, benefit from government guarantees, and do not have commercial objectives. However, Veemen, Fulton, and Larue (1999) make a very strong argument that STEs can, in some situations, improve market competition. They argue that STEs often operate on a commercial basis while private companies can also have monopoly power, use the commercial practice of differential pricing, and may receive government assistance during financial difficulties. Specific disciplines should apply to all enterprises, public and private.

Other issues relating to exporting STEs are discrimination among destinations ("pricing-to-market"), and price pooling between domestic and export sales (possibly leading to consumer-only-financed export subsidies dealt with above). Pricing-to-market is a very difficult issue both to analyze and to discipline because it often covers normal commercial practices related to transport costs, quality differences, and other similar factors. However, pricing-to-market can also function as predatory pricing. In principle, this should be subject to discipline, although it may be difficult in practice to agree on workable mechanisms for bringing that about.

## Options for Strengthening Disciplines on Export Subsidies in the Negotiations

The successful conclusion of the Doha Development Round will depend on a complex mix of politics and economics, but the prospects for success can certainly be enhanced by a close retrospective look at what went right and wrong in the implementation of the URAA with respect to disciplines on export subsidies. The analysis above finds the agreement's intent was undermined during the implementation period (1995–2001 for developed countries), as countries took advantage of a number of omissions and loopholes. This has implications for the current negotiations, since an objective is "reductions of, with a view to phasing out, all forms of export subsidies."

Some of the factors affecting the effectiveness of the value and volume commitments in the URAA originated from the excessive flexibility allowed in choosing some key parameters. Countries were allowed their choice of base period from which reduction commitments would be measured (front-loading), an option that allowed them to postpone reductions. They were also given the option of "banking" unused allowances in one period, to use them in a later period. This enabled an increase in the levels (value) of export subsidies in some periods during the overall implementation period. In addition, the per unit export subsidy was not regulated so the reduction commitments did not limit distortions in prices. This is because the same value of subsidy can lead to different per unit subsidies, and different impacts on export supply and therefore on world prices. The data on export subsidy equivalents confirm that these differences are significant across countries, commodities, and over time.

Export subsidies take a wide variety of direct and indirect forms. Agreement on specific limitations will be difficult to reach because of the variety of institutions and programs involved. Notwithstanding the difficulty, the analysis in this chapter indicates that meeting the following targets would help the Doha Round Agreement to more fully meet the goal of minimizing the unfavorable effects of export subsidies on the world trading system and on developing countries in particular:

- Establishing a firm deadline for eliminating export subsidies.
- Establishing modalities to ensure significant reductions in MFN tariffs (since reductions in import barriers will automatically strengthen disciplines on export subsidies).
- Introducing *ad valorem* (percentage) limits on the per unit subsidy on a commodity-by-commodity basis (as a percentage of the world price), combined with a ceiling on the total value of exports that may be subsidized. The *ad valorem* limit would place a constraint on the difference between domestic and world prices, and limit the distortions of relative prices across different products, while the value limit would constrain the impact of export subsidies on world markets. The value limit became less binding during the Uruguay Round implementation period, so new commitments need to "squeeze out some of the water" in the current level of commitments (in other words, reduce the commitment levels to make them binding) as a minimal starting point.
- Strengthening the monitoring of export subsidies by coordinating data collection with other organizations (for example, the OECD), and possibly the WTO Trade Policy Review, providing an annual evaluation of the effects of export subsidies, focusing in particular on developing countries.
- Improving the rules governing food aid. With the potential adverse impacts on domestic producers from food aid that is not targeted (WTO 2002) ("targeted" aid is only available to the poor via some kind of means testing), a formula should be developed for estimating the subsidy element of food aid. This could be counted against the export subsidy limits for purposes of meeting reduction commitments. Efforts could be made to encourage the use of cash aid in place of food aid to minimize adverse effects on markets. For these rules to produce their desired results, countries would also have to untie their aid (that is, refrain from imposing requirements that the food be purchased from the country giving the aid)—otherwise they would have no effect.

### *Improving Rules on Circumvention*

The current rules on export subsidies can be strengthened to deal with the key problems and make the reduction commitments more effective by:

a. Banning the banking (or "rollover" to subsequent years) of export subsidies and agreeing on annual targets for reductions. Without such limits, countries have excessive flexibility in meeting their commitments, which can lead to destabilization of world markets through higher subsidization when world prices are low.
b. Making all commitments on a per product basis, with a uniform agreed system of classifying products, to ensure that countries cannot use "tailor made" product aggregation in the baseline as a means to circumvent commitments. The current rules attempt to do this, in that products are aggregated into 23 commodity groups (22 groups plus "other agricultural products"). However, the aggregation differs across countries, as well as the units reported. The aggregation of different products into the same group (as "fruits and vegetables," for example) poses problems when comparing figures across countries that may refer to completely different products. The units used to report volumes for meats can be carcass weight or product weight, for instance, and for eggs they can be units, dozens, tons, or tons of shell-equivalents. Such nonstandardization opens possibilities for circumvention.
c. Banning front-loading (the practice of using different bases from which export subsidy reductions are measured), used in the Uruguay Round Agreements to postpone reductions.

d. Subjecting all expenditures involving direct in-kind disposal of public stocks in export markets to the same rules as export subsidies.[6]

Some holes left by the URAA need to be plugged by:

a. Establishing rules that directly constrain export credit and payment guarantees and direct financing, as these have the effect of subsidizing exports. Such rules are needed as part of the disciplines on export subsidies. A methodology could be developed to include the export subsidy component of these measures, and this could be counted against reduction commitments.
b. Establishing stronger disciplines on STEs by at a minimum subjecting them to the same rules on export subsidies that apply to private sector enterprises, using notification and transparency requirements to prevent disguised export subsidies. An option would be to strengthen and extend the disciplines of GATT Article XVII and Article II on state trading imports to include limits on the *ad valorem* subsidies.
c. Establishing rules to constrain consumer-financed export subsidies (for example, revenue-pooling arrangements).

## Chapter Annex: Volume versus Expenditure Limits on Export Subsidies

In a static analysis, excess supply and demand curves do not shift over time. As figure 3.A.1 depicts, baseline exports of $Q_0$, which receive a per unit export subsidy of $P_d^0 - P_w^0$, represent the price gap between domestic and world prices. Assume that in the baseline, both the volume of subsidized exports ($Q_0$) and the value of export subsidy expenditures (represented by the area $P_d^0$ A B $P_w^0$) are binding. Note that a reduction in the quantity of subsidized exports to $Q_{ft}$ (possibly a rather small reduction and certainly less than 100 percent) will result in a free-trade equilibrium, in which the "price gap" is zero and both the world price and the quantity exported are the same as if no export subsidies were offered. If the reduction commitment was made in terms of expenditure, it would require a 100 percent reduction to reach this point, since any subsidy (without a volume constraint) would produce an equilibrium level of exports higher than $Q_{ft}$.

Assuming that both volume and value reductions are equally binding after the reductions have occurred, for exogenous shifts in excess supply and excess demand, volume constraints are always binding in the case of a positive shift (that is, a shift that moves the free trade equilibrium to the right, or alternatively stated, a shift that reduces the per unit subsidy necessary to achieve a given level of exports), and expenditure constraints are always binding in the case of a negative shift.

Consider first a positive shift. In figure 3.A.1, suppose that originally both volume constraints are binding; that is, the country's commitments do not allow it to increase export volume above $Q_0$, nor its export subsidy expenditure above ($P_d^0$ A B $P_w^0$). Now suppose that the excess supply curve shifts outward from $ES_0$ to $ES_1$. If there was no constraint on the volume of exports subsidized, but there was a constraint on expenditure, the government could increase exports, while lowering or holding constant its expenditure. For example, it could reduce the per unit subsidy such that the new expenditure level ($P_d^2$ D E $P_w^2$) would be the same as the previous level, while increasing the exports subsidized to $Q_1$, causing the world price to decline to $P_w^2$. In contrast, if there was a constraint on volume subsidized, the government could not affect the world price (since it could not increase the supply of the product on world markets), regardless of whether there is an expenditure constraint or not. It would, in fact, have to lower the subsidy to ($P_d^1 - P_w^0$) to keep exports from exceeding their limit. In this case with a positive shift of the free-trade equilibrium, the volume constraint is necessary and sufficient to prevent an increase in subsidized exports and a consequent adverse impact on world prices, whereas an expenditure constraint alone would not be effective in meeting this objective. The expenditure limitation is not binding. That is, there can be water in this limit.

Next consider a negative shift, in which the excess supply curve shifts inward to $ES^2$ in figure 3.A.2. With no constraint on expenditure, but with a constraint on volume subsidized, the government could increase the per unit subsidy to ($P_d^3 - P_w^0$),

**FIGURE 3.A.1 Excess Supply Curve Shifts Outward from $ES_0$ to $ES_1$**

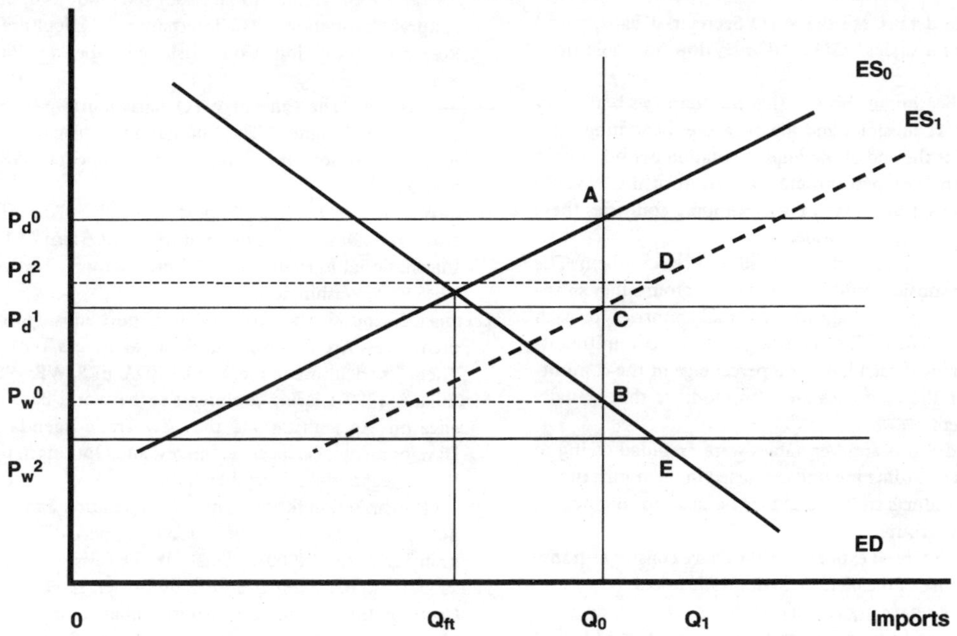


*Note:* $(P^0_d - P^0_w) < (P^2_d - P^2_w)$

**FIGURE 3.A.2 Excess Supply Curve Shifts Inward from $ES_0$ to $ES_2$**

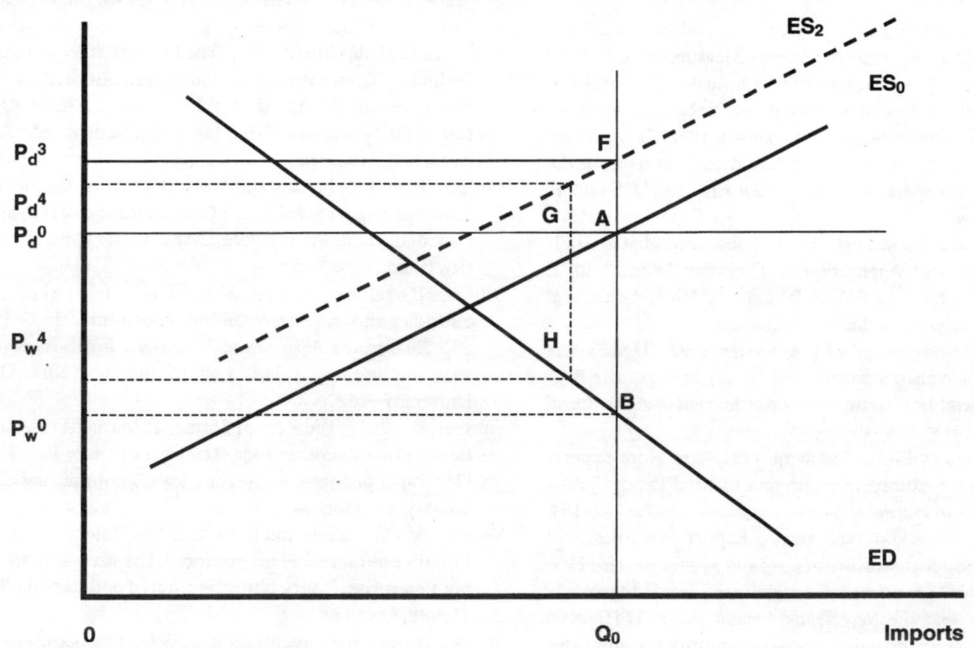


maintain the same level of exports, and keep the world price depressed. On the other hand, if there was a constraint on expenditure, the government would be forced to reduce the volume of exports that it subsidizes (such that the area $P_d^4$ G H $P_w^4$ equals the original expenditure $P_d^0$ A B $P_w^0$), thereby allowing the world price to rise. In this case, it is the expenditure constraint that is necessary and sufficient to enforce a reduction in subsidized exports and cause the world price to be higher than it otherwise would be. Again, the volume limitation is not binding. There can be water in this limit.

## Notes

1. For more details, see the WTO Secretariat background paper, "Export Subsidies," G/AG/NG/S/5, downloadable from wto.org.

2. The implication of this was that the country's budgetary outlays for export subsidies and the quantities benefiting from such subsidies, at the end of the implementation period, should be no greater than 64 percent and 79 percent of the 1986–90 base period levels, respectively. For developing countries these percentages were 76 and 86, respectively.

3. Not all the countries that have allowances use them. The countries using subsidies and the commodity groups they subsidize are less than the total allowances of all countries for each commodity. Therefore, the percentage use of commitments would be different if calculated as a percentage of the commitments only for the countries and commodities that actually make use of them.

4. Eggs, and Fruits and Vegetables were excluded owing to inconsistencies regarding the units reported in the notifications. Incorporated products are also excluded because no volumes are reported for this group.

5. Taxpayer-financed export subsidies have consumer transfers as well because of the increase in domestic prices.

6. Economists have argued that such schemes can decrease domestic prices and hence not act like an export subsidy, but these types of analyses focus only on the effects of *disposing* public stocks on the world market and exclude *acquisition* costs.

## Select Bibliography


ABARE (Australian Bureau of Agricultural and Resource Economics). 2001. "Agricultural Export Measures in the WTO Negotiations." Research Report 01.12, Australian Bureau of Agricultural and Resource Economics, Canberra.

Abraham, F., I. Couwenberg, and G. Dewit. 1992. "Towards an EC Policy on Export Financing Subsidies: Lessons from the 1980s and Prospects for Future Reform." *World Economy* 15(3): 389–405.

Alston, J. M., and R. Gray. 1998. "Export Subsidies and State Trading: Theory and Application to Canadian Wheat." In T. Yildirim, A. Schmitz, and W. H. Furtan, eds., *World Agricultural Trade.* Westview Press: Boulder, Colo.

Anania, G., M. Bohman, and M. A. Carter. 1992. "U.S. Export Subsidies in Wheat: Strategic Trade Policy or Expensive Beggar-Thy-Neighbor Tactic." *American Journal of Agricultural Economics* 74(3): 534–45.

Chambers, R. G., and R. L. Paarlberg. 1991. "Are More Exports Always Better? Comparing Cash and In-Kind Export Subsidies." *American Journal of Agricultural Economics* 73: 142–154.

de Gorter, H. 1999. "Market Access, Export Subsidies, and Domestic Support Measures: Issues and Suggestions for New Rules in the Agreement on Agriculture." In M. Ingco, ed., *Agriculture and the New Trade Agenda in the WTO 2000 Negotiations.* Forthcoming in 2003, Cambridge: Cambridge University Press.

Gardner, B. L. 1996. "The Political Economy of U.S. Export Subsidies for Wheat." In Anne Krueger, ed., *The Political Economy of American Trade Policy.* Chicago: University of Chicago Press.

Houck, J. P. 1986. "The Basic Economics of an Export Bonus Scheme." *North Central Journal of Agricultural Economics* 8(2): 227–35.

IATRC (International Agricultural Trade Research Consortium). 2001a. "Export Competition: Issues and Options in the Agricultural Negotiations." The International Agricultural Trade Research Consortium Commissioned Paper 15, Washington, D.C.

———. 2001b. "The Current WTO Agricultural Negotiations: Options for Progress." The International Agricultural Trade Research Consortium Commissioned Paper 18, Washington, D.C.

Leetmaa, S. 1997. "EU Export Subsidy Commitments Not Yet Binding, But Future Uncertain." Europe-International Agriculture and Trade Report, USDA, ERS, WRS 97-5, Washington, D.C.

Leetmaa, S., and K. Ackerman. 1998. "Export Subsidy Commitments: Few Are Binding, But Some Members Try to Evade Them." Agriculture in the WTO, USDA, ERS, WRS-98-44.

McCalla, A. 1999. Closing comments at the World Bank conference on "Agriculture and the New Trade Agenda from a Developmental Perspective: Interest and Options in the Next WTO Negotiations." October 2, Geneva.

OECD (Organisation for Economic Co-operation and Development). 2000. "An Analysis of Officially Supported Export Credits in Agriculture." (200)91/Final. OECD: Paris.

Peterson, J. M., B. J. Minten, and H. de Gorter. 1999. "Economic Costs of the U.S. Wheat Export Enhancement Program: Manna from Heaven or from Taxpayers?" International Agricultural Trade Research Consortium Working Paper 99-2, Washington, D.C.

Ruiz, L. 2000. "The Impacts of Export Subsidy Reduction Commitments in the Agreement on Agriculture on International Trade: A General Assessment." M.S. thesis, August, Cornell University, Ithaca, New York.

Ruiz, L., and H. de Gorter. 2001. "The Impacts of Export Subsidy Reduction Commitments in the Agreement on Agriculture on International Trade." In Lyn Kennedy, ed., *Global Agriculture in the New Millennium.* Dordrecht, Netherlands: Kluwer Academic Publishers.

Schluep, I. 1999. "The Law and Economics of 'Consumer Only' Financed Export Subsidies: A Context for the WTO Panel on Canadian Dairy Pricing Policy." M.S. thesis, Cornell University, Ithaca, New York.

Schluep, I., and H. de Gorter. 2001. "The Definition of Export Subsidies and the Agreement on Agriculture." In G. Peters, ed., *Tomorrow's Agriculture: Incentives, Institutions, Infrastructure and Innovations.* Oxford and New York: Oxford University Press.

Sumner, D. 1996. "The Role of Domestic Market Price Regulations in International Trade: The Case of Dairy Policy in the U.S." Paper presented to the American Economic Association, January, San Francisco.

Veeman, M., M. Fulton, and B. Larue. 1999. "International Trade in Agricultural and Food Products: The Role of State Trading Enterprises." Agriculture and Agri-Food Canada Report #1998E, Ottawa.

WTO (World Trade Organization). 1999–2000. "Country Notifications on Export Subsidies" G/AG/N. Office of the Secretary General, Geneva.

———. 2002. "Submission of the World Bank, Response to the Proposal of the Least-Developed and Net Food-Importing Countries." In Report of the Interagency Panel on Short-Term Difficulties in Financing Normal Levels of Commercial Imports of Basic Foodstuffs. WT/GC/62, G/AG/13. Geneva.

4

# MARKET ACCESS: ECONOMICS AND THE EFFECTS OF POLICY INSTRUMENTS

*Harry de Gorter, Merlinda D. Ingco, and Laura Ignacio*

## Introduction

This chapter aims to analyze and underline key points for future action on the negotiating issues for market access in agriculture in the context of the current World Trade Organization's (WTO) Doha Development Round negotiations. Market access was at the core of past trade negotiating rounds, but agricultural import barriers remain high with an average global bound tariff of 62 percent in 2000 (the end of the implementation period of the Uruguay Round Agreement on Agriculture [URAA]), and a large variation of import protection rates among commodities and countries.[1] The Agreement itself did not lead to much liberalization of agricultural trade,[2] but it limits the type of border instruments countries can use. Quantitative commitments have also made market access issues more easily negotiable in the current negotiations. The conversion of all nontariff measures into bound tariffs and the introduction of access commitments in the form of current and minimum access import quotas (as a share of domestic consumption) are two of the most important achievements of the URAA (Tangermann 1996; IATRC 2001a, 2001b). Establishing rules for acceptable agricultural policy measures and requiring future mandatory reductions of these measures was an important step for the liberalization of agricultural trade. Bound tariffs are considered more transparent, allow trade to adjust to changes in market conditions, limit the scope for protection (including export subsidies), and can be disciplined through tariff reduction commitments. Hence, current negotiations can make decisive progress for the future.

The next tasks in the negotiations are to agree on formulas and other "modalities" for countries' commitments. The purpose is to establish a fair and market-oriented trading system through a program of fundamental reform that encompasses strengthened rules, and specific commitments on government support and protection for agriculture. In this way, restrictions and distortions in world agricultural markets can be disciplined and prevented. Developing countries as a whole have sizable potential gains from improved market access, but both the size and the distribution depend on the extent to which developing countries will be active in the negotiations.

Current negotiations should focus on creating meaningful market access that would overcome the limitations of the URAA and this will require the identification of a set of feasible and effective modalities. Market access issues that should be addressed in the current negotiations and that are particularly relevant for developing countries can be categorized as follows:

1. Lowering tariffs, tariff escalation, effective protection, tariff peaks, and tariff dispersion across commodities and countries.
2. Increasing tariff rate quotas.
3. Limiting the application of special safeguard tariffs, antidumping laws, countervailing duties, and other contingent measures so that they are not used to restrict market access unfairly.
4. Improving the rules on tariff rate quota administration methods (including those concerning state trading enterprises) to make them more transparent, to improve fill rates so that imports are not discouraged or blocked, and to ensure access by lowest-cost suppliers so that countries are not discriminated against.
5. Rationalizing product regulations (such as sanitary and phytosanitary [SPS] rules, labeling laws, and other nontrade concerns) so that they cannot be formulated as nontariff barriers.
6. Developing rules for special and differential treatment measures for developing countries that provide greater benefits from a more liberalized trading environment and protection from instability and food security concerns.[3]

### *The Plan of This Chapter*

This chapter analyzes the first three issues identified above. The fourth issue, on tariff rate quota administration, is covered in the following chapter, while the fifth and sixth issues are dealt with in other chapters on SPS (chapter 11), multifunctionality (chapter 8). Concerns specific to developing countries are covered in later chapters too, such as special and differential treatment (chapter 14), managing low and volatile prices (chapter 10), and food security concerns (chapter 9). The next section describes the issues and present empirical evidence of tariff dispersion, tariff peaks, tariff water, preferential tariffs, and tariff rate quota fill rates. This is followed by a section that provides an explanation of the basic economics of tariff rate quotas (TRQs), including the effects of water in the tariff (the difference between applied tariff rates and the tariff equivalent of the binding quota[4]), binding overhang (the difference between bound and applied tariffs), and over-quota versus out-of-quota import tariffs (the former has in-quota tariffs applied to imports above the quota). Another section provides empirical analysis of alternative modalities in liberalizing tariff quotas using the Policy Evaluation Matrix (PEM) model of the Organisation for Economic Co-operation and Development (OECD). The last section provides conclusions and policy recommendations.

## Background: Evidence of Market Access Barriers in Agriculture

Barriers in market access were collapsed into two forms by the URAA: import tariffs and tariff rate quotas; and remaining contentious nontariff barriers such as SPS standards. The tariffication process converted quantitative barriers into tariffs in the URAA and ensured access at bound tariffs for all commodities. Tariffs could be simple, specific, *ad valorem*, or a combination. Each country was also able to designate TRQs for most commodities where quantitative barriers were tariffied. TRQs are commitments to allow access at least up to a quota level at an in-quota tariff rate. The quota is either the level of imports in the 1986–88 base period or 3 percent of domestic consumption (increasing to 5 percent by the year 2000), whichever is larger. Out-of-quota imports can occur but only at the (often much) higher out-of-quota tariffs that are bound in the agreement. The out-of-quota tariffs were reduced by an unweighted simple average of 36 percent (minimum of 15 percent per tariff line) by 2000–01 (and four years later for developing countries). Requiring an average cut in tariffs rather than a cut in average tariffs meant that a country could make a large cut in a tariff that was already low (from 2 percent to 1 percent, representing a 50 percent reduction) or in sectors with low political sensitivity, while making only minimal cuts in sensitive product categories.

Developing countries were not required to undertake tariffication but instead could opt for ceiling bindings. To address the concern of sudden import surges or depressed import prices, a special safeguard for agriculture was introduced for those who tariffied. However, the effectiveness of URAA market access commitments was compromised because the out-of-quota tariffs were bound at such high levels by both developed and developing countries as to effectively prevent all imports above the TRQ levels (ABARE 1999, Martin 2000). TRQs were sometimes understated to prevent a significant increase in market access relative to the status quo that prevailed before the 1994 agreement. On the other hand, countries with TRQs were allowed to follow significantly less restrictive import regimes than their commitment specifies by allowing over-quota imports. Applied in-quota tariffs (that is, the actual tariff) may be less than the official in-quota or out-of-quota tariff rates.

### *Import Protection Levels*

Agricultural trade regimes have changed in the recent past. Developed countries have moved away from domestic support and border protection to a reliance on domestic support, while many developing countries have reformed agricultural policies resulting in low rates of protection. Several middle-income countries, however, have provided more protection in agriculture.

The absolute level of support to agriculture in OECD countries has not changed very much since the conclusion of the Uruguay Round. Figure 4.1 compares market price support (MPS)—that is from border protection—from 1986 to 2001 with both the total producer support estimate (PSE) and the total support estimate (TSE).[5] The gap as a fraction of MPS for either the TSE or PSE has shown a downward trend, however, implying a re-instrumentation toward domestic policy measures. During 1986–88, the market price support from border protection accounted for 77 percent (61 percent) of the PSE (TSE), while by 2001 the shares had fallen to 63 percent (47 percent).

The shift away from border support in OECD countries is mainly concentrated in the grains and oilseeds sectors (figure 4.2) with the overall rate of protection—support as a percent of farm revenues at world prices—dropping rapidly after 1986 and 1987 when world prices were low, and has since stabilized. The overall percentage of protection started at close to 120 percent in 1986 and fell to 50 percent in 1996; it stood at 77 percent as of 2001. The cyclical component of protection over time reflects changes in world prices more than changes in policy. Average protection for grains and oilseeds is 80 percent for the time period 1986–2001. The move away from MPS and toward the various forms of direct payments, especially area payments and historical entitlements, is also evident. Agricultural support, although still dominated by MPS, is declining, with the growing components being area payments and historical entitlements. Purchased input subsidies and output price subsidies have been fairly constant.

**FIGURE 4.1 Evolution of Border versus Total Support in OECD Agriculture (US$ Billions)**

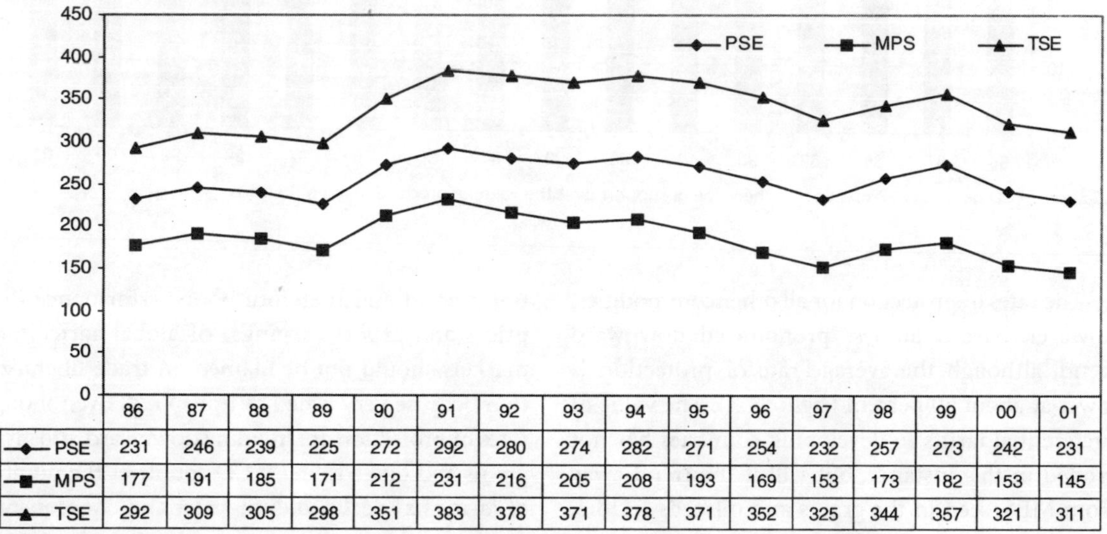


| | 86 | 87 | 88 | 89 | 90 | 91 | 92 | 93 | 94 | 95 | 96 | 97 | 98 | 99 | 00 | 01 |
|---|---|---|---|---|---|---|---|---|---|---|---|---|---|---|---|---|
| PSE | 231 | 246 | 239 | 225 | 272 | 292 | 280 | 274 | 282 | 271 | 254 | 232 | 257 | 273 | 242 | 231 |
| MPS | 177 | 191 | 185 | 171 | 212 | 231 | 216 | 205 | 208 | 193 | 169 | 153 | 173 | 182 | 153 | 145 |
| TSE | 292 | 309 | 305 | 298 | 351 | 383 | 378 | 371 | 378 | 371 | 352 | 325 | 344 | 357 | 321 | 311 |

PSE: Producer support estimate, MPS: Market price support, TSE: Total support estimate.
*Source:* OECD PSE/CSE Database 2002.

**FIGURE 4.2 OECD: Grains and Oilseeds**

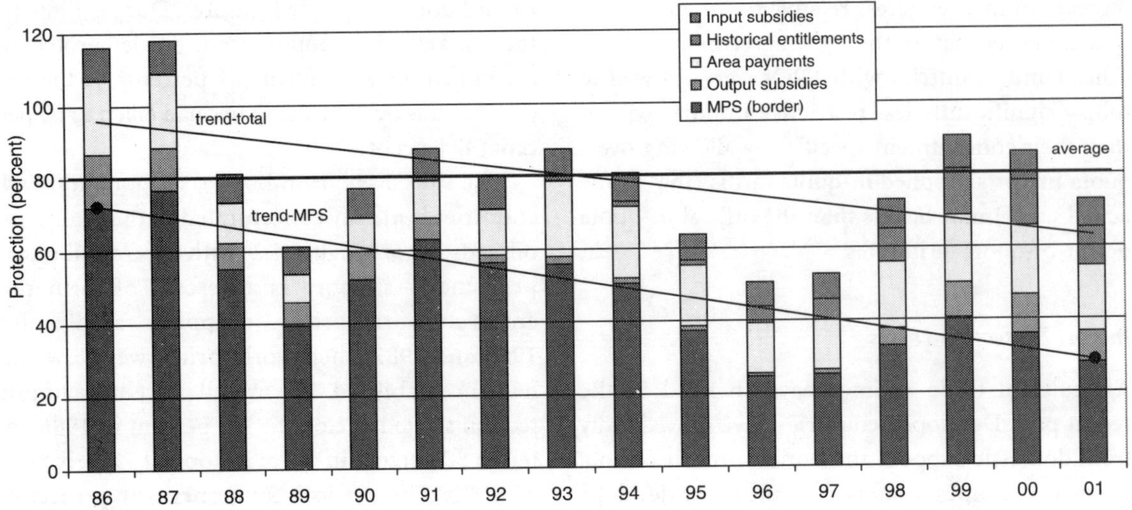


*Source:* OECD database. "Protection" is the value of support over the value of production at world prices.

**FIGURE 4.3 OECD: Other Commodities**

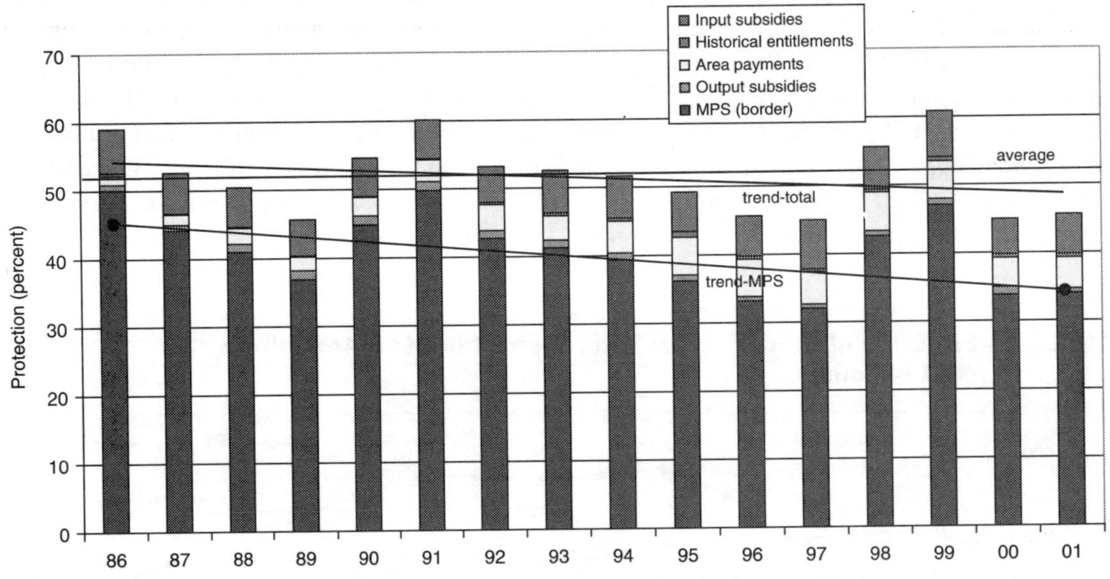


*Source:* OECD database. "Protection" is the value of support over the value of production at world prices.

The rates of protection for all other commodities, however, have a far less pronounced downward trend, although the average rate of protection is lower at about 50 percent (figure 4.3). The value of preferential tariffs to developing countries has not eroded in this instance, but will if the trend away from MPS, seen in the grains and oilseeds sectors, spreads to other sectors. The significance of the foregoing discussion is that very little trade liberalization seems to have occurred in the URAA implementation period and therefore poor performance (low prices and export earnings) of global agricultural markets should not be blamed on trade liberalization because very little has transpired. Even though rates of protection are trending downward, mostly in grains and oilseeds, in OECD countries the number of farms has declined even faster and consequently per farm subsidies have increased (Messerlin 2002).

The distribution of bound "most favored nation" (MFN) tariffs across regions is summarized in fig-

**FIGURE 4.4 Average Agricultural Bound Tariffs by Region 2001 (in percent)**

| Region | South Asia | Non-EU West Europe | Caribbean Islands | Sub-Saharan Africa | North Africa | Central America | Eastern Europe | Middle East | Southern Africa | South America | Asia-Pacific | European Union-15 | North America |
|---|---|---|---|---|---|---|---|---|---|---|---|---|---|
| Tariff | 113 | 104 | 86 | 75 | 71 | 54 | 49 | 48 | 39 | 39 | 34 | 30 | 25 |

Average Agricultural Tariff (62%)

*Source:* Gibson and others (2001).

**FIGURE 4.5 Applied Versus Bound Tariffs (Percentage of Overhang) in Developing Countries**

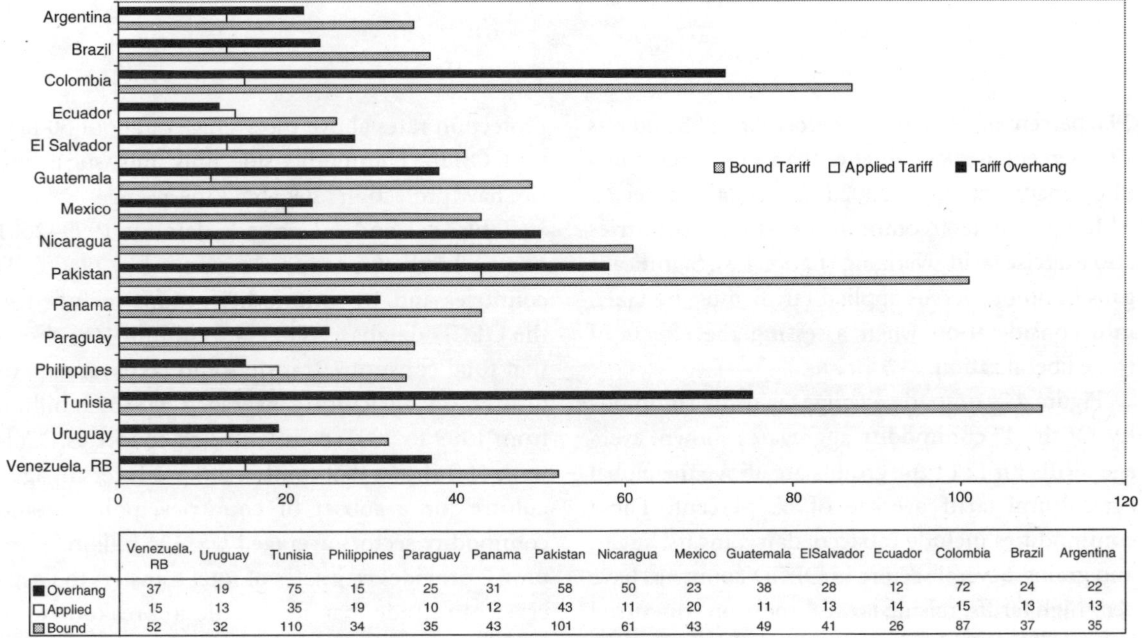


| | Venezuela, RB | Uruguay | Tunisia | Philippines | Paraguay | Panama | Pakistan | Nicaragua | Mexico | Guatemala | ElSalvador | Ecuador | Colombia | Brazil | Argentina |
|---|---|---|---|---|---|---|---|---|---|---|---|---|---|---|---|
| Overhang | 37 | 19 | 75 | 15 | 25 | 31 | 58 | 50 | 23 | 38 | 28 | 12 | 72 | 24 | 22 |
| Applied | 15 | 13 | 35 | 19 | 10 | 12 | 43 | 11 | 20 | 11 | 13 | 14 | 15 | 13 | 13 |
| Bound | 52 | 32 | 110 | 34 | 35 | 43 | 101 | 61 | 43 | 49 | 41 | 26 | 87 | 37 | 35 |

*Source:* Authors' calculations from ATPSM, OECD, TRAINS, and AMAD databases.

ure 4.4.[6] Regional average tariffs for WTO members range from an *ad valorem* equivalent of 25 percent to 113 percent. With the exception of Non–European Union Western Europe, the regional groups with the highest average tariffs are developing countries. However, this comparison is not indicative of their actual protection because these "bound" tariffs are much higher than "applied" tariffs ("tariff binding overhang") and fewer TRQs are used. Figure 4.5 gives the level of tariff binding overhang for a selected group of developing countries. The average tariff for agricultural products in developing countries declined from

**FIGURE 4.6 Applied versus Bound Tariffs in Developed Countries (Tariffs Binding Overhang)**

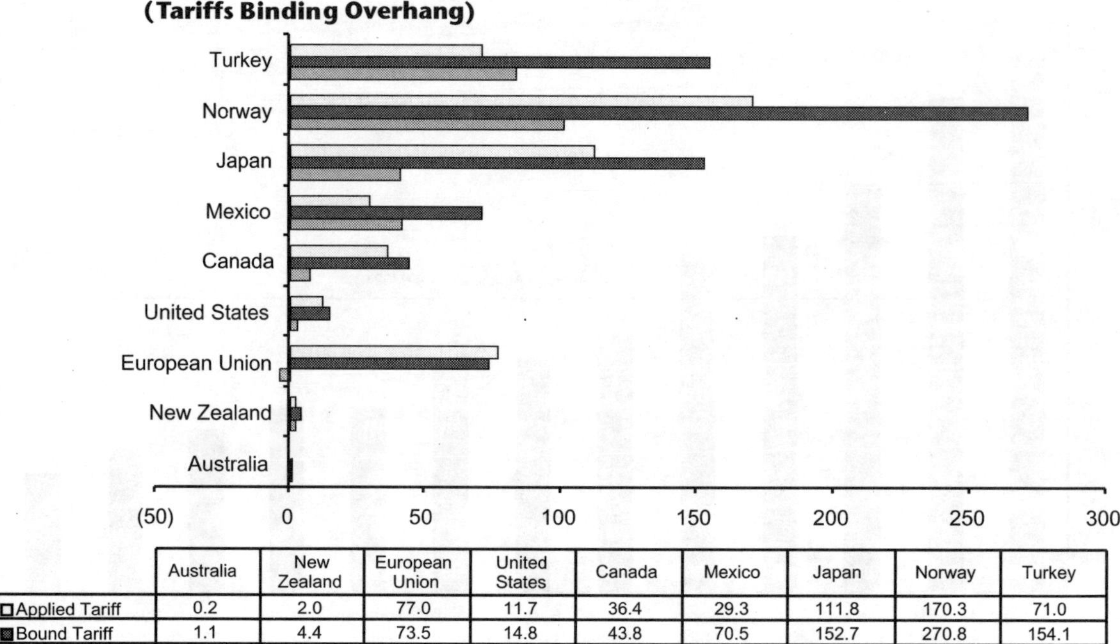


| | Australia | New Zealand | European Union | United States | Canada | Mexico | Japan | Norway | Turkey |
|---|---|---|---|---|---|---|---|---|---|
| Applied Tariff | 0.2 | 2.0 | 77.0 | 11.7 | 36.4 | 29.3 | 111.8 | 170.3 | 71.0 |
| Bound Tariff | 1.1 | 4.4 | 73.5 | 14.8 | 43.8 | 70.5 | 152.7 | 270.8 | 154.1 |
| Tariff Overhang | 0.9 | 2.3 | (3.5) | 3.1 | 7.4 | 41.2 | 40.9 | 100.5 | 83.1 |

*Note:* EU estimated overhang is –3.5 because although a large majority of EU tariff lines have zero overhang, special circumstances cause some applied tariffs to exceed the bound rates, and there may also be some errors in the reported data.

*Source:* Authors' calculations from ATPSM, OECD, and AMAD databases.

29.6 percent in 1990 to 22.9 percent in 1995 and was 18.4 percent in 2000—higher than 11.4 percent tariff on manufactures in 2002 (GEP 2004, chapter 3). Although far less common, developed countries also exercise tariff overhang (figure 4.6). Significant gaps in bound versus applied tariffs must be taken into consideration when assessing the effects of trade liberalization.

Figure 4.7 compares average tariffs by commodity. Of the 47 commodity aggregates shown, average tariffs on 12 of the groups are above the global agricultural tariff average of 62 percent. These commodities include tobacco, dairy, meats, sugar, and grains. Several sectors in OECD countries have very high tariffs, raising tariff dispersion (discussed below). The incidence of non–*ad valorem* tariffs and the implications for measuring protection and transparency is discussed in box 4.1.

Figures 4.8 and 4.9 present the nominal protection coefficient (by country and commodity, respectively, in the OECD countries and commodity groupings). A value of 1.0 means no protection. The Republic of Korea, Norway, Iceland, Switzerland, and Japan have protection rates above the average of about 50 percent. On the commodity side, only milk, sugar, and rice have protection rates above the average.

Tables 4.1 and 4.2 provide data for 1999–2001 on the level of producer support for 29 OECD countries and 10 commodity groups included in the OECD database. Table 4.1 column 1(a) shows that total consumer transfers and taxpayer expenditures on agriculture averaged US$329 billion from 1999 to 2001, mostly in rich countries.[7] Column 1(c) shows that transfers to producers in agriculture for a subset of countries, policies, and commodity sectors averaged US$126 billion.[8] Column 2 provides estimates of total transfers to farmers from trade barriers, with a breakdown of import quota rents and tariff revenues. Annual average quota rents and tariff revenue column 2(b) are in the order of US$49 billion. Column 3 at US$25 billion gives an estimate of transfers derived from domestic agricultural policy and indicates the significance of domestic support. Nontrade transfers represent about 20 percent of total or consumer/taxpayers transfer to farmers. The final

**FIGURE 4.7 Average Bound Tariffs by Commodity, 2001**

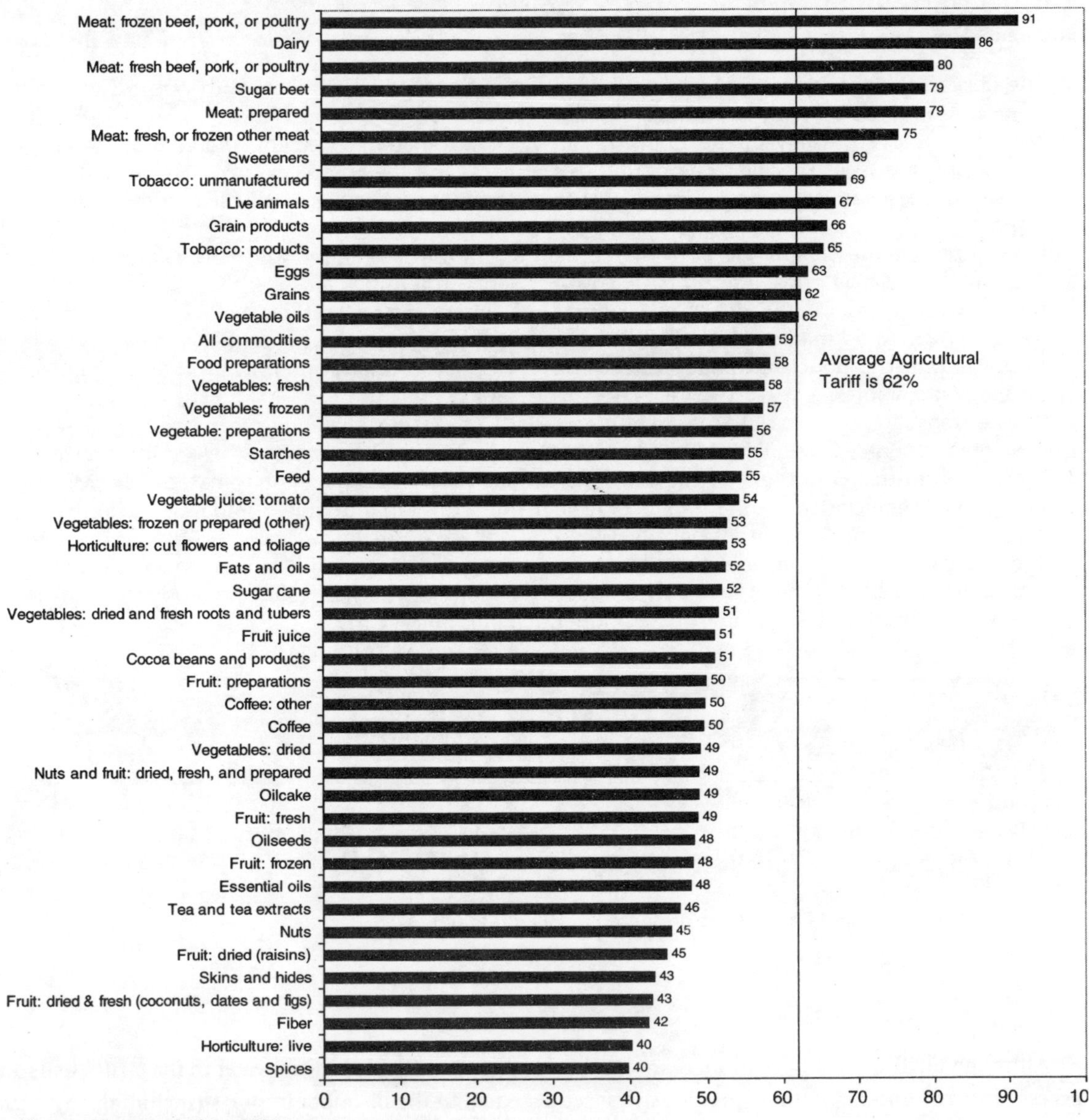


*Source:* Gibson and others 2001.

column shows the proportion of transfers that are self-defeating because world prices decline due to the country's own policies and the policies of other countries. Much of these measured transfers simply offset the deleterious effects of the policies themselves, and the remaining transfers that appear to go to farmers may be at least partially dissipated because of economic inefficiencies and rent-seeking behavior by market participants. This occurs less in Japan and the Republic of Korea because these two countries have extraordinarily high levels of total trade-distorting support as well as high levels of agricultural imports.

Table 4.2 presents the data by commodity group. Surprisingly, milk and sugar, among others, have trade transfers that are less than nontrade transfers. Most of the wheat and oilseed transfers are offset by the reduction in world prices caused by wheat and oilseed policies themselves, while sugar and rice transfers are mostly real increases in transfers to farmers because the latter two commodities have high levels of market price support and are heavily traded.

## BOX 4.1 Transparency and Tariffication

The objective of providing greater transparency of protection levels through tariffication has not been fully realized. Many of the tariffs within agriculture are still specific, compound, or mixed. For these tariffs it is almost impossible to estimate the real protection levels because the level of protection will change both over time and with the relative price of imports. The protection will increase as the prices of products decline in the world markets and will be higher for lower-priced products originating from the developing countries.

The transparency of tariffs in agriculture in developing countries is significantly higher than those in industrial countries. Of the 24 developing countries included in this sample, 14 have no non–ad valorem; 2 countries have less than 1 percent of their tariff lines; 4 have less than 5 percent of their tariff lines; and only 6 countries, all of them middle income, have higher proportion of tariff lines with non–ad valorem rates. On the other hand, Japan has 15 percent, Canada 28 percent, United States 43 percent, and the European Union 44 percent of all tariff lines that are specific, compound, or mixed.

In the sample reporting ad valorem equivalents, the duties are much higher than the ad valorem rates (see table below). This suggests that tariffs are seriously underestimated in those cases with a large number of non–ad valorem tariffs.

Tariffs are also nontransparent because of many bilateral agreements to fix import prices—such as those concerning tomatoes from Mexico into the United States and apples from the United States into Mexico. These agreements are a result of antidumping or countervailing actions and end up not being reported as official tariffs in the WTO.

| | *Ad Valorem and Specific Duty Rates* | | |
|---|---|---|---|
| | **Average ad Valorem Tariff** | **Average ad valorem Tariff Equivalent** | **Percentage of non–ad Valorem Lines** |
| Australia | 1.2 | 5.0 | 1.0 |
| United States | 8.8 | 12.3 | 43.8 |
| European Union | 10.6 | 35.2 | 43.6 |
| Jordan | 22.5 | 58.0 | 0.9 |

*Source:* WTO Integrated Database as presented in GEP 2004 (ch. 3).

Although tariff quotas were to increase market access for commodities that previously faced quantitative barriers, the high in-quota and out-of-quota tariffs still remain for these commodities with quotas. Across all WTO members, the average out-of-quota tariff is 123 percent, while the simple in-quota average tariff is 63 percent (approximately equal to the 62 percent average bound MFN tariffs for all countries and agricultural commodities including non-quota commodities, Gibson and others 2001). The average tariff difference of out-of-quota tariffs over in-quota tariffs is 336 percent.

Out-of-quota tariffs are overstated because during the Uruguay Round negotiations, countries were given considerable discretion in calculating these tariffs, resulting in water in the tariff. Rents are equal to the in-quota imports (including any over-quota imports) times the difference between either the out-of-quota applied tariff or the tariff equivalent of the binding quota (depending on which regime—quota, out-of-quota tariff, or in-quota tariff regime—is the effective constraint) and the in-quota tariff.

Figures 4.10 and 4.11 calculate the water in the tariff using values of the applied tariffs, and the MPS as tariff equivalent protection for the product from binding TRQs. Although the data are rough estimates of world price gaps and do not include all countries or commodities that have TRQs, there is evidence that water in the tariff is an issue that can dilute the effects of any tariff liberalization.

**FIGURE 4.8 Nominal Protection Coefficient by OECD Country**

| | Mexico | Poland | New Zealand | Australia | Hungary | Turkey | United States | Slovak Republic | Canada | OECD All | Czech Republic | EU | Japan | Korea, Rep. of | Norway | Iceland | Switzer land |
|---|---|---|---|---|---|---|---|---|---|---|---|---|---|---|---|---|---|
| ■ 2000 | 1.18 | 1.11 | 1.01 | 1 | 2 | 1.31 | 1.14 | 1.11 | 1.13 | 1.34 | 1.06 | 1.33 | 2.45 | 2.9 | 2.31 | 2.27 | 2.71 |
| ▨ 86–88 | 0.91 | 1 | 1.02 | 1.05 | 1.14 | 1.15 | 1.19 | 1.29 | 1.4 | 1.58 | 1.74 | 1.87 | 2.51 | 3.36 | 3.38 | 3.78 | 3.85 |

*Source:* OECD PSE/CSE Database 2002.

**FIGURE 4.9 Nominal Protection Coefficient by Commodity (OECD)**

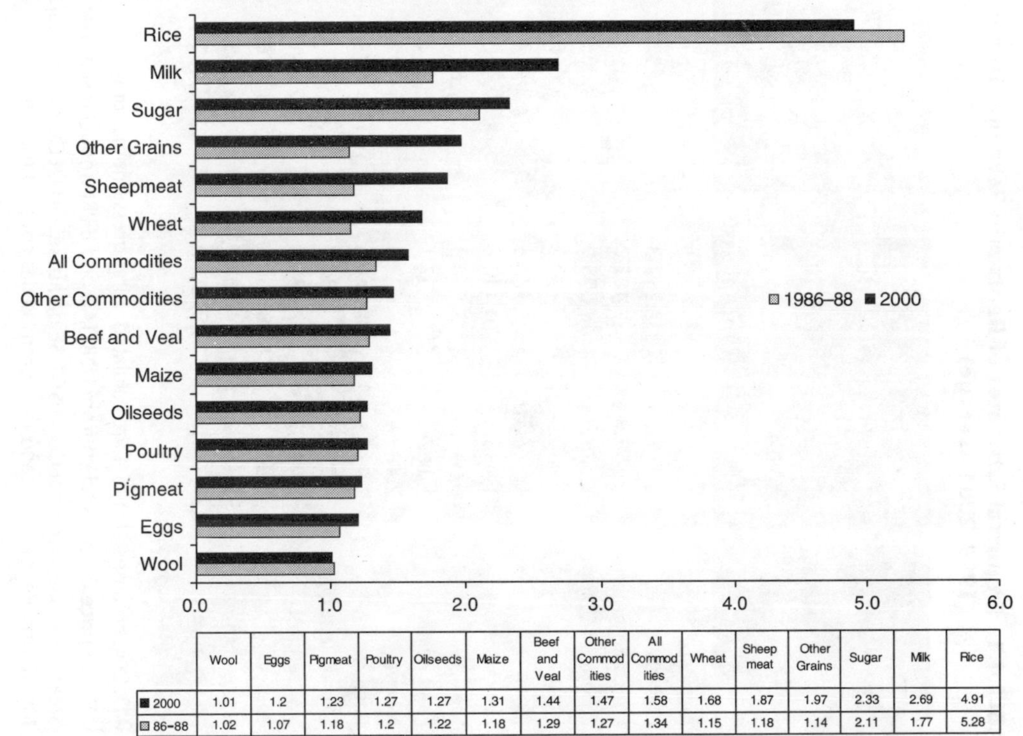


| | Wool | Eggs | Pigmeat | Poultry | Oilseeds | Maize | Beef and Veal | Other Commod ities | All Commod ities | Wheat | Sheep meat | Other Grains | Sugar | Milk | Rice |
|---|---|---|---|---|---|---|---|---|---|---|---|---|---|---|---|
| ■ 2000 | 1.01 | 1.2 | 1.23 | 1.27 | 1.27 | 1.31 | 1.44 | 1.47 | 1.58 | 1.68 | 1.87 | 1.97 | 2.33 | 2.69 | 4.91 |
| ▨ 86–88 | 1.02 | 1.07 | 1.18 | 1.2 | 1.22 | 1.18 | 1.29 | 1.27 | 1.34 | 1.15 | 1.18 | 1.14 | 2.11 | 1.77 | 5.28 |

*Source:* OECD PSE/CSE Database 2002.

**TABLE 4.1 Empirical Estimates of Rents and Revenues Due to Policies in World Agriculture, US$ Millions (1999–2001 average)**

| Country | 1 *Total Transfers* | | | 2 *Transfers from Trade Barriers* | | 3 | 4 |
|---|---|---|---|---|---|---|---|
| | (a) TSE (total support) | (b) Trade-distorting support | (c) Trade-distorting support w/ gross imports[a] | (a) Total MPS | (b) Tariff revenues and import Quota rents[a] | *Non-trade Transfers* OPS+IPS | Reduction in Transfers created by world price decreases owing to policies[b] |
| Australia | 1,375.9 | 470.5 | 263.7 | 72.9 | 2.6 | 190.7 | 42.4% |
| Canada | 5,231.5 | 2,232.3 | 2,232.3 | 1,462.8 | 62.1 | 769.6 | 54.6% |
| Czech Republic | 759.9 | 402.0 | 398.4 | 326.8 | 15.1 | 71.6 | 48.3% |
| European Union | 112,629.9 | 48,008.0 | 48,008.0 | 42,852.0 | 2,373.8 | 5,156.0 | 44.8% |
| Hungary | 1,080.3 | 703.8 | 690.2 | 384.3 | 15.5 | 306.0 | 54.1% |
| Japan | 64,777.5 | 28,472.3 | 28,472.3 | 25,520.4 | 34,362.7 | 2,951.9 | 20.0% |
| Korea, Rep. of | 21,488.8 | 10,440.8 | 10,440.8 | 10,187.4 | 9,701.2 | 253.5 | 16.0% |
| Mexico | 6,999.1 | 3,550.3 | 2,840.3 | 2,401.2 | 1,023.4 | 439.0 | 53.4% |
| New Zealand | 162.2 | 37.1 | 11.4 | 0.0 | 0.0 | 11.4 | 44.7% |
| Norway | 2,489.4 | 1,629.0 | 1,101.6 | 499.4 | 62.5 | 602.1 | 51.0% |
| Poland | 1,934.3 | 1,144.6 | 1,023.4 | 746.7 | 39.7 | 276.7 | 60.5% |
| Slovak Republic | 332.3 | 238.7 | 220.6 | 81.7 | 6.2 | 138.9 | 48.4% |
| Switzerland | 5,047.3 | 2,681.8 | 2,681.8 | 1,991.1 | 508.2 | 690.7 | 48.7% |
| Turkey | 9,649.5 | 3,960.9 | 2,726.7 | 2,222.0 | 161.6 | 504.7 | 54.3% |
| United States | 95,455.2 | 24,969.7 | 24,969.7 | 12,152.0 | 595.8 | 12,817.7 | 51.4% |
| All Countries | 329,413.1 | 128,942.0 | 126,081.3 | 100,900.7 | 48,930.4 | 25,180.6 | 39.0% |

a. Data in columns 1(c) to 4 are calulated using gross imports only.

b. World price changes taken from UNCTAD and IFPRI model results presented at IATRC Conference, Whistler, Canada, June 2002.

*Source:* Estimates from OECD's PSE/CSE database and OECD's Agricultural Outlook database. Data correspond to the 15-country coverage of the OECD Monitoring Report 2002 and the commodities covered therein.

**TABLE 4.2 Empirical Estimates of Rents and Revenues Due to Policies by Commodity in World Agriculture, US$ Millions (1999–2001 average)**

| | 1 *Total Transfers* | | 2 *Transfers from Trade Barriers* | | 3 | 4 |
|---|---|---|---|---|---|---|
| Commodity | (a) Trade-distorting support | (b) Trade-distorting support w/ gross imports[a] | (a) Total MPS | (b) Tariff revenues and import quota rents[a] | Nontrade Transfers OPS+IPS[b] | Reduction in Transfers created by world price decreases owing to policies[b] |
| Beef and veal | 19,736.8 | 19,426.9 | 16,108.3 | 4,389.1 | 3,318.6 | 40.3% |
| Coarse grains | 8,665.4 | 8,638.1 | 3,735.1 | 26,443.8 | 4,903.0 | 43.1% |
| Milk | 40,642.6 | 40,635.7 | 36,334.6 | 2,523.4 | 4,301.1 | 50.0% |
| Oilseeds | 4,897.4 | 4,892.9 | 390.7 | 3,207.2 | 4,502.2 | 72.0% |
| Pigmeat | 9,769.9 | 9,730.7 | 8,384.8 | 1,692.6 | 1,345.9 | 38.8% |
| Poultry meat | 5,543.5 | 5,232.6 | 4,257.7 | 462.7 | 974.9 | 60.2% |
| Refined Sugar | 6,217.0 | 4,509.1 | 4,108.8 | 1,777.0 | 400.3 | 8.0% |
| Rice | 25,744.4 | 25,744.4 | 23,221.6 | 1,599.7 | 2,522.8 | 2.4% |
| Sheep meat | 2,026.0 | 1,686.8 | 1,296.0 | 388.1 | 390.8 | 52.4% |
| Wheat | 5,691.3 | 5,584.0 | 3,063.0 | 6,446.6 | 2,521.0 | 90.0% |

a. Data in columns 1(b) to 4 are calculated using gross imports only.

b. World price changes taken from UNCTAD and IFPRI model results presented at IATRC Conference, Whistler, Canada, June 2002.

*Source:* Estimates from OECD's PSE/CSE database and OECD's Agricultural Outlook database. Data correspond to the 15-country coverage of the OECD Monitoring Report 2002 and the commodities covered therein.

**FIGURE 4.10 Water in the Tariff—Applied Tariffs *versus* Tariff Equivalent of Binding TRQs for Selected OECD Countries (%)**

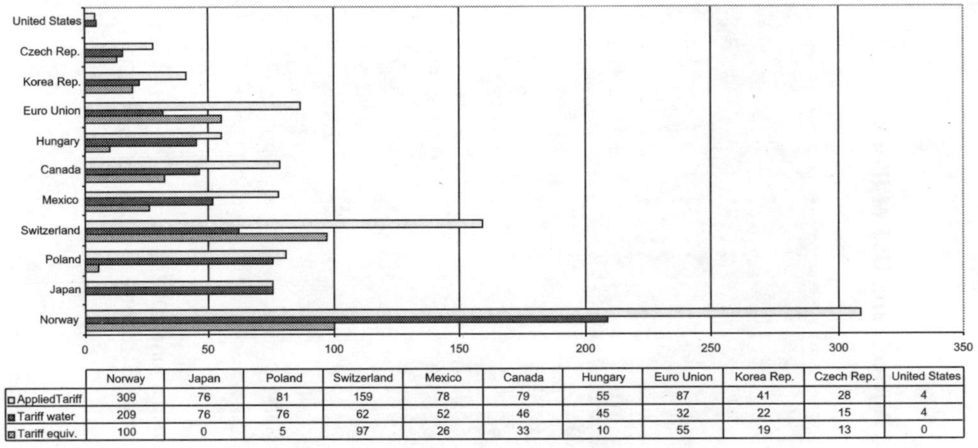


| | Norway | Japan | Poland | Switzerland | Mexico | Canada | Hungary | Euro Union | Korea Rep. | Czech Rep. | United States |
|---|---|---|---|---|---|---|---|---|---|---|---|
| AppliedTariff | 309 | 76 | 81 | 159 | 78 | 79 | 55 | 87 | 41 | 28 | 4 |
| Tariff water | 209 | 76 | 76 | 62 | 52 | 46 | 45 | 32 | 22 | 15 | 4 |
| Tariff equiv. | 100 | 0 | 5 | 97 | 26 | 33 | 10 | 55 | 19 | 13 | 0 |

*Source:* Applied tariffs data are from UNCTAD's ATPSM database. Tariff equivalent tariffs of binding TRQs are from the OECD's PSE/CSE database 2002. Because of different data sources and an arbitrary selection of countries and commodities, the estimates of water in the tariff are very imprecise and are meant only for illustrative purposes.

**FIGURE 4.11 Water in the Tariff—Applied Tariffs *versus* Tariff Equivalent of Binding TRQs for Selected OECD Commodities (%)**

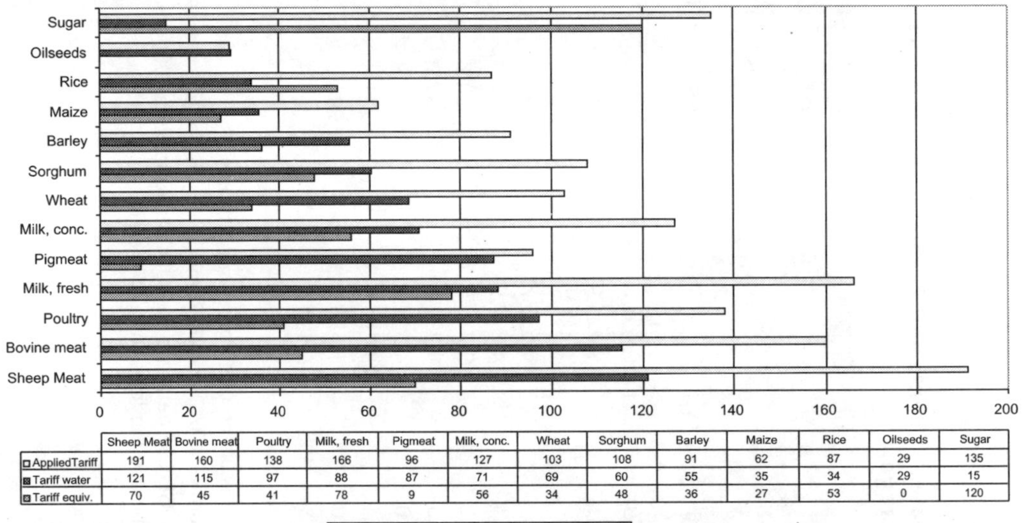


| | Sheep Meat | Bovine meat | Poultry | Milk, fresh | Pigmeat | Milk, conc. | Wheat | Sorghum | Barley | Maize | Rice | Oilseeds | Sugar |
|---|---|---|---|---|---|---|---|---|---|---|---|---|---|
| AppliedTariff | 191 | 160 | 138 | 166 | 96 | 127 | 103 | 108 | 91 | 62 | 87 | 29 | 135 |
| Tariff water | 121 | 115 | 97 | 88 | 87 | 71 | 69 | 60 | 55 | 35 | 34 | 29 | 15 |
| Tariff equiv. | 70 | 45 | 41 | 78 | 9 | 56 | 34 | 48 | 36 | 27 | 53 | 0 | 120 |

*Source:* Applied tariffs data are from UNCTAD's ATPSM database. Tariff equivalent tariffs of binding TRQs are from the OECD's PSE/CSE database 2002. Because of different data sources and an arbitrary selection of countries and commodities, the estimates of water in the tariff are very imprecise and are meant only for illustrative purposes.

### *Tariff Peaks and Dispersion*

Data in table 4.3 demonstrate the high dispersion in tariff rates, with a large number of tariff peaks for products of interest to developing countries (Cernat, Laird, and Turrini 2002). Gibson and others (2001) show that there is a large difference between the median and mean tariffs in rich countries, indicating mega-tariffs (tariffs over 100 percent) or tariff peaks, accompanied by a wide dispersion in tariff rates. The United States (U.S.) has 24 mega-tariffs with the mean tariff four times the median tariff. The European Union (EU) has 141 mega-tariffs and the mean

**TABLE 4.3 Examples of Tariff Peaks and Dispersion in Agriculure**

| Product | Standard Deviation | MFN-weighted average tariff | Maximum MFN tariff | Domestic peaks (percent) | International peaks (percent) |
|---|---|---|---|---|---|
| Beef | 16.16 | 12.89 | 41.35 | 52.11 | 29.58 |
| Sheep meat | 9.02 | 0.84 | 21.25 | 3.45 | 3.45 |
| Poultry | 33.33 | 8.16 | 134.30 | 2.52 | 2.52 |
| Milk | 56.33 | 22.70 | 140.00 | 17.78 | 17.78 |
| Milk concentrates | 105.02 | 19.59 | 308.50 | 22.15 | 22.15 |
| Butter | 100.54 | 249.97 | 336.25 | 32.47 | 19.48 |
| Barley | 41.73 | 22.12 | 101.50 | 11.43 | 11.43 |
| Maize | 13.19 | 3.99 | 50.00 | 4.00 | 4.00 |
| Wheat | 28.93 | 39.51 | 81.50 | 13.11 | 9.84 |
| Banana | 9.07 | 4.27 | 27.95 | 22.73 | 13.64 |
| Citrus fruits | 7.1 | 4.62 | 25.65 | 6.10 | 8.54 |
| Other tropical fruits | 8.57 | 10.68 | 33.25 | 14.86 | 8.11 |
| Nontropical fruits | 5.6 | 0.77 | 17.75 | 1.45 | 2.90 |
| Chocolate | 40.55 | 22.72 | 276.50 | 34.21 | 14.33 |
| Tobacco | 97.97 | 44.86 | 350.00 | 6.25 | 6.25 |
| Cigarettes | 10.78 | 2.67 | 30.00 | 4.17 | 4.17 |
| Cigars | 6.95 | 10.14 | 17.00 | 0.00 | 10.00 |
| Other tobacco products | 115.49 | 168.57 | 350.00 | 16.46 | 17.72 |
| Tea | 5.96 | 3.82 | 17.75 | 11.11 | 11.11 |
| Oilseeds | 24.84 | 9.56 | 171.00 | 1.02 | 1.02 |
| Vegetable oils | 4.99 | 1.40 | 19.95 | 3.74 | 1.15 |

*Source:* UNCTAD TRAINS by Cernat, Laird, and Turrini (2002).

tariff is over two and one-half times the median tariff while Japan has 142 mega-tariffs with the mean tariff almost six times the median tariff. These mega-tariffs differ across countries for the same commodity.

A uniform tariff structure is preferred by economists and policymakers if maximizing the benefits of trade liberalization is the goal because misallocation of resources (land, capital, labor, consumption, investment, and so on) is exacerbated with an increasing degree of tariff dispersion. Tariff peaks increase the economic inefficiency stemming from protection as they reduce competition and specialization according to comparative advantage, and distort consumption. Uniform tariff rates are also more transparent and easier to administer than nonuniform tariffs, and less likely to be determined by the relative political power of domestic industries, bribery of customs officials, and administrative inefficiency. Data presented in table 4.3 reveal the degree to which applied tariff peaks affect various agricultural products. The highest tariff dispersion was found in tobacco products, milk concentrates, and butter. The highest standard deviation products are also the ones where the highest maximum tariffs are found (between 300 and 350 percent).

In terms of frequency of tariff peaks across agricultural products (expressed as the percentage of tariff lines affected by tariff peaks in the total number of lines), the most affected sectors by domestic tariff peaks are beef (more than 52 percent) and chocolate (more than 34 percent). The highest frequency of international tariff peaks is also found in beef, followed by dairy products (milk and butter). Very high weighted out-of-quota tariffs are applied to butter and other tobacco products, which also have record maximum out-of-quota tariffs. Other products with high tariffs have lower weighted average, probably as a result of a large value of trade in items that have zero or very low *ad valorem* tariff rates. In summary, the data show that although average tariff rates in developed countries have been reduced to low levels, tariff peaks on products of interest to developing countries are of concern. One way developing countries may gauge success in the Doha Round negotiations is if tariff peaks on products of interest are reduced, thereby improving market access.

### *Tariff Escalation*

Average tariffs on processed agricultural products are found to be consistently higher than average tariffs on raw or low levels of processing, although bulk agricultural products have higher tariff rates than intermediate products in the U.S. and the EU (Wainio, Gibson, and Whitley 2001). An increase in tariffs with each stage of processing is termed tariff escalation and affects trade flows in a number of products of interest to developing countries. Tariff escalation biases exports toward unprocessed resource-based commodities, characterized by low value-added. This may cause difficulties for commodity-dependent developing countries in their attempt to diversify their agricultural export base. A number of important commodities have been categorized according to primary, intermediate, and processed stages in production chains, and table 4.4 provides the tariff levels by product and by processing stage in the Quad markets (U.S., EU, Japan, and Canada). Tariffs can escalate between raw and semifinished products and also between semifinished and finished products. On average, the escalation in Canada, Japan, and the EU is higher between raw and finished goods, while in the U.S. the average highest escalation is found between semifinished and finished goods.

A more detailed analysis of tariff escalation, distinguishing between markets of developing and developed countries, shows that tariff escalation is not just a feature of developed markets but in fact is present (sometimes even more prominently) in developing countries as well. Tariff escalation also impedes South–South trade.

### *Special Safeguard Tariffs*

Safeguards are contingent restrictions on imports adopted temporarily to deal with special circumstances such as a sudden surge in imports (WTO 2002c). They normally come under the WTO Safeguards Agreement, but the URAA has additional special provisions (Article 5) on safeguards that apply only to tariffied agricultural products. In agriculture, unlike safeguards provisions that apply to manufactured products, higher safeguards duties can be triggered automatically when the import volume of the agricultural products rises above a certain level, or if prices fall below a certain level; and it is not necessary to demonstrate that serious injury is being caused to the domestic industry.

The special agricultural safeguards (SSG) can only be used on products that were tariffied—which amount to less than 20 percent of all agricultural products (as defined by "tariff lines"). They cannot be used on imports within the tariff quotas, and they can only be used if the government reserved the right to do so in its schedule of commitments on agriculture. Most developing countries cannot use these safeguards because few TRQs were adopted by them and most opted for tariff ceiling bindings rather than for tariffication. In practice, the special agricultural safeguard has been used in relatively few cases. Ten WTO members have notified the WTO as required that, from 1995 to 2001, they have taken such action under the SSG. Thirty-eight WTO members that have reserved the right to use a combined total of 5,043 special safeguards on agricultural products are shown in table 4.5.

Taking U.S. dairy as an example, two types of special safeguards apply—price-based and quantity-based. Price-based special safeguards allow additional duties (over and above the out-of-quota tariff rate) to be imposed on out-of-quota imports when prices fall below a fixed trigger price (based on average prices during 1986–88), and are invoked automatically on a shipment-by-shipment basis. Price-based special safeguards duties operate like a variable levy scheme whereby duties increase as the value of imports declines. According to WTO notifications, price-based special safeguards were invoked on a significant volume of out-of-quota imports during 1995–98 on butter and cheese. Quantity-based special safeguards allow additional duties to be imposed on out-of-quota imports if actual imports exceed a certain trigger level. The trigger import level for each product is based on imports over the previous three years, so these are announced annually and decline 15 percent during the URAA implementation period.

## The Basic Economics of Barriers to Market Access

Import barriers such as tariffs and quotas reduce the level of imports, thereby increasing the price in the importing country and reducing world prices to exporters and other importers. Treasuries

**TABLE 4.4 Tariff Escalation (Weighted Average MFN Applied Tariffs in Percentage) in the Quad Markets (US, EU, Japan, and Canada)**

| Product Group | *Canada* | | | *Japan* | | | *United States* | | | *European Union* | | |
|---|---|---|---|---|---|---|---|---|---|---|---|---|
| | Raw | Semifinished | Finished | Raw | Semifinished | Finished | Raw | Semifinished | Finished | Raw | Semifinished | Finished |
| Meat products | 0.11 | 10.25 | 18.83 | 0.88 | 12.92 | 10.66 | 0.60 | 6.15 | 3.38 | 1.53 | 5.16 | 12.95 |
| Dairy and egg products | 1.94 | — | 9.00 | 18.77 | — | 17.39 | 2.82 | — | 11.56 | 6.27 | — | 7.70 |
| Fish products | 0.01 | 1.53 | 0.01 | 3.91 | 5.10 | 11.58 | 0.15 | 1.88 | 1.96 | 9.34 | 14.64 | 13.31 |
| Sugar products | 0.00 | 6.25 | 5.76 | 25.50 | 1.00 | 15.40 | — | 5.82 | 7.48 | 17.30 | — | 13.07 |
| Cereal products | 2.75 | 3.85 | 4.43 | 6.37 | 12.86 | 20.79 | 0.87 | 4.32 | 3.12 | 1.35 | 11.56 | 11.65 |
| Vegetable oils | 0.00 | 3.00 | — | 0.14 | 4.20 | — | 35.42 | 1.83 | — | 0.00 | 1.10 | — |
| Coffee, tea, and spices | 0.08 | 0.00 | 5.14 | 1.63 | 10.60 | 20.02 | 0.37 | 0.07 | 5.35 | 0.11 | 8.63 | 8.00 |
| Fruits and vegetables | 0.89 | 4.56 | 3.16 | 7.07 | 8.44 | 17.92 | 2.94 | 6.07 | 3.95 | 8.12 | 8.02 | 19.15 |
| Tobacco | 7.79 | — | 8.17 | 0.00 | — | 0.07 | 68.26 | — | 350.00 | — | — | 24.81 |
| Other food | — | 5.70 | 7.90 | — | 13.43 | 16.51 | — | 13.00 | 6.98 | — | 8.58 | 10.47 |
| Animal food | 0.01 | 3.17 | 0.26 | 0.00 | 0.20 | 0.00 | 0.61 | 2.27 | 0.00 | 0.71 | 4.55 | 0.00 |
| Hides and skins | 0.00 | 0.00 | 13.05 | 0.00 | 0.64 | 19.47 | 0.00 | 0.25 | 12.49 | 0.00 | 0.00 | 8.54 |
| Average | 1.23 | 3.83 | 6.88 | 5.77 | 6.94 | 13.62 | 11.20 | 4.17 | 36.93 | 4.47 | 6.93 | 11.79 |

*Source:* UNCTAD TRAINS by Cernat, Laird, and Turrini (2002).

**TABLE 4.5 Special Safeguards Tabled in the URAA**

| Country/Entity | Number | Country/Entity | Number | Country/Entity | Number |
|---|---|---|---|---|---|
| Australia | 10 | Iceland | 462 | Phillipines | 118 |
| Barbados | 37 | Indonesia | 13 | Poland | 144 |
| Botswana | 161 | Israel | 41 | Romania | 175 |
| Bulgaria | 21 | Japan | 121 | Slovak Republic | 114 |
| Canada | 150 | Korea, Rep. of | 111 | South Africa | 166 |
| Colombia | 56 | Malaysia | 72 | Swaziland | 166 |
| Costa Rica | 87 | Mexico | 293 | Switzerland-Lctn | 961 |
| Czech Republic | 236 | Morocco | 374 | Thailand | 52 |
| Ecuador | 7 | Namibia | 166 | Tunisia | 32 |
| El Salvador | 84 | New Zealand | 4 | United States | 189 |
| European Union | 539 | Nicaragua | 21 | Uruguay | 2 |
| Guatemala | 107 | Norway | 581 | Venezuela, RB | 76 |
| Hungary | 117 | Panama | 6 | | |

*Source:* WTO (2002c).

accumulate tariff revenues and product quota holders (such as companies, state trading enterprises, and others) obtain excess profits ("rents"). Farmers in the protected import market increase supply and consumers reduce their demand. The opposite occurs in exporting and other importing countries. Hence, import barriers reduce economic efficiency by distorting relative prices in both the importing and exporting countries, and also impose an externality in the form of lower world prices that adversely affects all farmers outside the protectionist importing countries. Inputs such as land prices are also adversely affected in other countries, along with foreign exchange earnings.

The analysis of alternative trade liberalization scenarios is somewhat more complex than simple tariffs or a simple import quota in the case of tariff quota schemes. It is important to understand that only one of the import tariffs or the quota can be effective in the sense that it controls or limits imports at any one time, rendering the other two policy instruments redundant. Hence, there are three possible regimes, depending on the level of the quota for a given market situation and relative tariff levels. Figure 4.12 summarizes these three regimes, where PW is the world price and the importer is assumed to be able to import as much as it needs without changing the level of the world price (Moschini 1991; de Gorter and others 2001). The import demand curve is given by ED (the horizontal difference between the domestic demand and supply curves). M denotes total imports and the import quota is depicted as Q. $P_d$ represents the resulting domestic price in each regime. The three regimes are as follows:

- The "in-quota tariff regime" where the lower in-quota tariff $t_1$ is effective, quota rents and out-of-quota revenues are zero, and in-quota tariff revenues are equal to $t_1$ times imports (figure 4.12a).
- The "quota-binding regime" where the import quota determines price, quota rents equal the difference between the domestic and world price plus $t_1$ times the quota, in-quota tariff revenues equal $t_1$ times the quota, and out-of-quota tariff revenues are zero (figure 4.12b).
- The "out-of-quota tariff regime" where the higher out-of-quota tariff $t_2$ is effective, quota rents equal the difference in the domestic and world price times the quota, out-of-quota tariff revenues equal the difference between domestic and world price times the difference in the total imports and the quota, and in-quota tariff revenues equal $t_1$ times the quota (figure 4.12c).

While only one policy instrument can be effective at a time, a change in world prices, a change in the policy instruments, or a change in domestic market conditions can result in a switch in the effective tariff or quota regime. However, a change in the redundant policy instrument may have no impact on the volume of trade or prices unless that change

**FIGURE 4.12 The Three TRQ Regimes**

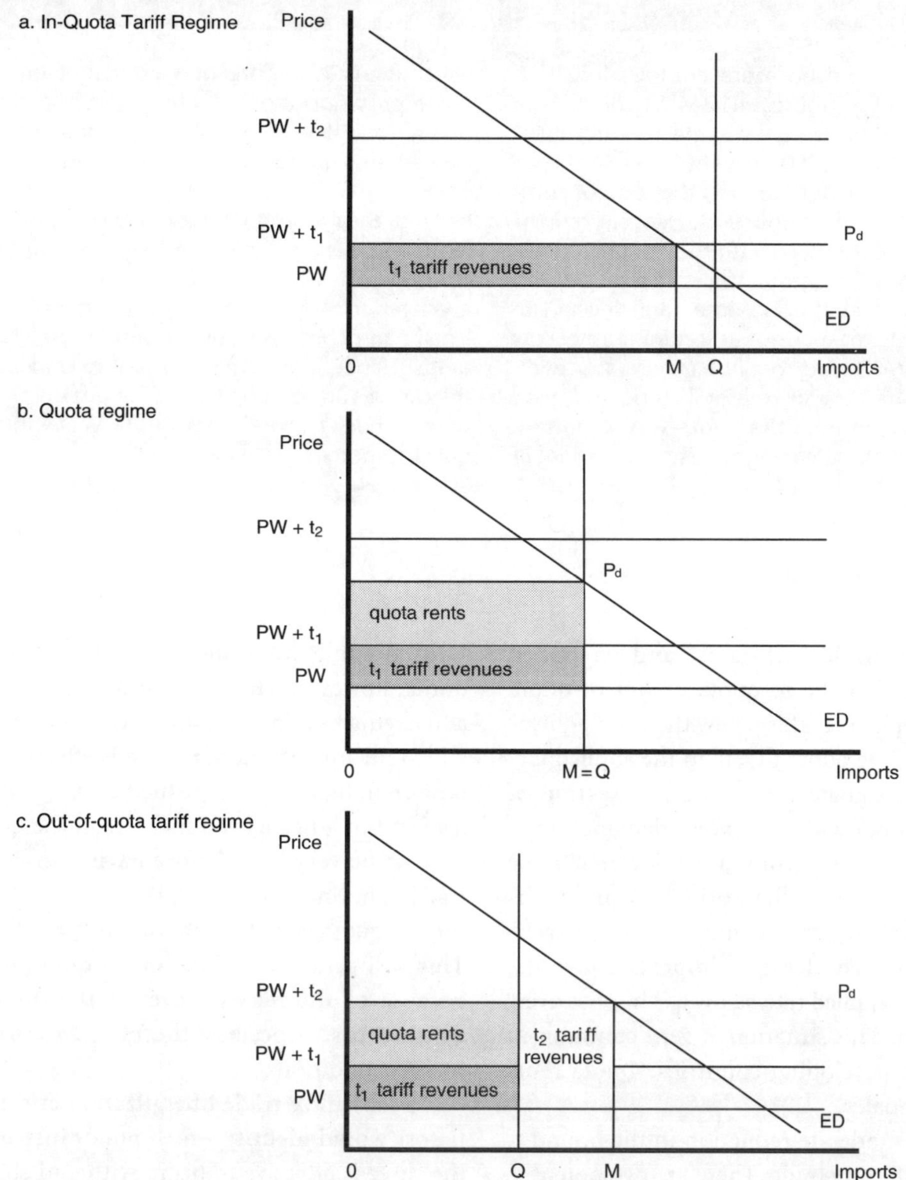


*Source:* Authors.

is sufficiently large to cause a switch in the effective regime (Boughner, de Gorter, and Sheldon 2000).

### *The Implications for the Trade Negotiations*

Other types of tariffs may be used by countries so that there are several variations of the in-quota and out-of-quota tariffs described above in terms of "applied" versus "bound" and "preferential" (see box 4.2 for further explanation). As described below, "applied" tariffs, often significantly lower than bound rates, are especially prevalent in developing countries. Most developed countries offer lower tariffs for developing countries under "preferential" tariff schemes with rates below either the in-quota or out-of-quota tariffs, and can be equal to zero.

The basic implications of bound versus applied tariffs are shown in figure 4.13 where there are over-quota imports at the applied tariff t. In-quota tariffs are not necessarily bound, therefore they are

## BOX 4.2 More on Tariff Quotas

Tariff quotas are even more complicated than that described in figures 4.12–4.14. Nonquota imports often occur in the same product category. For example, 50 percent of U.S. cheese imports are nonquota products that do not compete with domestic production. Hence, comparing data on total imports with the quota level will be misleading. Governments also import beyond the quota but at the in-quota tariff level. The quota is not a maximum but a minimum access level. The WTO data do not report any over-quota imports, so a fill rate of 100 percent may mean that more than the quota was imported. Another type of misleading statistics is the case in which the WTO reports quota under-fill but does not report out-of-quota imports at the out-of-quota tariff levels, which may equal or even exceed the quota under-fill reported. In these cases, rents are foregone by quota holders because their costs are too high and out-of-quota tariff revenues are collected by the importing country in their stead. Some countries do not even report any imports beyond quota levels. Finally, some imports come in under preferential tariffs. Hence, it is very important to understand the details surrounding the definitions of imports, quota under-fill, and over-quota versus out-of-quota imports.

referred to here as the "official $t_1$," and an applied tariff can be either the in-quota or out-of-quota tariff. If the applied tariff is below the tariff equivalent of the binding quota $t_eQ$, then the applied tariff is simply designated as t. The intersection of the implied quota with the excess demand curve ED of the importer determines the domestic price PW + $t_eQ$ (where PW is the world price and $t_eQ$ is the tariff equivalent of the binding quota with over-quota imports). The level of imports above the quota but at an applied rate below $t_eQ$ implies over-quota imports. This situation is very common in both rich and developing countries. Quota rents can be substantial.

A small or moderate reduction in the bound $t_2$ can have no effect on trade. There are two potential sources for this: the gap between bound and applied tariffs (tariff binding overhang) and the gap between the domestic price and world price plus applied $t_2$ (water in the tariff). Many tariff quotas operate in a quota-binding regime protected by very high levels of out-of-quota $t_2$ tariffs. Under these circumstances, only a very large reduction in $t_2$ will generate a switch to an out-of-quota regime. A small reduction in the out-of-quota tariff rate will have no impact. Only if $t_2$ falls below the price gap (the tariff equivalent when the quota is binding) will it have an impact on liberalizing trade rather than simply reducing water in the tariff or tariff binding overhang. A small change in the quota, however, will cause an increase in imports and a reduction in domestic prices. The situation in which the out-of-quota regime is effective initially is given in figure 4.14. A reduction in $t_2$ will have an impact but a negotiated increase in the quota will need to be very large before having an impact on trade. The in-quota tariff is effective only if the import quota is to the right of point *a* in the figure. This will generate a situation of quota under-fill because of the relative level of the three policy instruments (especially the effective tariff t) or market conditions.

To maximize trade liberalization effects, negotiators would identify which policy instrument of the three is effective to begin with and change the corresponding policy instrument. They could focus on reducing out-of-quota tariffs, in those cases with out-of-quota imports or if the out-of-quota tariff $t_2$ is close to the tariff equivalent of the binding quota. If the tariff equivalent of the binding quota is far below $t_2$, increasing the quota will have a greater chance of liberalizing trade in the short run. A reduction in $t_1$ will liberalize trade only if $t_2$ is close to and below $t_1$, in which case both tariffs need to be reduced, or if under-fill is significant because $t_1$ is effective—otherwise, quotas will also have to be increased to obtain trade-liberalizing effects. Because governments may try

**FIGURE 4.13 Definitions of Alternative Tariffs**

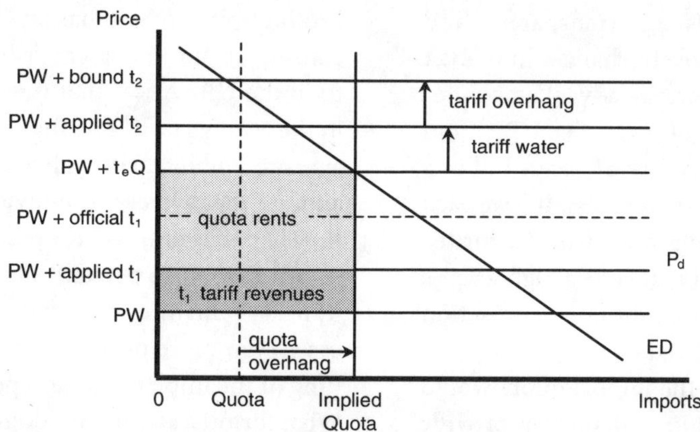


*Notes:* The applied $t_2$ can be below $t_eQ$ or anywhere below bound $t_2$ (if applied $t_2 < t_eQ$, no water in the tariff exists but tariff binding overhang remains). There can be quota underfill and out-of-quota imports.
*Source:* Authors.

**FIGURE 4.14 Out-of-Quota Imports with Quota Underfill and Out-of-Quota Imports**

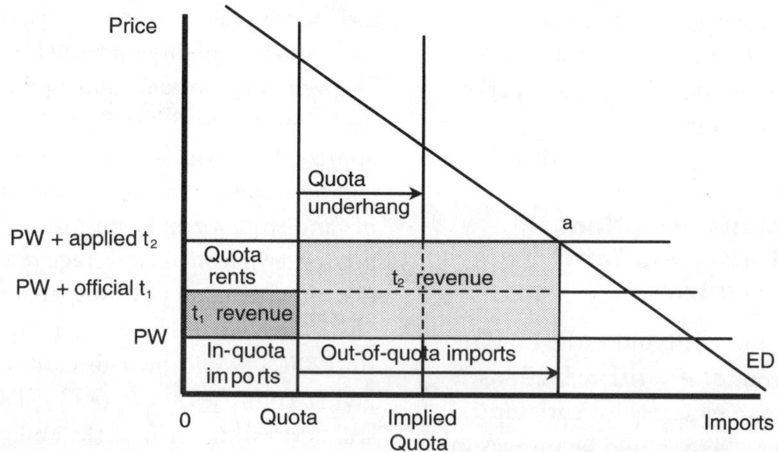


*Source*: Authors.

to protect farmers, they should not be given the choice of a trade-liberalizing instrument because a redundant policy instrument might be chosen, thereby thwarting the objective of increasing market access. Such an approach relies on information about each commodity sector and country, and the resulting tariff policy conclusions may rapidly become obsolete. A switch in regimes can occur with changes in market conditions—for example, in a case in which the quota is initially effective and analysis would therefore have determined that an increase in the tariff quota was the effective means of liberalizing trade. An increase in world prices can cause a switch to the $t_1$ regime. A downward trend can put trade into a $t_2$ regime (although tariff water and overhang are so large in some cases that this switch would be extremely unlikely). In either case, the tariff quota is no longer the effective way of liberalizing trade.

A broader approach to tariffs and quotas that focuses on more macro indicators such as minimum quotas relative to size of market (for instance, consumption) and maximum prices as a percentage of world prices (tariff) may be desired. The WTO gives primacy to tariffs over quotas as the more effective instrument because tariffs are transparent and because they are more flexible to changes in market conditions and allow comparative advantage to prevail with changing volumes of trade. The URAA did provide for a minimum quantity of access but at a very low level, except for current access. It gave each country flexibility in setting out-of-quota tariffs; most countries therefore set $t_2$ at such a high level as to effectively perpetuate the quantitative restriction on imports that quotas replaced.

A very large increase in the import quota would result in in-quota tariff regimes that often provide much lower levels of domestic protection. A very large decrease in out-of-quota tariffs (comparable to commodities not protected by tariff quotas) could also result in out-of-quota tariff regimes with significantly lower levels of protection. The "Swiss formula" approach used for industrial products in the Tokyo Round caps out-of-quota tariffs and this would be effective in reducing peak tariffs and tariff dispersion in agriculture. Such an approach offers the prospect of a substantial increase in market access for agricultural commodities.

## An Empirical Analysis of Options for Liberalizing Tariffs and Tariff Quotas in OECD Countries

Because of water in the tariff and tariff binding overhang, another round of tariff reductions is needed to improve market access for agricultural products. In principle, there should be no reason why the same overall rate of reduction could not be achieved that was agreed to in the URAA, namely a reduction by 36 percent and a minimum of 15 percent per tariff line (for developed countries) over a six-year implementation period (2001 to 2006), but with more effective modalities than were used in the URAA. This approach raises the following questions:

1. What should the starting point be for calculating the reductions? Zero tariffs are never reached if percentage reductions are always made from existing tariffs.
2. What tariff rates should be disciplined? Bound or applied tariffs? And what should be done about tariff equivalents of binding quotas—simply expand quotas?
3. Should a reduction formula be negotiated on a product-by-product basis? One major shortcoming of the 36 percent reduction rate agreed to in the URAA was that it was not a reduction in the average tariff rate for each country, but an average cut in tariffs. Hence, countries could allocate that average to individual tariff lines, as they liked (as long as they reduced no single tariff by less than 15 percent). As a result, many tariff peaks remain, and tariff dispersion is in many cases even more pronounced than at the beginning of the implementation period.[9]
4. What formula should be adopted to reduce average tariffs across products and reduce tariff peaks and dispersion? The Swiss formula has been used for industrial products in previous rounds and has been proposed for agriculture by the U.S. and the Cairns Group.[10] Because higher tariffs inevitably contain more water and binding overhang than lower tariffs, a formula that results in more uniform tariffs is likely to be the most effective.
5. How much flexibility on reducing tariffs should be given to individual countries? An interesting variation on the Swiss formula is a "cocktail" approach by which countries are allowed to choose among (a) a flat rate reduction of all tariffs and (b) a formula cut that yields an agreed but somewhat smaller average reduction of tariffs, but attenuates tariff dispersion. A modified Swiss formula developed by Francois and Martin (2002) would be a disciplined method of giving countries more political flexibility yet still addressing tariff peaks and dispersion, as well as tariff escalation.

There are a variety of possible liberalization scenarios for tariffs, applied or bound (including the tariff equivalents of quota binding situations):

1. Proportional cuts;
2. The Swiss formula;
3. Continuation of the URAA formula;
4. Across-the-board tariff cuts; and
5. Reduction of bound tariffs to applied tariffs (including tariff equivalents of binding quotas).

We analyze two empirical simulations here:

- OECD data on market price support (MPS) that reflect effective average tariffs or tariff equivalents for each commodity group (in *ad valorem* equivalents) for 29 countries and 11 commodity groups (see "initial *ad valorem* tariffs" in the first part of table 4.6).

- OECD's PEM model with a subset of the commodities (4) and countries (20) but where the effects of a binding quota are taken into account explicitly as well as world price changes with liberalization.

### *Analyzing the Swiss Formula Approach to Tariff Reductions*

The Swiss formula (SW) is defined as follows:

$$T_1/T_0 = a/(a + T_0)$$

where $T_1$ is the new tariff, $T_0$ is the initial tariff and *a* is the maximum tariff that is determined in advance by the WTO agreement.

There are several properties of the SW if a common parameter *a* is negotiated:

1. There exists a common maximum tariff for all countries and commodities determined by the value of the parameter *a* chosen by the world body politic (WTO) where $0 \leqslant a \leqslant \infty$.
2. High tariffs are brought down faster than low tariffs (in terms of percentage reduction in *ad valorem* tariffs) across commodities and across countries. Data in table 4.6 show:

    a. A high-tariff country's reduction in average tariffs is higher than that of a low-tariff country;
    b. A high-tariff country's final average tariff is higher than a low-tariff country's final average tariff;
    c. A high-tariff country's average tariff reduction is higher than a low-tariff country's average tariff reduction; and
    d. A high-tariff country's average of tariff reductions is higher than a low-tariff country's average of tariff reductions.

3. There cannot be a common reduction in average tariffs across commodities and countries because of different initial tariffs but the final tariffs will have greatly reduced dispersions and similar maximum tariffs.
4. There cannot be a common average tariff for all countries but the differences *ex post* will be greatly reduced.

Note that some tariffs are reduced by more than 25 percent when *a* = 0.25 (and some less than 25 percent) but the maximum tariff is less than 25 percent for any $T_0 < \infty$. The average tariff must be less than *a*. If the average initial tariff is more than 100 percent, the reduction will be greater than 50 percent in this example of *a* = 0.50.

For each $T_i < \infty$, the maximum tariff will be less than *a*. For $a = T_0$, there is a 50 percent reduction in tariffs. The country with very high tariffs will have the highest average tariff *ex post* (but still less than *a*). Note that specific tariffs cannot be disciplined using the SW because the parameter *a* will vary depending on the units and therefore will vary across countries and commodities with currencies, units used, and so on.

The Agreement on Agriculture formula (AA) is as follows:

$$\left(\frac{T_{1,1} - T_{0,1}}{T_{0,1}} + \frac{T_{1,2} - T_{0,2}}{T_{0,2}} + \cdots \frac{T_{1,j} - T_{0,j}}{T_{0,j}}\right)/N \geq 0.36$$

where j = 1 to N countries.

In this case, there is an average reduction in tariffs (not a reduction in average tariffs as in the SW approach).

### *Analyzing Liberalization Scenarios Using the PEM Model*

There are tariff rate quota regimes for wheat and coarse grains in Mexico, Switzerland, and Japan in the OECD's Policy Evaluation Model (PEM—see OECD 2001a, appendix A, for detailed descriptions of the PEM). There is also a tariff quota regime for rice in the EU and Japan.[11] Table 4.7 shows the level and value of production as well as tariff-quota-related protection for grains and oilseeds in the six combined regions in the PEM. Total world production ranges from 236 million tonnes (mmt) for oilseeds to 904 mmt for coarse grains. The total amount of grains and oilseeds import quota in all six regions is only 43 mmt, ranging from 0 percent of production for oilseeds to 3 percent for coarse grains. The total value of production of tariff-quota-related market price support due to import barriers (MPS) is US$15.9 billion, which was about 7.3 percent of the value of production (net of market price support). Other market nontariff-quota-related protection amounted to US$0.7 billion, which indicates that tariff quotas are the

**TABLE 4.6 Analyzing Tariff Equivalents Using the Swiss Formula (maximum tariff of 25%)**

| | Australia | Canada | Czech Rep. | EU | Hungary | Iceland | Japan | Korea, Rep. of | Mexico | New Zealand | Norway | Poland | Slovak Rep | Switzerland | Turkey | U.S. | Average |
|---|---|---|---|---|---|---|---|---|---|---|---|---|---|---|---|---|---|
| *1. Initial ad valorem tariffs* | | | | | | | | | | | | | | | | | |
| Wheat | 0.0% | 0.0% | 0.0% | 0.8% | 0.0% | n.a. | 538.5% | n.a. | 33.3% | n.a. | 122.5% | 20.4% | 0.0% | 48.2% | 4.5% | 0.0% | 59.1% |
| Maize | n.a. | 0.0% | n.a. | 12.3% | 0.0% | n.a. | n.a. | n.a. | 50.2% | n.a. | n.a. | 0.0% | 0.0% | 59.6% | 15.5% | 0.0% | 15.3% |
| Other grains | 0.0% | 0.0% | 0.0% | 1.1% | 0.0% | n.a. | 405.2% | 316.1% | 5.3% | n.a. | 89.9% | 0.0% | 0.0% | 98.4% | 5.4% | 0.0% | 65.8% |
| Rice | 2.0% | n.a. | n.a. | 53.3% | n.a. | n.a. | 564.4% | 409.4% | 14.5% | n.a. | n.a. | n.a. | n.a. | n.a. | n.a. | 0.0% | 173.9% |
| Oilseeds | 0.0% | 0.0% | 0.0% | 0.0% | 0.0% | n.a. | 0.0% | 734.6% | 23.2% | n.a. | n.a. | 34.7% | 0.0% | 332.5% | 57.1% | 0.0% | 90.9% |
| Refined sugar | 0.0% | n.a. | 8.8% | 651.7% | 19.9% | n.a. | 398.9% | n.a. | 58.5% | n.a. | n.a. | 94.6% | 38.9% | 237.5% | 143.3% | 56.2% | 155.3% |
| Milk | 0.0% | 96.8% | 16.1% | 59.6% | 28.6% | 74.6% | 274.9% | 182.1 % | 74.9% | 0.0% | 99.8% | 9.7% | 4.1% | 153.8% | 29.0% | 93.4% | 74.8% |
| Beef and veal | 0.0% | 0.6% | 33.4% | 120.0% | 22.2% | 98.4% | 38.5% | 152.7% | 2.8% | 0.0% | 136.6% | 0.0% | 5.8% | 202.8% | 71.1% | 0.0% | 55.3% |
| Sheep meat | 0.0% | n.a. | n.a. | 116.7% | 43.5% | 11.8% | n.a. | n.a. | n.a. | 0.0% | 93.3% | 0.0% | n.a. | 267.0% | 18.1% | 9.9% | 56.0% |
| Wool | 0.0% | n.a. | n.a. | n.a. | n.a. | 115.7% | n.a. | n.a. | n.a. | n.a. | 0.0% | n.a. | n.a. | n.a. | n.a. | 1.8% | 29.4% |
| Pigmeat | 0.0% | 0.0% | 3.5% | 22.9% | 0.0% | 17.2% | 80.9% | 18.8% | 6.3% | 0.0% | 18.3% | 0.0% | 0.0% | 34.9% | n.a. | 0.0% | 13.5% |
| Poultry meat | 0.0% | 1.2% | 46.7% | 3.4% | 16.5% | 431.6% | 11.7% | 42.6% | 0.0% | 8.1% | 162.0% | 23.1% | 31.9% | 415.8% | 5.6% | 0.2% | 75.0% |
| Eggs | 0.0% | 17.3% | 58.6% | 0.0% | 160.7% | 212.6% | 17.0% | 14.3% | 0.0% | 50.6% | 91.6% | 73.3% | 0.0% | 318.6% | 50.0% | 0.0% | 66.5% |
| Average | 0.2% | 12.9% | 18.6% | 86.8% | 26.5% | 137.4% | 233.0% | 233.8% | 24.5% | 9.8% | 90.4% | 23.3% | 8.1% | 197.2% | 40.0% | 12.4% | 71.6% |
| Variance | 0.0% | 10% | 5% | 336% | 22% | 214% | 526% | 612% | 7% | 4% | 27% | 11% | 2% | 166% | 19% | 8% | 22% |
| *2. Final ad valorem tariffs* | | | | | | | | | | | | | | | | | |
| Wheat | 0.0% | 0.0% | 0.0% | 0.7% | 0.0% | n.a. | 23.9% | n.a. | 14.3% | n.a. | 20.8% | 11.2% | 0.0% | 16.5% | 3.8% | 0.0% | 7.0% |
| Maize | n.a. | 0.0% | n.a. | 8.2% | 0.0% | n.a. | n.a. | n.a. | 16.7% | n.a. | n.a. | 0.0% | 0.0% | 17.6% | 9.6% | 0.0% | 5.8% |
| Other grains | 0.0% | 0.0% | 0.0% | 1.1% | 0.0% | n.a. | 23.5% | 23.2% | 4.3% | n.a. | 19.6% | 0.0% | 0.0% | 19.9% | 4.4% | 0.0% | 6.9% |
| Rice | 1.9% | n.a. | n.a. | 17.0% | n.a. | n.a. | 23.9% | 23.6% | 9.2% | n.a. | n.a. | n.a. | n.a. | n.a. | n.a. | 0.0% | 12.6% |
| Oilseeds | 0.0% | 0.0% | 0.0% | 0.0% | 0.0% | n.a. | 0.0% | 24.2% | 12.0% | n.a. | n.a. | 14.5% | 0.0% | 23.3% | 17.4% | 0.0% | 7.0% |
| Refined sugar | 0.0% | n.a. | 6.5% | 24.1% | 11.1 % | n.a. | 23.5% | n.a. | 17.5% | n.a. | n.a. | 19.8% | 15.2% | 22.6% | 21.3% | 17.3% | 16.3% |
| Milk | 0.0% | 19.9% | 9.8% | 17.6% | 13.3% | 18.7% | 22.9% | 22.0% | 18.7% | 0.0% | 20.0% | 7.0% | 3.5% | 21.5% | 13.4% | 19.7% | 14.3% |
| Beef and veal | 0.0% | 0.6% | 14.3% | 20.7% | 11.8% | 19.9% | 15.2% | 21.5% | 2.5% | 0.0% | 21.1% | 0.0% | 4.7% | 22.3% | 18.5% | 0.0% | 10.8% |
| Sheep meat | 0.0% | n.a. | n.a. | 20.6% | 15.9% | 8.0% | n.a. | n.a. | n.a. | 0.0% | 19.7% | 0.0% | n.a. | 22.9% | 10.5% | 7.1% | 10.5% |
| Wool | 0.0% | n.a. | n.a. | n.a. | n.a. | 20.6% | n.a. | n.a. | n.a. | n.a. | 0.0% | n.a. | n.a. | n.a. | n.a. | 1.7% | 5.6% |
| Pigmeat | 0.0% | 0.0% | 3.1% | 12.0% | 0.0% | 10.2% | 19.1% | 10.7% | 5.0% | 0.0% | 10.6% | 0.0% | 0.0% | 14.6% | n.a. | 0.0% | 5.7% |
| Poultry meat | 0.0% | 1.1% | 16.3% | 3.0% | 9.9% | 23.6% | 7.9% | 15.8% | 0.0% | 6.1% | 21.7% | 12.0% | 14.0% | 23.6% | 4.5% | 0.2% | 10.0% |
| Eggs | 0.0% | 10.2% | 17.5% | 0.0% | 21.6% | 22.4% | 10.1% | 9.1% | 0.0% | 16.7% | 19.6% | 18.6% | 0.0% | 23.2% | 16.7% | 0.0% | 11.6% |
| Average | 0.2% | 3.5% | 10.7% | 10.4% | 7.6% | 17.6% | 17.0% | 18.7% | 9.1% | 3.8% | 17.0% | 7.6% | 3.7% | 20.7% | 12.0% | 3.5% | 9.5% |
| Variance | 0.00% | 0.49% | 0.52% | 0.86% | 0.62% | 0.37% | 0.71% | 0.37% | 0.50% | 0.46% | 0.52% | 0.64% | 0.36% | 0.10% | 0.41% | 0.48% | 0.12% |

**TABLE 4.6 (continued)**

| | Australia | Canada | Czech Rep. | EU | Hungary | Iceland | Japan | Korea, Rep. of | Mexico | New Zealand | Norway | Poland | Slovak Rep | Switzerland | Turkey | U.S. | Average |
|---|---|---|---|---|---|---|---|---|---|---|---|---|---|---|---|---|---|
| *3. Percent reduction in tariffs* | | | | | | | | | | | | | | | | | |
| Wheat | 0.0% | 0.0% | 0.0% | −3.0% | 0.0% | n.a. | −95.6% | n.a. | −57.1% | n.a. | −83.1 % | −44.9% | 0.0% | −65.8% | −15.2% | 0.0% | −28.1 % |
| Maize | n.a. | 0.0% | n.a. | −32.9% | 0.0% | n.a. | n.a. | n.a. | −66.8% | n.a. | n.a. | 0.0% | 0.0% | −70.5% | −38.3% | 0.0% | −23.2% |
| Other grains | 0.0% | 0.0% | 0.0% | −4.4% | 0.0% | n.a. | −94.2% | −92.7% | −17.4% | n.a. | −78.2% | 0.0% | 0.0% | −79.7% | −17.7% | 0.0% | −27.4% |
| Rice | −7.4% | n.a. | n.a. | −68.1 % | n.a. | n.a. | −95.8% | −94.2% | −36.7% | n.a. | n.a. | n.a. | n.a. | n.a. | n.a. | 0.0% | −50.4% |
| Oilseeds | 0.0% | 0.0% | 0.0% | 0.0% | 0.0% | n.a. | 0.0% | −96.7% | −48.2% | n.a. | n.a. | −58.2% | 0.0% | −93.0% | −69.5% | 0.0% | −28.1 % |
| Refined sugar | 0.0% | n.a. | −25.9% | −96.3% | −44.3% | n.a. | −94.1 % | n.a. | −70.1 % | n.a. | n.a. | −79.1% | −60.9% | −90.5% | −85.1 % | −69.2% | −65.0% |
| Milk | 0.0% | −79.5% | −39.1 % | −70.4% | −53.4% | −74.9% | −91.7% | −87.9% | −75.0% | 0.0% | −80.0% | −27.9% | −14.1% | −86.0% | −53.7% | −78.9% | −57.0% |
| Beef and veal | 0.0% | −2.3% | −57.2% | −82.8% | −47.0% | −79.7% | −60.6% | −85.9% | −10.2% | 0.0% | −84.5% | 0.0% | −18.8% | −89.0% | −74.0% | 0.0% | −43.3% |
| Sheep meat | 0.0% | n.a. | n.a. | −82.4% | −63.5% | −32.1 % | n.a. | n.a. | n.a. | 0.0% | −78.9% | 0.0% | n.a. | −91.4% | −42.0% | −28.3% | −41.9% |
| Wool | 0.0% | n.a. | n.a. | n.a. | n.a. | −82.2% | n.a. | n.a. | n.a. | n.a. | 0.0% | n.a. | n.a. | n.a. | n.a. | −6.8% | −22.3% |
| Pigmeat | 0.0% | 0.0% | −12.4% | −47.8% | 0.0% | −40.8% | −76.4% | −42.9% | −20.1 % | 0.0% | −42.3% | 0.0% | 0.0% | −58.2% | n.a. | 0.0% | −22.7% |
| Poultry meat | 0.0% | −4.6% | −65.1 % | −12.1% | −39.7% | −94.5% | −31.8% | −63.0% | 0.0% | −24.5% | −86.6% | −48.0% | −56.1 % | −94.3% | −18.2% | −0.7% | −40.0% |
| Eggs | 0.0% | −40.9% | −70.1 % | 0.0% | −86.5% | −89.5% | −40.5% | −36.4% | 0.0% | −66.9% | −78.6% | −74.6% | 0.0% | −92.7% | −66.7% | 0.0% | −46.5% |
| Average | −0.6% | −14.1% | −30.0% | −41.7% | −30.4% | −70.5% | −68.1% | −75.0% | −36.5% | −15.2% | −68.0% | −30.2% | −15.0% | −82.8% | −48.1% | −14.1% | −38.1% |
| *4. Tariff reduction as a % of average tariff reduction* | | | | | | | | | | | | | | | | | |
| Wheat | 0.0% | 0.0% | 0.0% | −89.5% | n.a. | n.a. | 240.7% | n.a. | 103.6% | n.a. | 196.1 % | 60.1% | n.a. | 134.7% | −45.7% | n.a. | 60.0% |
| Maize | n.a. | 0.0% | | 42.1% | n.a. | n.a. | n.a. | n.a. | 188.2% | n.a. | n.a. | n.a. | n.a. | 204.2% | 65.6% | n.a. | 100.0% |
| Other grains | 0.0% | 0.0% | 0.0% | −84.1 % | n.a. | n.a. | 243.1 % | 237.6% | −36.6% | n.a. | 185.1 % | n.a. | n.a. | 190.5% | −35.6% | n.a. | 70.0% |
| Rice | −85.3% | n.a. | | 35.2% | n.a. | n.a. | 90.1% | 87.1% | −27.1 % | n.a. | n.a. | n.a. | n.a. | n.a. | n.a. | n.a. | 20.0% |
| Oilseeds | 0.0% | 0.0% | 0.0% | 0.0% | n.a. | n.a. | n.a. | 243.9% | 71.3% | n.a. | n.a. | 106.8% | n.a. | 230.7% | 147.3% | n.a. | 88.9% |
| Refined sugar | 0.0% | n.a. | −60.1% | 48.0% | −31.9% | n.a. | 44.7% | n.a. | 7.7% | n.a. | n.a. | 21.6% | −6.4% | 39.1% | 30.9% | 6.4% | 9.1% |
| Milk | 0.0% | 39.4% | −31.4% | 23.5% | −6.4% | 31.3% | 60.7% | 54.2% | 31.5% | n.a. | 40.2% | −51.1% | −75.3% | 50.8% | −5.8% | 38.3% | 13.3% |
| Beef and veal | 0.0% | −94.6% | 32.2% | 91.3% | 8.8% | 84.3% | 40.2% | 98.7% | −76.5% | n.a. | 95.4% | n.a. | −56.5% | 105.8% | 71.0% | n.a. | 30.8% |
| Sheep meat | 0.0% | n.a. | n.a. | 96.8% | 51.7% | −23.4% | n.a. | n.a. | n.a. | n.a. | 88.4% | n.a. | n.a. | 118.4% | 0.3% | −32.3% | 37.5% |
| Wool | 0.0% | n.a. | n.a. | n.a. | n.a. | 269.5% | n.a. | n.a. | n.a. | n.a. | n.a. | n.a. | n.a. | n.a. | n.a. | −69.5% | 66.7% |
| Pigmeat | 0.0% | 0.0% | −45.4% | 110.5% | n.a. | 79.3% | 236.1 % | 88.6% | −11.5% | n.a. | 86.2% | n.a. | n.a. | 156.3% | n.a. | n.a. | 70.0% |
| Poultry meat | 0.0% | −88.5% | 63.0% | −69.7% | −0.6% | 136.6% | −20.4% | 57.7% | n.a. | −38.7% | 116.8% | 20.2% | 40.3% | 136.1 % | −54.5% | −98.3% | 13.3% |
| Eggs | 0.0% | −12.0% | 50.9% | 0.0% | 86.3% | 92.6% | −12.9% | −21.6% | n.a. | 44.1% | 69.1% | 60.5% | n.a. | 99.6% | 43.5% | n.a. | 38.5% |
| Average | −7.1% | −17.3% | 1.0% | 17.0% | 18.0% | 95.8% | 102.5% | 105.8% | 27.8% | 2.7% | 109.7% | 36.3% | −24.5% | 133.3% | 21.7% | −31.1% | 37.0% |

**TABLE 4.6 (continued)**

| | Australia | Canada | Czech Rep. | EU | Hungary | Iceland | Japan | Korea Rep. of | Mexico | New Zealand | Norway | Poland | Slovak Rep. | Switzerland | Turkey | U.S. | Average |
|---|---|---|---|---|---|---|---|---|---|---|---|---|---|---|---|---|---|
| *5. Percentage reduction in average tariffs for each country* | | | | | | | | | | | | | | | | | |
| Average Tariff | −7.4% | −72.5% | −42.6% | −88.0% | −71.3% | −87.2% | −92.7% | −92.0% | −62.7% | −61 .1 % | −81.2% | −67.5% | −53.6% | −89.5% | −69.9% | −71.5% | −69.4% |
| *6. Percentage reduction in average tariff for each country relative to average of all countries' tariff reductions* | | | | | | | | | | | | | | | | | |
| AverageTariff | −89.3% | 4.5% | −38.6% | 26.8% | 2.7% | 25.6% | 33.5% | 32.5% | −9.7% | −12.0% | 17.0% | −2.8% | −22.8% | 28.9% | 0.7% | 3.0% | 0.0% |
| *7. Each country's initial tariff as a percentage of average initial tariff* | | | | | | | | | | | | | | | | | |
| Wheat | n.a. | n.a. | n.a. | −98.7% | n.a. | n.a. | 811.4% | n.a. | −43.6% | n.a. | 107.3% | −65.5% | n.a. | −18.5% | −92.4% | n.a. | 85.7% |
| Maize | n.a. | n.a. | n.a. | −19.8% | n.a. | n.a. | | n.a. | 228.4% | n.a. | n.a. | n.a. | n.a. | 289.8% | 1.7% | n.a. | 125.0% |
| Other grains | n.a. | n.a. | n.a. | −98.3% | n.a. | n.a. | 515.7% | 380.3% | −92.0% | n.a. | 36.6% | n.a. | n.a. | 49.5% | −91.8% | n.a. | 100.0% |
| Rice | −98.9% | n.a. | n.a. | −69.4% | n.a. | n.a. | 224.5% | 135.4% | −91.7% | n.a. | n.a. | n.a. | n.a. | n.a. | n.a. | n.a. | 20.0% |
| Oilseeds | n.a. | n.a. | n.a. | n.a. | n.a. | n.a. | n.a. | 707.9% | −74.4% | n.a. | n.a. | −61.8% | n.a. | 265.6% | −37.3% | n.a. | 160.0% |
| Refined sugar | n.a. | n.a. | −94.4% | 319.6% | −87.2% | n.a. | 156.9% | n.a. | −62.3% | n.a. | n.a. | −39.1 % | −74.9% | 52.9% | −7.7% | −63.8% | 10.0% |
| Milk | n.a. | 29.3% | −78.5% | −20.4% | −61.7% | −0.3% | 267.4% | 143.3% | 0.1% | n.a. | 33.4% | −87.1 % | −94.5% | 105.5% | −61 .2% | 24.8% | 14.3% |
| Beef and veal | n.a. | −98.9% | −39.7% | 116.9% | −59.8% | 78.0% | −30.4% | 176.2% | −94.9% | n.a. | 146.9% | n.a. | −89.5% | 266.7% | 28.5% | n.a. | 33.3% |
| Sheep meat | n.a. | n.a. | n.a. | 108.3% | −22.3% | −78.9% | n.a. | n.a. | n.a. | n.a. | 66.5% | n.a. | n.a. | 376.5% | −67.7% | −82.3% | 42.9% |
| Wool | n.a. | n.a. | n.a. | n.a. | n.a. | 293.8% | n.a. | n.a. | n.a. | n.a. | n.a. | n.a. | n.a. | n.a. | n.a. | −93.8% | 100.0% |
| Pigmeat | n.a. | n.a. | −73.8% | 69.5% | n.a. | 27.2% | 498.3% | 38.7% | −53.4% | n.a. | 35.6% | n.a. | n.a. | 157.9% | n.a. | n.a. | 87.5% |
| Poultry meat | n.a. | −98.4% | −37.7% | −95.4% | −78.1% | 475.3% | −84.5% | −43.2% | n.a. | −89.2% | 115.9% | −69.2% | −57.5% | 454.3% | −92.6% | −99.8% | 14.3% |
| Eggs | n.a. | −74.0% | −11.9% | | 141.5% | 219.4% | −74.5% | −78.5% | n.a. | −23.9% | 37.7% | 10.1% | n.a. | 378.8% | −24.8% | n.a. | 45.5% |
| Average 7' | −99.8% | −82.0% | −74.1% | 21.2% | −63.0% | 91.9% | 225.4% | 226.5% | −65.8% | −86.3% | 26.3% | −67.5% | −88.7% | 175.3% | −44.2% | −82.7% | 64.5% |
| Col. Ave. | −98.9% | −60.5% | −56.0% | 21.2% | −27.9% | 144.9% | 253.9% | 182.5% | −31.5% | −56.5% | 72.5% | −52.1% | −79.1 % | 216.3% | −44.5% | −63.0% | |

**TABLE 4.6 (continued)**

| | Australia | Canada | Czech Rep. | EU | Hungary | Iceland | Japan | Korea Rep. of | Mexico | New Zealand | Norway | Poland | Slovak Rep. | Switzerland | Turkey | U.S. | Average |
|---|---|---|---|---|---|---|---|---|---|---|---|---|---|---|---|---|---|
| *8. Each country's final tariff as a % of average final tariff of all countries* | | | | | | | | | | | | | | | | | |
| Wheat | n.a. | n.a. | n.a. | −89.5% | n.a. | n.a. | 240.7% | n.a. | 103.6% | n.a. | 196.1 % | 60.1% | n.a. | 134.7% | −45.7% | n.a. | 85.7% |
| Maize | n.a. | n.a. | n.a. | 42.1% | n.a. | n.a. | n.a. | n.a. | 188.2% | n.a. | n.a. | n.a. | n.a. | 204.2% | 65.6% | n.a. | 125.0% |
| Other grains | n.a. | n.a. | n.a. | −84.1 % | n.a. | n.a. | 243.1 % | 237.6% | −36.6% | n.a. | 185.1 % | n.a. | n.a. | 190.5% | −35.6% | n.a. | 100.0% |
| Rice | −85.3% | n.a. | n.a. | 35.2% | n.a. | n.a. | 90.1% | 87.1% | −27.1 % | n.a. | n.a. | n.a. | n.a. | n.a. | n.a. | n.a. | 20.0% |
| Oilseeds | n.a. | n.a. | n.a. | n.a. | n.a. | n.a. | n.a. | 243.9% | 71.3% | n.a. | n.a. | 106.8% | n.a. | 230.7% | 147.3% | n.a. | 160.0% |
| Refined sugar | n.a. | n.a. | −60.1 % | 48.0% | −31.9% | n.a. | 44.7% | n.a. | 7.7% | n.a. | n.a. | 21.6% | −6.4% | 39.1% | 30.9% | 6.4% | 10.0% |
| Milk | n.a. | 39.4% | −31.4% | 23.5% | −6.4% | 31.3% | 60.7% | 54.2% | 31.5% | n.a. | 40.2% | −51.1 % | −75.3% | 50.8% | −5.8% | 38.3% | 14.3% |
| Beef and veal | n.a. | −94.6% | 32.2% | 91.3% | 8.8% | 84.3% | 40.2% | 98.7% | −76.5% | n.a. | 95.4% | n.a. | −56.5% | 105.8% | 71.0% | n.a. | 33.3% |
| Sheep meat | n.a. | n.a. | n.a. | 96.8% | 51.7% | −23.4% | n.a. | n.a. | n.a. | n.a. | 88.4% | n.a. | n.a. | 118.4% | 0.3% | −32.3% | 42.9% |
| Wool | n.a. | n.a. | n.a. | n.a. | n.a. | 269.5% | n.a. | n.a. | n.a. | n.a. | n.a. | n.a. | n.a. | n.a. | n.a. | −69.5% | 100.0% |
| Pigmeat | n.a. | n.a. | −45.4% | 110.5% | n.a. | 79.3% | 236.1 % | 88.6% | −11.5% | n.a. | 86.2% | n.a. | n.a. | 156.3% | n.a. | n.a. | 87.5% |
| Poultry meat | n.a. | −88.5% | 63.0% | −69.7% | −0.6% | 136.6% | −20.4% | 57.7% | n.a. | −38.7% | 116.8% | 20.2% | 40.3% | 136.1 % | −54.5% | −98.3% | 14.3% |
| Eggs | n.a. | −12.0% | 50.9% | n.a. | 86.3% | 92.6% | −12.9% | −21.6% | n.a. | 44.1% | 69.1% | 60.5% | n.a. | 99.6% | 43.5% | n.a. | 45.5% |
| Average 8' | −98.4% | −62.9% | −11.7% | 9.3% | −20.3% | 85.0% | 78.5% | 96.6% | −4.3% | −60.0% | 78.4% | −20.7% | −60.7% | 117.2% | 26.0% | −62.9% | 7.0% |
| Col. Ave. | −85.3% | −38.9% | 1.5% | 20.4% | 18.0% | 95.8% | 102.5% | 105.8% | 27.8% | 2.7% | 109.7% | 36.3% | −24.5% | 133.3% | 21.7% | −31.1% | |
| *9. Each country's average tariff reduction as a percentage of average tariff reduction of all countries* | | | | | | | | | | | | | | | | | |
| Wheat | n.a. | n.a. | n.a. | −89.5% | n.a. | n.a. | 240.7% | n.a. | 103.6% | n.a. | 196.1 % | 60.1% | n.a. | 134.7% | −45.7% | n.a. | 85.7% |
| Maize | n.a. | n.a. | n.a. | 42.1% | n.a. | n.a. | n.a. | n.a. | 188.2% | n.a. | n.a. | n.a. | n.a. | 204.2% | 65.6% | n.a. | 125.0% |
| Other grains | n.a. | n.a. | n.a. | −84.1 % | n.a. | n.a. | 243.1 % | 237.6% | −36.6% | n.a. | 185.1 % | n.a. | n.a. | 190.5% | −35.6% | n.a. | 100.0% |
| Rice | −85.3% | n.a. | n.a. | 35.2% | n.a. | n.a. | 90.1% | 87.1% | −27.1 % | n.a. | n.a. | n.a. | n.a. | n.a. | n.a. | n.a. | 20.0% |
| Oilseeds | n.a. | n.a. | n.a. | n.a. | n.a. | n.a. | n.a. | 243.9% | 71.3% | n.a. | n.a. | 106.8% | n.a. | 230.7% | 147.3% | n.a. | 160.0% |
| Refined sugar | n.a. | n.a. | −60.1 % | 48.0% | −31.9% | n.a. | 44.7% | n.a. | 7.7% | n.a. | n.a. | 21.6% | −6.4% | 39.1% | 30.9% | 6.4% | 10.0% |
| Milk | n.a. | 39.4% | −31.4% | 23.5% | −6.4% | 31.3% | 60.7% | 54.2% | 31.5% | n.a. | 40.2% | −51.1 % | −75.3% | 50.8% | −5.8% | 38.3% | 14.3% |
| Beef and veal | n.a. | −94.6% | 32.2% | 91.3% | 8.8% | 84.3% | 40.2% | 98.7% | −76.5% | n.a. | 95.4% | n.a. | −56.5% | 105.8% | 71.0% | n.a. | 33.3% |
| Sheep meat | n.a. | n.a. | n.a. | 96.8% | 51.7% | −23.4% | n.a. | n.a. | n.a. | n.a. | 88.4% | n.a. | n.a. | 118.4% | 0.3% | −32.3% | 42.9% |
| Wool | n.a. | n.a. | n.a. | n.a. | n.a. | 269.5% | n.a. | n.a. | n.a. | n.a. | n.a. | n.a. | n.a. | n.a. | n.a. | −69.5% | 100.0% |
| Pigmeat | n.a. | n.a. | −45.4% | 110.5% | n.a. | 79.3% | 236.1 % | 88.6% | −11.5% | n.a. | 86.2% | n.a. | n.a. | 156.3% | n.a. | n.a. | 87.5% |
| Poultry meat | n.a. | −88.5% | 63.0% | −69.7% | −0.6% | 136.6% | −20.4% | 57.7% | n.a. | −38.7% | 116.8% | 20.2% | 40.3% | 136.1 % | −54.5% | −98.3% | 14.3% |
| Eggs | n.a. | −12.0% | 50.9% | n.a. | 86.3% | 92.6% | −12.9% | −21.6% | n.a. | 44.1% | 69.1% | 60.5% | n.a. | 99.6% | 43.5% | n.a. | 45.5% |
| Average 9' | −98.4% | −62.9% | −21.4% | 9.3% | −20.3% | 85.0% | 78.5% | 96.6% | −4.3% | −60.0% | 78.4% | −20.7% | −60.7% | 117.2% | 26.0% | −62.9% | 5.0% |
| Col. Ave. | −91.8% | −43.7% | −1.8% | 19.4% | 12.5% | 94.4% | 100.1 % | 104.8% | 24.6% | −18.2% | 106.2% | 28.2% | −31.7% | 131.9% | 22.1% | −36.4% | 60.2% |
| *10. Each country's average of tariff reductions as a percentage of average of all countries' tariff reductions* | | | | | | | | | | | | | | | | | |
| Ave. Reducting | −119.2% | −146.8% | -97.3% | −54.0% | -51.4% | 159.0% | 177.2% | 186.1% | -24.7% | -92.7% | 196.6% | -1.7% | -166.2% | 260.5% | -41.3 % | -184.0% | 0.0% |

*Source:* Calculated using hte tariff equivalents of border protections ("market price support"—MPS) as published by the OECD 2002.

**TABLE 4.7 World Production and Value of Production and Tariff-Quota-Related Protection for Grains and Oilseeds in the Six Regions of the PEM Model**

| | *Production* | | | *Value of Production* | | |
|---|---|---|---|---|---|---|
| Commodity | Total (mmt) | Quota (mmt) | Quota/Prod (%) | Total US$Bn | Quota MPS US$Bn | MPS/VOP (%) |
| Wheat | 603 | 5 | 0.8 | 63.5 | 0.3 | 0.4 |
| Coarse grains | 904 | 27 | 3.0 | 74.6 | 1.3 | 1.7 |
| Oilseeds | 236 | 0 | 0.0 | 39 | 0.0 | 0.0 |
| Rice | 405 | 12 | 2.9 | 39.8 | 14.4 | 36.2 |
| Total | 2,148 | 43 | 2.0 | 216.9 | 15.9 | 7.3 |

*Source:* Authors' calculations using PEM (see Short 2002).

**TABLE 4.8 Import Quotas in PEM**

| | *Imports in 2001* | | *Tariff-quota* | | |
|---|---|---|---|---|---|
| Crop/Region | Amount (mmt) | Share of Consumption | Quota (mmt) | Over-Quota Imports (mmt) | Over-Quota Imports Quota |
| ***Mexico*** | | | | | |
| Wheat | 3.003 | 51% | 0.605 | 2.398 | 397% |
| Maize | 11.1 | 31% | 2.501 | 8.6 | 344% |
| ***EU*** | | | | | |
| Rice | 1.848 | 75% | 0.084 | 1.764 | 2100% |
| ***Switzerland*** | | | | | |
| Wheat | 0.300 | 33% | 0.180 | 0. 120 | 67% |
| Coarse grains | 0.151 | 19% | 0.630 | −0.479 | −76% |
| ***Japan*** | | | | | |
| Wheat | 5.396 | 84% | 5.740 | −0.344 | −6% |
| Coarse grains | 2.280 | 92% | 1.369 | 0.911 | 67% |
| Rice | 0.763 | 8% | 0.682 | 0.081 | 12% |

*Source:* Authors' calculations using PEM (see Short 2002).

overwhelming form of border protection for grains and oilseeds in these regions.

Table 4.8 shows the levels of quotas as well as the level of gross imports in 2001. Imports are shown in million metric tonnes as well as a share of consumption. In many instances, imports are a significant share of consumption. The last two columns in table 4.8 show the degree of quota overhang reflecting the difference between total imports and the tariff quota level at the applied tariff t (which is below $t_eQ$). Tariff quotas and total imports are almost identical in Japan, indicating that Japan is fully applying its tariff quota entitlements. The over-quota imports show that imports exceed tariff quotas for Mexico and for wheat in Switzerland but the $t_1$ regime is effective for coarse grains in Switzerland, resulting in quota under-fill. Over-quota imports subject to the official in-quota rates or less are allowed at the discretion of the importing country. This is a practice followed by many countries. However, if current negotiations are phrased in terms of each country's existing commitment, it may have a significant impact on both the amount and the equity of additional market liberalization. Nevertheless, as shown in table 4.9, the applied tariff is $t_1$ in both cases in Switzerland but the economics of trade liberalization will be very different.

The significance of over-quota imports is that it affects how a country will or will not have to adjust

**TABLE 4.9 Tariffs Applicable to Tariff Quota Commodities**

| Crop/Region | Bound $t_1$ | Bound $t_2$ | World Price[c] (US$/mt) | Bound $t_1$ (US$/mt) | Bound $t_2$ (US$/mt) |
|---|---|---|---|---|---|
| *Mexico* | | | | | |
| Wheat | 50%[b] | 67%[b] | 119.6 | 59.80 | 80.13 |
| Maize | 50%[a] | 200%[a] | 142.94 | 71.47 | 208.09 |
| Other grains | 50%[a] | 119%[a] | 99.42 | 49.71 | 118.31 |
| *EU* | | | | | |
| Rice | 21[b,d] | 376[b,d] | 169.4 | 18.81 | 336.74 |
| *Switzerland* | | | | | |
| Wheat | 222[b,e] | 740[b,e] | 224.12 | 131.6 | 438.67 |
| Coarse grains | 323[b,e] | 500[b,e] | 146.23 | 191.48 | 296.40 |
| *Japan* | | | | | |
| Wheat | 9.5%[a] | 546.9%[a] | 256.26 | 24.34 | 1,401.47 |
| Coarse grains | 0[a] | 399.9%[a] | 219.75 | 0.00 | 878.76 |
| Rice | 5%[a] | 1291%[a] | 277.38 | 13.87 | 3,580.99 |

*Notes:*

a. Agricultural Market Access Database (AMAD) reported in the OECD Outlook database and described as follows: "The tariff and TRQ data are based on Most Favored Nation rates scheduled with the WTO and exclude those under preferential or regional agreements, which may be substantially different. Tariffs are averages of several product lines. Specific rates are converted to *ad valorem* rates using world prices in the outlook."

b. The AMAD database directly, using weighted averages where this was appropriate.

c. Reference prices are from the OECD PSE tables.

d. In ECU/mt.

e. In SF/mt.

*Source:* Authors' calculations using PEM (see Short 2002).

to increased trade pressure in the negotiations. For example, if quotas were increased by 20 percent as suggested by the U.S., there would be no impact on either Mexico or Switzerland because their over-quota imports are already much larger than 20 percent of their current quota.

An increase in quotas of 20 percent in Japan would have an impact on wheat because there is no overhang but *a priori* the impact on rice would be small even though there are some over-quota imports, because the current quota is a small share of total consumption. (In this case a 20 percent increase in the quota would be less than 2 percent of current consumption, so the world market adjustments to this change alone would be small.)

Table 4.9 sets out tariffs applicable for the tariff quota commodities in the PEM. (The bound $t_1$ tariff rates are applicable to tariff quota imports while the bound $t_2$ rates are applicable to out-of-quota imports.) The third data column of the table shows the OECD reference prices in 2001. The last two columns show tariffs in U.S. dollars per metric tonne that result from applying the tariff rates in the first two data columns to the OECD reference prices.

The tariff equivalent rates ($t_eQ$) in the first data column of table 4.10 are derived from the market price support reported in the OECD PSE tables. It is necessary to have an estimate of the average tariff actually charged for in-quota and over-quota imports to divide the tariff equivalent rates into benefits accruing to taxpayers in the form of duties collected and those accruing to quota holders in the form of quota rents. In some cases, the bound $t_1$ tariff rates are assumed to be the applied rates, while in other cases the applied rates are below the bound rates. The applied tariffs for Switzerland were set at the $t_eQ$ rates since these were slightly less than the bound $t_1$ tariff rates estimated. The applied tariffs in Mexico were 3 percent, 3 percent, and 2 percent on

**TABLE 4.10 Tariff Rates (US$/mt)**

| Crop/Region | Tariff Equivalents | In-Quota Applied Tariff | Quota Rental Rate | Water and Overhang | Water and Overhang as a % of PW |
|---|---|---|---|---|---|
| *Mexico* | | | | | |
| Wheat | 39.85 | 3.59 | 36.26 | 97.69 | 82% |
| Maize | 52.25 | 4.29 | 16.51 | 149.31 | 104% |
| Other grains | 5.23 | 1.99 | 3.24 | 193.90 | 195% |
| *EU* | | | | | |
| Rice | 90.31 | 18.81 | 71.50 | 246.43 | 146% |
| *Switzerland* | | | | | |
| Wheat | 107.90 | 107.90 | 0.00 | 330.77 | 147% |
| Coarse grains | 113.52 | 113.52 | 0.00 | 182.88 | 129% |
| *Japan* | | | | | |
| Wheat | 1 09.73 | 24.34 | 85.39 | 1,291.73 | 504% |
| Coarse grains | 878.98 | 351.10 | 527.88 | 0.00 | 0% |
| Rice | 1,565.40 | 13.87 | 1,551.53 | 2,015.59 | 727% |

*Note:* The $t_eQ$ rates are the rates of MPS derived from the PSE tables.
*Source:* Authors' calculations using PEM (see Short 2002).

an *ad valorem* basis for wheat, maize, and other grains, respectively.

The case of coarse grains in Japan is somewhat unusual in that $t_eQ$ in table 4.10 is almost exactly identical to the bound $t_2$ tariff in table 4.9. There are significant over-quota tariffs for coarse grains in Japan. This suggests that the bound $t_2$ tariff is determining Japanese coarse grain prices rather than applied tariff quotas. The applied tariff in this case is a combination of the in-quota tariff (table 4.9) applied on the first 1.369 mmt of imports (the quota) and US$878.98/mt (the $t_eQ$) thereafter.

The difference between the applied tariffs and the $t_eQ$ rates are the quota rental rates listed in the third data column of table 4.10.

Table 4.10 also contains an estimate of water in the tariff and binding overhang, found by subtracting the $t_eQ$ rates from the $t_2$-bound rate (from table 4.9).

### *The Swiss Formula for Improving Market Access in Tariff Rate Quota Regimes*

The main features of the Swiss Formula for tariff reductions are as follows:[12]

- Reduction of all non-tariff-quota tariffs by application of the Swiss (25) formula;
- Reduction of all tariff-quota bound $t_2$ tariffs by application of the Swiss (25) formula;
- Reduction of tariff-quota bound $t_1$ tariffs to zero; and
- Increase in tariff quotas by 20 percent.

The Swiss formula achieves a reduction in the average tariffs (unlike the average 36 percent cut in the URAA, which allows members to meet the target through large cuts in trivial tariffs, and small cuts in the highest and most important tariffs). It also achieves a reduction in the highest rates by relatively more than others.

Here the tariff-equivalent version of the model is used first, in which all commodities are modeled as though they are subject to a simple quota set at the MPS rate in the baseline scenario but quotas are adjusted to ensure that the $t_eQ$ of binding quotas decline with the MPS of nonbinding quota situations. This scenario strips away any tariff quota protection. The following two scenarios are run with this "tariff" model: Swiss (25) and Swiss (50).

The other scenarios were created using the PEM adapted to simulate the operation of the tariff rate quotas with imports restricted to the import quota and price determined nationally (the TRQ model). Regimes switch automatically in the TRQ model

**TABLE 4.11 Impact of Tariff Quota Border Protection (US$/mt)**

| Crop/Region | Base | Swiss (25) | Swiss (50) |
|---|---|---|---|
| *Mexico* | | | |
| Wheat | 39.85 | 17.08 | 23.91 |
| Maize | 5.23 | 4.36 | 4.76 |
| Other grains | 52.25 | 17.49 | 26.21 |
| *EU* | | | |
| Rice | 90.31 | 29.80 | 45.04 |
| *Switzerland* | | | |
| Wheat | 107.90 | 36.89 | 54.96 |
| Coarse grains | 113.52 | 27.80 | 44.64 |
| *Japan* | | | |
| Wheat | 109.73 | 40.44 | 59.10 |
| Coarse grains | 878.98 | 51.89 | 97.91 |
| Rice | 1,565.40 | 67.77 | 129.78 |

*Note:* The $t_eQ$ rates are the rates of MPS derived from the PSE tables.
*Source:* Authors' calculations using PEM (see Short 2002).

(Short 2002). In this way, the U.S. proposal can be analyzed directly.

However, if the national price becomes greater than the world reference price for the country plus the bound $t_2$ ($PW + t_2$), imports increase above the quota and price is $PW + t_2$. The second scenario in which the bound $t_2$ rates are determined by the Swiss formula with $a = 0.25$ is meant to simulate the U.S. proposal for market access. The last two scenarios show more liberal versions obtained by increasing the $a$-parameter in the Swiss formula to 0.50.

Table 4.11 demonstrates the impacts on border protection by showing the specific tariff equivalents that would result in all three scenarios together with the levels of $t_eQ$ rates in the base for comparison. All scenarios result in large changes in Japanese and Swiss agriculture because of the current extraordinarily high rates of effective protection. Mexico would also be in a position of making extremely large changes except for the high degree of over-quota imports in the baseline.

There are perhaps two especially noteworthy results from this simulation of the U.S. proposal with the TRQ version of the PEM:

- All commodities switch from a quota-binding regime in which prices are determined nationally by the volume of imports to a $t_2$-binding regime in which prices are determined by the world prices and the tariff bounds. This is true even in Mexico where there are considerable over-quota imports.[13]
- The final level of border protection is very similar to that resulting from the tariff-equivalent model.

Because there is so little increase in world market prices, producer prices decline almost entirely by the amount of the reduction in MPS. There is some offset with rice but baseline protection rates are so large for rice that this is hardly noticeable.

## Policy Options for Market Access Commitments

This chapter provides a broad overview of the ways in which market access improvements as a result of the URAA have been limited across countries and commodities worldwide. Although policy data are only available on a comprehensive basis for developed countries and some middle-income developing countries, it can be concluded that most developing countries have reduced protection in the past decade by reducing tariffs. In the meantime, the absolute value of total transfers from consumers and taxpayers to agriculture has not changed very much for all developed countries and has even increased for some middle-income developing countries. Not only does import protection remain very high, it varies across countries and commodities in terms of levels and the type of instrument used (tariffs versus tariff quotas), tariff escalation, special safeguards, and tariff peaks and dispersion.

This means that the URAA in and of itself has done very little in liberalizing trade. The agreement is widely credited for bringing transparency through the process of tariffication, limiting the type of instruments that can be used, and making it easier for future negotiations to bring about meaningful trade liberalization. Nevertheless, the analysis in this chapter shows that transparency is not complete as many non-*ad valorem* tariffs and complicated import quota schemes remain.

Import protection rates have gone down for developed countries, particularly in the grains and oilseeds sectors as a re-instrumentation away from border protection to domestic support has occurred. However, declines in protection rates otherwise may be due more to world price changes and exchange rate realignments than to policy changes. The share of total trade-distorting support from import protection *versus* production and input subsidies (excluding area and historical entitlement payments) has declined from 77 to 61 percent in OECD countries. However, empirical analysis in this paper indicates total trade rents and tariff revenue amount of approximately US$50 billion, implying that revenues and rents for governments and quota holders may decline with trade liberalization.

Empirical analysis of a variant of the Swiss formula shows that tariff peaks and dispersion can be reduced significantly—therefore this is a useful approach that should be taken seriously in the negotiations. Using the PEM model, it was shown that reducing tariffs is not enough because of gaps in the applied versus bound tariffs (tariff binding overhang) and applied versus tariff equivalent of binding quota (water in the tariff). Hence, significant increases in quotas along with large tariff cuts are required for significant trade liberalization to occur. The Swiss formula with a maximum tariff of 25 percent was used here as an illustration of such an effective mechanism.

Some of the key options for the Doha Round negotiations are summarized below that would enable it to more fully meet the goal of minimizing the unfavorable effects of import protection on the world trading system and on the developing countries in particular. A basic set of principles that should be incorporated in any deliberation of market access disciplines in the WTO negotiations is presented.

### *Tariff Reductions*

1. Current tariff reduction commitments based on unweighted average tariff reductions have allowed countries to have larger tariff reductions on commodities with low tariffs, which are of little importance to exporters, and politically less sensitive domestically. This shortcoming can be mitigated if all tariff reduction commitments are made on an individual product basis or using a formula approach.
2. Tariff levels need to be reduced substantially because of gaps between bound tariffs and applied tariffs and between applied tariffs and tariff equivalents of binding import quotas.
3. Non-*ad valorem* tariffs should be converted to *ad valorem* equivalents to increase transparency and then be reduced to levels consistent with reduction commitments for current *ad valorem* tariffs.
4. Tariff dispersion should be dealt with by lowering higher tariffs faster. For example, using a Swiss formula–type approach, significant improvements were shown to occur.
5. Tariff escalation should be dealt with by immediately lowering all tariffs on processed foods to current tariffs on imported intermediate or farm bulk products using a Swiss formula–type approach.
6. Discretionary duties in the EU and special safeguard duties for rich countries should be eliminated.
7. No tariffs should be employed to fulfill "non-trade" concerns.

### *Expanding Quotas Versus Reducing Tariffs*

Given that only minimal market access was ensured by the implementation of quotas, negotiators may want to ensure a significant increase in access. The analysis of this chapter suggests that the best strategy to meet this goal depends on the conditions of the market and the relative values of the quota and various tariff levels. Negotiators should especially focus on reducing out-of-quota tariffs, in those cases with out-of-quota imports, or if the out-of-quota tariff is close to the tariff equivalent of the binding quota. If there are no out-of-quota imports, increasing the quota will have a greater chance of liberalizing trade in the short run. A reduction in in-quota tariffs will liberalize trade only if the out-of-quota tariff is close to and below the in-quota tariff, in which case both tariffs need to be reduced, or if under-fill is significant because the in-quota tariff is binding. Otherwise, quotas will also have to be increased to obtain trade-liberalizing effects.

While reducing the extremely high out-of-quota tariffs may seem an attractive political option to negotiators, the net result will be little or no increase in the degree of trade liberalization if either the quota or in-quota-tariff is actually the binding instrument—because there is a significant amount of "binding overhang" and "water" in many of these tariffs. But as long as a two-tiered tariff rate quota regime remains, so does the possibility of quotas and consequent rent seeking. Therefore, it may be better to reduce the out-of-quota tariff significantly and eliminate quotas all together. For example, reducing the out-of-quota tariff will expand imports in those cases in which the tariff equivalent of the quota is very close to it—and even then, decreasing tariffs and increasing quotas will maximize the gains from liberalization. If, however, the tariff equivalent of the quota is significantly below the out-of-quota tariff, increasing the size of the quota will have an immediate effect.

## Notes

1. In contrast, most industrial tariffs are about 5 percent, with many manufacturing tariffs now traded duty-free. Textiles and a few other goods join agriculture as the last sectors with very high import protection levels.

2. For such a critical assessment, see Ingco (1996), Ingco and Hathaway (1996), and OECD (2001b), as well as chapters 3 and 6 of this volume.

3. As described in chapter 8 on food security, trade policy is usually not the best means to achieve food security goals.

4. This is only one of several possible definitions of "water in the tariff." In the literature, water in the tariff is the amount by which a tariff charged exceeds the prohibitive tariff, with the "prohibitive tariff" defined as the difference between the border price at which imports would be 0 and the domestic price; in other words, that portion of the tariff which is beyond what is necessary to cut off all trade. Other definitions of water in the tariff allow for the possibility that the domestic product is differentiated from imports, and so is marked up by less than the tariff. Still others include situations where the country imposes an import tariff, but is an exporter and the domestic price is lower than the border price without tariff (in which case the entire tariff is water). This chapter discusses—and measures—those cases where the product is imported and is subject to a binding tariff rate quota. These are the cases that are relevant for policy discussions.

5. "Total support" is a measure of all transfers from taxpayers and consumers, regardless of objectives and impact, while the "producer support" is that intended to enhance farm incomes. However, most of these affect farm income indirectly—such as environmental payments, which can act as input subsidies, or expenditures on marketing and promotion (the latter alone amounting to US$20 billion).

6. For those tariff quota commodities, these tariffs are the bound out-of-quota tariff levels.

7. The OECD country coverage includes only three developing countries (the Republic of Korea, Mexico, and Turkey) and four transition economies (Czech Republic, Hungary, Poland, and Slovak Republic).

8. The difference between column 1(b) and 1(c) represents an estimate of non-import-barrier protection—for instance, export subsidies.

9. As shown earlier, uneven rates of protection among products closely related in production and/or use can distort the use of resources in world agriculture even more than a slightly higher but more uniform level of protection.

10. A Swiss formula tariff cut will result in a common maximum tariff across countries and high tariffs will be cut more than lower tariffs.

11. The EU tariff quota regime for wheat was in effect in 2001 but the EU was a net exporter so it was not modeled in the PEM.

12. Note that the recent Cairns proposal has similar characteristics while Japan and the EU have failed to provide numbers with respect to tariff-quota liberalization scenarios.

13. There is some uncertainty in designing scenarios for countries such as Mexico. Since these countries utilize only a fraction of the tariff quota protection available to them, it is difficult to know how much protection they would choose to use when the maximum protection is much reduced, as it would be with the U.S. proposal. The high degree of over-quota imports gives them significant discretion in some instances. Their $t_eQ$ rates are around US$40/mt for wheat and US$52/mt for maize at the current levels of imports. Applying the Swiss formula with $a = 25$ to their $t_2$-bound rates and allowing world prices to adjust results in border protection of US$22/mt for wheat and US$23/mt for maize. In other words, they are forced out of the quota-binding regime for these commodities. Their effective protection for other grains is much lower, however, so they may continue to allow over-quota imports at low tariffs and keep the lower degree of protection they had in the base. Note that the tariff quotas for Mexico are to be nonbinding by 2008.

## Select Bibliography

ABARE (Australian Bureau of Agricultural and Resource Economics). 1999. "WTO Agricultural Negotiations: Important Market Access Issues." Research Report 99.3, Canberra.

AMAD (Agricultural Market Access Database—www.amad. org).

Boughner, D., H. de Gorter, and I. Sheldon. 2000. "The Economics of Tariff-Rate Quotas in the Agricultural Agreement in the WTO." *Agricultural and Resource Economics Review* 20(April): 58–69.

Cernat, Lucian, Sam Laird, and Alessandro Turrini. 2002. "Back to Basics: Market Access Issues in the Doha Agenda." Trade Analysis Branch, DITC, UNCTAD draft.

de Gorter, H., and D. Boughner. 1999. "U.S. Dairy Policy and the Agreement on Agriculture in the WTO." *Canadian Journal of Agricultural Economics* 47(5): 31–42.

de Gorter, H., and I. Sheldon, eds. 2001. "Issues in Reforming Tariff-Rate Import Quotas in the Agreement on Agriculture in the WTO." International Agricultural Trade Research Consortium (IATRC) Commissioned Paper 13, University of Minnesota, St. Paul. iatrcweb.org/Publications/commiss.html.

Francois, Joseph, and Will Martin. 2002. "Formula Approaches for Market Access Negotiations." *World Economy* 26(1): 1–28.

Gibson, Paul, John Wainio, Daniel Whitley, and Mary Bohman. 2001. "Profiles of Tariffs in Global Agricultural Markets." Agriculture Economic Report No. 796, USDA Economic Research Service, Washington, D.C.

IATRC (International Agricultural Trade Research Consortium). 2001a. "Market Access: Issues and Options in the Agricultural Negotiations." Commissioned Paper 14, May.

———. 2001b. "The Current WTO Agricultural Negotiations: Options for Progress." Commissioned Paper 18, May. IATRC, Washington, D.C.

Ingco, M. D. 1996. "Tariffication in the Uruguay Round: How Much Liberalization?" *The World Economy* 19(4) (July): 425–47.

Ingco, M. D., and D. E. Hathaway. 1996. "Implementation of the Uruguay Round Commitments in Agriculture: Issues and Practice." Paper for the Roundtable Discussion of the Uruguay Round Agreement on Agriculture, "Rural Well-Being: From Vision to Action," sponsored by the Environment and Sustainable Development Department, World Bank, Washington, D.C., September 25–27.

Josling, T., S. Tangermann, and T. K. Warley. 1996. *Agriculture in the GATT*. Houndmills, U.K. and New York: Macmillan and St. Martin's Press.

Martin, W. 2000. "What Has the GATT/WTO Agricultural Agreement Actually Done?" *American Journal of Agricultural Economics* 82(August): 729–30.

Messerlin, Patrick A. 2002. "Agriculture in the Doha Round." Paper presented at the World Bank's Wilton Park Conference on Prospects for the New Trade Round, July.

Moschini, G. 1991. "Economic Issues in Tariffication: An Overview." *Agricultural Economics* 5: 101–20.

OECD. 2001a. "Market Effects of Crop Support Measures." OECD, Paris.

———. 2001b. "The Uruguay Round Agreement on Agriculture: An Evaluation of Its Implementation in OECD Countries." OECD, Paris.

———. 2002. "Agricultural Policies in OECD Countries: Monitoring and Evaluation 2002." OECD, Paris.

Short, C. 2002. "Distributional Effects of Agricultural Policy Reforms: Results from the Policy Evaluation Model." Report to ARD, World Bank, Washington, D.C. August 2.

Tangermann, S. 1996. "Implementation of the Uruguay Round Agreement on Agriculture: Issues and Prospects." *Journal of Agricultural Economics* 47: 315–37.

Wainio, J., P. Gibson, and D. Whitley. 2001. "Options for Reducing Agricultural Tariffs." In M. Burfisher, ed., "Agricultural Policy Reform in the WTO—The Road Ahead." USDA ERS Agricultural Economics Report No. 802., Washington, D.C.

World Bank. 2003. "Agricultural Policies and Trade." Chapter 3 in *Global Economic Prospects 2004*. Washington, D.C.: World Bank.

WTO (World Trade Organization). 2002a. "Tariff Quota and Other Quotas." Background paper TN/AG/S/5, March 21.

———. 2002b. "Tariff Quota Administration Methods and Tariff Quota Fill." Background paper TN/AG/S/6, March 22.

———. 2002c. "Special Agricultural Safeguard." Background paper G/AG/NG/S/9, February 19.

5

# QUOTA ADMINISTRATION METHODS: ECONOMICS AND EFFECTS WITH TRADE LIBERALIZATION

***Harry de Gorter and Jana Hranaiova***

## Introduction

Since 1995, 1,425 tariff quotas have come into effect as a result of the World Trade Organization's (WTO) Uruguay Round Agreement on Agriculture (URAA). Rents generated by import quotas provide an opportunity for firms to spend resources in competing for these rents, with the degree of dissipation depending critically on the method by which import quota licenses are allocated. Allocating the importing rights directly to higher-cost importing firms with nontransferable licenses can also dissipate rents.

In 1995, the URAA put in place a set of rules that can have significant effects on the conditions for market access for agricultural products. In most cases, bound tariffs replaced nontariff barriers such as quotas, embargoes, and licenses. From that point on, rules facing exporters were to be more transparent. In addition, minimum access commitments were made through the use of tariff rate quotas (TRQs), with a lower tariff (in-quota tariff) for imports within the quota, and a higher tariff rate (out-of-quota tariff) for imports exceeding the quota. A total of 43 countries including the Organisation for Economic Co-operation and Development (OECD) member countries (except Turkey) have TRQs in their Schedules annexed to the URAA. Quotas have resulted in the institutionalization of preexisting rents for specific countries and firms or state trading enterprises (STEs), thereby potentially maintaining resistance by these stakeholders to any further trade liberalization initiatives.

The purpose of this chapter is to assess the problems and issues related to administering the large number of TRQs. No specific provisions were approved in the URAA regarding administration of the quotas, although relevant General Agreement on Tariffs and Trade (GATT) rules were to apply. Trade liberalization with TRQs is very complex, involving two tariffs, a quota, and occasionally multiple situations like over-quota imports, quota under-fill, and preferential quotas and tariffs. In terms of administering TRQs, WTO members use different methods, such as applied tariffs; auctioning; licenses on demand; and first-come, first-served (FCFS). Each method can lead to differing inefficiencies and inequities. In addition, other conditions placed on TRQ administration by WTO members such as domestic purchase requirements (even though these are prohibited by existing GATT rules) or quota limits per firm have the potential to generate inefficiencies.

Quota administration can have a direct influence on both trade flows and the distribution of rents originating under the quotas, and is, therefore, a highly political issue. In the debate about the URAA's implementation, members' dissatisfaction has been voiced regarding TRQ administration in many specific cases, and, in some instances, disputes have been brought before the WTO. There is an urgent need to provide more information on how TRQs are currently administered, what the economic implications are for TRQ reform and trade liberalization, and what better rules for TRQ administration might look like.

TRQs at low or minimal tariffs provide market access opportunities in agriculture, beyond the expected effects of the scheduled reduction in tariffs. TRQs were put in place to mitigate the fact that tariffication of then-existing quantitative restrictions would have shut off all trade in many cases. All countries with quotas were expected to allow access to their domestic markets for imports equivalent to at least 3 percent of domestic consumption in the 1986–88 base period. This proportion was to rise to 5 percent by 2000 (2004 for developing countries). These provisions refer to "minimum access." When the normal level of imports did not represent a sufficient percentage of domestic consumption, TRQs were applied to meet the URAA minimum access commitments.

In addition to minimum access requirements, the URAA stated that pre-existing market access also had to be preserved. That is, access conditions for historically established import quantities would be maintained by a provision referred to as "current access." Hence, for a number of products, countries established TRQs to meet the obligations of current and minimum access. Quotas for these products may be allocated on a yearly, half-yearly, or quarterly basis.

TRQs under minimum access are not always allocated on a nondiscriminatory basis, as was specified in the URAA's modalities. Countries have used the lack of rules to fill not only current access TRQs but also, sometimes, minimum access TRQs with imports under preferential agreements. In such cases, one or a few countries are allowed access to the TRQ concerned and can take advantage of the new trade opportunities. When this is the case, it considerably limits the scope of the current functioning of these URAA provisions in terms of trade liberalization. In some cases, quotas are allocated to countries that are unlikely to be able to export the relevant commodity. In other cases, tariffs under preferential agreements are lower than the in-quota most-favored-nation (MFN) tariffs, so those minimum access quotas are, *de facto*, filled with preferential imports from particular countries.

TRQs have various institutional designs with respect to the distribution of quota shares among countries and licenses (allocated by both importing and exporting countries) among importing and exporting firms or to STEs. A *global quota* has imports determined by market forces (provided there are no biases in the licensing schemes) while *country-specific allocations* allow the importing country to assign shares to specific exporting countries. In the latter case, WTO rules state that all *substantial suppliers*—defined as countries with a market share of over 10 percent—have to receive a share (see paragraph 7 of Article XXVIII:1, GATT 1994). *Licenses* are often used as a means of administering TRQs and can be assigned to importing or exporting firms (or to both such that an importing firm needs to present both an import and an export license to customs authorities). The share of rent going to importing or exporting countries will depend on the bargaining power resulting from any licensing requirements.

An efficient TRQ administration method will be one that allows for full utilization of the import quota (where all quotas are allocated to importing firms, which then fully use their allocation). Rules such as the tradability of quotas and/or licenses (for example, selling or renting) will affect the incentives for utilizing TRQs. An understanding of the implications of allocating nontradable, country-specific export quotas and licenses to importing or exporting firms is important. The method of allocating quotas can have important implications for the impact of trade liberalization. For example, if export licenses are allocated to high-cost producers, a reduction of in-quota tariffs may result in increased quota fill, whereas an increase in the quota limit may result in quota under-fill. Other factors affecting the efficient administration of TRQs include simplicity, transparency, and certainty.

This chapter provides a conceptual analysis of the negotiating issues for evaluating options for the reform of import quota administration methods in agriculture and thereby increasing trade liberalization. Improving the rules on quota administration methods (including STEs) is important as this will make them more transparent, improve fill rates so that imports are not discouraged or blocked, and ensure access by lowest-cost suppliers so that these countries are not discriminated against.

## The Plan of This Chapter

The first section below describes import quota administration methods. The next section provides an overview of TRQs and WTO rules, using the WTO bananas dispute as an example. This is followed by sections that discuss quota fill rates and an overview of the basic economics of the alternative methods and the potential effects on trade. The last section provides conclusions and policy recommendations for tariff quota administration reform.

## Alternative Quota Administration Methods

As of 2002, 43 WTO members showed 1,425 individual tariff quota commitments in their URAA Schedules.[1] These tariff quotas originate from a number of sources, including the Uruguay Round's "tariffication" methodology (current-access or minimum-access commitments), in place prior to the conclusion of the 1994 negotiations (such as sugar quotas in the United States [U.S.]). Accession negotiations by new members since the Uruguay Round Agreements came into force determine their commitments.

The WTO has classified tariff quotas by means of broad product categories. Table 5.1 lists the product categories and the number of tariff quotas in each category (for all members combined). Fruits and vegetables have the highest number (370 tariff quotas), followed by meat products (258) and cereals (226). Tobacco (13) ranks last among the 12 categories. Table 5.2 provides a breakdown of the total number of tariff quotas by WTO member country, with the number of tariff quotas by member ranging from 1 (Chile) to 232 (Norway).

During 1995–2001, the principal administration method of about half of all applicable tariff quotas was Applied Tariffs, as shown in table 5.3. For a detailed description of each administration method, consult box 5.1. An applied-tariff regime means no quota shares are allocated and imports are allowed in unlimited quantities at the in-quota tariff rate or lower. The second most frequently used method (324 quotas) is License on Demand—where import licenses are allocated in relation to quantities demanded and requests are typically reduced pro rata if they exceed the quota volume—is used 25 percent of the time.[2] First-Come, First-Served (FCFS), the third most commonly used administration method (153 quotas),

**TABLE 5.1 Tarriff Quotas by Product Category**

| Product Category | Number of Tariff Quotas |
|---|---|
| Cereals | 226 |
| Oilseeds Products | 129 |
| Sugar and Sugar Products | 59 |
| Dairy Products | 183 |
| Meat Products | 258 |
| Eggs and Egg Products | 21 |
| Beverages | 35 |
| Fruits and Vegetables | 370 |
| Tobacco | 13 |
| Agricultural Fibers | 20 |
| Coffee, Tea, Spices, and Processed Agricultural Products | 58 |
| Other Agricultural Products | 53 |
| **Total** | **1,425** |

*Source:* WTO 2002a, 2002b.

**TABLE 5.2 Number of Tariff Quotas by Member Country**

| Member | Number of Tariff Quotes | Members | Number of Tariff Quotas |
|---|---|---|---|
| Australia | 2 | Latvia | 4 |
| Barbados | 36 | Lithuania | 4 |
| Brazil | 2 | Malaysia | 19 |
| Bulgaria | 73 | Mexico | 11 |
| Canada | 21 | Morocco | 16 |
| Chile | 1 | New Zealand | 3 |
| China | 10 | Nicaragua | 9 |
| Colombia | 67 | Norway | 232 |
| Costa Rica | 27 | Panama | 19 |
| Croatia | 9 | Phillippines | 14 |
| Czech Republic | 24 | Poland | 109 |
| Dominican Republic | 8 | Romania | 12 |
| Ecuador | 14 | Slovak Republic | 24 |
| El Salvador | 11 | Slovenia | 20 |
| EC-15 | 87 | South Africa | 53 |
| Guatemala | 22 | Switzerland | 28 |
| Hungary | 70 | Taiwan, China | 22 |
| Iceland | 90 | Thailand | 23 |
| Indonesia | 2 | Tunisia | 13 |
| Israel | 12 | United States | 54 |
| Japan | 20 | Venezuela, RB | 61 |
| Korea, Rep. of | 67 | **All members (43)** | **1,425** |

*Source:* Data from WTO 2002a, 2002b.

**TABLE 5.3 Tariff Quotas by Principal Administration Method, 1995–2001**

| Method | Number of Tariff Quotas | | | | | | |
|---|---|---|---|---|---|---|---|
| | 1995 | 1996 | 1997 | 1998 | 1999 | 2000 | 2001 |
| Applied Tariffs | 654 | 642 | 673 | 665 | 656 | 639 | 631 |
| First-Come, First-Served (FCFS) | 101 | 103 | 147 | 147 | 146 | 153 | 153 |
| Licenses on Demand | 290 | 299 | 302 | 298 | 310 | 297 | 324 |
| Auctioning | 41 | 39 | 59 | 59 | 59 | 52 | 52 |
| Historical Allocation | 68 | 82 | 88 | 97 | 97 | 119 | 100 |
| Imports Undertaken By State Trading Enterprises | 22 | 22 | 20 | 19 | 20 | 20 | 21 |
| Producer Groups or Associations | 8 | 8 | 7 | 7 | 7 | 9 | 8 |
| Other | 12 | 13 | 7 | 7 | 7 | 9 | 8 |
| Mixed Allocation Methods | 54 | 55 | 58 | 59 | 60 | 60 | 60 |
| Nonspecified | 9 | 10 | 6 | 6 | 14 | 7 | 20 |
| **Total Number of Applicable Tariff Quotas** | **1,259** | **1,273** | **1,367** | **1,364** | **1,376** | **1,365** | **1,377** |

*Source:* WTO 2002a, 2002b.

**BOX 5.1 Tariff Quotas: Categories of Principal Administration Methods**

**Applied Tariffs**: No shares are allocated to importers. Imports of the products concerned are allowed into the territory of the member in unlimited quantities at the in-quota tariff rate or below.

**First-Come, First-Served (FCFS)**: No shares are allocated to importers. Imports are permitted entry at the in-quota tariff rates until such time as the tariff quota is filled; then the higher tariff automatically applies. The physical importation of the good determines the order and hence the applicable tariff.

**Licenses on Demand**: Importers' shares are generally allocated, or licenses issued, in relation to quantities demanded and often prior to the commencement of the period during which the physical importation is to take place. This includes methods involving licenses issued on a first-come, first-served basis and those systems under which license requests are reduced pro rata when they exceed available quantities.

**Auctioning**: Importers' shares are allocated, or licenses issued, largely on the basis of an auctioning or competitive bid system.

**Historical Allocation**: Importers' shares are allocated, or licenses issued, principally in relation to past imports of the product concerned.

**Imports Undertaken By State Trading Entities**: Import shares are allocated entirely or mainly to a state trading entity that imports (or has direct control of imports undertaken by intermediaries) the product concerned.

**Producer Groups or Associations**: Import shares are allocated entirely or mainly to a produce group or association that imports (or has direct control of imports undertaken by the relevant member) the product concerned.

**Other**: Administration methods that do not clearly fall within any of the above categories.

**Mixed Allocation Methods**: Administration methods involving a combination of the methods as set out above with no one method being dominant.

**Nonspecified**: Tariff quotas for which no administration method has been notified.

*Source:* WTO 2002a, 2002b.

allows imports at the in-quota tariff rate until the quota is filled. Historical Allocation is a method where the licenses are issued in relation to past imports while Auctioning results in licenses allocated on the basis of a competitive bid system. Imports directly controlled by STEs (21) and Producer Groups (8) are the remaining types of administration methods of tariff quotas. Other administration methods (8) are those that do not fall into the aforementioned categories, Mixed Allocation (60) refers to procedures that are a combination of methods, and Nonspecified refers to tariff quota administration regimes that have not been notified. Notwithstanding these administrative methods, products can still come into a quota-using country but the tariff is paid at the out-of-quota rate. This tariff may be prohibitive. As a result, effective entry of the product is usually limited to the TRQ.[3]

In a number of cases, it proved difficult to identify the principal administration method, because several methods were in place. For example, most dairy tariff quotas of the U.S. are administered by allocating a large share of the tariff quota concerned to historical importers, but significant shares are also allocated by lottery or through an "exporter designated" method, both of which fall into the Other category. These tariff quotas, and similar cases, were assigned to the Mixed category since the administration methods are a mix of the Historical Importers and the Other categories.

Additional conditions are also often specified (box 5.2), such as a domestic purchase requirement (a condition requiring the purchase of domestic production of the product in order to be eligible), limits on tariff quota shares (which limits the maximum share or quantity of the quota allowed), export certificates (a condition that requires an export certificate administered by the exporting country), and past trading performance (which limits eligibility to established importers of the product concerned). About 20 percent of the quotas were subject to additional conditions, with 19 countries using conditions. The most

**BOX 5.2 Tariff Quotas: Categories of Additional Conditions**

**Domestic Purchase Requirement:** An additional condition requiring the purchase or absorption of domestic production of the product concerned to be eligible to secure a share of the tariff quota.

**Limits on Tariff Quota Shares per Allocation:** An additional condition involving the specification of a maximum share or quantity of the tariff quota for each importer or shipment.

**Export Certificates:** An additional condition requiring the submission of an export certificate, certificate of authenticity, certificate of origin, or any kind of export license issued by the exporting country concerned in order to be eligible to secure a share of the tariff quota.

**Past Trading Performance:** An additional condition limiting eligibility to secure a share of the tariff quota to established importers of the product concerned, although allocations are not made in proportion to past trade shares.

**No Other Conditions:** None of the above were identified.

*Source:* WTO 2002a, 2002b.

frequently used additional condition was "limits on tariff quota shares per allocation."

## Characteristics of More Efficient TRQ Administration Methods

Three broad objectives of TRQ administration are important. The first one, from an international perspective, is to allow market access opportunities up to the full amount of the TRQ level.[4] This is how the URAA intended to deal with the remaining high tariffs. The second objective, from a domestic perspective of making the most efficient use of domestic resources, is to ensure that the lowest-cost firms do the importing. In other words, allocate TRQs to those firms that can make the best use of them by generating the highest profits from the importing activity. Finally, the third objective is to operate efficiently—in other words, the TRQ should not waste the country's resources.

Given these objectives, the following describes what would constitute an efficient regime for administering TRQs by discussing the means for achieving each objective.

### *Full Utilization of the TRQ*

To ensure full use of the TRQ, many methods and procedures can be followed. The full use of TRQs has two aspects: the aggregate TRQ for a country should be fully allocated to importing entities (firms), and the entities receiving TRQs should fully use their allocation. For the first aspect, the main means of ensuring full utilization is for the administering agency to fully distribute import quotas to importers, and to do so relatively early in the quota period. Additional rules for operating the TRQ administrative system must be designed to facilitate a full, rapid, and transparent distribution of the quota.

In terms of the second aspect, there are many means of ensuring that importers holding the quota make full use of it. In a market economy, with the intention to preserve the profit motive for importers, the quota would be imported as long as domestic prices are higher than world prices by more than the cost of importation. This can be accomplished by having private firms receive the import quotas or by allowing firms to compete to obtain these import rights. Under these conditions, the TRQ system should involve many importers and not create a situation in which there is a monopoly importer.

Similarly, allowing quotas to be rented or bought and sold openly will create strong incentives for the firms that obtain the quotas to use them fully. The application of carefully constructed additional regulations can also strengthen the incentives for firms to make full use of their quotas. One example is the widely observed rule, for all types of quota systems, that the quota holder must "use it or lose it." The regulation removes the quota from holders if they do not use an agreed-upon percentage of it. Whether such added regulations are necessary is a separate question, but most countries seem to believe so because this type of regulation is almost universal across and within countries.[5]

### *Giving TRQs to Firms That Make Best Use of Them*

The second objective is to ensure that those importers receiving the quota are the most efficient ones in terms of net profit (lowest costs, highest revenues). One widely suggested method of achieving this is to use quota auctions to allocate the TRQ. Although this allocation mechanism is economically efficient, there may be legal WTO issues that inhibit its use. The fee that is paid in such an auction, although it is bid by the would-be buyer, could be seen as a breach of the tariff binding, the in-quota tariff in this case, and that fee is not related to the cost of import service. Under allocation by auction, those firms that make the highest net importing profit will acquire the quota.

However, other methods can achieve this same end. One effective but overlooked mechanism is to allow quota resale and transfer.[6] However the quota is initially allocated, if there is a well-developed (and legal) market in quota resale and transfer, a firm that is unlikely to utilize its quota fully can sell it and realize the quota profits. In the process, the quota passes along to a firm that will necessarily use it to recoup the costs of buying it. The point is often lost that resale provisions will result in the quota ending up in the same hands (in other words, that it is as economically efficient) as with an auction. This point has practical importance because many jurisdictions find some reason for *not* allowing quota transfer and sale.

### *An Efficient TRQ Operating System*

The third objective is to have efficient quota administration and regulations. This can be accomplished most effectively by following a basic rule in regulating quota use: *keep the regulatory system as simple as possible.* All firms (existing ones or newcomers) should be allowed to acquire the quota; there is no reason for narrowly stipulating the quota validity window (that is, firms should be able to use the full quota whenever they wish within the full quota period); and buying and renting of licenses should be allowed for all firms regardless of the size of their facilities. Put differently, the rules state which commodity can be imported and that imports must be completed by the end of the quota period. The quota administration system can be kept as simple as possible by *minimizing the uncertainty* and rule changes associated with the regime. Even if there are several rules, if these rules are transparent, well publicized, and stable, the uncertainty factor facing quota users is substantially reduced. This is particularly an issue in developing countries where quota regimes are often characterized by little information and lack of transparency—and this can facilitate corruption.

An additional useful rule concerns a *distribution of quota rents* and whether the recipient should *pay* for the quota. (There are possible legal issues surrounding any payment for the quota, beyond the in-quota tariff and a cost of service, as already mentioned.) The government may judge it desirable to tax some of the profits (quota rents) accruing to quota holders. This can be done effectively by an auction, or less thoroughly by imposing a tax to acquire the quota. Imposing a tax on quotas has the advantage of generating some public revenue as well as leaving some profits in the hands of the quota recipient (although reducing those profits by the amount taxed). And the tax can be varied to achieve any desired split in revenues (quota rents) between the quota recipients and the government treasury. One disadvantage is the difficulty in knowing, at least at the outset, the amount of the tax that will fully extract all the rents. Observations on the transfer price prevailing in private transactions can be a guide to the total rents and to an appropriate tax to levy on initial allocations.

One advantage of quota taxes is that they have the effect of reducing *rent seeking* or corruption by those wishing to obtain quotas. Rent seeking induced by a quota allocation scheme, especially when quota values are high, can make the system extremely inefficient in terms of the expense of time and money spent in lobbying. This can be reduced or prevented by making the receipt of quotas less lucrative by auctioning them or charging a fee for them that is close to the auction price. In general, rent seeking can be reduced by keeping the quota allocation system rules-based, with clear reallocation criteria and a mechanical reallocation process with no scope for case-by-case adjustments or individual subjective judgments. (Keeping the system rules-based is still consistent with imposing penalties for quota-holder behavior that is considered undesirable by quota administrators. The key issue is that these penalties—which may result in quota reallocations—be specified in advance and not be discretionary.)

Another way to make the quota system work more efficiently is to define *two types of quotas*—permanent and annual. Tariff rate quotas are usually valid for only one year. In some cases, it may be more efficient for a firm to own the quota outright, so that the amount of quota the firm will have in future years is known with certainty. This can be accomplished by defining a permanent quota, according to which the firm would receive the annual import rights every year in perpetuity (subject to the possible future demise of the regime, of course, and subject to "use it or lose it" provisions). Yet to have *only* such a "permanent" quota is less efficient than giving the permanent quota owner the flexibility of being able to rent out (or in) some permanent quota from year to year. In other words, an efficient quota system will involve both permanent quotas (for acquisition for long-term reasons) and one-year quotas or the rental of permanent quotas (for short-term reasons of fluctuating markets and general flexibility). Several other issues regarding TRQ systems concern the efficiency of the quota administrative system, the profitability (size of quota rents) of the export opportunities opened up or restricted by the TRQ, and the equity of quota allocations. This allocation issue is as much about which entities within a country receive import rights as it is about which countries gain the right to export into the importing region through the TRQs.

Four issues must be addressed. First, how aggregated are TRQ commitments and at what level of commodity aggregation are TRQs administered? Second, should TRQs be targeted partly or completely to specific countries' exports ("country reserves")? Third, should import allocations be restricted to industry segments, firms, and product end-uses? And fourth, are there administrative matters concerning the handling of TRQs, such as validity periods and unfilled quota provisions, that lead to fewer imports or lower-valued imports that lower the value of the TRQ to the exporting country?

**Aggregation** On the subject of aggregation, to maximize the value of the TRQs, commitments defined as broad aggregates and administered similarly are desirable. However, if the TRQ is defined broadly (for instance, as "eggs"), yet administrative terms only allow the import of processed eggs, not table eggs, the TRQ will be valid only for low-valued egg products. This mix of commitment and administration detail effectively reduces the market access for the product under the TRQ. To maximize the value of market access for a given TRQ, the commitment should be made across a broad commodity category, without further administrative constraint, and the private trade should determine which products to import within that broad commodity category.

**Country Reserves** The country reserve or preferential trade issue is one of equity in the distribution of TRQs among different countries' exports. But limiting a TRQ to a specific country's exports lowers the benefit in terms of trade liberalization of the TRQ compared with allowing any country to export under that quota, as in the previous case discussed. Certain country quota allocations existed prior to the URAA, sometimes under preferential-type arrangements, and these were continued to ensure that those countries would not lose access as a result of an importer's URAA commitments under the guidelines for establishing current access commitments.

**Restrictions** Restricting import allocations to industry segments, firms, and product end-uses will also reduce the value of the market access represented by the TRQ. In effect, compared with unrestricted, open market allocation of those imports, such a restriction reduces the demand for them. Although this restriction puts allocations into the hands of those who will use them, the recipients are willing to pay less to get the allocations than others would be. If that were not the case, the restriction would be unnecessary.

Consequently this type of restriction has the same effects as do country allocations and, arguably, allocating TRQs to state traders. Any restrictions on who can use or receive TRQs will reduce the demand for and lower the implicit value of that TRQ, to the disadvantage of would-be exporters. There are several examples of this kind of TRQ allocation and it has usually arisen for historical reasons, whereby pre-URAA end-use allocations have been preserved in the current TRQ allocations.

**Administrative** With regard to administrative restrictions in the handling of TRQs, such as limited validity periods for the quota and unfilled quota provisions, the tighter those restrictions, the more costly it is to comply and the lower the demand for TRQ imports. This could lead to fewer or lower-valued imports, or to a reduction in import quota rents (or in the implicit value to the importing country of the TRQ). This situation can harm the importing country as much as the exporting country, as discussed earlier.

## Tariff Rate Quotas: GATT, WTO, and URAA Rules

Article 4 of the URAA specifies disciplines for market access, one of the three key provisions or pillars of the agreement.[7] Paragraph 2 of Article 4 states that "members shall not maintain, resort to, or revert to any measures of the kind which have been required to be converted into ordinary customs duties."

While Article 4 established an obligation to convert nontariff barriers into customs duties, the URAA left WTO members considerable discretion over how to effect this conversion. Guidelines or "modalities" for establishing tariffs and tariff rate quotas were drafted but never formally adopted. Various economic studies show that several WTO members engaged in "dirty tariffication," that is, at the time of the negotiations, they established higher tariffs on sensitive agricultural products than the suggested method would have allowed. There are also guidelines for calculating minimum access volumes, that is, how to determine the 3 percent of base period domestic consumption. These constructed tariffs and in-quota volumes were included in Members' Schedules of concessions and commitments. A window for challenging them existed between the time the country Schedules were submitted and when the URAA was signed. If a member submitted a tariff that was "too high" or an in-quota volume that was "too low" and it was not successfully challenged, once it was accepted as part of the Member's URAA Schedule, it was too late to be challenged. The tariffs and in-quota volumes became new WTO obligations. These obligations are the starting point for disputes over how the obligations are implemented and administered.

Article XIII of the GATT 1994 "Non-discriminatory Administration of Quantitative Restrictions" governs the administration of quantitative restrictions, including TRQs. Article XIII can be interpreted as being inherently contradictory. It advocates nondiscrimination and the use of tariffs rather than quantitative restrictions, yet it also allows supplier tariff quotas to be allocated on a historical basis, a method that is inherently discriminatory. The WTO, established in 1995, administers trade agreements negotiated by its members. In the enforcement of Article XIII, fair market access is the relevant provision and there is no provision relating to quota rents. However, it is the distribution of rents that drives many trade conflicts and is the source of disputes over TRQs.

Tariff quota administration concerns how the rights to import at the in-quota tariff are distributed. This determines the volume and distribution of trade, as well as the distribution of quota rents. It is important to keep the distinction clear between the volume and distribution of *trade* and the volume and distribution of *rents*. The WTO is concerned only with how quota administration influences the volume and distribution of *trade;* it has no direct interest in the distribution of rents. However, it is the distribution of *rents* that motivates the politics of TRQ administration. The choice of how to administer a tariff quota becomes a political decision; many competing interests claim entitlements to quota rents, which are on the order of US$48 billion (as shown in chapter 4).

Historically, four positions have been put forward by various countries:

a. Quantitative restrictions are *per se* inconsistent with MFN status (the principle of nondiscrimination).
b. MFN status requires that each country be assigned an *equal* share of the global quota.
c. MFN status can be approximated by allotting the global quota in *proportion* to the trade shares of current suppliers.
d. Quantitative restrictions should be filled on a First-Come, First-Served basis.

Because of conflicting interpretations of MFN status, there was no consensus, but most agreed that "global, race-to-the-border quotas (now permitted by Article XIII, GATT 1994) was inconsistent with MFN because it unduly favored countries with geographical proximity and/or better transport facilities" (Hudec 1988, p. 178, n. 14). The first position claims there is no just way to solve the quota allocation problem. The second position argues for strict parity. The third position advocates proportionality, defined as the observed volume of trade in some recent representative period. The fourth position asserts (literal) priority in the form of first-come, first-served. The universal choice of the best tariff quota administration method remains unresolved.

Instead of advocating one principle of distributive justice and proscribing all others, Article XIII allows a conflicting set of distributive principles. Predictably, this leads to trade conflicts over TRQ administration. The interpretation is as follows: quantitative restrictions are inconsistent with MFN principles; however, if quota restrictions are administered as if they were tariffs, they can be MFN-consistent. Two means of administering TRQs as tariffs are auctioning TRQ rights and allowing current TRQ holders to lease TRQ rights to other suppliers. Actions and transfers have radically different distributions of rent, but identical expected distributions of trade. The expected distributions of trade are also identical to that generated by a tariff, and thus consistent with MFN principles.

The economic interpretation of GATT Article XIII advanced here, and in Skully (1999, 2001a), concludes that the GATT advocates two criteria for judging whether the quotas under TRQs are being properly administered: (1) quota fill and (2) distribution of trade. Quota fill requires that imports of the in-quota volume be allowed if market conditions permit. That is, TRQ administrators should impose no impediments to imports beyond payment of the in-quota tariff. If apparent profitable arbitrage opportunities are not realized, it may be because of the TRQ administration method. Of course, there may be other legitimate costs that have not been observed, thus zero-fill or under-fill does not necessarily mean TRQ administration is the cause.

As for the distribution of trade, GATT Article XIII, paragraph 2 states:

> In applying import restrictions to any product, contracting parties shall aim at a distribution of trade in such product approaching as closely as possible the shares which the various contracting parties might be expected to obtain in the absence of such restrictions. . . .

In other words, one determines what the distribution of trade (supplier market shares) would be if there were no trade restrictions. The allocation of the TRQ is then evaluated by how closely the observed distribution of the restricted volume of trade (that is, under-tariff quota) approaches the counterfactual distribution. The economic principle underlying the distribution of trade criterion is the minimization of trade distortions given the TRQ constraint. The GATT principle of nondiscrimination asserts that trade shares should be determined by the relative efficiency of suppliers and not by alternative, discriminatory criteria.

Subparagraphs in XIII:2 (c) and 2 (d), on supplier quotas, are clearly contradictory in advocating both nondiscrimination and tolerance (if not advocacy) of discrimination. The subparagraphs allow for "supplier tariff quotas," TRQs that are allocated to supplying countries and require that "the imported product originate from a particular country or source." Thus, they allow importing countries a GATT-consistent means of discrimination. As for how the supplier tariff quota shares are apportioned, GATT Article XIII:2 (d) states that agreement should be sought among all interested WTO members but that if this is "not reasonably practicable,"

> . . . the contracting party concerned shall allot to contracting parties having a substantial interest in supplying the product shares based upon the proportions, supplied by such contracting parties during a previous representative period, of the total quantity or value of imports of the product, due account being taken of any special factors which may have affected or may be affecting the trade in the product.

The passages quoted in this section have been the subject of further definition by the GATT in a series of interpretative notes to Article XIII. The convention has been to use an average of the three years prior to the imposition of a restriction as the representative period. Several disputes have arisen over base periods during which there were other restrictions on trade. The GATT recommends that shares be allotted according to the trade shares "which would correspond to what could reasonably have been expected in the absence of restrictions." Once again, this is the free trade counterfactual distribution of trade, the operational equivalent of nondiscrimination.

With regard to the meaning of *special factors*, the GATT interpretation includes "changes in relative productive efficiency" that may have occurred since the representative period "as between the various foreign producers." Clearly, changes in competitive advantage are viewed as an appropriate cause for reapportioning supplier shares.

Thus, XIII:2(c) and 2(d) instruct member governments that they are allowed to transfer TRQ rights to incumbent exporters, but that they should do so in such a way as to approximate the free trade counterfactual distribution of trade. This is not a simple task. The passage above elucidating the term "special factors" gives the impression that exporter shares can be (and, indeed, should be) reallocated in line with changing economic conditions. Logically this reapportionment should be without compensation. If quota rights are granted partially to compensate for lost market access due to the imposition of a quota, quota rights should go to those suppliers actually harmed by the quota. If a supplier-granted quota suffers a loss of competitive advantage and is incapable of exporting without the quota rent, the quota clearly no longer denies market access and there is no basis for compensation. It is the lower-cost entrants that are impaired. However, once vested with quota rights, suppliers aggressively defend what they view to be their property rights to quota rents.

There is no case in which this kind of reallocation has occurred in accordance with Article XIII. The lack of such reallocations is hardly surprising. First, Article XIII:2(d) instructs the country imposing the quota to "seek agreement with . . . all other contracting parties having a substantial interest in supplying the product concerned." As share reapportionment is a zero-sum game from the quota holders' point of view, unanimous agreement among them is unlikely. Second, the primary reason the government imposing the quota chooses to allocate "supplier quota" is to appease suppliers harmed by the quota. In this regard, it is similar to a voluntary export restraint whereby the quota-constrained exporter is partially compensated by the transfer of rents from the importing country. For example, the U.S. tobacco, peanut, and sugar TRQs (and some in dairy) transfer quota rents from the U.S. to the holders in exporting countries of TRQ rights. The quota rights are nontransferable, and the product delivered in-quota must be the domestic product of the exporter. Such compensation might have been reasonably and nondiscriminatorily apportioned when the quota was imposed, but with the passage of time and changes in the relative comparative advantage of potential suppliers of the control product, the distribution of shares can become increasingly malapportioned. The allocation of the right to export via "country-specific" TRQs is also contentious because an exporting firm has the potential to obtain the rents available through bargaining power, imperfectly competitive practices, and/or the issuance of an export license.

An example of a dispute over the method by which country-specific export quotas are allocated is the "Banana Dispute" (WTO 1997a). Exporters such as Ecuador argued that the methods used by the European Union (EU) in allocating export quotas were discriminatory and did not reflect recent trade patterns. Export quotas were allegedly allocated to some countries but not others with comparable or even greater historical trade levels. As upheld by the WTO Appellate Body in the Banana Dispute, this is inconsistent with Article XIII, although the latter rules that importers allocating export quotas may "seek agreement with respect to the allocation of shares of the quota with all other contracting parties having a substantial interest in supplying the product concerned."

If an agreement is not possible, export quotas are to be allocated to those countries having a "substantial interest" based on shipments during a "previous representative period." The EU was accused of not allocating quotas consistent with exports in the "representative period," with some countries receiving higher quotas than historical exports and other countries less. The EU also allocated export quotas to non-WTO members; provided additional amounts to Lomé countries above and beyond that "required" by the preferential agreement between the EU and African, Caribbean, and Pacific (ACP) countries (agreement known as the Lomé Convention and its successor, the Cotonou Agreement); and assigned shares to some, but not all, countries that did not have a "substantial interest."

The WTO Appellate Body also ruled on the issue of the EU requiring only some countries to issue export licenses to exporting firms for the country-specific export quota. The EU was found to be in violation of Article I of GATT, which requires that ". . . all rules and formalities in connection with importation and exportation . . . be accorded immediately and unconditionally to the like product. . . ." Hence, not requiring export licenses for all countries with export quotas was not in accordance with the MFN clause. Countries with export licenses were given preferential bargaining power because the licenses allowed them to extract a share of the quota rents.

The Banana Dispute also highlighted the problems of allocating import licenses. There are inconsistencies across countries in regard to the period of validity for the import license, the size of the licenses, eligibility requirements for an import license, reallocation of unused licenses, and requirements for the use of the license. Overall, firms importing from Latin America faced very complicated licensing procedures in comparison to firms importing from the ACP countries. The first group of firms had unnecessary burdens imposed on them; they were deemed to have been treated in a discriminatory, trade-restrictive, and trade-distorting manner. These importing firms faced nonautomatic licensing and had to apply many times, which often delayed imports (sometimes for the first three weeks of every quarter, according to claims filed by Ecuador, a non-ACP country). The panel ruled that licensing rules are generally covered by Article 1 GATT as ". . . rules and formalities in connection with importation and exportation . . ." and therefore, the EU was again found in violation of this GATT article.

The Agreement on Import Licensing in the GATT requires that the application process for obtaining and renewing a license be as simple as possible, and that all rules and information concerning the procedures should be published. The Licensing Agreement provides for two types of import licensing: automatic and nonautomatic. Rules applied by importing countries for licensing procedures should ". . . be neutral in application and administered in a fair and equitable manner." No licensing procedures should be trade distorting or restrictive and ". . . no more administratively burdensome than absolutely necessary to administer the measure."

However, the importing country gets to decide what is "fair and equitable" and which methods are least "administratively burdensome." The Licensing Agreement sets only vague guidelines, many of which are open to the interpretations of the importing countries. In the Banana Dispute, the EU's import licensing scheme was deemed to be "highly complex" for imports from Latin America (WTO 1997b).

The licensing procedures were found to be inconsistent not only with GATT Article I but also with GATT Article III (national treatment clause) and Article X (applying different sets of rules) as well as with General Agreement on Trade in Services (GATS) rules. Even though it is true that Article XIII of the GATT is not concerned with the distribution of rents, rents cannot be arbitrarily distributed in a way that alters competitive conditions for firms in a discriminating manner. That is what the dispute around GATS was all about. Even though the EU had claimed that the distribution of quota rent was at its discretion and not within the scope of WTO rules, the panel stated precisely the fact that firms of complainants' origin, which were mostly category A operators (firms importing from Latin America), had to purchase licenses from EU/ACP firms, which were mostly category B operators (firms importing from the EU/ACP countries), to maintain their previous market share within the Latin American region. The price of these licenses sometimes usurped the entire quota rent. The European Commission had reported to the Panel that the licensing regime was designed to "cross-subsidize" bananas of EU and ACP origin, which means it intended this distribution effect. To sum up, this panel decision makes clear that quota rent cannot be used by the importing country to manipulate competitive conditions in a discriminating way in service sectors that are tied to the supply of the import-restricted good.

These issues surrounding country-specific export quotas, exporting firm licenses, and import-licensing procedures highlight the problems of discrimination and exemplify the inefficiencies that can arise in the administration of tariff quotas.

## Import Quota Fill Rates

The WTO publishes average quota fill rates across commodity groupings, countries, and quota administration methods (WTO 2002b). These average fill rates can be misleading because of aggregation, whereby some products within a group have high fill rates and others do not because of market conditions. The fill rates reported are also biased because trade volume or value is not used to weight them (that is, the fill rate of a commodity with a large volume of trade is averaged in with those that are insignificant). Notification procedures also vary, with some countries reporting in-quota imports only, while others report imports under licenses only.

Data provided by the WTO (2002a, 2002b) indicate that the fill rates are constant for the period 1995–2001 (table 5.4). However, these fill rates are not directly comparable. First, the total number of *applicable* tariff quotas varies on a yearly basis, as can be seen from the last column. This is principally due to (a) the accession of new members to the WTO over this period, (b) the opening of additional tariff quotas as a result of negotiations, and (c) the phasing out of certain tariff quotas. Second, the number of tariff quotas *included* in, or *excluded* from, the calculation of fill rates also varies, as shown in the third and fourth columns, because of data availability problems. Nevertheless, with no changes in the fill rates over time, it can be argued that imports have at least kept up with the mandated increase in the minimum access quota over the implementation time period.

For the purposes of calculating fill rates by product category and by member country, simple averages of fill rates have been used. It should be noted that this measure is only a very broad indicator of fill rates. The simple average does not differentiate in any way between tariff quotas on the basis of size or economic importance. For example, a tariff quota of 200 kg. obtains the same weighting as another with a quantity of 6,000,000 tonnes. Likewise, low-valued products are not differentiated from high-valued products.

As already noted, for reasons of consistency the fill rates are calculated up to 100 percent; that is, they do not take into consideration any "over-fill" of a tariff quota. The fill rate represents imports as a percentage of the volume of the tariff quota as notified in the WTO notifications rather than the scheduled quantity, in cases in which there is a difference between the two.[8]

The spread of tariff quota fill in percentage terms over five distinct ranges of fill rates is described in table 5.5 for the implementation period 1995–2001. For all implementation years, 52 percent of the tariff quotas for which notified data are available fall in the upper range of fill, that is, 80–100 percent. Twenty-seven percent were less than 20 percent filled, and 21 percent were between 20 and 80 percent filled.

There is no difference in the fill rate between global and country-specific export allocations, and only a small difference across commodity groups, with fibers and beverages having the lowest fill rates (approximately 40 percent) and oilseeds, sugar, and tobacco having the highest fill rate of 67 percent. The fill rates do vary significantly across countries, with Australia, Brazil, and Indonesia showing 100 percent fill rates and Costa Rica, Malaysia, and the Slovak Republic below 40 percent. Again, substantive conclusions cannot be reached from these data because of the many caveats regarding how the data are constructed, plus the fact that almost 50 percent of the administration methods are applied tariffs, in which a 100 percent fill rate would not be expected because the quota is greater than the imports under the in-quota tariff binding scenario.

The URAA did not mandate that each quota be filled but GATT XIII considers quota fill to be associated with proper TRQ administration. Nonetheless,

**TABLE 5.4 Tariff Quotas: Simple Average Fill Rates, 1995–2001**

| Implementation Year | Simple Average Fill Rate (%) | *Number of Tariff Quotas* | | |
|---|---|---|---|---|
| | | Included | Excluded | Total |
| 1995 | **66** | 1,028 | 231 | **1,259** |
| 1996 | **63** | 1,081 | 192 | **1,273** |
| 1997 | **62** | 1,166 | 201 | **1,367** |
| 1998 | **63** | 1,134 | 230 | **1,364** |
| 1999 | **62** | 849 | 527 | **1,376** |
| 2000 | **60** | 700 | 5 | **1,365** |
| 2001 | **54** | 71 | 1,306 | **1,377** |

*Source:* WTO 2002a, 2002b.

**TABLE 5.5 Distribution of Fill Rates, 1995–2000**

| | Percentage of the Number of Tariff Quotas Included | | | | | |
|---|---|---|---|---|---|---|
| | 0–20% | 20–40% | 40–60% | 60–80% | 80–100% | All |
| 1995 | 23 | 7 | 7 | 7 | 55 | **100** |
| 1996 | 27 | 7 | 6 | 7 | 52 | **100** |
| 1997 | 28 | 7 | 7 | 7 | 51 | **100** |
| 1998 | 27 | 7 | 6 | 7 | 53 | **100** |
| 1999 | 28 | 8 | 7 | 6 | 51 | **100** |
| 2000 | 30 | 8 | 6 | 6 | 50 | **100** |

*Source:* WTO 2002a, 2002b.

a low quota fill rate does not necessarily imply inefficiency. There may be unavailable supply or insufficient demand such that the in-quota tariff is effective. A fill rate of 100 percent or more does not necessarily imply efficiency. Filled quotas may occur even if suppliers are high-cost importing firms or export countries/firms, or STEs may have fulfilled WTO commitments but have imported low-quality product or destroyed imports (as in the case for rice in the Republic of Korea and Japan, respectively). Either way, inefficiencies in the administration of quotas can be associated with fill rates greater than 100 percent. Independent of export quotas or nontradability of licenses, the method of allocation of the import license itself can have a direct impact on the quota fill rate and hence on economic efficiency. An important indicator of administrative inefficiency is when there is a fill rate of less than 100 percent and there are out-of-quota imports (de Gorter and Boughner 1999). Situations such as this raise the question of whether imports will increase with an increase in the level of the quota. In other words, the issue is whether the fill rate is proportionate to the quota, or whether in-quota imports are limited by other and non-economic factors, independent of the quota level. This becomes an important question when determining the effectiveness of alternative trade liberalization scenarios.

While the numbers of tariff lines under tariff quotas are few, they cover some of the main commodities produced in the OECD countries. According to OECD data, almost 28.5 percent of domestic agricultural production is protected by tariff quotas (figure 5.1). These rates range from a high of 50 percent in Eastern Europe to zero percent in Australia and New Zealand. The large economies, such as the EU and the U.S., have 39.2 percent and 26.2 percent of their production, respectively, protected by tariff quotas. These numbers underestimate the true importance of OECD tariff quota commodities for at least three reasons: (a) the reported value of production for tariff quota commodities in figure 5.1 is valued at world prices, while total value of agricultural production includes market price support; (b) many commodities not included as tariff quota regimes have policies that are very similar, if not identical (for example, rice in Korea, sugar in Japan, and fruits and vegetables in the EU); and (c) total value of production in some instances includes services and forestry. Of the total value of production at world prices for all commodity aggregates tracked by the OECD, 85 percent of the sectors have at least one tariff line with an import quota.

## Inefficiency of Quota Administration Methods

The chapter now outlines the incentives for inefficiencies with each tariff quota administration type. Tariff quotas create economic rents, so the importing country must develop procedures to administer the quota. There are various institutional designs with respect to the distribution of quota shares. Some countries require licenses for trading firms. A global quota has imports determined by market forces (provided there are no biases in the licensing schemes), while country-specific allocations involve the importing country assigning shares to specific exporting countries. In the latter case, WTO rules state that all substantial suppliers (defined as countries with a market share of over 10 percent) must receive a share (see paragraph 7 of Article XXVIII:1 of GATT 1994). Licenses are often used as a means of administering tariff quotas, and can be assigned to importing firms or exporting firms, or to both

**FIGURE 5.1 Share of Output under Tariff Quotas**

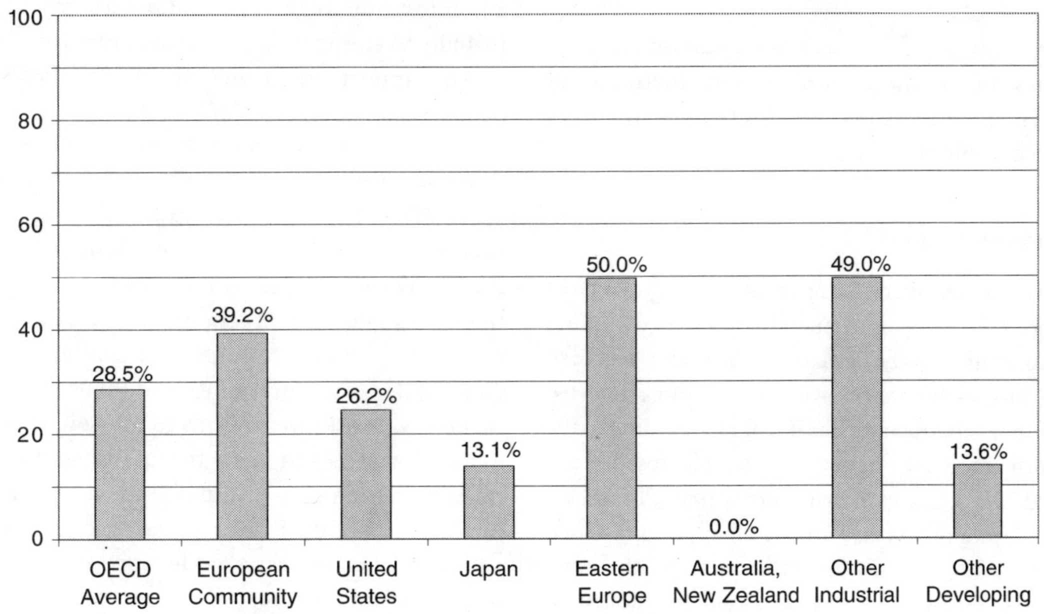

*Source*: OECD, Agriculture Market Access Database (AMAD).

(such that an importing firm needs to present both an import and an export license to import authorities). The share of rent going to importing or exporting countries will depend on the bargaining power between trading firms resulting from any licensing requirements.

Controversy surrounds quota administration, as many quotas remain unfilled. As was shown earlier, quota under-fill does not necessarily mean the quota is the cause of economic inefficiency, nor does a 100 percent quota fill rate necessarily imply that there is no inefficiency associated with the quota itself. Rules such as tradability of quotas and/or licenses (for instance, selling or renting) will improve the incentives for utilizing tariff quotas. The method of allocating quotas can have important implications for the impact of trade liberalization. High transaction costs exceeding the rent or allocating export licenses to high-cost producers can result in quota under-fill. A reduction of in-quota tariffs may result in increased quota fill, whereas an increase in the quota may result in quota under-fill. Other factors affecting the efficient administration of tariff quotas include simplicity, transparency, and certainty, and many exporters have demanded new rules or guidelines for tariff quota administration.

Almost 50 percent of the total 1,425 tariff quotas scheduled in the WTO are administered by Applied Tariffs. Licenses on Demand are used 25 percent of the time. Higher-cost firms and exporting countries are therefore guaranteed quotas, wasting economic resources. FCFS is the third most commonly used administration method. In FCFS regimes, firms waste resources racing to, or lining up at, the border, so the uncertainty and increased transaction costs generate economic waste.

Historical Allocation is the next most common method and has licenses issued in relation to past imports. It is not responsive to changing cost conditions, allowing inefficient traders to operate. Auctioning is one of the least common methods used, yet economists deem it to be the most efficient and fair method of disbursing licenses.

Imports directly controlled by STEs and Producer Groups are the remaining major types of administration methods of tariff quotas. The URAA has no precise rules on STEs, and control of imports by STEs and producer groups can discriminate across suppliers and reduce total imports. In a number of cases, combinations or Other Methods are used (for example, U.S. dairy quotas are Historical Importers, but lottery and "exporter designated" fall into the "other" category. Additional conditions are also often specified (box 5.2).

The following sub-sections analyze the economics of quota administration methods in greater depth to assess the effects on rent shares and economic efficiency.

### *Licenses on Demand*

Licenses are required to import at the in-quota tariff under a licenses-on-demand method of quota administration. If the demand for licenses is less than the quota, each firm receives the amount requested and the system operates like it would according to the FCFS method (see below). If demand for licenses exceeds the quota, each firm's allocation of licenses is reduced proportionately among all applicants, based on the ratio of each firm's request to the total requests. Firms behave strategically by adjusting requests for licenses to be as close as possible to their individual desired quantities of imports.

With no penalty for unused licenses, no bidding costs, and knowledge of cost structures among competing firms common, the lowest-cost firms receive amounts less than their desired quantities while the highest-cost firms receive exactly the amounts desired (Hranaiova, Falk, and de Gorter 2002). Each firm requests the maximum equal to the quota. If the firm receives more licenses than its optimal level of imports, some licenses will be unused. Each firm is allocated the same number of licenses, 1/N, where N is the number of trading firms requesting licenses. This outcome is independent of the underlying cost structures of the participating firms. Inefficiency results because low-cost firms on average get fewer licenses than is optimal, and quota under-fill also results.

Allocation of licenses to the high-cost firms increases the gap between the desired and actual number of licenses for the low-cost participants. In addition, these allocated licenses are left unused by high-cost firms, which use licenses only up to their desired levels of imports. This implies inefficiency in resource allocation. Allocating licenses by demand enables high-cost firms to remain in business and achieve license allocation that under an efficient outcome would be assigned to low-cost firms. The inefficient distribution of licenses across firms generates economic waste of quota rents with the extra costs associated with importation. Thus, relative to the auction, a license-on-demand administration method generates waste through its inability to eliminate the inefficient firms.

The import quota will be filled if firms are penalized for nonuse of awarded licenses. A good example of such a scheme is the EU regime for eggs. Any importer can apply for a license, but licensees are required to pay 20 percent of the value of the product in advance once a license is awarded. The down payment acts as a deterrent for firms to let the licenses go unused—inducing the same result as under auctions, through which quota is completely filled. But uncertainty and imperfect information with risk-averse firms may result in license demand that is less than the quota, and consequently the remaining imports are subject to the inefficiencies of the FCFS method described later.

Inefficiency increases under this scenario with larger variance of cost structures of importing firms. This is because a higher cost variation in the industry implies more high-cost firms. The difference between the desired quantity and the allocated quantity is larger for high-cost firms, generating more unused licenses than otherwise would have been allocated to lower-cost firms had there been a minimum penalty for unused licenses.

The above results are established in a one-period setting when only bona fide importing firms participate in the bidding. As a consequence, no rent seeking occurs under licenses on demand. Being a bona fide importing firm ensures a firm the right to compete for licenses. Therefore no other firm has an incentive to spend resources in the effort to obtain this right. However, this is not the case in practice, where new higher-cost firms will enter the industry to be able to bid on licenses. Also, no resources are assumed to be expended when competing for licenses, as bidding is assumed to be costless. This result is the same for a one-time auction, since only the participants that can bid the highest amount receive and pay for the licenses and there is no incentive to rent seek.

The presence of fixed costs has an indeterminate effect on economic inefficiency under a license-on-demand system. If the fixed costs prevent the highest-cost importers from bidding, inefficiency may decrease. Compared with zero fixed costs and identical variable cost functions among firms, fixed costs add to the deadweight cost because they constitute an additional cost for the firms that would not be in business under an efficient auctioning system. The same reasoning applies when there is an exogenous decrease in the per unit quota rent caused by either an increase in the in-quota tariff (for tariff quotas) or the world price, or a decrease in the domestic price owing to an economic shock. The absolute level of inefficiency may decrease because of an elimination of the highest-cost importers, but relative distortion for the remaining firms still exists.

An increase in the quota, on the other hand, decreases inefficiency by reducing the relative distortion. The high-cost firms that originally received their optimal amount will maintain imports at their optimal profit-maximizing levels and the additional quota will be transferred to lower-cost firms. In addition, a decline in the per unit rent increases the probability that the highest-cost firm will not participate. Hence, trade liberalization by reducing in-quota tariffs or expanding quotas will reduce the inefficiency of the licenses-on-demand method. When a limit on the licenses received by each firm is imposed, inefficiency increases because the limit would be more binding on low-cost firms. As will be noted later, this result is in sharp contrast to that of nontransferable rents with the historical allocation method.

If marginal costs of importing firms are constant, each firm again bids the maximum amount equal to the quota and receives 1/N licenses. If fixed costs are also present, deadweight costs increase by the fixed costs of the high-cost firms remaining in the bidding that otherwise would not be there, and decrease by the deadweight cost of the highest-cost firms that exit. A decrease in the per unit quota rent brought about by either an increase in the in-quota tariff or change in world or domestic prices will result in a decline in deadweight costs if the highest cost firm is forced to exit the bidding process. The per firm deadweight costs of the remaining higher-cost firms increase, but total deadweight costs decline. The identical effect on deadweight costs occurs if a license fee is imposed that forces the highest-cost firm to exit.

An increase in the quota through trade negotiations will have an indeterminate effect on deadweight costs because the increase causes domestic prices to fall (and world prices increase if the party is a large importer) and as a result high-cost importers may exit the bidding process (the outcome depends on the elasticity of excess demand—and excess supply if the entity in question is a large-country importer). If there is no exit, deadweight costs increase. A limit on the import licenses received by a firm can increase (but not decrease) deadweight costs but quota underfill never occurs under the assumptions of this model unless the total quantity demanded is less than the quota. Note that the variance of costs is important in addition to the level of costs among importing firms in determining the degree of economic inefficiency.

To summarize, the following factors decrease the inefficiency of the licenses-on-demand method:

- Fixed costs
- Decrease in per unit quota rent because of:
  - an increase in the in-quota tariff
  - an increase in world price
  - a reduction in excess demand
- Nonuse license penalties
- Increasing license fees
- Reducing the limit on number of licenses per firm
- Allowing trade in licenses

### *Historical Allocation*

Allocating import licenses to importing firms or "country-specific" export quotas on the basis of historical shares can lead to a waste of global resources if the lowest-cost exporting country or importing firm does not receive the rights to import. Historical import allocation enables high-cost importing firms and/or high-cost exporting countries to operate, leading to the partial dissipation of quota rents (provided licenses and quotas are nontradable). If licenses are known to be allocated as a share of historical imports, firms may act strategically to increase market share. The U.S. company Chiquita is purported to have expanded banana imports in the EU in 1992 in anticipation of the new Common Market Organization for Bananas (CMOB), which would have led to import licenses (and export quotas) being allocated as a proportion of historical imports. Chiquita's resources were therefore wasted in rent-seeking activities to obtain more licenses.

In summary, inefficiency results with high-cost firms when historical shares is the method of allocation because market conditions change over time across trading firms or exporting countries, historical importers may not be competitive in the first place, and strategic behavior in the form of "rent seeking" may occur. The effects of trade liberalization are as follows: a reduction of in-quota tariff increases quota fill rate, and an increase in the quota reduces quota fill rate. These results are the opposite of those yielded by Licenses on Demand because reducing a tariff increases high-cost firm participation while increasing the quota reduces high-cost firm shares for a fixed rent (because the quota is less of a constraint to low-cost firms under this scheme) and rent also declines.

### *First-Come, First-Served*

A majority of tariff quotas in agriculture do not require import or export licenses (WTO 2002a). With no property rights assigned to these import quota rents, rent seeking can occur to the extent that rents are dissipated. The WTO reports that almost 50 percent of the quotas are not binding in that a tariff is operational (that is, applied tariff). However, of the remaining administration methods under which the quota is binding, the WTO lists 147 official FCFS situations. FCFS, along with Licenses on Demand and Historical Allocation (accounting for the bulk of the other administration methods), are allocation methods that require some form of inefficient rationing (unlike well-defined assignment of quota rights such as those determined through auctions).

With no import rights allocated to either the importer or the exporter, an exporter may not risk the costs of shipping the product and finding that the quota has been filled, as this would result in having to pay the costs of storage until the following quota season, of paying the higher out-of-quota tariff, or of shipping the product elsewhere. The costs for traders of establishing a business relationship over time with importers are also a factor contributing to quota under-fill. Exporters do not have information on who holds the import license. The FCFS method is prone to wasting resources by concentrating imports at the beginning of the season; increasing costs for importers that have to store the product; and discriminating against exporters farther from the import market and with different seasons, generating higher exporting costs at the beginning of the quota year. FCFS can also encourage low-value bulk shipments as exporters cannot guarantee customers regular shipments of finished products throughout the year.

The waiting in line literature implies rent dissipation through rent seeking if the value of the product does not vary with the timing of the sales—imports in this case (Barzel 1974; Suen 1989). Barzel shows that with perfect information rents are completely dissipated through waiting in line if agents are identical. Firms compete to be first, therefore, by arriving before the market opens with the product and forming a queue. The waiting time rises, that is until in equilibrium, the money-plus-time price clears the market. Thus when firms are homogenous, waiting dissipates the rent completely. Every firm arrives at the same optimal time—that is, before the supply is gone—and no unnecessary waiting occurs (each firm chooses an optimal arrival time, given arrival times of all others). With zero serving time, the queue forms immediately such that the marginal valuation equals the price plus cost of waiting.

Actions to mitigate costs of waiting—such as paying storage costs or paying others to wait—may induce overdissipation of rents (Deacon and Sonstelie 1991). When firms are asymmetric (for example, with different opportunity costs of time), every firm still waits for the same length of time but only the marginal firm dissipates the rent completely. The inframarginal participants are still able to earn a part of the rent, resulting in underdissipation of total rents. Suen (1989) argues that the extent to which rent is dissipated depends upon the degree of heterogeneity in individual valuations.

Both the rent-seeking and waiting-in-line literatures assume that the marginal valuation (the price or per unit rent) of the rationed good is fixed. This will not be the case for FCFS import quotas in agriculture where the rent is reduced as imports occur earlier in the year and domestic prices fall as a result. Rent can still be dissipated in wasteful activities (for example, seasonality in prices—and hence, rents—results in rent dissipation) but more likely they will be transferred to (or "appropriated" by) domestic consumers because imports are "hurried up," causing domestic prices to fall. Therefore, the economics of FCFS import quotas for agriculture differ from these models in the literature because rents are endogenous. Skully (1999, 2001a) provides empirical evidence of imports mostly in the first month and domestic prices falling with FCFS import quotas. In addition, agricultural products will have opportunity costs, including storage costs on ship and cost of spoilage. If there is "serving time" (for example, clearing customs, unloading, and so on), importing firms still wait the same amount of time but come at times of the day (week or month) that differ by the length of the serving time (Chau, de Gorter, and Hranaiova 2002). In the meantime, domestic producers receive only the world price and consumers enjoy lower prices for this part of domestic production as well. This continues as long as imports occur. Once the import quota has been filled, the domestic price goes up and is above the level compared to when the quota was binding in traditional analysis. Rents to farmers are now higher compared to the case of a standard import quota but only for the time period after the quota is filled.

There can be full rent appropriation by consumers when the domestic price is being reduced to world price levels as importers compete for the rents by racing to the border. Once the quota limit is reached, the domestic price rises again but in the meantime domestic consumers have appropriated the entire quota rent—rents are not dissipated in wasteful rent-seeking activities. The same situation arises when the product in question is nonperishable but storage costs are prohibitive. Box 5.3 provides a summary of the economics of FCFS and the factors affecting the degree of rent appropriation versus dissipation. Factors affecting the outcome include the degree of perishability, storage costs, heterogeneity of firms, and time sensitivity of domestic production (some production is continuous and cannot be delayed—for example, milk consumed fresh). The amount of rent appropriated by consumers from domestic producers depends on the supply and demand elasticities, the level of the quota relative to free trade levels, and the level of domestic production (annual production at world prices) relative to the level of imports under free trade.

### *State Trading Enterprises*

The matter of STEs handling tariff quotas remains contentious. One argument is that the STE, often less influenced compared to firms or other commercial enterprises by market considerations, may have no incentive to fill the quota. Another complaint is that the STE, especially if it represents producer interests, will choose to limit the quota to lower-valued imports within that category or to pay the exporter lower prices for the good in question than would be paid under a private market transaction. Therefore, allocating quotas to STEs can reduce market access, even with 100 percent fill rates, by discriminating across countries or choosing low-quality products. Some STEs deliberately allocate export quotas to higher-cost exporters for political reasons (ABARE 1999), resulting in inefficiencies and inequities.

Many factors, as summarized in box 5.4, need to be taken into account when analyzing the effects of an importing STE. Take for example an STE that favors domestic producers and controls imports. If the quota rents are given to producers, then it is a "producer group" STE. In theory, an exclusive right to purchase from producers and sell in the domestic market should give monopoly power to such an STE. In practice, political pressure and other factors may curb this market power and the degree of the power remains an empirical question. Also, there remains a problem of distributing the rents to farmers, which if blended with revenues from sales from domestic production would cause an increase in domestic production and consequently reduce welfare to both producers and society.

The control over imports leads the STE to trade off the benefits from owning the quota rents and the loss in producer surplus through competition from imports. Failing to fill the quota is advantageous only if the quota rents are smaller than the loss in producer surplus due to increased imports. When relative levels of $t_1$ (in-quota tariff), $t_2$ (out-of-quota tariff), and quota are such that quota would be binding under perfect competition, the STE will either choose to prevent imports completely (autarky outcome) or fill the quota (quota-binding outcome). The relative surpluses of these two choices depend on elasticities of demand and supply and relative levels of TRQ instruments (that is, relative tariff levels, world prices, and quota levels), as well as the degree of market power of the STE in the domestic market.

The out-of-quota inclusive price ($Pw + t_2$) constitutes an upper boundary on the price the STE can charge. The STE cannot charge a higher price

**BOX 5.3 Tariff Quotas: Economics of First-Come, First-Served (FCFS)**

*Situation 1:* nonperishable product with zero storage costs

- Race to border and rents dissipated by waiting in line
- Money-plus-time price clears the market (all arrive at same time except if serving time, order of arrival is affected)
- If heterogeneous importing firms, some inframarginal rents retained
- Positive storage (fixed) costs can result in over-dissipation of quota rents

*Situation 2:* perishable product or cost prohibitive storage

- No queuing and domestic price falls to world price

*Case A:* production not time sensitive (instant at world price)

- Consumers appropriate all quota rents and most of rents to farmers due to a standard import quota
- Imports and domestic consumption at world price and then domestic prices spike normal quota levels

*Case B:* both production and consumption constant flow (for example, milk)

- Imports and domestic consumption and production at world price until quota filled; then domestic prices spike above normal quotal level
- Quota rents appropriated by consumers and producer rents for production at world prices; however, price higher than normal for end-of-year production, consequently producers get more rents than in Case A above

*Source:* Chau, de Gorter, and Hranaiova (2002).

because the demand would be filled by out-of-quota imports. Once Pw + $t_2$ becomes an effective upper boundary price—that is, at lower levels of $t_2$—it reduces the surplus from the autarky outcome and increases the probability of filling the quota. A switch to the quota-binding outcome then implies a discrete increase in social welfare.

A decrease in $t_1$ also increases the benefits to farmers of the quota-binding case as it lowers the cost of purchasing the quota and thus increases the quota rents. Trade liberalization through quota expansion has ambiguous welfare effects. On the one hand, it increases the quota rents by increasing the amount the STE can purchase at the low Pw + $t_1$, but on the other hand the larger amount of imports has a dampening effect on the domestic price. The aggregate effect may be negative for the quota-binding outcome and may lead the STE to switch back to the socially inferior autarky solution.

If the STE is obliged to fill the quota (market conditions permitting), the autarky solution becomes less attractive as the STE is forced to incur the extra cost of purchasing in-quota imports. However, demand and supply elasticities may be such that it pays for the producers (if the STE acts on behalf of producers' interests) to destroy the imports rather than include them in the domestic market. Or the STE could import a product that is of inferior quality, thereby fulfilling the quota and at the same time maintaining income from domestic production, provided that the cross elasticity of demand is low.

The quota may be under-filled under the STE, and the level of underfill depends on the degree of market power in the domestic market. The closer the STE is to a monopoly, the lower the proportion of the quota that will be filled. Liberalizing through lowering $t_1$ increases social welfare, while a decrease in $t_2$ again has no trade and welfare effects until Pw + $t_2$ becomes an effective upper boundary price—that is, Pw + $t_2$ falls below the $t_1$-binding price. Further decreases of $t_2$ result in a decrease in producer welfare but no change in the social welfare.

Positive out-of-quota imports occur in the $t_2$-binding case, which in the case of STE coincides with perfect competition. That is, when Pw + $t_2$ is below the quota-binding competitive price, it is forced to behave competitively, acting as a price taker at Pw + $t_2$. It is always optimal for the producers (domestic) to fill the quota as producers gain rents from the in-quota imports. Otherwise, the demand would be filled by the out-of-quota imports that do not generate rents for producers. Trade liberalization has the usual positive trade and welfare effects as analyzed for perfect competition.

**BOX 5.4 Tariff Quotas: Factors Affecting the Impacts on Trade with an STE in Importing Country**

*Objective Function*[a]

- Maximize producer welfare
- Maximize consumer welfare
- Maximize regulatory intermediary welfare

*Degree of Control*

- Control of imports
- Control of domestic market

*Obligation to Fill Quota*

- No obligation to fill quota
- Obligation to fill quota if $t_1$ not binding (option to destroy)

*Appropriation of Quota Rents*

- Quota rents redistributed to the favored group
- Quota rents appropriated by taxpayers
- Quota rents accrue to foreign country

*Relative Levels of $t_1$, $t_2$, and Quota*

- Effect of STE depends on what instrument is binding initially under perfect competition (quota, $t_1$, $t_2$, or autarky)
- Effect of trade liberalization depends on what instrument is binding initially under the STE equilibrium (quota, $t_1$, $t_2$, or autarky)

[a] The list of objective functions is not meant to be exhaustive and may include job creation, revenue maximization, and the like.

*Notes:* $t_1$ = in-quota tariff. $t_2$ = out-of-quota tariff. STE = State trading enterprise.
*Source:* Hranaiova, Falk, and de Gorter 2002.

Many STEs have both monopsony and monopoly power (for instance, grain STEs in China, especially in the past, and BULOG in Indonesia). The monopsony/monopoly power effectively prevents competitive imports from entering the country at Pw + $t_2$ and allows prices to rise above Pw + $t_2$ as much as the residual demand faced by the STE (net domestic demand) allows via "surcharges," as is done in Japan, for example with rice. The domestic price ceiling, therefore, is above Pw + $t_2$ in these cases.

What if the STE could not appropriate the in-quota rents and could not efficiently redistribute them to producers? It would then never be optimal to purchase the in-quota imports, or in the case of the obligation to fill the quota, it would be optimal for producers (with the STE acting on behalf of producers or a producer organization and hence STE) to destroy the imports. This option is viable because no benefits accrue to domestic producers from including the in-quota imports in the domestic sales, while it costs them in terms of a lower domestic price. If the STE is obliged to purchase the quota imports and $t_2$ is binding, the STE will be indifferent between including the quota in domestic sales and letting the demand be filled by out-of-quota imports, provided that the in-quota imports can be destroyed at no cost, or re-exported.

It should be noted that there is also some unnotified state trading *cum* TRQ activities in the Japanese sugar market as reported by Fukuda, Dyck, and Stout (2002). The Japanese government uses sugar import targets and two-tiered "surcharges" while keeping official tariffs low, but there is no official TRQ. There may be other instances of policies that act like TRQ schemes but are not reported as such.

### *Lottery*

An option not discussed in the WTO's documents is issuing import licenses by lottery. This does occur (some U.S. butter and milk powder import licenses, for example) and is efficient in that a firm cannot affect the likelihood of obtaining the license *a priori*. Nevertheless, under this option each firm would have to comply with application procedures, and assuming each firm is allowed only one draw in the lottery, there are incentives to break the firm down into many small firms to increase the probability of receiving a license. Such rent-seeking activities involve economic inefficiencies. Furthermore, high-cost firms may win the lottery and this, if the licenses are nontradable, results in economic waste.

### *Additional Conditions*

Additional conditions associated with the administration methods discussed above can lead to wasteful rent-seeking activities as well. A domestic purchase requirement increases the cost for some importing firms that otherwise would not be involved in domestic production.[9] Thus, part of the quota rents is dissipated and fill rates would be lower as domestic consumption declines and production increases. Limits on quota shares do not allow for economies of size and coordination, again resulting in the dissipation of quota rents. Limits on quota shares discriminate against more distant suppliers for whom shipload amounts are the economic size of shipment, rather than truckload lots, for example.

## Policy Options for Reforming Tariff Quota Administration Methods

The objective of this chapter was to provide a conceptual analysis of the negotiating issues for market access through the use of tariff rate quotas, and evaluate options for their reform to improve market access in agriculture. Governments use different methods to administer tariff quotas, affecting the distribution of quota shares among countries and licenses among importing and exporting firms. A global quota has imports determined by market forces (provided there are no biases in the licensing schemes), while country-specific allocations involve the importing country assigning shares to specific exporting countries. In the latter case, WTO rules state that all substantial suppliers—defined as countries with a market share of over 10 percent—have to receive a share (see paragraph 7 of Article XXVIII:1). Licenses are often used as a means of administering tariff quotas and can be assigned by the government authority to importing or exporting firms (or to both, such that an importing firm needs to present both an import and an export license to import authorities or to STEs). The share of rent going to importing or exporting countries or firms will depend on the bargaining power resulting from any licensing requirements.

An efficient tariff quota administration method will be one that allows for full utilization of the import quota (in terms of quotas allocated to importing firms and of the latter fully using their allocation). Rules such as the tradability of quotas and/or licenses (for example, sold or rented) will affect the incentives for utilizing tariff quotas. The lack of transparency in the administration of the TRQs has been magnified by their variety, which could be reduced by broader product definitions. A broader definition of products would reduce tariff dispersion—and yield one tariff rate for several products under one category. The likelihood of using the URAA special safeguards provision may also be affected by the definition of broader categories.

The method of allocating quotas can have important implications for the impact of trade liberalization. For example, if export licenses are allocated to high-cost producers, a reduction of in-quota tariffs may result in increased quota fill, whereas an increase in the quota may result in quota under-fill. Other factors affecting the efficient administration of tariff quotas include simplicity, transparency, and certainty.

To make quota administration rules more transparent, to improve quota fill rates, and to ensure access by low-cost suppliers, negotiators could consider the following options:

1. All countries should adopt auctions of quotas to the highest bidder (lowest-cost trading firms and exporting countries) and eliminate all other methods. The license auction has a significant advantage over other schemes because it ensures quotas are allocated to the lowest-cost producers and are fully utilized.
2. All quotas and licenses should be tradable between firms and countries. This has the same advantages as explained in item 1 above.
3. All preferential agreements should be collapsed into the proposed “development box” put forward by a number of developing countries as an

outcome of the current trade negotiations. This would ensure that only developing countries benefit—but in a fair way.

4. State trading enterprises (STEs) should be disciplined to provide greater transparency in their quota administration activities. Control over domestic prices and production can indirectly affect imports. The degree to which STEs affect market access also depends on whether they control exports, whether they control imports and/or own import quotas, and whether they feel obligated to fill the quota. The objective of STEs is also critical, whether they want to help domestic consumers or producers or maximize quota rents.
5. All "additional conditions" should be eliminated in the administration of tariff quotas.

## Notes

1. This paper draws on two good surveys of the issues related to TRQs: IATRC Commissioned Paper 13 (de Gorter and Sheldon 2001) and the special issue of the *Agricultural and Resource Economic Review* (de Gorter and Sheldon 2000).

2. Some license-on-demand regimes allocate licenses on a first-come, first-served basis.

3. FCFS and Historical Allocation have shown the greatest percentage increases since 1995, suggesting that countries opt for administrative and political simplicity when selecting quota administration methods.

4. This section relies heavily on chapter 2 in de Gorter and Sheldon (2001).

5. A "use it or lose it" stipulation could have firms importing when it is not economical to do so, because the import license has capitalized value for future use. This can cause economic waste.

6. There is a strong similarity between the TRQ and production quotas formerly used in U.S. agriculture (tobacco and peanuts). For an interesting paper analyzing ways to improve the efficiency of the production quota allocation and the market for production rights, see Rucker, Thurman, and Sumner (1995).

7. This section relies heavily on Skully (2001b).

8. For a certain number of scheduled tariff quotas, the information notified by Poland covers specific tariff quota subitems only, both in terms of notified quantities and notified imports. To ensure consistent treatment among members, these partial data are not included in the analysis.

9. Domestic purchase requirements could have in the past been considered a GATT Article XI quantitative restriction, which is now prohibited by the URAA.

## Select Bibliography


ABARE (Australian Bureau of Agricultural and Resource Economics). 1999. "WTO Agricultural Negotiations: Important Market Access Issues." Research Report 99.3, Canberra.

Barzel, Y. 1974. "A Theory of Rationing by Waiting." *Journal of Law and Economics* 17(11): 73–95.

Bergsten, C. F., K. A. Elliott, J. J. Schott, and W. E. Takes. 1987. "Auction Quotas and U.S. Trade Policy." *Policy Analyses in International Economics* No. 19. Institute of International Economics, Washington, D.C.

Chau, N., H. de Gorter, and J. Hranaiova. 2002. "Rent Dissipation versus Consumer Appropriation of Rents with First-Come, First-Served Import Quotas in Agriculture." Unpublished manuscript, Cornell University, Ithaca, N.Y.

Deacon, R. T., and J. Sonstelie. 1991. "Price Controls and Rent Dissipation With Endogenous Transaction Costs." *American Economic Review* 81(5): 1361–73.

de Gorter, H., and D. Boughner. 1999. "U.S. Dairy Policy and the Agreement on Agriculture in the WTO." *Canadian Journal of Agricultural Economics* 47(5): 31–42.

de Gorter, H., and I. Sheldon. 2000. "Issues in the Administration of Tariff-Rate Import Quotas in the Agreement on Agriculture in the WTO: An Introduction." *Agricultural and Resource Economic Review* 20 (April): 52–7.

de Gorter, H., and I. Sheldon, eds. 2001. "Issues in Reforming Tariff-Rate Import Quotas in the Agreement on Agriculture in the WTO." International Agricultural Trade Research Consortium (IATRC) Commissioned Paper 13, University of Minnesota, St. Paul.iatrcweb. org/Publications/commiss.html.

Fukuda, H., J. Dyck, and J. Stout. 2002. "Sweetener Policies in Japan." USDA-ERS Electronic Outlook Report SSS-234-01. USDA Economic Research Service, Washington, D.C. ers.usda.gov/publications/SSS/sep02/sss23401/

Hillman, A. L. 1989. *The Political Economy of Protection.* London: Harwood.

Hillman, A. L., and J. G. Riley, 1989. "Politically Contestable Rents and Transfers." *Economics and Politics* 1: 17–39.

Holt, C. A. 1980. "Competitive Bidding for Contracts under Alternative Auction Procedures." *Journal of Political Economics* 88(3): 433–45.

Holt, C. A., and R. Sherman. 1982 "Waiting-Line Auctions." *Journal of Political Economics* 90(2): 280–94.

Hranaiova, J., and H. de Gorter. 2002. "The Economics of Tariff Quotas with Imperfect Competition." Unpublished manuscript, Cornell University, Ithaca.

Hranaiova, J., J. Falk, and H. de Gorter. 2002. "The Economics of Administering Import Quotas With Licenses-on-Demand." Unpublished manuscript, University of New Mexico, Albuquerque.

Hudec, R. E. 1988. "Tiger, Tiger in the House: A Critical Appraisal of the Case Against Discriminatory Trade Measures." In M. Hilf and E.U. Petersmann, eds., *The New GATT Round of Multilateral Trade Negotiations: Legal and Economic Problems.* Deventer, Netherlands: Kluwer.

Krishna, Kala. 1993. "Theoretical Implications of Imperfect Competition on Quota License Prices and Auctions." *World Bank Economic Review* (7): 113–36.

Krishna, Kala, and Ling Hui Tan. 1998. *Rags and Riches: Implementing Apparel Quotas Under the Multi-Fibre Arrangement.* Ann Arbor: The University of Michigan Press.

Krueger, A. O. 1974. "The Political Economy of the Rent-Seeking Society." *The American Economic Review* 64(3): 291–303.

Lott, J. R. 1987. "Licensing and Nontransferable Rents." *American Economic Review* 7(3): 453–55.

McCorriston, S., and I. M. Sheldon. 1994. "Selling Import Quota Licenses: The U.S. Cheese Case." *American Journal of Agricultural Economics* 76(November): 818–28.

Rucker, R., W. Thurman, and D. Sumner. 1995. "Restricting the Market for Quota: An Analysis of Tobacco Production Rights With Corroboration from Congressional Testimony." *Journal of Political Economy* 103(1): 142–75.

Skully, D. 1999. "Economics of TRQ Administration." International Agricultural Trade Research Consortium, Working Paper 99–6.

———. 2001a. "Economics of Tariff-Rate Quota Administration." U.S. Department of Agriculture, Economic Research Service, Technical Bulletin Number 1893, Washington, D.C.

———. 2001b. In de Gorter, H., and I. Sheldon, eds., "Issues in Reforming Tariff-Rate Import Quotas in the Agreement on Agriculture in the WTO." Chapter 3. International Agricultural Trade Research Consortium (IATRC): Washington, D.C.

Suen, W. 1989. "Rationing and Rent Dissipation in the Presence of Heterogeneous Individuals." *Jounral of Political Economics* 97(6): 1384–94.

Tullock, G. 1980. "Efficient Rent Seeking." In J. M. Buchanan, R. D. Tollison, and G. Tullock, eds., *Toward a Theory of the Rent-Seeking Society.* College Station: Texas A&M Press.

WTO (World Trade Organization), ed. 1994. The Legal Texts: The Results of the Uruguay Round of Multilateral Trade Negotiations. Cambridge and New York: Cambridge University Press.

WTO (World Trade Organization). 1997a. "European Communities-Regime for the Importation, Sale and Distribution of Bananas." Report of the Appellate Body, 9 September, WT/DS27/AB/R. Office of the Secretary General, Geneva.

———. 1997b. "European Communities—Regime for the Importation, Sale and Distribution of Bananas, Complaint by Ecuador." Report by the Panel. 22 May, WT/DS27/R/ECU. Office of the Secretary General, Geneva.

———. 2002a. "Tariff Quota and Other Quotas." Background paper. March 21, TN/AG/S/5. Office of the Secretary General, Geneva.

______. 2002b. "Tariff Quota Administration Methods and Tariff Quota Fill." Background paper. March 22, TN/AG/S/6. Office of the Secretary General, Geneva.

# 6

# DOMESTIC SUPPORT: ECONOMICS AND POLICY INSTRUMENTS

*Harry de Gorter, Merlinda D. Ingco, and Laura Ignacio*

## Introduction

The objective of this chapter is to provide a conceptual analysis of the negotiating issues related to government-provided domestic support to agriculture, and to evaluate options in the current World Trade Organization (WTO) trade negotiations to reform or discipline such government action. In an unprecedented act, the 1994 Uruguay Round Agreement on Agriculture (URAA) introduced disciplines on domestic agricultural support programs that encouraged production. Countries made commitments to bind their level of support using the Aggregate Measurement of Support (AMS). This provided a measure of domestic trade-distorting policies (classified as "amber box" policies). Developed countries agreed to reduce this support by 20 percent by 2000, and developing countries by 13 percent by 2004. Trade-distorting domestic policies that were below a *de minimis* standard (5 and 10 percent of value of production in developed and developing countries, respectively) were exempt in two separate categories: non-product-specific and product-specific support. In addition, other domestic support policies exempted from disciplines were certain direct payments with production-limiting characteristics (classified as "blue box" polices) and policies that were considered to have no or "minimally" trade-distorting effects (classified as "green box" policies). For developing countries a wider list of policies was exempt and all least-developed countries were exempt from all subsidy reduction commitments. Finally, the URAA provision described as "the Peace Clause," and due to expire in 2004, specified that green box policies were nonactionable (for example, from countervailing duties) while amber and blue box subsidies were mostly protected, under specific circumstances.

Several outstanding issues on domestic support relate to its measurement and the URAA disciplines. Reduction commitments on amber box policies apply to total agricultural support and are not related to any specific agricultural sector. Hence, governments can reduce support in one sector and increase it in another without changing total support for agriculture. The *de minimis* provisions for domestic support were large; they have created the potential for the continuation of subsidies or an increase in support of commodity production at high levels.

The AMS has two components: (1) price support, which is the difference between an "administered" price support and a fixed world "reference" price; and (2) nonexempt domestic subsidies. In the first component, the domestic "administered" support price does not represent the domestic market price while the fixed-base world reference price does not represent the actual world market price. The price support element of the AMS also depends on the existence of the administered price as some countries simply did not report the reference price (or abandoned it), but kept the border protection. Hence, there was no change in the level of trade or prices. In addition, the quantity chosen varied among countries, some using production and others' exports. These facts mean that the method of measuring the AMS specified in the URAA—which relies on these measures of domestic and world prices—can be somewhat inaccurate.

As will be further elaborated below, the AMS also includes support derived from border protection (such as tariffs or export subsidies), which results in double counting.[1] In addition to including a substantial proportion of support already counted in the AMS market access and export subsidy support, the baseline AMS is overestimated because it includes blue box support, but this support is not measured in the AMS reduction requirements. The AMS is, therefore, a misleading indicator of domestic support and penalizes some countries when policy reforms are undertaken and favors others when they are not, depending entirely on how programs are designed.

The blue box is for support that is directed at production-limiting programs for payments based on no more than 85 percent of the base level of production. However, blue box support can be trade distorting, depending on how the program is designed and implemented.

Green box policies include expenditures on domestic food aid and food security, environmental programs, regional assistance, and infrastructure investments, and can also be trade-distorting. For example, green box payments that are based on historical entitlements but require "land to be kept in agricultural use" induce higher production because fixed costs are covered (which induces less exit by farmers); production risk is reduced; input market constraints are removed; and expectations are formed for more support in the future (especially when payment criteria are updated, as in the case of the 2002 United States (U.S.) Farm Bill). Rules on eligibility for decoupled payments have changed in some instances, making them coupled payments in practice. The green box is also being used for payments to farmers for reducing the negative impacts on the environment and for providing social amenities such as rural landscape. Government support for these "nontrade" concerns can actually be disguised protection. Therefore, disciplines are also required for policies supporting these multifunctional aspects of agriculture.

The URAA contains exemptions for developing countries on domestic support but does not provide specific criteria for determining a country's development status or details on what domestic support policies should go in the "development box."

For most countries, the AMS has been the least binding element of the URAA commitments because of an extremely high base period (1986–88) upon which reduction commitments were made and the ease with which commitments have been circumvented. (The base period support was high due to low world prices and the inclusion of blue box support in the base period only.) This, combined with the deficiencies of the AMS mentioned previously, implies that a major reform will be required in the way the AMS is defined and measured.

Reform of domestic support is particularly important because a significant shift from border protection to domestic support has occurred, as discussed in chapter 4. Furthermore, subsidies on inputs and outputs can almost be as trade-distorting as import barriers (OECD 2001). The purpose of the URAA was to define, quantify, and reduce trade-distorting policies, but we argue here that the URAA has not properly defined and quantified (and hence reduced) trade-distorting domestic support measures in many instances. Hence, a major challenge is to address the imbalances in the definition and quantification of agricultural support so that a level playing field is established and effective reductions in trade distortions are ensured. This will then make it possible to focus on trade-distorting policies, negotiate reductions in their magnitude, and provide an incentive for governments to change their domestic policies toward nondistorting measures.

### *The Plan of This Chapter*

This chapter provides an overview of the amber, blue, and green boxes. The importance of domestic support versus border support is emphasized by presenting the results of the Organisation for Economic Co-operation and Development's

(OECD) Policy Evaluation Matrix (PEM) model for the grains and oilseeds sectors. The theory of decoupling is then discussed and its weaknesses are analyzed. The basic economics of the blue box as it pertains to the European Union's (EU) use of it for area and headage payments is explained, followed by a section on the specific issues and problems of the AMS such as sector-wide aggregation, double counting, insensitivity to changes in policy reform, and the role of *de minimis* and non-product support. Only limited attention is given to other issues such as how to reduce amber box support, the status and future of the blue box, the definition of green box policies, how to accommodate non-trade concerns and multifunctionality (see chapter 8 in this volume), the role and future of the Peace Clause, the role of Special and Differential treatment for developing countries, and the development box (see chapter 14 of this volume).

## Brief Overview of Domestic Support

Carefully constructed estimates of domestic support to agriculture are provided by the OECD, and are presented in table 6.1. Much of the total support in agriculture is either border protection or so-called nondistorting domestic support. Data in table 6.1 show that border support averaged US$160 billion from 1999 to 2001, representing 65 percent of the producer support estimate (PSE) and less than 50 percent of the total support estimate (TSE). Payments based on output and input use, while significant, represented only US$36.6 billion, followed by area/headage payments and historical entitlements. The category "other" includes payments based on input constraints and farm income, and general services such as infrastructure and marketing costs. Table 6.1 also shows that several countries or regions have large shares of protection derived from border support, especially Japan, the Republic of Korea, and Turkey, while the U.S., the Slovak Republic, Norway, and Australia have above average shares of domestic support. Only 10.2 percent of Australia's total support is from border protection—the rest is domestic support.

Figure 6.1 shows that trade-distorting domestic support (defined only as output and input subsidies) has trended up slightly since 1986–88 at around US$40 billion, but the share of trade-distorting domestic support as a percentage of total support (including general services and the like) has trended downward over time.[2] This can be construed as evidence of a move toward nondistorting support in agriculture among OECD countries. On average from 1986 to 1991, approximately 12 percent of total support is classified as trade-distorting domestic support (figure 6.1). Tables 6.2 and 6.3 provide data on domestic support as a share of trade-distorting support by country and commodity, respectively. The domestic support share varies widely across countries, with Australia, New Zealand, the Slovak Republic, and the U.S. having trade-distorting domestic support above 50 percent. The EU, for example, has a low level of trade-distorting domestic support, but these payments exclude blue box expenditures (discussed later). Among the commodities, wheat, coarse grains, and oilseeds have the highest proportion of trade-distorting support in the form of domestic subsidies (table 6.3).

The composition of the URAA's measure of domestic support by box and country is given in table 6.4. The green box is the largest (undisciplined) box, followed by the amber box.

### *The Aggregate Measurement of Support (AMS)*

The AMS is calculated for specific commodities receiving "market support," nonexempt direct payments, or any other non-product-specific support to producers. The last of these measures is aggregated into a non-product-specific AMS. Amber box policies include transfers from consumers such as government-administered price supports and taxpayer-funded subsidies for both inputs and outputs. The accounting method is either government expenditures or price gaps calculated as the difference between a fixed external reference price and the applied administered price using the Equivalent Measurement of Support (EMS). AMS includes market price support defined as a gap between the official administered price and the fixed world reference price (1986–88 average) times current production.[3] The fixed world reference price means that market support as defined by the AMS does not change with world prices or with changes in the domestic market price. Product-specific support that is less than 5 (10) percent of value of production in developed (developing) countries is not included in the AMS—neither is non-product-specific domestic support that does not exceed 5 (10) percent of the total value of production.

At least 30 WTO members made commitments to reduce their trade-distorting domestic supports in the amber box as measured by their AMS. Members without these commitments have to keep within 5 percent of the value of production (that is, the *de minimis* level)—10 percent in the case of developing countries. Table 6.5 summarizes the values for key countries and outcomes for 1995–2001. The EU, Japan, and the U.S. account for over 85 percent of total domestic support under the AMS. Table 6.6 shows that all countries except Argentina and Iceland are below the baseline for 1995–2001. With a few exceptions, most countries have changed their domestic support policies to comply with the URAA. The U.S. converted amber box subsidies into green box policies for crops by eliminating the target price, while Canada made major changes in its domestic income support policies. Several countries are between 80 and 100 percent of commitment levels for 1995–2001 (see table 6.7) including Brazil, the Republic of Korea, Slovenia, Switzerland, and Tunisia (last three not shown) (Nelson and others 1998). Although the AMS level is under the limit, the potential for governments to reach their ceilings may have pressured them to re-instrument their policies towards green box policies. It is important to note that the baseline AMS includes blue box payments. However, these payments are excluded from discipline and are therefore not included in the reduction commitments for the amber box support during the implementation period.

The AMS provision was meant to focus on and distinguish distortions in border policies (which were subject to other reduction commitments) from those of domestic support. In the case of taxpayer-financed government payments, such as loan deficiency payments in the U.S. and area payments in the EU, measurement of the AMS is straightforward (but the AMS is still unable to distinguish among policies with different degrees of trade-distorting effects). On the other hand, consumer-financed transfers to farmers in the form of price supports pose measurement problems for the AMS resulting in misleading comparisons and conclusions.

For example, the EU's intervention price is considered an administered price, so there is market price support for many products in the EU's calculation of the AMS. The reason for measuring market price support using administered prices (rather than basing it on market prices) is that WTO

**FIGURE 6.1 Trends in Domestic Support**

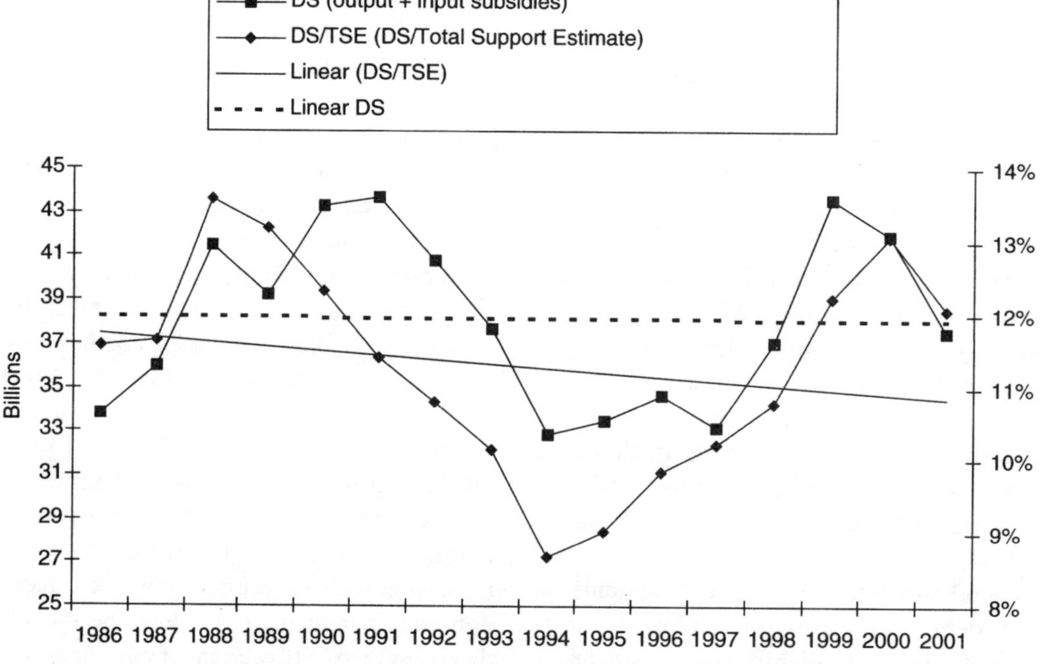


*Source:* OECD Monitoring Report 2002.

**TABLE 6.1 Agricultural Support in OECD Countries, 1999–2001 Average (million $)**

| | Total Support Estimate | Total Producer Support Estimate | Border Protection | % Border Protection | *Payments Based on* | | | |
|---|---|---|---|---|---|---|---|---|
| | | | | | Output and Input Use | Area Planted/ Animal Numbers | Historical Entitlements | Other |
| Australia | 1,376 | 946.7 | 96.7 | 10.2 | 640.3 | 13.7 | 49.0 | 147.0 |
| Canada | 5,231 | 3,892.1 | 1,997.8 | 51.3 | 644.8 | 303.5 | 356.3 | 589.7 |
| Czech Republic | 760 | 655.3 | 366.1 | 55.9 | 113.5 | 92.4 | 78.4 | 4.9 |
| EU | 112,628 | 99,556.4 | 60,863.2 | 61.1 | 10,184.3 | 24,733.4 | 597.0 | 3,178.5 |
| Hungary | 1,080 | 878.6 | 427.5 | 48.7 | 373.7 | 55.0 | — | 22.5 |
| Iceland | 156 | 135.9 | 65.6 | 48.2 | 50.3 | — | 20.1 | — |
| Japan | 64,775 | 51,979.3 | 46,973.9 | 90.4 | 3,982.4 | — | — | 1,023.1 |
| Korea, Rep. of | 21,489 | 18,169.8 | 17,233.8 | 94.8 | 496.0 | 75.4 | — | 364.4 |
| Mexico | 6,999 | 5,692.6 | 3,624.8 | 63.7 | 83 1.1 | 61.0 | 1,112.2 | 63.5 |
| Norway | 2,489 | 66.7 | 46.7 | 69.9 | 19.3 | — | — | 0.8 |
| New Zealand | 162 | 2,274.1 | 891.4 | 39.2 | 885.1 | 377.5 | — | 120.0 |
| Poland | 1,934 | 1,672.7 | 1,162.4 | 69.5 | 491.8 | 17.2 | — | 1.3 |
| Slovak Republic | 332 | 290.7 | 48.2 | 16.6 | 117.6 | 96.6 | — | 28.2 |
| Switzerland | 5,047 | 4,354.4 | 2,588.6 | 59.4 | 396.9 | 530.3 | 744.9 | 93.7 |
| Turkey | 9,649 | 6,522.0 | 5,092.7 | 78.1 | 1,293.7 | — | 135.7 | — |
| United States | 95,455 | 51,255.7 | 18,662.0 | 36.4 | 16,162.0 | 2,722.1 | 10,085.4 | 3,624.1 |
| **Total OECD** | **329,564** | **248,343.0** | **160,141.2** | **64.5** | **36,682.8** | **29,078.2** | **13,179.0** | **9,261.9** |

*Source:* OECD Monitoring Report 2002.

**TABLE 6.2 Domestic Producer Support Relative to Total and Traded Distorting Support in World Agriculture, US$ Millions (1999–2001 average)**

| Country | (1) TSE (total support) | (2) TDS (Trade-distorting Support) | (3) *Trade-distorting Domestic Support-DS (input & output price subsidies)* (a) Total Value | (b) % of TSE | (c) % of TDS |
|---|---|---|---|---|---|
| Australia | 1,375.9 | 263.7 | 190.7 | 13.9% | 72.3% |
| Canada | 5,231.5 | 2,232.3 | 769.6 | 14.7% | 34.5% |
| Czech Republic | 759.9 | 398.4 | 71.6 | 9.4% | 18.0% |
| EU | 112,629.9 | 48,008.0 | 5,156.0 | 4.6% | 10.7% |
| Hungary | 1,080.3 | 690.2 | 306.0 | 28.3% | 44.3% |
| Japan | 64,777.5 | 28,472.3 | 2,951.9 | 4.6% | 10.4% |
| Korea, Rep. of | 21,488.8 | 10,440.8 | 253.5 | 1.2% | 2.4% |
| Mexico | 6,999.1 | 2,840.3 | 439.0 | 6.3% | 15.5% |
| New Zealand | 162.2 | 11.4 | 11.4 | 7.1% | 100.0% |
| Norway | 2,489.4 | 1,101.6 | 602.1 | 24.2% | 54.7% |
| Poland | 1,934.3 | 1,023.4 | 276.7 | 14.3% | 27.0% |
| Slovak Republic | 332.3 | 220.6 | 138.9 | 41.8% | 63.0% |
| Switzerland | 5,047.3 | 2,681.8 | 690.7 | 13.7% | 25.8% |
| Turkey | 9,649.5 | 2,726.7 | 504.7 | 5.2% | 18.5% |
| United States | 95,455.2 | 24,969.7 | 12,817.7 | 13.4% | 51.3% |
| **All Countries** | **329,413.1** | **126,081.3** | **25,180.6** | **7.6%** | **20.0%** |

*Note:* Data correspond to the 29-country coverage of the OECD Monitoring Report 2002 and the 11 commodity groups.

*Source:* Estimates from OECD's PSE/CSE database and OECD's Agricultural Outlook database.

**TABLE 6.3 Empirical Measures of Domestic Support by Commodity in World Agriculture, USD Millions (1999–2001 Average)**

| Commodity | (1) Trade Distorting Support (TDS) | (2) *Trade Distorting Domestic Support* (a) Total | (b) % of TDS |
|---|---|---|---|
| Beef and Veal | 19,736.8 | 3,318.6 | 16.8% |
| Coarse grains | 8,665.4 | 4,903.0 | 56.6% |
| Milk | 40,642.6 | 4,301.1 | 10.6% |
| Oilseeds | 4,897.4 | 4,502.2 | 91.9% |
| Pigmeat | 9,769.9 | 1,345.9 | 13.8% |
| Poultry meat | 5,543.5 | 974.9 | 17.6% |
| Refined sugar | 6,217.0 | 400.3 | 6.4% |
| Rice | 25,744.4 | 2,522.8 | 9.8% |
| Sheep meat | 2,026.0 | 390.8 | 19.3% |
| Wheat | 5,691.3 | 2,521.0 | 44.3% |
| Total | 128,934.3 | 25,180.6 | 28.7% |

Data correspond to the 15-country coverage of the OECD Monitoring Report 2002 and the commodities covered therein.

*Source:* Estimates from OECD's PSE/CSE database and OECD's Agricultural Outlook database.

**TABLE 6.4 Composition of Domestic Support by Country, 1995–1998 (%)**

| Country | Total AMS | Green Box | Blue Box | *de minimis* | S&D[a] |
|---|---|---|---|---|---|
| Australia | 11 | 89 | 0 | 0 | n.a. |
| Canada | 21 | 51 | 0 | 28 | n.a. |
| Czech Republic | 21 | 79 | 0 | 0 | n.a. |
| EU | 55 | 22 | 23 | 1 | n.a. |
| Hungary | 0 | 39 | 0 | 61 | n.a. |
| Iceland | 82 | 16 | 2 | 0 | n.a. |
| Japan | 48 | 51 | 0 | 1 | n.a. |
| Korea, Rep. of | 26 | 67 | 0 | 6 | 0 |
| Mexico | 30 | 58 | 0 | 0 | 24 |
| New Zealand | 0 | 100 | 0 | 0 | n.a. |
| Norway | 48 | 18 | 34 | 0 | n.a. |
| Poland | 14 | 86 | 0 | 0 | n.a. |
| Slovak Republic | 39 | 1 | 60 | 0 | 0 |
| Switzerland | 55 | 45 | 0 | 0 | n.a. |
| United States | 12 | 83 | 3 | 2 | n.a. |
| OECD | 38 | 46 | 12 | 1 | 0 |

*Source:* WTO (2002).

members could not commit to reducing something over which they did not have direct control. Setting an administered price at a particular level requires a government decision of some kind.[4] However, such reasoning leads to difficulties in comparing the AMS across commodities and countries because it is conflated with import barriers and export subsidy measures, and consequently, the actual market price may not be equal to the support price.

The URAA requires each country to identify market price supports in the form of administered prices, which must be included in the calculation of the AMS. On the other hand, if there are import barriers in place that keep domestic prices high but there is no administered price, no market price support is estimated for the AMS. For example, Canada has not been able to identify an administered price for chicken, turkey, or eggs, so there is no market price support for Canada's AMS for these products. Japan simply eliminated an administered price for one commodity, even though the commodity's level of protection did not change. This is arbitrary action on whether an official price is reported or not. The U.S. reported an administered price support for dairy products but these were mostly inoperative because market prices were well above administered price support in the implementation period (1995–2001), owing to export subsidies on dairy products and import barriers. As a result, in the 2002 total AMS the U.S. has US$4.3 billion in "unused" dairy support.

Figure 6.2 shows how the trend in the AMS is down even as the total producer support estimate—as well as trade-distorting support, as shown in figure 6.1—is going up. Table 6.7 shows the evolution of the AMS versus the PSE over time and by country. In some instances, the AMS is greater than the PSE, as is the case for Mexico during 1986–88, which in principle should not be possible. This occurs even more often when comparing PSEs and AMSs at the commodity level (Diakosavvas 2002). Looking at the world, the AMS was 71 percent of the PSE in the baseline and averaged only 38 percent of the total domestic support reported in the amber, blue and green boxes (plus *de minimis*) for 1995–98 (WTO 2000).[5] It is therefore possible that the double counting with border support and the resulting overestimation of the AMS could be such that the sum of the three domestic support boxes plus *de minimis* support exceeds the total PSE. Indeed, for the EU alone in 1996, total domestic support (the sum of the three boxes) was US$115 billion as measured by the WTO, while the total PSE as measured

**TABLE 6.5 Use of Total Aggregate Measurement of Support (AMS) Commitments by Member, 1995–2001 (percent)**

| Member | 1995 | 1996 | 1997 | 1998 | 1999 | 2000 | 2001 |
|---|---|---|---|---|---|---|---|
| Argentina | 144 | 100 | 100 | 99 | 100 | — | — |
| Australia | 27 | 26 | 25 | 23 | 13 | — | — |
| Brazil | 28 | 35 | 30 | 8 | — | — | — |
| Bulgaria | n.r. | n.r. | 1 | 3 | 2 | — | — |
| Canada | 15 | 12 | 11 | 17 | — | — | — |
| Chinese Taipei | n.r. | n.r. | n.r. | n.r. | n.r. | n.r. | n.r. |
| Colombia | 15 | 1 | 4 | 3 | 2 | — | — |
| Costa Rica | 0 | 0 | 0 | 0 | 9 | — | — |
| Croatia | n.r. | n.r. | n.r. | n.r. | n.r. | n.r. | — |
| Cyprus | 63 | 63 | 45 | 39 | 53 | 43 | — |
| Czech Republic | 7 | 11 | 7 | 7 | 31 | 35 | — |
| EC | 64 | 67 | 68 | 65 | — | — | — |
| Hungary | 51 | — | — | — | — | — | — |
| Iceland | 79 | 71 | 74 | 178 | — | — | — |
| Israel | 71 | 79 | 83 | 66 | 42 | — | — |
| Japan | 73 | 72 | 71 | 18 | 18 | — | — |
| Jordan | n.r. | n.r. | n.r. | n.r. | n.r. | — | — |
| Korea, Rep. of | 95 | 93 | 95 | 80 | 83 | — | — |
| Lithuania | n.r. | n.r. | n.r. | n.r. | n.r. | n.r. | — |
| Mexico | 5 | 3 | 11 | 14 | — | — | — |
| Moldova | n.r. | n.r. | n.r. | n.r. | n.r. | n.r. | — |
| Morocco | 12 | 33 | 12 | 17 | 24 | — | — |
| New Zealand | 0 | 0 | 0 | 0 | 0 | 0 | — |
| Norway | 71 | 79 | 82 | 88 | 90 | 90 | — |
| Papua New Guinea | n.r. | — | — | — | — | — | — |
| Poland | 6 | 6 | 8 | 8 | 7 | — | — |
| Slovak Republic | 58 | 59 | 73 | 70 | 66 | 78 | — |
| Slovenia | 93 | 91 | 87 | 97 | 85 | 25 | — |
| South Africa | 67 | 82 | 97 | 38 | 38 | — | — |
| Switzerland-Liecht | 83 | 74 | 72 | 71 | — | — | — |
| Thailand | 72 | 60 | 79 | 79 | — | — | — |
| Tunisia | 87 | 77 | 81 | 94 | 46 | — | — |
| United States | 27 | 26 | 29 | 50 | — | — | — |
| Venezuela, RB | 42 | 26 | 36 | 17 | — | — | — |

*Note:* n.r. = not reported.
*Source:* WTO 2002.

by the OECD was US$109 billion. If only OECD data are used for both domestic support and the PSE, total domestic support exceeds the total PSE for the EU in 1996 by US$12 billion (OECD 2000b). This erroneously implies that protection afforded EU agriculture from import access and export subsidies was negative and of the order of $12 billion.[6]

Trade negotiations need to single out amber box policies that are truly domestic support policies and therefore are not conflated with market access or export subsidy policies. In this way, AMS reduction commitments can have a maximum effect. To distinguish policies that have a market impact but are *not* part of the import access or export subsidy commitments, it would be fruitful to designate a new amber box for such policies. At the present time, the only way a reduction in the AMS can have an impact is if it comes from a reduction in this kind of new amber-type policy intervention, or an

**TABLE 6.6 AMS) Commitments Versus Actual**

| Member | Currency | 1995 | | 1996 | | 1997 | | 1998 | | 1999 | | 2000 | | 2001 | |
|---|---|---|---|---|---|---|---|---|---|---|---|---|---|---|---|
| | | Total AMS Commit-ment Level | Current Total AMS | Total AMS Commit-ment Level | Current Total AMS | Total AMS Commit-ment Level | Current Total AMS | Total AMS Commit-ment Level | Current Total AMS | Total AMS Commit-ment Level | Current Total AMS | Total AMS Commit-ment Level | Current Total AMS | Total AMS Commit-ment Level | Current Total AMS |
| Argentina | US$ Million | 85 | 123 | 84 | 84 | 83 | 83 | 82 | 81 | 81 | 80 | 80 | n.a | 80 | n.a |
| Australia | $A Million | 570 | 152 | 551 | 144 | 531 | 132 | 511 | 120 | 492 | 62 | 472 | 214 | 472 | n.a |
| Brazil | US$ Million | 1039 | 295 | 1025 | 363 | 1011 | 307 | 997 | 83 | 983 | n.a | 969 | n.a | 969 | n.a |
| Bulgaria | ECU Million | n.a | n.a | 650 | n.a | 635 | 5 | 520 | 14 | 520 | 10 | 520 | n.a | 520 | n.a |
| Canada | Can$ Million | 5197 | 777 | 5017 | 619 | 4838 | 522 | 4659 | 790 | 4480 | 939 | 4301 | n.a | 4301 | n.a |
| Chinese Taipei | NT$ Million | n.a | n.a | n.a | n.a | n.a | n.a | n.a | n.a | n.a | n.a | n.a | n.a | n.a | n.a |
| Colombia | US$ Million | 392 | 58 | 387 | 4 | 382 | 14 | 377 | 10 | 371 | 7 | 366 | n.a | 361 | n.a |
| Costa Rica | US$ Million | 18 | 0 | 18 | 0 | 18 | 0 | 17 | 2 | 17 | 2 | 17 | n.a | 17 | n.a |
| Cyprus | £C Million | 58 | 37 | 57 | 36 | 56 | 26 | 55 | 22 | 55 | 29 | 54 | 23 | 53 | n.a |
| Czech Republic | Kè Million | 16 | 1 | 16 | 2 | 15 | 1 | 15 | 1 | 14 | 4 | 14 | 5 | 14 | 5 |
| EC | ECU Billion | 79 | 50 | 76 | 51 | 74 | 50 | 72 | 47 | 69 | 48 | 67 | n.a | 67 | n.a |
| Hungary | Ft Million | 41 | 21 | 39 | 11 | 38 | 12 | 37 | 98 | 35 | n.a | 34 | n.a | 34 | n.a |
| Iceland | SDR Million | 157 | 124 | 152 | 108 | 146 | 109 | 141 | 250 | 136 | 135 | 130 | 134 | 131 | n.a |
| Israel | US$ Million | 645 | 461 | 637 | 501 | 628 | 524 | 620 | 412 | 611 | 257 | 603 | 325 | 603 | n.a |
| Japan | ¥ Billion | 4801 | 3508 | 4635 | 3330 | 4470 | 3171 | 4304 | 767 | 4138 | 748 | 3973 | n.a | 3972 | n.a |
| Jordan | Jordanian Dinar | n.a | n.a | n.a | n.a | n.a | n.a | n.a | n.a | n.a | n.a | 2 | n.a | 1 | n.a |
| Korea, Rep. of | W Billion | 2183 | 2075 | 2106 | 1967 | 2029 | 1937 | 1952 | 1563 | 1875 | 1552 | 1798 | 1691 | 1798 | n.a |
| Lithuania | US$ Million | n.a | n.a | n.a | n.a | n.a | n.a | n.a | n.a | n.a | n.a | n.a | n.a | 113 | n.a |
| Mexico | Mex$1991 Million | 29 | 1 | 28 | 1 | 28 | 3 | 27 | 4 | 27 | n.a | 27 | 0 | 26 | n.a |
| Moldova | SDR Million | n.a | n.a | n.a | n.a | n.a | n.a | n.a | n.a | n.a | n.a | n.a | n.a | 15 | n.a |

**TABLE 6.6 (Continued)**

| Member | Currency | 1995 | | 1996 | | 1997 | | 1998 | | 1999 | | 2000 | | 2001 | |
|---|---|---|---|---|---|---|---|---|---|---|---|---|---|---|---|
| | | Total AMS Commit-ment Level | Current Total AMS | Total AMS Commit-ment Level | Current Total AMS | Total AMS Commit-ment Level | Current Total AMS | Total AMS Commit-ment Level | Current Total AMS | Total AMS Commit-ment Level | Current Total AMS | Total AMS Commit-ment Level | Current Total AMS | Total AMS Commit-ment Level | Current Total AMS |
| Morocco | DH Million | 779 | 94 | 769 | 250 | 758 | 91 | 748 | 126 | 737 | 180 | 727 | 155 | 716 | n.a |
| New Zealand | NZ$ Million | 348 | 0 | 336 | 0 | 324 | 0 | 312 | 0 | 300 | 0 | 288 | 0 | 288 | 11 |
| Norway | NOK Million | 14 | 10 | 13 | 11 | 13 | 11 | 12 | 11 | 12 | 11 | 11 | 10 | 11 | n.a |
| Papua New Guinea | US$ Million | 39 | n.a | 38 | n.a | 38 | n.a | 37 | n.a | 37 | n.a | 36 | n.a | 36 | n.a |
| Poland | US$ Million | 4022 | 255 | 3883 | 227 | 3745 | 296 | 3606 | 301 | 3457 | 237 | 3329 | 336 | 3316 | n.a |
| Slovak Republic | Sk Million | 12 | 7 | 12 | 7 | 11 | 8 | 11 | 8 | 11 | 7 | 10 | 8 | 10 | 8 |
| Slovenia | ECU Million | 75 | 70 | 72 | 66 | 70 | 60 | 67 | 65 | 64 | 55 | 62 | 16 | 61 | 14 |
| South Africa | R Million | 2435 | 1640 | 2351 | 1938 | 2267 | 2198 | 2183 | 820 | 2099 | 790 | 2015 | 439 | 2015 | n.a |
| Switzerland-Liecht. | Sw F Million | 5143 | 4287 | 4966 | 3663 | 4789 | 3445 | 4611 | 3273 | 4434 | n.a | 4257 | n.a | 4257 | n.a |
| Thailand | B Million | 22 | 16 | 22 | 13 | 21 | 17 | 21 | 16 | 21 | n.a | 20 | n.a | 20 | n.a |
| Tunisia | D Million | 67 | 59 | 67 | 51 | 66 | 53 | 65 | 61 | 64 | 29 | 63 | 0 | 62 | n.a |
| United States | US$ Million | 23 | 6 | 22 | 6 | 21 | 6 | 21 | 10 | 20 | 17 | 19 | n.a | 19 | n.a |
| Venezuela, RB | US$ Million | 1287 | 542 | 1270 | 331 | 1252 | 457 | 1235 | 211 | 1218 | n.a | 1200 | n.a | 1183 | n.a |

*Note:* With respect to Argentina's Current Total AMS figure of 1995 see G/AG/N/ARG/4 and WT/Let/292. With respect to Iceland's Current Total AMS figure for 1998 see G/AG/N/ISL/14 regarding the unadjusted and adjusted Current Total AMS for 1998.

*Source:* WTO (2002).

**TABLE 6.7 Evolution of Aggregate Measure of Support (AMS) and Producer Support Estimate (PSE) US$ billion**

| Country | *1986–88* | | | *1995* | | | *1996* | | | *1997* | | | *1998* | | |
|---|---|---|---|---|---|---|---|---|---|---|---|---|---|---|---|
| | (1) AMS | (2) PSE | (3) (2)/(1) | (1) AMS | (2) PSE | (3) (2)/(1) | (1) AMS | (2) PSE | (3) (2)/(1) | (1) AMS | (2) PSE | (3) (2)/(1) | (1) AMS | (2) PSE | (3) (2)/(1) |
| Australia | 0.4 | 1.8 | 22.1 | 0.1 | 2.3 | 5.0 | 0.1 | 2.2 | 5.1 | 0.1 | 2.3 | 4.3 | 0.1 | 2.0 | 3.7 |
| Canada | 4.1 | 7 5 | 54.8 | 0.6 | 5.5 | 10.2 | 0.5 | 5.0 | 9.0 | 0.4 | 4.4 | 8.6 | 0.5 | 5.2 | 10.3 |
| Czech Republic | 1.2 | 62.9 | 1.9 | 0.0 | 24.7 | 0.2 | 0.1 | 26.2 | 0.2 | 0.0 | 7.9 | 0.4 | 0.0 | 31.9 | 0.1 |
| EU | 80.7 | 85.0 | 94.9 | 0.1 | 96.1 | 0.1 | 0.1 | 91.7 | 0.1 | 0.1 | 92.7 | 0.1 | 0.1 | 102.3 | 0.1 |
| Hungary | 0.9 | 123.9 | 0.7 | 0.2 | 93.8 | 0.2 | 0.0 | 104.5 | 0.0 | 0.0 | 67.2 | 0.0 | 0.0 | 227.6 | 0.0 |
| Iceland | 0.2 | 7.9 | 2.5 | 0.0 | 9.3 | 0.0 | 0.0 | 8.2 | 0.0 | 0.0 | 9.1 | 0.0 | 0.0 | 11.4 | 0.0 |
| Japan | 33.8 | 7.2 | 467.7 | 37.3 | 7.1 | 524.1 | 30.6 | 6.5 | 472.6 | 26.2 | 5.9 | 447.2 | 5.9 | 6.2 | 94.0 |
| Korea | 2.1 | 9.7 | 21.7 | 2.7 | 19.4 | 13.8 | 2.4 | 18.8 | 13.0 | 2.0 | 19.2 | 10.6 | 1.1 | 17.6 | 6.3 |
| Mexico | 9.6 | -0.6 | -1648.3 | 0.2 | -7.9 | -2.7 | 0.1 | 11.0 | 1.1 | 0.4 | 31.6 | 1.3 | 0.4 | 37.8 | 1.1 |
| New Zealand | 0.2 | 0.9 | 23.4 | 0.0 | 0.2 | 0.0 | 0.0 | 0.2 | 0.0 | 0.0 | 0.2 | 0.0 | 0.0 | 0.1 | 0.0 |
| Norway | 2.1 | 18.0 | 11.7 | 1.5 | 18.4 | 8.4 | 1.6 | 17.7 | 9.2 | 1.5 | 18.4 | 8.1 | 1.4 | 20.0 | 7.2 |
| Poland | 4.2 | 0.1 | 5282.6 | 0.3 | 4.7 | 5.4 | 0.2 | 7.1 | 3.2 | 0.3 | 6.6 | 4.5 | 0.3 | 12.4 | 2.4 |
| Switzerland | 3.4 | 7.9 | 42.8 | 3.6 | 7.5 | 48.4 | 3.0 | 7.1 | 41.7 | 2.4 | 7.2 | 33.2 | 2.3 | 7.3 | 31.1 |
| United States | 23.9 | 41.8 | 57.1 | 6.2 | 22.9 | 27.2 | 5.9 | 29.9 | 19.8 | 6.2 | 30.7 | 20.3 | 10.4 | 48.6 | 21.4 |
| All OECD | 166.8 | 238.9 | 69.8 | 52.8 | 271.2 | 19.5 | 44.6 | 254.1 | 17.5 | 39.6 | 231.8 | 17.1 | 22.5 | 256.7 | 8.8 |

*Note:* n.a.=Not applicable.
*Source:* OECD Secretariat calculations

**FIGURE 6.2 Trends in AMS versus PSE (1986–2001), US$ Billions**

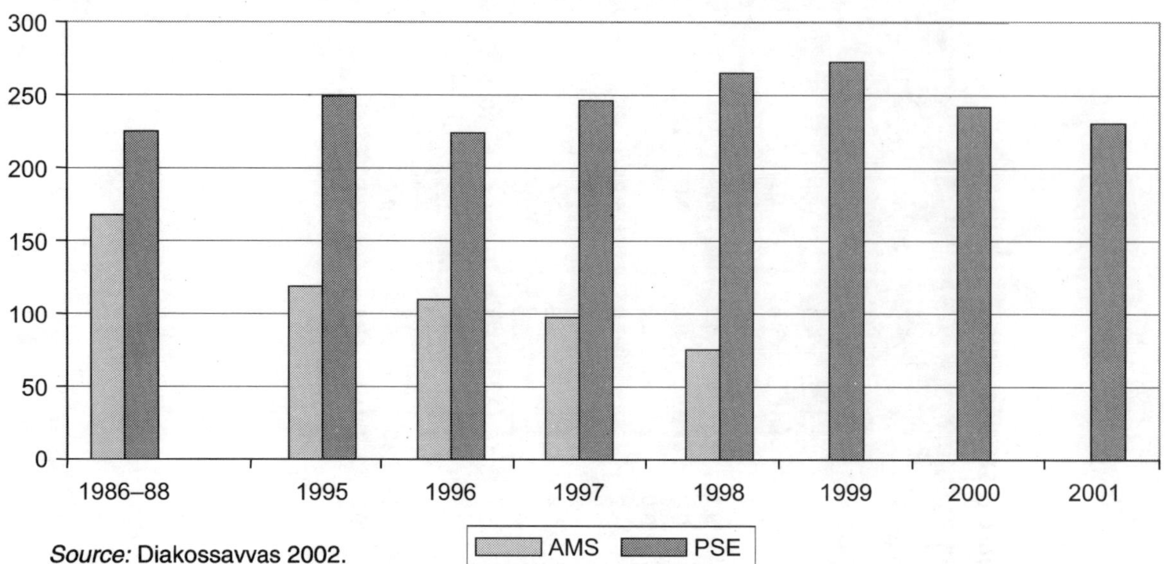


*Source:* Diakossavvas 2002.

increase in market access or a reduction in export subsidies (because AMS measures are often conflated with the latter type of commitments).

Another AMS issue requiring attention is that the world price is fixed at the 1986–88 base period and as a result, the AMS does not vary with world prices but instead with changes in domestic production and support prices. Consequently, if the world commodity prices continue their decline, the implied support from administered price supports (with consumer transfers and border protection) will increase, but measured support in the AMS will not. This may have implications for the effectiveness of AMS reduction commitments as negotiated in the URAA.

The aggregation of all policies and commodity sectors (including sector-wide policies) into a single AMS has limited the effectiveness of amber box policy reductions. Countries have flexibility not to reduce support in some sectors and even increase it in other sectors. The incentive to do this is constrained somewhat by the Peace Clause, which states that policies are exempt from WTO policy challenges such as countervailing duties, provided that support does not exceed the 1992 levels for that particular sector (see box 6.1). Support reduction commitments on a policy type and commodity sector basis rather than on a single AMS for all policies and sectors should be considered. This will secure a more meaningful reduction in trade distortion arising from amber box policies and prevent countries from shifting support from sector to sector as market conditions change.

### *Blue Box*

The blue box is an exemption from the general rule that all subsidies linked to production must be reduced or kept within defined minimal (*de minimis*) levels. It covers payments directly linked to acreage or animal numbers, but under schemes that also limit production by imposing production quotas or requiring farmers to set aside land. Only the EU, Iceland, Norway, Japan, the Slovak Republic, Slovenia, and the U.S. have used these subsidies. The U.S. has since changed its blue box policies so that they fall in the green box category. Blue box payments were included in the baseline AMS only and were excluded from the AMS for the implementation period. The result is that the base AMS is overstated, which makes it easier for countries to reach their AMS reduction requirements.

The distinguishing feature of blue box policies is payments based on fixed acreage, yields, or livestock numbers on no more than 85 percent of baseline production. Paying farmers not to produce can be trade-distorting by either reducing

## BOX 6.1 The Peace Clause and Domestic Subsidies

The "Peace Clause" (Article 13 of the URAA) precludes most WTO dispute settlement challenges against a country in compliance with the Agreement, but ends after 2003. Many agricultural subsidies will then be vulnerable to legal challenge under Article XVI of GATT 1994, Articles 6.3(a)–(c) and 6.4 of the WTO Agreement on Subsidies and Countervailing Measures (SCM) or with claims of nullification or impairment. Nonsubsidizing developing countries will then be able to bargain using dispute settlement panels (or direct negotiations) to contest the compatibility of domestic farm policies with these more strict disciplines generally available to nonagricultural sectors in the WTO. The remedy would require elimination of the subsidy or reduce its adverse effects. The various subsidy provisions of the WTO, therefore, represent potentially powerful disciplines on agricultural subsidies.

Agricultural subsidies hitherto have been sheltered under various conditions from the application of several WTO provisions on subsidies. However, amber and blue box policies have not been entirely immune from countervailing duties and GATT 1994 Article XVI:13 even with the Peace Clause in effect. The dispute between New Zealand and the United States and Canada over the impact of Canadian dairy policy, together with the complaint by Brazil over U.S. cotton subsidies and the challenge by Australia, Brazil, and Thailand of the EU sugar regime reflects the reduced protection from actionability relative to green box and export subsidies.

For a detailed analysis of the Peace Clause and its implications, read Richard H. Steinberg and Timothy E. Josling (2003), "When the Peace Ends: The Vulnerability of EC and U.S. Agricultural Subsidies to WTO Legal Challenge," *Journal of International Economic Law*, Spring.

production or even increasing production (the latter because farmers have an incentive to stay in production and even expand in order to receive more payments in the future). The EU employs production controls (production quotas and acreage constraints including acreage set-asides) for major field crops, and deficiency payments are given for sectors such as oilseeds and sheepmeat. Acrerage premia are given for area set-asides and areas that are planted. There are slaughter premia for beef cattle and calves and "headage payments" for beef and dairy (with the latter requiring land density targets to protect the environment). Even though there are acreage constraints, production may be distorted because farmers may increase production by using inputs more intensively. Farmers may also be encouraged to plant more area—up to the ceiling—than they otherwise would. Acreage payments are based on a fixed regional base area but individual farmers still have an incentive to increase acreage to maximize their share of the regional payments. It will be shown later that the EU program is fully coupled in acreage decisions, rendering the supply-reducing impact of the base acreage constraint ineffective.

A similar situation occurs for livestock headage payments and all payments that require farmers to continue to remain in agriculture. Hence, the EU compensatory payment scheme appears to be at best only partially decoupled. Similar conclusions could be made for the original (that is, pre-1996 Farm Bill) policies of the U.S. that were included in the blue box but have since been transferred to the green box with the use of the production flexibility payment program.

EU compensatory payments are blue box and, although regarded as trade-distorting-type policies, are exempt from reductions. With the Peace Clause set to expire and blue box policies under consideration in the current trade negotiations, it is important to understand the trade-distorting effects of blue box provisions for the EU relative to that of decoupled taxpayer-financed programs such as historical entitlements in the U.S.

Area (formerly called compensatory) payments for cereals totaled 14.6 billion Euro in 1999. However, acerage set-aside (both a mandatory minimum and a voluntary set-aside with a maximum) along with set-aside payments (1.3 billion Euro in 1999) restricted to a base level of acres (with penalties if exceeded) are designed to reduce or even nullify the trade-distorting effects of such producer subsidies. Nevertheless, acreage set-aside has a cost, in that it can reduce production at the same time by idling a valuable resource, as has been the experience with the U.S. Conservation Reserve Program (CRP).

There is a need to identify the impacts of direct income or "compensatory" payments for acres planted and diverted by cereal producers in the EU. Commentators argue that these payments fulfill several criteria of Annex 2 of the URAA defining non-trade-distorting subsidies in that they are taxpayer-financed and do not provide price support to producers (Cahill 1997; Guyomard, Baudry, and Carpentier 1996; Moro and Sckokai 1998). However, payments are based on acres planted and farmers are obligated to produce cereals on those acres. Because payments are made on a fixed base acreage, economists thus far have assumed that the effects are akin to those of inframarginal production subsidies.

However, area payments in the EU are not decoupled because they are made on an aggregate fixed area base that is set at the national or regional level. Individual farmers do not have a base area—just eligible acres for which to receive payments—and have area set-asides. If the regional base area is exceeded, the per unit subsidy is prorated downward proportionately for all farmers. This means that the area payments are fully coupled in plantings because there is no constraint for an individual farmer not to plant up to the level of production at which marginal costs equal market price plus the per unit subsidy (de Gorter, Hranaiova, and Tsur 2000). The penalty of the reduced subsidy due to the aggregate base area being exceeded is applied to all farmers, even if another farmer or other farmers are responsible for the excess acreage. Area payments with a national base area are therefore not a limit on total acres planted.

For EU cattle, the headage payments that are under "production limiting" arrangements are anything but production limiting because: (a) claims for payments are the only limiting feature, not production; and (b) the number of animals eligible is not limited to numbers on farms prior to the payments being instituted in 1992. Where numbers of animals were below the maximum that could be claimed per farm, farmers have had an incentive to expand their stock of animals held up to the limits on which payments are made. As such, the incentives in the program have been to encourage expansion of animal numbers initially and then to lock in production near levels that are consistent with the maximum number of animals eligible for payments. Those numbers reflect the very high levels of support for several decades as well as the incentives inherent in the headage payments (Roberts 2003).[7]

### *Green Box*

Green box policies include decoupled payments (which purportedly do not affect production decisions) and general policies such as environmental programs, research, food aid, crop insurance, and income safety net programs to correct for market failures. These policies are generally taxpayer-funded and do not involve consumer transfers.

Green box policies are supposed to meet the criteria of "no, or at most minimal, trade-distorting effects or effects on production." It will be shown later that the green box also encompasses some policies that are not fully decoupled.

The URAA uses the term "decoupled" only in connection with direct payments to producers called "decoupled income support." These provide domestic support exempt from reduction commitments. The issue is whether the rationale for the policy is to correct for market failures or to redistribute income.[8] If the rationale for the policy is to redistribute income, the policy should be designed to fulfill the criteria for decoupling. Policies correcting for market failures, on the other hand, inevitably require a change in production (for example, pollution reduction policies), so these polices are not required to meet the definition of decoupling as presented in the URAA. Of course, politicians like to mix the two motives in their call for multifunctionality. Hence, the URAA definition of decoupling may need to be expanded for other motives of subsidies to ensure minimally trade-distorting policies (see discussion below).

The green box also includes programs that are not directed at particular commodities or products, such as income insurance programs, as well as environmental protection and regional development programs. Table 6.4 provides the composition of domestic support with green box support as the largest category. Expenditures by

**TABLE 6.8 Total Green Box Expenditures by Category, US$ Million, 1995–98**

| Green Box Category | *Total Green Box Expenditures (US$ million)* | | | |
|---|---|---|---|---|
| | 1995 | 1996 | 1997 | 1998 |
| Research | 3,251.5 | 3,428.9 | 2,660.3 | 713.1 |
| Pest & Disease Control | 1,339.7 | 2,705.7 | 620.1 | 368.3 |
| Training Services | 2,330.7 | 2,047.4 | 623.7 | 385.3 |
| Extension & Advisory Services | 2,620.4 | 3,264.5 | 2,923.8 | 597.8 |
| Inspection Services | 326.2 | 660.9 | 295.6 | 140.1 |
| Marketing & Promotion Services | 991.9 | 1,008.3 | 201.8 | 75.0 |
| Infrastructural Services | 28,507.3 | 23,664.4 | 18,834.0 | 3,179.5 |
| Other General Services | 6,020.1 | 4,173.6 | 3,514.2 | 364.5 |
| Non-separated General Services | 9,396.8 | 7,625.5 | 7,475.0 | 242.6 |
| Public Stockholding for Food Security | 2,927.3 | 1,375.4 | 1,202.8 | 264.5 |
| Domestic Food Aid | 40,771.1 | 40,131.2 | 37,718.2 | 351.5 |
| Direct Payments to Producers[a] | 339.8 | 349.4 | 0.0 | 0.0 |
| Decoupled Income Support | 2,586.5 | 7,316.4 | 7,254.3 | 793.4 |
| Income Insurance/Safety Net Programs | 39.8 | 53.9 | 8.3 | 0.0 |
| Natural Disaster Relief | 1,766.7 | 1,401.0 | 1,096.9 | 765.8 |
| Producer Retirement Programs | 1,505.5 | 2,035.2 | 757.3 | 7.4 |
| Resource Retirement Programs | 3,167.7 | 3,589.5 | 1,706.8 | 7.9 |
| Investment Aids | 12,065.7 | 9,847.2 | 3,751.3 | 2,019.5 |
| Environmental Programs | 5,237.9 | 7,459.4 | 2,292.0 | 1,056.5 |
| Regional Assistance Programs | 4,205.9 | 4,571.7 | 685.3 | 539.9 |
| Other Measures | 3,916.0 | 383.4 | 320.0 | 289.0 |
| Total Green Box, of which (in %): | 133,331.7 | 127,091.9 | 93,980.9 | 12,161.8 |
| **Shares by Category (in %):** | | | | |
| Total General Services (para. 2 of Annex 2) | 41.1 | 38.2 | 39.5 | 49.9 |
| Total Public Stockholding & Domestic Food Aid (paras. 3–4 of Annex 2) | 32.8 | 32.7 | 41.4 | 5.1 |
| Total Direct Payments (paras. 6–13 of Annex 2) | 23.2 | 28.8 | 18.7 | 42.7 |
| Total Other Measures | 2.9 | 0.3 | 0.3 | 2.4 |
| Member Countries Covered | 46 | 47 | 43 | 26 |

*Note:* "Direct Payments to Producers" relates to measures covered by the second sentence of paragraph 5 of Annex 2 of the Agreement.
*Source:* WTO (2002).

category of green box support are shown in table 6.8.

Green box policies may require tighter definitions for the requirement that "no production shall be required in order to receive . . . payments," as stated in Annex 2 of the URAA. Do payments that require that eligible farmers keep their land in agricultural use meet that condition? The current negotiations will have to address the questions of whether the programs listed in Annex 2 are truly non- or minimally trade-distorting, how green box definitions can be tightened, what the criteria should be to reduce the loopholes provided for continuing output-increasing subsidies, and whether another category of green or nonactionable subsidies should be established. Stricter rules, definitions, and monitoring arrangements will be required.

**TABLE 6.9** ***de minimis* Support**

| Country | Total AMS | | | Total *de minimus* | | | Total AMS w/o *de minimus* | | | *de minimus* % of Total AMS | | |
|---|---|---|---|---|---|---|---|---|---|---|---|---|
| | 1995 | 1996 | 1997 | 1995 | 1996 | 1997 | 1995 | 1996 | 1997 | 1995 | 1996 | 1997 |
| United States | 6.31 | 5.94 | — | 0.11 | 0.04 | — | 6.2 | 5.9 | — | 2% | 1% | — |
| EU | 61.07 | — | — | −1.06 | — | — | 62.13 | — | — | −2% | 0% | — |
| Japan | 37.42 | — | — | 0.13 | — | — | 37.29 | — | — | 0% | 0% | — |
| Canada | 0.79 | — | — | 0.22 | — | — | 0.57 | — | — | 28% | 0% | — |
| Korea, Rep. of | 3.06 | 2.87 | 2.73 | 0.04 | 0.07 | 0.28 | 3.01 | 2.81 | 2.45 | 1% | 2% | 0.1 |
| Mexico | 0.21 | — | — | — | — | — | 0.21 | — | — | 0% | 0% | — |
| Switzerland | 3.63 | 2.96 | 2.38 | — | — | — | 3.63 | — | — | 0% | 0% | — |
| Norway | 1.56 | 1.64 | — | — | — | — | 1.56 | — | — | 0% | 0% | — |

*Source:* WTO (2002).

Finally, *de minimis* subsidies are defined as those that fall within small limits. The levels of these subsidies are summarized in table 6.9. Many countries have expressed a general willingness to reconsider *de minimis* levels for developing countries and possibly transition economies (most are bound by *de minimis* levels rather than AMS reduction commitments). A possible loophole in the AMS are *de minimis* rules that allow for an exemption of 5 percent (10 percent for developing countries) of total value of production for each commodity plus another 5 percent (10 percent for developing countries) for non-commodity-specific support. In the case of Canada in 1995, *de minimis* support accounted for 28 percent of the total AMS (table 6.9). Unlike the AMS itself, the *de minimis* clause operates on an individual commodity basis only. It is not possible to offset support above the *de minimis* level for one product by transferring it to another commodity that is below its *de minimis* level.

## The Economics of Domestic Support and Trade Distortions

### *The Effect of Domestic Versus Border Support on Trade Distortion*

Economists generally argue that domestic support is less trade-distorting than border protection because the latter reduces consumption as well. But because the supply curve is very likely to be elastic and the demand for food inelastic in developed countries, the difference in trade-distorting effects between domestic and border support may not be large. Analysis by the OECD (2001) using the PEM model for grains and oilseeds indicates that border protection does not distort trade much more than does domestic support. Input subsidies on purchased inputs, for example, can have a large distortion on production. This is more likely with a more elastic supply curve for purchased inputs and a more inelastic supply curve of other inputs (for instance, land). If purchased inputs are also a large share of input costs, if the value of returns to scale in agricultural production is close to one, and if the substitutability between inputs is high, then an input subsidy will be more output distorting. These conditions do characterize much of agricultural production.

According to OECD estimates of income transfer efficiency (that is, the actual amount that farmers receive from consumer and taxpayer transfers), no support policy linked to agricultural activity succeeds in delivering more than half the monetary transfers from consumers and taxpayers as additional income to farm households. In the case of market price support due to border protection and production subsidies, the share is one-fourth or less; for input subsidies it is less than one-fifth. On average, only 25 percent of producer support actually finds its way into the producer's pocket. Most of the market price support is paid back to input suppliers, capitalized into land values, or compensates for the market-depressing effects of government policies (that is, offsetting the world price declines owing to all countries' policies). Hoekman, Ng, and Olarreaga (2002) find that high levels of protection and domestic support for farmers in developed countries significantly affect many least-developed countries, both directly and indirectly through the price-depressing effect of agricultural support policies. In assessing the impact of reducing domestic support for a sample of 119 countries, significant differences are found in the impact of a 50 percent cut in tariffs and a 50 percent cut in domestic support for developing countries compared to developed countries. However, for both groups tariff reductions have a much greater positive effect on exports and welfare. In the following analysis, the relative trade-distorting effects of domestic versus border support are analyzed using the OECD's PEM model for grains and oilseeds.[9]

**PEM Analysis** Border support is implemented through import tariffs/quotas and export subsidies while domestic support refers to subsidies on outputs and inputs that are classified as amber in the WTO. Other payments such as historical entitlements or area payments depend on historical land uses and may be classified as green or blue.

There is a great deal of variation in the relative reliance on market price support derived from border protection and from direct payments to provide support across countries and even across commodities (wheat, coarse grains, oilseeds, and rice) within a country (table 6.10). All six countries/entities in the model (Canada, Mexico, the U.S., the EU, Switzerland, and Japan) use domestic support.

**TABLE 6.10 2001 Baseline Support by Commodity Region and Type (US$/tonne)**

| | Canada | Mexico | USA | EU | Switzerland | Japan |
|---|---|---|---|---|---|---|
| ***Border*** | | | | | | |
| Wheat | 0.00 | 39.85 | 0.00 | 0.83 | 107.90 | 109.73 |
| Coarse grains | 0.00 | 38.84 | 0.00 | 6.27 | 113.52 | 878.98 |
| Oilseeds | 0.00 | 42.37 | 0.00 | 0.00 | 653.01 | 0.00 |
| Rice | — | 20.80 | 0.00 | 90.31 | — | 1,565.40 |
| ***Domestic*** | | | | | | |
| Wheat | 15.96 | 54.97 | 68.77 | 83.53 | 165.75 | 980.28 |
| Coarse grains | 12.85 | 46.93 | 28.97 | 77.84 | 101.10 | 135.84 |
| Oilseeds | 35.81 | 173.82 | 53.70 | 131.60 | 812.02 | 840.56 |
| Rice | — | 47.04 | 81.38 | 39.53 | — | 197.14 |

*Source:* See appendix A.

Support levels per tonne are lowest in Canada in all cases. Domestic support for oilseeds tends to be high in all countries except the U.S. and Japan.

Canada and the U.S. used no border protection and the EU used very little border protection except for rice. Mexico had moderate levels of border protection for all four crops; Switzerland had high levels of both border protection and direct payments for wheat and coarse grains, and extremely high border protection and direct payments for oilseeds.

Japan employed extremely high border protection combined with high direct payments for rice and coarse grains. It used the reverse combination for wheat and oilseeds—extremely high direct payments with high levels of border support.

Table 6.11 shows the effect of removing border protection (setting the market price support [MPS] = 0). The world price of wheat increased by less than 0.5 percent because only a very small amount of border protection was used in 2001. OECD countries had net exports in 2001 without extensive use of export subsidies. The three countries that relied on MPS for wheat—Mexico, Switzerland, and Japan—accounted for 4.6 million tonnes (mmt) of production, which is less than 2 percent of world production. Wheat production in Mexico and Switzerland declined by 20 and 21 percent, respectively.

Unbalanced baseline support patterns are very important in affecting the outcome of reducing just one type of support (border protection or direct payments). Removing border protection in Japan results in movement of productive resources away from the commodity receiving extremely high levels of border support (rice and coarse grains) toward the commodity still receiving extremely high levels of direct payments (wheat and oilseeds) and vice versa. The opposite happens for removing direct payments only. Production of wheat therefore increases by 0.9 mmt in this scenario because input market adjustment from the even greater changes is affecting rice and coarse grains.

The world price of coarse grains increases by 3 percent while the price of oilseeds and rice increases by 1 and 7 percent, respectively. The resulting patterns of adjustment are fairly easy to follow. The commodity most affected is rice because production in two regions, Japan and the EU, declines dramatically. Rice production increases in the U.S., which relies on extensive direct payments support for rice, and in the rest of the world.

The most significant impact for Mexico is in terms of wheat and coarse grains (maize) since these are the staple crops. Reduction of MPS reduces production by 20 and 18 percent, respectively. Switzerland also has a large reduction in production following the pattern of its MPS.

The impact of removing domestic support on increased world prices (from 5 percent for rice to 18 percent for oilseeds) is greater than that of reducing border support (0 percent for wheat to 7 percent for rice)—compare the last column of table 6.11 to that of table 6.12. Two primary reasons account for this: domestic support is higher (table 6.10); and direct payments based on use of inputs with elastic supply

**TABLE 6.11 Effect of Removing All Border Protection on Effective Producer Price* and Production**

| | Canada | Mexico | USA | EU | Switzerland | Japan | ROW |
|---|---|---|---|---|---|---|---|
| *Effective Producer Price* | | | | | | | |
| Wheat | 0% | −21% | 0% | −1% | −32% | −9% | 0% |
| Coarse grains | 2% | −25% | 2% | −4% | −43% | −78% | 3% |
| Oilseeds | 1% | −14% | 1% | 1% | −77% | 0% | 1% |
| Rice | 0% | −8% | 4% | −32% | 0% | −80% | 7% |
| *Production* | | | | | | | |
| Wheat | −1% | −20% | −1% | 1% | −21% | 128% | 0% |
| Coarse grains | 3% | −18% | 3% | −6% | −48% | −96% | 0% |
| Oilseeds | 0% | −4% | 0% | 3% | −97% | 66% | 0% |
| Rice | 0% | 2% | 6% | −46% | 0% | −90% | 3% |

*Note:* ROW = Rest of World.
*Source:* See Appendix A.

**TABLE 6.12 Effect on Effective Producer Price and Production of Removing All Direct Payments Support**

| | Canada | Mexico | USA | EU | Switzerland | Japan | ROW |
|---|---|---|---|---|---|---|---|
| *Effective Producer Price*[a] | | | | | | | |
| Wheat | 13% | −10% | 8% | 11% | 4% | −68% | 12% |
| Coarse grains | 9% | 4% | 8% | 11% | 5% | −1% | 16% |
| Oilseeds | 15% | −16% | −7% | 14% | 3% | −43% | 18% |
| Rice | 0% | −8% | −35% | 2% | 0% | −5% | 5% |
| *Production* | | | | | | | |
| Wheat | 5% | −37% | 5% | −9% | −18% | −100% | 0% |
| Coarse grains | 1% | 3% | 5% | −9% | −22% | 66% | 1% |
| Oilseeds | 9% | −15% | −16% | 4% | −14% | −43% | 5% |
| Rice | 0% | −15% | −74% | −10% | 0% | −6% | 2% |

a. The effective producer price is the world price adjusted for transportation and quality differentials (OECD world price for each country) plus the MPS rate plus the rate of output price support in the form of direct payments.
*Note:* ROW = Rest of World.
*Source:* See Appendix A.

curves generate larger increases in production (OECD 2001).

Table 6.13 shows the impacts of agricultural trade liberalization according to how each major category of people participates in these markets (as taxpayers, consumers, farm operators, land owners, and other input suppliers) and by region.

Economic efficiency is measured by deadweight loss and determined by the total welfare sum across the six countries. As expected, this number is small relative to the transfers that take place among the categories. Reduced deadweight loss from eliminating direct payments is US$4.2 billion, US$11.9 billion from eliminating MPS, and US$14.9 billion from eliminating both.

Deadweight loss is primarily a result of the very large distortion of consumer prices in Japan. The consumer benefit of eliminating MPS is US$22.7 billion. There is a benefit of US$1.7 billion in Mexico. As Japan, Mexico, and Switzerland rely on MPS, the

**TABLE 6.13 Effect of Trade Liberalization (US$ Millions)**

| | Canada | Mexico | US | EU | Switzerland | Japan | Welfare Sum |
|---|---|---|---|---|---|---|---|
| ***No Border Support*** | | | | | | | |
| Taxpayers | −4 | −450 | −133 | 202 | −194 | −3,039 | −3,618 |
| Consumers | −53 | 1,704 | −551 | 580 | 583 | 22,658 | 24,921 |
| Other Farmer Owned | 16 | −186 | 214 | −114 | −34 | −3,218 | −3,322 |
| Land | 22 | −494 | 320 | −218 | −28 | −2,718 | −3,115 |
| Hired Labor | 0 | 0 | 8 | −16 | −2 | 0 | −9 |
| Purchased Inputs | 13 | −272 | 189 | −248 | −36 | −2,579 | −2,932 |
| Welfare sum | −5 | 302 | 47 | 187 | 290 | 11,105 | 11,925 |
| ***No Domestic Payments*** | | | | | | | |
| Taxpayers | 806 | 1,444 | 16,288 | 17,461 | 175 | 3,437 | 39,611 |
| Consumers | −504 | −135 | −4,598 | −3,116 | −8 | −158 | −8,519 |
| Other Farmer Owned | 111 | −4 | −243 | −43 | −13 | −547 | −738 |
| Land | −307 | −1,140 | −8,559 | −13,111 | −106 | −1,005 | −24,228 |
| Hired Labor | 0 | 0 | −27 | −10 | −1 | 0 | −37 |
| Purchased Inputs | 91 | −51 | −617 | −637 | −22 | −608 | −1,844 |
| Welfare sum | 197 | 115 | 2,245 | 543 | 25 | 1,119 | 4,244 |
| ***100% Liberalization*** | | | | | | | |
| Taxpayers | 806 | 846 | 16,288 | 17,446 | −63 | −1,142 | 34,181 |
| Consumers | −555 | 1,028 | −5,139 | −2,526 | 502 | 22,325 | 15,636 |
| Other Farmer Owned | 127 | −170 | −20 | −132 | −36 | −3,669 | −3,900 |
| Land | −285 | −1,471 | −8,324 | −13,252 | −147 | −2,906 | −26,385 |
| Hired Labor | 0 | 0 | −18 | −26 | −2 | 0 | −46 |
| Purchased Inputs | 104 | −296 | −431 | −872 | −45 | −2,958 | −4,498 |
| Welfare sum | 198 | −63 | 2,356 | 638 | 210 | 11,651 | 14,989 |

*Notes:* Mexico: 1991 U.S. dollars, n.a. = not available.
*Source:* See Appendix A.

benefits of MPS elimination in Japan are more or less evenly split among farm operators, landowners, input suppliers, and taxpayers (through tariffs collected), but the benefits to all these are about half the cost to consumers. A similar pattern of beneficiaries is seen in both Mexico and Switzerland.

The main beneficiaries of eliminating direct payments are taxpayers, particularly taxpayers in the U.S. and the EU because of the size of these regions and because of their reliance on direct payments in the form of historical entitlements and acreage payments. In Mexico, Farmers Direct Support Program (PROCAMPO) payments result in a large transfer from taxpayers to landowners. Consumers benefit somewhat from these policies and from other purchased input subsidies and deficiency payments that reduce world prices.

### *The Theory of Decoupling*

Re-instrumentation or change away from border protection to domestic support and partially decoupled support accelerated in the mid-1980s, especially in the major field crop sectors. For example, the U.S. introduced a "freeze" on payment yields in the 1985 Farm Bill. The EU followed with similar direct payments in the major reform of the Common Agricultural Policy (CAP) in 1992. Mexico replaced price supports with decoupled payments in 1994, as did the U.S. in the Federal Agricultural Improvement and Reform Act of 1996. Aided by a World Bank loan, Turkey replaced price supports and input subsidies by phasing in a decoupled payment scheme beginning in 2001.

Decoupling is of interest to developing countries because a number of mostly middle-income countries support agriculture. If effective decoupling is adopted worldwide, world commodity prices will increase. For net commodity exporter developing countries, higher prices, due to decoupling would increase their share of world markets, increase rural income, and reduce dependence on tropical commodity exports.

A broadly accepted definition of decoupling in production is when transfers to farmers are made on inframarginal output only or are paid independent of current or future production. But the concept of decoupling has different meanings among economists, policymakers, and trade negotiators. Some define it in terms of trade distortions, others in terms of production distortions alone. Decoupling is sometimes defined only for those programs that are designed to transfer income to producers; others define it in terms of all programs including those, for example, to improve the environment. Still others define decoupling to include the way in which the policy is implemented—that is, there is also no change in the underlying production structure. Sometimes commentators evaluate the degree of decoupling to include the dynamic, long-term effects of a policy in increasing output owing to the policy's impact on such factors as uncertainty, investment, and expectations.

The URAA uses the term "decoupled" in connection with taxpayer-financed payments to producers that satisfy the following conditions (URAA Annex 2.6):

> determined by clearly-defined criteria such as income, status as a producer or landowner, factor use or production level in a defined and fixed base period, and the amount . . . shall not be related to, or based on, the type or volume of production . . . undertaken . . . in any year after the base period . . . nor on the price, domestic or international, applying to any production undertaken in any year after the base period.

The OECD defines a policy to be *effectively fully decoupled* if:

> . . . it results in a level of production and trade equal to what would have occurred if the policy were not in place . . . The shape of the supply or demand curves could be changed . . . even if the equilibrium production and consumption are not changed.

or to be *fully decoupled* if:

> . . . it does not influence production decisions of farmers receiving payments . . . both the shape and the position of the supply and demand curves should not be changed.

The concept of *full decoupling* is more restrictive. Full decoupling requires that there be no impact on the underlying supply response and adjustment process—not just effects on equilibrium quantities, as in the first definition. It should be noted that measuring equilibrium quantities is very difficult in practice.

The URAA defines decoupling in terms of policy design, whereas the OECD defines decoupling in terms of policy effects. Policy design and policy effects are obviously interconnected but not the same. Goodwin and Mishra (2002) offer an alternative definition of a fully decoupled payment whereby the payment level is fixed and guaranteed and thus is not influenced by *ex post* realizations of market conditions (for example, low prices or area yields). This is a definition in terms of rules, like that of the URAA, but is more restrictive in that payments cannot change.

Decoupling is important because most of the existing income transfer mechanisms fall short of meeting one of their main objectives: boosting farm household income. Three sources explain the gap between intended and actual transfers: (a) economic inefficiencies; (b) distributive leakages, whereby some of the benefits of support accrue to groups (such as input suppliers) other than the intended beneficiaries; and (c) the self-defeating effects of all countries' policies in lowering world prices. As a result, a large amount of support in most OECD countries has been transferred to producers but average farm household income has not increased as much. A major problem is that much of the transfers go to farm households that do not need them because the measures are still predominantly based on production or factors of production that fail to change the income distribution in any significant way.

From an efficiency point of view, budgetary payments that are decoupled from agricultural activity altogether would transfer income to selected farm households most efficiently. Economic distortions and distributive leakages would be minimized, providing a compelling case for further reform of agricultural policies, and for increased market openness. The benefits would be substantial, and include reduced costs to consumers and taxpayers, improved trade opportunities for competitive suppliers, less stress on the environment, and more effective policies to achieve goals.

In order to design agricultural policies that are decoupled from production, it is necessary to understand the mechanisms through which decoupling may affect the farmer's production decision. Decoupled payments may affect the farmer's production decision in a dynamic dimension or in the presence of uncertainty. Producers make decisions about future production and what investments to undertake based on expectations of future prices, policies, and output. Several mechanisms or categories of incentives can be identified whereby production increases as a result of direct payments to producers: fixed costs, risk reduction and wealth effects, government credibility problems with expectations about changes in future decoupled payments or criteria to receive them, and imperfect input markets.

**Fixed Costs** Even if direct income payments are on inframarginal output only, fixed costs can be offset. Often market revenues do not cover total costs. But the addition of government payments covers full economic costs in many cases. Hence, production beyond the amount for which the payments are determined (for example, base or quota) can occur because government payments deter exiting from farming or crop production.

Taxpayer- or consumer-financed inframarginal (or decoupled) production subsidies to farmers can effectively cross-subsidize production through their effects on farmers' ability to cover fixed and/or variable costs. When production is required to receive the payments, the farmers' ability to cover these costs is improved, thereby allowing a farmer who would otherwise have to exit the industry to instead stay in business, and perhaps even expand output beyond the quota or base acreage.

Four broad categories of policies can be identified that encompass most "direct farm income payment schemes" in agriculture worldwide: (a) inframarginal income payments financed by consumers (for instance, the EU's sugar quotas, California's fluid milk quotas in the U.S.); (b) inframarginal taxpayer-financed income payments (for instance, former U.S. crop policy with fixed payment yield and base acreage); (c) inframarginal direct income payments with fixed per unit production subsidies financed by taxpayers (for example, EU oilseeds and cereals); and (d) inframarginal income payments financed by taxpayers with the income payments fixed per farm (based on historical production, which means farmers do not have to produce to get payments—for example, U.S. production flexibility contract payments).[10, 11, 12] The first three of these categories require production in order to receive decoupled payments. Chau and de Gorter (2001) model several consequences of domestic support payments such as (a) inducing exit or entry; (b) biasing production incentives in domestic markets; and (c) cross-subsidizing production and exports.

Consumer-financed inframarginal production subsidies may also be referred to as decoupled payments. Like milk and sugar quotas in California and the EU, respectively, and supply management programs in Canada, consumer-financed inframarginal production subsidies can act like a production subsidy because higher domestic prices imply an expansion in production owing to the role of payments in improving farmers' ability to cover costs.[13]

Taxpayer-financed decoupled payments in the U.S. are not linked to current market prices and are presumed to have little or no direct effect on production decisions. Furthermore, program benefits are tied to the land,[14] and farmers have flexibility in what and how much to plant, except for some limitations on planting fruits and vegetables. There are implicit costs to remaining eligible to receive payments, however, in that recipients of decoupled payments may not use contract acreage for nonagricultural commercial or industrial purposes. Decoupled payments can also distort production because, to receive these payments, farmers are required to keep the land in "agricultural uses." This serves as an incentive to prevent some land from being converted to nonagricultural use. In addition, as the schemes are currently designed in some countries, farmers may not get direct payments if they plant fruit and vegetable crops on their historical base area.

Chau and de Gorter (2001) analyze the distribution of fixed costs across individual wheat farms in the U.S. The output and export consequences of three policy scenarios are studied: the removal of coupled payments, removal of decoupled payments, and removal of both. The removal of coupled payments alone decreases exports by 56 percent while the removal of decoupled payments alone reduces exports by 41 percent. Hence, decoupled payments can have a relatively large impact on the exit decision on low-profit farm units. The aggregate impact on output of the removal of both can remain quite limited so long as the output level of the marginal farm is relatively small. If existing income payments (both coupled and decoupled) generate expectations of future payments that compensate short-term losses, the reservation profit of the marginal farm may take on a negative value and the aggregate output and export distortion of decoupled payments can accordingly be considerably larger.

**Risk and Wealth** Agricultural production is characterized by a high degree of uncertainty; therefore the policies discussed here may affect a risk-averse farmer's production decision by either mitigating the farmer's response to risk or reducing the amount of risk.[15]

Two sources of output response can be identified with a reduction in uncertainty as a result of direct government payments:

1. The income effect, whereby higher incomes due to direct government payments make farmers less risk-averse, thereby leading them to assume more risk and increase production with uncertainty in the marketplace.
2. The risk effect, whereby direct payments reduce the farmer's perception of the variability of farm revenue and hence degree of risk. The degree of risk is only affected if total income varies with market prices and subsidies compensate at least partially for price declines.

Hennessy (1998) describes how programs in the U.S. affect both the variance of total income and risk aversion of farmers, thus affecting their output decisions. Empirical studies by de Gorter and Tsur (1995), Hennessy (1998), and Mullen and others (2001), provide estimates of the absolute effects of the mean (subsidy) versus variance (stabilizing) effects of direct government payment programs in Canada and the U.S. In all of these studies, the variance effect on output was approximately three times that of the mean effect. The absolute change in total output was 3 percent in the Hennessy study and 10 to 20 percent in the de Gorter and Tsur study. The impact of these direct payments on absolute levels of output depends on the level of price or income stabilization, the variance of prices and income, the degree of risk aversion on the part of the farmer, and the level of subsidy provided. Because de Gorter and Tsur evaluated two different stabilization policies in Canada and Hennessy evaluated an input subsidy for the U.S., changes would not necessarily be expected in the absolute level of output to be equal between the two studies. But it is very interesting that both studies find the relative magnitude of the stabilization effect on output to be about three times as great as that of the subsidy effect. The latter is usually debated in international trade negotiations, while the stabilization effects on output because of farmers' risk aversion are ignored.

The intuitive explanation for the empirical result that the stabilization effect can have three times the subsidy effect revolves around the relative magnitude of the mean versus variance effect. A policy may not change the mean price very much but stabilizes the price considerably. This depends on the design of the government program, the variability of market prices, and the level of risk aversion on the part of farmers. It is possible that the subsidy component is relatively large and the reduction in price variance very low (because of the design of the policy or because there is not very much variability in the price in the first place). In this case, the subsidy effect would be expected to be higher than the stabilization effect.

Young and Westcott (2000) evaluate the U.S. crop and revenue insurance programs that provide catastrophic coverage and subsidize premiums, reimbursing costs of selling and servicing policies, and underwriting risk protection. Government insurance reduces the variability of expected farm revenues by reducing risk associated with crop production variability. Subsidies encourage greater participation in insurance programs and consequently increase hectares planted because of the greater level of revenue and lower variance (in other words, again, the mean/variance components of risk-reducing policies). Because subsidies are calculated as a percentage of the total premium, which varies across crops and farms to reflect different risks of loss associated with each crop and insurable hectare, premium subsidies are higher for production on riskier crops and hectares. This subsidy structure favors production on hectarage with higher yield variability and thus encourages production on land that might not otherwise occur.

Young and Westcott report that crop insurance subsidies averaged US$1.4 billion during 1995–98, resulting in an increase of 600,000 hectares planted, with wheat and cotton showing the largest percentage gains. Beginning in 2001, U.S. crop insurance subsidies almost doubled to about US$3.0 billion owing to the reform passed by Congress to improve the "safety net" for U.S. farmers.

**Expectations About Future Policies and Dynamic Considerations** Most disaster payments and "emergency market loss" payments are made after the production decision has been made. Nevertheless, producers will develop expectations of future assistance based on past government actions, thereby affecting current production decisions. As Barry (1999) comments: "It is not hard to plan on government assistance when it comes so easily." Furthermore, when market prices decline and "emergency market loss" subsidies increase, farmers build that into their expectations. Hence, production is inevitably increased not only through fewer exits and more entry of farms into crop farming such that land is not otherwise left idle or used for nonagricultural purposes, but also through acreage expansion by existing farmers.

A combination of a coupled payment and a quantity constraint that achieves an effectively decoupled outcome will thus not qualify for the green box under the heading "decoupled income support." However, this policy under current rules may well qualify for the blue box, which would exempt it from the requirements to reduce domestic support. This would, for instance, be the case if farmers expect the government to update the base year used for determining the amount of support each farmer receives. This problem is explicitly dealt with in the URAA, as green box decoupled income support payments may not be based on "output, prices or factors used in any year after a fixed base year" (OECD 2001). Taking dynamic aspects and uncertainty into consideration suggests additional channels through which agricultural policies may affect the farmer's production decision.

For example, after the U.S. Federal Agricultural Improvement and Reform Act of 1996, American farmers were to receive generous transition payments to compensate for the removal of the price support. But the credibility of the government is now in question because of the additional emergency programs added since 1996 and the 2002 Farm Bill, which adds additional commodities to the price support program and allows both payment yields and base acreage to be updated. When future agricultural policies are considered as a whole policy package evolving over time, new programs adding to old programs confirms an impression that one needs to be a farmer to receive these benefits. It appears politically impossible to design truly decoupled programs such as that purported in the last two U.S. Farm Bills without affecting farmers' expectations for future subsidies in the event of adverse market conditions. Uncertainties over future farm legislation in the U.S. about reinstating direct payments cause farmers to stay in business and produce cereals even if it is not economical, because of the capitalized value of holding a base for future payments.

**Imperfect Input Markets** Fully decoupled support in a static framework will not affect the farmer's investment decision if markets are perfect. However, if input markets are imperfect, even decoupled income support will affect the decision through the investment mechanism. Farmers will therefore have an incentive to retain more resources in agricultural use and possibly produce more than justified by current market conditions. Hence, current policies can affect future production.

Direct payments can affect farmers' investment and exit decisions if there are constraints facing them in capital and labor markets. For example, credit constraints because of imperfect information may prevent farmers from investing under normal market conditions. However, direct payments allow banks to make loans that they otherwise would not, thereby allowing farmers to stay in agriculture and even increase their investment in production capital and capacity. Another example of how imperfections in input markets can result in direct payments affecting output is through the labor market. Farmers have specialized skills, and therefore have a difficult time finding off-farm employment that would remunerate them enough to exit farming or to farm part-time. Government payments allow farmers to stay in agriculture and thus avoid any costs associated with participating in nonagricultural labor markets.

## Toward an Ideal Decoupling Scheme

The primary motivation for decoupling is to compensate farmers with transitional adjustment assistance to free markets while at the same time making the move politically palatable and transparent. The ideal would be compensation programs that are universal (open to all sectors in the economy, not just agriculture) or at least nonsector-specific within agriculture, such as the all-farm income or gross revenue stabilization programs used in Canada. Decoupling on a sector-specific basis is clearly a third-best option because it is sector-specific within agriculture, is not based on tax data (so targeting is not achieved), and there are no effective limits per farm. A non-product-specific payment scheme covering all farmers dilutes the maximum payment per farm and as a consequence minimizes inefficiencies and inequities.

Several features are necessary to make a decoupling policy work at the sector level (if universal or whole-farm income insurance schemes for all of agriculture are not available). The simplest way is a one-time unconditional payment to all in farming or considered in need of compensation (equal to the difference between current income and income under free markets) as an annuity (bond), which is nontransferable to successors (Beard and Swinbank 2001). Any other scheme should meet the following conditions:

- No production is necessary.
- Land, labor, or other inputs do not have to be in "agricultural use."
- Eligibility rules are clearly defined and not allowed to change.
- A permanently fixed base period is established.
- Maximum number of years is required as a farmer to get payments (or if the farmer reaches retirement age).
- Payments are capped and vary inversely with farm size, and farm size or numbers cannot be manipulated.
- Any other coupled support for agriculture is eliminated.
- Level of payments in aggregate and per farm and the terms described above must be bound in the WTO to prevent changes in policies by governments.

## Concluding Remarks and Options for the Negotiations

The URAA has not defined and quantified trade-distorting measures in an optimal manner. Several categories of support are inappropriately categorized as nondistorting. A major reform is needed in the way in which the "aggregate measurement of support" (AMS)—a measure for trade-distorting domestic support policies—is defined and measured. These trade-distorting policies were assigned to the amber box category of support. URAA reduction commitments were supposed to measure domestic support, independent of support due to import barriers and export subsidies. In reality, however, the AMS is double-counted with support derived from trade policies. Total support as measured by the OECD's "producer support estimate" (PSE) is often less than domestic support, as measured by the AMS. If each of these calculations measured what it was supposed to measure, this would not be possible. Hence, a new amber box should be created that includes only domestic support that is trade-distorting (with perhaps adjustments downward for output-reducing measures), and is not conflated with trade border measures.

The method of measuring domestic support through the AMS is somewhat misleading and penalizes some countries. Furthermore, some green box government payments induce higher production because fixed costs are covered (which induces less exit by farmers); production risk is reduced; input market constraints are removed; and expectations are formed for more support in the future. Hence, a major challenge in the current negotiations is to address the imbalances in the definition and quantification of agricultural support so that a level playing field can be established and effective reductions in trade distortions are consequently ensured. The baseline AMS is overestimated not only because it includes a substantial proportion of support already counted in market access and export subsidy measures, but also because it ignores the fact that farm prices often diverge from the administered price support defined in the URAA.

In general, reduction commitments in the URAA suffered from over-emphasis on border support in relation to the amber box and under-emphasis on green box support. With the end of the URAA implementation (2001), the Peace

Clause set to expire on January 1, 2004, and new negotiations, it is important to put the issues associated with domestic support into perspective. With that outlook, the disparities in support levels and trade-distorting effects can be addressed in such a way as to strengthen the reform process in general, and improve the fairness and effectiveness of future support reduction commitments. Effective and balanced support reductions can be negotiated only if new categories of domestic support and major changes in the current methods of measuring and classifying support are introduced.

In the current WTO agricultural trade negotiations, negotiators must be aware of the following:

- The AMS has measurement problems.
- Two categories of *de minimis* reduces the effectiveness of support reduction commitments.
- Blue box support is trade-distorting.
- Some direct income payment policies in the green box are trade-distorting.
- The Peace Clause allows countries to circumvent disciplines on domestic subsidies in the WTO in general.

The following suggestions are designed to make reduction commitments meaningful, measurable, and effective.

**1. Abandon or significantly modify the AMS.**

The AMS has the following problems:

- The aggregation of the AMS commitment into a single measure covering all products and non-product-specific support maximizes the flexibility to avoid reducing support in some sectors and even to increase it.
- Double counting with market access and export subsidy measures makes reduction commitments less effective.
- Fixed baseline world reference prices rather than actual world prices in the implementation period results in over-counting or under-counting of true domestic support—with measured support very high when world prices are high (which means reductions in support are not that pressing) and vice versa if world prices are low.
- "Administered" or "official" domestic prices rather than actual domestic prices used in the implementation period result in over-counting or under-counting of true domestic support.
- Inclusion of "official" prices by some countries results in countries being penalized if they do report domestic administered prices or have more conflation with border support than do other countries.

**2. Abandon the "Peace Clause," which exempts countries from countervailing duties under certain conditions (see box 6.1).**

**3. Abandon the Blue Box.**

Collapse the blue box into the new amber box and give no provision for supply controls—each country should be on its own on this and payments to have farmers idle resources should be counted as decoupled payments as described above.[16] The EU's acreage decisions are fully coupled while yields upon which payment amounts are calculated are decoupled, but the latter have output-distorting features such as decoupled inframarginal production support and decoupled direct payments.

**4. Introduce a New Amber Box.**

A new amber box covering domestic support with market effects (independent of market access and export subsidy support) will ensure that reductions in domestic support will result in meaningful trade liberalization. Recommendations include the following:

- Establish a new baseline of agreed-upon levels at the end of the URAA's implementation period.
- Include so-called decoupled inframarginal production support financed either by consumers or taxpayers because such support induces exit or entry, biases production incentives in domestic markets, and cross-subsidizes exports in global markets.
- Include currently blue box support (the blue box should be abandoned with no credits given for inputs that are idled or restricted).
- Include so-called decoupled direct payments (including crop insurance). These may reduce

both risk and risk aversion owing to the reduction in uncertainty and an increase in wealth, respectively, resulting in higher levels of production than what otherwise would be. Direct payments can also reduce imperfections in the input markets, thereby affecting exit/entry and investment decisions, and increasing production in those countries that are only able to afford the large direct payments to farmers. In addition, to make them truly minimally trade-distorting, the program design of decoupled payments should be disciplined so that expectations for future payments are not based on the status of being a farmer, of land being in agricultural use for particular crops (and perhaps even the level of planting), or on previous levels of "emergency" payments, so production decisions are not distorted.

**5. Revise other domestic support rules.**

- Revise and expand the URAA definition of domestic support to include tax concessions and other transfers of value to agricultural production.
- Introduce a per unit support subsidy reduction commitment along the lines of a tariff (not only total value) to make reductions more effective.
- Maintain the green box with defined limits for expenditures that provide for public goods or prevent negative externalities (but limit both the level of product and nonproduct expenditures)—and provide tighter definitions of programs listed in URAA Annex 2 as truly non- or minimally trade-distorting. Strict rules, definitions, and monitoring arrangements should be required. Cap green box expenditures as a percentage of market value of output.

## Notes

1. In some instances, total support as measured by the OECD's "producer support estimate" (PSE) is less than total domestic support.

2. Data in figure 6.1 and tables 6.2 and 6.3 refer to 29 countries covered by the OECD database and 11 commodity groups. Trade-distorting domestic support refers to output and input subsidies only. TSE refers to "Total Support Estimate" and includes expenditures on general services, etc.

3. The quantity eligible is also not well defined and therefore open to manipulation (for example, one may use quantities purchased by the government instead of total production).

4. The specifics of how to measure "Market Price Support" for AMS are in Annex 3 of the Agreement on Agriculture, in paragraph 8.

5. The AMS is not the same as the "Producer Support Estimate" (PSE) as measured by the OECD. Only part of the border support is included in the AMS for some countries and is excluded for others. In addition, fixed baseline reference prices are used to measure the current AMS (unlike for the PSE), and the AMS excludes *de minimis* support as well as support contained in the blue and green boxes.

6. The AMS can be greater than the PSE if world prices are above or below the AMS world reference price because the outcome also depends on the relative value of the domestic market price to the "Market Price Support".

7. These results need to be further refined to include minimum mandatory acreage set-aside requirements (farmers get paid the same as that for the minimum acres set aside) and maximum voluntary acreage set-aside, and "extra-ordinary" set-aside that has no financial compensation and is in proportion to the excess acres. The historical and fixed character of yield payments per hectare also affects the production decision.

8. Some economists argue that income inequality is a market failure.

9. The PEM is described in detail in Appendix A on the distributional effects of OECD policy reforms.

10. "Inframarginal" means the marginal cost for output-receiving income payments is below the world price and farmers may or may not have to produce in order to receive payments (an example of not having to produce is the production flexibility contract payment scheme of the 1996 U.S. FAIR Act).

11. Standard analysis of consumer-financed inframarginal subsidies for the U.S. peanut sector (with and without quota transfers) is given by Borges and Thurman (1994); Rucker and Thurman (1990); and Rucker, Thurman, and Sumner (1995); and for the U.S. dairy sector by Sumner and Wolf (1996).

12. The approach also allows for the potential effect of decoupled payments on investment, given the specialized skills of farmers and imperfect labor, information, and capital markets (Roberts 1997; Skees 1999a, 1999b).

13. The recent WTO Dispute Settlement Panel on Canadian dairy policy illustrates the issues related to consumer-financed inframarginal subsidies. The panel ruled that milk sold at the world price below domestic prices was an export subsidy for reasons other than those discussed in this paper. For a critique on the WTO ruling, see Schluep and de Gorter (2001) and Annand, Buckingham, and Kerr (2001).

14. Eligibility requires one of the following: (a) land is enrolled in acreage reduction programs for any of the crop years 1991 through 1995; (b) land is planted to program crops under program rules; or (c) land is enrolled in the Conservation Reserve Program (CRP) and has a crop acreage base associated with it.

15. Several variables can be stabilized such as price, output, revenue, revenue net of costs (gross margins), and the like. Stabilization can also affect the choice of technique in production.

16. Paying farmers not to produce is like paying polluters not to pollute—more firms enter the industry than would otherwise and existing firms produce (pollute) more so as to get more money later to produce (pollute) less.

## Select Bibliography

The word *processed* describes informally reproduced works that may not be commonly available through libraries.


ABARE (Australian Bureau of Agricultural and Resource Economics). 1998. "Decoupling Farm Income Support." OECD Workshop on Emerging Trade Issues in Agriculture, Paris.

———. 2001. "US and EU Agricultural Support: Who Does It Benefit?" *Current Issues* no. 2, Canberra.

Annand, M., D. Buckingham, and W. Kerr. 2001. "Export Subsidies and the World Trade Organization." Estey Centre Research Papers, Number 1, Estey Centre for Law and Economics in International Trade, Saskatoon, Canada.

Barry, P. 1999. "Risk Management and Safety Nets for Farmers." *Choices* 14(3): 22–28.

Beard, Nick, and A. Swinbank. 2001. "Decoupled Payments to Facilitate CAP Reforms." *Food Policy* 26(2): 121–46.

Blandford, D. 2000. "Are Disciplines Required on Domestic Support?" Paper Presented at the Canadian Agri-Food Trade Research Network Workshop on Agricultural Trade Liberalization, "Can We Make Progress?" 27–28 October, Quebec City, Canada.

Borges, R., and W. Thurman. 1994. "Marketing Quotas and Random Yields: Marginal Effects of Inframarginal Subsidies on Peanut Supply." *American Journal of Agricultural Economics* 76(4): 809–17.

Brink, L. 2000. "Domestic Support Issues in the Uruguay Round and Beyond." Trade Research Series, Agriculture and Agri-Food Canada, Ottawa.

Cahill, S. A. 1997. "Calculating the Rate of Decoupling for Drops under CAP/Oilseeds Reform." *Journal of Agricultural Economics* 48(3): 349–78.

Chau, N., and H. de Gorter. 2001. "Disentangling the Consequences of Direct Payment Schemes in Agriculture on Fixed Costs, Exit Decisions and Output." Working Paper 2001-16, Cornell University Department of Applied Economics and Management, Ithaca.

Collins, K., and J. Vertrees. 1988. "Decoupling and U.S. Farm Policy Reform." *Canadian Journal of Agricultural Economics* 36(4): 733–45.

de Gorter, H., J. Hranaiova, and Y. Tsur. 2000. "Understanding the Production Effects of EU Direct Payments for Acres Planted and Diverted." Processed. Department of Applied Economics and Management, Cornell University, Ithaca.

de Gorter, H., and Y. Tsur. 1995. "Supply and Welfare Effects of Income Stabilization Programs: NISA versus NTSP." Report to Policy Branch, Industry Performance and Analysis Directorate, Agriculture and Agri-Food Canada, Ottawa.

Diakosavvas, D. 2002. "How to Measure the Level of Agricultural Support: Comparison of the Methodologies Applied by OECD and WTO." Workshop on Agricultural Policy Adjustments in China after WTO Accession, May 30–31, Beijing.

Gardner, B. L. 2001. "Benefit-Cost Economics of the FAIR Act." Paper presented at the Fixing the Farm Bill Conference, 27 March, Washington, D.C.

Gisser, M. 1993. "Price Support, Acreage Controls and Efficient Redistribution" *Journal of Political Economics* 101(4): 584–611.

Goodwin, B., and A. Mishra. 2002. "Are 'Decoupled' Farm Program Payments Really Decoupled? An Empirical Evaluation." Processed. Ohio State University, Columbus.

Guyomard, H., M. Baudry, and A. Carpentier. 1996. "Estimating Crop Supply in the Presence of Farm Programmes: Application to the Common Agricultural Policy." *European Review of Agricultural Economics* 23(4): 401–20.

Hennessy, D. A. 1998. "The Production Effects of Agricultural Income Support Policies under Uncertainty." *American Journal of Agricultural Economics* 80(1): 46–57.

Hoekman, B., F. Ng, and M. Olarreaga. 2002. "Reducing Agricultural Tariffs versus Domestic Support: What's More Important for Developing Countries?" Processed. World Bank, Washington, D.C.

Innes, R. 1995. "An Essay on Takings: Concepts and Issues." *Choices* 10(1): 4–7.

Kuhn, B., and S. Offutt. 1999. "Farm Policy in an Era of Farm Diversity." *Choices* 14(3): 37–38.

Moro, D., and P. Sckokai. 1998. "Modeling the 1992 CAP Reform: Degree of Decoupling and Future Scenarios." Paper presented at AAEA Annual Meeting, 2-5 August, Salt Lake City, Utah.

Moschini, G., and P. Sckokai. 1994. "Efficiency of Decoupled Farm Programs under Distortionary Taxation." *American Journal of Agricultural Economics* 76(3): 362–70.

Mullen, K., N. Chau, H. de Gorter, and B. Gloy. 2001. "The Risk Reduction Effects of Direct Payments on U.S. Wheat Production." Paper presented at the IATRC meeting, May 14, Washington D.C.

Nelson, F., E. Young, P. Liapis, and R. Schnepf. 1998. "Domestic Support Commitments: A Preliminary Evaluation." In "Agriculture in the WTO" WRS-98-44, U.S.D.A. Economic Research Service, Washington, D.C.

Orden, D. 2001. "Should There Be a Federal Farm Income Safety Net?" Paper presented at the Agricultural Outlook Forum, 22-23 February, Arlington, Virginia.

OECD (Organisation for Economic Co-operation and Development). 1997. "Environmental Benefits from Agriculture: Issues and Policies." The Helsinki Seminar, OECD, Paris.

———. 1999. "A Matrix Approach to Evaluating Policy: Preliminary Findings from PEM Pilot Studies of Crop Policy in the EU, the U.S., Canada and Mexico." COM/AGR/CA/RD/TC(99)117/Final. OECD, Paris.

———. 2000a. "Decoupling: A Conceptual Overview." COM/AGR/APM/TD/WP(2000)14. OECD, Paris.

———. 2000b. "A Preliminary Report of Domestic Support Aspects of the Uruguay Round Implementation." COM/AGR/APM/TD/WP(2000)9. OECD, Paris.

———. 2001. "Agricultural Policies in OECD Countries: Monitoring and Evaluation 2001." OECD, Paris.

Roberts, I. 1997. "Australia and the Next Multilateral Trade Negotiations for Agriculture." ABARE Research Report 97.6, Canberra.

———. 2003. "Three Pillars of Agricultural Support and Their Impact on WTO Reforms." ABARE report 03.5, Abareconomics, Canberra.

Rucker, R., and W. Thurman. 1990. "The Economic Effects of Supply Controls: The Simple Analytics of the U.S. Peanut Program." *Journal of Law and Economics* 33(2): 483–515.

Rucker, R., W. Thurman, and D. Sumner. 1995. "Restricting the Market for Quota: An Analysis of Tobacco Production Rights with Corroboration from Congressional Testimony." *Journal of Political Economy* 103(1): 142–75.

Rude, J. 2000a. "An Examination of Nearly Green Programs: Case Studies for Canada, the U.S. and the EU." Agriculture and Agri-Food Canada, Economic and Policy Analysis Directorate Policy Branch, Publication 2010/E Ottawa.

———. 2000b. "Green Box Criteria: A Theoretical Assessment." Agriculture and Agri-Food Canada, Economic and Policy Analysis Directorate Policy Branch, Publication 2007/E Ottawa.

Schluep, I., and H. de Gorter. 2001. "The Definition of Export Subsidies and the Agreement on Agriculture." In G. Peters, ed., *Tomorrow's Agriculture: Incentives, Institutions, Infrastructure and Innovations.* Oxford: Oxford University Press.

Schmitz, A., and J. Vercammen. 1995. "Efficiency of Farm Programs and Their Trade-Distorting Effect." In G. Rausser, ed., GATT *Negotiations and the Political Economy of Policy Reform,* pp. 35–36. Berlin: Springer-Verlag.

Skees, J. R. 1999a. "Agricultural Risk Management or Income Enhancement?" *Regulation* 22(1): 35–43.

———. 1999b. "Policy Implications of Income Insurance: Lessons Learned from the U.S. and Canada." Paper presented to the European Association of Agricultural Economists meetings, Summer 1999, Warsaw, Poland.

Sumner, D., and C. Wolf. 1996. "Quotas Without Supply Control: Effects of Dairy Quota Policy in California." *American Journal of Agricultural Economics* 78(2): 354–66.

U.S. Department of Agriculture. 1997. "Agricultural Resources and Environmental Indicators, 1996–97." USDA, Economic Research Service, Natural Resources and Economics Division Agricultural Handbook 712. Washington, D.C.

Vavra, P., and D. Coleman. 2000. "Land Allocation Under Arable Area Payment Scheme." Paper presented at the International Association of Agricultural Economists Conference, August, Berlin.

Westcott, P. C. 1999. "Ag Policy: Marketing Loans Benefits Supplement Market Revenues for Farmers." Agricultural Outlook, December, AGO-267. UDSA Economic Research Service, Washington, D.C.

WTO (World Trade Organization). 2000. "Members' Usage of Domestic Support Categories." 15 June, G/AG/NG/S/12. Office of the Secretary General, Geneva.

———. 2002. "Domestic Support Background Paper by the Secretariat." March 20, TN/AG/S/4. Office of the Secretary General.

Young, E., and J. Westcott. 2000. "How Decoupled is U.S Agricultural Support for Major Crops?" *American Journal of Agricultural Economics* 82(3): 762–67.

7

# THE DISTRIBUTIONAL EFFECTS OF AGRICULTURAL POLICY REFORMS

*Harry de Gorter, Merlinda D. Ingco, and Cameron Short*

## Introduction

There has been dramatic growth in total world trade as successive rounds of multilateral trade negotiations have progressively reduced trade barriers, providing an important engine of growth in the world economy. Nonetheless, very high barriers to trade remain in agriculture where markets are still heavily protected, especially in rich countries. The grains and oilseeds sector is a good example of extensive trade on the one hand, and high levels of domestic subsidies and border protection (including export subsidies) on the other. However, a major transformation in terms of changes in policy intervention or re-instrumentation has also occurred in this sector over the past 15 years, from border to domestic support and from coupled subsidies to land area payments and historical entitlement payments.

Several key questions emerge: What are the impacts of alternative policy interventions on consumers, taxpayers, farm operators, and land owners? Does this impact vary across countries, commodity, or policy types? Is border protection or are domestic subsidy programs more important than other policy interventions? What are the effects of unilateral versus multilateral trade liberalization negotiated in the World Trade Organization (WTO)? What is the impact on poverty and income inequality on both urban consumers and rural farmers in a developing country? These and other issues will be assessed in this chapter by using the Organisation for Economic Co-operation and Development (OECD) "Policy Evaluation Matrix" model (PEM) for grains and oilseeds (see Appendix A for complete details of this model).[1]

Such an analysis allows an evaluation of how poverty in both urban and rural areas should affect attitudes toward trade liberalization in agriculture and its implementation. There is overwhelming evidence that trade generates higher economic growth and reduces poverty.[2] However, income distribution is inevitably affected, and although overall poverty declines, some people become poor and some among the existing poor get poorer because of trade liberalization (at least in the short run, before general equilibrium adjustments occur in the labor markets). The other side to this is that additional aggregate income gives society more resources to tackle poverty.

The purpose of this chapter is to illustrate how agricultural policy reforms affect income distribution both in high-income OECD countries and in a sample developing country, Mexico (also an OECD member). This comparison can help policymakers understand the effects on poverty and the need to consider complementary and sometimes compensatory policies to alleviate some of these effects. The broad policy implication of this analysis is that, in most cases, trade liberalization would yield aggregate gains to a country and that analysis of its poverty consequences should be used to determine how these gains can be used to benefit the poor.

Agriculture is the key sector for nearly all studies on poverty analysis: the poor in developing countries are predominantly rural; food accounts for a major share of their expenditure; agriculture is their major source of income; and farm incomes have large spillovers to others in the rural sector and hence increases in farm incomes help to relieve poverty throughout the rural economy. Many developing countries have a comparative advantage in agriculture because of their relatively large endowments of land and unskilled labor. For these countries, access to the large markets of the developed countries and the prices received there are of central importance to their economic well-being.

Agricultural trade liberalization affects poverty in many ways.[3] Changes in prices of agricultural outputs and inputs affect farm profits, land prices, demand for rural laborers, off-farm labor opportunities for farm households, and rural wages. The relative impact of these price changes on consumers, farmers, landowners, laborers, and input suppliers depends on the structure of the economy—share of consumer budget spent on food, income levels, demand elasticities, the production technology, input shares in production, and the like. But the outcome also depends on farm size distribution and whether farm operators own their land or not. Trade liberalization effects can also be affected by domestic policies.

### *The Plan of This Chapter*

This chapter begins by describing some of the different types of agriculture policies in the grains and oilseeds sectors in OECD countries. Trends in protection levels and changes in the policy mix are documented for the grains and oilseed sector in relation to all other commodities for the OECD as a whole and for the six OECD regions covered in the PEM. The chapter then outlines the agricultural policy reforms in Mexico that are in many respects representative of such developing-country reforms. The PEM framework is then used to analyze the effects of these policies on the sample developing country, Mexico, for which the required data are available. The various scenarios analyzed include different types of policy reforms that might arise out of the Doha Round trade negotiations—reforms of rich-country policies, as well as reforms in Mexico's policies. The chapter reports the distributional impacts by income level within Mexico for both consumers and producers, as well as some selected results for other groups in other OECD countries. This analysis is intended to be illustrative of the methodology, rather than representative of developing countries as a group. Several further considerations of trade liberalization and poverty are discussed including imperfect markets and price transmission, and the implications for subsistence farmers. The final section of the chapter presents a summary and concluding remarks.

## Policy Developments in the Grains and Oilseeds Sector

The OECD identifies five major categories of support used in the PEM (see Appendix A):

- Market price support (MPS) due to border protection (including export subsidies).
- Output price support (OPS) such as deficiency payments.
- Input price subsidies (IPS) such as fertilizer subsidies.
- Area payments such as those in the EU.
- Historical entitlements such as those associated with grains and oilseeds in the U.S.

The PEM has six regions (the OECD-6): Canada, the European Union (EU), Japan, Mexico, Switzerland, and the United States (U.S.). Appendix A summarizes the support for grains and oilseeds in the OECD-6 in the PEM and all OECD countries compared to all other commodities. Grains and oilseeds MPS represents 27 percent of total OECD MPS, but grains and oilseeds receive a far higher share of total support in each of the other four policy categories of domestic support. Support across all policy types is far more uniform in the grains and oilseeds sector in all OECD countries as a group.

The OECD-6 represents most of the support for grains in the OECD. In OPS, IPS, area payments, and historical entitlements, grains and oilseeds dominate in terms of amount of support relative to other commodities—and these policies dominate within the grains and oilseeds sector itself. This means that the various types of payments are atypically far more important for wheat, coarse grains, and oilseeds. The six regions analyzed comprise most of the support for each of the four commodity groups (wheat, coarse grains, oilseeds, and rice) except for oilseeds (only 9.7 percent of total OECD support). A significant feature of area payments and historical entitlements is its concentration in the grains and oilseeds sector in the countries and regions in the PEM—especially the U.S., the EU, and Mexico. Both the U.S. and the EU will have a major influence on the Doha Round because of the size of their economies.

Appendix A shows that the rates of protection resulting from domestic policies are very low for Canada in all policy categories, while the EU has significant MPS for rice and high rates of support in area payments and IPS for all commodities. Japan has very high MPS and significant OPS and IPS in oilseeds and rice only. Mexico uses all policies except area payments while the U.S. relies heavily on OPS and historical entitlement payments.

The trend downwards over time for MPS is significant and slightly more than that of total support. Overall protection started at close to 120 percent in 1986 and fell to 50 percent in 1996—it stood at 77 percent in 2001. The move away from MPS and toward the various forms of direct payments, especially area payments and historical entitlements, is also very evident. Purchased input subsidies and output price support have been fairly constant.

One question this chapter seeks to address is whether changing the composition of support away from border protection will make a major difference to developing countries. The alternative policy framework proposed in the WTO by the 17-member Cairns Group of major nonsubsidizing agricultural exporting countries, and more recently by other developing countries, calls for a substantial reduction in support. The PEM's strength is its ability to analyze the differential effects of alternative policies on farmers, landowners, input suppliers, taxpayers, consumers, and world prices and trade.

### *Agricultural Policy Reform in Mexico*

Prior to the 1980s, Mexico, like most developing countries, followed the import substitution industrialization model of development with fixed and overvalued exchange rates and import tariffs on agricultural inputs. This imposed a tax on agriculture and was typical of developing countries (the so-called "urban bias"—see Krueger, Schiff, and Valdés 1988). But governments also intervened directly in agricultural markets using: (a) guaranteed prices to farmers enforced by parastatal or state trading purchases and food reserve purchases and fixed prices to consumers that were often lower than producer prices (with either producer or consumer prices above or below world prices, depending on the commodity, country, or year); (b) trade controls (import licenses and import tariffs, or direct controls by a state trading enterprise); and (c) subsidized inputs. Because of the focus on degree of self-sufficiency for the import-competing staple foods, policies promoted technical change and often subsidized purchased inputs such as fertilizers and improved seeds and other modern-sector purchased inputs.[4]

Most developing countries including Mexico committed to major economy-wide and sectoral reforms in the 1980s. This included trade liberalization, structural adjustment, deregulation, and privatization of state-run commodity bodies to increase the role of market forces. The recent history of agricultural policy transformation in Mexico for the import-competing staple field crops is a good example of developing-country policy transformation.

In general, governments intervened through price controls, trade barriers, and marketing policies. In Mexico, direct government intervention in agriculture was heavily influenced by the National Company of Popular Subsistence (CONASUPO) in its multiple roles in shaping food production, consumption, and rural incomes. It was a typical developing-country parastatal enterprise whose activities began to be reformed after the 1982 debt crisis and devaluation, and then further reformed and finally eliminated in the context of domestic economic reforms, trade liberalization processes, and commitments under the

1994 North American Free Trade Agreement and the URAA. By 1999, the elimination of subsidies to consumers for cornbread (or *tortilla*) consumption preceded the liquidation of CONASUPO and completed the liberalization of crop markets—which are now protected by modest import tariffs and import quotas that are binding for maize, barley/malt, and dry beans only. There are no export subsidies. Farmers currently receive three major categories of taxpayer-financed subsidies:

- Area payments whereby farmers are required to plant (but both the acreage receiving payments and the payments themselves are not based on current production decisions, and therefore payments are on inframarginal—that is, for the first units of output only, not for the last units of output—acreage and hence deemed decoupled).
- Production subsidies (farmers are guaranteed "concerted prices" through deficiency payments).
- Input subsidies.

Consumers are now subsidized only for maize. A summary of policy developments since 1980 is given in Appendix A, table A.6.

Parallel to the elimination of guaranteed crop prices, a major reform in Mexican state intervention in staple food production was implemented in 1991 through the creation of an agricultural marketing agency, ASERCA (Support Services for Agricultural Marketing). Its functions are directed toward marketing, but the agency does not buy or store agricultural commodities (now carried out by the states, farmer organizations, or the private sector). ASERCA is also in charge of a pilot hedging program for grains and oilseeds producers.

In 1992, extensive land reforms were implemented including the elimination of restrictions on land transactions (previously, land in "*Ejidos*"—a form of communal ownership—could not be sold, rented, mortgaged, or subdivided). Usufruct rights were contingent on occupation and cultivation of the land. With these restrictions removed, land titling allowed decoupled payments to be implemented. Some feared that poor, small farmers would be forced to sell their land in the face of capital constraints, but small farmers in fact rent approximately 10 percent of their land to larger farmers (Olinto, Deininger, and Davis 2000).

There are two other important features about direct payment policies in Mexico that have a significant impact on improving incomes of low-income and small farmers and hence on the distribution of income. Neither decoupled payments nor output subsidies are distributed proportionately to production and therefore farm size. Decoupled payments are given for a minimum of 1 hectare (regardless of the actual size of the farm) and a maximum of 100 hectares. Data furnished by the government of Mexico indicate that 1.2 million maize farms have less than one hectare of maize plantings, representing 36 percent of the total number of farmers but only 9 percent of total area planted.[5]

Furthermore, output subsidies increase the farther away a farm is from the major consumption or market center—and average farm size decreases with distance from major markets. These policy details can have significant positive impacts on income distribution compared to historical guaranteed prices with a parastatal enterprise (where many small farmers did not benefit because they were often net buyers, sold goods at distressed prices at harvest, or were not integrated with market price centers owing to transactions costs and the like).[6]

Consumer subsidy programs varied over the years but a subsidy to *nixtamaleros* (makers of corn dough to produce tortillas) and corn millers (producers of flour to make tortillas), the two major corn processing industries in Mexico, was significant. These two industries represented 63 percent of the corn industry in 1996, and the subsidy allowed corn processors to sell flour and tortillas to final consumers and to government retail shops at low prices. In order to support the subsidy to tortilla consumers, CONASUPO sold maize to *nixtamaleros* at a price that permitted a "reasonable" profit from tortilla sales at subsidized prices. Corn millers received a cash subsidy for the corn that they bought directly in the domestic market. ASERCA, which administered the subsidy, has now been replaced by a single targeted consumer subsidy program.

## Some Empirical Results

In this section, results are presented on the following two themes:

1. Effects of an equal reduction in support rates in all regions.
2. Trade liberalization in Mexico versus trade liberalization in rich countries.

It is clear, for example, that since Mexico is a net importer of grains and oilseeds, its citizens can in the aggregate be made worse off by external measures that cause global prices of these commodities to increase. In this sense at least, Mexico is not representative of developing countries as a whole, which are net exporters of agricultural products. But what is interesting is that this aggregate effect masks important differences in how these policies affect different classes of citizens and Mexico illustrates the benefits of a model that is capable of disaggregating the impacts within groups.

### *Trade Liberalization in All Regions*

Some of the material presented in the preceding sections illustrates the problem that government support is highly variable from one region to another, both in terms of level and type. This diversity makes it extremely difficult to design a "fair" result for support reduction. How much of a reduction in U.S. historical entitlements is equivalent to a 10 percent reduction in EU area payments or a 10 percent reduction in Japanese MPS? There are many other similarly possible deals that could be constructed—and interpreting fairness would still be subjective.

Instead of trying to construct equivalent support reductions across regions, this chapter considers simply reducing support rates proportionately in all regions by 10, 50, and 100 percent. Reducing support rates rather than the amount of support per unit or the total amount of support implies larger reductions in regions with higher initial rates of support. It does not take into account whether the type of support is normally associated with a high degree of trade distortion or not.

Tables 7.1–7.4 summarize impacts by region for wheat, coarse grains, oilseeds, and rice, respectively. These tables also give a good idea of the overall responsiveness of the model by sector and region. The response in the wheat market is described in

**TABLE 7.1 Liberalization Effects on Wheat Price, Production, and Exports by Region, Base Levels, and Percentage Change**

| Region | Canada | Mexico | United States | EU | Switzerland | Japan | ROW |
|---|---|---|---|---|---|---|---|
| ***Baseline*** | | | | | | | |
| Producer price (US$/mt) | 92 | 190 | 108 | 110 | 332 | 1,192 | 105 |
| Production (mmt) | 20.7 | 3.4 | 53.3 | 97.6 | 0.5 | 0.7 | 426.7 |
| Net exports (mmt) | 12.6 | −2.6 | 19.3 | 13.6 | −0.4 | −5.7 | −36.8 |
| ***10% liberalization*** | | | | | | | |
| Producer price | 1% | −3% | 1% | 1% | −3% | −8% | 1% |
| Production | 0% | −4% | 0% | 0% | −4% | −11% | 0% |
| Net exports | 1% | −7% | 1% | 1% | −2% | −1% | 0% |
| ***50% liberalization*** | | | | | | | |
| Producer price | 6% | −15% | 4% | 5% | −14% | −39% | 6% |
| Production | 2% | −23% | 1% | −3% | −19% | −53% | 0% |
| Net exports | 4% | −37% | 5% | 3% | −7% | −5% | −2% |
| ***100% liberalization*** | | | | | | | |
| Producer price | 13% | −30% | 9% | 11% | −29% | −77% | 13% |
| Production | 5% | −50% | 2% | −7% | −30% | −92% | 0% |
| Net exports | 9% | −81% | 14% | −4% | −3% | −4% | −3% |

*Notes:* ROW = Rest of world, mt = metric tonne, mmt = million metric tonnes.
*Source:* Calculated using the OECD's Policy Evaluation Model (PEM).

some detail. Only a brief description is provided of the response for the other three commodities, since to do more would be repetitive.

Of the six regions, Mexico, Switzerland, and Japan tend to have high rates of MPS and OPS for wheat, which is reflected in the baseline producer prices (of US$190/mt, US$332/mt, and US$1,192/mt, respectively) shown in the first row. Results for wheat in table 7.1 show that as a consequence, a proportional reduction in all support rates will have the greatest impact in these regions. The producer price of wheat with 100 percent liberalization falls by 30, 29, and 77 percent, respectively in these three regions, but increases in Canada, the U.S., and the EU. The last column, for the rest of the world ("ROW" in the table), shows that the underlying world price increases by 1, 6, and 13 percent as the level of liberalization increases to 10, 50, and 100 percent, respectively.

Wheat production generally falls most in the regions that experience the greatest fall in producer prices, but this too is moderated by the impact of other types of support. Wheat production decreases the most in Japan (from 11 percent to 92 percent) in the 100 percent liberalization scenario; production decreases by 50 percent in Mexico and 30 percent in Switzerland even though producer prices decline by almost the same amount in both regions. The differences in the response among the three regions that were not using high levels of MPS and OPS are also instructive. EU wheat production declines by 7 percent despite the increase in commodity price because of the effect of the reduction in area payments. Production in both Canada and the U.S. increases slightly. Exports increase proportionately more from the U.S. because baseline exports are a much larger share of production in Canada.

Finally, it is perhaps worth noticing that there is a fairly high degree of linearity in the results for prices and production within each region. The change in prices in the 50 percent liberalization scenario, for example, is about five times the change in prices in the 10 percent liberalization scenario in each region. This suggests that interpolating model results might give a good approximation of these results.

**TABLE 7.2 Liberalization Effects on Coarse Grains Price, Production, and Exports by Region, Base Levels, and Percentage Change**

| Region | Canada | Mexico | United States | EU | Switzerland | Japan | ROW |
|---|---|---|---|---|---|---|---|
| ***Baseline*** | | | | | | | |
| Producer price ( ) | 90 | 149 | 85 | 109 | 260 | 1,123 | 79 |
| Production (mmt) | 19.3 | 26.0 | 261.6 | 94.5 | 0.5 | 0.2 | 502.2 |
| Net exports (mmt) | −1.5 | −9.5 | 49.6 | 9.9 | −0.3 | −2.3 | −45.9 |
| ***10% liberalization*** | | | | | | | |
| Producer price | 1% | −3% | 1% | 1% | −4% | −8% | 2% |
| Production | 0% | −3% | 1% | −1% | −6% | −7% | 0% |
| Net exports | 6% | 0% | 1% | −14% | −13% | −2% | 2% |
| ***50% liberalization*** | | | | | | | |
| Producer price | 6% | −14% | 5% | 4% | −19% | −40% | 9% |
| Production | 2% | −13% | 3% | −6% | −31% | −39% | 1% |
| Net exports | 31% | 0% | 8% | −75% | −69% | −11% | 9% |
| ***100% liberalization*** | | | | | | | |
| Producer price | 12% | −27% | 11% | 8% | −38% | −79% | 20% |
| Production | 5% | −25% | 7% | −15% | −62% | −81% | 1% |
| Net exports | 68% | 0% | 21% | −169% | −140% | −32% | 17% |

*Notes:* ROW = Rest of world, mt = metric tonne, mmt = million metric tonnes.
*Source:* Calculated using the OECD's Policy Evaluation Model (PEM).

**TABLE 7.3 Liberalization Effects on Oilseeds Price, Production, and Exports by Region, Base Levels, and Percentage Change**

| Region | Canada | Mexico | United States | EU | Switzerland | Japan | ROW |
|---|---|---|---|---|---|---|---|
| ***Baseline*** | | | | | | | |
| Producer price ($/mt) | 187 | 302 | 204 | 201 | 849 | 1,205 | 162 |
| Production (mmt) | 6.4 | 0.1 | 79.6 | 13.4 | 0.0 | 0.2 | 136.5 |
| Net exports (mmt) | 1.5 | −4.4 | 29.5 | −20.7 | −0.2 | −4.8 | −0.9 |
| ***10% liberalization*** | | | | | | | |
| Producer price | 1% | −3% | −1% | 1% | −7% | −4% | 2% |
| Production | 1% | −4% | −2% | 1% | −8% | −1% | 0% |
| Net exports | 4% | 0% | −4% | 1% | −10% | 0% | 110% |
| ***50% liberalization*** | | | | | | | |
| Producer price | 7% | −15% | −3% | 7% | −37% | −22% | 9% |
| Production | 5% | −19% | −8% | 3% | −44% | −3% | 2% |
| Net exports | 22% | −2% | −21% | 5% | −70% | 2% | 559% |
| ***100% liberalization*** | | | | | | | |
| Producer price | 16% | −29% | −5% | 15% | −73% | −43% | 20% |
| Production | 10% | −43% | −17% | 8% | −96% | 27% | 5% |
| Net exports | 46% | −4% | −44% | 11% | −306% | 9% | 1153% |

*Notes:* ROW = Rest of the world. mt = metric tonne. mmt = million metric tonnes.
*Source:* Calculated using the OECD's Policy Evaluation Model (PEM).

**TABLE 7.4 Liberalization Effects on Rice Price, Production, and Exports by Region, Base Levels, and Percentage Change**

| Region | Canada | Mexico | United States | EU | Switzerland | Japan | ROW |
|---|---|---|---|---|---|---|---|
| ***Baseline*** | | | | | | | |
| Producer price ($/mt) | | 184 | 151 | 260 | | 1,950 | 94 |
| Production (mmt) | 0.0 | 0.4 | 9.5 | 2.5 | 0.0 | 9.0 | 383.1 |
| Net exports (mmt) | −0.3 | −0.7 | 4.0 | 0.0 | −0.1 | −0.8 | −2.3 |
| ***10% liberalization*** | | | | | | | |
| Producer price | | −2% | −3% | −3% | | −9% | 1% |
| Production | | −2% | −6% | −6% | | −7% | 0% |
| Net exports | 0% | −1% | −15% | −423% | 0% | −106% | 68% |
| ***50% liberalization*** | | | | | | | |
| Producer price | | −9% | −16% | −16% | | −43% | 5% |
| Production | | −8% | −33% | −28% | | −39% | 2% |
| Net exports | 0% | −8% | −77% | −2122% | 0% | −621% | 376% |
| ***100% liberalization*** | | | | | | | |
| Producer price | | −16% | −30% | −30% | | −85% | 12% |
| Production | | −16% | −67% | −55% | | −91% | 5% |
| Net exports | 0% | −16% | −156% | −4193% | 0% | −1773% | 936% |

*Notes:* ROW = Rest of the world. mt = metric tonne. mmt = million metric tonnes.
*Source:* Calculated using the OECD's Policy Evaluation Model (PEM).

The high variability in results for net exports is also evident in the three tables for the other three commodities (tables 7.2–7.4). It is interesting to note that the EU switches from being a net exporter to a net importer of coarse grains in the 100 percent liberalization scenario but not in the 50 percent liberalization scenario. The increase in oilseeds production in Japan (by 27 percent with 100 percent liberalization) should probably be regarded as a quirk resulting from the extremely high levels of support in the base and the model searching for some way of using land in Japan. The U.S. does relatively less well in oilseeds (decrease by 17 percent with 100 percent liberalization) because of the OPS in its base.

Results for rice are the most dramatic and probably the least reliable, especially for the 100 percent liberalization scenario (table 7.4). Rice production in the four regions declines drastically, while production from the rest of the world increases by 5 percent in response to 12 percent increase in average price. This is possible because the rest of the world accounts for 95 percent of production in the base, leaving only 5 percent from the endogenous regions. Nearly all of the rest-of-the-world rice production comes from developing countries. The high levels of OPS and/or MPS in the base for the endogenous regions is evident from a comparison of base prices.

Table 7.5 shows the welfare implications by level of liberalization and region. It shows the impact on

**TABLE 7.5 Welfare Effects of Liberalization by Region (US$ Millions)**

| Region | Canada | Mexico | United States | EU | Switzerland | Japan | All six regions |
|---|---|---|---|---|---|---|---|
| *10% liberalization* | | | | | | | |
| Taxpayer | 81 | 129 | 1,749 | 1,853 | 15 | 1,279 | 5,106 |
| Consumer | −53 | 103 | −487 | −237 | 32 | 1,807 | 1,166 |
| Farm operator | 12 | −22 | −35 | −16 | −5 | −598 | −665 |
| Landowner | −33 | −163 | −853 | −1,439 | −15 | −645 | −3,148 |
| Hired labor | 0 | 0 | −3 | −2 | 0 | 0 | −5 |
| Other purchased inputs | 10 | −32 | −65 | −79 | −6 | −398 | −572 |
| Sum | 16 | 16 | 305 | 80 | 20 | 1,445 | 1,882 |
| Percent PSE | 16% | 35% | 27% | 41% | 60% | 84% | 39% |
| *50% liberalization* | | | | | | | |
| Taxpayer | 403 | 554 | 8,487 | 9,086 | 41 | 3,885 | 22,455 |
| Consumer | −275 | 510 | −2,537 | −1,243 | 178 | 9,485 | 6,118 |
| Farm operator | 62 | −98 | −127 | −68 | −24 | −2,543 | −2,798 |
| Landowner | −151 | −783 | −4,102 | −7,028 | −69 | −2,503 | −14,636 |
| Hired labor | 0 | 0 | −13 | −8 | −1 | 0 | −22 |
| Other purchased inputs | 51 | −155 | −295 | −388 | −27 | −1,823 | −2,638 |
| Sum | 90 | 26 | 1,414 | 350 | 98 | 6,501 | 8,478 |
| Percent PSE | 10% | 22% | 16% | 27% | 47% | 74% | 24% |
| *100% liberalization* | | | | | | | |
| Taxpayer | 806 | 846 | 16,288 | 17,446 | −63 | −1,142 | 34,181 |
| Consumer | −591 | 980 | −5,474 | −2,733 | 498 | 22,310 | 14,990 |
| Farm operator | 141 | −158 | −69 | −114 | −37 | −3,669 | −3,905 |
| Landowner | −262 | −1,488 | −7,669 | −13,166 | −133 | −2,906 | −25,624 |
| Hired labor | 0 | 0 | −20 | −21 | −2 | 0 | −43 |
| Other purchased inputs | 116 | −283 | −467 | −806 | −46 | −2,957 | −4,443 |
| Sum | 211 | −105 | 2,590 | 606 | 218 | 11,636 | 15,156 |
| Percent PSE | 3% | 1% | 1% | 0% | 10% | 0% | 1% |

*Note:* Percent PSE is the ratio of total transfers directly to producers and total farm revenues.
*Source:* Calculated using the OECD's Policy Evaluation Model (PEM).

economic welfare for each group of economic agents with a different role in the economy: taxpayers, consumers, farm operators, landowners, hired labor, and purchased input suppliers. Farmers are both farm operators and landowners, and of course there are landowners who are not farmers. Similarly, farmers are also consumers. Though the consumer role can be ignored for farmers in the developed countries, consumption to fulfill own needs is a significant factor for poor farmers in developing countries—the chapter will return to this issue below. Table 7.5 shows the impact on each role without regard to the interactions among the roles.

Agricultural support in Japan chiefly consists of a large transfer from consumers to farm operators and landowners. In the U.S. and the EU, the transfer is from taxpayers to landowners, with a small share going to farm operators. Mexico and Switzerland are more even-handed on the financing side of this operation, taking from consumers and taxpayers about equally but delivering most of the benefits to landowners.

The concentration of program benefits on landowners raises some important questions about the distribution of agricultural land ownership. About half the land in the U.S. and Canada is owned by farm operators with a significant portion of nonfarmer landowners, probably retired farmers or their children. If land ownership becomes skewed toward nonfarmers—and there are certainly tax and cultural incentives favoring this type of distribution of land ownership—the distributional equity of agricultural support linked to land (area payments and historical entitlements—that is, land payments) needs to be seriously reconsidered. The situation in Mexico is probably somewhat unique because of the effect of the *Ejido* land tenure system. The interaction of the reform of *Ejido* tenure in 1992 and the Farmers Direct Support Program (PROCAMPO) historical entitlements introduced in 1994 on the distribution of land ownership and the issue of who ultimately benefits from Mexican agricultural policy is an intriguing question, but it will not be considered here.

Tables 7.6 and 7.7 show that the deadweight loss of support for grains and oilseeds in these six

**TABLE 7.6 Distribution of the Effects of Global Liberalization on Mexico: Base Income Levels and Percentage Change**

| Income Decile | 1 | 2 | 3 | 4 | 5 | 6–10 |
|---|---|---|---|---|---|---|
| ***Annual income per capita*** | | | | | | |
| Farmer (US$/person) | 365 | 466 | 687 | 954 | 1,526 | |
| Nonfarmer (US$/person) | 362 | 656 | 859 | 1,089 | 1,217 | 3,799 |
| ***10% liberalization*** | | | | | | |
| Farmer | | | | | | |
| Income effect | 0% | −1% | −2% | −2% | −1% | |
| Consumer surplus | 0% | 0% | 0% | 0% | 0% | |
| Total | 0% | −1% | −2% | −2% | −1% | |
| Nonfarmer | 0% | 0% | 0% | 0% | 0% | 0% |
| ***50% liberalization*** | | | | | | |
| Farmer | | | | | | |
| Income effect | −3% | −7% | −12% | −8% | −5% | |
| Consumer surplus | 1% | 1% | 1% | 1% | 0% | |
| Total | −1% | −6% | −11% | −8% | −5% | |
| Nonfarmer | 1% | 1% | 1% | 0% | 0% | 0% |
| ***100% liberalization*** | | | | | | |
| Farmer | | | | | | |
| Income effect | −7% | −15% | −22% | −16% | −10% | |
| Consumer surplus | 3% | 2% | 1% | 1% | 1% | |
| Total | −4% | −13% | −20% | −15% | −9% | |
| Nonfarmer | 2% | 1% | 1% | 1% | 1% | 0% |

*Source:* Calculated using the OECD's Policy Evaluation Model (PEM).

**TABLE 7.7 Welfare Effects of Liberalization by Region (US$ Millions)**

| Region | *Liberalization in Mexico* | | *Liberalization in Rich 5* | | *100% liberalization (all regions)* | |
|---|---|---|---|---|---|---|
| | Rich 5 | Mexico | Rich 5 | Mexico | Rich 5 | Mexico |
| Taxpayer | −83 | 846 | 33,336 | −120 | 33,336 | 846 |
| Consumer | −519 | 1,749 | 14,479 | −755 | 14,011 | 980 |
| Farm operator | 146 | −232 | −3,884 | 89 | −3,747 | −158 |
| Landowner | 286 | −1,652 | −24,368 | 260 | −24,135 | −1,488 |
| Hired labor | 9 | 0 | −51 | 0 | −43 | 0 |
| Other purchased inputs | 174 | −379 | −4,309 | 108 | −4,160 | −283 |
| Sum | 14 | 332 | 15,203 | −418 | 15,261 | −105 |

*Source:* Calculated using the OECD's Policy Evaluation Model (PEM).

regions amounts to about US$15 billion per year. Landowners are invariably losers from liberalization and this probably means that farmers also lose from liberalization, with the one exception of farmers in Canada who own about 50 percent of the land they operate. This means Canadian farmers on average probably do not lose from liberalization.

All regions gain from liberalization as shown in table 7.5, but there is an important exception: Mexico gains at the 10 and 50 percent levels of liberalization but loses at the 100 percent level. Mexico's position here is probably atypical of developing countries because its agricultural policy currently has a farm bias transferring large sums from taxpayers and consumers to farmers.

The welfare results in table 7.5 also provide an interesting insight into the interpretation of the commodity market results for rice in table 7.4. Even if there is a lack of confidence in the numerical predictions in the latter, the quantitative result is clear. Rice policy in the developed countries results in a large shift of income among four groups of people: *from* consumers in the rich countries and farmers in the poor countries, and *to* rich country farmers and developing-country consumers. Since developing-country farmers are the poorest of these groups and rich-country farmers the richest, this is a particularly regressive policy framework.

Finally, table 7.6 shows distributional effects in Mexico. This table is particularly affected by data problems as the authors have not yet been able to identify the distribution of land ownership in terms of the households in the model. Including hired labor and a landless rural labor household class would also provide better results. Currently all households involved in production on the commercial farms are treated the same when in reality there is a division of benefits among farmers, landowners, and hired operators that would be available with better data.

The columns in table 7.6 show the effects on both farmers and nonfarmers by income decile. Results for deciles 6–10 are combined. The first two rows show baseline per capita income in U.S. dollars per person per year. There is a small benefit to consumers from cereals liberalization in Mexico but it is at most equivalent to 2 percent of income for the lowest-income urban consumer. (This result assumes that these consumers will continue to receive the same level of targeted food subsidies.)

Farmers in income decile 1 are subsistence maize producers; in fact they are net maize buyers and maize is a relatively large part of their budget—so they too benefit as consumers. But they lose as farmers. The biggest losers are the small-scale commercial farmers in income deciles 2–4. They are net maize sellers, they receive a lot of their income from maize production, and they find it more difficult to adjust to lower subsidies.

### *Trade Liberalization in Developed Versus Developing Countries*

Tables 7.7 and 7.8 contrast what happens when trade liberalization occurs only in the rich countries in the model, with trade liberalization in Mexico only. Again, these results are highly influenced by

**TABLE 7.8 Distribution of the Effects of Liberalization on Mexican Base Income Levels and Percentage Change**

| Income Decile | 1 | 2 | 3 | 4 | 5 | 6–10 |
|---|---|---|---|---|---|---|
| *Annual income per capita* | | | | | | |
| Farmer (US$/person) | 365 | 466 | 687 | 954 | 1,526 | |
| Nonfarmer (US$/person) | 362 | 656 | 859 | 1,089 | 1,217 | 3,799 |
| *Liberalization in Mexico* | | | | | | |
| Farmer | | | | | | |
| Income effect | −7% | −17% | −24% | −17% | −11% | |
| Consumer surplus | 4% | 3% | 2% | 1% | 1% | |
| Total | −4% | −14% | −22% | −16% | −10% | |
| Nonfarmer | 3% | 2% | 2% | 1% | 1% | 0% |
| *Liberalization in Rich 5* | | | | | | |
| Farmer | | | | | | |
| Income effect | 0% | 1% | 4% | 3% | 2% | |
| Consumer surplus | −1% | −1% | −1% | 0% | 0% | |
| Total | −1% | 0% | 3% | 2% | 2% | |
| Nonfarmer | −1% | 0% | 0% | 0% | 0% | 0% |
| *100% liberalization (All regions)* | | | | | | |
| Farmer | | | | | | |
| Income effect | −7% | −15% | −22% | −16% | −10% | |
| Consumer surplus | 3% | 2% | 1% | 1% | 1% | |
| Total | −4% | −13% | −20% | −15% | −9% | |
| Nonfarmer | 2% | 1% | 1% | 1% | 1% | 0% |

*Source:* Calculated using the OECD's Policy Evaluation Model (PEM).

the baseline position with very high levels of support in Mexico.

Elimination of support in Mexico has an enormous distributional effect within that country. There is a net benefit overall of US$332 million and only a very small impact on the rich countries. Farm operators and landowners in the rich countries benefit because of increased market access while consumers lose from high prices and taxpayers from greater subsidies resulting from the small increase in production.

Consumers and taxpayers in Mexico benefit by about US$2.5 billion per year while the landowners are the main losers. Of course, many of the landowners are farm operators at the same time. Table 7.8 shows that if all land benefits are attributed to the farm operators, income for the small-scale commercial farmers drops by as much as 22 percent. This group is hit the hardest by the policy change. The consumer benefit ranges from 0 to 4 percent of income, with the greatest benefit for the lower-income deciles.

As might be anticipated, liberalization by only the rich countries has the opposite effects. Results in table 7.7 show that this makes a small difference only to the rich countries in the results of the 100 percent liberalization scenario already discussed. There is a huge difference in the distribution of benefits in Mexico. Mexican farm operators and landowners benefit modestly from the liberalization in the rich countries because of higher commodity prices. Table 7.8 shows that it is the large-scale commercial producers who benefit most within the agricultural sector. Consumers and taxpayers lose and the net effect is a modest negative.

### Implications of Mexico's Change in the Policy Mix

The effects of Mexico's shift in policy away from input subsidies and border protection to historical entitlements are illustrated by simulating the effect of a US$1 billion increase in each of the four major policy instruments: MPS, OPS, IPS, and historical entitlements in the form of area payments. The results are summarized in table 7.9. Among the most interesting are the following:

- A purchased input subsidy is the most inefficient policy (even more so than MPS). This is consistent with the argument earlier that elastic purchased input supply curves can distort production more than border protection.
- Not surprisingly, therefore, a purchased input subsidy distorts trade more than any other policy.
- Small farmers benefit more from historical entitlements in the form of area payments. It is likely that these results actually underestimate the degree to which the system disproportionately benefits small farmers, since the model does not include three characteristics that increase progressivity: (1) the impact on the incomes of small farmers renting their land to large ones; (2) the floor on payment so that those with land under one hectare receive payment for a full

**TABLE 7.9 Impacts of Hypothetical Changes in Maize Policies in Mexico (US$ million)**

| Measure | Subcategory | Change in Maize Farm Household Income by Decile: 1 | 2 | 3 | 4 | 5 | Total |
|---|---|---|---|---|---|---|---|
| **Purchase input subsidy (extra $1 billion)** | | −7.3 | −21.3 | 62.4 | 93.9 | 185.4 | 313.0 |
| (all crops) | *Farm Operators* | −3.1 | −8.8 | 16.5 | 24.8 | 49.0 | 78.4 |
| | Landowners | −4.2 | −12.5 | 45.9 | 69.1 | 136.4 | 234.6 |
| **Output price subsidy (extra $1 billion)** | | 0.0 | 6.3 | 47.7 | 72.5 | 142.9 | 269.4 |
| (maize only) | *Farm Operators* | −0.2 | 0.6 | 6.9 | 10.4 | 20.6 | 38.3 |
| | *Landowners* | 0.2 | 5.6 | 40.9 | 62.0 | 122.4 | 231.1 |
| **Market price support (extra $1 billion)** | | 0.6 | 13.2 | 90.9 | 136.5 | 269.5 | 510.7 |
| (maize only) | *Farm Operators* | 0.0 | 4.1 | 25.8 | 38.8 | 76.5 | 145.3 |
| | *Landowners* | 0.6 | 9.1 | 65.0 | 97.7 | 193.0 | 365.4 |
| **Historical entitlements (extra $1 billion)** | | 10.1 | 50.2 | 103.7 | 155.5 | 307.1 | 626.7 |
| (area payments) | *Farm Operators* | 0.4 | 1.5 | 1.6 | 2.5 | 4.9 | 10.8 |
| (all crops) | *Landowners* | 9.7 | 48.7 | 102.1 | 153.1 | 302.3 | 615.9 |

| Measure | Subcategory | Trade Distortion Maize | Grains and Oilseed Sectors*: Taxpayers | Consumers | Purchased Input Suppliers | Inefficiency Costs |
|---|---|---|---|---|---|---|
| **Purchased input subsidy (extra $1 billion)** | | 58.2% | −1,287.8 | 32.0 | 342.6 | −439.0 |
| (all crops) | *Fram Operators* | | | | | |
| | *Landowners* | | | | | |
| **Output price subsidy (extra $1 billion)** | | 5.5% | −1084.6 | 15.5 | 177.8 | −235.5 |
| (maize only) | *Farm Operators* | | | | | |
| | *Landowners* | | | | | |
| **Market price support (extra $1 billion)** | | 60.4% | −42.0 | −1040.4 | 194.4 | −328.6 |
| (maize only) | *Farm Operators* | | | | | |
| | *Landowners* | | | | | |
| **Historical entitlements (extra $1 billion)** | | 6.9% | −1033.0 | 3.7 | 18.0 | −81.7 |
| (area payments) | *Farm Operators* | | | | | |
| (all crops) | *Landowners* | | | | | |

1. The sum of transfers and inefficiency costs do not add up to US$1 billion because of indirect effects on other grains and oilseeds sectors (where policy intervention is held constant).

*Source:* Calculated using the OECD's Policy Evaluation Model (PEM).

hectare; and (3) output subsidies that increase with distance from markets.

- Farmers in the lower two deciles lose from an input subsidy because land prices are bid up and used by larger farm sizes.

## Further Considerations

This chapter has shown that heterogeneity across households means that the effect of price declines are felt differentially across household types—surplus growers are adversely affected. The immediate impact of eliminating the government-guaranteed price of staples in Mexico is to decrease the profitability of growing staples by farm households that have access to the high price. However, to see the full impact on these households, food staples must be seen in the context of the households' other income activities. In rural Mexico, households, including those producing staples, tend to be highly diversified. As a result, decreases in the staple price would be expected to have small impacts on income.

The analysis with the PEM, however, does not incorporate the effects of several very important details of Mexico's agricultural policy and economic structure. For example, the characteristics of the demand linkages among firms and households depend on the answers to several questions:

- Is price transmission imperfect because of market failures (transactions costs), owing to the market power of intermediaries, government policy, or lack of rural infrastructure for transportation, information, credit, and the like?
- Is the household a net consumer? Or do farmers facing high storage and transport costs need to sell immediately because of a lack of credit, so that prices are depressed at harvest (and farmers purchase for consumption later at higher prices)?
- Is there a surplus pool of rural laborers or full employment?
- What are the opportunities of crop diversification?[7]
- Are complementary policies relating to infrastructure and information available to establish markets, improve competition, and deepen market integration?

### *Imperfect Price Transmission*

Market failures (that is, transaction costs) create a buffer for subsistence producers (about half of all maize producers in Mexico) from the change in the market price. Market imperfections, created by high transaction costs, mean many of Mexico's staple farmers did not sell to the market. Transportation costs, marketing uncertainties, storage costs, and lack of credit often lead to harvest-time sales at distressed prices. Being isolated from regional staple markets by poor infrastructure and high transaction costs makes people rely on local production to satisfy their consumption demands—and producers, finding it too costly to market their output outside of the area, must seek markets for their surplus production within the local economy. These conditions create a local market for the staple; the staple price is determined by local supply and demand, not by outside markets or government policy.

The implication for trade liberalization and policy reform is that guaranteed market prices are not good instruments to improve efficiency or income distribution among farmers and consumers. Direct income payments such as those through PROCAMPO do get to the smaller farms farther away from market centers. Furthermore, the new deficiency payment program based on "concerted" prices, that have payments increasing inversely with farm size (because farms on average become smaller and poorer with distance from market centers), also improves the distribution of income.

## Imperfect Markets

Constraints exist owing to a variety of market failures, including missing or incomplete (that is, not functioning) capital, insurance, and labor markets. However, market imperfections result in household-specific "shadow prices" that transmit income impacts to the production side of the household-farm economy. If the household is liquidity-constrained (that is, lacks capital), the PROCAMPO payments generate benefits relative to the constrained situation by increasing the amount of inputs used or investments in human or physical capital (and they also can be used as collateral).

To understand the impact of the transfer on incomes and investments, it is necessary to follow expenditure linkages to the labor-supplying household. Government payments (for decoupled income payments under PROCAMPO) stimulate income growth in households that sell consumption goods or services to the household receiving the transfer. A PROCAMPO payment increases a household's demand for staples (directly or indirectly, for example, through demand for livestock or other products). The local staple price increases. The higher staple price transmits benefits from the transfer-receiving household to local staple surplus producers. Sadoulet, de Janvry, and Davis (2001) estimate the income multiplier for PROCAMPO payments to range from 1.5 to 2.6. Hence, these market structures not taken into account by the PEM are critical in shaping local economy-wide impacts of government policy.

### *Net Suppliers or Demanders?*

The empirical results show that all farm sizes for maize in Mexico lose from price declines even though many of the decile 1 farmers are net buyers of food. Data limitations currently prevent the authors from having a net buyer category but it is an important issue for those cases in which farmers are net buyers. The traditional, neoclassical agricultural household model used here assumes perfect markets with decoupled payments and other exogenous income shocks. Direct payments or exogenous income changes do not affect production, because an income transfer (from government) leaves the conditions for farm profit maximization unchanged.

The welfare effects of low prices of food have been a contentious issue in numerous debates on development policy. A commonly held view is that low food prices benefit urban groups but hurt the rural population because they depend primarily on agriculture. However, many of the rural poor are actually net demanders of food, even in Mexico. A great many among the poor do not produce sufficient food for their own consumption, typically supplementing their own farm incomes with agricultural labor earnings. Under regular partial equilibrium conditions, such persons cannot benefit from high food prices. This conclusion is contentious when other welfare-relevant prices and quantities are responsive to changes in food prices. In particular, it has been argued that by stimulating food production and the demand for agricultural labor, high food prices may benefit the rural poor through the induced wage response, even when the poor are net demanders of food.

But there has been little agreement on how responsive agricultural wages are to food prices. Contrast the results of Sah and Stiglitz (1984) with those of de Janvry and Subbarao (1986). Both studies model the distributional effects of food pricing policies in economies when the rural poor depend heavily on their earnings from supplying agricultural labor. Sah and Stiglitz contend that the food price elasticity of the agricultural wage rate is close to one, implying that a movement in the terms of trade against agriculture hurts everyone in the sector, whether rich or poor.

On the other hand, de Janvry and Subbarao assume that the nominal wage rate in agriculture is exogenously fixed, implying zero food price elasticity, and, hence, quite adverse effects on the rural poor of higher food prices. Neither study presents sufficient empirical evidence to support its assumptions.

Ravallion (1990) examines the rural welfare distributional effects of changes in food prices under induced wage responses for rural Bangladesh. He identifies the critical value of the elasticity of the agricultural wage rate with respect to the price of food necessary for an increase in food price to be welfare-improving. There can be little doubt that many poor households in rural areas are highly vulnerable to at least the initial impact of an increase in the price of staple foods. But the welfare effects of price changes have often focused on a single relative price or income, whereas a better indicator would be the food purchasing power of the agricultural wage.

A complete analysis of the welfare effects of a food price change, therefore, would require information on how nonfood prices and incomes as well as agricultural wages respond. It is not implausible, for example, that higher food prices would increase village-level demand for the petty trading and service activities typically supplied by the poor. In a relatively closed economy the prices of nonfood goods can also be expected to respond. The price elasticity of the wage rate that is necessary for the household (net supplier or demander of food) and farm laborer to benefit from a food price increase depends on several factors not analyzed here, including the ratio of the worker's net food expenditure (after deducting the value of the worker's own production) to labor earnings, elasticities of supply and demand for labor, and the share of income from alternative income sources.

### *Incorporating Off-Farm Labor Decisions*

The above discussion points to an important aspect of trade liberalization regarding its impact on the allocation of labor to nonagricultural activities (including labor migration and income remittances). This would require the PEM to be extended to a full household model that incorporates exogenous income sources and labor allocation to off-farm and noncrop agricultural activities. This would incorporate multiple sources of income outside of agriculture, multiple crops within agriculture, off-farm versus farm labor decisions, and endogenous rural wage. The results discussed earlier would be that much more complete with exogenous income changes due to policy affecting labor decisions.

### *Complementary Policies*

For long-run benefits to accrue in terms of poverty alleviation, rural households will need to adjust their production patterns and farm/off-farm labor activities.[8] Trade liberalization should be accompanied by sound domestic policies in areas such as transport and communications infrastructure, market facilitation, competition, education, and governance. Otherwise, it will fail to generate the investment and productivity improvements needed for growth. More specifically, progress should be made in: investment in irrigation and rural roads to ensure that agricultural production can be connected to world markets; property rights to encourage investment in the land; appropriate agricultural extension and mechanisms for the dissemination of market and technical information; and the development of markets for credit, agricultural inputs and services.

Trade liberalization almost inevitably involves costs of adjustment, notably job losses in formerly protected sectors. The best way to ease the pain of transition is to protect social expenditure and ensure appropriate targeting of the poor, providing a cushion without undermining their incentives to adjust. Trade liberalization can change the nature of the risk and uncertainty that poor households face, although not always for the worse. It can also affect their ability to cope with risk and uncertainty. Policies such as improving access to credit markets can help a great deal here, along with improvements in land asset distribution and in the flexibility of local labor markets.

## Summary and Concluding Remarks

This chapter highlighted some important implications of alternative OECD policies on income distribution, economic efficiency, and trade distortion across countries and commodity groups. Specific emphasis on Mexico was to illustrate the impacts on a developing country. The grains and oilseeds sector was chosen as an example using the OECD PEM framework. The countries and commodities explored are good examples because of the importance of grains and oilseeds for the six regions in terms of policy intervention levels and value of production and trade. There is also a wide range of policy instruments used and a major transformation of the sector in terms of policy re-instrumentation that has occurred over the past 15 years, from border to domestic support and from coupled subsidies to land area payments and historical entitlement payments. The policy mix also differs across both countries and commodities, allowing a wide range of policy effects to be examined.

Several key questions were addressed in this chapter by analyzing the impacts of the alternative policy interventions on consumers, taxpayers, farm operators, and landowners and across countries, commodities, and policies. With high barriers to trade in agriculture, the impact of trade liberalization and policy re-instrumentation has taxpayers and consumers generally gaining from lower domestic prices and trade distortion declining as world prices rise.

The effects on landowners, purchased input suppliers, and farm operators were shown to depend critically on the policy instrument type used. Purchased input subsidies and market price supports were found to be inefficient, trade distorting, and ineffective in transferring income to farmers (the primary goal of agricultural policies) while historical entitlements and area payments were found to be the best (with output subsidies falling in-between).

It is worth underscoring that OECD policy is particularly regressive in that it results in a large shift of income from farmers in the poor countries (and rich-country consumers) to rich-country farmers (and developing-country consumers). The authors found substantial differences in the effects of unilateral versus multilateral trade liberalization. Full trade liberalization in the PEM countries would result in a net savings of US$15 billion per year, with the largest part of this savings being made in Japan. Agricultural support in all regions involves much larger transfers from consumers and taxpayers to farm operators and especially to landowners.

Mexico would not benefit from a full trade liberalization. Atypical for a developing country, Mexico has farmers who now receive most support in the form of historical entitlements (that is, PROCAMPO), and less in terms of output price support, input subsidies, and market price support. Eliminating these latter policies would benefit poor consumers but hurt small-scale commercial farmers by much more.

All regions gain from liberalization, but there is a small, important caveat. Mexico gains at the 10 and 50 percent level of liberalization while losing at the 100 percent level. Mexico's position here is probably atypical of developing countries because its agricultural policy currently has a farm bias transferring large sums from taxpayers and consumers to farmers.

Elimination of support in Mexico has a large distributional effect within the country. There is a modest net benefit overall of US$332 million and only a very small impact on the rich countries. Farm operators and landowners in the rich countries benefit because of increased market access while consumers lose from high prices and taxpayers lose because of greater subsidies resulting from the small increase in production.

Mexican consumers and taxpayers benefit by about US$2.5 billion per year while landowners are the main losers. Of course, many of the landowners are also farm operators. If all land benefits are attributed to the farm operators, income for the small-scale commercial farmers drops by as much as 24 percent, making this group the hardest-hit by the policy change. The consumer benefit ranges between 0 and 4 percent of income with the greatest benefit for the lower-income deciles.

As might be anticipated, liberalization by only the rich countries has the opposite effects. The results show that this makes a small difference to the rich countries compared to the full multilateral liberalization. There is a large difference in the distribution of benefits in Mexico. Farm operators and landowners in Mexico benefit modestly from the liberalization in the rich countries because of higher commodity prices, and small-scale commercial producers benefit most within the agricultural sector. Consumers and taxpayers lose and the net effect is a modest negative.

The analysis demonstrates the importance of accurately simulating and fully evaluating the likely consequences of partial liberalization of policies such as tariffs, tariff rate quotas, input or output subsidies, area payments, and historical entitlements. The results here were highly sensitive to details of market structure and the importance of other support measures.

Mexico's policy reform shifted away from fixed and overvalued exchange rates, import tariffs on and subsidies to farmers for purchased agricultural inputs, and direct intervention in agricultural markets with guaranteed prices to farmers and fixed lower prices to consumers, to direct area payments (PROCAMPO) and production subsidies (ASERCA), which improved the efficiency and incomes of smaller farms. Consumer subsidies are also now more targeted and therefore more effective.

Furthermore, income distribution among farms has improved because land reforms allow small farms to rent out approximately 10 percent of their land to larger farmers. Decoupled area payments and output subsidies are distributed disproportionately to smaller farm sizes. Decoupled payments are given for the minimum of 1 hectare (regardless of the actual size of the farm) and a maximum of 100 hectares. Output subsidies increase the farther away a farm is from the major consumption or market center (and average farm size decreases with distance from major markets). These policy details can have significant positive impacts on income distribution compared to historical guaranteed prices with a parastatal enterprise—where many small farmers did not benefit because they were often net buyers, sold prices at distressed prices at harvest, or were not integrated with market price centers owing to transactions costs and the like.

## Notes

1. PEM is a multimarket policy model of the grains and oilseeds sectors for OECD countries including Mexico.

2. See Frankel and Romer (1999); Dollar and Kraay (2001); and Ravallion and Chen (2001). For a critique of the empirical results in the literature on the links between trade and growth, see Rodrik (2000); and Nye, Reddy, and Watkins (2002).

3. Inequality can have an adverse impact on growth, especially if there is inequality in asset distribution and education. It is also well known that inequality can adversely affect political feasibility of policy reforms to liberalize trade.

4. As will be shown later, analysis of the OECD's PEMs suggests that this type of support is extremely trade-distorting, but therefore also effective in promoting self-sufficiency.

5. Data furnished by Patricia Aguilar through personal communication.

6. Payments vary by distance through the use of concerted prices (prior to 2001, these payments were given to buyers). Payments are calculated through the "Local Prices of Indifference" mechanism because in receiving the deficiency payment, the buyer is indifferent between purchasing the domestic and imported crop. Prices of indifference vary according to the region in which commodities are consumed or produced: there is a different deficiency payment for each origin–destination combination. The subsidy also serves as compensation to farmers for selling at distressed prices at harvest owing to lack of credit, storage costs, and transportation costs.

7. Coffee serves as an example here. Large, soft bean coffee in lowlands ("robusta") with lower costs in humid tropical regions—for instance, Brazil and Vietnam—could easily switch to cotton/sugar/beef/grains and oilseeds if desired, while hard bean, high altitude, high quality coffee such as grown in Central America and Malawi/Kenya have economic conditions for coffee producers who cannot switch to cotton/sugar/beef/grains because their land and climate make growing these crops unprofitable (although some would migrate to lowlands if possible to plant these commodities subsidized by OECD countries).

8. The ability of poor households to respond to the new opportunities presented by trade liberalization will be influenced by their location and demographic structure, and the gender, health status, education, and assets of their members. In addition, benefits from trade liberalization will be minimal unless there is a sound investment climate, macroeconomic stability and openness, governance and sound institutions and the rule of law, legal and judicial support for property rights, financial regulation, and competition policy.

## Select Bibliography

The word *processed* describes informally reproduced works that may not be commonly available through libraries.


de Janvry, A., and K. Subbarao. 1986. *Agricultural Price Policy and Income Distribution in India.* Delhi: Oxford University Press.

Dollar, D., and A. Kraay. 2001. "Trade, Growth, and Poverty." World Bank Policy Research Working Paper 2615. World Bank, Washington, D.C.

Frankel, J., and D. Romer. 1999. *Does Trade Cause Growth? American Economic Review* 89(3): 379–99.

Krueger, A. O., M. Schiff, and A. Valdés. 1988. "Agricultural Incentives in Developing Countries: Measuring the Effect of Sectoral and Economywide Policies." World Bank Economic Review 1988, vol. 2(3): 255–71.

OECD (Organisation for Economic Co-operation). 2001. "Market Effects of Crop Support Measures." OECD, Paris.

——. 2002a. "Agricultural Policies in OECD Countries: Monitoring and Evaluation 2002." OECD, Paris.

——. 2002b. "The Transfer Efficiency of Farm Support for Farm Household Income." OECD, Paris.

Nye, H., S. Reddy, and K. Watkins. 2002. "Dollar and Kraay on 'Trade, Growth, and Poverty': A Critique." Paper, International Development Economics Associates, New Delhi. networkideas.org/themes/human/jun2002/hd19_Trade_Growth_Poverty.htm.

Olinto, P., K. Deininger, and B. Davis. 2000. "Land Market Liberalization and the Access to Land by the Rural Poor: Panel Data Evidence of the Impact of the Mexican *Ejido* Reform." Processed. World Bank, Washington, D.C.

Ravallion, M. 1989. "Do Price Increases for Staple Foods Help or Hurt the Rural Poor?" Policy Research Working Paper WPS167. World Bank, Washington, D.C.

——. 1990. "Rural Welfare Effects of Food Price Changes under Induced Wage Responses: Theory and Evidence for Bangladesh." *Oxford Economic Papers* 42(3): 574–85.

Ravallion, M., and S. Chen. 2001. "Measuring Pro-Poor Growth," Working Papers—Macroeconomics and Growth; Stabilization; Monetary/Fiscal Policy, 2666, World Bank, Washington, D.C.

Robilliard, A., F. Bourguignon, and S. Robinson. 2001. "Crisis and Income Distribution: A Micro-Macro Model for Indonesia." Paper prepared for the ESRC Development Economics/International Economics Conference, April 5–7, Nottingham University.

Rodrik, D. 2000. "Comments on 'Trade, Growth, and Poverty,' by David Dollar and Aart Kraay." http://ksghome.harvard.edu/~.drodrik.academic.ksg/papers.html.

Sadoulet, E., and A. de Janvry. 1995. *Quantitative Development Policy Analysis.* Baltimore: Johns Hopkins University Press.

Sadoulet, E., A. de Janvry, and B. Davis. 2001. "Cash Transfer Programs with Income Multiplier: PROCAMPO in Mexico." *World Development* 29(6): 1043–56.

Sah, R. K., and J. E. Stiglitz. 1984. "The Economics of Price Scissors." *American Economic Review* 74(1): 125–38.

———. 1987. "Price Scissors and the Structure of the Economy." *Quarterly Journal of Economics* 102(1): 109–34.

Singh, I., L. Squire, and J. Strauss. 1986. "A Survey of Agricultural Household Models: Recent Findings and Policy Implications." In *Agricultural Household Models: Extensions, Applications and Policy.* Baltimore: Johns Hopkins University Press.

Winters, L. A. 2001. "Trade, Trade Policy and Poverty: What Are the Links?" Centre for Economic Policy Research Policy Paper No. 2382, London.

Winters, P., B. Davis, and L. Corral. 2001. "Assets, Activities and Income Generation in Rural Mexico: Factoring in Social and Public Capital." Graduate School of Agricultural and Resource Economics Working Paper 2001-1, School of Economics, University of New England, Armidale, Australia.

8

# THE "MULTIFUNCTIONALITY" OF AGRICULTURE AND ITS IMPLICATIONS FOR POLICY

*David Vanzetti and Els Wynen*

## Introduction

The Uruguay Round Agreement on Agriculture (URAA), in its built-in agenda for future negotiations, and the Doha Ministerial Declaration explicitly confirm that nontrade concerns will be taken into account in the current round of negotiations. Such concerns relate to nonfood outputs including the environment, food security, rural amenities, and viable rural communities. The major issue concerning negotiators is the extent to which these benefits are jointly produced. The additional production has provided an incentive for several highly protective developed-country members to raise concerns about the multifunctional benefits of agriculture that may be lost if further erosion of coupled or trade-distorting agricultural support were to occur. Countries most active in espousing government support for the provision of these multifunctional benefits are Japan, the Republic of Korea, Norway, and Switzerland, as well as the European Union (EU). These countries have, coincidentally or not, highly protected agriculture.

Multifunctionality conceivably presents itself as a stumbling block to the World Trade Organization (WTO) agricultural negotiations. The various benefits, such as landscape values, are notoriously difficult to value. It is thus tempting for proponents to use inflated values to justify support to agriculture. One can imagine negotiations stalled on valuing cultural heritage, biodiversity, or animal welfare. Continued support to agriculture in developed countries distorts trade and may have detrimental effects on many developing countries.

## The Plan of This Chapter

The aim of this chapter is to use some economic concepts to explore the issue of multifunctionality. In the next section, the positions of some of the major players on each side of the debate are briefly described and analyzed. Legal dimensions are then described, followed by an economic perspective and some policy implications. Some implications and conclusions draw the chapter to a close.

## Positions of the Parties

WTO members agreed in the Uruguay Round to cut domestic support to agriculture. Support was divided into three categories (so-called "boxes") depending on the degree of trade distortion.

Support measures that are nondistorting, in the sense that they have no or minimal effects on production and trade, are grouped in the green box (set out in Annex 2 of the URAA) and are not subject to reduction disciplines. These include measures such as general services (research, pest and disease controls, infrastructure), food security stocks, domestic food aid, decoupled farm income support, income insurance, provision of safety nets, and environmental and regional assistance programs. This covers many of the nontrade concerns.

The blue box covers domestic support measures of direct government payments to farmers under production-limiting programs.

More relevant, the amber box contains the most production-distorting measures (such as government support for prices), which are subject to reductions. Some members argue that some production-stimulating measures should be permitted precisely because of the need to stimulate agricultural production to provide the multifunctional benefits and that some of the amber box measures need to be relocated to the green box, not subject to reduction commitments.

As previously stated, the countries that most heavily promote the concept of multifunctionality are Japan, the Republic of Korea, Norway, and Switzerland, as well as the EU. Perhaps coincidently, as the U.S. Department of Agriculture (USDA) has observed, it is also these countries (along with Slovenia) that have high levels of amber box support relative to what they are permitted under the URAA (Bohman and others 1999, p. 6). Although the data used in the USDA study are dated, with the EU switching support from the amber to the blue box in recent years, the point is well-made that further negotiated reductions in permitted amber box support may act as a constraint on its support of agriculture.

The Norwegian government has produced perhaps the best-articulated position in favor of multifunctionality (see, for example, Norway Ministry of Agriculture 2001). Its argument progresses as follows: the reform process agreed to in the Uruguay Round should not necessarily be finalized in the current negotiations; countries are diverse, with differing concerns and production conditions; production is required to supply the nontrade concerns; low-potential areas need government support to sustain production; and finally, green box measures may be insufficient. The key to this argument is the jointness of production. Elsewhere the government maintains, "The value of the agricultural landscape . . . [is] closely contingent upon the landscape's authenticity as a food producer" (Ministry of Agriculture, cited in Bohman and others 1999, p. 7). The crucial word here is "authenticity." Would agriculture become less authentic if the intensity of production were to fall following reductions in support? Assessing values is also difficult. Many taxpayers may prefer wilderness to an agricultural landscape.

The Japanese government has offered flood mitigation as a justification for subsidies to paddy rice production. The water-buffering effect prevents erosion and the potential destruction of valuable urban areas (ABARE 1999, p. 3). Opponents argue that this hardly justifies raising rice prices to six times world levels, provided to all farmers regardless of their impact on flood mitigation. Furthermore, alternative methods (dams, forestry) may be equally as effective without stimulating agricultural production.

Japan's government also stresses food security as an important component of multifunctionality. It maintains that short-term food insecurity may increase in the future, owing to El Niño and other climate changes. Furthermore, increasing global demand for food, coupled with feed and supply constraints, may push up world prices (Japan Ministry of Foreign Affairs 2000). The Japanese government emphasizes self-sufficiency as a means of enhancing food security.

The EU proposal to the WTO negotiations gives multifunctionality a central role in addressing societal concerns related to agriculture (WTO 2002b). The proposal claims that this is necessary to gain public support to further trade liberalization. The EU's claim is based on the notion that the European public fears the effects of trade liberalization on rural communities. Nonetheless, according to the proposal, policies to achieve the multifunctional benefits of agriculture represent a much more targeted approach than the others discussed so far. For example, the EU proposal states that environmental policies should be used to tackle environmental problems. Moreover, these should be written into the URAA. The EU proposal also emphasizes animal welfare and food safety issues, claiming that compensation for additional costs of meeting animal welfare standards should be exempt from reduction commitments. Recent developments, including bovine spongiform encephalopathy and foot-and-mouth disease in livestock, and genetically modified organisms in crops, have made food safety issues a concern in the EU. The EU proposal favors clarification of the precautionary principle as a guide to food safety issues.[1]

The Republic of Korea and Switzerland are the other two countries best known for espousing the concept of multifunctionality as a means of obtaining flexibility in providing support to agriculture. The Republic of Korea puts forward the additional view that agricultural productive capacity should be maintained to allow for the possible reunification of the two Koreas. (The Democratic People's Republic of Korea's agricultural capacity is currently depleted.)

Although all countries have some multifunctional aspects associated with their agriculture, most oppose the use of the concept to justify production-distorting government support. The United States (U.S.) position on multifunctionality is articulated in a USDA publication, "The Use and Abuse of Multifunctionality" (Bohman and others 1999). The title signals the flavor of the discussion, which emphasizes that the nonfood outputs from agriculture can be provided without additional production-linked subsidies. Targeted measures to provide these multifunctional outputs are already included in the green box. This study makes the point, mentioned earlier, that a country's support for the multifunctional agenda is related to its level of protection for agriculture. Where the amber box policies are a constraint, countries transfer their production-linked support to the blue box or preferably to the unregulated green box. According to the authors, the concept has been misused by countries claiming that the nonfood outputs are "jointly produced"—and therefore production-linked, rather than targeted, policies are necessary to increase production of these outputs.

As leader of the Cairns Group of agricultural exporters, Australia holds a position that is rather similar to that of the United States (U.S.) (see Roberts, Podbury, and Hinchy 2001, p. 35 for a detailed discussion). A note by the Australian Bureau of Agricultural and Resource Economics (ABARE 1999) claims that multifunctionality is "a pretext for protection." These studies point to the need for targeted support, raise the question of whether separate markets can be established to determine the real values of environmental and cultural products, and emphasize the role of diversifying supply to ensure food security. They also emphasize the importance of considering negative as well as positive externalities. Finally, the dangers of overvaluing hard-to-value multifunctional externalities are stressed. The valuation problems allow proponents to justify any expenditure and make "wild and exaggerated claims as to the magnitude of the valuation of non-market rural goods," according to an Australian government representative (OECD 2000, p. 171). The Australian government is concerned that the concept of multifunctionality may be used to stifle reform of domestic support for agriculture. In contrast to the U.S. and the EU, Australia believes the production-stimulating effects of support, even blue and green box support, are significant (Roberts, Podbury, and Hinchy 2001, p. 5). The Cairns Group proposes a review of green box criteria to ensure that they are indeed minimally distorting.

The Cairns Group contains several agricultural-exporting developing countries that support the Group view with varying levels of enthusiasm. Some of these countries claim that domestic support outside the green box is a form of special and differential support for rich countries (WTO 2002c). Outside the Cairns Group, developing countries are a disparate grouping but in general they oppose the use of the concept of multifunctionality to justify domestic support. Relatively few developing countries have submitted negotiating proposals to the WTO emphasizing non-trade concerns. Mauritius has proposed that developing countries, and in particular small island states, be given greater scope to provide production-distorting support to agriculture (WTO 2002a). Jordan has proposed domestic support for its olive and sheep producers. The Democratic Republic of Congo, Croatia, and Poland have also made proposals to the WTO concerning non-trade concerns. The various African, Caribbean, and Pacific countries that currently receive preferential access to the EU markets tend to be sympathetic to the EU's negotiating position.

Many developing countries are concerned about food security, one aspect of multifunctionality. The problem they face is not so much inadequate flexibility to provide production-distorting domestic support to agriculture as it is the inability to finance it on a wide scale. For this reason, border measures rather than domestic support are commonly used to encourage agricultural production. Thus the EU, Japan, and other European countries appear to have had little success as yet in building a substantial coalition of supporters of multifunctionality.

## Legal Dimensions

Trade negotiations are concerned with changing the rules governing world trade. It is pertinent then to outline what the current rules say on multifunctionality and related issues. Article 20 of the URAA, which contains an agenda for further negotiations and uses the term "non-trade concerns," an alternative phrase for multifunctionality: "Commitments under the reform program should be made in an equitable way among all Members, having regard to non-trade concerns, including food security and the need to protect the environment. . . ."

The WTO Secretariat elaborates on this list, specifying "non-trade concerns such as food security, the environment, structural adjustment, rural development, poverty alleviation and so on" (WTO 2002c, p. 24). In 1947, GATT Article XX (General Exceptions) gave the then–GATT members the right to implement measures to protect the life or health of humans, animals, and plants and to conserve natural resources. This applies particularly to multifunctional outputs of an environmental nature. However, recognizing the pitfalls, Article XX specifically mentions that these measures should not be applied in an arbitrary or discriminatory fashion, or be applied to restrict trade (Raney and Tschirley 1999).

Some multifunctional outputs of agriculture have specific rules. Food security is one.[2] The WTO agreements include the "Decision on the Possible Negative Effects of the Reform Programme on Least-Developed and Net-Food Importing Developing Countries," which is aimed at enhancing agricultural productivity and infrastructure in these developing countries (WTO 2002c, p. 23). However, most of the countries espousing food security as a multifunctional benefit of agriculture are in fact developed countries, such as Japan, Norway, and Switzerland.

The issue of multifunctionality can be described as a "bandwagon" that has attracted numerous fellow travelers hoping to use trade negotiations on this issue to further their particular interests, legitimate or otherwise. Animal welfare issues are not covered under existing rules, but the WTO has received proposals allowing member countries to compensate farmers for the extra costs of meeting more stringent animal welfare standards (WTO 2002c, p. 24). Food safety[3] is another issue that sometimes finds a place on the multifunctionality bandwagon, the view being that domestic production ensures safe food (TAED 2000). The URAA does not cover this, but Article 5.7 of the WTO Agreement on the Application of Sanitary and Phytosanitary Measures refers to it, and sets out specific conditions under which such measures may be implemented.

In essence, negotiations concerning multifunctionality hinge on whether production-distorting support (including amber and blue box domestic support and border measures) should be maintained or perhaps increased to guarantee benefits indirectly provided by agricultural production. Opponents of that view claim that these external benefits from agriculture, if desired, can be provided without increasing production. The next section reviews some economic concepts to help the reader assess these conflicting claims.

## Economic Perspectives

### *General Characteristics of Multifunctionality*

There may be an economic justification for governments to provide key goods and services when market failure exists. Where the output of one good or service is directly related to the production of another, in certain circumstances it may be desirable to subsidize the second to obtain the benefits from the first. This is more likely to be the case if the two goods are jointly produced, and the production of the second involves externalities of such a nature that government intervention is desirable. For example, if a farmer's row of walnut trees provides some welcome shade along a dusty public road, it may be desirable to subsidize production of walnuts from those particular trees to encourage the farmer to maintain the shade-producing trees. These essential concepts relating to multifunctionality are explained in turn below.

**Joint Production** The main feature of multifunctionality, in any industry, is that the secondary benefits are jointly produced and would not be available without the primary output. Wool is a joint product of sheep meat. Although quality may vary, it is not feasible to have one product without the other. If strong jointness exists, the multifunctional benefits cannot be produced separately from the agricultural output. If strong jointness does not exist, there may be a lower-cost means of producing the multifunctional benefit without subsidizing agricultural output.

A recent Organisation for Economic Co-operation and Development (OECD) study synthesized information from 17 countries on the question of degree of jointness between commodity and noncommodity outputs (Abler 2001, esp. p. 31). The report focused on physical rather than economic links and attempted to assess the scope for de-linking agricultural production and its multifunctional benefits, and concluded that among the positive multifunctional benefits only food security is strongly linked to commodity production.

**Externalities** Externalities refer to beneficial or harmful effects occurring in production, distribution, or consumption of a good or service that are not captured by the buyer or seller. This implies that no market exists or that markets function poorly and hence externalities are difficult to value. Jointly produced goods are not necessarily externalities. Wool is jointly produced but is not an externality because both buyers and sellers of sheep know the value of wool, and it can be capitalized into the value of a sheep. There is thus a market for the by-product. The market for external benefits may not exist because of an absence of property rights or high transaction costs. Agricultural pollution is a common externality that has come about because farmers, historically, have had the right to pollute. This has evolved from the days when farm pollution (for instance, water runoff containing pesticides) was minimal. A further example is landscape values. Farmers are aware that passersby may enjoy the scenery provided by their farm, but they find it difficult to charge them for this benefit.

It is not clear how much agricultural output is necessary to provide the desired secondary benefits. Does a decrease in agricultural output at the margin lead to a fall in these positive externalities? A review (Burrell 2001, esp. p. 16) for the OECD of reports from 17 countries has examined the issue of market failure, and concludes that almost no cases are reported in which the level of multifunctional benefits is directly related to agricultural output. The author notes that these benefits are more closely related to input use, that is, if the land remains in farming most of the secondary benefits are retained.

**Government Intervention** Government intervention depends on the nature of the externalities and the possibility of market failure. This intervention is more likely to be appropriate in cases in which the jointly produced multifunctional benefits are a public good, having the characteristics of nonrivalry in consumption and nonexcludability. The earlier example used shade from walnut trees on a public road to illustrate this. The consumption by one person does not affect availability to others (at least until congestion occurs), nor can pedestrians be easily excluded and hence charged for the service. In the absence of a well-functioning market, public goods (for example, shade) tend to be undersupplied. A government may respond in several ways: (a) alter property rights to create a market (for instance, privatizing the road and allowing the farmer to charge a toll); (b) regulate (for instance, requiring farmers to grow trees along roads); (c) impose taxes or subsidies to alter the behavior of buyers or sellers (for instance, subsidizing tree planting along roads); or (d) provide the service itself (for instance, planting trees along roads). The appropriate response depends on the precise nature of the public good, the degree of jointness, the value of the benefits, transaction costs, the availability of alternatives, and perhaps various location-specific issues.

### *An Analytical Framework*

The OECD has attempted to provide a comprehensive analytical framework to assist policymakers in deciding whether government intervention for the provision of positive multifunctional benefits is justified (OECD 2001).[4] This framework sets out a series of questions for decisionmakers:

1. Is there a strong degree of jointness between commodity and noncommodity outputs?
2. Is there some market failure associated with the noncommodity outputs?
3. Is government action required or are there better alternatives?

### BOX 8.1 Aspects of Valuation

Valuing multifunctional benefits is evidently likely to be difficult, yet policymakers must make decisions using explicit or implicit valuations. Apart from the absence of markets, there are several additional difficulties relating to nonuse valuations.

***Existence values*** refer to the satisfaction gained from knowing that a good or resource exists. Many people who have never seen whales or tigers nonetheless benefit from their continued existence. An obvious example is agriculture's role in preserving biodiversity.

***Bequest values*** are the benefits to one generation of knowing that a resource will be passed down to the next generation. Forests may have this characteristic. Rather than converting a forest for agricultural use, there is some value in preserving it to future generations.

***Option values*** are the benefits of preserving a resource so that it can be used for an alternative purpose later.

Various methods exist to obtain nonmarket valuations. Unfortunately, in most cases none are entirely satisfactory. Travel costs methods attempt to value an attraction by measuring how much people will pay to travel to it. Hedonic pricing involves measuring a particular characteristic of a good. For example, housing situated near scenic agricultural land may have a different value from otherwise identical housing situated elsewhere. Finally, contingent valuation involves asking people hypothetical questions concerning their willingness to pay.

In the absence of reliable economic valuations, policymakers have other indicators to assess the desirability of a good or service. This may range from polling individuals to media coverage to visible protests (both in support or opposition). The danger here is that particular interest groups may claim to represent a larger section of society than is in fact the case. Farmers may claim that the bulk of society is in favor of preserving farmland, on the basis that taxpayers have supported farmers for a generation. In reality, many nonfarmers may prefer that the land be returned to its natural state.

All three questions must be answered in the affirmative to justify government support. The OECD emphasizes the scope to de-link commodity and noncommodity outputs by changing farming practices and technologies, or by pursuing low-cost nonagricultural provision of noncommodity outputs. Even in the presence of strong jointness and market failure, the OECD questions whether options not linked to government (such as market creation or voluntary provision) may not be a more efficient strategy than government subsidies, given the transaction and administrative costs and risk of policy failure associated with government intervention.

The OECD also notes the importance of negative externalities associated with agriculture. Although it is obvious that they are significant, these negative effects are rarely introduced into discussions of multifunctionality. The point that further subsidization of agriculture may generate net negative rather than positive externalities is sometimes overlooked.

#### *Valuation of Multifunctional Benefits*

A final conceptual point in setting up an economic framework helpful in analyzing multifunctionality as it relates to valuation, the estimation of demand. Multifunctional benefits are commonly characterized by externalities. By their nature, externalities are difficult to value (see box 8.1). How much of a service should a government provide, given there is no market to indicate its value to taxpayers who pay for the service?

This is an important point. When a valuation of a service is not available, groups in society that want the service are likely to claim that it is much more valuable to society as a whole than others who might favor alternative services. Governments have to assess competing claims before providing the service, and given the conflicting advice from stakeholders, bureaucrats, scientists, opinion polls, and various interest groups, it is not clear how such assessments can best be made.

The OECD (2000) recently examined the question of valuation and concluded that valuation studies can help policymakers. However, the OECD warns that in many cases the results from hypothetical contingent valuation studies should not be taken literally, and values should not be summed across locations or different types of amenities. Nor should comparisons across countries be attempted. While of use, such studies should be used with care and in conjunction with other approaches (OECD 2000, p. 176). With particular reference to the impact of further reductions in domestic support for agricultural production, the OECD claims that it is not clear whether these valuation techniques shed any light on the impact of changes at the margin, and whether changes affect several multifunctional outputs simultaneously. Finally, the techniques have yet to gain the credibility required for their use in international trade negotiations (OECD 2000, p. 172). So far, the major elements of the debate on multifunctionality would seem to center on the need for government intervention, given the absence of a market of multifunctional goods and the valuation of these goods. If governments are to intervene, it is desirable that their policies meet certain criteria.

### *Policy Implications*

Policies applying to agriculture should be subject to the same criteria as other industries. Sound policies are effective, efficient, equitable, transparent, and administratively simple. This means that such policies actually work (effective), do so at least cost (efficient), are fair to providers and beneficiaries (equitable), easily understood (transparent), and can be implemented at a reasonable cost (administratively simple). There are obviously tradeoffs among these criteria, but policies meeting the first three criteria are usually well-targeted. Targeting implies limiting the number of people affected by the policy but may impose additional costs of transparency and administrative simplicity. If these criteria are not taken into consideration, it is likely that policy failure will occur, or at least that alternative policies would work better.

Several policy implications can be drawn from economic analysis of the multifunctional nature of agriculture:

- There are both positive and negative externalities associated with agriculture production. It is desirable to internalize their effects, so that the negative effects are minimized and the positive effects maximized. This does not, of course, mean that the negative effects should be removed altogether—for example, agricultural production will inevitably involve some pollution. Nor does it mean that there should be no upper limit to the external benefits, as these will become increasing costly to provide, and at some point additional benefits will be unappreciated.
- In circumstances involving more than one objective, multiple instruments are required. For example, rather than using domestic support to influence the level of output, additional instruments are required to control pollution and to encourage the provision of rural amenities.
- Sound policies imply targeting the problem as accurately as possible. Controlling agricultural output may be one way of controlling nitrate emissions, for instance, but a better way is to regulate or tax emissions directly. In that way, farmers change farming practices to sustain production and still meet the pollution objective.

In some countries, input constraints have been used to control output: farmers may be limited to a given area. Area controls have been used in the U.S. for this purpose. This policy is effective in limiting output only so long as there is a fixed relationship between output and the limiting input (land, in this case). The typical response is for farmers to increase the use of inputs that are not limited and thus raise the yields substantially, undermining the policy objective.

In general, negative externalities are related to input use rather than output, in particular the use of fertilizer and chemicals. These pollutants can be controlled most effectively by focusing directly on the emissions. This would not be the case where inputs and outputs are in direct proportions, but usually there is scope to vary the mix of inputs to meet environmental objectives at minimum cost.

Measures that influence output, such as tariffs and other trade measures and output-related domestic support measures, are not the most effective instrument for tackling output-related positive or negative externalities. Environmental policies are needed to achieve environmental outcomes. This implies that to generate the optimal level of environmental benefits, a specific instrument is likely to be required, unless the externality is generated in fixed proportion to output. If apple blossoms are considered scenic, a subsidy should apply to the generation of blossoms and be related to their duration and beauty, and the location of admirers. There is little value in having scenery with nobody to behold it (although some gain satisfaction for just knowing that it is there; see "existence values" in box 8.1).

### *Three Multifunctional Outputs from Agriculture*

All industries have multifunctional benefits to some degree, but this does not imply they should all be subsidized. Some claim that agriculture is special or different in ways that justify government support. Three aspects of particular interest are environmental benefits, food security, and rural amenities. These are examined in more detail.

**Agriculture and Environmental Benefits** Agricultural production is inevitably associated with positive and negative environmental externalities or spillovers. The negative spillovers are familiar; they include nutrient and pesticide runoff, soil erosion, methane emissions, loss of biodiversity, noise, odor, and increased likelihood of flooding. Positive environmental externalities are less obvious but real nonetheless. These include scenic vistas, wildlife habitat, open spaces, recreational amenities, and opportunities for peace and solitude. One important attribute in countries with steep terrain is flood control (Japan Ministry of Foreign Affairs 2000). Some WTO members claim, for example, that rice paddies have an important function in preventing floods (Roberts, Podbury, and Hinchy 2001, p. 39).

A feature of these externalities is the absence of a market. One response of government may be to set up a market. This might involve, for example, licensing landowners to charge fees to those wishing to walk over their land. In this way land prices would more closely reflect their scenic value. Market-based solutions may not be the entire answer because nonuse values are hard to quantify (see box 8.1).

A second approach taken by governments may involve the payment of subsidies to encourage production of the externality. The problem here is that the government performs the function of the market, and there is some question as to how well it can provide the service where, when, and in the appropriate quantity that consumers desire and are willing to pay for. Switzerland provides scenic alpine landscapes, of value to locals and tourists alike, and these are enhanced by the presence of livestock. There is little point in providing a scenic agricultural landscape in a valley where there are few people to see it, or at a time when most consumers (tourists) are elsewhere, or in quantities that are too few or too great. If this were the case then governments could do better by subsidizing extensive livestock operations alongside railways and motorways.

**Agriculture and Food Security** Food security is an issue normally associated with developing countries where food supplies are inadequate because of low production or inability to import and distribute adequate amounts.[5] Perhaps somewhat surprisingly, food security is also an issue in developed countries that can readily afford to import much of the food they consume. Japan, the Republic of Korea, and Norway, for example, claim to be concerned that their supplies of imports may be disrupted because of wars, embargoes, price shocks, and perhaps, natural disasters.

Food security can be defined as a situation in which "all households have both physical and economic access to adequate food for all members, and where households are not at risk of losing such access" (FAO 1996). At the global level, food security is obviously a distributional issue. In spite of some 800 million malnourished individuals, there is enough grain produced to feed all the people in the world, as well as livestock. Furthermore, policies such as production quotas, schemes to set aside productive land, and taxes are in place in many countries to limit production.

Food security fits rather uncomfortably with the other multifunctional benefits of agriculture, such as environmental goods, for several reasons:

- Food security is not a nonfood item, which is what multifunctional outputs of agriculture are generally considered to be.
- It is questionable whether food security is a public good, with the properties of nonrivalry and nonexcludability, given that a functioning market exists.
- Food security is not a joint product with production, as it can be attained through trade and storage (Bohman and others 1999, p. 18).

Arguments in favor of domestic support to increase food production, and hence food security, emphasize the insurance aspect of maintaining the capacity to produce food domestically (Norway Ministry of Agriculture 2001). Taken to the extreme, evidence of self-sufficiency is obtained only when all consumption is domestically produced.

A second argument in favor of food security relates to the instability of international prices. For example, the Japanese view is that international prices of staple commodities are likely to become increasingly unstable with the El Niño effect on climate and increasing pressure on grain prices from population and income growth in developing countries (Japan Ministry of Foreign Affairs 2001).

The arguments against using domestic support to provide food security are along the lines that domestic production does not necessarily provide security, nor is it the best way to do so. Domestic production may be subject to disruption in the supply of imported inputs such as fuel, fertilizer, and chemicals that would limit the ability of countries to produce their own food in times of an embargo. Other means of achieving continuity in supplies include holding stocks and long-term contracts, and maintaining a diversity of suppliers. In the case of Japanese rice, in which the market for the favored Japonica rice grown in temperate climates is relatively thin, opening up the market would encourage suppliers to diversify into other production, thereby increasing market liquidity. A further strategy could be for wholesalers to have contracts directly with foreign producers, perhaps even jointly owning the production facilities.

**Agriculture and Rural Amenities** Some, perhaps most, countries place value on maintaining viable rural communities. This task is made more difficult by the exodus of labor from the agricultural sector, a secular decline that has been going on since the 1800s, when the industrial revolution made wages more attractive in industries located in urban areas. As farm consolidation occurs, rural populations fall and the demand for services is reduced. As services such as hospitals, schools, bus routes, and banks are reduced or removed, the local populations must find substitutes. At the extreme, rural areas may depopulate altogether and countries may be concerned about invasion from foreign powers. Populating the land is seen as a means of discouraging this (Norway Ministry of Agriculture 2001).

This natural decline in farm populations is viewed by some policymakers as detrimental, and they wish to subsidize agricultural production to reverse this development. It is likely that subsidizing agricultural output is a very indirect means of supporting rural communities, as most of the support goes to the large farmers. Even domestic support directed to inputs such as livestock and land, such as that provided in the EU, is relatively ineffective because 50 percent of it finds its way to only 17 percent of the EU's farmers—those with the largest capacity (ABARE 2000). And in the U.S., 9 percent of farms receive 41 percent of the government's support, according to ABARE.

If it is thought desirable to support rural communities, the most appropriate means is to directly provide missing services. This may mean governments subsidizing medical practitioners in remote rural areas, providing infrastructure for wireless telephony (mobile phones), facilitating Internet banking, and perhaps subsidizing or cross-subsidizing transport services. Such policies can be targeted to the specific areas that need assistance.

Another approach is to encourage rural employment. Agricultural support encourages agricultural output, but its impact on employment is lessened by capital-labor substitution and increasing productivity. In many heavily populated developed countries—for example, Japan and the EU countries—rural communities are not highly dependent on agricultural incomes, as off-farm incomes are a high proportion of total incomes. The share of agricultural employment in predominantly rural regions ranges from 2 percent in Germany to 8 percent in Norway, 11 percent in France, and 14 percent in Japan (Bohman and others 1999, p. 19).

The relatively small share of agricultural employment may be due to the proximity of urban employment opportunities. Governments can encourage the location of nonagricultural industries in particular rural areas through regulation or the provision of infrastructure. As technology changes work habits in countries, the need for physical proximity in many occupations is lessening. As branch offices are replaced by technology call centers, the need to place employees in a specific location is reduced. In rural areas there is a natural subsidy available to industry through low-cost rent on housing and office accommodations, but the need for high quality transport and communications is paramount. Governments have a role in facilitating the provision of this infrastructure. Social infrastructure, such as education, training, and health, will help agricultural workers to find employment in other industries in rural areas.

Thus far the main characteristics of multifunctionality—environmental benefits, food security, and rural viability—have been discussed. Some claim that there are additional benefits, including cultural and heritage values (TAED 2000). These will not be discussed here explicitly; suffice to say that the principles relating to their provision by governments are similar to those covered above in the context of the main benefits.

## Implications and Conclusions

National sovereignty is a fundamental right of WTO members. This provides members with the right to choose the nature of their agricultural policy objectives, with the proviso, agreed among members, that the policies to achieve these objectives are non-trade-distorting. In the run-up to the current round of multilateral trade negotiations, several developed countries began emphasizing the need for output-supporting policies to ensure that the external benefits of agriculture were provided in sufficient quantities. These external benefits, by their nature difficult to measure, include environmental goods, food security, rural development, and other less concrete externalities such as cultural and heritage values. And as noted above, coincidentally or otherwise, members in favor of multifunctionality—Japan, the Republic of Korea, Norway, Switzerland, and countries of the EU—are those with high levels of government support for agriculture.

Opponents of multifunctionality maintain that claims for the existence of the difficult-to-measure external benefits of agriculture are merely a pretext for additional support. Furthermore, they maintain that these claims represent a substantial threat to further trade reform, that negative externalities should also be considered, and that there are better ways of providing the public goods that people want. Indeed, the WTO has provision for such policies (that is, the green box) and many such polices are already being used (Freeman and Roberts 1999, p. 5).

In analyzing the competing claims, perhaps the major issue is the degree of jointness: the extent to which output of agriculture and provision of the externality is jointly produced. If the requirement was solely to generate the benefit, would it be necessary to produce the same level of agricultural output as at present? If the degree of jointness is somewhat weak, a policy targeting the external benefit specifically will very likely be superior.

A second issue is the valuation of the benefits, as this determines the quantity to be provided. Although by their nature externalities are difficult to measure in the absence of market valuations, measures to encourage the provision of the benefits should be in proportion to the likely gains. For example, it may not be sound policy to subsidize all of agriculture forever to help prevent a flood once in a lifetime or a price spike in a commodity once every 50 years.

Developing countries have long been concerned about limited access to developed-country markets because subsidized agriculture reduces market opportunities. Support to agriculture in OECD countries amounted to US$327 billion in 2000, more than half the farm-gate value of production (OECD 2002). In many cases, the subsidies exceed the value added. Estimates by ABARE suggest that developing countries would enjoy static welfare gains of US$14 billion from a 50 percent reduction in agricultural support levels and are likely to enjoy more stable world prices (Freeman and Roberts 1999, p. 38). While all modeling results should be used with caution, it can be said that developing countries as a group are likely to be disadvantaged if the concept of multifunctionality leads to much agricultural support in some developed countries being reassigned into the green box in a way that locks in existing distortions in their potential markets.

Multifunctional benefits apply to all industries and have done so for many years. Sound policy involves identifying those benefits and seeing that they are supplied in the right quantities, in the right places, and at the right time.

## Notes

1. Food safety covered under the Sanitary and Phytosanitary Measures (known as the "SPS agreement") is not strictly a multifunctionality issue, although some commentators regard it as such. This issue is addressed later.

2. See also chapter 9.

3. See also chapter 11.

4. The Abler (2001) and Burrell (2001) studies quoted above use this analytical framework to provide an empirical assessment.

5. See also chapter 9.

## Select Bibliography

ABARE (Australian Bureau of Agricultural and Resource Economics). 2000. "US and EU Agricultural Support: Who Does It Benefit?" Current Issues 2000.2, Canberra.

Abler, D. 2001. "A Synthesis of Country Reports on Jointness between Commodity and Non-Commodity Outputs in OECD Agriculture." Paper presented at the Workshop on Multifunctionality, OECD Directorate for Food, Agriculture and Fisheries, July 2–3, Paris.

Bohman, M., J. Cooper, D. Mullarkey, M. A. Normile, D. Skully, S. Vogel, and E. Young. 1999. "The Use and Abuse of Multifunctionality." Economic Research Service, USDA, Washington, D.C.

Burrell, A. 2001. "Synthesis of the Evidence on the Possible Impact of Commodity Price Decreases on Land Use and Commodity Production, and the Incidence on the Provision of Non-Commodity Outputs." Paper presented at the Workshop on Multifunctionality, OECD Directorate for Food, Agriculture and Fisheries, Workshop on Multifunctionality, July 2–3, Paris.

FAO (Food and Agriculture Organization of the United Nations). 1996. "World Food Summit: Technical Background Document No. 12." World Food Summit, 13–17 November. FAO, Rome.

Freeman, F., and I. Roberts. 1999. "Multifunctionality: A Pretext for Protection?" Australian Bureau of Agricultural and Resource Economics (ABARE), Current Issues 1999.3, Canberra.

Japan Ministry of Foreign Affairs. 2000. "Negotiating Proposal by Japan on WTO Agricultural Negotiations." Committee on Agriculture Special Session. www.mofa.go.jp.

Norway Ministry of Agriculture. 2001. "Coexistence in a World of Agricultural Diversity—The Right of Every Country to Safeguard Non-Trade Concerns." Paper presented at the International Conference on Non-Trade Concerns in Agriculture, May 28–31, Mauritius. http://odin.dep.no.

OECD (Organisation for Economic Co-operation and Development). 2000. "Valuing Rural Amenities—Territorial Economy." Workshop Proceedings, June 5–6, Paris.

———. 2001. "Multifunctionality: Towards an Analytical Framework." OECD Directorate for Food, Agriculture and Fisheries, Workshop on Multifunctionality, July 2–3, Paris. www.oecd.org.

———. 2002. *Agricultural Policies in OECD Countries: Monitoring and Evaluation 2001.* Paris: OECD.

Podbury, Troy. 2000. "US and EU Agricultural Support: Who Does It Benefit?" Australian Bureau of Agricultural and Resource Economics (ABARE) Current Issues 2000.2, Canberra.

Raney, T., and J. Tschirley. 1999. "Environment, Trade and SARD: Concepts, Issues and Tools, Cultivating Our Futures Background Paper 4." Paper prepared for The FAO/Netherlands Conference on "The Multifunctional Character of Agriculture and Land (MFCAL)." September 12–18, Maastricht, The Netherlands. www.fao.org.

Roberts, I., T. Podbury, and M. Hinchy. 2001. "Reforming Domestic Agricultural Support Policies through the WTO." ABARE Research Report 2001.2, RIRDC Publication no. 01/07, Canberra.

TAED (Transatlantic Environmental Dialogue). 2000. "World Trade, Production and Multifunctionality." Prepared by the Food and Agriculture Working Group. www.tiesweb.org

WTO (World Trade Organization). 2002a. "Negotiating Proposal by Mauritius." G/AG/NG/W/90. Office of the Secretary General, Geneva.

———. 2002b. "EC Comprehensive Negotiating Proposal." G/AG/NG/W/90. Office of the Secretary General, Geneva.

———. 2002c. "WTO Agriculture Negotiations: The Issues, and Where We Are Now." Office of the Secretary General, Geneva.

9

# FOOD SECURITY AND AGRICULTURAL TRADE POLICY REFORM

*Merlinda D. Ingco, Donald Mitchell, and John D. Nash*

## Introduction

Article 20 of the Uruguay Round Agreement on Agriculture (URAA), and the paragraphs of the Doha Declaration dealing with the present negotiations on agriculture focus on the continuation of reforms begun in the Uruguay Round, with "the long-term objective of substantial progressive reductions in support and protection." Of the objectives and concerns mentioned in the URAA's Preamble, Article 20 refers specifically to "non-trade concerns, special and differential treatment to developing country Members, and the objective to establish a fair and market-oriented agricultural trading system." Paragraph 13 of the Doha Declaration elaborates on these points and confirms that all three considerations will figure in the new negotiations.

## The Plan of This Chapter

This chapter considers the objective of food security, one of the cluster of objectives collectively referred to as "nontrade concerns." It first looks at several conceptual levels of "food security" and examines how they have been or might be affected by multilateral trade reforms. It next examines more concretely and empirically the question of whether and to what extent the URAA has had the effect—as some allege—of reducing the food security of some least-developed and net food-importing countries by structurally raising the cost of food imports. The chapter finally considers what alternatives might be useful to reduce vulnerability to shocks that threaten food security, whether the shocks originate from trade policy reforms or other sources. In particular, it considers whether there are ways in which trade rules can be developed to offset the possible harmful effects, especially in developing countries; or whether there are additional international actions that can be taken (either in the context of the World Trade Organization [WTO] negotiations or elsewhere) that would contribute to greater food security for these countries.

## Whose Food Security?

Among all the "nontrade concerns," the issue of food security is by far the most frequently mentioned. This is especially true of developing countries, but a significant number of developed countries also mention it.[1]

Food security can be addressed at several levels: food security of the individual or family, national food security, and international food security.

### *Individual and Family Food Security*

Although the issue is not often framed in this way, the most important level at which long-term structural food insecurity occurs is the household.[2] Hundreds of millions of individuals, largely in developing countries, lack food security. The fundamental cause of this is poverty, that is, inadequacy of buying power. There are ample supplies of food in global markets to feed the poor, and a well-established trading system to ensure that it gets to areas where there is demand. If the poor had sufficient incomes, this would translate into effective demand, and food insecurity would not be a problem except in certain transitory situations, discussed later in the chapter.

Poverty in urban areas is due to scarcity of employment opportunities and lack of human capital to earn an income sufficient to purchase an adequate diet. In rural areas, which still account for the bulk of employment in most developing countries, poverty is due to the lack of productive resources, poor technology, and inadequate infrastructure, coupled with the need to use marginal land that often suffers from inadequate rainfall and other natural disasters. Civil strife, ethnic violence, and corrupt or ineffective public institutions sometimes compound these problems. Moreover, in many cases government policies exacerbate poverty in rural areas by holding down internal prices of food and agricultural products via the use of state trading enterprises, export taxes, and overvalued exchange rates.

Seen in this light, long-term structural food insecurity exists primarily because of a demand-side problem—lack of purchasing power by the poor—and must be addressed by raising incomes. Global trade negotiations can affect food security in two ways. First, if the agreements result in a structural supply shift that increases the average price of food, this could increase the long-term incidence of food insecurity by causing more of the poor to be unable to purchase an adequate supply of food, or to do so only at the cost of diverting so much of their income into food that they have inadequate income remaining to meet their other basic needs. Such a structural supply shift could also increase food insecurity by increasing the budgetary requirement of any government or privately-funded safety net programs that provide food to the needy. This possibility is discussed later in the chapter.

The second channel through which the negotiations could affect food security is through their effect on the policies and conditions that alleviate poverty, that is, policies aimed at economic development—especially rural development—and targeted programs of poverty alleviation to increase the buying power of those most at risk. The question that must therefore be answered is whether the URAA or further reforms that are likely in the new trade negotiations tend to inhibit or encourage these kinds of policies.

A strong case can be made that further reforms that remove support and protection that distorts international agricultural markets will provide strong positive support for the necessary national policies needed to increase rural development and economic growth in developing countries. This is true for two reasons.

First, most of the major distortions in world agricultural markets arising from protection and supports occur in developed countries. This has two adverse impacts on developing countries. For food-exporting developing countries, access to markets is limited, and the prices of their products in international markets are depressed by unfair competition from developed-country export practices. At the same time, developing countries that are not food exporters face international price signals that undervalue their internal production and may provide serious disincentives for necessary investment in their agricultural development. Moreover, these international policies that adversely affect markets unwittingly support the flawed policies of developing countries that tax, rather than support, their agricultural sectors. While there is good evidence that the URAA did not have as large an impact in disciplining the use of these policies as intended, one result of successful current negotiations will be to reform these policies of developed countries, which will certainly improve incomes in rural areas in the developing countries.

Second, careful examination of the policies that were disciplined by the URAA—namely export subsidies, certain kinds of domestic support, and market access barriers—and that will be further disciplined in the new round, suggests that the new agreement is not likely to discourage developing countries from adopting policies that would foster rural development and poverty reduction.

The URAA prevents all countries that did not declare the use of export subsidies during the base period (1986–90) from introducing subsidies in the future. However, these subsidies represent a policy that makes food available to foreign buyers at a lower price than to a country's own population. It is hard, therefore, to see how a policy of using export subsidies would be an optimal development policy in poor developing countries. In addition, the fiscal cost of significant subsidies is beyond the fiscal capacity of most developing-country governments. The case against export subsidies is strengthened by the fact that expenditures on export infrastructure and internal transport costs—which have many benefits in addition to lowering export costs—are exempt from export subsidy limits for developing countries.

Likewise, URAA constraints placed on domestic support to agriculture do not inhibit sound rural development policies in developing countries. Of the three categories of domestic support defined in the URAA, green box support measures are those considered least-trade-distorting. They include spending on general agricultural services including research, education, and payments to producers not tied to current production. At present, there are no limits to the expenditures that can be made in the green box category, although certain countries have called for some limits to the level of decoupled direct payments that can be made to farmers. However, even if such limits were adopted, they should not reduce the policy options of developing countries, which generally do not use such direct payments to producers because they are both expensive and difficult to administer. Possible changes to domestic support measures in the blue box are even less relevant to developing countries. It is difficult to imagine that developing countries facing food supply constraints would adopt such production-control policies that reward producers for limiting production.

The remaining category of trade-distorting domestic support is the one classified in the URAA as the amber box. These are commodity-specific subsidies that support internal prices, are paid on the basis of prices, subsidize commodity-specific inputs, and otherwise distort the incentives to produce and consume specific products. In general, they are not appropriate policies for rural development. They are also extremely inadequate tools for poverty alleviation, since payments are proportional to output or input use and therefore are greatest for large farmers and leave out the poorest (landless laborers) entirely.

Apart from the fact that such domestic support policies are not good policies for rural development and poverty alleviation, there are good reasons to believe that developing countries have not been constrained in their use of amber box measures. Countries were required to declare the level of amber box support they were using during the base period and were required to reduce their aggregate expenditures on subsidies in this category by the end of the URAA implementation period. Developing countries had few amber box subsidies to declare. The small number of developing countries providing some subsidies classified as amber box did not have to make reductions as large as those required of developed countries, and were allowed to make their cuts over a longer period—of up to 10 years. In addition, a *de minimis* exemption was included that exempted product-specific support by developing countries if it did not exceed 10 percent of the value of total agricultural production (compared with 5 percent of the value of production for developing countries). Least-developed countries (LDCs) were not required to make reduction commitments.

It is sometimes asserted that tariffs are preferable to domestic support as a way of encouraging agricultural sector growth in developing countries, since these countries cannot afford the kinds of subsidies given to farmers in developed countries. The argument usually proceeds that the URAA did not provide developing countries sufficient flexibility in this regard. However, it is not clear that poor consumers in these countries can "afford" to pay higher prices any more than the governments can "afford" to pay farmers directly. Like subsidies, and for the same reasons, tariffs are a poor and untargeted policy for rural development and poverty alleviation. In any case, tariffs also were not well-disciplined by the URAA because of the large margin between the bound and applied rates in developing-country tariffs (see chapter 4).

In summary, it is difficult to make a case that the URAA rules on domestic support impose constraints on the ability of developing countries to push forward with policies and programs that will promote agricultural growth, improve agricultural incomes, and thus contribute to a significant increase in food security at the personal and family levels, especially in rural areas.

In the new round, a number of developing countries have suggested that a development box be established. While this might be necessary or desirable (the question is discussed further in chapter 14), clear analysis is needed regarding what a development box could include that is not permitted under the present green box rules, in combination with the higher *de minimis* rules and other special and differential treatment given to developing countries by the URAA.

Stronger arguments may exist for revisiting the WTO rules on notification of existing subsidies by developing countries, and for promulgating rules that would prevent the unintended imposition of real limits on policies by domestic inflation and currency fluctuations, outside the sphere of agricultural policy. But the major implication for negotiations of this view of structural food security—that it is mainly a household level issue—is that food security concerns are best addressed in the negotiations through a focus on ensuring that green box agricultural support measures and targeted poverty programs are not constrained.

### *National Food Security*

Most discussions of food security are focused on food security at the national level, not at the individual level. Food security at the national level concerns having an adequate total food supply to enable the population of the country on average to maintain a reasonable level of consumption. (See box 9.1 on Food Security Indicators that are considered proxies for measures of food security at the national level.) This approach to food security is not focused on internal income distribution or individual food security. What is often obscured by looking at food security in this way is that under normal circumstances—barring war, natural disasters, artificial barriers to trade, and macroeconomic disruptions sufficiently severe to impede imports—if individual households have adequate purchasing power, national food security follows automatically.

Households of course can purchase food of either domestic or foreign origin. However, there is a tendency for governments, especially in countries with large populations, to believe that they can only

**BOX 9.1 Food Security Indicators**

Food security can be analyzed at the global, regional, national, household, or individual level. The focus of this chapter is at the national level, which is the level at which World Trade Organization (WTO) negotiating categories are defined. In a study done by International Food Policy Research Institute (IFPRI), "Food Security and Trade Negotiations in the World Trade Organization: A Cluster Analysis of Country Groups," the authors describe key indicators of food security that are considered proxies for three measures of food security at the national level: food availability, access, and utilization. The indicators are summarized below

(a) *Food production per capita* is a measure of a country's ability to feed its population. The Food and Agriculture Organization (FAO) defines this variable as the total food production in every year multiplied by the 1989–91 world price in U.S. dollars, divided by the total population of the corresponding year. The definition of food is the one provided by the FAO Statistical Database.

(b) *The ratio of total exports to food imports* is a measure of a country's ability to finance its food imports from its total export revenues. The ratio of the cost of food import to the value of total exports is a more accurate food security indicator than the net food trade position, which is determined by subtracting a country's total food imports from its food exports.

(c) *Calories per capita and protein per capita* are used to estimate consumption levels and therefore food availability at the national level. It is understood that national averages are limited in reflecting household and individual food and nutrition security levels. However, national calorie-aggregates are important in explaining changes in malnutrition as defined by anthropometrical measures of children.

(d) *Nonagricultural population* is used to analyze the nonagricultural sector in assessing how a country may be affected by changes in trade and agricultural policies and the potential distributive impact on the urban/rural population. This indicator, however, is not as straightforward in its implications as the others.

achieve food security in the national sense by maintaining a high degree of self-sufficiency in all of the basic foodstuffs. The argument is that the demands of their populations are so great that food imports are in some sense more costly than domestic production. While the rationale is seldom made explicit, this line of thinking could have two possible bases. One is that the shadow value (social value) of foreign exchange is higher than its market value. This was undoubtedly true in many countries in the past, when currency controls caused major distortions in foreign exchange markets, but is not an issue in the overwhelming majority of countries today. A second possible rationale is that the elasticity of supply of basic foodstuffs is higher in these countries with large populations than it is in the major food-exporting countries. Many developing countries with large populations have, however, already extended agricultural production to less favorable areas, and often have less developed infrastructure and support to expand agricultural output. It is clear that for these countries, the pursuit of food security via self-sufficiency will be an expensive route to food security.

Governments hoping to achieve food security via self-sufficiency generally want to maintain high border protection and high internal prices to encourage increased domestic output. This, however, has some adverse impacts on the food security of at least some groups.

First, the consumers of the country pay a consistently higher price for the products, undermining the food security of the poor by reducing their purchasing power. This acts as a regressive tax, since the proportion of income spent on food is inversely related to income. Consequently, poorer consumers tend to be hit hardest by the higher prices. This is especially troubling in light of evidence that there may be a shift in poverty to urban areas (Haddad, Ruel, and Garrett 1999; Garrett and Ruel 2000), and that the poorest of the poor in rural areas are landless laborers. Neither the urban poor nor landless laborers derive any benefit from the higher food prices, so clearly their structural food security is adversely affected by such policies.

But second, even many members of the farming community may be hurt or at best not be helped by protectionist measures. The poorest farmers in the developing world are subsistence farmers, and these by definition have no marketable surplus and therefore do not benefit from higher prices. Farmers in the commercial sector who are in a position to grow the staples may benefit in the short run. But even they may lose out from the protection of these crops in the long run because of the disincentives this creates for diversifying into nontraditional exports, which may be a better road to escape from poverty (Christiaensen, Demery, and Paternostro 2002; Kherallah and others 2000). Diversion of resources from export production also reduces the long-term foreign exchange earning capacity of the country and thereby undermines its structural capacity to import food and other products. And finally, supporting the agricultural sector through trade protection diverts attention from methods of support that in the long run could be more productive. Simulations in a computable general equilibrium (CGE) world model by the IFPRI (Diaz-Bonilla, Diao, and Robinson 2003) of the alternative of raising cereal tariffs by half in different groups of developing countries (mostly net food-importers), versus transforming the mainly implicit and privately collected tax on consumption in the first scenario into an equivalent explicit tax, and investing that money in agricultural research, found the latter to be enormously more beneficial in increasing employment, income, and consumption in general—including, particularly, food.

While it is clear that policies aiming to increase self-sufficiency are in many ways counterproductive to the goal of structural food security, other justifications for policies to increase self-sufficiency are based on more short-term concerns—disruptions to trade from hostile actions of other countries or from barriers to exports imposed by the exporting countries themselves in times of international shortages or high prices. Such concerns tend to be exaggerated; serious trade disruption would require concerted action by a large number of competitive exporters, which is most unlikely. The effects of temporary disruptions could also be mitigated through other measures—stockpiling of reserves, for example—that would be much less costly than efforts to achieve self-sufficiency. But in any case, the preoccupation with self-sufficiency has diverted attention from the question of how the trading system could be used to prevent these short-term concerns. Too little attention has been given to the obligations of food-exporting countries to make supplies available to all food-importing countries without export restrictions, taxes, or other discriminatory policies. This issue has been raised in the context of the current negotiations, and its resolution could give some comfort to countries concerned about disruptions and therefore make them more amenable to shifting their focus away from self-sufficiency.

More attention should also be given to the special problems of developing countries that may have difficulties in meeting their food import bills because of unusual increases in import requirements or because of increases in agricultural commodity prices, either cyclical or longer-term structural increases. This latter issue underlies the Marrakesh Decision on "Measures Concerning the Possible Negative Effects of the Reform Programme on Least-Developed and Net Food-Importing Developing Countries," discussed later in this chapter. The implementation—or lack thereof—of this Decision has increased the concern of many developing countries and may drive their policies even further in the direction of expensive attempts at national food self-sufficiency. However, it is not clear that WTO agricultural negotiations are the forum in which to address this issue in a definitive way. The WTO is neither a multilateral financial institution nor an international development assistance agency. Attempts to address the problem within the context of the WTO are likely to lead to frustration and/or further problems, with the implementation of agreements falling outside the WTO's purview.

Finally, while not a food security issue *per se,* the related argument that cyclically low commodity prices or import surges can damage the relatively fragile agricultural structure in developing countries may have some weight and is examined separately (chapter 10). A relevant issue would be whether such a mechanism should be available only to developing countries in the name of food security, or on a broader basis.

### *International Food Security*

The concept of international food security is rarely if ever discussed, yet it may be the most important element of national food security.

International food security means that the aggregate supply of food produced in the world is adequate to provide sufficient calories to feed the world population at levels consistent with their demands. Periodically agricultural commodity prices rise substantially, notwithstanding a secular downward trend. Whenever this occurs, there is concern about the ability of the world's agricultural producers and the resources they command to continue to meet world demand at constant or declining real prices. Land and water resources available for agricultural production are finite. However, the output from those resources has steadily increased with the development and adoption of new technology, greater investment, and improved human resource skills engaged in agricultural production.

Global food security depends on the continued increase in the efficiency with which global agricultural resources are used, on continued market incentives to develop and adopt improved technology, and on continued public investments in the necessary institutions to support sustained agricultural growth. Further reduction of the major distortions in agricultural markets can undoubtedly make a significant contribution to the continued achievement of global food security in two ways. First, it can encourage distribution of production among countries based on true comparative advantage. Second, trade barriers that inhibit the spread of new technologies that are embedded in agricultural inputs can significantly reduce global food security in the long term, and these barriers to technology diffusion should be dismantled through successful negotiations.

## Aftermath of the URAA: The Marrakesh Decision

The Decision on "Measures Concerning the Possible Negative Effects of the Reform Programme on Least-Developed and Net Food-Importing Developing Countries" was adopted by the Ministerial conference in Marrakesh in 1994 that concluded the Uruguay Round. It was intended to respond to the fears of the LDCs, as well as of a number of other developing countries that are net importers of food (NFIDCs), that subsidy cuts imposed on their food suppliers by the URAA reforms would have the effect of raising the price of their food imports. The requirements of the Marrakesh Decision focus on regular review of food aid commitments and flows, the adoption of guidelines to ensure that food aid is given in grant form or on appropriate concessional terms, and technical assistance. Motivated in particular by a spike in grain prices in the mid-1990s, there was a proposal by 16 LDCs and NFIDCs for the establishment of a revolving fund to help meet short-term difficulties in financing normal levels of commercial imports. This proposed fund was intended to fulfill the terms of the Marrakesh Decision. The proposal would establish a countercyclical subsidy mechanism whereby food and financial aid are automatically triggered by commodity price increases owing to agricultural trade liberalization agreed to under the Uruguay Round. In this context, it is useful to examine retrospectively the evidence on the effects of the URAA on world food prices.

Research into the real and potential effects of trade liberalization on world grain prices leads to five important conclusions, summarized below.

### *Cereal Import Prices for NFIDCs and LDCs Have Not Risen Significantly during the 1990s*

The proposal for a revolving fund was based on the contention that NFIDCs and LDCs are facing much higher cereal import prices following the URAA, and that these higher prices are due to the agreement. The basis of this is a comparison of cereal import prices during 1993–94 with 1995–96, and the attribution of the change to the URAA. Cereal prices were low during 1993–94 and high during 1995–96, as table 9.1 shows. However, prices have declined since 1996 and average import prices are now below the levels of 1993–94 for the LDCs and slightly above for the low-income food-deficit countries.

### *The Evidence Does Not Support the Argument That Cereal Prices Rose during 1995–96 Because of the URAA*

Cereal prices rose in 1995 and 1996 primarily because of low world grain stocks, which followed from a 3.2 percent decline in world production in 1995–96 (see figure 9.1). Because of a poor United States (U.S.) harvest, cereal stock relative to use fell to an unusually low level at the end of the 1995–96 marketing year (13.4 percent compared to an average of 18.8 percent in the previous five years). High fertilizer prices and strong economic growth

**TABLE 9.1 Average Cereal Prices (US$/ton)**

| | 1993–94 | 1995–96 | Price Difference 95–96 vs 93–94 | 1997–1999 | Price Difference 97–99 vs 93–94 |
|---|---|---|---|---|---|
| Low-Income Food Deficit | 175.3 | 229.5 | 30.9 | 193.0 | 10.1 |
| Least-Developed Countries | 224.9 | 252.1 | 12.1 | 203.0 | −9.7 |
| Developing Countries | 180.6 | 229.7 | 27.1 | 181.3 | 0.3 |
| Trade Weighted Cereal Price (free on board) | 137.1 | 184.4 | 34.5 | 125.7 | −8.3 |

*Source:* World Bank Databases.

**FIGURE 9.1 Cereal Import Costs per Ton**

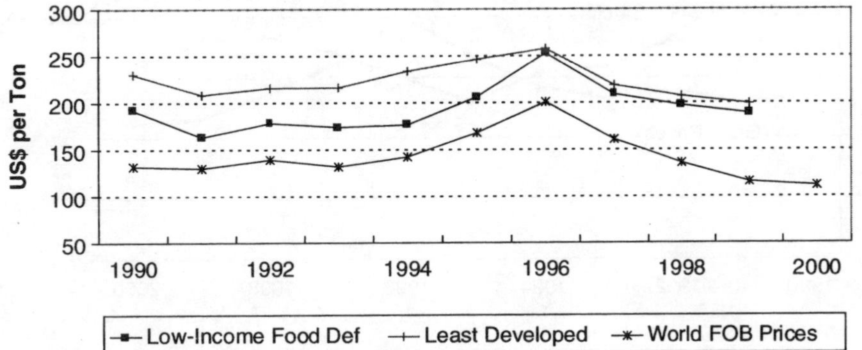

during that period contributed to the sharp price increases. Stock levels recovered in 1996 and continued to increase through 1998, driving world cereal prices lower. The URAA was not directly related to the price increases during 1995 and 1996, nor the price declines since. The fact that grain import bills in some countries continue to be higher despite the price declines is another indicator that trade liberalization is not the cause.

It is, of course, possible that the URAA increased food prices relative to what they would have been in its absence, even though they fell relative to past levels. That is, it may be true that without the URAA, prices would have fallen further than they in fact did. This is plausible, but even by this standard of comparison, price "increases" attributable to the URAA are estimated to be quite small. One estimate suggests that enough liberalization was achieved in wheat, for example, to raise estimated world wheat prices by only 3.8 percent (Goldin and van der Mensbrugghe 1996, p. 169). By contrast, the same study estimated that the prices of coarse grains and sugar would rise by only around 2 percent, and dairy products by a little over 1 percent. For a number of other agricultural commodities, including rice and cotton, the study estimates that there was so little overall liberalization that prices would actually fall relative to the prices of manufactures exports.

One reason for this limited impact on food prices is that the URAA did not achieve a great deal of agricultural liberalization. While it achieved an enormous amount in terms of establishing rules, the liberalization that it achieved was much less than the target cuts in protection included in the agreement, for reasons discussed elsewhere in this volume.

### *Real Cereal Prices Have Shown a Strong Secular Declining Trend*

Primarily because of the tremendous increase in productivity and yields in the past decades, the long-run prices of cereals (at least wheat and rice) have shown a downward trend. Real prices of cereals are near extremely low levels as figure 9.2 shows.

### *Prices Are Unlikely to Increase in the Near Term*

The failure of the Uruguay Round to achieve substantial agricultural liberalization implies that much is left to be done, so a successful current round of negotiations could potentially achieve a great deal of liberalization, which in turn could potentially raise world agricultural prices. Yet the impact is likely to be felt only gradually and in the medium term. The round itself is scheduled to be concluded only in 2005, and it appears likely that any significant steps in sensitive areas such as agriculture would be phased in over an even longer period. Other structural supply and demand shifters are also at work, the net impact of which is difficult to predict. But judging from the experience of the last decades, it would appear likely that these will operate to depress prices. In addition, to the extent that trade barriers have been reduced (or will be reduced in the future), this implies reduced world price variability and therefore better ability to plan and to hedge against price hikes.

**FIGURE 9.2 World Grain Stocks and Price, 1990–2000**

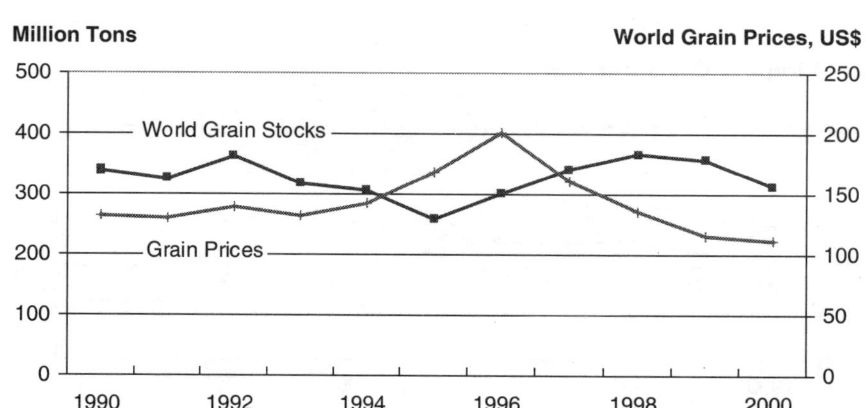


*Source:* World Bank Databases.

### *Research Suggests That Multilateral Trade Liberalization Produces Benefits to Net Food-Importing Countries That in Some Cases Offset the Costs from Higher Food Prices*

Several World Bank studies that examined the impacts of Uruguay Round liberalization on least-developed and net food-importing countries focused on the impacts of round-induced changes in external prices on these countries.[3] These studies divided the impacts of changes in world prices into two components—terms-of-trade effects and distortion impacts. The terms-of-trade effects of liberalization are well known and have frequently featured in policy discussions, but the distortion impacts have only received attention in a small number of studies,[4] none of which focused on the least-developed and net food-importing countries.

The terms-of-trade impacts resulting from changes in world prices are relatively straightforward. They are the impacts of changes in world prices on the costs of net food imports, or the benefits obtained from net exports. For a net importer, an increase in prices will raise costs, with the size of the additional cost depending on the level of imports. For a net exporter, an increase in prices will increase returns, with the magnitude of the benefits depending on the level of net exports. The distortion impacts are more complex, because they depend on the nature of an entire array of policy distortions in the economy. They arise from the impact of changes in world prices on the extent to which countries undertake activities that are worth less (or more) than their true costs. If, for example, a country has an export tax on a particular commodity, the resulting depressed domestic prices will lead producers to produce less of the good than is socially optimal, and consumers to consume more than is socially optimal. Both increases in production and reductions in consumption of such a good will make the country better off. A rise in the world price of this export good will, assuming it is passed on to the domestic market, lead to such a net gain. An increase in the import bill (caused, for example, by an increase in import prices) may contribute to an exchange rate depreciation, which will have the same kind of effect in the market for this export, tending to offset the adverse terms-of-trade effect for the country from the higher import prices.

A key finding of the studies is that the distortion impacts, which have typically been ignored in the past, can be extremely important in least-developed and net food-importing countries. One of the studies, which covers a wide range of low-income and net food-importing countries, shows that in a number of cases, including Bangladesh, the Arab Republic of Egypt, and Tanzania, the distortion effects operated in the opposite direction to the terms-of-trade impacts, and converted an apparent negative impact of the URAA into a substantially larger gain.[5] The distortion impacts are extremely complex however, and sometimes worked against the country. In India, for example, the distortion impacts were negative, primarily because the world prices of some its commodities on which the country's own policies imposed a net tax, such as rice and cotton, were estimated to fall. These price declines reduced India's output of these commodities, which was already too low because of the use of export restrictions. On the other hand, in Kenya and Zimbabwe the distortion effects greatly reinforced an initial gain from the changed terms of trade.

Overall, the results of these studies suggest that the policy-related impacts increased the gains from the URAA to most low-income and net food-importing countries. However, the impacts in any future liberalization will clearly depend on the specific nature of the agricultural policies used in the country and on the impacts on world prices of the resulting liberalization.

The overall conclusion from the above points, taken together, is that any substantial increase in international agricultural prices that could potentially result from the international agreements (a) has not occurred yet, (b) is probably a number of years away, and (c) could well be offset by other economic factors at work in the meantime. Furthermore, any losses to net food-importing countries would not be uniform across countries, and may be partially or completely offset in individual countries by other gains from the overall agreement.

## Measures to Ameliorate the Impact of Shocks That Threaten Food Security

Apart from the long-term structural food security issues on which previous sections of this chapter focused, transitory food insecurity at the household level can arise because of shocks on either the demand or supply side, or both. Wars, political disturbances, economic crises, or natural disasters may temporarily disrupt the income-earning capacity of the population (demand side), as well as productive capacity and commercial channels for delivering food (supply side). Short-term but dramatic spikes in international food prices may also disrupt import channels by exhausting the lines of credit of importers. In the section below, the existing and potential mechanisms for dealing with this kind of shock are examined.

### *IMF and World Bank Facilities*

The IMF's Compensatory Financing Facility (CFF) is the only international mechanism that is specifically designed to help alleviate adverse effects of certain commodities' price movements that result in balance-of-payments difficulties. This facility was used by only four countries during 1993–99. A number of developing countries have noted that the CFF has several shortcomings,[6] including limited commodity coverage (the only import commodities that are eligible are grains), perceived requirements of "policy conditionality," and the lack of concessionality in terms. With respect to the last point, it is worth noting that the terms are almost certainly better than commercial terms, though not as good as those of the IMF's concessional facilities. Perhaps a more relevant criticism in the context of a discussion of food security is that the loan is taken by the government, and without some additional internal distribution mechanism, the benefits may not be shared with the individuals within the country whose food security is put at risk by the high food prices. This may then require that the government rely on direct distribution to needy individuals, which undermines the development of efficient private marketing channels. Nonetheless, use of the facility could at a minimum reduce the magnitude of the disruption of imports and increase the aggregate supply of food in a country.

Most of the World Bank's lending and nonlending services are aimed at the root cause of long-term food insecurity: poverty. Some investment projects are also aimed at improving trade and distribution facilities, or improving a country's trade finance infrastructure, thereby reducing vulnerability to disruptions of imports. The World Bank has no facilities that are specifically designed to help countries cope with price shocks, as is the CFF, but it does have several instruments to provide urgent assistance when a country is struck by an emergency that seriously dislocates its economy and calls for a quick response. Several types of emergency loans, as well as adjustment loans, work by quickly disbursing funds to a government's budget, thereby making foreign exchange available for additional food imports. This mechanism shares most of the shortcomings and the advantages of the CFF, though the trigger is not intended to be price movements.

### *Commodity Price Risk Management Measures*

A wide range of instruments is now available commercially to protect against price movements in the short term. Options can be used by economic agents with large exposure to risk from price movements either to lock in a specific price or to ensure that price will not be greater (or lower) than a specified level. These could be readily used by large purchasers of foodstuffs—either private sector commercial importers or government agents (food corporations or state-owned enterprises). They could also be used by governments to insulate safety nets (that is, targeted poverty programs such as food stamps) from budgetary crises arising from food price increases. In other words, a government agency that knows that its expenditures will increase when food prices rise (either because it provides food in-kind and must procure the higher-priced food itself, or because it must give higher income support to the poor) can purchase options that would pay out when import prices increase beyond a certain level. This would then ensure that a country would have the budgetary resources required without creating an unanticipated fiscal burden on the government. The price insurance would protect against short-term fluctuations in price, but not against long-term downward trends.

The International Task Force on Commodity Price Risk Management, with its secretariat in the World Bank, is currently implementing pilot projects to provide commodity price insurance to smallholder farms in developing countries, and this could possibly be extended to consumers in food importing countries as well. This insurance scheme, while varied in its specific application by country, is focused on adapting the commodity price risk management tools available on international markets to provide a form of price insurance to producers (and consumers in the case of import prices). The World Bank also has developed instruments to support the development of crop yield insurance and has one operational pilot project in Morocco, with others under preparation.

### *Commodity Swaps*

The World Bank began offering commodity swaps in 1999, to help borrowing countries address commodity price risk. Bank members whose debt-servicing capacity is heavily exposed to specific commodities may benefit from financial terms that link the debt-servicing costs of their loans from the World Bank to movements in the price of a specific commodity or basket of commodities. Managing the risks associated with commodity prices is a major challenge for many developing countries, and most commodity-dependent countries have inadequate access to risk-hedging instruments. It was to address this need that the World Bank began offering commodity swaps on a pilot basis to its borrowers with a demonstrated need to reduce exposure to commodity price changes. Such swaps are individually negotiated transactions to exchange two sets of cash flows at certain dates in the future, whereby one set of cash flows is linked to the market price of a commodity or index and the other is a pre-agreed fixed cash flow or a cash flow based on a floating or fixed rate of interest. Hedges could be structured to reduce commodity price–related risks for both producers and consumers of energy, minerals, and agricultural products.

### *Food Aid and Subsidized Credit*

Food aid is often the response of the international community to disruptions of domestic supply in developing countries. While food aid has served a valuable function in cases of disasters when normal supply channels are disrupted, it has in many cases had undesirable and unintended consequences. In general, food aid provides significant quantities that have a potentially large impact on the local market price. While an increase in supply will lower the market price, even if it is sold at "market prices," this effect of distorting the market is often magnified because distribution is free or actual sales prices are far below local prices. This tends to depress prices for local producers, lowering their incomes, reducing incentives for production, and thereby increasing the country's future reliance on food imports. In addition, the price reductions created by food aid distort seasonal (interharvest) price movements and discourage the development of private storage facilities. Finally, food aid is in many cases distributed through governmental channels, thereby undermining private sector development in marketing infrastructure. While such adverse effects may on specific occasions be acceptable costs to pay for mitigating or avoiding famine, they should be evaluated on a case-by-case basis.

Many of these same shortcomings are true of subsidized credit for food imports (including export credit from the exporting countries): the subsidized imports depress farmers' prices and discourage production; if not done on a purely commercial basis, they can be poorly timed (for instance, in conformity with the requirements of the export credit agency, not with the demands in the importing country) and thereby distort seasonal price movements; and they are often channeled through government agents, undermining private sector market development.

Both food donations and concessional credit programs also obscure the real value of the grant element involved and run counter to the principle of transparency. If a grant is justified, it should be transparent and not disguised through an unknown grant element embedded in in-kind food aid or subsidized interest rates.

### *New Approaches to Handling Short-Term Threats to Food Security*

Two other mechanisms have been proposed to meet the concerns addressed in the Marrakesh Decision, but not yet implemented, to deal with short-term food supply disruptions. These, summarized below, could be useful in meeting these concerns in the new round.

**Food Vouchers** One proposal that would not entail several of the shortcomings of direct food aid is to establish a system to distribute food vouchers to the needy when food prices increase.[7] These vouchers could be redeemed through normal commercial import and distribution channels and therefore would not undermine private sector development. They would also operate to increase demand, not supply, and as a result they would not distort domestic prices for either producers or consumers. The difficulty in this is that it requires a system for identifying target recipients and distributing the vouchers to them. (This problem is not unique to this scheme; any compensatory mechanism that does not identify those most in need will have a very high cost relative to the benefits it provides to the poor.) Many countries already have at least some existing mechanisms that could be adapted for this. Experience with similar programs such as food stamps or other income support mechanisms is accumulating as more countries begin to use them as part of their safety net programs. Since there is significant lead time before any structural price increases would be felt from the new round of trade negotiations, there is some time to install such programs in countries that may be vulnerable.

**An Ex Ante Fund for Trade Finance** Sudden increases in the international food prices may disrupt imports if this causes the demand for trade finance to exceed the credit available to the importers in the country.[8] One way of dealing with this would be to establish a fund to make available to importers, guarantees that would enable them to access the necessary financing. The availability of these guarantees would be triggered by objective criteria—agreed to in advance—that are outside the control of the governments. (Granting access based on an increase in the import bill for food would reward poor economic policies—for example, food subsidies or macroeconomic mismanagement—which could trigger a sharp increase in food imports.) An example of such an objective trigger would be some indicator of world wheat prices rising above a specified level or objective warning indicators of famine. In such cases, importers could access the guarantees up to an established limit. The feasibility of such a facility is being explored by a WTO panel.

## Notes

1. Diaz-Bonilla, Diao, and Robinson (2003) have a good discussion of the various submissions to the WTO on this subject by both developed and developing countries.
2. Some analysts distinguish between household and individual food security, but this distinction has little relevance for a discussion of trade policy.
3. Anderson (1998a, b, c); Ingco (1997). These studies were undertaken using a relatively simple numerical model designed so that it could be applied to countries where data availability is limited. These models allow the evaluation of the impacts on least-developed countries of different world price changes resulting from future liberalization proposals.
4. These include Anderson and Tyers (1993); Tyers and Falvey (1989); and Alston and Martin (1995).
5. See Ingco (1997, p. 16, Scenario II).
6. For a more detailed discussion, see WTO (2002).
7. See WTO (2002, annex 8, Submission by the World Bank).
8. See WTO (2002, annex 7, Submission by UNCTAD).

## Select Bibliography


Alston, J. M., and W. J. Martin. 1995. "Reversal of Fortune: Immiserizing Technological Change in Agriculture." *American Journal of Agricultural Economics* 77: 251–259.

Anderson, K. 1998a. "Economic Reform in Nepal and WTO Accession." Adelaide: Centre for International Economic Studies, Adelaide, Australia.

Anderson, K. 1998b. "Vietnam's Transforming Economy and WTO Accession." Adelaide: Centre for International Economic Studies and Singapore: Institute of Southeast Asian Studies, Adelaide, Australia.

Anderson, K. 1998c. "Lao Economic Reform and WTO Accession." Adelaide: Centre for International Economic Studies and Singapore: Institute of Southeast Asian Studies, Adelaide, Australia.

Anderson, K., and R. Tyers. 1993. "More on Welfare Gains to Developing Countries from Liberalising World Food Trade", *Journal of Agricultural Economics* 44(2): 189–204.

Christiaensen, L., L. Demery, and S. Paternostro. 2002. "Growth, Distribution, and Poverty in Africa: Messages from the 1990s." Processed. The World Bank, Washington, D.C.

de Janvry, A., Graff, G., Sadoulet, E. and D. Zilberman. (1999). "Agricultural Biotechnology and Poverty: How to Make the Promise a Reality?" Preliminary draft, University of California at Berkeley.

Diaz-Bonilla, E., X. Diao, and S. Robinson. 2003. "Thinking Inside the Boxes: WTO Agricultural Negotiations and the Development and Food Security Boxes." Paper presented to joint IATRC/USDA-ERS/UC Davis/University of Calabria "International Conference: Agricultural policy reform and the WTO: Where are we heading?" June 23–26, Capri.

Ferreira, F. H.G., and P. Lanjouw. 2000. "Rural Non-Farm Activities and Poverty in the Brazilian Northeast." Draft Mimeo. Development Economics Group, World Bank, Washington, D.C.

Garrett, J. L., and M. Ruel. 2000. "Achieving Urban Food and Nutrition Security in The Developing World." IFPRI 2020 Focus 3. IFPRI: Washington, D.C.

Goldin, I., and D. van der Mensbrugghe. 1996. "Assessing Agricultural Tariffication Under the Uruguay Round." In W.J. Martin, L.A. Winters, eds., *The Uruguay Round and the Developing Countries.* Cambridge: Cambridge University Press.

Haddad, L., M. Ruel, and J. L. Garrett. 1999. "Are Urban Poverty and Undernutrition Growing? Some Newly Assembled Evidence." Food Consumption and Nutrition Discussion Paper 63. IFRPI: Washington, D.C.

Ingco, M. D. 1997. "Has Agricultural Trade Liberalization Improved Welfare in the Least-developed Countries? Yes." Policy Research Working Paper 1748, International Trade Division, International Economics Department, World Bank. Washington, D.C.

Kherallah, M., C. Delgado, E. Gabre-Madhin, N. Minot, and M. Johnson. 2000. "Agricultural Market Reforms in Sub-Saharan Africa: A Synthesis of Research Findings." Markets and Structural Studies Division, IFPRI. Washington, D.C.

Longhurst, R. and M. Lipton. 1989. "The Role of Agricultural Research and Secondary Food Crops in Reducing Seasonal Food Insecurity." In D. Sahn (ed.), *Seasonal Variability in Third World Agriculture: The Consequences of Food Security.* Baltimore and London: John Hopkins University Press.

Sutherland, P. D. 1998. "Answering Globalization's Challenges," ODC Viewpoint, October. Washington, D.C.: Development Council.

Tyers, R., and R. E. Falvey. 1989. "Border Price Changes and Domestic Welfare in the Presence of Subsidised Exports," Oxford Economic Papers, 41(2): 434–451.

World Bank. 2001. "Rural Poverty Reduction in Brazil: Towards an Integrated Strategy." Processed. Washington, D.C.

WTO (World Trade Organization). 1999. Annual Report, 1999. International Trade Statistics. Geneva: WTO.

———. 2002. "Report of the Interagency Panel on Short-Term Difficulties in Financing Normal Levels of Commercial Imports of Foodstuffs." 28 June, WT/GC/62/G/AG/13. Office of the Secretary General, Geneva.

10

# MANAGING POTENTIAL ADVERSE IMPACTS OF AGRICULTURAL TRADE LIBERALIZATION

*William Foster and Alberto Valdés*

## Introduction

When a country's agricultural sector is integrated more closely into the world economy by reducing its trade barriers, its producers are exposed to greater downside price risk. Policymakers in developing countries have few instruments available to cushion farmers from episodes of very low world prices, which in many countries has made them reluctant to make a serious commitment to significantly reduce tariffs and maintain them at low levels. This may help explain why so many developing countries bound their agricultural product tariffs at extremely high levels in the Uruguay Round. It would clearly be in the interests of both developed and developing countries for all participants to make commitments to significantly reduce their import barriers in the Doha Round, but to induce developing countries to participate fully in the Doha process may require some creative thinking on how to meet this political concern over increased price risk when tariff walls are lowered.

In this paper several questions surrounding continuing trade reform will be addressed as they relate to the management of the price risk originating in world markets that affects farmers in developing countries. The paper considers national border measures particularly related to international price fluctuations. Other chapters address questions relating to safety-net policies (such as revenue insurance), international assistance measures (such as food aid and compensatory financing), and the concerns regarding the effects of food price movements on real wages and their potential macroeconomic repercussions. We take the perspective that the price risk management problem is not so much the instability of international prices *per se*, but the difficulties associated with periods of low and politically unsustainable price levels. The governments of many developing countries understandably distrust the present state of their domestic markets and institutions to manage the risks to farmers of extended periods of low prices. Such distrust and the associated political pressures from farm groups—especially those competing with imports—would have the effect of reducing any enthusiasm for further trade liberalization. It is in this context that the distortions in world prices and the issue of the transmission of price risk become critical in the political commitment to deepen trade reforms in developing countries.

### *The Plan of This Chapter*

The structure of this paper follows what are, in the authors' opinion, the central, politically sensitive issues[1] from the perspective of a developing country in the process of expanding or deepening trade liberalization:

- The enhanced transmission to domestic markets of international price movements due to trade reforms, especially the elimination of quantitative restrictions (QRs), and the limited policy tools available in the present environment of trade commitments.
- The definition of price risk in terms of periods of very low prices facing producers in import-competing sectors.
- The resistance in developing countries to lowering trade barriers on imports caused by developed-country subsidies that artificially lower world prices, which are in turn transmitted to domestic developing-country markets. One argument made in developing countries is that activities that would otherwise be competitive at world prices without distortions are not sustainable in the current environment of distorted international prices.
- The stochastic nature of world prices is characterized by occasional periods of persistently low prices below trend. This persistence characteristic limits the type of policies that might be used to manage price risk.
- The practical relevance of enhanced price transmission. The price risk facing farmers is not merely caused by world price movements, but by other factors, such as exchange rate fluctuations. That price transmission is not the only question of significance implies the reduced effectiveness of border instruments to manage price risk.
- Policy implications of price risk management, in the present environment of World Trade Organization (WTO) commitments and the functioning of world markets.

## The Move to World Price Regimes: Greater Price Transmission and the Limits to Managing International Price Variability

In the mid-1980s, several developing countries, particularly in Latin America, began a series of economic reforms. Continuing through the 1990s, larger numbers of developing countries—eventually including the transition economies of Eastern and Central Europe—adopted trade liberalization, privatization, and deregulation. The degree and depth of these reforms, of course, varied significantly. Chile was an early and deep reformer, beginning with a radical change in its trade regime around 1976. In contrast, Venezuela and Caribbean countries, for example, began reforms late, in the mid-1990s, coinciding with the emergence else-where of the transition from command socialism policies.

The move toward the adoption of a world price regime—trade liberalization—meant (particularly in Latin America) the reduction in direct price interventions, the lowering of tariff levels, and the convergence of previously disparate tariffs across commodities. And—perhaps most critically in terms of enhancing price transmission—trade liberalization meant the elimination of all but a few quantitative restrictions on imports and the removal of state trading in most countries. In the past these policies had the effect of insulating domestic consumers and producers from the vicissitudes of world markets and international trade. The decline of trade-restricting policies magnified the effects on domestic markets of changes in border prices—that is, it magnified the transmission of price signals across borders as the determinants of a country's allocation of resources. (This is what is meant when reference is made to developing countries coping with a "world price regime.") Consequently, the arguments surrounding both price risk and the selection of policies to counteract possible distortions in international prices have grown in importance in domestic policy debates.

In the more protectionist economic environment of the past—especially with quantitative restrictions related to import licenses and quotas, variable levies, and state trading monopolies—logically there should have been less transmission of international price variability than under the present and evolving system, which emphasizes the use of tariffs only. And even where no quantitative restrictions existed, high tariffs would have tended both to reduce the practical importance of international price fluctuations, and to cushion the effect of those shocks to whatever extent they were transmitted from international to domestic markets.

Today the set of policy instruments available to governments is largely restricted to tariffs and surcharges (including safeguards), and the levels of those tariff instruments are limited.[2] For many developing and transition economies, the present trade and policy environment has amplified political pressures—in a situation of falling world prices—to counteract the transmission to internal markets of the debilitating effects generated by perceived distortions in world prices caused by external interventions. Particularly worthy of attention are the pressures arising in import-competing sectors.

The implications of low-price periods to producers in import-competing sectors, however, are what is really important about price risk in the context of trade reform.

The adverse effect of high levels of protection in developed, industrial countries (addressed below) is a widely recognized problem for developing countries as exporters of agricultural products. But what is likely an undervalued question (especially by economists in the "North"), and what generates the most complex domestic policy debates in many developing countries, surrounds the pricing of importables. In practical political terms, for these countries, the problem of access to foreign markets is not a contentious issue in internal debates over domestic policies, although it is clearly an important issue in terms of foreign relations.

The question of access is certainly central to the international diplomatic debate over trade with Organisation for Economic Co-operation and Development (OECD) members. Nevertheless, as we observe in the analysis of countries that have opened their markets significantly to trade, the dilemma today is dealing with the episodes of "excessively low" border prices affecting some import-competing activities. Moreover, the concerns over low price episodes are reinforced by the undeniable long-term declining historical trend in world agricultural prices. Often in economic literature, price risk is understood, in the simplest terms, as the variance of prices. But in the context of trade liberalization and efforts to encourage governments to move toward a world price regime, that definition is too narrow. Price risk should be considered in terms of price levels, and not simply by some measure of the variance of prices.

Trade liberalization did two things: it reduced border protection on importables and it removed export taxes and restrictions of many developing countries on exportables. This had the combined effect of reducing the bias against export agriculture. So while the same characteristics of world prices of importables also apply to exportables, the beneficiaries of trade liberalization tended to be producers in export-oriented sectors (and of course consumers). Furthermore, it appears to be a widely noted fact that, with respect to policy issues, producers of importables usually are better-organized, more vocal, and stronger lobbyists than producers of exportables.

This political reality reinforces the prominence of importables in policy debates over that of exportables. Simply put, the political economies of the two types of products are different. On top of all of this, the present policy tools (for example, increasing tariffs) for the protection of importables are straightforward and bureaucratically remunerative. For exportables there is not much that fiscally limited developing countries can realistically do, unlike the case of richer economies, such as the United States (U.S.) and the European Union (EU), where export subsidies represent a relatively minor and often inconspicuous burden on taxpayers.

## Greater Price Transmission Is Perceived as Increasing Producer Vulnerability

What evidence is there that greater price transmission is perceived as increasing producer vulnerability? The 1992 study of the political economy of agricultural price policies in 18 developing countries by Schiff and Valdés shows that governments tend to insulate domestic sectors to a greater degree during periods of volatile world prices. If attaining price stability was the purpose for such interventions, then in overall terms governments succeeded in achieving the objective, primarily through direct interventions. Relative to world prices, protective policies managed to reduce domestic price variability by an average of 25 percent, and even more so in products for which world prices were highly volatile. Quiroz and Soto's 1995 cross-country analysis of the transmission of world agricultural price shocks reinforce these conclusions. In 67 of 76 countries examined, it took at least two years to transmit 50 percent of international price shocks to domestic markets.

The historical policy decisions of governments could be interpreted as evidence, in the sense of revealed preference, that they think reductions in price transmission effectively reduce the vulnerability of producers. This is what should be expected from a welfare and public choice perspective, where commodity prices are politically sensitive. In terms of farmers in developing countries, governments tend to be sensitive to price instability because farmers tend to be risk averse, there are also fewer opportunities to hedge risk, credit markets are less developed, and governments do not have the fiscal resources to provide nonborder support to farmers in years of low prices. In terms of consumers and labor markets, without the fiscal wherewithal to provide broad coverage of safety net programs, variation in food prices can have significant effects on real wages and real household income.[3]

As emphasized earlier, from the perspective of politicians and farmers in import-competing sectors, the policy problem is not so much the volatility of domestic prices *per se*, as those are influenced by world price fluctuations. It is rather the difficulties associated with periods of exceptionally low price levels falling below the long-term trends. Aggravating the political pressures to "do something," producers and politicians in developing countries tend to attribute these episodes to the distortions in world prices brought about by the continued subsidies of developed countries.

## The Role of Developed-Country Subsidies in Lowering World Prices

From an economic perspective, the world price of a product, however determined, represents the true cost of that product to an economy, and—abstracting from dynamic considerations—the welfare of the economy as a whole is unambiguously maximized if the world price is also the domestic market price for both consumers and producers. In the political realm, however, the underlying determinants of the international market conditions may matter a lot. The resistance in developing countries to lowering trade barriers on imports arises owing in part to the widely held assumption that developed-country subsidies artificially and significantly lower world prices. Lower prices are in turn transmitted to domestic developing-country markets. Many industries in developing countries argue that they would be competitive in world markets without distortions, but that they are unprofitable in the current environment of distorted international prices. In terms of political decisions in these countries, the implication of this argument to the selection of price risk management tools is to mix policy objectives. The political imperative is that such instruments should not merely guard against low prices, but simultaneously compensate for an artificially caused downward shift in the long-term pattern of prices owing to developed-country subsidies.

Is this a reasonable argument? What then is known about the manner in which developed-country policies distort the levels of prices around their long-term trends? In the context of the policy debate in many developing countries, reference is often found to the billions of dollars given to agriculture in developed nations. But it is an open question as to the degree to which current commodity price levels and the declining trend in prices are due to protection and government support in developed countries—and to what degree they are the result of productivity levels, factor use, income growth, and population.[4]

Often explicitly, there is the presumption that international prices are so distorted by external subsidies that they do not represent a sound basis for the determination of the true competitiveness of domestically produced importables. Moreover, there is often the confusion in the policy debate that the producers in developing countries should be compensated for the absolute value of the export subsidies, without a clear distinction between measurable subsidy levels and their overall final effect on world prices. From an economist's perspective, of course, what should matter is the final effect of subsidies on world prices, not absolute subsidy levels. The focus on absolute levels of subsidies leaves the question of the appropriate compensating tariff or surcharges with an unrestricted upper limit.[5]

What should be considered most relevant for the discussion, in terms of the familiar steady-state comparisons derived from modeling efforts, is that practically all quantitative analyses on agricultural protection conclude that such protectionist subsidy policies depress world prices relative to what would otherwise be the case with lower protection. This point is concisely made by McCulloch, Winters, and Cirera (2002, 175–6): "Agricultural markets are among the most distorted in the world, with both developed and developing countries maintaining high levels of intervention."

But first one should keep in mind the importance of distinguishing between the impacts of distortions from developing countries and those from developed countries. The evidence indicates that the direction of the effects of intervention differs between developed and developing countries. Developed countries usually protect their agricultural sectors, and developing countries usually tax their agricultural sectors. Certainly the historical evidence suggests that developed countries' policies have depressed world prices, while developing countries' policies have increased those prices.[6] In addition, complicating the issue in the case of developing countries, the effects of exchange rate misalignment and industrial protection have been shown to be influential in depressing the internal prices of agricultural tradables, unlike the situation in developed countries.

Regardless of past opinions, it is well recognized today that domestic price and trade interventions among the major producing and trading countries continue to have a significant effect on world prices. The higher the level of protection on importables and the higher the export subsidies, the lower will be the world price. From a welfare-analysis point of view, it is recognized that consumers of the country imposing these policies suffer the main costs of intervention. For agriculture sectors, however, developed-country policies can also impose high costs, particularly in developing economies where agriculture is relatively more important and where rural poverty is of considerably greater social importance.

There have been several efforts to quantify the present effects of these interventions on world prices and trade flows. This literature is discussed in publications including Goldin and Knudsen (1989) for the OECD, and various other sources. The modeling efforts currently undertaken by the Global Trade Analysis Project and the OECD are worth mentioning as the most significant in terms of recent work. While there are some methodological caveats to keep in mind,[7] these studies can be used as points of reference that offer a sense of the orders of magnitude involved in world price distortions.

What can be concluded from the literature? Two comparable papers, Valdés and Zietz (1995) and Ingco (1996) summarize the findings of various published studies on predicting the world price effects of partial agricultural trade reform. In Ingco, for rice and coarse grains, world price effects on the order of 5 percent or less are a good approximation. For wheat, the estimates range from 1.2 percent to 10 percent, where three of the six estimates are—for all intents and purposes—approximately 6 percent. For tropical products the effects are lower.

Goldin, Knudsen, and van der Mensbrugghe (1992) use the RUNS model[8] to simulate both "partial" and "full" agricultural reforms and multisectoral reforms. For partial agricultural reforms, tariff equivalents are reduced by 30 percent; for full agricultural reforms all tariffs are eliminated, including those for inputs. Partial reforms are similar to those mentioned above, but for full agricultural reforms the world price effects are considerably and surprisingly higher, especially when compared to studies that address similar simulations. For example, sugar prices rise from 10.2 percent in the case of partial agricultural reform to 59.3 percent in the case of full agricultural reform. Wheat prices rise 5.9 percent for partial reform to 39.2 percent for full reform. For multisectoral reform, the price effects in general are lower, owing to both demand and supply effects in a hypothetical world of more efficient use of resources. Notably, practically all studies conclude that the largest effects appear to be for sugar and dairy, on the order of at least 10 percent in the case of partial reform, and higher for full agricultural reform.[9]

## The Stochastic Nature of World Prices

What is known about price variability and the persistence of low prices? The measurement of price instability in world agricultural markets is a relatively well-researched area. In recent years Alexander Sarris' (1997b) work on measurement, for example, has been comprehensive in the case of cereals. He arrives at several conclusions. With respect to the question of whether or not there has been an increase in interyear and intrayear price variability for cereals, the evidence shows no trend toward greater world price instability. Harwood comes to the same conclusion for corn, using data from 1920 to 1996. Apparently, no other comparable studies have been applied to other commodities of interest to developing countries.

**TABLE 10.1 Coefficients of Variation of World Prices of Selected Commodities**

| Period | Corn | Rice | Sugar | Wheat |
|---|---|---|---|---|
| **1960–1972** | 0.11 | 0.09 | 0.60 | 0.25 |
| **1973–1985** | 0.31 | 0.44 | 0.81 | 0.42 |
| **1986–1997** | 0.18 | 0.20 | 0.22 | 0.17 |
| **1960–1997** | 0.37 | 0.46 | 0.90 | 0.44 |

*Source:* Valdés 2000, p. 21.

Table 10.1 presents the coefficients of variation of world prices for four selected commodities for 1960 through 1997 (reproduced from Quiroz, Foster, and Valdés 1999). The results show that sugar is considerably more unstable than the three cereals throughout the period. Also notable is that the sub-period 1973–85 shows a much higher coefficient of variation than the preceding and following sub-periods. Evidently the coefficient of variation of these commodities changes with time, and moreover, for wheat and sugar, there has been a decline in price instability for the period 1986–97 (which is consistent with the conclusions of Sarris).

A related question is whether the instability is caused by the "system" of protection (see, for example, Josling 1980). Certainly establishing variable levies and quotas with a targeted domestic price on importables results in a shift of domestic instability to world markets. With the move toward removal of quantitative restrictions and variable levies, it would be expected that the contribution of developed countries' distortions on world price instability would be less. As a result of the Uruguay Round tariffication by developed and developing countries, one expects to see reduced price instability but increased transmission of price instability to domestic producers and consumers. Tyers and Anderson (1992) conclude from policy simulations of tariffication in industrial countries that "[t]he effect of tariffication is to reduce [world] price volatility substantially" during the 1990s (p. 264). Tariffication in developed countries helps reduce instability in wheat, dairy products, and beef, among others. For some commodities, however, reduced instability would derive primarily from the tariffication policies of developing countries, such as in the case of rice and sugar.

Instability *per se* is one issue, but more important to understanding the price risk facing agricultural producers in developing economies is the question of the persistence of low prices. In the context of an open economy, a central problem of the design for policy instruments to deal with instability is understanding the nature and duration of price cycles in world markets. Do shocks to international prices dissipate rapidly, or are they phenomena that persist for several years? There is now a rich literature on the times-series properties of commodity prices. Early research, often framed within the context of unit-root analysis, led to the conclusion that prices exhibited a significant degree of shock persistence. The results presented by Gersovitz and Paxson (1990) show that the hypothesis of a unit root could not be rejected for a number of commodity prices of African exports. Later studies have been more cautious in coming to the strict conclusion of unit roots deduced from simple measures of persistence (Caner and Hansen 1997; Perron 1989; and Zivot and Andrews 1992). León and Soto (1995) conclude that real world prices do not exhibit unit roots, but rather they are trend-stationary processes. Nevertheless, there remains the stylized fact that commodity prices exhibit considerable shock persistence (see also Deaton 1992).

Especially pertinent—and in the authors' opinion most convincing—is the 1999 study by Cashin, Liang, and McDermott on the half-life of shocks to world commodity prices. In the case of wheat, for example, international price shocks have a median half-life of 44 months, with a 90 percent confidence interval that implies a range from an extreme low half-life of 14 months to an extreme high of "infinity." It is significant that there is a 50 percent probability of prices prevailing below the expected value (declining over time) for more than 44 months. The empirical evidence from Cashin, Liang, and McDermott (see also table 10.2) is that the distribution of prices is not symmetric—low prices endure for more months than high prices.

As figure 10.1 amply demonstrates, the nature of price movements is such that low prices have

**TABLE 10.2 Descriptive Statistics for Selected Commodities**

| | *Corn* | | | *Rice* | | |
|---|---|---|---|---|---|---|
| Period | Skewness | Kurtosis | Jarque-Bera | Skewness | Kurtosis | Jarque-Bera |
| 1960–72 | –0.34 | 2.34 | 5.87 | –0.51 | 1.87 | 15.14 |
| 1973–85 | 1.01 | 3.58 | 28.5 | 1.59 | 5.53 | 107.3 |
| 1986–97 | 1.14 | 4.73 | 47.76 | 1.25 | 4.73 | 51.64 |
| 1960–97 | 0.65 | 3.77 | 42.6 | 1.21 | 6.3 | 310.64 |
| | *Sugar* | | | *Wheat* | | |
| Period | Skewness | Kurtosis | Jarque-Bera | Skewness | Kurtosis | Jarque-Bera |
| 1960–72 | 1.88 | 6.47 | 170.7 | 0.35 | 1.65 | 14.39 |
| 1973–85 | 2.05 | 8.51 | 306.98 | 1.69 | 6.06 | 134.79 |
| 1986–97 | 0.62 | 3.12 | 8.85 | 0.43 | 2.22 | 7.86 |
| 1960–97 | 3.25 | 17.66 | 48.35 | 1.41 | 6.1 | 325.08 |

*Source:* Quiroz, Foster, and Valdés 1999.

**FIGURE 10.1 Real Price of Selected Commodities (1960–97, US$ of July 1997)**

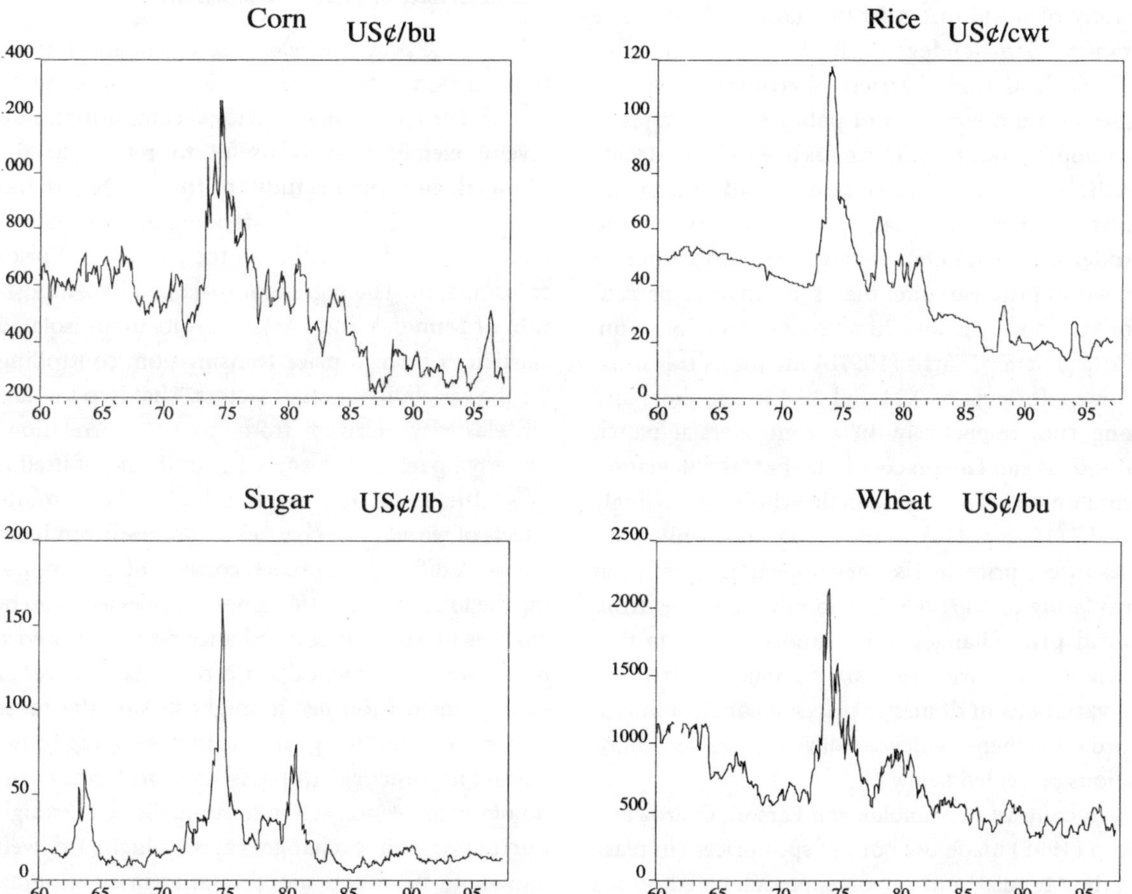


*Notes:* bu = bushels, cwt = hundred weight, lb = pound. Years are represented on the X axis.
*Source:* Quiroz, Foster, and Valdés 1999.

the tendency to persist for many months, with occasional spikes of shorter duration. These characteristics of world price movements lead to notable difficulties in the design of policies. The use of futures markets would reduce the effect of short-term uncertainty but could not guard against the effects of consecutive years of low prices. In the past, minimum import price schemes were popular, and several developing countries still have in place systems of price bands. Safeguards (increased tariffs) are always an applicable contingency measure, but under WTO rules they are limited in duration, involve compensation, and are restricted in their frequency of application.

## The Practical Relevance of Price Transmission in the Determination of Price Risks Facing Farmers

The degree of world price distortion due to developed-country subsidies and the stochastic nature of world prices set the stage in which price transmission—endogenously determined by policies such as trade barriers—becomes a relevant question in the context of policy controversies in developing countries. There has been a lively debate in the literature regarding the degree of price transmission. For European producers, Tyers and Anderson (1992) demonstrate a transmission rate of world price variation that is less than 10 percent for the short run, and 20 percent for the long run. More generally, Sarris (1997b) mentions transmission coefficients of 0.24 and 0.58 in the short and long run, respectively. In a controversial paper, Mundlak and Larson conclude that "the deviation from unitary elasticity is, on the whole, surprisingly small" (1992, p. 419). In their judgment, while policies affect price levels, they appear ineffective at insulating to a great degree domestic prices from world price changes. The authors also note that variations in world prices are the major contributor to variations in domestic prices, a conclusion discordant with the evidence from the price decompositions presented below.

In contrast to Mundlak and Larson, Quiroz and Soto (1995) made use both of spot prices (in place of the Mundlak and Larson approach based on the Food and Agriculture Organization [FAO] average unit export values) and of an error-correction specification of the relationship between world and domestic prices. Covering 78 countries, Quiroz and Soto conclude, "In an overwhelming majority of cases transmission of international price signals in agriculture is either non-existent or low, by any reasonable standard." But the degree of price transmission, of course, ranges across countries. For Australia, Canada, New Zealand, and Uruguay, 50 percent or more of any given shock from world prices is transmitted within a year. But these few countries are in contrast to 30 countries that exhibit price transmission characteristics such that it takes five years or longer to transmit half of any world price shocks. Surprisingly, another group of 30 countries appears "virtually isolated from international price signals."

One major caveat of these mentioned studies is that the data correspond to trade regimes that applied before the Uruguay Round. So with tariffication and the removal of QRs, transmission could be higher today, and this offers a rich area of study.

### *The Relevance of Price Transmission*

What is the practical relevance of enhanced price transmission to the determination of real domestic prices? The answer lies in price decomposition into several elements. It is useful to return to the Mundlak and Larson study (or that of Quiroz and Soto 1995) to aid in understanding the alternatives for specifying the question of the relevance of price transmission. The regression-oriented decomposition of Mundlak and Larson results in an isolated elasticity of world price transmission, controlling for the variability of other factors. That is to say, it is an elasticity derived from partial correlations underlying regression analysis, but in and of itself it says little about the magnitudes of the absolute effects of world price changes on domestic producer prices. A different approach consists of decomposing the total variation of domestic prices as a sum of changes in world prices, exchange rates, and border protection. In a practical sense, the isolated effect of price transmission *per se* might not be the most important issue facing farmers in developing countries. The practical impacts of world prices on domestic prices are, at a minimum, filtered through fluctuations in exchange rates, which are well known to be much more volatile in developing economies. In addition, historically, changes in border protection have been of significant importance during the 1990s in many countries, influenc-

**TABLE 10.3 Decomposition of Real Producer Price for Wheat in Transition Economies**

| | | *Percent Change in* | | | |
|---|---|---|---|---|---|
| Country | Period | Domestic Price | Border Price | Real Exchange Rate | Residual Policies |
| **Bulgaria** | 1994–95 | 2 | 6 | –8 | 4 |
| | 1995-96 | 25 | 6 | 20 | –1 |
| | 1996–97 | –2 | –18 | 22 | –6 |
| | 1994–97 | 25 | –6 | 34 | –3 |
| **Poland** | 1994–95 | –8 | –14 | –8 | 14 |
| | 1995–96 | 13 | 28 | –2 | –13 |
| | 1996–97 | –9 | –24 | 3 | 12 |
| | 1994–97 | –4 | –10 | –7 | 13 |
| **Romania** | 1994–95 | –8 | –6 | –1 | –1 |
| | 1995–96 | 13 | 3 | 4 | 5 |
| | 1996–97 | –13 | –13 | –3 | 3 |
| | 1994–97 | –8 | –16 | 0 | 8 |
| **Russia** | 1995–95 | 17 | 14 | –4 | 7 |
| | 1995–96 | 16 | 7 | –2 | 11 |
| | 1996–97 | –6 | –12 | 2 | 4 |
| | 1994-97 | 27 | 9 | –4 | 22 |
| **Ukraine** | 1994–95 | –30 | –5 | –35 | 10 |
| | 1995–96 | –9 | 7 | –20 | 4 |
| | 1996–97 | –4 | –12 | –5 | 12 |
| | 1994–97 | –43 | –10 | –60 | 27 |
| **Germany** | 1994–95 | –4 | 14 | –5 | –12 |
| | 1995–96 | 1 | 11 | 3 | –12 |
| | 1996–97 | –4 | –10 | 6 | –1 |
| | 1994–97 | –7 | 14 | 4 | –26 |

*Source:* Valdés 2000, p. 21.

ing the ultimate effects of changes in world prices on domestic producers.

It is relevant to consider the extreme case of countries that have fixed exchange rates and dollar convertibility, such as Argentina, until recently. In such a case, and where the rate of inflation would be close to zero, a price transmission elasticity of one is expected. Moreover, any decomposition of domestic price changes would show a near one-to-one total correlation between domestic prices and world prices (abstracting from marketing margin changes). In contrast, in Chile, the real exchange rate fluctuated significantly in spite of a stable macroeconomic environment (with an inflation rate of less than 3 percent, a fiscal deficit that is less than 1 percent of GDP, and with ample foreign exchange reserves). This has been due mainly to movements in capital accounts and also to the inherent instability associated with emerging economies related to the "neighborhood effect" of the various economic crises—the Asian Crisis, the Tequila (or Mexico) Effect, the Brazilian devaluation, and most recently the Argentinean crisis. Even if the price transmission elasticity were one for Chilean exported fruits and wine (which is likely the real case), the final effect of world price changes on real domestic prices might be overwhelmed by the accumulated influence of exchange variation.

In the example of real price trends of wheat in the transition economies of Bulgaria, Romania, the Russian Federation, and Ukraine (Valdés 2000), these countries have experienced large yearly real producer price variations. The decomposition of these fluctuations is presented in table 10.3 for the period 1994–97, permitting an examination of the contribution of price changes from changes in border prices, real exchange rates, and policy interventions. What is notable from the data is

**TABLE 10.4 Decomposition of Producer Price Changes: Argentina**

| | | *Cumulative Percentage Change in* | | | | | |
|---|---|---|---|---|---|---|---|
| Product | Period | Real Domestic Prices | Real Border Prices | Real Exchange Rate | (1+Ti) | Others | (1 + Ti) + Others |
| *Exportables* | | | | | | | |
| Beef | 1960–69 | −43.55 | −30.97 | −244.19 | | | 231.61 |
| | 1970–79 | 22.29 | 43.58 | −67.67 | | | 46.38 |
| | 1980–84 | −33.97 | −104.29 | 87.20 | | | −16.88 |
| | 1985–89 | 32.68 | 13.16 | 39.36 | −19.62 | −0.22 | −19.84 |
| | 1990–93 | −91.35 | 13.28 | −132.01 | 27.75 | −0.38 | 27.38 |
| | 1994–95 | 2.45 | −3.31 | −2.02 | | | 7.78 |
| Maize | 1960–69 | 2.57 | −21.54 | −14.42 | | | 38.52 |
| | 1970–79 | −102.78 | 4.04 | −83.34 | | | −23.49 |
| | 1980–84 | 54.93 | −33.69 | 89.39 | | | −0.77 |
| | 1985–89 | −38.40 | −38.74 | 14.36 | 4.65 | 3.52 | 9.23 |
| | 1990–93 | −68.28 | −38.88 | −61.98 | 28.61 | 3.97 | 32.58 |
| | 1994–95 | 25.97 | 13.08 | −2.02 | | | 14.92 |
| Sorghum | 1960–69 | −4.51 | −24.07 | −14.42 | | | 33.98 |
| | 1970–79 | −38.49 | 4.86 | −58.54 | | | 15.19 |
| | 1980–84 | −4.69 | −23.41 | 64.60 | | | −45.88 |
| | 1985–89 | −15.72 | 1.86 | −35.62 | 2.65 | 15.39 | 18.04 |
| | 1990–92 | −89.00 | −47.73 | −54.70 | 25.28 | −11.85 | 13.43 |
| Soybeans | 1960–69 | — | — | — | — | — | — |
| | 1977–79 | −112.07 | −51.20 | −55.40 | | | −5.47 |
| | 1980–84 | 7.60 | −60.75 | 80.42 | | | −12.07 |
| | 1985–89 | −41.02 | 10.87 | −48.30 | −3.52 | −0.07 | −3.59 |
| | 1990–93 | −58.64 | −39.38 | −61.98 | 38.67 | 4.04 | 42.72 |
| | 1994–95 | −41.36 | −52.61 | −2.33 | | | 13.58 |
| Sunflowers | 1960–69 | — | — | — | — | — | — |
| | 1977–79 | −89.08 | −24.34 | −55.40 | | | −9.33 |
| | 1980–84 | 22.02 | −59.88 | 80.42 | | | 1.48 |
| | 1985–89 | −56.64 | −17.50 | −35.62 | −2.01 | −1.51 | −3.52 |
| | 1990–92 | −67.65 | −46.14 | −54.70 | 32.93 | 0.27 | 33.19 |
| Wheat | 1960–69 | −3.77 | −18.09 | −14.42 | | | 19.51 |
| | 1970–79 | −87.73 | 6.85 | −92.60 | | | −33.80 |
| | 1980–84 | −64.03 | −62.15 | 9.18 | | | −11.06 |
| | 1985–88 | −3.72 | −19.11 | −12.32 | 20.18 | 7.53 | 27.71 |
| | 1991–93 | −24.76 | −35.94 | −26.64 | 31.64 | 1.42 | 37.82 |
| | 1994 | −2.61 | −5.93 | −1.44 | | | 4.77 |

*Source:* Valdés 1996.

the imperfect correlation (sometimes negative) between border price changes and domestic producer prices. For example, in the case of wheat in Bulgaria during the period 1994–97, domestic prices increased 25 percent while border prices fell 6 percent, the increase owing primarily to a 34 percent increase in the real exchange rate.

The evidence for various agricultural commodities in Argentina, Chile, and Colombia (tables 10.4, 10.5, and 10.6, respectively) shows a similar pattern with respect to the alternating relative weight of border prices movements to the final determination of domestic real producer prices. In short, price transmission *per se* is not the whole story.

**TABLE 10.5 Decomposition of Producer Price Changes: Chile**

| | | *Cumulative Percentage Change in* | | | | |
|---|---|---|---|---|---|---|
| Product | Period | Real Domestic Prices | Real Border Prices | Real Exchange Rate | (1+Ti) | Others |
| ***Exportables*** | | | | | | |
| Apples, red | 1960–70 | 133.77 | 41.02 | 30.94 | 17.14 | 44.67 |
| | 1971–74 | −2.40 | −21.22 | 44.77 | −10.38 | −15.58 |
| | 1975–83 | 6.40 | −8.40 | 46.47 | −6.77 | −24.90 |
| | 1984–89 | 30.48 | −4.10 | 36.11 | 0.00 | −1.53 |
| | 1990–93 | −429.10 | −64.88 | −14.79 | 0.00 | −349.43 |
| Grapes, Thompson | 1960–70 | 99.29 | 21.53 | 30.94 | 17.14 | 29.67 |
| | 1971–74 | 54.35 | 4.37 | 44.77 | −0.59 | 5.80 |
| | 1975–83 | 41.51 | 20.91 | 46.47 | −16.55 | −9.31 |
| | 1984–89 | −4.70 | −30.47 | 33.67 | 0.00 | −7.91 |
| | 1990–94 | 22.24 | 21.37 | −16.80 | 0.00 | 17.67 |
| ***Importables*** | | | | | | |
| Beef | 1960–70 | 41.20 | 9.57 | 30.94 | 0.00 | 0.69 |
| | 1971–74 | 87.27 | 42.14 | 44.77 | 0.00 | 0.36 |
| | 1975–83 | −51.72 | −76.06 | 46.47 | 0.00 | −22.12 |
| | 1984–89 | 136.69 | 64.93 | 33.67 | 13.98 | 24.12 |
| | 1990–95 | −30.05 | 16.88 | −26.84 | −3.54 | −16.54 |
| Maize | 1960–70 | — | — | — | — | — |
| | 1971–74 | — | — | — | — | — |
| | 1975–83 | — | — | — | — | — |
| | 1984–89 | −4.24 | −45.12 | 25.27 | −7.84 | 23.46 |
| | 1990–93 | −22.18 | −23.84 | −16.25 | −3.54 | 21.44 |
| Milk | 1960–70 | 3.29 | −5.37 | 30.94 | 0.00 | −22.28 |
| | 1971–74 | 77.44 | 14.27 | 44.77 | 0.00 | 18.40 |
| | 1975–83 | −0.18 | −2.39 | 46.47 | 0.00 | −44.26 |
| | 1984–89 | −6.25 | 9.46 | 33.67 | 13.98 | −63.35 |
| | 1990–93 | −16.51 | −19.66 | −16.25 | −3.54 | 22.94 |
| Sugarbeets | 1960–70 | — | — | — | — | — |
| | 1971–74 | — | — | — | — | — |
| | 1975–83 | — | — | — | — | — |
| | 1984–89 | −1.35 | 39.16 | 25.27 | −7.84 | −57.93 |
| | 1990–93 | −7.57 | 18.72 | −16.25 | −3.54 | −6.50 |
| Wheat | 1960–70 | 6.33 | −13.15 | 26.76 | 0.00 | −7.28 |
| | 1971–74 | 53.81 | 80.13 | 9.89 | 0.00 | −36.21 |
| | 1975–83 | 35.51 | −88.39 | 81.35 | 0.00 | 42.55 |
| | 1984–89 | −0.42 | −32.83 | 37.84 | −7.84 | 2.41 |
| | 1990–95 | −27.80 | −12.84 | −26.84 | 7.84 | 4.04 |

*Source:* Valdés (1996).

**TABLE 10.6 Decomposition of Producer Price Changes: Colombia**

| | | Cumulative Percentage Change in | | | | |
|---|---|---|---|---|---|---|
| Product | Period | Real Domestic Prices | Real Border Prices | Real Exchange Rate | (1+Ti) | Others |
| *Exportables* | | | | | | |
| Beef | 1960–69 | — | — | — | — | — |
| | 1970–79 | — | — | — | — | — |
| | 1980–89 | −6.45 | −40.26 | 63.16 | −29.22 | −0.13 |
| | 1990–92 | 27.68 | −35.73 | 4.94 | 75.43 | −16.96 |
| | 1993–95 | −24.77 | 15.87 | −32.89 | — | −7.74 |
| Coffee | 1960–69 | −6.12 | −27.89 | 20.90 | −6.76 | 7.63 |
| | 1970–79 | 47.24 | 78.81 | −21.43 | −34.88 | 24.75 |
| | 1980–89 | −33.07 | −108.98 | 65.31 | 61.82 | −51.22 |
| | 1990–92 | −47.12 | −61.91 | 4.94 | 28.45 | −18.60 |
| | 1993–95 | 28.07 | 74.80 | −32.89 | — | −13.83 |
| Cotton | 1960–69 | −7.30 | −20.82 | 20.90 | 0.13 | −7.52 |
| | 1970–79 | 13.46 | 40.04 | −21.43 | −0.09 | −5.06 |
| | 1980–89 | 4.43 | −52.62 | 65.31 | 0.11 | −8.37 |
| | 1990–92 | −25.87 | −38.25 | 4.94 | 13.02 | −5.58 |

Source: Valdés 1996.

## Policy Implications for Managing Price Risk in the Context of WTO Commitments

In summarizing the concerns in developing countries with respect to managing price risk, there are five points to keep in mind:

- Perhaps the central political concern in developing countries is the question of whether or not prices levels are very distorted—and excessively low—owing to OECD subsidies. This preoccupation is intensified in the context of falling prices in real terms.
- From a perspective of developing and transition countries, as the result of their trade liberalization (the reduction in price distortions and the removal of QRs) and thus enhanced price transmission, world price distortions and the possibility of facing periods of low world prices are now more important in determining domestic producer price risk. The reduction in protection and the change in the system of protection brought about by decisions in developing countries have augmented the importance of the possibly distorted levels and the stochastic nature of world prices.
- While there might be a concern about world price instability *per se* and while it is likely more of a concern in developing countries, the real possibility of extended periods of "low prices" is the biggest political difficulty in these countries. And the persistence problem makes more difficult any attempt to resolve that low price problem without resorting to border measures.
- What can be done to deal with the low price problem for developing countries? Special agricultural safeguards (SSGs) were conceived as an instrument, but most developing countries in the present WTO environment cannot use them, because they undertook tariffication before the Uruguay Round (see Konandreas 2000).
- What is emphasized is direct price transmission, but there are other effects of trade liberalization on the welfare of the poor, which go uncaptured by simply looking at price effects. It should be recognized that there are also questions surrounding what constitutes the important definition of "transmission." Normally price transmission refers to the transmission from border prices to domestic prices of tradables. But what is also important from the perspective of poorer farm-

ers is the second-order transmission of world market changes through labor markets, capital markets, and the influence of missing or poorly functioning markets for staples (Taylor 2002). Imperfectly functioning capital markets and high transactions costs—including those associated with access to markets for new products—tend to isolate poorer farmers and rural areas. Rural households that would lose under trade liberalization could conceivably move their resources—primarily labor—to other economic sectors in which transactions costs are lower and access to capital is less expensive. Many do, but for some the net benefits of migration are low, especially for older persons and those with human capital specific to farming and lower levels of education that might otherwise provide skills transferable to other sectors.

That world prices have been affected by government policies in both developed and developing countries appears to be a historical fact, although the degree to which such policies have distorted prices is subject to debate. Perhaps these distortions have changed with the recent overall movements toward liberalization, but certainly not the direction of their negative effect on world prices. Liberalization in developing and transition economies has certainly enhanced the transmission of world prices to their economies, and thus the importance of the distortions that continue to exist.

Particularly in the context of ongoing WTO negotiations, what can be said briefly about the policy implications for managing price risk that one can draw from this environment of price distortion and price transmission? In this period of major policy reforms toward more open economies, there are valid political and economic arguments for governments and the farming community in developing countries to find effective interventions to deal with enhanced price transmission, especially in the context of the persistence of low world prices. The movement toward trade liberalization, toward allowing market price signals to determine the use of resources, could be frustrated by the reluctance of governments to expose further their farming constituents, especially those in the import-competing sectors, to the risks of price instability and periods of persistent low prices that would result from the enhanced price transmission associated with additional reforms. Obviously, those who believe in the benefits of freer world trade have an interest in facilitating policy adjustments in developing economies. But these adjustments must be designed in such a way so as to overcome the potential political resistance likely to result from the exposure of large agricultural sectors, in which a large share of the poor are concentrated, to the risks of sustained price decreases.

Perhaps the first question an economist would ask is, "What about making use of market-oriented policies?" If problems associated with price risk were merely related to year-to-year resource allocations, futures and other derivative markets would be the easiest and likely the most efficient solution to overcoming the risk-related political costs of further trade reform that arises in countries that are risk averse and have underdeveloped capital markets, and other possible institutional problems. If private hedging was not feasible, then a government policy based on a futures market would serve as a solution. An expected low price would simply signal a decrease in resource use devoted to the commodity. And if a realized low price in the previous year led to an expectation that low prices would eventually increase, resources would merely wait to reenter production of the commodity until such a time that price realizations signal their expected profitable use.

Resource decisions, however, are usually matters of multiyear commitments, and it can be concluded from the above discussion of the stochastic nature of world prices that there is a high probability that low-price events come grouped together in distinct episodes of series, or clusters, of months, if not years. This implies that futures and options markets would be inadequate to insure completely against the unfavorable effects of exposing import-competing farm sectors to world price declines. Certainly politicians have insisted on providing some stabilization during the course of transition toward integration into the world price regime. Although in the case of New Zealand some 15 years ago, there was little government support to soften the transition from government support of farming to life without such support (see box 10.1). Other strategies are called for to smooth income fluctuations across years, such as the use of credit or equity markets, long-term contracts, vertical integration, and other means. Nevertheless, in developing

## BOX 10.1 Farming Without Subsidies: The Experience of New Zealand

New Zealand has a vibrant, diversified, and sustainable rural economy. Government handouts were discontinued some 15 years ago. Left to face the market, family farmers have succeeded by their own efforts. Their experience provides a message of reassurance to farmers, policy makers, and others facing change. The New Zealand experience has debunked the myth that the farming sector cannot prosper without government subsidies.

With agriculture based largely on pastoral farming, New Zealand had just over 80,000 farm holdings. Sheep and/or beef farms and dairy farms account for 58% and 29% of the total number of farms respectively. Horticulture, forestry, cropping, and rural tourism contributed to its agricultural sector, which employed 11.4% of the work force. New Zealand exported about 80% of its farming outputs, and agricultural exports—especially sheep meat and dairy products—accounted for over 50% of total merchandise exports.

New Zealand has the lowest level of agricultural support for industrialized countries, which was around 2% of the value of output in 1999 compared with an OECD average of 40%. Most of this support relates to agricultural research funding. However, this has not always been the case. In the mid-1980s the situation was quite different. In 1984 nearly 40% of the average New Zealand sheep and beef farmer's gross income came from government subsidies. With the New Zealand economy almost on the brink of bankruptcy and faced with deteriorating external markets, inflation, historically high interest rates, and agricultural support at 33% of output value in 1983, the government suddenly removed all subsidies and took other market reform measures. In the November 1984 budget, the government abolished almost 30 different production subsidies, including fertilizers, taxation schemes, production, and livestock support. These subsidies had caused long-term damage to agriculture by corrupting market signals, reducing innovation, and misusing resources with their damaging effects on the environment.

Since 1986–1987 the value of economic activity in New Zealand's farm sector has grown by over 40% in constant dollar terms, and its contribution to the economy has risen from 14.2% of GDP in 1986–1987 to 16% in 1990–2000. The removal of farm subsidies has proven to be a catalyst for productivity gains from 1% in 1986 to the current average annual 5.9%.

The change was not achieved without significant effort. Early predictions of large numbers of farmers leaving the land did not occur. Only about 1% of the total number of farms faced bankruptcy and were forced to sell. Land prices, kept artificially high by subsidies, plummeted with their removal. Marginal land reverted to bush, and subsidy-driven land management problems ended. Today farmland values have more than recovered and farm profitability has been restored. Farmers reduced costs and focused on producing higher value products. Many restructured debts and continued farming, adjusting farm practices to reduce input costs. With investment decisions now subject to commercial and good farming disciplines, agricultural input suppliers were forced to become more competitive, thereby contributing to the competitiveness of the agricultural sector.

The government's financial assistance to farmers to make the transition to an unsupported market was minimal: a one-off "exit" grant—the equivalent to about two-thirds of their previous annual income, some access to social welfare income, and limited financial advice. There was no substantive effort to soften the effect of change. New Zealand farmers have proved far more resilient and adaptive than expected when subsidies were first removed. They have proved to the rest of the world that, for family farming, there is a life after subsidies.

*Source:* Adapted from *Life After Subsidies: The New Zealand Farming Experience—15 Years Later,* Federated Farmers of New Zealand (Inc), (revised March 2001).

countries the resources for implementing these market-based strategies are likely missing, or only slowly becoming available. Therefore, to reduce the resistance to reform, it would be worthwhile to consider the development of other government price stabilization plans that would reduce the effects of what seems to be the most disturbing characteristic of world commodity prices: their periodic tendency to persist at values below trend.

Although there is a variety of possible instruments currently in use, there is the question of both their effectiveness and legality under the current WTO legal framework. In a relevant technical note, Konandreas (2000) of the FAO discusses the current framework, classifying permissible policies into two broad categories: border measures through tariffs (within the tariff ceiling bounds) and domestic support measures (price and nonprice programs within the limits of WTO commitments).

With respect to the current state of border measures, most developing countries have bound their agricultural tariffs at a relatively high rate—100 percent and sometimes more. Several countries, such as the Philippines, Chile, Thailand, Argentina, and Malaysia, have bound their tariffs around 30 percent. In many countries, the actual rates or applied tariffs are lower than the bound tariff (so-called dirty tariffication). In Konandreas's assessment, a high bound tariff might be insufficient to avoid the politically difficult situation of very low prices. But more significantly, it is likely that the lack of other instruments under the WTO has encouraged governments to cynically set overly high bound tariffs. This permits considerable discretion in the selection of tariff levels, and thus a greater degree of uncertainty with regard to the effective trade regime at any point in time.

In practical political terms, currently very few countries have access to the SSG provision, an exemption to tariff ceiling levels. Eligibility to this safeguard process is limited because the majority of developing countries did not "tariffy." Instead, they offered ceiling bindings, or made pre-WTO commitments.

With respect to domestic support policies, there are both bound supports under nonexempt policies subject to the commitments of aggregate expenditure ceilings (the aggregate measurement of support—AMS—established during the Uruguay Round), and nonbound supports, exempt from limits, operating within the green box. In addition, developing countries have access to a special category of exempted supports under the "Special and Differential Treatment" provision of the Uruguay Round Agreement on Agriculture—investment subsidies, input subsidies to low-income farmers, and so on. Most developing countries (61 of 71) reported zero AMS levels—and in the remaining 10, these levels are very small. In part this was due to fiscal limitations (Konandreas). The implication is that most developing countries are limited in their support options to deal with price risk to action under the *de minimis* provisions and the definitions of government support contained in the green box, and are thus restricted in their use of nonborder support policies. In contrast, developed countries (and a few developing countries) reported high AMS.

Therefore, here is the situation: Developing countries have fewer fiscal resources to manage price risk and aid their farmers through domestic supports, and have fewer alternative market instruments to compensate for the higher probability of periods of low domestic prices that might result from further moves toward trade liberalization. This leaves many governments in developing countries with the temptation to seek protection of their import-competing sectors through border measures. From an economist's perspective of the welfare gains from trade, and from a practitioner's perspective of facilitating the liberalization process, current WTO negotiations might well consider providing greater flexibility to developing economies with respect to well-defined and disciplined tariffs and surcharges. Such flexibility might come through permitting the application of price bands or price floors, the modification of the general WTO safeguards, and—perhaps the most promising—the alteration or adaptation of the special safeguard clause for countries with low bound tariffs.

### *Price Bands*

An instrument that has been used in several countries in Latin America is a system of price bands. Price bands function in a similar manner to the use of a simple price floor, although important points of difference exist. Price bands stabilize prices between a floor and a ceiling—both of which typically are based on moving averages of past world prices, not a domestic target price. For example, in the case of Chile, the moving average for wheat is based on 60 months, and for sugar 120 months.[10] Such a scheme implies a moving floor price level that would trigger government intervention. In the past the analytical justification of price bands has been on stabilization *per se* rather than on the avoidance of extremely low price events. In fact, the automatic, reflexive nature of determining the price bands can lead to levels of floor prices that would be difficult to justify in terms of protecting against the risk of unsustainable low prices. For

**FIGURE 10.2 Price Band of Sugar in Chile**

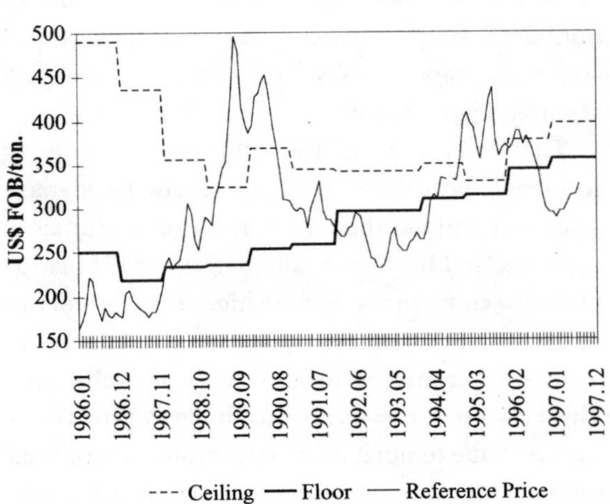


**FIGURE 10.3 Price Band of Edible Oil in Chile**

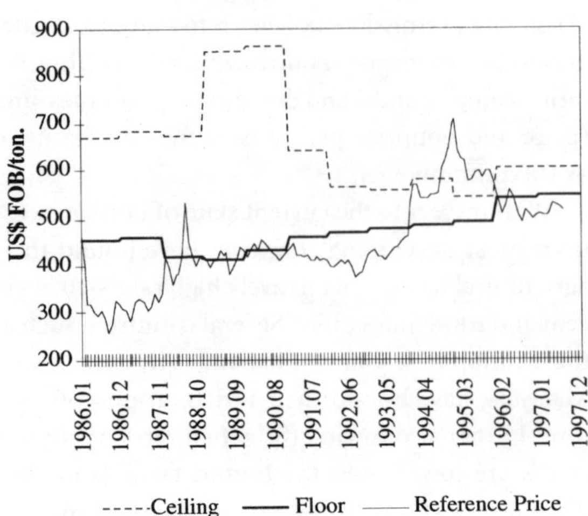


example, in the case of Chilean sugar, there have been periods in which the floor price in dollars has exceeded the price ceilings in other periods (see figure 10.2). Figures 10.2 and 10.3 show the evolution of the price floor and ceiling for sugar and edible oil in Chile. It is difficult to rationalize the narrowing over time of the price bands in these cases, except by reference to the manner by which the dynamics of international price formation affect the mechanical determination of the floor and ceiling.

The price floors associated with price bands as they have been typically applied are simply moving averages, reducing near-term volatility but not offering an assured minimum level as a fixed point of reference. Indeed, the adjusting price floor in a price band scheme is in many cases merely a means of deferring, or delaying price changes that inevitably must occur. For example, the 1998 floor price for Chilean wheat was US$150 per ton, implying a minimum cost, insurance, and freight price of US$175 per ton, well above the long-term minimum average production cost of the commodity in neighboring Argentina. Certainly there is nothing in price band schemes that involves moving-averages price that guarantees some long-term worst-case scenario for producers' incomes and ability to service debt. From recent experience with a relatively high price, supported in the short term by the price floor, it is difficult to assess whether or not the policy has caused investment in the wheat sector (or generated the long-term financing) greater than what would otherwise have been the case. Productivity certainly has grown in wheat and sugar, but not notably at a faster rate than in non-protected commodities such as maize.

### *Price Floors*

In place of price bands as traditionally applied, one policy option that might be worthy of consideration is a simplified fixed price floor scheme for the elimination of the worst-case scenarios associated with several concurrent years of especially low world prices. For specific "sensitive" commodities, a minimum world price or threshold level might be defined, below which a government would commit itself to intervention in order to maintain the domestic price received by producers.[11] In terms of international acceptability, this threshold price should be based on the minimum-average cost of the least-cost international exporter, and therefore be unmistakably transitory, in the sense that prices in the future would almost certainly rise. For example, when sugar prices reached US$250 per ton in 1985, sugar production was unprofitable even in Australia, one of the most cost-efficient producers in the world; one could have concluded that world prices were unmistakably low and resources would certainly move from sugar production, and price would rise in the future. In fact, two years later, prices increased to approximately US$400 per ton.

It is worth emphasizing that the objective of the type of price-floor policy discussed here is more narrowly defined than that of price stabilization as pursued by most current stabilization schemes. A price floor that is based on some fixed, internationally recognized, most-efficient average cost of production would be meant to provide a safety net against the lowest prices, as a form of price insurance. While this would likely reduce the variance of domestic price, the objective would not be to insulate domestic prices in any general sense. Indeed, a simple floor policy would allow the flow of information between international and domestic markets through price signals in all periods except those with extremely low and certainly transitory low prices. A policy based on the free transfer of price signals except at the lowest of prices would leave unhindered the development of risk markets, the use of futures, and other activities that "price stabilization" programs have tended to impede.

While the principal advantage of a price floor would be the protection of producers in long-run viable sectors that might not otherwise survive extremely low prices in the short run, there are some other advantages worth mentioning. From an economic perspective, in the present environment of immature markets in which agriculture finds itself in many developing countries, the elimination of "worst-price scenarios" could provide incentives to investment in promising sectors. While eliminating the worst-price risk, which a developing-country economy is not yet able to diversify away by other means, a price floor based solely on the most efficient world producer would not distort long-run returns to investment and would not protect long-run uncompetitive sectors. Moreover, in terms of credit and the ability of lenders to securitize producers' cash flows, variance-stabilizing policies, such as moving-average price bands, do not have the advantage of an easily referenced and guaranteed forecast of a minimum worst-case scenario that would result from a fixed price floor.

In terms of practical implementation, for import-competing commodities, a price floor policy could be implemented through a system of variable surcharges that are only triggered by a predetermined, international reference price along the lines of the safeguard mechanisms of the WTO.[12] Unlike a variable levy, there would be no domestic target price. It appears clear that a basic principle or criterion for establishing a feasible floor price policy should be the limited nature of the interventions. The record of most ad hoc price stabilization programs is one of a proliferation of distortions and indiscriminate protections that are difficult to justify.[13] A second criterion would also be important: a product selected for special treatment with a price floor should be a standardized commodity of the type that has a near-perfect substitute on international markets.[14] The application of these two criteria would guard against both the protection of goods that are not economically profitable in the long run and the tendency of governments to complicate and manipulate for short-term objectives programs that ought to be transparent and based on long-term economic feasibility.

It must be recognized, however, that this kind of scheme would not be free of practical difficulties. One difficult issue would be the determination of the internationally lowest production cost. This was tried before in Australia, with the result that the process became tainted by political influence. Some mechanism would need to be used to guard against a similar outcome, and it is not clear how this could feasibly be done. This concern would need to be considered in the calculus of the decision on what option is most likely to lower political resistance to dismantling high tariff barriers without putting in their place something equally as protectionist, or worse.

## General WTO Safeguards and Contingency Measures

When there is either an abrupt and large surge of imports, or a sudden decline in import prices that threaten a country's import-competing sector, WTO safeguards or contingency measures are applicable. These relatively well-known measures permit the suspension of WTO obligations, at least temporarily and in some cases permanently. General safeguard measures can be classified in the following manner (see Konandreas; Hoekman and Kostecki 1996):

- Antidumping measures that counteract the effects of private firms using price discrimination that lowers export prices below home market prices. The legal test is that of material injury to a domestic industry. The most notorious use of antidumping measures has been by the U.S.; however, such measures have been used by some developing countries, although with only partial success. Paz Caferata and Valdés (2000) observe that in Latin American and Caribbean countries, of the 469 antidumping investigations initiated during the period 1987–97, 60 were related to agriculture—but only 199 (of 469) investigations were adopted, and among those, only three (of 60) applied to agricultural products. While overall, 42 percent of the investigations led to the adoption of antidumping measures, only 5 percent of the requests in agriculture were adopted at the country level.[15]

- Countervailing duties, which are also based on material injury to a domestic industry, but apply to the subsidization by the exporting country's government.
- Emergency safeguards, which are explicitly temporary and limited in frequency of use. These are immediately applicable without formalities in the event of imports threatening serious injury to domestic industries. The use of this measure does not presume any "unfair" behavior on the part of exporting firms or governments, but is restrictive both in time and repeatable application.[16]
- Measures related to balance of payments to safeguard a government's external financial position.
- "General waivers," which enable countries to ask for these. This requires formal authorization by the WTO Council.
- Modifications of schedules and renegotiations of tariffs.

### *The Special Safeguards Provision (SSG)*

Special safeguards are applicable to agricultural producers under the Agreement on Agriculture, restricted to products that were included in the Uruguay Round tariffication process. Many developing countries simply are not eligible to use the SSG provision because they set bound tariffs outside of the tariffication mechanism. Of course, the future status of special safeguards is questionable, as they are especially vulnerable to the criticisms from the Cairns Group. Nevertheless, it is possible to adapt or modify the special safeguard clause to allow effective border measures in the management of the low-price risk relevant to developing-country import-competing sectors.

The clearly stated impetus for modifying the special safeguard scheme would have to be to permit countries to apply tariffs beyond their bound ceilings in the event that otherwise-competitive domestic producers face severe injury during periods of extremely low prices. This justification for any modification would be moot for commodities for which bound tariffs are already high. But as Konandreas notes, "There is no apparent relationship between access to the existing SSG and low bound tariffs. Eligibility to the existing SSG clause has very little relationship to the problem that it presumably was meant to address" (p. 12).

In practical terms, how might the special safeguard clause be adjusted so that it would be oriented toward protecting farmers from the risk of low world prices in the absence of a sufficiently flexible (and WTO-legitimate) standard tariff system, or where domestic supports are inadequate? The first modification is to allow special safeguards only for commodities and countries for which bound tariffs are below some threshold (Konandreas suggests 70 percent, although the authors would suggest a limit of 35 percent). As a variation on this theme, the upper limit to variable safeguards could be inversely related to the bound tariff. This would induce the governments to set lower bound tariffs, because they would have access to additional border protections triggered in emergencies.

But how would one define such emergencies? The triggering of variable safeguards would have to be specified in terms of well-defined low price events, universally applicable to all countries, developed and developing. This would necessarily involve a negotiation process within a WTO-established framework, which would have to determine coverage of importables that qualify for variable special safeguards and would have to establish a process of registration.

A third possible modification of the special safeguards clause would be to make access to it contingent on domestic support transfers. Countries with the ability to use other safety net mechanisms, such as farm revenue insurance along the lines of Canada's Net Income Stabilization Account, to protect producers during periods of low prices would be excluded. Konandreas suggests, for example, that special safeguards be limited to countries with domestic support below 15–20 percent of the value of domestic production.

There is a technical discussion ongoing in Geneva and in the United Nations system on these issues. The specificity of these measures, their legality, their operational implementation, and their relative effectiveness are questions that would be major research efforts in and of themselves, and which are certainly worthy of the professional attention of economists and others committed to improving the performance of the international trade system.

## Notes

1. In this paper, we put emphasis on price risk and developing-country farmers in terms of further policy reforms. Nevertheless, we recognize that the topic of price risk is relevant to consumers as well, particularly low-income consumers. With trade reforms and world prices determining to a greater extent domestic prices, consumers could benefit from lower food prices, although these might be more volatile. On the negative side, however, there is a perceived problem of increased import dependence. This is in essence a food supply management issue, and often examined in the context of food security.

2. With policies restricted to tariffs, an important choice is between differentiated and uniform tariffs. While most trade economists favor low, uniform tariffs, one can always find technical economic arguments for applying higher or lower tariffs in some products. But the process is almost always corrupted, a captive of special interests. Harberger concludes his 1984 edited volume, *World Economic Growth*, with several policy lessons, one of which is entitled, "Some types and patterns of trade restrictions are far worse than others" (p. 431). The author notes that "[t]he only sure way to guarantee against catastrophic variations in rates of effective protection—even with moderate-looking rates of nominal protection on final products—is to make the rate of nominal protection uniform across all products. . . . For only when all nominal rates of protection are equal are all effective rates equal to this same nominal rate. Only a given uniform rate of tariff can automatically avoid capricious and distorting variations in the effective rates of protection actually achieved. Modification of tariff schedules in the direction of greater equality is thus one of the most important reforms advocated by professionals." And again in *Frontiers of Development Economics*, edited by Meier and Stiglitz (2001), Harberger states: "Yet, I have not the slightest doubt that, asked to choose between Ramsey tariffs and uniform tariffs, or between a Ramsey-style differentiated value-added tax and a broadly based, uniform one, my practicing professionals and Williamson's consensus members would vote overwhelmingly in favor of the uniform-rate alternatives. In doing so they would be expressing not the implications of neoclassical theory but rather what they think of as practical wisdom derived from long experience. This is a political-economy argument for uniformity, not a neoclassical one" (Harberger 2001, p. 549).

3. Another aspect, which we do not consider here, is the effect of trade liberalization and price transmission on agricultural value added, and not simply on prices. The case of Brazil after the 1991 reforms is very interesting: border protection on tradable inputs fell rapidly and significantly, benefiting the producers of exportables (whose export taxes were eliminated) and partially compensating producers of importables who confronted tariff reductions on their products. The data suggest that the reduction in price of purchased inputs and machinery tended to favor mid-size and larger farmers.

4. Of course, productivity and factor use are endogenous and not independent of policy, but this issue is beyond the scope of the present discussion.

5. Recently in Chile farm lobbies proposed, with considerable political support from legislators, a surcharge on imported milk product prices that would compensate one-for-one the EU export subsidy on milk. If adopted, this proposal would lead to internal Chilean prices approximately equal to the internal European price. This would grossly overestimate the true distortion in world prices.

6. See, for example, Zietz and Valdés (1989) for the OECD (in Goldin and Knudsen, eds.), and Tyers and Anderson (1992) for work on developed and developing countries.

7. A number of methodological questions can be raised regarding the particular estimates of the effects of trade liberalization derived from these models. There are three notable themes:

- There is a complex interaction between domestic distortions and the transmission of these distortions into domestic markets. What is assumed in estimation models about price transmission is an important issue in and of itself (Coleman 1995; Taylor 2002). For example, prices in remote areas tend to exhibit independence from prices in major trading centers. Notwithstanding, one can draw on various parameters to estimate export demand and supply in order to predict the overall sector's response—even if there are various subsets of producers that are not well integrated in the markets for tradables. This question is one of distributional welfare implications, and we return briefly to this issue below.
- How realistic are the assumptions about transmission? Some earlier work (for example, Valdés and Zietz 1980) assumed perfect transmission, but more recent studies (such as Tyers and Anderson 1992) have allowed for the possibility of lower transmission elasticities. This is an empirical question grounded in the nature of the data available and the econometric subtleties required to give flexibility to the analysis.
- What about the interdependence across products, both horizontally and vertically, extending upward through processed products? Processed agricultural products (for instance, orange juice concentrate, tomato paste, processed frozen and canned products, and wine) are rarely considered. It is a complex analytical problem, involving a proliferation of parameters that might adequately account for cross-product effects. Some authors consider a fixed-proportion world, others are inclined to an Armington-style approach. In our opinion this has not been solved in a satisfactorily rigorous way.

8. RUNS is an acronym for Rural-Urban North-South. This model was developed as a joint OECD and World Bank project, and includes 22 regions and 20 sectors, 15 of which are agricultural, covering the years 1985–2002.

9. For further analysis of a more recent nature, we refer the reader to the OECD (2001) report on export subsidies, "A Forward-Looking Analysis of Export Subsidies in Agriculture," and the ERS/USDA study edited by Burfisher (2001).

10. Also for the application of the bands, 25 percent of the highest and lowest prices are eliminated for calculation of the moving average.

11. A government's commitment to intervene at very low prices should likely be reserved for one or only a few commodities, the long-term international competitiveness of which is highly probable. This basic criterion of long-term comparative advantage of selected commodities would preclude encouraging commodity production for the purposes of self-sufficiency or other goals inconsistent with developing patterns of free trade based on underlying differences in costs of production. For example, supporting rice production in Chile would not be consistent with this criterion, nor would promoting the production in tropical climates of commodities associated with temperate zones, as has been the case with crops such as wheat in Colombia or sorghum in Venezuela.

12. For exported commodities, a fund built of producer contributions during periods in which the floor policy is dormant could finance producers in periods of extremely low prices. In the case of exportables, the use of put options could complement a price floor policy and be useful in the initial years of operation before fund reserves could cover a string of low-price events.

13. Not only does the floating nature of price bands undermine the use of any floor for guaranteeing medium-term agricultural loans (and tend to preclude alternative market developments that could reduce the consequences of price risk), as a broad rule bands have been applied indiscriminately to various commodities and products. This has been notable in the cases of Colombia, Republica Bolivariana de Venezuela, and Ecuador, where more than 120 importable goods are covered by the policy. The administration of such a system of price bands has been cumbersome at best and has tended to make the structure of incentives and effective protection almost unpredictable (Quiroz 1996, 1997).

14. This criterion precludes stabilization programs for agroindustrial products derived from basic commodities, which in effect become indistinguishable from crude protectionism, as has been the experience during the 1990s with price bands for "derivatives" in Ecuador, Colombia, and Venezuela.

15. Argentina, Brazil, and Mexico initiated 87 percent of Latin America and the Caribbean region's antidumping investigations during 1987–97, and 88 percent of the investigations related specifically to agriculture (Paz Caferata and Valdés 2000).

16. Notification to the WTO is required.

## Select Bibliography

Burfisher, M. E., ed. 2001. "Agricultural Policy Reform in the WTO—The Road Ahead." Market and Trade Economics Division, ERS, USDA, Agricultural Economic Report no. 802, Washington, D.C.

Caner, M., and B. Hansen. 1997. "Threshold Autoregression with a Unit Root." Boston College Working Papers in Economics, no. 381, Boston, Mass.

Cafferata, P., and A. Valdés. 2000. "Interests and Options in the WTO 2000 Negotiations: Latin America and the Caribbean." In M. D. Ingco and L. A. Winters, eds., *Agricultural Trade Liberalization in a New Trade Round: Perspectives of Developing Countries and Transition Economies.* Washington, D.C.: World Bank.

Cafferata Paz, J., and A. Valdés. 2001. "Agricultural Trade Liberalization in a New Trade Round." In M. D. Ingco and L. A. Winters, eds., World Bank Discussion Papers No 418, World Bank, Washington, D.C.

Cashin, P., H. Liang, and J. McDermott. 1999. "How Persistent Are Shocks to World Commodity Prices?" IMF Working Papers, IMF, Washington, D.C.

Coleman, D. 1995. "Problems of Measuring Price Distortion and Price Transmission: A Framework for Analysis." *Oxford Agrarian Studies* 23(1): 3–13.

Deaton, A. 1992. "Commodity Prices, Stabilization, and Growth in Africa." Research Program in Development Studies, Discussion Paper 166. Princeton University.

Gersovitz, M., and C. Paxson. 1990. "The Economics of Africa and the Prices of Their Export." *Studies in International Finance,* 68, Princeton University Department of Economics, Princeton, New Jersey.

Goldin, I., and O. Knudsen. 1989. *Agricultural Trade Liberalisation: Implications for Developing Countries.* Paris and Washington, D.C.: Organisation for Economic Development and Co-operation and the World Bank.

Goldin, I., O. Knudsen, and D. van der Mensbrugghe. 1993. *Trade Liberalisation: Global Economic Implications.* Paris and Washington, D.C.: Organisation for Economic Development and Co-operation and the World Bank.

Harwood J., R. Heifner, K. Cable, J. Perry, and A. Somwaru. 1999. "Managing Risks in Farming: Concepts, Research, and Analysis." *Agricultural Economics Report* 774, U.S.D.A. Economic Research Service, Washington, D.C.

Harberger, A. C., ed. 1984. "World Economic Growth: Case Studies of Developed and Developing Nations." Institute of Contemporary Studies, San Francisco.

———. 2001. "The View from the Trenches: Development Processes and Policies as Seen by a Working Professional." In G. M. Meier and J. E. Stiglitz, eds., *Frontiers of Development Economics: The Future in Perspective.* New York: Oxford University Press.

Hoekman, B., and M. Kostecki. 1996. "The Political Economy of the World Trading System: From GATT to WTO." Oxford and New York: Oxford University Press.

Ingco, M. D. 1996. "Progress in Agricultural Trade Liberalization and Welfare of Least-Developed Countries." International Trade Division, World Bank, Washington, D.C.

Josling, T. 1980. "Developed Country Agricultural Policies and Developing Country Food Supplies: The Case of Wheat." (Research Report). International Food Policy Research Institute (IFPRI), Washington, D.C.

Konandreas, P. 2000. "The Need for Effective Safeguards against Very Low World Market Prices in the Context of the WTO Negotiations on Agriculture." United Nations Food and Agriculture Organization (FAO) Informal Expert Consultation, December 7–8, FAO, Rome.

León, J., and R. Soto. 1995. "Structural Breaks and Long-Run Trends in Commodity Prices." Policy Research Working Paper 1406, World Bank, Washington, D.C.

McCulloch, N., L. A. Winters, and X. Cirera. 2002. Trade Liberalization and Poverty: A Handbook. London: Centre for Economic Policy Research.

Mundlak, Y., and D. Larson. 1992. "On the Transmission of World Agricultural Prices." *World Bank Economic Review,* 6(3): 399–422.

OECD (Organisation for Economic Co-operation and Development). 2001. "A Forward-Looking Analysis of Export Subsidies in Agriculture." Paris, OECD. oecd.org.

Perron, P. 1989. "The Great Crash, the Oil Price Shock and the Unit Root Hypothesis." *Econometrica* 57(6): 1361–1401.

Quiroz, J., and R. Soto. 1995. "International Price Signals in Agricultural Prices: Do Governments Care?" Documento de Investigación no. 88, Programa de Postgrado en Economía, ILADES/Georgetown University, Santiago, Chile.

Quiroz J., W. Foster, and A. Valdés. 1999. "Agricultural Price Instability and Price Floors: A Proposal." World Bank, Washington, D.C.

Sarris, A. 1997a. "¿Ha aumentado la inestabilidad de los mercados internacionales de cereales?" Revista Española de Economía Agraria, 181 (September– December): 157–82.

———. 1997b. "Risk Management in Cereal and Oilseed Markets." Paper prepared for the Commodity Risk Management Group, World Bank, Washington, D.C.

———. 1999a. "Commodity Risk Management for Developing Countries: Towards Implementing a New Approach." Paper prepared for the Commodity Risk Management Group, World Bank, Washington, D.C.

———. 1999b. "Price and Income Variability." Paper prepared for the Commodity Risk Management Group, World Bank, Washington, D.C.

Schiff, M., and A. Valdés. 1992. *A Synthesis of the Economics in Developing Countries.* Vol. 4 of *The Political Economy of Agricultural Pricing Policy.* Baltimore and London: Johns Hopkins University Press.

Taylor, J. E. 2002. "Trade Integration and Rural Economies in Less Developed Countries: Lessons from Micro Economy-Wide Models with Particular Attention to Mexico and Central America." Working Paper, Latin America and Caribbean Office of the World Bank, Washington, D.C.

Tsetsekos, G., and P. Varangis. 1999. "The Structure of Derivatives Exchanges: Lessons from Developed and Emerging Markets." Paper prepared for the Commodity Risk Management Group, World Bank, Washington, D.C.

Tyers, R., and K. Anderson. 1992. *Disarray in World Food Markets, A Quantitative Assessment.* Cambridge: Cambridge University Press.

Valdés, A. 1996. "Surveillance of Agricultural Price and Trade Policy in Latin America during Major Policy Reforms." Discussion Paper 349, World Bank, Washington, D.C.

———. 2000. "Measures of Agricultural Support in Transition Economies: 1994–1997." In A. Valdés, ed., *Agricultural Support Policies in Transition Economies,* World Bank Technical Paper 470, Europe and Central Asia Environmentally and Socially Sustainable Development Series, Washington, D.C.

Valdés, A., and W. Foster. 2002. "Reflections on the Policy Implications of Agricultural Price Distortions and Price Transmission for Producers in Developing and Transition Economies." Paper presented at the OECD Global Forum on Agriculture, Agricultural Trade Reform, Adjustment and Poverty, May 23–24, Paris.

Valdés, A., and J. Zietz. 1980. "Agricultural Protection in OECD Countries: Its Cost to Less-Developed Countries." International Food Policy Research Institute, Washington, D.C.

Valdés, A., and J. Zietz. 1995. "Distortions in World Food Markets in the Wake of GATT: Evidence and Policy Implications." *World Development 23*(6): 913–26.

Zietz, J., and A. Valdés. 1989. "International Interactions in Food and Agricultural Policies: The Effect of Alternative Policies." In I. Goldin and O. Knudsen, eds., *Agricultural Trade Liberalization: Implications for Developing Countries.* Paris: OECD.

Zivot, E., and D. Andrews. 2002. "Further Evidence on the Great Crash, the Oil Price Shock and the Unit Root Hypothesis." *Journal of Business and Economic Statistics* 20(1): 25–44.

11

# THE SANITARY AND PHYTOSANITARY AGREEMENT, FOOD SAFETY POLICIES, AND PRODUCT ATTRIBUTES

*Simonetta Zarrilli*[1] *with Irene Musselli*[2]

## Introduction

The issue of human and animal health and plant protection is high on the agenda of several developed countries, fueled by recent cases of food poisoning, the spread of pests among animals, and environmental contamination. International trade is perceived as a magnifier of such problems. Developing countries appreciate that, in several cases, these concerns are genuine, but they fear that developed countries may use sanitary and phytosanitary (SPS) measures for protectionist purposes. Their concern is well founded, since the major difficulty in dealing with SPS measures is likely to lie in distinguishing those measures that are justified by a legitimate goal, and have a scientific justification, from those that are applied to shield domestic producers from other-country agricultural exports.

Developing countries are not well positioned to address this issue. They lack complete information on the number of SPS measures that affect their exports, they are uncertain whether these measures are consistent or inconsistent with the World Trade Organization's (WTO's) SPS Agreement, and they have no reliable estimate of the impact of such measures on their exports.

Most developing countries are unable to participate effectively in the international standard-setting process relating to SPS measures and therefore face difficulties when requested to meet requirements in the importing markets, based on international standards. Transparency-related requirements usually represent a burden for developing countries, and they are often unable to benefit from them, owing to lack of appropriate infrastructure. With the relative lack of scientific and technical expertise, they experience serious problems with testing and conformity assessment. The regional conditions provision of the SPS Agreement, which greatly benefits developing countries, has been little used because of difficulties related to its scientific aspects. The provisions relating to special and differential treatment in favor of developing countries remain rather theoretical, and apparently have not led to any concrete steps.

The need for specialist scientific or technical knowledge makes restrictions imposed for health and safety reasons much more difficult to challenge than some other barriers to trade. While the requirement that SPS measures be based on scientific evidence helps secure trade policy objectives, it is perceived by some environmental and consumer protection groups in some developed and developing countries as a dangerous limitation on the right of governments to take precautionary measures to protect their citizens and the environment against risks that can have irreversible effects. Differences between "sound science" and the "precautionary approach" to health and safety are causing acute tensions among countries.

The situation is further complicated by the emergence of biotechnology, and international trade in biotechnology products. Because of the scientific uncertainty related to the impact of biotechnology products on health and on the environment and strong consumer resistance in some countries to these products, restrictive trade measures are increasingly being implemented by a number of governments. While the same rules apply to all countries, developing countries are facing several challenges in this field. As exporters, they may have to prove that their products do not contain any bioengineered inputs. This may imply a system of certification and segregation that can be costly and burdensome. As importers, they have to justify the scientific basis for their trade measures.

Equivalence of SPS measures is of special relevance to developing countries when one takes into account the share and destination of their agricultural exports, and considers that they face climatic, developmental, and technological conditions that often differ from those prevailing in developed countries. However, equivalence has not yet been recognized in a significant number of trade transactions.

The Doha Ministerial Decision on Implementation-Related Issues and Concerns provides some flexibility to developing countries in relation to the timeframe for compliance with the SPS measures,[3] to the interval between the publication of an SPS measure and its entry into force, to the issue of equivalence, to developing-country participation in the international standard-setting activities, and to technical assistance.

### *The Plan of This Chapter*

This chapter aims to recall the main features of the SPS Agreement and its purposes and negotiating history, stress some of the main difficulties encountered by developing countries in this area, and formulate a number of suggestions on how to improve developing countries' ability to use and benefit from the agreement. The chapter also proposes some actions that developing countries may wish to consider in the course of the current trade negotiations.

For developing countries, the most promising option to maintain and expand their agricultural and food exports is to respond to opportunities in their target markets by providing high-quality, safe products. This implies building up knowledge, skills, and capabilities. Strengthening domestic capacities in the SPS domain would also help developing countries to identify products that they may wish to keep out of their markets because of the actual or potential negative impact on human health and safety, animal health, or the environment. However, for this goal to materialize, developing countries need the support of their developed partners, international trade organizations, and technical organizations. They also need a multilateral legal framework that will facilitate achievement of such a result.

## The SPS Agreement

### *Negotiating History*

When the Uruguay Round started, there was a consensus that the time had come for reform of international agricultural trade (Stewart 1993). The Punta del Este Declaration, which launched the Round in September 1986, called for increased disciplines in three areas in the agricultural sector: market access, direct and indirect subsidies, and sanitary and phytosanitary measures. On the lattermost, the negotiators sought to develop a multilateral system that would allow simplification and harmonization of SPS measures, as well as elimination of all restrictions that lacked any valid scientific basis.

At the outset of the Round the negotiating positions were as follows: the United States (U.S.) and the European Communities (EUs) proposed broad harmonization efforts, based on the expertise of international organizations; and the European Communities called for all standards to be based on scientific evidence. The Cairns Group endorsed the broad recommendations toward harmonization and suggested that the burden of justification of SPS measures should be placed on the importing country. Japan supported harmonization efforts based on the work of international organizations, giving preference to the development of guidelines rather than standards; the improvement of notification and consultation procedures and of the dispute settlement mechanism;

and special allowances for developing countries. Developing countries strongly advocated the removal of sanitary and phytosanitary measures that acted as nontariff barriers to trade. They supported the international harmonization of SPS measures to prevent developed countries from imposing arbitrarily strict standards.

At the Mid-Term Review of the Uruguay Round (December 1988), it was agreed that the priorities in the area of SPS were international harmonization on the basis of the standards developed by international organizations, development of an effective notification process for national regulations, establishment of a system for the bilateral resolution of disputes, improvement of the dispute settlement process, and provision for the necessary input of scientific expertise and judgment, relying on relevant international organizations.

The Working Group on Sanitary and Phytosanitary Regulations, formed in 1988, produced a draft text in November 1990. Its central feature was the proposal to establish disciplines for SPS measures in an agreement separate from the draft Agreement on Agriculture. The negotiators reached consensus on a number of points: SPS measures should not represent disguised trade barriers; they should be harmonized on the basis of international standards, guidelines, and recommendations and of generally accepted scientific principles; special consideration should be taken of developing countries and their difficulties in meeting standards; transparency should be ensured in setting regulations and in solving disputes; and an international committee should be established to provide for consultations regarding standards. Some areas, however, remained unsettled.

As a result of deadlock in the agricultural negotiations, the Uruguay Round was not concluded in December 1990. A year later, however, the Director-General of the General Agreement on Tariffs and Trade (GATT) put forward a package of proposals (the so-called Dunkel draft) that incorporated both newly negotiated text and personal proposals by chairpersons of the negotiating groups. For SPS measures, the Dunkel text closely followed the draft text produced by the working group in November 1990. The final text of the SPS Agreement, as approved at the end of the Uruguay Round, was largely based on the Dunkel text and fulfills the general objectives of the Punta del Este Declaration.

### *Salient Features of the SPS Agreement and the Legal Framework*

The main goal of the SPS Agreement is to prevent SPS measures from having unnecessary negative effects on international trade and from being misused for protectionist purposes. However, the agreement fully recognizes the legitimate interest of countries in setting up rules to protect food safety and animal and plant health, and in fact allows countries to give these objectives priority over trade, provided there is a demonstrable scientific basis for their food safety and health requirements.

More specifically, the agreement covers measures adopted by countries to protect human or animal life from food-borne risks; human health from animal- or plant-carried diseases; animals and plants from pests and diseases; and the territory of a country from the entry, establishment, or spread of pests. In sum, SPS measures are meant to ensure food safety and to prevent the spread of diseases among animals and plants.

Sanitary and phytosanitary measures are typically applied to both domestically produced and imported goods, may address the characteristics of final products, and may take the form of residue limits, conformity assessment certificates, inspections, quarantine requirements, designation of disease-free areas, and import bans.

The agreement states that countries should base SPS measures on science, and establish them on the basis of an assessment of the risk involved. Sanitary and phytosanitary measures should ensure that the appropriate level of protection (as determined by the country in question) is achieved. If international standards, guidelines, and recommendations exist, the agreement urges countries to base their SPS measures on them. It encourages countries to play a full part in the activities of international organizations to promote the harmonization of SPS regulations on an international basis; to accept the SPS measures of exporting countries as equivalent to their own if they achieve the same level of SPS protection; and, where possible, to conclude bilateral and multilateral agreements on recognition of the equivalence of specific SPS measures.

**BOX 11.1 The Joint FAO/WHO Codex Alimentarius Commission (CAC)**

The CAC is an intergovernmental body that reports to the Directors-General of FAO and WHO. It is open to all members of these two organizations, and currently has 166 members. It meets every two years. Its primary function is protecting the health of consumers while ensuring fair practices in the food trade. The commission's organizational structure comprises 23 Codex Committees and Task Forces, responsible for drafting food standards; six Regional Coordinating Committees to ensure regional coordination; and an Executive Committee that oversees the commission's work. The Codex Alimentarius is the complete collection of standards, codes of practice, guidelines, and recommendations adopted by the commission to achieve its objectives. The standards, guidelines, and recommendations established by the CAC on food additives, veterinary drug and pesticide residues, contaminants, methods of analysis and sampling, and codes and guidelines of hygienic practice are recognized by the SPS Agreement as the international reference for food safety requirements."

*Source:* Information provided by the relevant organization at the Meeting of the SPS Committee held on March 14–15, 2001.

The agreement requires countries to choose those measures that are no more trade restrictive than required to achieve domestic SPS objectives, provided these measures are technically and economically feasible (for example, applying a quarantine requirement instead of an import ban). The SPS Agreement recognizes that, owing to differences in geographical, climatic, and epidemiological conditions prevailing in different countries or regions, it would often be inappropriate to apply the same rules to products coming from different regions or countries. This flexibility should not, however, lead to any unjustified discrimination among foreign suppliers or in favor of domestic producers. On the same lines, governments should recognize disease-free countries, or disease-free areas within countries, and adapt their requirements to products originating in such countries or areas.

The agreement allows countries to introduce SPS measures that result in a higher level of protection than would be achieved by measures based on international standards, if there is a scientific justification or if a country determines on the basis of an assessment of risks that a higher level of sanitary and phytosanitary protection would be appropriate. In carrying out risk assessment, countries are urged to use techniques developed by the relevant international organizations. Since the entry into force of the SPS Agreement, a substantial amount of work has been undertaken in the area of risk analysis by the Food and Agriculture Organization (FAO)/World Health Organization (WHO) Joint Codex Alimentarius Commission (CAC) (see box 11.1), the Secretariat of the International Plant Protection Convention (IPPC) (see box 11.2), and the International Office of Epizootics (OIE) (see box 11.3).[4] The SPS Agreement permits governments to decline international standards and adopt lower standards. The agreement also permits the adoption of SPS measures on a provisional basis as a precautionary step, in cases in which there is an immediate risk related to the spread of diseases, food contamination, biodiversity damage, and so on, but where the scientific evidence is insufficient.

All countries must maintain an "enquiry point"—an office to receive and respond to requests for information regarding domestic SPS measures, including new or existing regulations and decisions based on risk assessment. Countries are required to notify the WTO Secretariat of any new SPS requirement, or modification of existing requirements, that they are proposing to introduce domestically, if the requirements differ from international standards and may affect international trade. The secretariat circulates the notifications to all WTO members. Notifications are to be submitted in advance of the implementation of the measure, so as to provide other countries with the opportunity to comment on them. In an emergency, governments may implement a measure prior to notification. Countries are also required—the original text of the paper uses the word "requested," but the agreement states that members

## BOX 11.2 The Office International des Epizooties (OIE)

The OIE, an intergovernmental organization with 158 member countries, is concerned with the occurrence and course of epizootics that could endanger animal or human health. Its objectives and functions include developing regulations designed to prevent the spread of transmissible diseases to humans and animals through trade in animals and animal products, and the harmonization of requirements for such trade, in order to avoid unjustified trade barriers. OIE standards are recognized by the SPS Agreement as international sanitary rules of reference. They are prepared by elected Specialist Commissions and by Working Groups bringing together internationally renowned scientists. Standards are adopted by the OIE's highest authority, the International Committee, meeting in General Session in May of each year. Standards, guidelines, and recommendations developed under the auspices of the OIE principally refer to standards for international trade in animals and animal products (International Animal Health Code, 10th Edition, 2001); standardized diagnostic techniques and vaccine control methods for use in international trade (Manual of Standards for Diagnostic Tests and Vaccines, 4th Edition, 2000); (International Aquatic Animal Health Code, 4th Edition, 2001; Diagnostic Manual for Aquatic Animal Diseases, 3rd Edition, 2000)."

*Source:* Information provided by the relevant organization at the Meeting of the SPS Committee held on March 14–15, 2001.

"shall ensure" that all SPS measures adopted are published promptly—to publish the sanitary and phytosanitary measures they have adopted and, except in urgent circumstances, to allow a reasonable interval between the publication of a new SPS measure and its entry into force.

The SPS Agreement provides for special and differential treatment in favor of developing countries and least-developed countries (LDCs). It includes, under certain circumstances, longer timeframes for compliance, time-limited exceptions from the obligations of the agreement, and facilitation of developing-country participation in the work of relevant international organizations.

The agreement includes provisions for a two-year grace period for all developing countries, which expired at the end of 1997. For LDCs, a five-year grace period expired at the end of 1999.

Prior to the entry into force of the SPS Agreement, health and safety regulations affecting imports were subject to the GATT and to the "plurilateral" 1979 Agreement on Technical Barriers to Trade ("Standards Code").[5]

The GATT recognizes, in Article XX(b) ("General Exceptions"), that protecting human, animal, and plant life and health is a legitimate objective of governments, and therefore exempts from GATT obligations, under specific and strict circumstances, measures designed to meet these objectives. The SPS Agreement provides detailed rules that supplement Article XX(b), especially relating to procedural obligations concerning appropriate risk assessment and proper scientific experimentation.

It is important to be able to distinguish measures that fall under the SPS Agreement from those falling under the Uruguay Round Agreement on Technical Barriers to Trade (TBT), which replaced the Standards Code. This distinction is relevant, as there are some significant differences in the provisions of the two agreements. Whether a specific measure is a technical regulation (and therefore within the scope of the TBT Agreement) or a sanitary/phytosanitary measure (under the SPS Agreement) depends on the objectives for which it has been adopted. As a general rule, if a measure is adopted to ensure the protection of human, animal, and plant life, and the health and protection of the territory of a country from damage caused by the entry, establishment, or spread of pests, it is an SPS measure. Measures adopted for purposes other than these are subject to the TBT Agreement. For instance, a pharmaceutical restriction would be a measure covered by the TBT Agreement (see WTO 1998). Labeling requirements related to food safety are usually SPS measures, while labels related to the nutrition characteristics or quality of a product fall under TBT disciplines.

As far as the legal relationship between the TBT and SPS Agreements and GATT 1994 is concerned, once SPS applies, TBT cannot apply. This is because

**BOX 11.3 The International Plant Protection Convention (IPPC)**

"The IPPC is a multilateral treaty deposited with the Director-General of the FAO. One hundred and seventeen governments are currently contracting parties to the IPPC. Amendments to the convention were unanimously adopted by the FAO Conference in 1997 (referred to as the 'New Revised Text of the IPPC') to update the convention and reflect the role of the IPPC in relation to the WTO-SPS Agreement. The convention is administered through the IPPC Secretariat located in FAO's Plant Protection Service. The Interim Commission on Phytosanitary Measures (ICPM), established as an interim measure by FAO until the IPPC (1997) comes into force, establishes priorities for standard setting and harmonization of phytosanitary measures. IPPC is named by the SPS Agreement as the international organization responsible for phytosanitary standard setting and the harmonization of phytosanitary measures affecting trade. To date, 17 international standards for phytosanitary measures (ISPMs) have been adopted. ISPMs 13 through 17 were adopted at the Fourth Session of the ICPM (March 11–15, 2002). Additionally, a number of standards are under development and revision."

*Source:* Information provided by the relevant organization at the Meeting of the SPS Committee held on March 14–15, 2001.

the SPS Agreement has a very well-defined but limited scope of application and is more rigorous than the TBT Agreement in its requirements. Either the SPS or the TBT Agreements and the GATT can apply concurrently. In the event of conflict between TBT/SPS and GATT, the specific agreement prevails over GATT, according to General Interpretative Note to Annex 1A of the the Marrakesh Agreement Establishing the World Trade Organization.

## Main Issues for Developing Countries in the SPS Agreement

### *Equivalence*

The November 2001 Doha Decision on Implementation-Related Issues and Concerns instructs the WTO SPS Committee "to develop expeditiously the specific program to further the implementation of Article 4 of the Agreement on the Application of Sanitary and Phytosanitary Measures" (WTO 2001a, para. 3.3).

Discussion on equivalency has been going on in the SPS Committee since 2000 and a decision on the implementation of equivalence was taken in October 2001 (WTO 2001b).

Article 4 of the SPS Agreement encourages countries to give positive consideration to accepting as equivalent the SPS measures of other WTO members, even if these measures differ from their own or from those used by other countries, if the exporting country demonstrates that its measures achieve the importing member's appropriate level of sanitary and phytosanitary protection. It also instructs countries to enter into consultations, upon request, with the aim of achieving bilateral and multilateral agreements on recognition of the equivalence of specified sanitary or phytosanitary measures.

Equivalence is the best option when harmonization of standards is not desirable or when international standards are lacking or are inappropriate. For developing countries—which face difficulties in trying to harmonize their standards with those of importing countries—the recognition of the equivalence of their SPS measures would represent a key instrument to enhance market access for their products. These countries face climatic, developmental, and technological conditions rather different from those prevailing in developed countries; recognition of the equivalence of their SPS measures to those applied by the importing countries would represent a key instrument to enhance market access for their products.

In this regard, the following issues might be of special concern to developing countries.

### *The Concept of Equivalence and Its Function*

The function of equivalence is to facilitate international trade by recognizing that different measures can achieve the same level of sanitary and phytosanitary protection. Therefore countries have flexibility about the kind of measures to adopt to ensure adequate SPS protection. Equivalence, then, is not about "duplication" or "sameness" of SPS measures. What is relevant is the achievement of the appropriate level of protection sought by the importing country. How this protection is achieved is not an autonomous issue. Methods might be relevant to the extent that the inquiry into methods is instrumental to assessing the achievement of the appropriate level of protection, but do not have any discrete relevance *per se.* The option of introducing additional requirements relating to how the level of protection is achieved would add an unnecessary burden to the recognition of equivalence.

### *Implementation of Equivalence*

The concept of equivalence lends itself to various applications (WTO 2000b and WTO 2001c). Variables on which the practical implementation of equivalence depends are, among others, the scope of the equivalence arrangement (specific products or product sectors, specific technical aspects of certain SPS measures, specific SPS measures, SPS systems, inspection and control systems, processing techniques); its level of formality (*ad hoc* recognition at the technical level,[6] unilateral determination of equivalence at the administrative level,[7] formal agreements); and the parties involved (bilateral or multilateral) (WTO 2000a). Equivalence arrangements on specific technical matters play an important role in building confidence between laboratories and certifying authorities in different countries and usually represent a necessary step toward the conclusion of broader arrangements. They may also represent crucial learning experiences, since they imply an intensive exchange of information and close contacts between relevant authorities.

### *Recognition of Equivalence versus Equivalence Agreements*

In the ongoing debate on equivalence, emphasis is increasingly placed on the "recognition of equivalence" rather than on formal "equivalence agreements." *Ad hoc* acceptance of the equivalence of particular SPS measures is largely recognized as the most effective way to apply the equivalence provisions. However, it might be worth considering some advantages associated with the negotiation of formal equivalence agreements. First, equivalence agreements can incorporate a general part establishing overall principles and long-term objectives, which might accommodate developing countries' attitudes and concerns on the issue of equivalence, and which might be reflected in the way specific equivalence arrangements are forged. Second, even if equivalence agreements are time consuming and resource intensive, developing countries might find it even more costly to seek equivalence on an *ad hoc* basis at the technical level. Argentina has proposed that equivalence agreements should contain a general part establishing overall principles, criteria, objectives, and long-term targets, and specific annexes for the products coming under the agreement (WTO 2001e).

### *Guidelines on the Recognition of Equivalence*

A related issue concerns the provision of guidance on the recognition of equivalence. International guidelines may be needed for the systematic application of equivalence. In particular, in the absence of guidelines on methodology for judging equivalence, specific bilateral issues are more likely to arise, and methodological concerns of developing countries are more likely to be neglected. International standard-setting bodies have been formally encouraged to elaborate guidelines, as appropriate, on the equivalence of SPS measures and equivalence agreements.[8] According to the March 2002 work program, draft guidance for the recognition of equivalence of products historically or previously traded, on the basis of categorization of trade patterns and risks, will be considered within the SPS Committee (WTO 2002a).

### *The North-South Dimension of Equivalence*

According to some WTO members, it might be desirable not to emphasize the North-South dimension of equivalence as this is seen as oversimplistic and not exhaustive, disregarding the reciprocal nature of equivalence arrangements and the fact that an increasing number of decisions are concerned with South-South trade. Even if equivalence cannot be reduced to a North-South issue, this dimension should not be underestimated. Equivalence is a particularly prominent issue for developing countries, reflecting their share and destination of agricultural and food exports,[9] their technical capability to comply with SPS requirements, and the diversity of conditions prevailing in developed and developing countries. Developing countries face climatic, developmental, and technological conditions that often differ from those prevailing in developed countries, and which might not be duly reflected in SPS systems designed and operated in developed countries. In these cases, equivalence could contribute considerably to sound results from a safety point of view, without unnecessary costs.

### *Equivalence and the Importing Member's Appropriate Level of Protection*

The concept of equivalence is linked to the determination of the appropriate level of protection. A crucial issue for the exporting country is therefore to identify the importing country's acceptable level of protection and the way the importing member sets it. It might be worth emphasizing that the determination of the level of protection is not an unquestionable sovereignty issue, being qualified by the wording of Article 5.4 (obligation to minimize negative trade effects) and Article 5.5 (obligation to avoid arbitrary or unjustifiable discriminations or disguised restrictions to international trade). The appropriate level of protection set by the importing country needs to be consistently met by domestically produced goods. SPS measures that are not enforced on domestic producers, but which are imposed on foreign ones, represent disguised trade restrictions. Another relevant issue concerns transparency and cooperation. In particular, the importing country should supply correct information on its acceptable level of risk so that the exporting country can meet the requirement of objectively demonstrating that its SPS measures are equivalent. In the salmon dispute (WTO 1998b), the WTO Appellate Body noted that although the determination of the appropriate level of protection is a prerogative of the member concerned, and there is no obligation to determine the appropriate level of protection in quantitative terms, this does not mean "that an importing member is free to determine its level of protection with such vagueness or equivocation that the application of the relevant provisions of the SPS Agreement, such as Article 5.6, becomes impossible" (WTO 1998b, paras. 199 and 206).

### *Burden of Proof and Costs Sharing*

A related issue is the division of responsibilities between the importer and the exporter in the determination of equivalence. According to the October 2001 Decision on the Implementation of Article 4 of the Agreement on the Application of Sanitary and Phytosanitary Measures (the "Decision on Equivalence") (WTO 2001g), the importing country should explain the objective and rationale of the SPS measure at stake, identify the risks that the measure is intended to address, indicate the appropriate level of protection that the measure is designed to achieve, and give full consideration to requests by developing countries for technical assistance to facilitate the implementation of Article 4. It is up to the importing country to analyze all relevant evidence provided by the exporting country on its SPS measures with a view to determining whether these measures achieve the appropriate level of protection. However, the importing country is not required to justify the refusal for equivalence, though it should respond, normally within six months, to any request of equivalence. A crucial issue in this respect is the impact on the competitiveness of the exported products of costs related to assessing equivalence of SPS measures and the sharing of such costs between the importer and exporter.

Equivalence at the regional level, in the framework of regional or subregional agreements, is easier to achieve. Developing countries may therefore have an interest in analyzing the possibility of including reference to the equivalency of SPS measures in the framework of regional and subregional groupings.[10]

A necessary precondition for implementing equivalence is the capacity of the exporting country to provide scientific and technical information to support the claim that its measures achieve the appropriate level of protection identified by the importing country. The latter may ask to check the laboratories and the testing facilities of the exporting country to be assured about the reliability of the information provided and the technical competence of the exporting country. Obviously a well-prepared case, adequately justified from a scientific point of view and supported by trustworthy certificates, will have more chance of being considered positively than an ill-prepared case. In this field, developing countries face enormous difficulties which could jeopardize their capacity to benefit from equivalence and from the specific work program. Operationalizing equivalence implies, therefore, the strengthening of developing-country scientific capacities, laboratories, and certification and accreditation authorities. The establishment of internationally financed national, regional, or subregional laboratories, certification bodies, and accreditation institutions could be explicitly included as one of the suitable outcomes of the work program on equivalence.

### *Special and Differential Treatment and Technical Assistance*

The SPS Agreement includes a specific article (Article 10) on special and differential treatment (S&D) for developing countries and LDCs, and another (Article 9) on technical assistance. The Doha Decision on Implementation-Related Issues and Concerns provided some instructions and clarifications aimed at operationalizing Article 10, and indicated July 2002 as the deadline for the identification of the S&D provisions that should be made mandatory and for examining additional ways in which S&D provisions can be made more effective (WTO 2001a, note 7, para. 3.1 and para. 12.1 (i) and (ii)).

The WTO Secretariat has identified six types of S&D provisions: (i) provisions aimed at increasing the trade opportunities of developing countries; (ii) provisions under which WTO members should safeguard the interests of developing countries; (iii) provisions concerning the flexibility of commitments, of actions, and use of policy instruments; (iv) provisions specifying transitional time periods; (v) provisions on technical assistance; and (vi) provisions related to LDCs. Provisions relating to flexibility and transition times tend to specify exceptions to rules to which developing countries may have recourse if they choose. Provisions relating to technical assistance, the safeguarding of the interests of developing countries, and measures to increase participation in world trade tend to specify positive actions to be undertaken by developed countries in favor of developing countries. According to this classification, Articles 10.1 and 10.4 of the SPS Agreement fall under the second category, Articles 10.2 and 10.3 fall under the fourth category, while Article 9 falls under the fifth category (WTO 2001g, pp. 5, 56–62). The WTO Secretariat has identified Article 10.1 and Article 9 as mandatory provisions and Articles 10.2 and 10.4 as nonmandatory provisions (WTO 2002b). Presumably, Article 10.3 is also a nonmandatory provision.

During the 1980s and in the early 1990s, the S&D principle came under criticism: instead of encouraging good polices and practices in the developing countries, it was seen as contributing to development-unfriendly policies. This perception influenced how S&D provisions were included in the Uruguay Round agreements: they reflect the trend toward reducing the scope for S&D, in particular for non-LDCs. The present rules and the related debate reflect a difficult equilibrium between the recognition of international asymmetries (implying that unequal countries cannot be treated as equals) and the notion of "leveling the playing field" (meaning that developing countries should not be shielded through discriminatory instruments in their favor, but helped to become more efficient and able to compete fairly in international markets). Special and differential provisions are included in two different areas of international economic cooperation: financial and monetary instruments as provided by the international and regional financial institutions; and trade disciplines at the multilateral and subregional levels. The latter are more prone to criticisms and challenges than the former (see UNCTAD Secretariat 2002; Breckenridge 2002).

Article 10.1 of the SPS Agreement states that the special needs of the developing and least-developed countries shall be taken into account in the preparation and application of SPS measures.

Article 10.2 states: "Where the appropriate level of sanitary or phytosanitary protection allows scope for the phased introduction of new sanitary and phytosanitary measures, longer time-frames for compliance should be accorded on products of export interest to developing country Members so as to maintain opportunities for their exports."

The Decision on Implementation clarifies that "longer time-frames for compliance" shall be understood to mean normally a period of not fewer than six months. Moreover, "Where the appropriate level of sanitary and phytosanitary protection does not allow scope for the phased introduction of a new measure, but specific problems are identified by a Member, the Member applying the measure shall upon request enter into consultations with the country with a view to finding a mutually satisfactory solution to the problem while continuing to achieve the importing member's appropriate level of protection" (WTO 2001a, note 7, para. 3.1).

Article 10.3 provides that specified, time-limited exceptions in whole or in part from the obligations under the SPS Agreement could be granted to developing countries by the SPS Committee, upon request, to ensure that developing countries are able to comply with the provisions of the agreement. To date, no request has been made under Article 10.3.

Article 10.4 refers to developing-country participation in the relevant international organizations. The issue is addressed in the following section.

It is worth stressing that developing countries' agricultural exports are concentrated in a few products and in a few markets and that the number of exporting enterprises is also limited. This situation should make it easier to implement Articles 10.1, 10.2, and 10.3 of the SPS Agreement and paragraph 3.1 of the Decision on Implementation. To further facilitate the functioning of such provisions, each developing and least-developed country could prepare a list of the main agricultural products it exports (perhaps a list of five to seven products), identify the principal countries of destination (again a list of five to seven markets), and circulate it among WTO members. Whenever new SPS measures affecting the listed products are introduced by a developed member, it should contact the developing countries concerned and ensure that the newly introduced measure is not going to disrupt traditional trade flows. For this to happen, the list should be "dynamic"—with products and markets added or deleted as necessary and detailed (for example, including pesticides used on exported products) to facilitate the task of the importing country in alerting the exporting country about new SPS measures that may have an impact on its exports.

If an importing country implements an SPS measure that is scientifically justified but disruptive, either the implementing country should reconsider the measure, or, if this proves impossible, provide assistance to the affected developing countries to meet the new requirements to preserve existing trade flows. The option of equivalence should also be considered. In this respect, developing countries have stressed that lack of adequate infrastructure, technology, finance, and skilled labor force, as well as lack of full understanding of the agreement, of appropriate administrative framework, and limited participation in the activities of the international standard-setting organizations and of the SPS Committee make it difficult for them to comply with the commitments under the agreement.[11]

As far as Article 10.3 is concerned, a delay in the implementation of the agreement would be worth pursuing under the condition that the transitional period is used to strengthen capacities in developing countries to satisfy their trade partners' SPS requirements, bring their domestic measures in conformity with international standards, and enter into equivalence agreements. For this to happen, international technical and financial support should be provided. Hence, developing countries will need longer time frames for compliance and technical assistance to make it possible for their products to meet the market requirements and for creating or strengthening the domestic institutional framework necessary to comply with the provisions of the agreement. In fact, granting a longer time frame for compliance without, at the same time, providing technical assistance, would have the effect only of postponing the problem. Transitional periods, longer time frames, and the like acquire a real meaning for development when they are accompanied by a policy package that facilitates the needed adjustments.

The provisions on S&D treatment are therefore very much linked to those on technical assistance. The SPS Agreement was apparently negotiated and concluded with little regard for the conditions necessary for its effective implementation, particularly in developing countries. Article 9.1 states that the assistance provided to developing countries, either bilaterally or through the appropriate international organizations, "may be, *inter alia,* in the areas of processing technologies, research, and infrastructure, including in the establishment of national regulatory bodies, and may take the form of credits, donations, and grants." This is a mandatory provision that, if carried out well, would create greater coherence in SPS policy because it would enable developing countries to establish the necessary infrastructural and other conditions needed for the effective implementation of the agreement. Technical cooperation and financial support, however, are not a panacea and should not be used to replace the removal of unnecessary SPS obstacles to trade.

Technical cooperation should be extended to cover capacity-building of the officials in charge of the enquiry points, as transparency is a key issue for the correct functioning of the agreement. It should be extended to upgrade the technical skill of personnel working in laboratories, certification bodies, and accreditation institutions, since their having a certain level of qualifications and training is a precondition for the international acceptance of certificates issued by them and represents the basis for the negotiation of equivalence agreements. Since developing countries experience difficulties in dealing with the scientific side of the agreement, in particular risk assessment, technical cooperation should be extended on this matter.

The Decision on Implementation addresses the issue of technical assistance, but only with reference to LDCs: it "(i) urges Members to provide, to the extent possible, the financial and technical assistance necessary to enable least-developed countries to respond adequately to the introduction of any new SPS measures that may have significant negative effects on their trade; and (ii) urges members to ensure that technical assistance is provided to least-developed countries with a view to responding to the special problems faced by them in implementing the Agreement on the Application of Sanitary and Phytosanitary measures" (WTO 2001a, note 7, para. 3.6).

According to Article 9.2, "where substantial investments are required in order for an exporting developing country Member to fulfill the sanitary or phytosanitary requirements of an importing Member, the latter shall consider providing such technical assistance as will permit the developing country Member to maintain and expand its market access opportunities for the product involved." Article 9.2 can be addressed along the same lines of Article 10. First, this provision should be strengthened by requesting the country implementing an SPS measure that creates particular difficulties for developing countries, to reconsider it. Second, if after reviewing its implications, the importing country reconfirms the measure, the provision of technical cooperation, including the transfer of the necessary technology, should follow, considering that Article 9.2 is a mandatory provision. Countries that experience the same trade problems in connection with a specific SPS measure may wish to join forces on proposed changes to a specific SPS measure. For developing countries, it may be useful to develop flexible alliances both among themselves and with developed countries, considering that the latter are often more experienced in bringing specific cases to the attention of other countries or to the attention of the SPS Committee. Since technical cooperation in the field of SPS measures is being provided by several international organizations and by a number of developed countries, better coordination among the different institutions would ensure that beneficiary countries fully benefit from these efforts.

The WTO Secretariat has identified four categories of technical assistance: information, training, "soft" infrastructure development, and "hard" infrastructure development, and has developed a questionnaire for submitting requests for technical cooperation (WTO 2001j). An informal meeting of the SPS Committee on technical assistance was held in July 2001 and some specific suggestions were put forward to improve the effectiveness of technical cooperation activities, namely: linking the private sector to all initiatives; taking a regional approach; integrating all forms of assistance into a coherent program regardless of the source of assistance; focusing on the development of human resources; and targeting assistance to help developing countries to comply with measures in their export markets as well as to develop their own regulatory control systems to ensure the safety of their domestic food supplies (WTO 2001i). As a general rule, the more specific a request is, the more likely it is to be satisfied promptly and adequately. On the other hand, vague and "shopping list" requests risk triggering actions that are rather unfocused and not particularly effective.

In conclusion, developing and least-developed countries may wish to request the establishment of a clear and mandatory link between the S&D provisions included in the SPS Agreement and those on technical assistance as one of the ways to make the S&D approach more effective, within the mandate included in the Decision on Implementation-Related Issues and Concerns, paragraph 12.1(ii). This goal could be achieved through a change in the language of the agreement, or through an authoritative interpretation of it, pursuant to Article IX:2 of the Marrakesh Agreement Establishing the World Trade Organization.

### *International Standards and International Standardizing Organizations*

The SPS Agreement aims to further the use of harmonized measures based on internationally agreed standards. Hence, SPS measures that conform to international standards "shall be deemed to be necessary to protect human, animal or plant life or health, and presumed to be consistent with the relevant provisions of this Agreement and of GATT 1994" (WTO 1999b SPS Agr., Art. 3.2). The standards, guidelines, and recommendations developed under the auspices of the CAC, OIE, and the Secretariat of the IPPC are explicitly referred to in the SPS Agreement as the international bodies respectively for food safety, animal health and zoonoses, and plant health (WTO 1999b SPS Agr., Annex A, para. 3(a)). For matters not covered by these organizations, standards established by other relevant international organizations, as identified by the SPS Committee, may be recognized (WTO 1999b SPS Agr., Annex A, para. 3(d)).

Harmonization of international standards entails major benefits. It facilitates trade: the same requirements applying in all countries that base their national measures on international standards. It reduces disputes: since measures based on standards are presumed to be WTO-consistent they are, in principle, not challenged by trading partners. And it fosters global dialogue on technical issues, with no single country bearing the burden of risk assessment. Conversely, the divergence of standards and regulations creates costs for international trade. Nevertheless, in some cases, these costs are justified, since they arise from legitimate differences in societal preferences, technological development, and environmental and health conditions. In these cases, standards harmonization would not be a desirable solution, while equivalence of SPS measures would provide a better option.

The benefits of harmonization may be impeded if the process is captured by special interests in order to exclude market participants, or if it is not adequately transparent. Against this, the adoption of consultative and participatory procedures in standard setting, in some cases including nontraditional stakeholders, makes the development and adoption of international standards more complex and time consuming, and implies that considerations of a nonscientific nature may play a role.

The efficiency and fairness of the international standard-setting process is crucial. It has occurred that standards developed by a limited number of countries or approved by a narrow majority of participants have achieved the status of international standards. Because of the simple majority rules, for instance, some Codex standards have been adopted or rejected by a relatively small majority of countries. This situation is well illustrated by the standard on maximum residue limits for growth hormones (beef) that was approved by 33 votes in favor, 29 against, and seven abstentions. The revised standard for natural mineral waters was approved by 33 votes in favor, 31 against, and 10 abstaining. As a result of increased criticism, international standard-setting bodies have adopted and are developing new procedures to ensure that standards truly reflect the view of all member countries. As regards the CAC, the Codex Committee on General Principles, at its 14th Session, (April 19–23, 1999), discussed various options to ensure greater fairness and efficiency in standard setting. Since then, the commission has committed itself to pursue consensus in the approval of its standards, as opposed to a simple majority of votes cast. The CAC, and specifically its 24th Session (July 27, 2001), continues to address the matter of developing-country participation. The issue of participation (and transparency) is being discussed in several areas, including as part of the commission's Strategic Framework, which sets out the strategic priorities for the CAC and provides the basis for the elaboration of the Medium-Term Plan for the period 2003–7.[12] The participation of developing countries in the Codex process is also likely to be considered within the current Review of the Joint FAO/WHO Food Standards Program, which was discussed at the extraordinary 49th Session of the Executive Committee in September 2001 (CAC 2001b, paras. 42–3). As to the IPPC, current procedures, entailing a nine-step elaboration and consultation process including review after adoption, were adopted by the Interim Commission on Phytosanitary Measures (ICPM) in 1999, based on interim procedures established by FAO (ICPM 1999). Current procedures and policies emphasize transparency, participation, and geographic representation in the IPPC's standard-setting processes. All standards submitted to the ICPM have been adopted by consensus. Standards can be adopted by a two-thirds majority vote if necessary; however, a vote cannot be requested for the adoption of a standard on the first occasion it is submitted to the ICPM. The OIE has adopted a consensus approach to the development and adoption of standards. However, it is reported that almost all written comments on draft Animal Health Code standards come from fewer than 10 countries, with oral comments from about the same number of countries.

Article 10.4 of the SPS Agreement states that "Members should encourage and facilitate the active participation of developing country Members in the relevant international organizations." However, developing countries have repeatedly expressed their concern about the way in which international standards are developed and approved, pointing out how their own participation is very limited in both number and effectiveness. This makes international standards irrelevant to them, inappropriate for use as a basis for their domestic SPS measures, and extremely difficult to comply with when incorporated by the importing countries in their national regulations. Developing countries' participation in international standards setting is an "implementation" issue that has been discussed in the WTO General Council. The "three sisters" (CAC, OIE, and IPPC) briefed members on participation in international standard-setting bodies in a workshop before the meeting of the SPS Committee (March 13–15, 2001). The information showed that developing countries are participating more than they were before, but not necessarily in the most adequate manner (see WTO 2001k, 2001l, 2001m).

The Doha Decision on Implementation-Related Issues and Concerns "(i) takes note of the actions taken to date by the Director-General [of the WTO] to facilitate the increased participation of Members at different levels of development in the work of the relevant international standard setting organizations as well as his efforts to coordinate with these organizations and financial institutions in identifying SPS-related technical assistance needs and how to best address them; and (ii) urges the Director-General to continue his cooperative efforts with these organizations and institutions in this regard, including with a view to according priority to the effective participation of least-developed countries and facilitating the provisions of technical and financial assistance for this purpose" (WTO 2001a, note 7, para. 3.5).

At the 2001 WTO Ministerial Conference in Doha, the WTO, FAO, OIE, WHO, and the World Bank issued a joint statement committing themselves to help developing countries participate more fully in setting international norms for SPS measures. The agencies are committed to coordinating the technical assistance they give to developing countries as part of this effort (WTO 2001h).

The costs of direct participation in standard setting pose a constraint to participation by developing countries. For the CAC, its subsidiary bodies responsible for drafting proposed standards meet either annually or biennially, creating a burden on all member countries regarding participation costs, but affecting developing countries more. Hence, their participation directly in the standard-setting activities of the CAC is mainly in the plenary commission sessions (where standards are formally adopted). Conversely, the participation of developing countries in the committees responsible for drafting proposed standards is still below the level that would be considered representative of the CAC as a whole.[13] The OIE bears the cost of experts' participation in the working groups and specialist commissions, as well as that of delegates attending the annual General Session of the International Committee, where draft standards are discussed and adopted. Funds are available for developed- and developing-country experts alike.

The most critical constraint, however, to effective participation by developing countries in international standards setting is the lack of capabilities at the national level for the evaluation of draft standards and the formulation of positions in consultation with all interested parties. This means that solutions such as sponsoring the participation of developing-country delegates in plenary meetings where international standards are formally approved are positive but far from sufficient. Adequate and effective participation of developing countries in the international standard-setting process relies on their technical capacity to contribute to the process by proposing solutions and criteria that are both scientifically sound and consistent with their technological and developmental conditions. It is to this end that efforts are needed. International cooperation aimed only at increasing the number of developing-country delegates present at the official meetings of the international standardization bodies would be inadequate, and even counterproductive, for developing countries, since it would make it possible to define as "genuinely international" activities that in reality are not.

The work of standard-setting organizations may also be of limited relevance to developing countries in the sense that standards are often developed for products that are not of export interest to them. This situation has not helped to make developing countries particularly interested and, in consequence, active in the process of international standardization. To a large extent, developing countries see the international standards as developed by and for the developed countries. An effort should therefore be made to develop standards on products that are of immediate relevance to developing countries, and that can facilitate their exports. Certain financial issues relating to directed funding for the development of standards should be taken into account when addressing this problem.

A recent development within the IPPC may well illustrate the case. Because of severe underfunding of the work program, financial assistance is provided for standard-setting through direct financial contributions from governments ("sponsorship of standards"). Concerns have been expressed by some members that if funds are provided to assist with the development of a specific standard, the standard might be afforded preferential treatment in the list of priorities. Hence, rules have been developed to ensure that no special treatment is given to the development of standards that are provided with financial assistance. In view of the 4th Session of the ICPM, held in Rome, March 11–15, 2002, the Informal Working Group recommended (ICPM 2002) that the provision of external resources for standard setting should be applied only for standards that are approved as priorities by the ICPM, and that it should follow the normal procedures, policies, and practices of standard setting with no modification according to the preferences of the funding entities. Accordingly, the ICPM has been invited to amend the existing criteria for setting the topics and priorities in standard setting by removing the last criterion listed—namely, the "availability of external resources to support preparation of a standard" (ICPM 1998, para. 13).

### *Transparency and Notification Provisions*

Transparency is vital to make sure that SPS measures are scientifically sound and do not have an unnecessary detrimental impact on international trade. However, variations in the quality and content of the information provided by countries in their notifications; short comment periods; delays in responding to requests for documentation; and absence, at times, of due consideration for the comments provided by other members are recurrent problems limiting the effective implementation of the transparency provisions.

Paragraph 2 of Annex B of the SPS Agreement mandates members to allow "a reasonable interval between the publication of a sanitary or phytosanitary regulation and its entry into force in order to allow time for producers in exporting Members, and particularly in developing country Members, to adapt their products and methods of production to the requirements of the importing Member." The Decision on Implementation-Related Issues and Concerns clarifies that "the phrase 'reasonable interval' shall be understood to mean normally a period of not less than 6 months." According to paragraph 5 of Annex B, an adequate time frame has also to be provided between the notification of a proposed regulation and its adoption, because this allows other members to provide comments on the draft.

Language may be an obstacle to the effective capacity of countries to comment on draft regulations; therefore members have agreed that at least a summary of the proposed regulation in one of the official languages of the WTO (English, French, and Spanish) should be made available by the notifying country, if the notifying country is a developed country. In accordance with paragraph 9 of Annex B of the SPS Agreement, the WTO Secretariat circulates copies of the notifications to all members and draws the attention of developing countries to any notification of special interest to them. Notifications are circulated both by hard copy and electronically. The ability of the enquiry points in developing countries to receive and provide information electronically is, therefore, crucial.

At times, even when countries are able to provide comments on the draft regulation, those comments are not taken into account by the notifying country and the whole exercise becomes pointless. A possible solution to this problem could be that when comments and suggestions are not reflected in the final text of the measure, the notifying country would have to explain the reason.

The SPS Committee is a forum in which countries can discuss the implementation of the agreement, bring their difficulties to the attention of other countries, and challenge specific SPS measures proposed or implemented by other members. Developing countries are still making limited use of this forum (though their participation is growing), as well as of the other transparency provisions included in the agreement. The limited use of the transparency provisions may be because links between the public authorities and the private sector are loose, with the result that public authorities are not fully aware of the difficulties that exporters face, while the private sector lacks appropriate channels to bring the difficulties it experiences to the attention of the competent authorities. Developing countries may, therefore, consider making the necessary efforts to strengthen these links.

### *Adaptation to Regional Conditions*

Within a given country, the situation regarding plant or animal disease may not be uniform. The importing country should, therefore, consider whether there are zones within the exporting country that represent a lesser danger, either as a result of the prevailing natural conditions or because the exporting country has made efforts to eradicate the disease from such zones and has taken the necessary measures to prevent its reintroduction.

The adaptation to regional conditions, including the recognition of pest- or disease-free areas or areas of low pest or disease prevalence (SPS Agreement Article 6), is of key relevance to developing countries, especially large countries where geographical, environmental, and epidemiological conditions may vary considerably from one region to another. In some cases, adaptation to regional conditions has facilitated trade in agriculture products. However, efforts to eradicate a pest or disease from a specific area may require a large investment and the procedures to prove that an area is pest-free or disease-free, or is an area of low pest or disease prevalence, are usually long and burdensome, and often require the provision of complex scientific evidence. As a result, developing countries have been unable to fully benefit from Article 6, despite the support provided by the relevant international organizations. Possible solutions include simplification of the procedures, while keeping them scientifically sound, and support for developing countries to prepare their submissions for the recognition of pest- or disease-free areas or of areas of low pest or disease prevalence. Developing countries have to determine when it is feasible and cost-effective to make efforts to eradicate a particular disease or pest from a zone and whether they can get an appropriate return on their investment. This is clearly an area where expert assistance would facilitate the actual implementation of the provision of the agreement by developing countries.[14] Once a country or an area within a country has been declared pest- or disease-free by the relevant international organizations, this status should not be questioned again by individual trade partners, which may, if necessary, request further evidence in terms of Article 6.3, but should refrain from requesting the concerned country to resubmit all the evidence. The nonrecognition by a trade partner of the status of "pest- or disease free area" declared by the competent international organization can be regarded as a trade-restrictive measure in terms of Article 2.3 of the agreement (see WTO 1999a, Art. 6(2), Annex A(3)(B)).

## The Precautionary Approach to Health and Safety and Biotechnology

In the present debate about health and safety, the "precautionary approach" is often opposed to a "sound-science approach." Varying perceptions about public health risks, different levels of acceptance of them, divergent priorities, and dissimilar economic interests have driven countries to take quite opposite positions in this field and have created acute tensions among them. International trade magnifies the problem.

Article 5 of the SPS Agreement permits the adoption of SPS measures on a provisional basis as a precautionary step in cases where there is an immediate risk of the spread of disease, but the scientific evidence is insufficient. However, it also provides that "Members shall seek to obtain the additional information necessary to a more objective assessment of risk and review the sanitary or phytosanitary measure accordingly within a reasonable period of time." The SPS Agreement thus includes a rather strict interpretation of the precautionary approach.

In the mid-1980s the precautionary approach started to appear in multilateral environmental agreements. Its use increased further in the 1990s, especially when it was included as one of the 27 principles of the Rio Declaration on Environment and Development (UNCED 1992). Principle 15 reads: "In order to protect the environment, the precautionary approach shall be widely applied by States according to their capabilities. Where there are threats of serious or irreversible damage, lack of full scientific certainty shall not be used as a reason for postponing cost-effective measures to prevent environmental degradation." By 1990, the precautionary approach was also appearing in regional declarations and treaties. Since 1992, it has also been reflected in the domestic legislation and case law of an increasing number of countries.[15]

The reference in multilateral, regional, and national legal texts to the precautionary approach does not make it less controversial in the context of international trade. Although it has been included in a number of legal instruments dealing with the environment, its status within the framework of the international trading system is still unclear.

The SPS Committee discussed the precautionary approach in several of its meetings in 2000 and 2001. While the EU has questioned the soundness of Article 5.7 of the SPS Agreement and suggested a possible revision or broader interpretation of it in order to give countries more flexibility to protect their markets against products whose health, safety, or environmental impacts are uncertain, several developed and developing countries have stressed that Article 5.7 is adequate to deal with cases where emergency measures are needed but related scientific evidence is not fully available. According to these countries, a broader application of the precautionary approach in international trade would lead to a situation of unpredictability in relation to market access, which would jeopardize the results of trade liberalization.

The debate about the precautionary approach, and the way it is reflected in the multilateral legal instruments, acquires a specific significance when the issue is trade in biotechnology products.[16] The precautionary approach is one of the main features of the Cartagena Protocol on Biosafety.[17] It allows importing countries to ban imports because of lack of scientific certainty. The ban may last until the importing country decides that it has arrived at scientific certainty about the effects of the genetically modified (GM) products on biodiversity and human health. However, since the importing country is not obliged to seek the information necessary for reaching scientific certainty, a trade-restrictive measure may be in force without time limits. The SPS Agreement, on the contrary, allows countries to provisionally adopt sanitary or phytosanitary measures when relevant scientific evidence is insufficient, but obliges them to seek the additional information necessary for a more objective assessment of risk and to review the SPS measure within a reasonable period of time (see Zarrilli 2000). The Preamble of the Biosafety Protocol states that it shall not be interpreted as implying a change in the rights and obligations of the parties under existing international agreements and that this recital is not intended to subordinate the protocol to other international agreements. This provision is, however, rather unclear and may prove not to be very helpful if a trade conflict arises between countries with divergent interests or perceptions in the area of biotechnology.

While some developing countries have embraced biotechnology and are becoming producers and exporters of bioengineered agricultural products, others are highly skeptical and fear that their lack of scientific knowledge and familiarity with biotechnology issues may lead them to risk importing products that, in the long run, may prove dangerous for health, safety, or the environment. Therefore they are putting in place restrictive trade measures regarding the production and import of GM products. However, if challenged, those countries may well face many problems in proving the scientific basis of their trade measures. Until the Cartagena Protocol enters into force, the SPS Agreement will probably remain the most adequate multilateral legal instrument to deal with trade in genetically modified agricultural products—and as mentioned above, its provisions on precautionary measures are quite strict.

Biotechnology is another field where developing countries would greatly benefit from the strengthening of their scientific and technical capacities. Once a better knowledge of biotechnology is acquired, developing countries would be able to assess the related risks and benefits as applied to them, and move from a situation of fear—and related refusal of GM products—to a situation in which they would decide which kinds of bioengineered products they may have an interest in producing and/or importing.

## Options

The benefits of trade liberalization in the agriculture sector achieved by the Uruguay Round negotiations, and those that may result from the Doha work program, could be undermined by the protectionist use of sanitary and phytosanitary measures. The SPS Agreement was negotiated to limit this danger, and represents a useful instrument for this purpose. However, this chapter has identified some shortcomings of the agreement. It could thus be worth considering the introduction of certain amendments to, or authoritative interpretations of, the agreement to ensure that the risk of SPS measures being used as border protection instruments is minimized, while all countries benefit equally from the agreement. The Doha work program and the Decision on Implementation-Related Issues and Concerns provide countries, especially developing countries, with a margin of flexibility in introduction and authoritative interpretation.

Since it is quite obvious that governments are not willing to compromise public health, the most promising option for developing countries to maintain and expand their exports of agricultural and food products is to be able to meet the mandatory requirements and the expectations of consumers in the target markets. At the same time, developing countries need to develop their own regulatory control systems to ensure the safety of their domestic production and of their imports, including those that result from the application of biotechnology. Any possible modification and interpretation of the SPS Agreement should keep these two goals in mind.

International standards should be developed through a fair process, based on consensus, where countries at different levels of development and from different geographical regions are effectively represented. To this end, support is needed to improve developing-country capacity to evaluate draft standards and formulate national, subregional, and regional positions. The development of standards for products that are of export interest to developing countries would increase the relevance of international standard-setting activities for them and could likely result in a more meaningful participation of developing countries in such activities.

Equivalence can facilitate international trade. Considering that it requires full confidence by the importing country in the laboratories and certifying authority of the exporting country, the establishment of internationally financed regional, subregional, or national laboratories, certification bodies, and accreditation institutions should be considered.

Special and differential provisions should help developing countries to adjust their products and process methods to the new requirements established by the importing countries, strengthen their institutional framework, upgrade their facilities, and become more capable of dealing with the scientific and technical aspects of SPS measures as exporters as well as importers. S&D provisions that only allow for longer time frames for compliance are insufficient and may prove self-defeating in the long run. Technical assistance and S&D are, therefore, closely linked.

Adaptation to regional conditions is of key relevance to developing countries. Clear reference should be made in Article 6 of the SPS Agreement to the scientific and administrative support needed by developing countries to facilitate implementation of the article. The disease-free status declared by the competent international organizations should be recognized by all trade partners.

The transparency provisions could be made more development-oriented by adding new language in Annex B to stress the expectation that comments provided on the drafts are reflected in the final texts and that, in the event they are not, explanations are provided. Electronic access to information should be made easier for developing countries.

## Notes

1. Simonetta Zarrilli is a legal officer of the Trade Negotiations and Commercial Diplomacy Branch, Division on International Trade and Commodities of the UNCTAD Secretariat. The views expressed in this paper are those of the author and do not necessarily reflect those of the UNCTAD Secretariat or of its member countries. E-mail: Simonetta.Zarrilli@UNCTAD.org. The author wishes to express her thanks to Gretchen Stanton, David Byron, and David Wilson for the information and comments provided. Any remaining errors are the author's responsibility.

2. Irene Musselli holds a UN Fellowship by the United Nations Department of Economic and Social Affairs.

3. Approved by Ministers at the 4th WTO Ministerial Conference in November 2001. It is separate from the Ministerial Declaration that launched the current round of multilateral trade negotiations.

4. Annex A of the SPS Agreement defines risk assessment as "the evaluation of the likelihood of entry, establishment, or spread of a pest or disease within the territory of an importing Member according to the sanitary or phytosanitary measures which might be applied, and of the associated potential biological and economic consequences; or the evaluation of the potential for adverse effects on human or animal health arising from the presence of additives, contaminants, toxins, or disease-causing organisms in food, beverages, or feedstuffs" (WTO 1999b).

5. The 1979 Standards Code is described as "plurilateral" because, like other "codes" negotiated during the Tokyo Round negotiations of the 1970s, it was an agreement that applied only to those countries that chose to sign it, rather than to the whole GATT membership (GATT 1979). Its successor, the TBT Agreement, applies to all WTO members (WTO 1999b).

6. New Zealand's experience on the implementation of equivalence (WTO 2001d) provides various examples of ad hoc recognition of SPS measures as equivalent: the acceptance of high-temperature forced air as effective fruit fly disinfestation treatment for paw-paw, mangoes, and eggplants from the South Pacific; acceptance of a "winter window" for cucurbit imported from Australia as equivalent to a postharvest chemical dip; and acceptance of tamperproof official stickers for accompanied consignments of fresh orchids from Singapore as equivalent to certificates to verify official inspection of the consignment.

7. For example, a determination of equivalence by the Food Safety and Inspection Service is a prerequisite for export of meat and poultry to the U.S. At the successful completion of an equivalence determination process, basically consisting of document review and an on-site audit, a country becomes eligible to export meat and poultry to the U.S. The determination of equivalence does not imply the stipulation of formal agreements between the parties concerned (WTO 2000a).

8. The Codex Alimentarius Commission (CAC) has adopted Guidelines for the Development of Equivalence Agreements Regarding Food Import and Export Inspection and Certification Systems (CAC 1999b). The Codex Committee on Food Import and Export Inspection and Certification Systems (CCFICS) is continuing work on the guidelines in the area of equivalence, mainly related to the judgment of equivalence of sanitary measures associated with food inspection and certification systems (and also equivalence of technical regulations). The primary intention is to assist countries, and especially developing countries, in the application of the SPS provisions. The guidelines did not advance in the Codex Step process at the recent 10th CCFICS meeting mainly because of ongoing discussions in the WTO/SPS Committee on Article 4 of the agreement. In other words, several delegations at the CCFICS meeting were trying to incorporate the rights and obligations of WTO members into the Codex Guidelines. A lot of the debate centered on the rights of exporters to obtain from the importers the basis for their risk assessment when trying to establish equivalence.

9. According to the World Bank, the value of agricultural exports as a proportion of total merchandise exports in Sub-Saharan Africa averaged above 25 percent over the period 1980–97. Concerning the destination of such export flows, developed countries still constitute the main recipients of agricultural and food export from developing countries (World Bank 1999). According to UNCTAD estimates, in 1997 developed-market-economy countries accounted for 54.8 percent of all food items exported from developing countries and territories (UNCTAD 1997). These figures are likely to be confirmed and strengthened should further trade liberalization occur in the agricultural and food products sectors.

10. Equivalence of regulations is at present taking place among the member states of the European Communities, among those of the North American Free Trade Agreement, and between Australia and New Zealand. The states that are parties to the Southern Common Market (MERCOSUR) have adopted three resolutions establishing the criteria, principles, and scopes for determining the equivalence of control systems in MERCOSUR. The issue is currently being discussed in the context of the Free Trade Areas of the Americas.

11. The WTO Secretariat has prepared a paper summarizing the positions taken by member countries, especially developing-country members, on S&D (see WTO 2001c).

12. See CAC 2001a Objective 5 Promoting participation figures among the objectives considered to be equally important to the overall achievement of the strategic vision.

13. Codex Committees are organized by host governments, which pay the operating costs of these meetings. The Rules of Procedure of the CAC specify that costs of delegates' participation are borne by the governments concerned. There have been several proposals to improve the participation of developing countries by holding Codex meetings in developing countries, paid for by the usual host country. The recent meetings of the Codex Committee on Food Additives serve to illustrate the potential of this option. Additionally, countries may still participate by correspondence. Although participation by accredited representatives to the parent organizations allows for greater nominal participation, the technical nature of the subject matter does not always ensure that the participation is as effective as it could be.

14. For example, the European Communities have stated in a communication on adaptation to regional conditions that, "When assessing the application of regionalization in an exporting country, the primary element to be taken into consideration is the quality of the service in charge of implementation and control of the policy. Acceptance of trade when a decision on regionalization is taken requires full confidence in the certifying competent authorities" (WTO 1998c).

15. For an in-depth analysis of the precautionary principle in regional and national legislation and in case law, see Stilwell (forthcoming). For an analysis of the precautionary principle in international trade, see Ward (1999).

16. The Convention on Biological Diversity defines biotechnology as "any technological application that uses biological systems, living organisms, or derivatives thereof, to make or modify products or processes for specific use." The biotechnology industry provides products for human health care, industrial processing, environmental bioremediation, and food and agriculture.

17. Negotiated under the auspices of the Convention on Biological Diversity (Rio de Janeiro, 1992) and adopted on 29 January 2000, the Cartagena Protocol provides rules for the safe transfer, handling, use, and disposal of "living modified organisms" (LMOs), defined by the protocol as "any living organism that possesses a novel combination of genetic material obtained through the use of modern biotechnology" [Article 3(g)]. Its aim is to address the threats posed by LMOs to biological diversity, also taking into account risks to human health. The protocol will enter into force 90 days after the 50th instrument of ratification is received. As of April 2003, 103 countries, including the countries of the European Community, had signed the protocol and 48 countries, including those of the European Community, had ratified it.

## Select Bibliography

The word *processed* describes informally reproduced works that may not be commonly available through libraries.


Breckenridge, A. 2002. "Developing an Issue-Based Approach to Special and Differential Treatment." Paper presented at the Third Meeting of the Integration and Trade Network organized by the Inter-American Development Bank, March 19–20. Washington, D.C.

CAC (Codex Alimentarius Commission). 1999a. "Guidelines for the Development of Equivalence Agreements Regarding Food Import and Export Inspection and Certification Systems." CAC/GL 34-1999. Codex Alimentarius Commission, Rome.

———. 1999b. "Improvement of Procedures for Adoption of Codex Standards and Measures to Facilitate Consensus." March 1999, CX/GP 99/5. Codex Alimentarius Commission, Rome.

———. 2001a. "Codex Alimentarius Commission Strategic Framework, Appendix II in Report of the Codex Alimentarius Commission, 24th Session." July 2001, ALINORM 01/41. Codex Alimentarius Commission, Rome.

———. 2001b. "Report of The Forty-Ninth (Extraordinary) Session of The Executive Committee of the Codex Alimentarius Commission." ALINORM 03/3. Codex Alimentarius Commission, Rome.

GATT (General Agreement on Tariffs and Trade). 1979. "Tokyo Round Codes, Agreement on Technical Barriers to Trade." LT/TR/A/5. Office of the WTO Secretary General, Geneva.

ICPM (Interim Commission on Phytosanitary Measures). 1998. "Report, Interim Commission on Phytosanitary Measures." 3–6 November 1998, ICPM-98/REPORT. FAO Headquarters, Rome.

———. 1999. "Report, Second Interim Commission on Phytosanitary Measures." 4–8 October 1999, ICPM-99 REPORT. FAO Headquarters, Rome.

———. 2002. "Directed Financial Assistance for Standard Setting (Sponsorship of Standards)." ICPM 02/15. Fourth Session of the ICPM. 11–15 March 2002. FAO Headquarters, Rome.

Stewart, T. P., ed. 1993. *The GATT Uruguay Round: A Negotiating History.* Deventer: Kluwer Law and Taxation Publishers.

Stilwell, M. T. Forthcoming. "The Legal Relationship between the Precautionary Principle and Multilateral Trade Rules." United Nations Environment Programme (UNEP), Geneva.

UN (United Nations). 2000. Cartagena Protocol on Biosafety to the Convention on Biological Diversity. Secretariat of the Convention on Biological Diversity, Montreal.

UNCTAD (United Nations Conference on Trade and Development). 2002. "Note on the Work on Special and Differential Treatment." Processed, March.

Ward, H. 1999. "Science and Precaution in the Trading System." Royal Institute of International Affairs and the International Institute for Sustainable Development, London.

World Bank. 1999. World Development Indicators 1998–99. World Bank, Washington, D.C.

WTO (World Trade Organization). 1998a. "WTO Agreements Series: Sanitary and Phytosanitary Measures." Office of the Secretary General, Geneva.

———. 1998b. "Report of the Appellate Body: Australia—Measures Affecting importation of Salmon." 20 October, WT/DS18/AB/R. Office of the Secretary General, Geneva.

———. 1998c. "Review of the SPS Agreement, Submission by the European Communities." 23 November, G/SPS/GEN/101. Office of the Secretary General, Geneva.

———. 1998d. "Review of the SPS Agreement, Submission by the European Communities." 23 November, G/SPS/GEN/101. Office of the Secretary General, Geneva.

———. 1999a. "Recognition of the Concept of Pest- or Disease-Free Area as an International Standard, Guideline, or Recommendation, Submission by South Africa." 2 November 1999, G/SPS/GEN/139. Office of the Secretary General, Geneva.

———. 1999b. *The Legal Texts: The Results of the Uruguay Round of Multilateral Trade Negotiations.* Cambridge: Cambridge University Press.

———. 2000a. "Equivalence, Submission from the United States to the Committee on Sanitary and Phytosanitary Measures." 7 November 2000, G/SPS/GEN/212. Office of the Secretary General, Geneva.

———. 2000b. "Report by the Chairman, Summary of the Discussions of the SPS Committee. 29 November, G/L/423. Office of the Secretary General, Geneva.

———. 2000c. "Special and Differential Treatment." 9 May, G/SPS/W/105. Office of the Secretary General, Geneva.

———. 2001a. "Decision on Implementation-Related Issues and Concerns." 20 November, WT/MIN(01)/17. Office of the Secretary General, Geneva.

———. 2001b. "Decision on the Implementation of Article 4 of the Agreement on the Application of Sanitary and Phytosanitary Measures." 26 October, G/SPS/19. Office of the Secretary General, Geneva.

———. 2001c. "Second Report by the Chairman, Summary of Informal Discussion on Equivalence." 21 March, G/L/445. Office of the Secretary General, Geneva.

———. 2001d. "Experience in Recognizing Equivalence of Phytosanitary Measures." Submission by New Zealand. 28 February, G/SPS/GEN/232. Office of the Secretary General, Geneva.

———. 2001e. "Equivalence, Communication from Argentina." 15 August, G/SPS/GEN/268. Office of the Secretary General, Geneva.

———. 2001f. "Decision on the Implementation of Article 4 of the SPS Agreement (Equivalence)." 26 October, G/SPS/19. Office of the Secretary General, Geneva.

———. 2001g. "Implementation of Special and Differential Treatment Provisions in WTO Agreements and Decisions, Mandatory and Non-Mandatory Special and Differential Treatment Provisions, Corrigendum." 4 February, WT/COMTD/W/77/Rev.1/Add.1/Corr.1. Office of the Secretary General, Geneva.

———. 2001h. "Agencies to Boost Developing Countries' Participation in Setting Food Safety and Related Norms." WTO Press Release. 12 November, PRESS/ 254. Office of the Secretary General, Geneva.

———. 2001i. "Discussion on Technical Assistance and Coordination-Informal meeting of the SPS Committee of 9 July 2001-Report by the Chairman." 16 July, G/SPS/GEN/267. Office of the Secretary General, Geneva.

———. 2001j. "Questionaire on Technical Assistance, Committee on Sanitary and Phytosanitary Measures, Note by the Secretariat." 15 October, G/SPS/W/113. Office of the Secretary General, Geneva.

———. 2001k. "Note on Developing Country Participation in Codex Bodies, Codex Alimentarius Commission." 9 March, G/SPS/GEN/236. Office of the Secretary General, Rome.

———. 2001l. "Developing Country Participation in IPPC Standard-setting—Statistical Summary, Internal Plant Protection Convention." 8 February, G/SPS/GEN/227. Office of the Secretary General, Rome.

———. 2001m. "Standard-setting Activities Related to the SPS Agreement, World Health Organization." 28 February, G/SPS/GEN/231.

———. 2002a. "Equivalence-Program for Further Work, Decision by the Committee." 21 March, G/SPS/20. Office of the Secretary General, Geneva.

———. 2002b. "Implementation of Special and Differential Treatment Provisions in WTO Agreements and Decisions, Mandatory and Non-Mandatory Special And Differential Treatment Provisions." 4 February,WT/COMTD/W/77/Rev.1/Add.1/Corr.1. Office of the Secretary General, Geneva.

Zarrilli, S. 2000. "Trade in Genetically Modified Organisms and Multilateral Negotiations: A New Dilemma for Developing Countries." UNCTAD/DITC/TNCD/1, October 20. UNCTAD, Geneva.

12

# AGRICULTURAL BIOTECHNOLOGY: A PRIMER FOR POLICYMAKERS

*Donald J. MacKenzie and Morven A. McLean*

## The Promise of Modern Biotechnology for Developing Regions

Even though global food production has outpaced population growth over the last four decades and there is a sufficient amount of food produced to adequately nourish the world's population (FAO 2000), hunger and malnutrition persist. More than one billion people, primarily in rural areas of developing countries, live in absolute poverty on less than US$1 per day (World Bank 2000). Solutions to this dilemma cannot rely solely on food redistribution—they must address sustainable food production and economic growth in the regions where these are needed.

Constraints on existing food production include the availability of arable land and water for irrigation, crop losses due to pests and disease, and the inherent productivity potential of agricultural crops. In addition, postharvest losses in tropical areas are higher than elsewhere, owing to fungal and insect infestations, and compounded by a lack of appropriate storage facilities. Despite efforts to prevent such crop losses, pests destroy more than half of the world food production. Except for recent decades, when rising crop yields have been the major factor, increases in agricultural production have historically been due to the expansion of land under cultivation. However, today most available arable land is already in use and any further expansion would mean incorporating fragile and marginal areas that represent an increased risk of lost biodiversity and environmental degradation.

## The Plan of This Chapter

This chapter discusses the meaning of modern biotechnology and the extent of global adoption of biotech crops with their benefits and concerns. The chapter outlines different government approaches for managing the use of biotech crops, both legislative and regulatory, and the issues that these approaches raise, including regulatory triggers, transparency and public involvement, labeling, and safety assessment in the context of both food and the environment. The trade implications of biotech crops are discussed by examining provisions in agreements on the environment (the Cartagena Protocol on Biosafety) and trade agreements in the World Trade Organization (WTO). The chapter also details the role of the Codex Alimentarius Commission (CAC). Given the important role of both the United States (U.S.) and the European Union (EU) in establishing rules on biosafety products, their trade dispute on these products has implications for future trade and is covered in this chapter.

It has been argued that modern biotechnology has the potential to contribute significantly to sustainable gains in agricultural productivity and to food security, especially in the developing world. In the broadest sense, biotechnology has been defined as the use of biological processes for the development of products such as foods, enzymes, drugs, and vaccines. In this view, biotechnology is simply a new label for a process that humans have used for thousands of years to ferment foods such as beer, wine, bread, and cheese, for the purposes of food preservation. Modern agricultural biotechnology, however, generally refers to the application of molecular biology, and more specifically, recombinant-DNA (deoxyribonucleic acid) technology,[1] to the genetic improvement of crop plants and livestock animals.

Using modern biotechnology, plant breeders are able to introduce specific genetic material taken from any species of plant, animal, or microorganism, or created synthetically within the laboratory, into many different species of plants or animals, to create so-called transgenic organisms.[2] The "first generation" of genetically modified (GM) products has generally included crop plants with new input traits, such as pest resistance or herbicide tolerance. These have included insect-resistant varieties of maize, potato, and cotton, containing a toxin-encoding gene from strains of the bacterium *Bacillus thuringiensis*; plants with tolerance to broad-spectrum herbicides, such as glyphosate (Roundup- tolerant canola, maize, and soybean), and glufosinate ammonium-tolerant canola, maize, rice, and soybean; and plants, such as melon, papaya, potato, and squash, with resistance to disease caused by specific plant viruses. In addition, there are a very few products with modified quality traits, such as high–oleic acid canola and soybean, and delayed-softening melon and tomato.[3]

To date there have been about 53 bioengineered foods reviewed by the U.S. Food and Drug Administration (FDA), and about 51 novel foods authorized for marketing in Canada by Health Canada.[4] A smaller subset of products has also been authorized for commercial use in a number of other countries, including Argentina, Australia, China, Japan, the Russian Federation, South Africa, and the countries of the EU.[5]

It is expected that over the coming years there will be a newer "second generation" of GM foods proposed for market introduction. These next-generation products will include plants with enhanced resistance to diseases caused by fungal and viral pathogens; improved tolerance to abiotic stresses such as drought, high-salt soils, and heavy metal contamination; increased yield potential; improved nutritional quality or medicinal value; vehicles for the delivery of oral vaccines and therapeutics; and factories for the production of pharmaceutical proteins or industrial polymers.

As an example of a solution to high-salt soils, a new GM tomato has been developed that is not only able to grow in 40 percent salt solution, but can also remove salt from the soil, thus combining the potential of increased income with environmental bioremediation.[6] Examples of nutraceutical products include the so-called golden rice, which has been bioengineered to express pro-vitamin A (beta-carotene) in the rice endosperm (Ye and others 2000), and tomatoes modified to contain four times the normal level of lycopene, a carotenoid pigment whose dietary intake has been correlated with a reduction in coronary heart disease and some types of cancer (Ausich 1997). There are a number of examples of food products that are being developed to act as edible vaccines to combat agents such as the hepatitis-B virus (Richter and others 2000); the Norwalk virus (Mason and others 1996) responsible for viral gastroenteritis, which comprises about 25 percent of the cases of traveler's diarrhea; and the rabies virus (Modelska and others 1998). These products have raised hopes of solving many of the problems associated with the delivery of safe, effective vaccines in developing countries (Mor and Arntzen 1999).

The application of transgenic animals for use in human food production has lagged behind applications in crop plants, and there are currently no bioengineered animal species that have been approved for food use. The first product likely to undergo regulatory assessment in the U.S. is transgenic Atlantic salmon that have been genetically engineered to grow faster.[7] Transgenic animals that have the potential to reduce the environmental impact of livestock food production are also being developed. For instance, transgenic pigs express a phytase enzyme that allows them to break down phytate,[8] which reduces phosphate contamination of agricultural soils. Bioengineered animals also have many potential applications in medical research as models of human disease, in the production of therapeutic products such as pharmaceutical proteins in milk, and as sources of organ and tissue xenografts for interspecies transplants.

Current global trade in products of agricultural biotechnology is almost exclusively limited to plant biotechnology products. The remainder of this chapter focuses on this class of GM products and does not address products such as recombinant vaccines or veterinary biologics.

## Global Adoption of Biotech Crops

For 2002, the International Service for the Acquisition of Agri-biotech Applications (ISAAA) has estimated that the global area of transgenic crops is 145 million acres—nearly 34-fold increase since 1996—grown by 5.5 million farmers in 16 countries (James 2002; see figure 12.1). Nearly all of this area is accounted for by four countries: the U.S. (66 percent), Argentina (23 percent), Canada (6 percent), and China (4 percent)—with 12 other countries making up the remaining 1 percent. It is noteworthy that the four principal countries growing transgenic crops are represented by two nations from the "North" and two nations from the developing world. Indeed, in recent years the rate of adoption of these crops in developing nations (50 percent between 2000 and 2002) has outstripped that of industrialized countries (30 percent between 2000 and 2002). For example, between 2000 and 2002, China increased its cultivation of insect-resistant Bt cotton fourfold, from 1.25 million acres to 6.25 million acres (see box 12.1).

Globally, the principal transgenic crops are herbicide-tolerant soybean (62 percent of total acreage in 2002), insect- and/or herbicide-tolerant maize (21 percent), insect- and/or herbicide-tolerant cotton (12 percent), and herbicide-tolerant canola (5 percent). Of the global aggregate area of these four crops (677.5 million acres), about 21 percent was used for planting transgenic varieties in 2002. Specifically, this represented 51 percent of total soybean acreage, 20 percent of total cotton acreage, 12 percent of total canola acreage, and 9 percent of total maize acreage.

According to ISAAA, there is "cautious optimism that global area and the number of farmers planting GM crops will continue to grow in 2002." Key events include the limited commercialization of insect-resistant Bt cotton in India during 2003 and the anticipated resolution of outstanding regulatory and legal issues surrounding the planting of herbicide-tolerant soybean in Brazil. In the fall of 2002, the Philippines authorized the commercial planting of Bt maize (MON 810), which represented a milestone event for Southeast Asia.

**FIGURE 12.1 Global Area of Transgenic Crops**

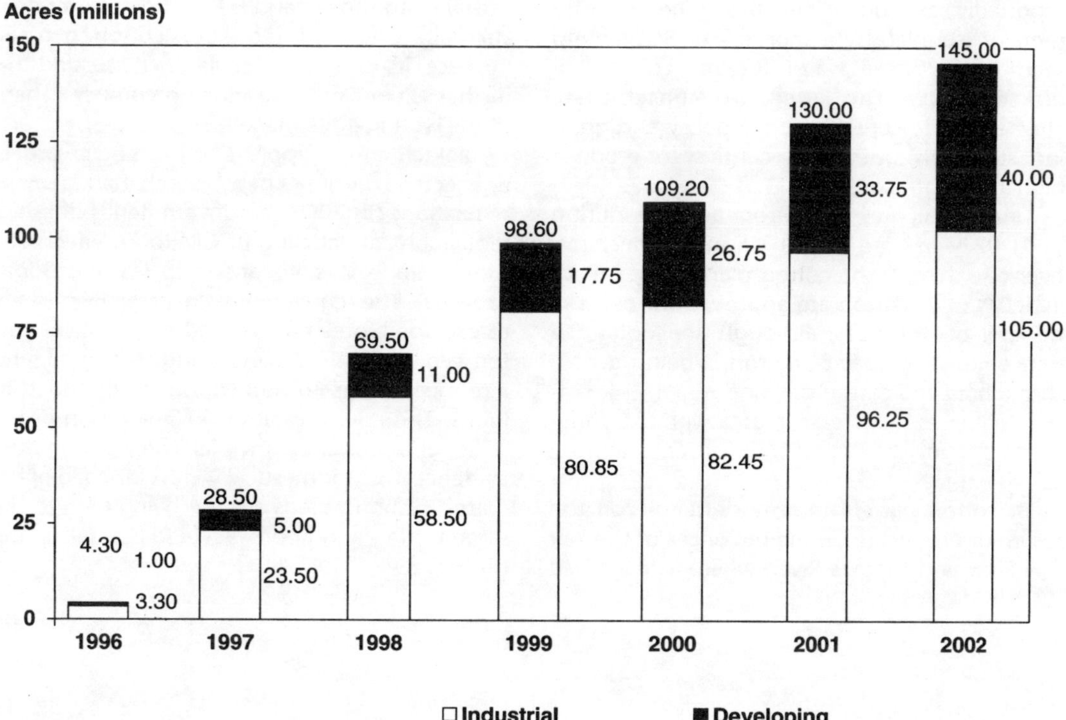


*Source:* Clive James 2002.

## BOX 12.1 The Global Trade Effects of China Bt Cotton

China attaches great importance to the application of biotechnology to agriculture, although recent developments relating to regulations, foreign investment in biotechnology, and criticism of genetically modified (GM) crops on environmental, food safety, and ethical grounds have created uncertainty. For the past 10 years in the cotton industry, China has focused on reducing its dependence on cotton imports and non-Chinese GM cotton technology. The impact of China's implementation of GM cotton goes well beyond its cotton crop sector to domestic textile production and foreign production of cotton, apparel, and textiles.

Since the 1980s China has invested significantly in biotechnology research to minimize dependence on foreign technology. Scientists have developed high-yielding, insect- and drought-resistant plant varieties of most major crops that have the potential to allow farmers to produce more food on China's limited land area. The Chinese Cotton Research Institute, an institute of the Chinese Academy of Agriculture Sciences (CAAS) in Henan Province, has developed several varieties of Bt cotton and a large proportion of the planting seed used in Xinjiang. Bt cotton produces its own pesticide through a gene borrowed from the bacterium *Bacillus thuringiensis.* Although earlier domestic varieties of Bt cotton were inferior, more recent types reportedly are quite effective. The industry remains troubled by a shortage of Bt planting seed quality issues, and foreign content in picked cotton. The latter two concerns are affected by procurement price policy and grading standards, with no incentive to produce higher strength cotton.

CAAS estimates Bt cotton acreage during 2001/02 Marketing Year at 1.5 million hectares, over one third of the cotton planted area. Four varieties of Bt cotton are approved for use in a number of provinces, although anecdotal evidence indicates that Bt cotton is being grown throughout the cotton-growing regions. Bt cotton continues to increase in area with the dominant varieties developed by Monsanto and by CASS.

Bt cotton played an important role on the return of production in the provinces of the Yellow River and Yangtze River, where acreage had declined. Indiscriminant use of insecticides had resulted in increased bollworm resistance to the agents, produced significant yield losses and resulted in cotton becoming unprofitable.

China is a significant importer of cotton and a net exporter of textiles and apparel. Changes in China's cotton production have the ability to affect both global cotton production and trade in textiles and apparel, which depends on continued liberalization of this trade.

Anderson and Yao have quantified the potential global economic effects when China adopts GM technology. The Global Trade Analysis Project trade model is used with projections to 2005 and assumptions relating to China's accession to the WTO and completion of the Uruguay Round undertakings in textiles and apparel trade. According to the study, without GM cotton technology, China was projected to be producing and using around one-quarter of the world's plant fibers. Use of GM technology by both China and outside of China can be expected to have a large trade impact on China and other cotton-producing countries, including other textile and apparel exporting countries. An increase in China's domestic GM cotton supply lowers cotton imports and decreases global cotton prices, as China's output is significant compared with total worldwide production. However, without China's voluntary export restraints to the US and EU, world cotton prices still fall, China's imports of cotton actually increase, its exports of textiles increase, and this further expands the developing country's share of the world textile market.

Biotech cotton appears to have been largely unaffected by China's new biotech management regulations (in 2002 the government published regulations on labeling of GM foods which disrupted trade in soybeans from US and South America). The regulations were carefully phrased to exclude biotech fibers, and to not affect cottonseed, which is processed into edible oil, and into meal that is consumed as feed or added to foods. This could result in WTO violation of the national treatment principle. There is also little evidence that domestically developed biotech cotton planting seeds are not being held to the same testing and approval standards set by the government.

**BOX 12.1 (Continued)**

The government now seems to be taking a more cautious approach to biotechnology. Despite the importance of GM cotton in its cotton production, China recently limited the development of the cotton industry by prohibiting foreign investment in biotechnology. This change of rules has placed existing biotech joint ventures in jeopardy.

*Sources:* Anderson and Yao 2001.

## Benefits and Concerns

As with any new technology, the potential benefits of applying modern biotechnology and genetic engineering to food production are balanced by concerns about potential adverse effects. All farmers, regardless of their economic status, are discerning judges of crop performance and the economic advantage that may or may not be offered by new varieties. Viewed in this light, the rapid adoption of transgenic crops, both in developed and developing regions, is testimony to the direct economic benefits to farmers. Based on data from 1999, it has been estimated that the global economic advantage to farmers planting transgenic crops is about US$710 million (James 2000). Transgenic soybean, cotton, and canola accounted for 61 percent, 35 percent, and 9 percent of the net economic benefit, respectively. The anomaly was the cultivation of Bt maize in the U.S., which represented a US$35 million loss to farmers in 1999.[9] Countering these apparent benefits to producers and technology providers are criticisms that consumers have yet to realize any direct benefits.

There are striking differences of opinion regarding the environmental risks posed by GM crops. Some argue that insect- and disease-resistant GM crops will reduce reliance on damaging pesticides, thus contributing to environmental sustainability, and could result in fewer cases of pesticide-related farm worker illness or injury and less groundwater contamination. On the other hand, there are many concerns about the impacts of GM crops on both agricultural and natural ecosystems, particularly in the long term. These include concerns that plants producing their own pesticides to combat insects could accelerate the development of resistant insect populations, thus reducing the effectiveness of these pesticides for other agricultural applications. There are also fears that outcrossing between herbicide-tolerant crop plants and closely related weeds could result in the creation of "superweeds," or in the movement of engineered traits into neighboring crops. Finally, there are concerns that animals and insects consuming transgenic plants will be harmed and that biodiversity will be diminished.

For developing countries, there are additional concerns that existing intellectual property rules will preclude access to the products of biotechnology research by resource-poor farmers, and that the new technology will lead to exploitation and monopoly control of seeds with novel and desirable traits.

If biotechnology is to contribute to rural development and the achievement of food security within developing countries, there must be increased emphasis on improving indigenous crops and agricultural practices, development of policies and programs to foster biotechnology developments as an adjunct to other agricultural practices, and establishment of adequate regulatory or oversight mechanisms to enable safe introduction of new technologies and products.

## Governance and Regulatory Oversight

The potential for adverse environmental and human health consequences arising from the introduction of GM plants into agriculture and food production has led to the development of regulatory regimes that are specifically applied to assessing the safety of these products and controlling their introduction into commerce. Based on the experiences of those industrialized nations with established regulatory systems, there is no consensus on a single best approach. There are no examples of existing biotechnology regulatory systems that were developed anew from a comprehensive plan designed from the outset to anticipate every contingency and to be integrated and coherent, both internally and with other national policies. Overall, these systems were developed in piecemeal fashion, usually beginning with voluntary guidelines and standards developed cooperatively by academia, industry, and government, and ending up incorporated over time into statutory instruments, either under existing legislation covering food and agricultural products, or under new legislation dealing specifically with gene technology.

Some countries have taken dramatically different approaches to regulating GM products, which can be particularly illustrated by comparing the U.S. and the EU. The U.S. has adopted an optimistic mindset and approaches the evaluation of new products and technologies by asking "Why not?" whereas the EU approach is more pessimistic and involves trying to predict the unknown and asking "Why?" Not surprisingly, these differences in philosophy have been translated into unique regulatory systems with significant differences in intent (product versus process), legislative basis (existing versus technology-specific laws), and location of decision-making authority (institutional versus political).

Notwithstanding the divergence of philosophical and/or political approach, at the scientific and technical level each country asks very similar questions when evaluating the potential environmental and human health risks of GM products. For example, in evaluating novel foods each country takes a comparative approach that focuses on the defined differences between the novel food and its traditional counterpart, and the effect these differences have on composition, nutritional quality, toxicology, and potential allergenicity. While it may not always be reflected in the regulatory decisionmaking process, the rate of approvals, or the ultimate decision to allow marketing, there is a high degree of consistency in the scientific opinion in different countries about the safety of novel foods that have been put forward for commercialization to date. Even in the EU, where there has been a moratorium on the approval of new GM products since 1998, the European Commission's scientific committees (for example, the Scientific Committee on Plants and the Scientific Committee on Foods) have continued to review new dossiers and publish their opinions, which are generally consistent with scientific assessments from other countries.

### *Legislative Basis*

Experiences from different countries have shown that effective regulatory frameworks can be based on nonstatutory guidelines,[10] statutory regulations entrenched in existing or new legislation, or some combination of these approaches. Generally within industrialized nations, the regulation of biotechnology was initiated as a system of voluntary information guidelines, codes of practice, and risk assessment criteria. The competent authorities[11] developed information guidelines, and technology developers abide by these. As examples, Argentina, Australia, Canada, Japan, and South Africa have all used nonstatutory guidelines to manage the environmental safety of GM plants before promulgating new acts or regulations.

The FDA provides an example of a regulatory management system for bioengineered foods that to date remains voluntary. The cornerstone of the FDA's 1992 policy for foods derived from new plant varieties is that foods produced through the application of genetic engineering techniques are not inherently riskier than foods produced through more conventional means (FDA 1992). Since publishing this policy, the FDA has conducted 53 voluntary (FDA 1997) consultations (FDA 2001) with companies about the safety and composition of new bioengineered food products.

The benefits of implementing voluntary guidelines include the speed with which the guidelines can be put in place and the flexibility they can afford. However, in the absence of a statutory instrument, there is a limited capacity for independent, legally enforceable auditing and monitoring of compliance. Depending on the discretionary power of the competent authority, there may be no legal basis for the imposition of penalties or other action in the event of noncompliance, or opportunities for the public to seek redress through the courts should negligence be suspected. As important, the public may not have confidence that the government is adequately regulating these products, or that developers are abiding by voluntary guidelines. In part because of political and public pressures to do so, both Australia (OGTR 2001) and South Africa[12] have implemented new acts to specifically regulate gene technology and genetically modified organisms (GMOs). In the U.S., the FDA has proposed a new rule requiring that all new foods derived from biotechnology be subject to mandatory review prior to marketing. This proposed new rule is subject to a public comment period (that is, the public is given time to comment on the proposed rule).

### *Regulatory Triggers*

With the exception of Canada,[13] some form of "process" trigger is the rule in all countries that have developed regulatory systems for GM foods. This is also the case for the United Nations Cartagena Protocol on Biosafety, which focuses specifically on living modified organisms (LMOs), defined as "any living organism that possesses a novel combination of genetic material obtained through the use of modern biotechnology." Very clearly, the protocol is limited to addressing biosafety concerns that may be associated with the products of modern biotechnology, irrespective of the trait or traits that an LMO may express.

While a "product-based" trigger for regulatory oversight is truest to the scientific principle that biotechnology is not inherently riskier than other technologies that have a long and accepted history of application in agriculture and food production, it is more difficult to implement than a "process-based" approach. In the absence of some form of *ex ante* risk assessment, it is extremely difficult to design a regulatory system that captures the products of concern without placing an undue burden on less risky products. Considering that it is the relatively new process of genetic engineering that causes the greatest public concern, regulatory oversight triggered by the application of this technology remains the most practical approach.

### *Transparency and Public Involvement*

Within the context of government regulatory systems, transparency refers to the extent to which governments provide information on why and how certain products are regulated, and how risk assessments are performed and decisions made as well as the conclusions and decisions that have been reached. Transparency can also involve the perceived independence and objectivity of the regulatory decisionmakers. Public involvement, on the other hand, refers to the extent to which the public has input either into the formulation of regulatory policy or into specific regulatory decisions. Although closely related, public information and participation are not synonymous, as it is certainly possible to have an open and transparent process that does not involve public input.

The degrees of transparency and public involvement vary greatly among countries. As a minimum, some countries publish information on the criteria for risk assessment and risk management so that developers, stakeholders, and the public can be confident that the biosafety system is both credible and predictable. Other jurisdictions have improved on this and additionally notify the public both when applications for the environmental safety assessment of a GMO are received by the competent authorities and when a regulatory decision is made.

Public participation may be sought at a number of levels throughout the development and implementation of a regulatory system. These include: representations to, or membership on, advisory committees, particularly those tasked with evaluating social, ethical, and economic dimensions of biosafety; input at public hearings during the development of policy or regulation; and comments during the risk assessment process. As exemplified by recent proposed changes by the FDA and the European Commission, the trend is toward increasing openness and public involvement.

### *Labeling Policies for GM Foods*

Notwithstanding the considerable scientific evidence supporting the safety of GM foods currently in the marketplace, there exists a level of consumer concern about these products.[14] For different people, these concerns may be precipitated by various factors, such as a lack of information about how these products are evaluated for safety, a lack of knowledge and/or trust in regulatory processes, or a philosophical opposition to the genetic engineering of food crops.

Provisions for the mandatory or voluntary labeling of GM foods have been perceived as the key means of providing consumers with the information they need to make choices in the marketplace. Some countries, such as Canada and the U.S., have taken a permissive approach and have not imposed a regulatory distinction between GM and non-GM foods when labeling for food safety. That is to say, there is a requirement for additional labeling only in cases of significantly altered nutritional composition, or potential for increased toxicity or allergenicity. In January 2001, the FDA announced its draft guidance to industry on "Voluntary Labeling Indicating Whether Foods Have or Have Not Been Developed Using Bioengineering."[15] The purpose of this guidance is to advise food manufacturers on the acceptability of various types of label claims and to reinforce the fact that labeling must be truthful and not misleading. Of particular importance, the FDA reiterates the requirement that manufacturers must be able to substantiate label claims, and that in labeling a food as "not a product of bioengineering" there should be no suggestion of superiority. In Canada, the Canadian Council of Grocery Distributors (CCGD)[16] and the Canadian General Standards Board (CGSB)[17] are currently developing a standard for the voluntary labeling of GM foods.

Other countries, such as Australia and New Zealand, the EU countries, Japan, the Republic of Korea, and Thailand have announced, or are beginning to implement, mandatory labeling requirements for GM foods that contain detectable amounts of novel DNA or protein (that is, GM content). While these requirements or schemes are similar in intent, there are notable differences with respect to which foods must be labeled (for example, whole foods versus processed foods versus restaurant foods), exemption thresholds for food additives that may have been derived from GM foods, and thresholds for the adventitious presence of GM foods in a processed product (see table 12.1).

The effective implementation of labeling provisions, whether mandatory or voluntary, is severely limited by the lack of objective, internationally accepted standards for verifying the presence or absence of a GM food in a food product. Without

**TABLE 12.1 Labeling Requirements for Genetically Modified Foods**

| Country/ Jurisdiction | Mandatory/ Voluntary (M/V) | Coverage |
|---|---|---|
| Australia and New Zealand | M | GM content in processed foods, fruits, vegetables; does not cover whole foods that do not otherwise carry labels; 1 percent tolerance for adventitious presence. |
| Canada | V | Mandatory labeling only for health and safety concerns, such as significantly altered nutritional composition or increased risk of toxicity or allergenicity; voluntary standard being developed. |
| European Union | M | GM content; 0.5 percent tolerance for adventitious presence and 0.9 percent threshold to trigger labeling; applicable to whole foods and to processed foods. |
| Japan | M | GM content; labeling of food ingredients only if the ingredient is one of the top three by weight and comprises at least 5 percent of the total weight of the product; no labeling on packages smaller than 30 $cm^2$; labeling of bulk shipments with more than 5 percent GM content ("may contain"); no labeling of bulk shipments if less than 1 percent GM content. |
| Korea, Rep. of | M | Processed foods with GM maize, soybean, or bean sprouts (and potatoes in 2002); if one of top five ingredients; 3 percent tolerance. |
| Thailand | M | GM content in all foods and raw products; 3 percent or 5 percent tolerance. |
| United States | V | Mandatory labeling only for health and safety concerns, such as significantly altered nutritional composition or increased risk of toxicity or allergenicity. |

*Source:* Adapted from Phillips and McNeill 2000.

adequate means of verification, the requirements imposed by any labeling protocol are difficult to enforce. The lack of standardization and verification methods has been a chief criticism of the EU's mandatory labeling of GM foods, which is viewed by some as arbitrary and trade-protectionist.

### *Safety Assessment*

Central to all biotechnology regulatory systems is a framework for risk assessment that evaluates the characteristics of the organism, the introduced trait, the environment into which the organism is introduced, the interaction between these, and the intended application.

**Food Safety Assessment and Substantial Equivalence** To date, the safety assessment of genetically engineered and novel foods has been based on the principle that these products can be compared with traditional foods that have an established history of safe use (OECD 1993). Furthermore, this comparison can be based on an examination of the same risk factors (that is, hazards) that have been established for the traditional counterpart. Keeping in mind that many conventional foods that are generally considered safe may present specific risks depending on conditions of processing, or to individuals within a population, the intent is not to establish absolute safety but rather whether the new food can be said to be "as safe as" its conventional counterpart.

This comparative approach has been embodied in the concept of substantial equivalence, which has been both endorsed as a useful risk assessment tool (FAO/WHO 1996) and criticized (Royal Society of Canada 2001), particularly for being subjective, inconsistent, and "pseudo-scientific" (Millstone, Brunner, and Mayer 1999). Even with its limitations, the substantial equivalence approach remains the most practical approach to addressing the safety of foods and food ingredients developed through modern biotechnology. In fact, there are at present no alternative strategies providing a better assurance of safety.

International discussion and expert consultations among Organisation for Economic Co-operation and Development (OECD) countries, and within the United Nations in the CAC of the FAO/WHO, have resulted in a consensus on the specific safety issues that should be considered when evaluating a novel food (OECD 2000). They include the following:

- A description of the host organism that has been modified, including information on nutrient composition, known antinutrients, toxicants and allergenic potential, and any significant changes in these that may result from normal processing.
- A description of the donor organism, including any known associated toxicities and allergenicities, and the introduced gene(s).
- Molecular characterization of the genetic modification, including a description of the modification process and the stability of the introduced trait.
- Identification of the primary and secondary gene products, including a description of the characteristics of the inserted gene.
- Evaluation of the safety of expected novel substances in the food, including an evaluation of any toxins produced directly by the modification.
- Assessment of the novel food's potential allergenicity.
- Evaluation of unintended effects on food composition, including (a) assessment of changes in the concentration of nutrients or naturally occurring toxicants, (b) identification of antinutrient compounds that are significantly altered in novel foods, and (c) evaluation of the safety of compounds that show a significantly altered concentration.

In evaluating these safety issues, due consideration is given to the processed version of the food (if the food normally undergoes manufacturing or processing), as well as food consumption issues including (a) identification of the potential human population consuming the genetically engineered foods and the amount they are expected to consume, and (b) assessment of any effects that may occur if intake of the modified food differs from intake of its conventional counterpart.

**Environmental Safety** Assessing the environmental safety of a transgenic plant requires familiarity with the biology of the plant itself and the agricultural practices employed in its cultivation. This concept of familiarity is a key approach used in identifying and evaluating environmental risks and also in informing practices that may be needed to manage recognized risks. For example, knowledge about the biology of the plant can identify species-specific characteristics that may be affected by the introduced trait and permit the transgenic plant to become "weedy," invasive of natural habitats, or be otherwise harmful to the environment.

Likewise, the introduction of a new trait may result in changed agricultural practices that affect the environment. The widespread cultivation of herbicide-tolerant rapeseed (*Brassica napus*, also known as canola) in the Canadian prairies has led farmers to switch to "no-till" cultivation. Farmers are able to seed herbicide-tolerant plants directly into the stubble of the previously harvested crop with no prior cultivation. This provides for both soil conservation (topsoil is held in place by the residue of the previous crop) and water conservation (the stubble cover allows for better water retention and inhibits evaporation).

Transgenic plants expressing stress tolerance genes are much sought after, particularly for production in soils damaged by salinization or alkalinization, or in environments where water is the limiting factor for food production. Stress tolerance may also be used to extend the typical zones of production of a crop plant. For example, cold tolerance is considered a desirable trait as it can be used to limit frost damage to crops and consequently extend production seasons. Cold tolerance may also permit the introduction of novel plants into areas where they have not previously been grown. This approximates the introduction of an exotic species and therefore necessitates the same close examination for potential ecosystem disruption.

Other ecological risks that must be assessed include the potential spread of introduced traits to related plant species through outcrossing, the potential build-up of resistance in insect populations to engineered insecticidal traits, unintended secondary effects on nontarget organisms, and potential effects on biodiversity. In this regard, it is important to distinguish between the biodiversity of natural populations and that of crops and other organisms within the agro-ecosystem. It is the latter context that is most relevant within the environmental risk assessment process for transgenic plants, which is designed to evaluate the incremental risks associated with replacing a conventional crop variety with a transgenic one.

In addition to evaluating the risks associated with the introduction of new transgenic varieties, consideration must be given to the risks associated with not using biotechnology to achieve desired goals. For example, the biodiversity of tropical rainforests can be maintained only if these natural ecosystems are not destroyed by the expansion of the agricultural land base.

## Trade Implications

The introduction of crop biotechnology products has had a profound effect on international trade in agricultural commodities. A dominating force behind changing agricultural trade policies has been consumers' opinions, primarily in the EU, on the safety or necessity of GM food products.

European fears over the introduction of GM crops and foods have been widely ascribed to a generalized lack of confidence in science and regulatory systems, largely as a result of food safety crises such as bovine spongiform encephalopathy (BSE—better known as "mad cow disease") and dioxin-tainted Belgian beef. In the BSE crisis, the attempts by U.K. government officials in 1990 to mollify initial public concern, which subsequently backfired, seriously eroded public confidence in the role of government in consumer protection. These issues, while not directly related to GM foods, have contributed to the belief among consumers that the whole story on GM foods is rarely told, and if it is, the risks are downplayed and the benefits accentuated.

These considerations, coupled with a highly organized campaign against GM products led by European-based activist organizations, contributed to the 1998 EU moratorium on new GM crop approvals, introduction of new regulations governing labeling and traceability of GM products, and the ascendancy of the Precautionary Principle within the risk analysis process for GM products.[18] The Precautionary Principle has been expressed and implemented by different countries in forms ranging from "weak" (that is, lack of full certainty is not a justification for preventing an action that might be harmful) to "strong" (that is, no action should be taken unless one is certain it will do no harm). It is when implemented in the "strong" form, as in cases where there is neither credible theoretical nor empirical evidence establishing the possibility of harm, that the Precautionary Principle has received its greatest criticism as a disguised trade barrier.

The lack of European acceptance of GM products affects not only the major growers of GM crops (U.S., Argentina, and Canada) but developing nations as well, which may be reticent to adopt the new technology for fear of losing export markets. Indeed, it could be argued that some countries, such as Brazil, maintained an official "GM-free" posture in order to capitalize on European and Japanese consumer preferences for GM-free soybeans.

The following discussion presents a brief overview of the Cartagena Protocol on Biosafety, the only international agreement to directly address international trade of GM seeds and plants, and longer-established trade agreements under the WTO. This discussion attempts to highlight the relationship between these agreements, particularly points of conflict. (Additional resources are detailed in table 12.2).

**TABLE 12.2 Online Resources**

| Resource | Description |
|---|---|
| Cartagena Protocol on Biosafety<br>(Convention on Biological Diversity)<br>393 Saint Jacques Street Suite 300<br>Montreal Québec, Canada H2Y 1N9<br>Tel: +1 (514) 288-2220<br>Fax: +1 (514) 288-6588<br>E-mail: secretariat@biodiv.org<br>URL: www.biodiv.org | Home page for the Biosafety Protocol and gateway to the Biosafety Clearing House mechanism. |
| Codex Alimentarius Commission<br>Secretariat of the Joint FAO/WHO Food Standards Program<br>Food and Agriculture Organization of the United Nations<br>Viale delle Terme di Caracalla<br>00100 Rome, Italy<br>Email: codex@fao.org<br>URLs: www.fao.org/ag/cgrfa/<br>www.codexalimentarius.net | International standards development with respect to food safety, including the risk assessment of foods derived from modern biotechnology. |
| Essential Biosafety<br>Essential Biosafety Press LLC<br>PO Box 475<br>Merrickville, Ontario<br>K0G 1N0 Canada<br>Email: info@essentialbiosafety.info<br>URL: http://essentialbiosafety.info | Information has been classified into three discrete areas that include a database of safety information on all GM plant products that have received regulatory approval; training tools in the form of case studies for food and environmental risk assessment; and a library of pertinent biosafety references and online documents. |
| Food and Agriculture Organization (FAO)<br>of the United Nations<br>URL: http://fao.org | Biotechnology in food and agriculture. Gateway to FAO documents and activities related to agricultural biotechnology. |
| Organisation for Economic Co-operation and Development (OECD)<br>OECD Environment Directorate<br>Environment, Health, and Safety Division<br>2 André-Pascal 75775 Paris Cedex 16, France<br>FAX: ** 33 1 45 24 16 75<br>E-mail: ehscont@ OECD.org<br>URL: http://www.oecd.org/EN/home/0,,<br>EN-home-27-nodirectorate-no-no—27,00.html | The main focus of the work program is on international harmonization of regulatory oversight in biotechnology that will ensure that environmental health and safety aspects are properly evaluated, while avoiding nontariff trade barriers to products of the technology. |

*Note:* This listing is not meant to be all-inclusive but rather to serve as a starting point.

### *The Cartagena Protocol on Biosafety*

Internationally, the need to ensure biosafety through national systems of risk assessment was recognized as a priority within the 1992 Convention on Biological Diversity, signed in Rio de Janeiro at the UN Conference on Environment and Development, and more explicitly within Chapter 16 of Agenda 21. Agenda 21 is a blueprint for sustainable development in the 21st century, and Chapter 16 requires governments to consider international cooperation on the "Environmentally Sound Management of Biotechnology" and to act appropriately to ensure that developing countries have effective participation in biotechnology research activities as well as priority access to the results and benefits of biotechnology on a fair and equitable basis (see table 12.3).

One result of the Convention has been the Cartagena Protocol on Biosafety, which was adopted in Montreal on January 29, 2000, and addresses the safe transfer, handling, and use of LMOs.[19] The protocol, which has been signed by 108 countries and ratified by 49, requires the ratification of 50 governments before coming into force. On June 13, 2003, the small Pacific nation of Palau became the fiftieth country to ratify the Protocol, triggering its implementation on September 11, 2003.

With its emphasis on the transboundary movement of LMOs, the protocol intersects directly with earlier (1995) international trade agreements made under the WTO. The specific agreements with significant overlap and potential for conflict with the protocol include the Sanitary and Phytosanitary (SPS) Agreement, intended to protect animal, plant, and human health; the Technical Barriers to Trade (TBT) Agreement, which sets out technical regulations and conformity procedures such as labeling; and the Trade Related Intellectual Property (TRIPS) Agreement, which defines basic intellectual property standards internationally.

Guidance as to the nature of the relationship between the protocol and trade agreements under the WTO is included only in the preamble to the protocol. Among other things, the preamble:

- Recognizes that trade and environment agreements should be mutually supportive.
- Emphasizes that the protocol does not change rights and obligations under existing agreements.
- Understands that the protocol is not subordinate to other international agreements.

The "soft" language of the preamble has left the relationship between the WTO and the Biosafety Protocol ambiguous and not likely to be resolved

**TABLE 12.3 The Cartagena Protocol on Biosafety**

| What It Does: | What It Does Not Do: |
|---|---|
| Establishes an Internet-based "Biosafety Clearing House" for information exchange | Does not address food safety issues; these are addressed in other international fora |
| Advance Informed Agreement (AIA) procedure requires exporters to seek consent of importers prior to shipments of LMOs destined for environmental release | Does not subject shipments of bulk commodities destined for direct processing or food use to the AIA procedure |
| Mandates bulk shipments of living modified organisms (LMOs) destined for food processing to be labeled as "may contain" LMOs and "not intended for intentional introduction into the environment" | Does not require segregation of bulk commodities that may contain LMOs and does not require detailed identification of bulk commodity shipments (these will be subject to further negotiation within two years of the protocol's coming into force) |
| Includes a "savings clause" stipulating that existing rights and obligations under the WTO or other international agreements are not altered | Does not require consumer product labeling |
| Assists developing countries in building capacity for managing modern biotechnology | |

*Source:* http://usinfo.state.gov/topical/global/biotech/00021601.htm.

until a measure is taken under it. The preamble asserts that the protocol would not alter countries' existing international rights and obligations, but the extent to which other agreements will preempt the Protocol has not been clarified (Swenarchuk 2000).

A number of the protocol provisions require an action by the Parties that could have consequences for trade. These include the advanced informed agreement (AIA) procedure to export GM products, risk management, confidential information, illegal transboundary movements, and socioeconomic considerations in risk assessment (WTO 2000). Dispute about a national measure taken pursuant to the Biosafety Protocol could possibly be resolved under the WTO, or under the dispute procedure of the Convention on *Biological Diversity (CBD) where parties must consent prior to* going to arbitration, or by submission to an International *Court of Justice (Cors 1999). Ongoing* discussions and analysis of the relationships between the WTO and multilateral environmental agreements, such as the CBD, are assisted by the United Nations Environment Programme (UNEP) to make trade and environment policies mutually supportive (WTO 2001).

The Biosafety Protocol entrenches a precautionary approach in the risk assessment process as it states that "lack of scientific certainty due to insufficient relevant scientific information and knowledge" should not prevent countries from taking precautionary import actions regarding LMOs. The related provision in the SPS Agreement is less restrictive as it emphasizes the provisional nature of such measures.

Although most developing countries are very supportive of the Biosafety Protocol, its implementation will pose both scientific and economic challenges to poorer countries. Parties to the protocol must develop or have access to "the necessary capacities to act on and respond to their rights and obligations." National, regional, and international agencies have recognized that successful implementation of the protocol is contingent on the development of national biosafety capacity in countries that have yet to establish, or are in the process of establishing, biosafety systems. Financial aid is being provided to parties, most notably by the UNEP/Global Environment Facility (GEF) global project on the development of National Biosafety Frameworks.[20]

The protocol provides considerable flexibility in terms of how importing countries may meet their obligations with respect to risk management decision-making and the implementation of these decisions. For example, under the Biosafety Protocol AIA, an importing country can request that the exporter conduct the risk assessment of an LMO or that the exporter pay for the cost of the assessment. While this appears to be an equitable approach to addressing the resource constraints (financial, scientific, and infrastructural) of developing-country exporters, it may be that those asked to bear the costs associated with risk assessments will choose to forgo the smaller markets, further constraining access to the technology in countries that may benefit the most from it. This is particularly true in that *the development of international standards for regulatory harmonization around GM crops and foods (for instance, by the OECD or the CAC) tends to be driven by industrialized countries, and* is resulting in ever more complex and expensive information and data requirements. These evolving criteria, which do not necessarily ensure a higher safety standard, may be practically unattainable for resource-poor countries and will affect their ability to import potentially useful products or technology as well as their opportunities to access desirable export markets with their own, domestically produced GM products.

### *WTO: The SPS and TBT Agreements*

Because they were negotiated prior to the commercialization of any GM plants or food commodities, the SPS Agreement and the TBT Agreement contain no provisions that are specific to these products.

The SPS Agreement sets out the basic rules for food safety and animal and plant health standards. Although it allows individual countries to set their own standards, it requires that regulations be based on science, and that they be applied only to the extent necessary to protect human, animal, or plant life and health.[21] Under the agreement, WTO Members are encouraged to adopt international standards (where they exist), but may define even higher standards provided these are based on a sound scientific risk assessment and do not discriminate against imports. Recognizing that a complete risk assessment may not be possible in the short term because of scientific uncertainty or the lack of sufficient evidence, Article 5.7 of the SPS Agreement allows member countries to adopt temporary restrictive measures. In such cases, members are expected to seek the additional information required to complete a full risk assessment within a reasonable period. Maintaining restrictive measures indeterminately in the absence of scientific evidence of risk solely for "precautionary" reasons is not allowed. The SPS Agreement would apply to regulations to protect the environment and biodiversity against introductions of harmful alien species and LMOs via trade, pursuant to Articles 8(g) and 8(h) of the CBD.

The TBT Agreement is intended to ensure that WTO Members do not use technical regulations and standards as disguised measures to protect domestic industries from foreign competition. In international trade law, health and environmental standards and regulations, labeling, symbols, and packaging markings can be considered as technical barriers to trade. In the agrifood sector, the TBT Agreement applies to all rules other than those specifically covered by the SPS Agreement. The TBT Agreement does not permit requirements for the labeling of some products whereby "like products" remain unlabeled (Article 2.1). For example, GM crop commodities that have been assessed and found to be "substantially equivalent" to their conventional counterparts would be considered "like products," and thus would not require specific labeling. Critics of the WTO stance argue that "substantially equivalent" is an unacceptable outcome of the risk assessment of GM products and assert that these products are not "like products" for purposes of labeling, and in fact, can be subjected to labeling. Traditionally within the WTO, a consumer desire for a measure such as mandatory labeling would not be viewed as a legitimate objective within the context of Article 2.2 of the TBT Agreement. This article states that regulatory measures that effectively disrupt trade must achieve a legitimate objective, and those regulations may restrict trade no more than what is necessary to accomplish the legitimate objective (WTO 1994).

### *WTO: Agreement on Trade Related Intellectual Property Rights*

One component of the TRIPS Agreement, Article 27:3(b), deals with plant variety protection, setting a minimum standard for the protection of plant varieties.[22] Countries have many options to fulfill this requirement. The U.S. and EU extend patent protection to plants, while most other countries have implemented a *sui generis* system, such as plant breeders' rights. In contrast, the CBD establishes the rights of indigenous communities to genetic and biological resources that are held in common, a concept that is largely ignored under intellectual property systems.

Market access and benefit-sharing are the two main crosscutting issues between the CBD and the TRIPS Agreement. It is not clear if or how these issues will impact on the Biosafety Protocol.

### *FAO/WHO: Codex Alimentarius Commission*

The CAC was created in 1962 by the Rome-based FAO and the Geneva-based WHO in order to establish internationally agreed-upon norms, directives, recommendations, or codes of practice designed to protect the health of consumers and ensure that procedures followed in trade of food products are fair. The CAC comprises representatives from 163 countries who meet every two years, in Rome and Geneva alternately, in order to make final decisions on the adoption of texts. The Codex Alimentarius process is based on reaching consensus, and a new standard or norm can only be adopted after eight stages of consultation.

The importance of the Codex Alimentarius process was heightened significantly when the new SPS Agreement came into force in 1995. Under the SPS Agreement, the CAC is responsible for maintaining international standards relevant to food safety that should be recognized by the WTO, and for determining whether national measures are sufficiently "based on scientific principles" to comply with WTO rules.

The CAC's Committees on Food Labeling, on Food Import and Export Certification and Inspection Systems, on General Principles, and a special Task Force on Foods Derived from Biotechnology are all currently considering issues relevant to GM foods.

Significant disagreements between the U.S. and the EU, particularly in the area of mandatory labeling of GM foods, threaten to paralyze the CAC's consensual approach. The U.S. supports mandatory labeling of GM foods only in situations of significantly altered composition or increased risk of toxicity or allergenicity. The EU, on the other hand, believes that labeling is required to inform consumers regarding processing and production methods (PPMs), such as the use of recombinant-DNA technology to produce new plants. This type of PPM labeling has not been previously permitted by the WTO, but in December 2001, the EU in a proposal to the WTO in the context of the current negotiations on agriculture proposed mandatory labeling for PPMs to address "societal values or concerns."[23]

Advocates of the Precautionary Principle, primarily from the EU, are pressing for incorporation of the principle within a revised Codex Alimentarius risk analysis framework, within the regulatory harmonization work of the OECD, and within anticipated revisions of the WTO SPS and TBT Agreements.

### *Future Developments*

Some of the most immediately visible impacts of changing European trade policies affecting GM products are likely to be seen in U.S.–EU agricultural trade. In 2001, the value of U.S. agricultural exports to the EU was US$6.3 billion, composed mainly of soybeans, tobacco, and animal feed (including corn gluten). The size of the reciprocal U.S. market for EU agricultural products was even larger, US$7.9 billion, and was accounted for primarily by exports of wine and beer.

The EU moratorium on new GM product approvals and labeling requirements has had a limited negative impact on U.S. corn exports to the EU. In 1999, the EU market represented about 4 percent (US$180 million) of total U.S. corn exports. However, the EU represents a much larger export market for corn byproducts, such as corn gluten used in livestock animal feed, and accounts for more than 85 percent of total exports. In July 2001, the EU proposed new rules requiring the labeling of animal feed products derived from GM plants or seeds that do not currently require specific labeling. These new labeling and traceability rules, which are viewed by many as clear violations of WTO trade rules, are certain to have a much greater impact on U.S.–EU trade.

In May 2003, the U.S., together with Canada and Argentina, announced its intent to challenge the EU's *de facto* moratorium on GM foods in the WTO. This action is being explicitly supported by a number of countries, including Australia, Chile, Colombia, El Salvador, Honduras, Mexico, New Zealand, Peru, and Uruguay, and unofficially by a number of others. Should the U.S. and its partner countries win their action under the WTO, it is unclear whether this will have the desired effect. Previous experience, such as the 1998 WTO ruling against the EU ban on hormone-treated beef, has not been encouraging. In that case, the EU decided to meet its WTO obligations by allowing the U.S. (and other complainants) to retaliate against an equivalent value of EU exports. There has been no change in EU policy, making this a less-than-satisfying WTO victory.

Resolution of the growing U.S.–EU trade impasse has broader impacts, and it may ultimately have its most profound effects on developing-country farmers. Notwithstanding the obvious economic benefits that GM crops may represent to farmers in industrialized countries, they can afford to do without them. The same may not be true of resource-poor farmers in developing regions, whose economic prosperity could be dramatically increased by the adoption of new GM varieties that are resistant to pests, disease, and drought.

## Notes

1. There are other techniques used in biotechnology, such as recombinant-RNA and cell fusion. The first recombinant deoxyribonucleic acid (DNA) molecule was created in 1972 by researchers at Stanford University. The group, led by Paul Berg, who received a Nobel Prize for the work, used enzymes found in bacteria called restriction endonucleases to cut DNA from two sources (a bacterium and a virus) and used a different enzymatic reaction to splice these two foreign pieces of DNA together into a functional, hybrid DNA molecule. In 1973, Stanley Cohen, also from Stanford, and Herbert Boyer, from the University of California at San Francisco, took this work to the next step by transferring a recombinant-DNA molecule into a bacterium where it functioned alongside the bacterium's own genes. In doing so, they created the first "genetically engineered" organism.

2. A transgenic organism is one into whose genome an isolated gene sequence usually, but not always, from another species has been integrated. In transgenic plants and animals, the introduced gene sequence must be transmitted through meiosis to allow its inheritance by the offspring.

3. "Essential Biosafety Crop Database Synopsis." Available on the Internet at http://www.essentialbiosafety.info/dbase.php?action=Synopsis.

4. Canada's regulatory framework for biotechnology products has a wider scope than just transgenic organisms produced via recombinant-DNA technology. For environmental release, the focus is on plants with novel traits, which are defined as plants that exhibit neither familiarity nor substantial equivalence that may have been produced by traditional plant breeding or genetic engineering. With respect to food products, Health Canada regulates novel foods, which could include any food without a history of safe use rather than just bioengineered foods.

5. A comprehensive database of crop biotechnology products that have received regulatory approval in various

jurisdictions can be accessed at http://www.essentialbiosafety.info/dbase.php.

6. High salinity affects about 20 percent of agricultural land overall and about 40 percent of irrigated land in particular. Most crop plants cannot tolerate high concentrations of salt, which leads to a decline in photosynthesis and an accumulation of deleterious metabolites (Zhang and Blumwald 2001).

7. These transgenic fish produce higher concentrations of growth hormone, causing them to increase their size and weight up to six times as fast as the conventional salmon. (Their final size is equivalent to that of normal Atlantic salmon, but they achieve that size in a shorter period of time.)

8. Seeds store phosphorus needed for germination in the form of phytate, a sugar molecule containing six phosphate groups. Because phytate also strongly binds iron, calcium, zinc, and other mineral ions, it acts as an antinutrient in the human diet (as well as the diet of livestock animals), making these substances unavailable for uptake.

9. This loss has been attributed to a record low level of infestation of European corn borer in 1999 that resulted in yields that were below the economic threshold for cost-effective control. Based on historical data, this can be expected to occur in one year out of four.

10. Voluntary guidelines may include standards for facilities and practices designed to prevent the unintended release of, or inadvertent exposure to, GMOs or recombinant DNA; conditions for ensuring reproductive isolation and site monitoring during the conduct of confined field trials; and standards for risk assessment that define criteria for conducting environmental or food safety assessments.

11. The competent authority is the body responsible for overseeing the development and implementation of, and compliance with, biosafety measures. It may be a government department or agency, or a statutory or nonstatutory committee.

12. S. R. Moephuli, Registrar, GMO Act, SA. Personal communication.

13. Canada's regulatory system is unique in that it was not designed to focus just on GM crops or GM foods, but rather on any new crop or food displaying novel, or unfamiliar, characteristics. Because of this different conceptual approach, Canadian regulators have adopted unique terminology and refer to plants with novel traits and novel foods, respectively.

14. The true level of consumer concern is difficult to ascertain precisely. In unprompted surveys, most consumers will identify issues such as microbial contamination or the presence of pesticide residues as their most immediate food safety concerns, with genetic modification of foods well down the list. In a recent study prepared for the Australia New Zealand Food Authority in 1999, it was estimated that the underlying consumer concern over genetically modified foods ranged between 0.25 percent and 5 percent, and that 87 percent of consumers made their buying decisions based on "price, brand, and use-by date."

15. "Voluntary Labeling Indicating Whether Foods Have or Have Not Been Developed Using Bioengineering." Draft guidance, U.S. Food and Drug Administration, Center for Food Safety and Nutrition, Washington, D.C. January 17, 2001. Docket Number 00D-1598. Available on the Internet at http://www.cfsan.fda.gov/~lrd/../ ~dms/biolabgu.html.

16. The CCGD is an organization representing about 80 percent of Canada's major food retailers and is involved in public awareness and education activities for biotechnology.

17. The CGSB is a standards-development organization in the federal Department of Public Works and Government Services.

18. In relation to biodiversity, the Precautionary Principle is listed as Principle 15 of the 1992 Rio Declaration on Environment and Development, which states that "In order to protect the environment, the precautionary approach should be widely applied by States according to their capabilities. Where there are threats of serious or irreversible damage, lack of full scientific certainty shall not be used as a reason for postponing cost-effective measures to prevent environmental degradation."

19. "Living modified organism" means any living organism that possesses a novel combination of genetic material obtained through the use of modern biotechnology. From the Cartagena Protocol on Biosafety, Article 3 (g).

20. The three-year-old UNEP/GEF project is designed to assist up to 140 countries to develop their National Biosafety Frameworks so that they can comply with the Cartagena Protocol on Biosafety. The project will also promote regional and subregional cooperation on biosafety. See http://www.unep.ch/biosafety/.

21. For a fuller discussion, see chapter 9 on "Food Safety" of this handbook.

22. See also chapter 13 of this handbook.

23. "EU Paper Calls for WTO Approval for Process-Based Labeling Schemes." *Inside U.S. Trade,* December 14, 2001, p. 13.

## Select Bibliography

Anderson, K., and S. Yao. 2001. "USDA Foreign Agriculture Attaché Reports: China, GMOS, and the World Trade in Agricultural and Textile Products." Centre for International Economics, Discussion Paper No. 0126, Adelaide, Australia.

Ausich, R. L. 1997. "Commercial Opportunities for Carotenoid Production by Biotechnology." *Pure and Applied Chemistry* 69(10): 2169–73.

Cors, T. A. 1999. "Biosafety and International Trade: Conflict or Convergence?" Prepared for the Centre for International Development at Harvard University. http://www.biotech-info.net/conflict_convergence.html.

FAO (Food and Agriculture Organization). 2000. "Agriculture: Towards 2015/2030." Technical interim report. FAO, Rome. fao.org/docrep/004/y3557e/y3557e00. htm.

FAO/WHO (Food and Agriculture Organization and the World Health Organization). 1996. "Biotechnology and Food Safety." Report of a joint Food and Agriculture Organization/World Health Organization Consultation. FAO/WHO, Rome.

———. 2000. "Safety Aspects of Genetically Modified Foods of Plant Origin." Report of a Joint Food and Agriculture Organization/World Health Organization Consultation. FAO/WHO, Rome.

FDA (U.S. Food and Drug Administration). 1992. "Statement of Policy: Foods Derived from New Plant Varieties." *Federal Register* 57: 22984–23001.

———. 1997. "Guidance on Consultation Procedures: Foods Derived from New Plant Varieties." FDA, Washington D.C. cfsan.fda.gov/~lrd/consulpr.html.

———. 2001. "List of Completed Consultations on Bioengineered Foods."cfsan.fda.gov/~lrd/biocon.html.

James, C. 2000. "Global Status of Commercialized Transgenic Crops: 2000." ISAAA Briefs No. 23. ISAAA, Ithaca.

———. 2002. "Global Status of Commercialized Transgenic Crops: 2002." ISAAA Briefs No. 27: Preview. ISAAA, Ithaca.

Mason, H. S., J. M. Ball, J.-J. Shi, X. Jiang, M. K. Estes, and C. J. Arntzen. 1996. "Expression of Norwalk Virus Capsid Protein in Transgenic Tobacco and Potato and Its Oral Immunogenicity In Mice." *Proceedings of the U.S. National Academy of Sciences* 93(11): 5335–40.

Millstone, E. P., E. J. Brunner, and S. Mayer. 1999. "Beyond 'Substantial Equivalence.'" *Nature* 401: 525–6.

Modelska A., B. Dietzschold, Z. F. Fu, K. Steplewski, D. C. Hooper, H. Koprowski, and V. Yusibov. 1998. "Immunization against Rabies With Plant-Derived Antigen." *Proceeding of the U.S. National Academy of Sciences* 95(5): 2481–85.

Mor, T. S., and C. J. Arntzen. 1999. "Pharmaceutical Foodstuffs: Oral Immunization With Transgenic Plants." In A. Altman, M. Ziv, and S. Izhar, eds., *Plant Biotechnology and in Vitro Biology in the 21st Century.* Dordrecht, Netherlands: Kluwer.

OECD (Organisation for Economic Co-operation and Development). 1993. "Safety Evaluation of Foods Derived by Modern Biotechnology, Concepts and Principles." OECD, Paris.

———. 2000. "Report of the Task Force for the Safety of Novel Foods and Feeds." C(2000)86/ADD1. OECD, Paris.

OGTR (Office of the Gene Technology Regulator). 2001. "Gene Technology Act, 2000." http://scaletext.law. gov.au/html/pasteact/3/3428/top.htm

Phillips, P. W. B., and H. McNeill. 2000. "Labeling for GM Foods: Theory and Practice." *AgBioForum* 3(4): 219–24. agbioforum.org.

Richter, L., Y. Thanavala, C. Arntzen, and H. Mason. 2000. "Production of Hepatitis B Surface Antigen in Transgenic Plants for Oral Immunization. *Nature Biotechnology* 18: 1167–71.

Royal Society of Canada. 2001. "Elements of Precaution: Recommendations for the Regulation of Food Biotechnology in Canada." Royal Society of Canada, Ottawa.

Swenarchuk, M. 2000. "The Cartagena Biosafety Protocol: Opportunities and Limitations. Canadian Centre for Policy Alternatives." Briefing Paper Series: *Trade and Investment* 1(3). April 1.

World Bank. 2000. *World Development Report 2000/2001: Attacking Poverty.* New York: Oxford University Press.

WTO (World Trade Organization). 1994. "The WTO Agreement on Technical Barriers to Trade (TBT Agreement)." Office of the Secretary General, Geneva.

———. 2000. "Response of the Executive Secretary of the Convention on Biological Diversity (CBD) to the Chair of the CTE." Communication from the CBD Secretariat. June 28, WT/CTE/W/149. Office of the Secretary General, Geneva.

———. 2001. "UNEP Meeting on Compliance, Enforcement, and Dispute Settlement in Multilateral Environmental Agreements and the WTO." Communication from UNEP. 20 July, WT/CTE/W/199. Office of the Secretary General, Geneva.

Ye, X., S. Al-Babili, A. Kloti, J. Zhang, P. Lucca, P. Beyer, and I. Potrykus. 2000. "Engineering the Provitamin A (Beta-Carotene) Biosynthetic Pathway into (Carotenoid-Free) Rice Endosperm." *Science* 287(5451): 303–5.

Zhang, H.-X., and E. Blumwald. 2001. "Transgenic Salt-Tolerant Tomato Plants Accumulate Salt in Foliage But Not in Fruit." *Nature Biotechnology* 19: 765.

13

# GLOBAL INTELLECTUAL PROPERTY RIGHTS: A NEW FACTOR IN FARMING

*Geoff Tansey*

## Why Intellectual Property Rights Matter

Since the early 1990s, the international rules affecting agriculture have been changing as a result of international negotiations ranging across issues of trade, the environment, food, and agriculture. The results of this process are only now emerging and are likely to affect farmers everywhere. One of the most hotly debated issues in these negotiations has been intellectual property rights (IPRs)—concerning among other things copyrights, patents, plant breeders' rights, and trade secrets. The most controversial set of rules on IPRs is contained in the Agreement on Trade-Related Aspects of Intellectual Property Rights (TRIPS). This is one of the 1995 World Trade Organization (WTO) agreements, with which all WTO Members must comply sooner or later.

Before the TRIPS Agreement, countries could decide whether or not to provide any form of IPRs in agriculture. Most developing countries did not. As a result of TRIPS, developed and developing members of WTO must adopt the same, relatively high, minimum levels of intellectual property protection. This removes from developing-country members options that were used historically by developed countries to adopt varying levels of IPRs, according to their needs. The agreement is one of the three pillars of the WTO—the others being trade in goods and trade in services. By placing IPRs in the WTO and making them subject to its binding disputes procedure, proponents of a strong IPRs regime have made it possible for non-compliant WTO Members to face trade sanctions in any area if they fail to live up to its rules. This is arguably the main reason why IPRs were put into the WTO instead of the existing body concerned with promoting IPRs, the World Intellectual Property Organization (WIPO). The TRIPS Agreement also includes rules on domestic enforcement procedures and remedies.

In the Uruguay Round negotiations (1986–94) TRIPS rules were developed with very little public involvement and introduced into the negotiations against strong, but in the end futile, opposition from developing countries. TRIPS originated from a small number of major business interests with a handful of corporations and lobbyists responsible for crafting its terms and pushing the agreement, via various developed-country governments (see Drahos 1995; Drahos and Braithwaite 2002).

Today IPRs increasingly underpin the new knowledge economy: their ownership and control will affect the distribution of wealth and power, and the direction of development. Intellectual property rights allow creators and inventors to exclude others from copying or using their work or invention without permission. The IPRs regime plays an important role in private sector-led innovation and establishing and maintaining market power.[1]

## The Plan of This Chapter

This chapter outlines the background to this change, the questions for development raised by IPRs, key features of the TRIPS Agreement, and in particular, the provisions on patents and plant variety protection most likely to affect agriculture. These provisions, initially reviewed in 1999, revealed wide divisions between developed and developing countries, and the review process became deadlocked. Other aspects of the TRIPS Agreement that may also affect agriculture—such as geographical indications and trademarks, and other relevant international agreements—are also discussed briefly, as are the decisions taken at the fourth Ministerial Conference of the WTO in Doha in November 2001. (See table 13.1 for a list of online resources.)

### *Tradeoffs Involved in IPRs*

Overall, the economic effects from stronger IPRs are far from simple, clear, or agreed. They are, as the World Bank's *World Development Report 1998/99* argued, "a compromise between preserving the incentive to create knowledge and the desirability of disseminating knowledge at little or no cost." In

**TABLE 13.1 Online Resources**

| Resource | Description |
|---|---|
| Convention on Biological Diversity<br>393 Saint Jacques Street, Suite 300<br>Montreal, Québec<br>Canada H2Y 1N9<br>Tel: +1 (514) 288-2220<br>Fax: +1 (514) 288-6588<br>Email: secretariat@biodiv.org<br>URL: www.biodiv.org/ | The Secretariat of the Convention on Biological Diversity works on developing access and benefit guidelines and the biosafety protocol among other issues. |
| Commission on Plant Genetic Resources for Food and Agriculture<br>Food and Agriculture Organization (FAO) of the United Nations<br>Viale delle Terme di Caracalla<br>00100 Rome, Italy<br>URL: www.fao.org/ag/cgrfa/ | The Commission deals with the International Treaty on Plant Genetic Resources for Food and Agriculture, and its secretariat is housed in FAO. |
| UNCTAD/ICTSD TRIPS and Development Capacity Building<br>URL: www.ictsd.org/iprsonline/ | This partnership is producing a range of resources to help developing countries deal with IPR issues, including a policy issues paper, series of case studies, annotated and updated bibliography on IPRs and sustainable development, and a detailed resource book on all aspects of the TRIPS Agreement. Drafts of these are put up on the Web site as the project progresses, with the final versions expected in mid-2003. It is also developing a portal to resources on IPRs available at www.ictsd.org/iprsonline/. |
| Commission on Intellectual Property Rights<br>URL: www.iprcommission.org/ | The Commission was set up by the British government to look at how intellectual property rights can work better for poor people and developing countries. It reported its findings in September 2002. Its report and all background papers are available online. |
| World Trade Organization (WTO)<br>URL: www.wto.org/ | WTO is the only global international organization dealing with the rules of trade between nations. At its heart are the WTO agreements, negotiated and signed by the bulk of the world's trading nations and ratified in their parliaments. The goal is to help producers of goods and services, exporters, and importers conduct their business. |

**TABLE 13.1 (Continued)**

| Resource | Description |
|---|---|
| The International Union for the Protection of New Varieties of Plants (UPOV)<br>Address: Boîte Postale (POB) 12, 34, chemin des Colombettes CH-1211 Geneva 20, Switzerland<br>Tel: +41-22 338 91 11<br>Fax: 41-22 733 03 36<br>Email: upov.mail@wipo.int<br>URL : www.upov.org | UPOV is an intergovernmental organization based on the International Convention for the Protection of New Varieties of Plants. It provides guidance on how to implement the system of Plant Breeders Rights. |
| World Intellectual Property Organization (WIPO)<br>URL: www.wipo.org/ | WIPO is an international organization dedicated to promoting the use and protection of works of the human spirit. It has established an intergovernmental committee on genetic resources, traditional knowledge, and folklore. |
| International Plant Genetic Resources Institute (IPGRI)<br>Via dei Tre Denari 472/a<br>00057 Maccarese (Fiumicino)<br>Rome, Italy<br>Tel: (39) 06 6112.1<br>Fax:(39) 06 61979661<br>Email: ipgri@cgiar.org<br>URL: www.cgiar.org/ipgri | IPGRI is an international research institute with a mandate to advance the conservation and use of genetic diversity for the well-being of present and future generations. It is a Centre of the Consultative Group on International Agricultural Research (CGIAR). It has produced a number of publications dealing with IPRs issues and is continuing to work on these. |
| International Seed Federation (ISF)<br>FIS/ASSINSELSecretariat<br>Chemin du Reposoir 7<br>1260 Nyon, Switzerland<br>Tel: +41 22 365 44 20<br>Fax: +41 22 365 44 21<br>Email: fis@worldseed.org or assinsel@worldseed.org<br>URL: worldseed.org/intellectual_property.htm | The ISF was created in May 2002 by the merger of the International Seed Trade Federation (FIS) and the International Association of Plant Breeders (ASSINSEL). ISF has a number of papers about its views on IPRs available online. |
| Genetic Resources Action International (GRAIN)<br>Girona 25, pral. E-08010<br>Barcelona, Spain<br>Tel: +34 933011381<br>Fax:+34 933011627<br>Email: grain@grain.org<br>URL: www.grain.org/ | GRAIN is an international nongovernmental organization that promotes the sustainable management and use of agricultural biodiversity based on people's control over genetic resources and local knowledge. It produces BIO-IPR, an irregular list serve to circulate information about recent developments in the field of intellectual property rights related to biodiversity and associated knowledge. BIO-IPR is a strictly noncommercial and educational service for nonprofit organizations and individuals active in the struggle against IPRs on life. The views expressed in each post are those of the indicated author(s). To join the mailing list, send the word "subscribe" (no quotes) as the subject of an email message to bio-ipr-request@cuenet.com. |
| The Action Group on Erosion, Technology and Concentration (ETC)<br>URL: www.etcgroup.org | The ETC group, formerly Rural Advancement Foundation International (RAFI), is an international civil society organization headquartered in Canada. It is dedicated to the advancement of cultural and ecological diversity and human rights, and monitors development in this area. |
| Quaker UN Office (QUNO)<br>13 Avenue du Mervelet, Geneva, Switzerland<br>URL: www.quno.org | QUNO represents worldwide Quaker concerns for peace and justice at the international level. It works with negotiators in Geneva to help develop their capacity to deal with IPRs, food, biodiversity, and health issues and produces papers dealing with Article 27.3(b), traditional knowledge, plant variety protection, and food security and biotechnology. All are available on the organization's Web site—click on the link to Geneva pages. |

theory, stronger IPRs should encourage more research and development (R&D) in countries where they exist, but there is "limited empirical evidence," even in industrial countries, that IPRs protection leads to increased investment in R&D. This is partly because of the difficulty of separating cause and effect—IPRs may stimulate more investment, but countries and firms that invest more in R&D may demand more protection.

Although IPRs restrict direct imitation, they can assist in the diffusion process of new knowledge within and among economies. Patents provide published information, which other researchers can also use to develop innovations. The World Bank report found that the level of IPRs protection appears to influence the degree of foreign direct investment (FDI), the vertical integration of multinational firms, and direct technology transfers through technology sales and licensing agreements, although the relationship between protection and FDI is not well established, according to other studies (UN 1993).

There are costs related to the granting of IPRs as they increase the market power of the right's owners, which may lead to higher consumer prices. They also, according to the World Bank report, "shift bargaining power toward the producers of knowledge, and away from its users." Stronger IPRs may lead to a higher cost of acquiring knowledge, and therefore may adversely affect follow-on innovations that draw on inventions whose patents have not yet expired. Tighter IPRs, notes the report, "may actually slow the overall pace of innovation. However, there is no systematic empirical evidence confirming this, just as there is none on the positive impact of IPRs on increased R&D."

Policymakers face the difficult task of defining the scope of IPRs—the length and breadth of protection—to maximize social welfare and to achieve certain distributional objectives. Protection that is too weak may lead firms to invest less than is socially desirable in the creation of new knowledge. Overly stringent protection may lead to wasteful R&D spending as firms compete to be first to innovate, which may make public R&D more socially desirable than private R&D. Only rarely, suggest Michael Trebilcock and Robert Howse (1995), will "a single level of protection for all technologies or sectors maximize domestic welfare," as the tradeoff between the economic benefits of innovation and imitation will depend on the sector involved.

### *Development Impacts*

The effects of IPRs protection become even more complex when producers and users of knowledge are in different countries with different economic levels of development. Theoretically, "it is far from clear that all countries should be required to maintain the same level of intellectual property protection," argue Trebilcock and Howse. If a country has limited innovative capabilities and primarily consumes foreign innovations, stronger IPRs protection may, they suggest, lead to "at least short-term consumer welfare losses and may discourage imitation and adaptation by competitors, which themselves constitute valuable economic activities." For example, in some developing countries with patent systems, the governments did not allow patent protection on certain products, such as pharmaceuticals. The absence of patents enabled these countries' infant industries to examine and copy products and develop local production capacities—as Swiss industry did in the 19th century. While this may have inhibited inward investment, it may also have produced net economic benefits for the country.

The World Bank report suggests that IPRs can disadvantage developing countries, however, "by increasing the knowledge gap and by shifting bargaining power toward the producers of knowledge, most of whom reside in industrial countries." While accepting the point, some analysts see such a view of IPRs as equating knowledge producers with commercial and research-based producers, and they focus on the role played by developing-country farming communities in producing knowledge about plants and animals (Tilahun and Edwards 1996). Intellectual property rights also pose developing countries with another challenge because "so many industrial-country firms are acquiring strong intellectual property positions, often covering fundamental research tools as well as marketable products, that it may prove hard for new firms and researchers to elbow into this new global industry." Firms and public research groups in developing countries need to be able to negotiate agreements to use these technologies and "to participate in the continuing debate about particular forms of intellectual property, to ensure that their interests and those of their country are taken into account," states the report.

## Intellectual Property Rights in International Agreements

TRIPS is not the only agreement concerned with IPRs and food. The Convention on Biological Diversity (CBD), agreed at the 1992 United Nations Conference on Environment and Development (also known as the Rio Earth Summit), and the International Treaty on Plant Genetic Resources for Food and Agriculture (ITPGRFA) both deal with IPRs. The latter agreement was finally reached in November 2001 after seven years of difficult negotiations. The International Union for the Protection of New Varieties of Plants (UPOV after its French title, "Union Internationale pour la Protection des Obtentions Végétales") and the WIPO are also relevant (see Tansey 2002). The most wide-ranging agreement, however, is TRIPS.

### *The WTO TRIPS Agreement*

The 1995 WTO TRIPS Agreement covers eight areas: copyright and related rights, trademarks, geographical indications, industrial designs, patents (and plant variety protection—PVP), layout designs (topographies) of integrated circuits, protection of undisclosed information, and control of anticompetitive practices in contractual licenses. Patents and PVP are the most important areas for agriculture.

Unlike other WTO agreements, the only special and differential treatment for developing countries in TRIPS concerns the timetable for implementation. While developed countries had to implement TRIPS within one year of the agreement's entry into force, developing countries had an extra four years, that is, until January 1, 2000. A similar delay applied to economies in transition (from centrally planned to market economies). Least-developed countries have a 10-year transition period, but may apply for extensions and thus could delay implementing TRIPS (Art. 66.1). New members acceding to the WTO generally do not benefit from the transitional arrangements.

Toward the end of the negotiations on TRIPS, as a result of strong resistance from a few developing countries, various modifications were made to provide some degree of flexibility in its implementation. These flexibilities include the lack of definition of any terms and exclusions to the all-encompassing patent requirements of Article 27. (This article states that "patents shall be available for any inventions, whether products or processes, in all fields of technology, provided that they are new, involve an inventive step and are capable of industrial application.")

There are concerns by a range of academics and nongovernmental organizations (NGOs) about the relatively high levels of IPRs protection and judicial interpretations in the United States (U.S.) and the European Union (EU), which provide broad patent protection in software and biotechnological inventions (Tansey 2002, p. 17). Recent moves in the EU to establish extensive rights in databases could also damage scientific research (Commission on Intellectual Property Rights 2002, p. 108). Whatever the concerns about the potentially damaging effects of excessive IPRs protection in developed countries, Keith Maskus in a major study of IPRs argues that it "is not too early to claim that they are inappropriate for developing economies and net technology importers" (Maskus 2000, p. 238).

### *TRIPS Section 5: Patents*

One reason for greater interest in patents, especially in the Organisation for Economic Co-operation and Development (OECD) countries, is the rapid development of biotechnology and its application in agriculture. A patent prevents someone from making commercial use of what is claimed in the patent without the authorization of the patent holder. To be patentable, an invention must be:

- Nonobvious for someone skilled in the art, that is, not simply be an extension of something that already exists—it must require some inventive step;
- Novel or not previously known; and
- Industrially applicable in some way.

Patents can be given for products and processes and are limited to a fixed period—at least 20 years under TRIPS—after which the invention moves into the public domain and can be used by anyone. Patents are territorial and apply only in the countries in which they are granted. Each country decides its own patent rules and how to interpret the meaning of different terms, but WTO Members must meet the minimum standards in TRIPS.

In return for the temporary monopoly granted by the patent, the inventor must make a full disclosure of the nature of his or her invention that is understandable to anyone else skilled in the necessary arts or sciences. In this way, inventions do not "die with the inventor." Moreover, others can try to invent something better, but sufficiently different so as not to infringe the claim of the original patent.

Clear evidence that the patent system has stimulated the development of new products and technologies, which otherwise would not have been developed, is available only for a few sectors (such as pharmaceuticals). In other sectors of the economy, patents are sometimes considered to have mainly anticompetitive effects: they serve to secure and strengthen the position of market leaders and limit the entry of new competitors. In the extreme, they may actually slow the pace of innovation if a dominant firm possesses a powerful group of patents that limits the ability of other firms to improve existing products and technologies.

Although policymakers have sought to limit such adverse effects of patents through various policies and regulations such as revised IPRs legislation, competition policy, and other business regulations, the anticompetitive implications remain a cause of concern. During the past decade such concerns have regained momentum with the emergence of patents on biotechnology products and processes that cover fundamental research tools, genetically engineered plants, human genes, and living organisms.

Patenting life-forms, or parts of them, has raised a range of concerns. Some are ethical, with various religious faiths and indigenous peoples rejecting the idea of intellectual ownership over life-forms. Some are environmental, linked to the role the patents play in underpinning the private sector-led development and in promoting the spread of genetically engineered plants and animals with its possible consequences for the environment, biodiversity, and human and animal health. Some argue that both patents and PVP systems favor commercial breeders at the expense of small, poor farmers who are the basis of traditional, community-based breeding—and fear that the adoption of these IPRs will promote more intensive farming, which will marginalize small farmers, cause social dislocation, and increase food insecurity.

Obtaining a patent can be quite expensive. Preparing a U.S. patent application in the early 1990s cost about US$20,000, while the cost in the EU was about twice that amount. Plant Breeder's Rights (PBRs), however, an alternative to patents discussed later in this chapter, are cheaper—about a tenth the cost of a patent (Lesser 1997). A patent applicant must apply for patents in every country where they will be used, pay an annual fee to maintain the patent, and pay patent agents' costs. The costs of filing a patent also vary greatly, ranging from US$355 to US$4,772 across 32 countries surveyed in the early 1990s (Helfgott 1993). For firms at the forefront of biotechnology research and use, establishing rights of ownership over new processes and plant varieties may also be a costly business as firms engage in litigation to determine rights ownership and to secure their markets.

### *TRIPS Article 27.3(b): Patentable Subject Matter and Exceptions*

Three subparagraphs in Article 27 of the TRIPS Agreement permit exceptions to the basic rule on patentability:

- Article 27.2 applies when members want to prevent the commercial exploitation of the invention to protect *ordre public,* or morality. This explicitly includes inventions that are dangerous to human, animal, or plant life or health, or are seriously prejudicial to the environment.
- Article 27.3(a) provides exemptions for diagnostic, therapeutic, and surgical methods for the treatment of humans or animals.
- Article 27.3(b) permits WTO Members to exclude from patentability "plants and animals other than micro-organisms, and essentially biological processes for the production of plants or animals other than non-biological and microbiological processes. However, Members shall provide for the protection of plant varieties either by patents or by an effective *sui generis* system or by any combination thereof. The provisions of this subparagraph shall be reviewed four years after the date of entry into force of the WTO Agreement."

The language of this exception is deliberately complex—described as "constructive ambiguity" by some negotiators—and continues to be subject to interpretation and legal argument among WTO members over its meaning (see Tansey 1999 for a more detailed discussion of this issue).

Members may also provide limited exceptions to the exclusive rights conferred by a patent, provided that such exceptions do not unreasonably conflict with a normal exploitation of the patent and do not unreasonably prejudice the legitimate interests of the patent owner, taking account of the legitimate interests of third parties (Art. 30).

Patents must also be available, and patent rights enjoyable, without discrimination as to the place of invention and whether products are imported or locally produced (Art. 27.1). According to Article 28.1(a) of the TRIPS Agreement, patents relating to products confer the right to prevent third parties from "making, using, offering for sale or importing for those purposes the product" without the patentee's consent. This last point is important for agricultural trade. For example, if something was patented in the U.S. but it was not patented elsewhere, then the holder of the U.S. patent could block imports of that product unless royalty payments were made. This has happened in a number of cases, for example, a contested yellow bean patent in the U.S., and has given rise to considerable controversy.[2]

In the case of process patents, the patentee may prevent the use of the process as well as the commercialization of a product "obtained directly by that process." Thus, if a process to produce a plant (for instance, by genetic engineering) is patented, exclusive rights would also apply with respect to the plants obtained with the process. Article 34.1 also places the burden of proof in process patents on the producer to show that it is not using the patented process.

### *TRIPS Article 27.3(b)*

The terms used in Article 27.3(b) are not defined in the TRIPS Agreement. The words that are open to interpretation are plants, animals, microorganisms, essentially biological processes, nonbiological, microbiological, plant varieties, effective, and *sui generis* (of its own kind) system. These disputed words are defined differently in different international and national legislation. Various authors argue that there is considerable scope for individual national interpretations to be attached to these words, and legal cases (which may be lengthy) are likely to determine which competing interpretation will prevail. Currently, patenting principles and practices on biotechnological inventions remains in a state of flux internationally, including in those countries that have already gained experience in patenting genes. According to Carlos Correa (see Correa 2000), where patenting is allowed, "the patenting of genes at the cell level extends the scope of protection to all plants which include a cell with the claimed gene." In general, patents give patentees the right to prevent any commercial use of the materials, including that for research and plant-breeding purposes. This could threaten commercial plant breeding, especially with broadly drafted patents—for example, those that seek rights over processes used in any plant species.

WTO Members may provide limited exceptions to the exclusive rights conferred by a patent (Art. 30). This provides some flexibility in drafting patent legislation and may allow members to include exemptions for research and breeding purposes. WTO Members are also free to determine what "invention" means, and many developing countries, including Argentina, Brazil, and the Andean Pact countries, "exclude the patentability of materials found in nature, even if isolated therefrom," notes Correa. Other areas of flexibility relate to the interpretation of the issues of novelty and inventive step and the scope of claims that will be admitted.

### *Plant Variety Protection—*Sui Generis *and UPOV*

A *sui generis* system of protection is a special system adapted to a particular subject matter, as opposed to protection provided by the existing patent or copyright systems or one of the other main systems of intellectual property protection. Thus, countries can make their own rules to protect new plant varieties with some form of IPRs provided that such protection is effective. The agreement does not define the elements of an effective system. In the last resort, it will be a WTO dispute settlement panel that will interpret the provision relating to an effective system.

One possible *sui generis* system likely to be recognized as effective is the UPOV system of PBRs. UPOV began in Europe in the 1960s and by early 2002 had 50 members, of which 14 were developing countries. PBRs were developed in Europe because plant breeders found it difficult or impossible to meet two of the fundamental requirements of patent law: inventiveness, and a written description of how to make and use the invention. PBRs were developed in response to the needs of commercial breeders and allow for the registration of a plant variety that has been discovered. UPOV defines a breeder as the person who bred, or discovered and developed, a variety. Such a variety must be distinct, stable, sufficiently uniform, and novel. Most plant varieties developed and used by small farmers in developing countries and by traditional and indigenous communities do not normally meet these criteria. Some countries such as India are developing their own systems of PVP, although there is considerable pressure for most to adopt the UPOV system.

Two major differences in terms of the level of protection offered made PBRs less restrictive compared to patents. PBRs provided a breeder's or researcher's exemption, which allowed use of the protected varieties for further R&D, and a farmer's exemption or "privilege," which allowed farmers to save and replant seeds from the first harvest of the protected crop. The scope of these exemptions has changed during various amendments to the UPOV convention. For example, the 1961 version prohibited both patents and PVP on a variety, but the 1991 version does not. It also no longer requires a farmer's exemption, but rather leaves it is an option.

The UPOV system, however, produces quite a strong IPRs regime for plant varieties geared to institutional breeding, which may not suit all countries. The alternative is for countries to develop their own solution with special legislation protecting plant varieties appropriate to their situation. Both are possible, but developing an appropriate *sui generis* system is a challenging task that may take some time (for a detailed discussion of this, see Dhar 2002). The Organization of African Unity has developed a model law, and India has introduced legislation that attempts to implement a new *sui generis* model and that encompasses farmers' rights as outlined in the International Treaty on Plant Genetic Resources for Food and Agriculture (ITPGRFA).

The International Plant Genetic Resources Institute (IPGRI), in producing a checklist for use in developing a *sui generis* system, argues that an IPR suitable for an industrialized system of production geared toward export is unlikely to be suitable or appropriate for an agricultural sector characterized primarily by subsistence farming (IPGRI 1999). Since both systems may exist in the same country, IPGRI suggests that it may be worthwhile for countries to explore how options can be mixed and matched, including the prohibition of double protection and providing different levels of protection for varieties of the same species, depending on their intended use.

IPGRI also stresses the need, whatever IPRs are used, for appropriate mechanisms to prevent any monopolistic effects of IPRs, particularly patents. Such mechanisms include: antitrust laws; shifting the burden of proof in patent law so that patent claimants have to prove that their wide-ranging claims will work, rather than challengers having to prove that their claims will not; rigorously applying the inventive step and industrial application requirements; mechanisms to balance the claims of initial and subsequent innovators; and limiting or prohibiting the use of functional claims.

### *Seed Provision and Plant Variety Protection*

Formal seed production systems encompassing public and private R&D with breeding companies dominate seed provision in industrialized countries. More informal seed production systems, with production largely by a mixture of farmers and public institutions, exist in many developing countries. With the exception of the U.S., and more recently the EU, in most countries plant varieties cannot be patented. There is now pressure from some developed countries for patents to be extended to plant varieties as well as PVP, and for PBRs to become more patent-like in their conditions.

With the introduction of PVP, in particular PBRs, the plant and seed industry argues that these will enable it to undertake breeding work and import seeds and breeding material into developing countries. The key questions, argues Dwijen Rangnekar in a background study for the United Kingdom's Commission on Intellectual Property Rights, are whether "the access to foreign-bred genetic material [has] enhanced national capacity in plant breeding, and what is the impact on food security. Existing literature on Kenya does not provide encouraging evidence on either of these two issues" (Rangnekar 2002). He finds that "(p)rivate sector breeding tends to limit itself to high value/low volume crops and hybrids.

Further, the agronomic qualities indicate that the target areas are characteristically the post–Green Revolution areas. Accordingly, it appears unlikely that the crop and agronomic needs of the wider farming populations, particularly low external-input use communities, are consistent with this research priority."

The Commission found that, based on evidence from developed countries on the impact of patents or PVP on research, PVP could be used in these countries as a marketing strategy for product differentiation as well as contribute to mergers in the seed industry (Commission on Intellectual Property Rights 2002, ch. 3). It is not only PVP legislation that affects seed provision but also national seed regulations and the effects of both on poor farmers that have to be considered.

The key to determining what impact the introduction of PVP required under TRIPS will have is whether the system adopted takes account of local conditions and provides a regulatory framework that will support the various farming systems in the country—rather than advantage some and disadvantage others. In a review of possible options, Biswajit Dhar concludes that "the *sui generis* legislation that developing countries must introduce has to take into consideration the interests of both the farming communities and the plant breeders in the formal sector" (Dhar 2002, p. 27). He argues that adopting the systems developed by the industrialized countries and embodied in UPOV is not adequate, and suggests approaches that take into account farmers' rights, as outlined in the ITPGRFA, and that allow seeds bred by farmers to be covered.

Under patent law there is no farmers' exemption to allow the use of farm-saved seed as allowed for in UPOV. IPGRI notes, "Breeders and modern biotechnology companies often perceive the farmers' exemption as potentially reducing the profit, or the expectation of profit. Consequently, there may be strong opposition on the part of breeders and modern biotechnology companies to this exemption in countries where patent-like protection for plant varieties is being considered" (see IPGRI 1999).

### *Research and Development Priorities*

The importance of patents and PVP is increasing partly because of changes in the funding of R&D for agriculture. Until relatively recently, agricultural R&D was largely publicly funded. Research results were given to farmers through extension services. The financial returns for publicly financed R&D into improved farming productivity are high for both developing and developed countries. The U.S. economy, for example, benefited from its long-term investment of US$134 million worth of support to international wheat and rice research aimed at developing countries by up to US$14.7 billion, according to research by the IPGRI.

In the OECD countries, private spending now accounts for about half of R&D. In many cases, governments have moved away from near-market research, which has immediate applicability on farms, to focus spending on basic research, which underpins future private R&D efforts. In some countries, resources have shifted into areas supporting agribusiness and food processing, which "may have reduced rather than increased the rate of return to public sector research," according to IPGRI researchers (Alston and others 1998).

One concern about patents is their effects on the movement of breeding materials—animals and plant germplasm. To date, the focus has been on plants. There is evidence that the strengthening of IPRs is leading to restrictions on the flow of germplasm and therefore inhibits the development of new plant varieties, particularly by publicly funded institutions such as those supported internationally by CGIAR. The seed industry itself is concerned about this reduced flow and recognizes the need to ensure that it is maintained.

The private sector, naturally, invests in areas in which it can hope for a return—with much work in agrochemicals. Today, former agrochemical companies have expanded to become biotechnology/seed companies (or life science companies, including pharmaceuticals), moving downstream to add value to their products. Huge investments have gone into this area—over US$8 billion per year in the U.S. alone, according to Ismail Serageldin, a vice president of the World Bank and former chairman of the CGIAR. Serageldin is concerned that this private proprietary science will focus on crops and innovations that will find rich markets, and ignore those of interest to poor, small farmers. Moves in developing countries to a greater private sector role in breeding would need to be balanced by continued public service activity geared to their needs.

There is some concern among researchers over the effects of the extension of copyright on access to educational materials and databases. More generally, since education is one of the prime areas for public investment that brings major returns in increasing productivity, if the extension of copyright affects access to education, especially by the poor, it may have deleterious effects. Therefore, special consideration may be necessary for knowledge that affects food security—to ensure that the flow of information is not inhibited to the detriment of farmers, researchers, and others involved in food production.

### *Market Structure and Farmers' Options*

Market structure is also very important in assessing the likely impact of changes in the IPRs regime and the role different participants can play, according to John Barton of Stanford Law School (Barton 1998). There is an increasing trend toward economic concentration of market power in larger and larger enterprises throughout the developed countries, including in the seed industry (Tansey and Worsley 1995). One argument for business mergers is that larger firms will be able to raise capital more easily than the small firms that make up the industry. Another is that there are economies of scale in R&D activities. The existence of an oligopoly also gives the firms greater pricing freedom and thus enables them to recover research costs. Such a structure provides an incentive for small firms to invest in biotech innovation in the expectation that they will recoup their costs and make money when they are sold to the large firms.

There are potential problems with this concentration of market power, however, and not simply of control over prices—it may produce declining incentives for research. According to Barton, "the incentives for the industry leaders to conduct research are now limited . . . new smaller firms may now find it impossible to enter the business because they face the assembled patent rights of the industry leaders and possibly also face contract restrictions on access to marketed materials that would once have been available for further breeding." Barton sees the key challenge as finding a way to reverse the oligopoly, while maintaining the use of intellectual property incentives to encourage research. Such incentives might include a tougher application of the nonobviousness principle (that is, inventions must not be obvious to one skilled in the art), restricting the scope of patent claims by making claimants prove the applicability over broad areas, and creating strong experimental use exemptions.

## Reviewing TRIPS Article 27.3(b) and Geographical Indications

### *Reviewing 27.3(b)*

There has been little progress in the WTO on the mandated review of Article 27.3(b) that began in 1999. There is a wide range of views on what should happen and whether specific interpretations or amendments are needed, and many countries have made proposals. Developing countries' proposals relate to the extension of exclusions from patentability to all life-forms and extension of the timetable for implementation, prevention of biopiracy, respecting use of traditional knowledge and farmers' rights, amendment to take account of the Convention on Biological Diversity (CBD) and International Understanding (now Treaty, see below), and what types of *sui generis* systems of PVP are effective. Developed countries' proposals include deletion of the exclusion and no lowering of standards of protection.[3]

### *Geographical Indications and Other IPRs*

Although patents and PVP are likely to have the most direct effects on agriculture, the major participants in the food system use a mix of IPRs in their businesses. Many companies make considerable use of trademarks, investing substantial amounts of capital in brand recognition to secure their markets. Greater efforts to protect brands and increase market share are increasingly likely by companies operating globally. Mergers and acquisitions in the food industry that have become common over the past decade are still continuing, as firms prepare to serve global markets and also to counter the growing power of multiple retailers. Achieving some kind of brand identity for products is a major challenge for small farmers and traditional knowledge-based producers as they try to differentiate and sell their products in markets dominated by brand advertising.

For some products, a combination of widely advertised branded (trademark) products and trade secrets can be used—Coca-Cola being the most famous generally and hybrids perhaps the most notable use of trade secrets in agriculture. For some producers, geographical indications defined as being linked to a region and a method of production provide a marketing tool that allows them to capitalize on their uniqueness—for example, Roquefort cheese and Parma ham. Such designations normally come out of a well-established agricultural and/or artisanal activity that has national recognition and produces items sought after by consumers. David Downes and others in a study of these issues with five case studies of niche products (kava, Rooibos tea, quinoa, Basmati rice, and neem) concluded that "(b)oth geographical indications and trademarks show the greatest potential [to benefit local producers] where traditional small-scale production is still present, on the supply side, and where end-use products are marketed directly to consumers. In other words, they are less likely to be appropriate when the product is a commodity traded primarily in bulk" (Downes and others 1999).

How far the use of geographical indications (GIs) will affect agricultural producers is unclear because the economic costs and benefits of any extension of stronger protection of GIs into food are not clear. GIs are likely to be of use to traditional communities producing products that could have a niche market domestically and abroad. They must first be protected locally, however (Art. 22 [Protection of Geographical Indications] of TRIPS). There is considerable disagreement among developing countries about the economic benefits of extending stronger protection to geographical indications for foodstuffs, and this is under discussion at the WTO TRIPS Council. Some countries, such as India, favor this, believing they will gain from having protection for a range of products such as Basmati rice. Others, such as Argentina, with a large segment of the population tracing their roots back to Europe and with tastes for European-type foodstuffs, fear that production of a local version of many products will become much more difficult if they are prevented from using terms associated with the foodstuff that are likely to be reserved for products such as cheeses from Europe.

Notwithstanding the latter concern, there remain problems of misappropriation of traditional knowledge of food crops, and the lack of a system for ensuring benefit sharing with traditional and indigenous communities, despite the CBD (see Correa 2001). Other kinds of instruments besides IPRs may be needed to protect these communities' knowledge as well as excluding plants and animals from patentability as allowed in TRIPS. Moreover, if indigenous crops such as quinoa, nuna, or yellow beans are patented in developed countries, in what is now called biopiracy, this may foreclose export markets there—or if other crops have look-alikes produced that are trademarked and widely marketed, this may also undermine the potential markets for developing-country crops.

### *The United Nations Convention on Biological Diversity*

The CBD is a framework agreement that leaves parties free to implement it through their own legislation. Its three objectives are the conservation of biological diversity, the sustainable use of its components, and the fair and equitable sharing of the benefits arising out of the utilization of genetic resources.[4]

The CBD recognizes, in Article 8(j), the need for *in situ* conservation of biodiversity and protection of indigenous knowledge. Article 8(j) requires states, subject to their national legislation, to preserve the knowledge, innovations, and practices of indigenous and local communities insofar as that knowledge, innovation, and practice serve the goals of conservation and sustainable use of biodiversity. In agriculture, this comes about through its use and development in farming communities. Thus the impact of changes brought about by IPRs-protected innovation in agriculture on those communities becomes an issue. The CBD also requires states to diffuse that knowledge, innovation, and practice with the cooperation of their holders, and encourages the sharing of any benefits that arise from such diffusion.

The CBD requires the equitable sharing of benefits arising from the commercial use of communities' biological resources and local knowledge (Art. 15.7). It also requires that access to generic resources be subject to "prior informed consent of the Contracting Party providing such resources, unless otherwise determined by that party" (Art. 15.5). At the sixth meeting of the Conference of the Parties (COP) in April 2002, parties agreed to a set of voluntary guidelines on access and benefit sharing (ABS) that aim to facilitate access to genetic resources on "mutually agreed terms" and on the basis of the country of origin's "prior informed consent" by providing guidance to parties in the development of ABS regimes, while promoting capacity building, technology transfer, and the provision of financial resources.[5]

Moreover, a section on the role of IPRs in implementing ABS arrangements, contained in the decision, invites parties to encourage the inclusion of disclosure requirements in IPRs applications and requests the CBD Executive Secretary and WIPO to provide further information on this issue.

In the CBD, which the U.S. has signed but not ratified, parties agree to undertake to provide and/or facilitate access to and transfer of technologies to other parties under fair and most favorable terms (Articles 16.1 and 16.2). Such technologies include biotechnology and others "that are relevant to the conservation and sustainable use of biological diversity or make use of genetic resources and do not cause significant damage to the environment" (Art. 16.1). Access to such technologies must be "on terms which recognize and are consistent with the adequate and effective protection of intellectual property rights" (16.2). This language mirrors that in the TRIPS Agreement.

The CBD also aims to enable these developing countries where genetic resources originate to have access to the technology that makes use of those resources on mutually agreed terms, including technology protected by patents and other IPRs (Art. 16.3). The parties to the treaty also are required to cooperate to ensure that patents and other IPRs "are supportive of and do not run counter to" the CBD's objectives (Art. 16.5). This reflects disagreement about whether or not IPRs support the CBD's objectives and implicitly accepts that conflicts may well arise between IPRs and the CBD. A study for the European Commission argued that legally TRIPS and the CBD are not in conflict but that conflicts may arise when the agreements are implemented, depending on how that is done (CEAS Consultants in association with Geoff Tansey and Queen Mary Intellectual Property Research Institute 2000). However, this congruence is not universally accepted.

### *The International Treaty on Plant Genetic Resources for Food and Agriculture*

Only in decisions of the COP to the CBD did members recognize the special needs of agriculture. The CBD developed from an approach that equated riches to be found in compounds in plants with minerals in the ground. Some developing countries felt that biodiversity-rich developing countries had undervalued wild biodiversity that was of use to developed countries and industries, which had been making use of them in patented products—such as pharmaceuticals—generating enormous returns. This winner-take-all, mining mentality toward the exploitation of wild biodiversity pays little attention to the differing nature of agricultural genetic resources that have been developed, exchanged, and bred around the globe for millennia. Indeed, some "wild" biodiversity-rich countries such as Brazil are agriculturally biodiversity-poor, depending for most of their agricultural production on nonindigenous crops such as soybeans.

The COP supported the renegotiation of the existing International Undertaking on Plant Genetic Resources for Food and Agriculture (IU). Agreed on in 1983 at the UN Food and Agriculture Organization (FAO), the IU was premised on the concept of germplasm as a common heritage of humankind, and needed to be restructured to be in harmony with the CBD. The IU recognized that today's crops had been developed by the activities of farmers over millennia. Renegotiating the IU began in 1994 and concluded in November 2001, when an International Treaty (ITPGRFA) was agreed to at the FAO conference in Rome.

The new treaty creates a mechanism that avoids the high transaction costs involved in bilateral exchanges of breeding material for food crops. It aims to ensure future food security by facilitating exchange of these materials through a multilateral system, which will use material transfer agreements. Such exchange is a necessity for future plant-breeding work. A rather limited range of 35 crops and 29 grasses and forages are included, as well as the *ex situ* collections of those crops held by the International Agricultural Research Centres belonging to the CGIAR. The treaty does not cover animals, although many breeds are threatened with extinction.

The treaty includes provisions on IPRs in Articles 12 and 13, which recognize that any germplasm taken out of the general pool available for further breeding, by having patents taken out on it, would create a loss to society as a whole—which should be compensated by some payment into a fund to promote the use of genetic resources for food and agriculture. Considerable work remains to be done to determine exactly how these and other articles of the treaty will be implemented. This also applies to farmers' rights, which the treaty recognizes in Article 9 but leaves to parties to realize as they wish. Governments should include at least three measures in their attempts to promote farmers' rights, according to Article 9.2:

- Protection of traditional knowledge relevant to plant genetic resources for food and agriculture.
- The right to equitably participate in sharing benefits arising from the utilization of plant genetic resources for food and agriculture.
- The right to participate in making decisions, at the national level, on matters related to the conservation and sustainable use of plant genetic resources for food and agriculture.

The negotiations associated with both the CBD and the ITPGRFA have had a wider range of participation from civil society in their deliberation, both domestically and internationally, than has been the case with the WTO TRIPS Agreement, or the other IP-related bodies of WIPO and UPOV. In keeping with the farmers' rights provisions of the ITPGRFA, wider consultation with farmers is also needed in framing IPRs in agriculture.

### *The World Intellectual Property Organization*

WIPO is the specialized UN agency whose mandate is "to promote the protection of intellectual property throughout the world through cooperation among States and, where appropriate, in collaboration with any other international organization."[6] Developments on patents and other IPRs at WIPO could provide the basis for additional issues to be included in the TRIPS Agreement. An Intergovernmental Committee on Intellectual Property and Genetic Resources, Traditional Knowledge and Folklore (IGC) was set up in 2001 to consider difficult issues such as IPRs relating to access to genetic resources and benefit sharing, as well as the protection of traditional knowledge and expressions of folklore. Following two meetings of the committee in 2001, the WIPO secretariat is preparing model IPR clauses for contractual agreements on ABS—although these will need to take into account both the CBD code and the ITPGRFA. The secretariat is also working on documenting public domain traditional knowledge to ensure that patent examiners can use such information to prevent misappropriation of this knowledge. This happened on a number of well-publicized occasions and gave rise to concern in developing countries about biopiracy—the unauthorized commercial exploitation of the knowledge and resources of traditional and indigenous communities in developing countries.[7]

Although the IGC is most directly concerned with genetic resources and traditional farming communities, other deliberations in WIPO could affect IPR use and remove the apparent flexibilities negotiated into TRIPS, for example, through moves to harmonize requirements in national patent regimes. Harmonization would make the patent system of countries more like one another in terms of administrative procedures and rules, enforcement standards, and substantive law.

A final area in which WIPO may affect the nature of IPRs in developing countries is through the technical assistance provided to countries to help them frame their laws and develop expertise in these areas. There have been concerns raised by a number of NGOs that this assistance is too narrowly focused and has not supported countries enough in using the flexibilities contained in TRIPS (MSF and others 2002).

### *A Confusion of Fora*

Different government ministries and interests are involved in negotiating at these many different fora and there is considerable difficulty in achieving coherence among them—or at least avoiding outright conflicts or contradiction. This was highlighted in an aptly titled report, "Why Governments Can't Make Policy—The Case of Plant Genetic Resources in the International Arena" (Petit and others 2001). The report reviewed decisionmaking in Brazil, France, Germany, India, Kenya, the Philippines, Sweden, and the U.S. and found policy coordination problems in all of these countries. According to the report, "(t)he combination of a complex international negotiation process and a complex set of issues with tremendous long term social, economic and political impact is the perfect setting for a breakdown of international consensus on the issues of genetic resources." The multiplicity of fora also poses a challenge in many countries to developing greater coherence among different ministries in formulating their polices and in the negotiations.

## The Development Dimension and TRIPS

A central concern about the current rules concerning IPRs is whether the one-size-fits-all approach of TRIPS rules, despite the apparent flexibilities, is adequate to deal with the diverse needs of communities worldwide. In 2001, speaking to the first meeting of the IGC, the U.S. delegate questioned whether "a comprehensive, uniform set of rules at the international level to govern the use of genetic resources, traditional knowledge and folklore" was either possible or desirable. Since many traditional knowledge farming communities are responsible for the development of agrobiodiversity, it is perhaps worth asking the same question about TRIPS when it comes to its impact on agriculture.

The fourth WTO Ministerial meeting in Doha in 2001 put a great deal of emphasis on there being a development dimension to the future work of the WTO. It made a number of specific comments relevant to the future work on TRIPS including the following:

In the Declaration on Implementation:

> 11.2. . . . developed-country Members shall submit prior to the end of 2002 detailed reports on the functioning in practice of the incentives provided to their enterprises for the transfer of technology in pursuance of their commitments under Article 66.2.

In the Ministerial Declaration:

> 12. . . . issues related to the extension of the protection of geographical indications provided for in Article 23 to products other than wines and spirits will be addressed in the Council for TRIPS pursuant to paragraph 12 of this Declaration. . . .
>
> 19. We instruct the Council for TRIPS, in pursuing its work program including under the review of Article 27.3(b), the review of the implementation of the TRIPS Agreement under Article 71.1 and the work foreseen pursuant to paragraph 12 of this Declaration, to examine, inter alia, the relationship between the TRIPS Agreement and the Convention on Biological Diversity, the protection of traditional knowledge and folklore, and other relevant new developments raised by Members pursuant to Article 71.1. In undertaking this work, the TRIPS Council shall be guided by the objectives and principles set out in Articles 7 and 8 of the TRIPS Agreement and shall take fully into account the development dimension.

There is a concern about how extension of the coverage of patents for inventions in all fields of technology, whether products or processes, will have an impact on agricultural R&D. While some of the concerns (for example, those over issuing overbroad patents) can be addressed within the terms of TRIPS through strict definitional and examination criteria, others, such as those over the length of protection, cannot. While Article 27.2 could be interpreted to exclude certain inventions from patentability, these inventions must be prevented from commercial exploitation. This might address the concerns of those who do not approve of patenting life-forms on a moral, ethical, religious, or customary-law basis. However, it would not address the concerns of those who would prohibit basic processes from being patented, but allow them to be used for commercial purposes—although the meaning of commercial exploitation is not given in TRIPS.

Article 27.3(b) provides the greatest scope for revisiting the provisions, as a review was mandated in 1999 and highlighted in the Doha Ministerial Declaration. However, this review has been deadlocked and would require significant movement among the members to achieve a consensus. If, however, any clarifications or interpretations are made acknowledging the special importance of food security and need for differentiation in that area—linked as it is to nutrition, which is specifically mentioned in Article 8 on Principles—this might be the place to make such clarifications. Moreover, since food security is a crucial issue for development, and the Doha Ministerial Declaration clearly required members to "take fully into account the development dimension" in their deliberations, there may be opportunity to do so in future. The thrust of many of the concerns about the impact of IPRs on food security, and the application of biotechnology, is that they will impede the developmental needs of the poorest people in many countries.

Given the many questions and uncertainties surrounding IPRs' impact on agriculture and different types of farmers, much more attention must be paid to these issues and a wider range of people must be involved in addressing the rules to different needs. As the United Kingdom's IPRs commission concludes, "the interests of developing countries are best served by tailoring their intellectual property regimes to their particular economic and social circumstances" (Commission on Intellectual Property Rights 2002, p. 155). In other words, one size does not fit all, especially in agriculture (see box 13.1).

**BOX 13.1 The U.K. Commission on Intellectual Property Rights' Recommendations on Agriculture and Genetic Resources**

The U.K. government set up an independent IPRs commission in May 2001 to see how IPR regimes could best be designed to benefit developing countries. Its six members came from Argentina, India, the United States, and the United Kingdom and their wide-ranging and challenging report was published in September 2002. The key recommendations for agriculture and genetic resources are summarized here.

- Developing countries should generally not provide patent protection for plants and animals, as is allowed under Article 27.3(b) of TRIPS, because of the restrictions patents may place on the use of seed by farmers and researchers. Rather they should consider different forms of *sui generis* systems for plant varieties.
- Those developing countries with limited technological capacity should restrict the application of patenting in agricultural biotechnology consistent with TRIPS, and they should adopt a restrictive definition of the term "microorganism."
- Countries that have, or wish to develop, biotechnology-related industries may wish to provide certain types of patent protection in this area. If they do so, specific exceptions to the exclusive rights, for plant breeding and research, should be established. The extent to which patent rights extend to the progeny or multiplied product of the patented invention should also be examined and a clear exception should be provided for farmers to reuse seeds.
- The continuing review of Article 27.3(b) of TRIPS should also preserve the right of countries not to grant patents for plants and animals, including genes and genetically modified plants and animals, as well as to develop *sui generis* regimes for the protection of plant varieties that suit their agricultural systems. Such regimes should permit access to the protected varieties for further research and breeding, and provide at least for the right of farmers to save and plant-back seed, including the possibility of informal sale and exchange.
- Because of the growing concentration in the seed industry, public sector research on agriculture and its international component should be strengthened and better funded. The objective should be to ensure that research is oriented to the needs of poor farmers; that public sector varieties are available to provide competition for private sector varieties; and that the world's plant genetic resource heritage is maintained. In addition, this is an area in which nations should consider the use of competition law to respond to the high level of concentration in the private sector.
- Developed and developing countries should accelerate the process of ratification of the FAO International Treaty on Plant Genetic Resources for Food and Agriculture and should, in particular, implement the treaty's provisions relating to the following:
  - Not granting IPR protection of any material transferred in the framework of the multilateral system, in the form received.
  - Implementation of farmers' rights at the national level, including the protection of traditional knowledge relevant to plant genetic resources for food and agriculture; the right to equitably participate in sharing benefits arising from the utilization of plant genetic resources for food and agriculture; and the right to participate in making decisions, at the national level, on matters related to the conservation and sustainable use of plant genetic resources for food and agriculture.

## Notes

1. For a more detailed discussion of the wide-ranging policy issues involved in IPRs, see the bibliography on IPRs and Sustainable Development as well as the draft policy issues paper on the UNCTAD–ICTSD Web site, listed in the online resources.

2. See the ETC Web site, http://etcgroup.org for details.

3. See http://www.grain.org/publications/trips-countrypos- en.cfm.

4. The CBD uses the following definitions: "Biological resources" includes genetic resources, organisms or parts thereof, populations, or any other biotic component of ecosystems with actual or potential use or value for humanity. "Genetic resources" means genetic material of actual or potential value.

5. Reported in *Bridges, Weekly Trade News Digest,* 6(15), April 23, 2002. Available on the Internet at ictsd.org.

6. Article 3, Convention Establishing WIPO. July 14, 1967.

7. See the Web site of the Action Group for Erosion, Technology and Concentration (ETC), formerly RAFI, for NGO coverage of biopiracy cases, at etcgroup.org.

## Select Bibliography


Alston, J. M., P. G. Pardey, and V. H. Smith. 1998. "Financing Agricultural R&D in Rich Countries: What's Happening and Why." *Australian Journal of Agricultural and Resource Economics* 42(1): 51–82.

Barton, J. H. 1998. "The Impact of Patent Law on Plant Biotechnology Research." *Intellectual Property Rights III—Global Genetic Resources: Access and Property Rights.* Crop Science Society of America, Madison, Wisconsin.

CEAS Consultants in association with Geoff Tansey and Queen Mary Intellectual Property Research Institute. 2000. "Study on the Relationship between the Agreement on Trade-Related Aspects of Intellectual Property Rights and Biodiversity Related Issues." Prepared for the Directorate-General for Trade of the European Commission. europa.eu.int/comm/trade/csc/dcs_trips.htm.

Commission on Intellectual Property Rights. 2002. "Integrating Intellectual Property Rights and Development Policy." Report of the UK Commission on Intellectual Property Rights, London. www.iprcommission.org.

Correa, C. M. 2000. "Access to Plant Genetic Resources and Intellectual Property Rights." Originally published by FAO-CGRFA in 1998. www.fao.org/ag/cgrfa and the author's book, *Intellectual Property Rights, the WTO and Developing Countries—The TRIPS Agreement and Policy Options.* London and Penang: Zed Books and Third World Network.

———. 2001. "Traditional Knowledge and Intellectual Property—Issues and Options Surrounding the Protection of Traditional Knowledge." Quaker UN Office, Geneva, November. geneva.quno.info/main/publication.php?pid=113 and GRAIN at www.grain.org/publications/trips-countrypos-en.cfm.

Dhar, B. 2002. "*Sui Generis* Systems for Plant Variety Protection: Options under TRIPS." Quaker UN Office, Geneva, April. geneva.quno.info/main/publication. php?pid=113.

Downes, D. R., and S. A. Laird, with contributions by Graham Dutfield and Wynberg. 1999. "Innovative Mechanisms for Sharing Benefits of Biodiversity and Related Knowledge—Case Studies on Geographical Indications and Trademarks." Paper prepared for the UNCTAD Biotrade Initiative, Geneva.

Drahos, P. 1995. "Global Property Rights in Information: The Story of TRIPS at the GATT." *Prometheus* 13: 6–19.

Drahos, P., with J. Braithwaite. 2002. *Information Feudalism—Who Owns the Knowledge Economy.* London: Earthscan.

Helfgott, S. 1993. "Patent Filing Costs Around the World." *Journal of the Patent and Trademark Office* 75(7): 567–80.

IPGRI (International Plant Genetic Resources Institute). 1999. "Key Questions for Decision-Makers—Protection of Plant Varieties under the WTO Agreement on Trade-Related Aspects of Intellectual Property Rights." IPGRI, Rome. ipgri.cgiar.org/system/page.asp?frame=publications/indexpub.htm

Lesser, W. 1997. "The Role of Intellectual Property Rights in Biotechnology Transfer under the Convention on Biological Diversity." ISAAA Briefs 3, Cornell University, Ithaca. isaaa.org.

Maskus, K. E. 2000. *Intellectual Property Rights in the Global Economy.* Washington, D.C.: Institute for International Economics.

Médecins sans Frontières, Consumer Project on Technology, Oxfam, and Health Action International. 2002. "Conference Report Implementation of the Doha Declaration on the TRIPS Agreement and Public Health: Technical Assistance—How To Get It Right." Conference Report on the March 28, 2002 meeting, Geneva.

Petit, M., C. Fowler, W. Collins, C. Correa, and C. G. Thornstrom. 2001. "Why Governments Can't Make Policy—The Case of Plant Genetic Resources in the International Arena." International Potato Centre (CIP) October, Lima.

Rangnekar, D. 2002. "Access to Genetic Resources, Gene-Based Inventions and Agriculture." Study Paper 3a, Commission on Intellectual Property Rights. iprcommission.org/papers/pdfs/study_papers/sp3a_rangnekar_study.pdf.

Tansey, G. 1999. *Trade, Intellectual Property, Food and Biodiversity: Key Issues and Options for the 1999 Review of Article 27.3(b) of the TRIPS Agreement.* Quaker Peace and Service, London. geneva.quno.info/ main/publication.php?pid=113.

———. 2002. *Food Security, Biotechnology and IPRs—Unpacking Some Issues around TRIPS.* Quaker UN Office, Geneva. geneva.quno.info/main/publication. php?pid=113.

Tansey, G., and T. Worsley. 1995. *The Food System—A Guide.* London: Earthscan.

Tilahun, S., and S. Edwards, eds. 1996. *The Movement for Collective Intellectual Rights.* Addis Ababa and London: Institute for Sustainable Development and The Gaia Foundation.

Trebilcock, M. J., and R. Howse. 1995. "Trade-Related Intellectual Property (TRIPS)." In *The Regulation of International Trade.* London: Routledge.

UN (United Nations). 1993. "Intellectual Property Rights and Foreign Direct Investment." Transnational Corporations and Management Division, Economic and Social Development Department. un.org/esa/

14

# RULES AND OPTIONS FOR SPECIAL AND DIFFERENTIAL TREATMENT

*Constantine Michalopoulos*

## Introduction

The Uruguay Round Agreement on Agriculture (URAA) has been hailed as a milestone because it started the process of subjecting agricultural trade to the same rules as trade in other products. Many have noted, however, that while the form of protection changed, little progress was made in actually reducing the level of protection used by some developed countries—and their export subsidies, while reduced, still remained at levels that undermined developing-country production and exports.[1] At the same time, the URAA's focus was on reform in developed countries' agriculture, not on how to increase agricultural production and trade in developing countries.

More broadly, the 1994 Uruguay Round (UR) agreements were supposed to usher in an international trade architecture in which all countries, developed and developing alike, would abide by the same rules—the notion that "one size fits all." This perception of the agreements has considerable merit, as all countries were expected to have participated in previous multilateral agreements under the General Agreement on Tariffs and Trade (GATT) such as that on Subsidies and Countervailing Measures—and in new agreements, such as the General Agreement on Trade in Services (GATS) resulting from the Uruguay Round and administered by the newly created World Trade Organization (WTO). But at the same time, all the agreements, including the URAA, contained a large number of provisions calling for special and more favorable treatment (commonly called special and differential treatment, or S&D) for developing countries—clearly not a "one size fits all" situation (WTO 2000c).

Soon after the URAA was signed, it came under considerable attack from developing-country critics who felt that it maintained an imbalance in trading rules which not only did not favor developing countries, but was actually tilted against them. They argued that the S&D provisions were not being implemented, or were not well conceived, or even that the URAA had continued, albeit on a reduced scale, the special and more favorable treatment of developed countries in the international trading system. It is fair to say that the URAA was always considered an interim agreement—a stepping stone—not a final one. It contained provisions for the initiation of new agricultural trade negotiations, which were duly started in 2000. Now, in the aftermath of the 2001 Doha Ministerial Conference which is supposed to result in a "Development Round," it is time to look carefully at the S&D

provisions of the URAA to ensure that indeed they further the process of development. The Doha Ministerial Declaration decided that the WTO Committee on Trade and Development (CTD) should review the implementation of all Uruguay Round S&D provisions and make recommendations to the WTO General Council by July 31, 2002 for changes that would make the provisions contribute more effectively to the achievement of development objectives. This and a subsequent deadline were missed, and in early 2003, the S&D discussions in the CTD were deadlocked, having achieved little beyond an agreement that future S&D implementation should be subject to regular review. At the same time, negotiations on agriculture continued, yielding in early 2003 a "Draft Modalities Text" containing many S&D provisions (WTO 2003).

## The Plan of This Chapter

This chapter reviews S&D provisions in the URAA, along with other aspects of the UR agreements that have a bearing on agriculture, with the aim of making recommendations that are meaningful and make developmental sense. It does not review all aspects of the agreement that have a bearing on developing countries, even though some issues—for example, market access—are inevitably closely related to S&D. One of the major problems addressed is that developing countries are not homogeneous and have widely differing interests in agriculture. Accommodating these varying interests when designing rules for S&D is a major challenge.

The chapter is structured in four parts, including this introduction. Part two discusses the conceptual basis of S&D, with special attention to the provisions concerning agriculture. The third part assesses implementation of S&D in the aftermath of the Uruguay Round and reviews new proposals for S&D presented by developing countries in the agriculture negotiations, in the run-up to the Doha meeting, and in the most recent negotiations on agriculture. The final part offers some preliminary conclusions on approaches that may be useful in structuring S&D provisions in the agriculture negotiations. An appendix lists all the S&D provisions in the UR agreements related to agriculture.

## Provisions Regarding Special and Differential Treatment

The provisions introduced into the WTO agreements to provide S&D fall into two broad categories:[2] positive actions by developed-country members or international institutions, and exceptions to the overall rules contained in the agreements—applicable to developing countries, with additional exceptions for least-developed countries (LDCs) in some cases.

Concerning agriculture, these provisions are included in three WTO texts: the URAA; the "Decision on Measures Concerning the Possible Negative Effects of the Reform Programme on Least-Developed and Net Food-Importing Developing Countries" (hereafter, referred to as the Decision); and the Agreement on the Application of Sanitary and Phytosanitary Measures (the SPS Agreement).

The fundamental principle underlying these provisions should be that developing countries are subject to the same rules and disciplines as all other countries, with certain well-defined exceptions designed to encourage development while having the least possible distorting effects on trade. The main topic of this chapter is how this overall principle can be made operational in agriculture.

### *Positive Steps to Be Taken by Developed Countries*

Developed countries have agreed to take three kinds of steps to support developing countries' participation in international trade:

a. Provide preferential access to developed-country markets.
b. Provide technical and other assistance to permit developing countries to meet their WTO obligations and otherwise enhance the benefits they derive from international trade.
c. Implement the overall agreements in ways that are beneficial or least damaging to the interests of developing and least-developed countries.

**Preferential Market Access** Developed countries have provided tariff preferences to exports from developing countries under the Generalized System of Preferences (GSP) schemes and, within that context, for special treatment of the LDCs. The GSP schemes were given a GATT waiver in 1971 and made a permanent feature of GATT provisions through the 1979 Enabling Clause. By and large, the

GSP programs of developed countries have focused on manufactures and have relatively limited coverage of agricultural products. However, substantial preferences on agricultural products have been included in autonomous trade preference schemes extended to smaller groups of developing countries. Examples include those provided by the European Union (EU) to the developing countries in Africa, the Caribbean, and the Pacific (ACP) on such products as beef, rum, sugar, and bananas (for which a WTO waiver was extended through 2007); as well as those provided by the United States (U.S.) to countries in the Caribbean and Central America. A recent EU decision will provide tariff- and quota-free access to all LDC products except armaments under a new agreement entitled "Everything But Arms" (EBA).

**Technical and Other Assistance** The WTO agreements contain numerous references to the desirability of developed-country members and to international institutions providing technical assistance to developing and least-developed countries. The main objective of such assistance is to strengthen the institutional capacity of developing countries and LDCs to enable them to meet the WTO obligations. Interestingly, there are no references to technical assistance in the URAA as such. Both the Decision and the SPS Agreement call for technical assistance to improve agricultural productivity and to meet the SPS standards. In addition, Article 10.4 of the URAA and the Decision make recommendations on food aid, and the latter addresses the possibility that developing countries may face financing difficulties as a consequence of the implementation of the URAA (because reduced export subsidies of developed countries might lead to higher prices and therefore to increased financing requirements for food imports).

### *Implementation of WTO Provisions in a Manner Favorable to Developing-Country Members*

In their preambles, as well as in the substantive provisions, the WTO agreements contain many references committing developed-country members to implement the agreements in ways that take into account the interests of developing and least-developed countries. These references are usually of a general nature and are expressed in broad "best efforts" terminology.[3] For example, the URAA's Preamble says that "in implementing their commitments on market access, developed-country members would take fully into account the particular needs and conditions of developing-country members by providing for a greater improvement of opportunities and terms of access for agricultural products of particular interest to these members" (see the chapter annex). There is a similar statement in Article 10.1 of the SPS Agreement.

### *Differential Commitments and Obligations by Developing Countries*

There are two fundamental ways in which developing and least-developed countries have accepted differential obligations under the WTO agreements. First, they enjoy freedom to undertake policies that limit access to their markets or that provide support to domestic producers or exporters in ways not allowed to other members—all of which can be viewed as exemptions from WTO disciplines. And second, they are provided with more time in meeting obligations or commitments under the agreements. In some cases, more favorable treatment involves a combination of the two.

**Exemptions from Disciplines** The most general and fundamental way in which developing countries continue to be exempted from WTO disciplines regarding market access policies is the recognition of the principle of nonreciprocity in trade negotiations with developed countries to reduce or remove tariffs and other barriers to trade. This principle is recognized in GATT (1994) Article XXXVI and in the Enabling Clause. Consistent with these provisions, in the Uruguay Round in their schedules of commitments developing countries were able to bind tariffs at levels much higher than applied rates—although in agriculture, unlike industry, they had to bind all tariffs.

The URAA also contains measures that exempt developing countries and, to an even greater extent, LDCs, from disciplines and obligations that apply generally. These measures may also provide for longer timetables or more modest reductions in government support and subsidies than those that apply to developed-country members. For example, investment subsidies or input subsidies to low-income producers are exempted from the calculation of aggregate measurement of support (AMS); reductions in export subsidies are targeted both to be smaller and to occur over a longer period of time; and there are specific provisions regarding the operation of government stockholding programs aimed at enhancing food security as well as less demanding minimum access provisions regarding primary agricultural products that are the predominant staple in the traditional diet of a developing-country (see the chapter annex).

A second way in which developing countries have been granted exemptions from general disciplines on the degree of protection is through the provisions of GATT Article XVIII, which give developing countries the freedoms to grant the tariff protection required for the establishment of a particular industry and to apply quantitative restrictions for balance-of-payments purposes. These have been little-used for agricultural products.

**Time Extensions** The second fundamental way in which special and differential treatment is provided in the WTO is through the extension of the time-frame over which certain obligations under the agreements are to be implemented by developing countries and LDCs. Flexibility in transition times is provided in practically all WTO agreements: the URAA, for example, permits developing countries to continue subsidizing exports for a period of time and in a variety of ways prohibited for other members, with flexibility taking the form of a longer implementation period.

The justification for the extension of additional time to implement agreed measures relates to weaknesses in the institutional capacity of developing countries and LDCs. It was assumed that, given additional time (as well as technical assistance, often expected to be provided), developing and least-developed countries would be able to strengthen their institutions in ways that would enable them to implement the agreements. In the case of subsidies, the presumption was that additional time would permit countries to develop the institutions and policies to implement alternative means of support (for agriculture or for exports in general) that were acceptable under the agreement. The main issues that arise in the implementation of this aspect of special and differential treatment have to do with the realism of the time extensions, relative to the actual time and cost required to build the institutional capacity needed.

### *Special Measures Concerning Least-Developed Countries*

The Enabling Clause of 1979 provided the basis for special treatment of LDCs "in the context of any general or specific measures in favor of developing countries." The UR agreements contain 17 provisions applicable specifically to LDC members, in addition to those applicable to all developing members. The URAA calls explicitly for exempting LDCs from all AMS and subsidy reduction commitments (see the chapter annex). A number of separate initiatives have also been adopted with regard to LDC members. Thus the 1994 WTO "Decision on Measures in Favour of Least Developed Countries" (WTO 1994) requires LDC members to undertake commitments and concessions only to the extent consistent with their individual development, financial, and trade needs, or administrative and institutional capabilities.

## Conceptual Issues Regarding Special and Differential Treatment in Agriculture

There are several conceptual problems related to S&D provisions that characterize all UR agreements, which are manifested in agriculture as well.

The first problem is that developed-country S&D commitments in the WTO agreements are either too broad and general in nature—such as those included in the many preambular statements, including those in the URAA and in SPS—to be of any practical significance, or are of the best-efforts variety, such as the provision of technical assistance, which means that they are not legally enforceable (Kessie 2000) and, therefore, that developed countries cannot be held accountable for not implementing them.

Underlying this problem is a second issue, which, unless addressed, is likely to undermine any future efforts to provide developing countries with meaningful differential treatment by developed countries. This is the failure of all agreements to recognize that the capacities of individual developing countries to export and compete in international markets, including for agricultural exports, are vastly different—as are their needs for support and assistance. Despite this difference, most WTO rules on the treatment of developing countries by developed countries—except those rules concerning the LDCs—are identical.[4] Singapore and the Republic of Korea are to be treated the same way as Ghana and Saint Lucia, Argentina and Brazil the same as the Maldives and Kenya, and so on.

On agricultural trade issues, at least four groups of developing countries can be identified, and this is often reflected in the support provided for different proposals in the agriculture negotiations. First, there is the group of major agricultural-commodity exporters, members of the Cairns Group. Second, there is a large group of the net food-importing developing countries (NFIDCs) along with others such as India, which have a significant agricultural sector and which produce but also import food, and export various agricultural products. A third group are countries with small nondiversified agricultural sectors that—either because of climatic conditions or land constraints (for example, the small island economies)—face significant difficulties in competing in agricultural trade. A fourth small group consists of generally higher-income developing countries that, like some developed countries, attach high priority to the many functions that agriculture plays in their society, irrespective of its efficiency or productivity.

Food security is one area in which some effort was made to apply the UR provisions in a somewhat differentiated fashion regarding the beneficiaries: there was recognition, for example, of the different needs of the NFIDCs. But the category itself does not adequately capture the groups of countries facing the largest food insecurity situations (Diaz-Bonilla and others 2000). In the context of export restraints, there was also recognition of the fact that some developing countries are major agricultural exporters. Most of the provisions, however, consider developing countries (except the LDCs) as a single group, which clearly they are not.

There is very little economic reason to suggest that some of the more developed of the developing countries cannot compete in the products in which they have comparative advantage with developed countries. And there is very little political support for extending S&D to them. Indeed, protectionist interests in developed countries frequently succeed in discriminating against these developing countries on products in which they enjoy comparative advantage. If S&D provisions are not differentiated to exclude developing countries that do not need them, there is very little likelihood that meaningful S&D commitments will be made by developed countries. They will continue to resort to general, best-efforts kinds of commitments whose implementation is hard to evaluate.

Developing countries have been treated differently by developed countries in the latter's unilateral implementation of their various GSP schemes. But leaving to developed countries the decisions on definition of which countries are to get what preferences and how much, invites the nonuniform treatment of countries in similar circumstances and the introduction of extraneous political considerations into the determination of benefits.

The final conceptual problem in the framing of S&D provisions is that the commitments aimed at addressing developing countries' institutional constraints have been made without serious consideration of how these will be implemented. This was seen in the setting of the transition periods for implementing the various agreements. These periods were part of the bargaining process at the late stages of the UR negotiations and without much involvement of developing-country officials familiar with how long it would take to build institutional capacity where it was inadequate or totally lacking. In some cases, the time limits for the extensions have already passed, and there is little evidence that countries have made sufficient progress in institution-building to permit them to implement their obligations fully. On the contrary, evidence gathered from the needs assessments undertaken in the context of implementing the Integrated Framework for Trade Related Technical Assistance for the Least Developed Countries suggests that many institutional weaknesses remain in these countries and in others where even shorter timeframes for implementation had been envisaged. While not all developing countries have given these issues the priority they deserve, it is clear that the transition time provided was far too short to do any meaningful institution building.

A different aspect of the same problem is evident in the commitments made by developing countries to implement various new standards called for by the UR agreements, including the SPS Agreement. These commitments were made without detailed consideration of the cost of their implementation or whether building the institutional capacity needed to permit developing countries to discharge their responsibilities was a high development priority for them.

### *Issues in the Implementation of Special and Differential Provisions in Agriculture*

**Market Access** The main market access problem in agriculture is that the present most-favored nation (MFN) tariffs in some developed countries, as well as the continuation of export subsidies, creates formidable barriers to developing-country exports and undermines the competitiveness of developing countries in third markets. In developed-country markets for some agricultural products tariffs are lower than overall agricultural tariffs, as this results from earlier liberalization in tropical products. Tariffication for some agricultural products under the UR provisions was often "dirty," resulting in higher levels of protection than existed previously. The remaining protection on developing-country agriculture exports such as rice (Japan), tobacco and groundnuts (U.S.), or grape juice (EU) is staggeringly high (UNCTAD 1997; UNCTAD/WTO 1997).

There is little evidence that the general hortatory language of the URAA regarding liberalizing products of particular interest to developing countries resulted in greater cuts in protection on such products in developed-country markets. It is unlikely that this central problem can be addressed by more verbiage and nonbinding differential treatment commitments in the future.

As noted earlier, there is relatively limited provision of S&D in favor of developing countries in agricultural products under GSP-type schemes. At the same time, a number of preferential schemes—most notably by the EU toward the ACP but also by the U.S. in favor of Caribbean and Central American countries and through a separate scheme for African countries—are providing much deeper preferences (that is, reduced tariffs) for the beneficiary countries.

The fact that in agriculture, unlike in industry, tariffs are high for some key agricultural products has led some developing countries to argue that this offers a large opportunity for preferences, presumably under GSP schemes. At the same time, a number of developing countries have argued for improvements in the existing GSP schemes, such as reducing the variability of product coverage from country to country and from year to year, simplifying the rules of origin to make these schemes more accessible, and binding tariff preference margins. Proposals have also been made to compensate developing countries for the losses they sustain when tariff or access preferences are eroded by reductions in MFN tariffs. These proposals have to be evaluated in light of past experience with GSP schemes, the potential benefits that they would yield to developing-country beneficiaries, and in the context of other developments that will affect developing countries' trade in agriculture.

The long experience with GSP schemes suggests that, while preferences can be and have been helpful to some countries for some products and through some periods, preferential approaches suffer from economic drawbacks when used as a means of improving generalized developing-country access to developed-country markets. First of all, the bulk of the benefits tends to accrue to a few countries—frequently those that need them the least. Second, preferential approaches tend to promote an attitude of dependency on particular products and markets that is inimical to change in response to changing market conditions or to promote competitiveness. And third, when aimed at a special group of countries, for example the LDCs, these preferences tend to impose certain costs on other developing countries—in some cases low-income and possibly equally deserving of similar treatment.[5]

The political economy of trade preferences also militates against generalized and unconditional approaches because the preference-giving countries wish to preserve the freedom to choose the recipients, often using conditionality that includes noneconomic criteria. The preferences offered to the LDCs by the EU's EBA initiative, and possibly by others in the future, are an exception to this rule that can be explained in part by the fact that the LDCs account for such a small portion of total trade as to have a very small possible impact on the economies of developed countries.

In judging the usefulness of preferences in the context of the negotiations on agriculture, other developments affecting agricultural trade in the near term should be taken into account. Most important is the provision of preferential treatment by the EU to the 80-odd ACP countries through Economic Partnership Agreements that essentially will involve the establishment of regional trade arrangements (that provide preferences for all members) to be put in place after 2007 and the expiry of the WTO waiver. Similarly, the U.S., in addition to the preferential scheme regarding African countries, is negotiating the establishment of a free trade area that would include all the developing countries in the Americas. The EU will also have the EBA in place favoring the 49 LDCs, and other developed countries may follow with similar programs for these countries.

Thus, a few years from now, the landscape in agricultural trade for LDCs may include the deep and mostly unconditional preferences in most developed-country markets, while regional trade agreements providing deep preferential margins for many developing countries may be in place in the two major developed-country markets, the EU and the U.S. This situation would leave a number of countries in South Asia without additional preferences except for GSP, while some countries in the ACP and some in Latin America would not enjoy preferences in the U.S. and EU, respectively. Included in this group would be a number of major developing-country agricultural exporters, such as Argentina, Brazil, Uruguay, the Philippines, and Thailand, which arguably do not need preferences in order to export.

In this setting, a "strengthened" GSP for agriculture is really not likely to be especially "generalized." At best, it could provide less deep preferences, and hence fewer benefits, for a relatively small group of developing countries that should in any case exclude those that do not need the preferences to export. Some of the proposals to strengthen GSP schemes, such as simplifying rules of origin, while useful in the case of agroindustries, are far less relevant for agriculture than for manufactures. Other proposals, such as assistance programs for countries—especially small economies dependent on only a few crops, which could be hurt substantially as a consequence of the elimination of preferences—may be implemented more easily in the context of regional arrangements that cover various aspects of economic integration. This leaves, as possibilities to be pursued by developing countries in the agriculture negotiations, such issues as including more products in GSP schemes and possibly also "binding" existing preference margins by expressing them as a fixed percentage of *ad valorem* tariffs.[6] Given, however, that GSP schemes would really be of potential benefit only to a relatively few countries, the question needs to be asked as to how much "negotiating capital" should be expended in this direction.

An alternative approach that would make much more economic sense is to expand the beneficiaries of the "deep" preferences now being extended to the LDCs to cover a larger group of low-income, vulnerable, or "food-insecure" developing countries that exhibit very similar problems to those of the LDCs but which are not included in the current list (Tangerman 2001). The problem with this approach is that it runs against the political economy of granting preferences to a list of countries unconditionally—and that the larger the group of countries included, the more difficult it is to cope with the developed-country domestic interests, affected by the expanded commodity and volume coverage. Finally, such an expansion of the LDC list would have to be accompanied with clear graduation criteria to ensure that countries do not continue to receive preferences when they do not need them.

These considerations suggest that by far the best way of addressing the issue of market access to developed-country markets in the current agriculture negotiations is not through efforts to expand generalized S&D treatment, but rather through a general effort by developing countries to push for substantial reduction of developed-country protection on an MFN basis and for total elimination of export subsidies at the earliest possible date. A variety of approaches may be used for cutting developed-country tariff protection, for instance by adopting a formula approach that would result in more than proportional cuts in the tariff peaks that are present in some developed-country agriculture (see FAO 2002a). At the same time, relatively slow liberalization in developing countries would have an impact on other developing countries that are major exporters, as trade among developing countries in agricultural products is important, especially in Asia (Ruffer 2002).

**Sanitary and Phytosanitary Issues** The implementation of the new SPS Agreement has raised significant problems for developing countries. Some result from the lack of capacity to develop the institutional arrangements that permit them to meet their SPS-related WTO commitments. Even if the capacity exists, these commitments are costly to implement: standards, along with testing and certification, represent between 2 and 10 percent of overall product costs. Thus they impose a burden on developing countries even when the standards are used for legitimate reasons and the countries are able to meet them.

The greatest potential costs of the SPS Agreement, however, may lie in the market access issues they raise. The agreement may serve to legitimize developed-country actions that result in substantial problems for developing-country trade, even if the actions appear to be justified, for example, on health grounds. Article 10.1 of the SPS Agreement says that "[i]n the preparation and application of sanitary and physosanitary measures, Members shall take account of the special needs of developing-country Members and in particular of the least-developed country Members" (see the chapter annex). A recent paper found that a 1998 European Commission regulation that raised the standards for the minimum level for certain types of aflatoxin (a toxic substance found in foodstuffs and animal feed), to levels higher than those required by the Codex Alimentarius (the food standards code) is estimated to cost close to US$700 million in lost revenue to African groundnut exporters, many of them LDCs (Otsuki, Wilson, and Sewadeh 2000).

It is difficult to argue against developed-country actions that aim to protect consumer health. But when such actions result in significant costs to developing-country exports, it would seem fair that the developed countries be legally committed to take steps that will help the developing country meet the problem that the developed-country regulation has created. There are examples of such assistance in the past: the EU has provided assistance to Senegal in order to help exporters meet EU fisheries standards. Yet a recent review by the WTO Secretariat showed no information regarding the implementation of technical assistance provision (WTO 2002a). Perhaps more assistance has been provided in this area bilaterally but has not been notified.

The existing provisions in the SPS Agreement on these issues are inadequate and need to be strengthened. Article 9.2 of the SPS Agreement states that where "substantial investments" are needed for a developing country to meet the SPS "requirements of an importing Member, the latter shall consider providing such technical assistance as will permit the developing country Member to maintain and expand its market access opportunities for the product involved." Developed-country members should have the obligation to provide the developing country with both the financial and technical assistance needed to permit the improvement in product quality until the product meets the standard. Ideally the obligation should be legally bound under the WTO, but even a broader "commitment" that makes the link may be a useful step. More broadly, there should be increased coherence between trade commitments and assistance to meet those commitments, a more general point that requires additional coordination of actions by the international community.

**Technical and Other Assistance** As noted earlier, the URAA itself is silent on issues of assistance, except in the case of food aid. The references to assistance related to agriculture are included in the Decision and in the SPS Agreement (discussed above). Regarding the provision of technical and financial assistance to improve "agricultural productivity and infrastructure," the WTO Secretariat prepared a compilation of such assistance provided since 1995 as notified by members. It is unclear whether this compilation includes all the assistance provided, including that by the international financial institutions. While the WTO is not the main international body where coordination of assistance in general, and on agriculture in particular, can be achieved, it is important that information regarding assistance flows available to the WTO be as complete as possible, especially on trade-related issues.

The Decision also called for a new food aid convention which was negotiated in 1999 and which stipulates that, when allocating food aid, priority should be given to LDCs and low-income countries. Other NFIDCs can also be provided with food aid "when experiencing food emergencies or internationally recognized financial crises leading to food shortage emergencies or when food aid operations are targeted on vulnerable groups." Donor performance regarding both food aid levels and allocations to LDCs and NFIDCs under the Food Aid Convention (FAC) 1999 has been monitored closely by the WTO Committee on Agriculture. These reviews have shown that donors collectively supplied food aid in excess of the commitments they had made under the FAC, and that they followed the guidelines regarding its concessionality. At the same time there continues to be a problem in that food aid is most available when international prices are lowest and, hence, financing needs of developing countries are less.

The main focus of developing-country discussions on topics covered by the Decision has been on the question of whether the URAA has resulted in additional financing needs for the NFIDCs and LDCs on account of higher import prices for food. Perhaps because the URAA did not change agricultural trade that much, some of the fears of NFIDCs about the possible adverse effect of the agreement did not materialize. The Decision called for a study by the World Bank and the International Monetary Fund (IMF) of the implications of the URAA on food import prices for these countries and the provision of appropriate compensatory finance to deal with the problem. The two institutions found little evidence that the export subsidy reductions of the URAA had led to an increase in import expenditures of poor NFIDCs and concluded that there was no need to provide financing over and above what could be obtained through their regular facilities. Both the IMF and the World Bank have reiterated this position in subsequent reviews of the issue in the WTO.

Even so, it is legitimate to ask what the proper international response would be if developed-country export subsidies were to decline. The problem relates to the possible adverse short-term effects of eliminating trade-distorting measures on poor NFIDCs. These short-term effects are likely to be outweighed by the longer-term worldwide efficiency gains in agricultural markets, and are in fact likely to spread over time, as the distortions are destined for phaseout rather than elimination at once. It would also be very difficult to isolate the impact of the resulting price increases from other factors, including the developing countries' own policies. It is for the price effect reason that the IMF did not provide automatic financing from its Compensatory Financing Facility (CFF) for cereals, but drawings from the CFF were included in the overall IMF program to individual countries. But there is nothing—and there should be nothing—automatic about the assistance provided. Indeed, if a need can be shown to exist, the international response should not be limited to food aid but should extend to all kinds of general-purpose financing on appropriate terms. The latter would be preferable to food aid, which is frequently tied to procurement from a particular donor and is determined by food stock availability in the donor rather than the needs of the recipient.

The new FAC could help, in a small way, in dealing with some of the food security problems many face, but it is not a substitute for further liberalization of agricultural trade. It should rather be considered as a supporting element for such liberalization. Reduced protection in developed-country markets will improve market access prospects for both existing and potential exporters, while reduced export subsidies by developed countries will reduce international market distortions that impede the expansion of developing-country agricultural production. Where appropriate, reductions in developing countries' own protection of agriculture, as part of the broader reduction in agricultural protection, could stimulate efficiency through improved allocation of their own resources.

Notwithstanding this experience, several developing countries have proposed the establishment of a revolving fund facility whose objective would be to stabilize international food prices to developing countries. Following Doha, a new group was set up to consider proposals in this area; its recommendations were submitted to the WTO General Council in June 2002 (WTO 2002c). This is discussed along with other food security issues in chapter 9. The most recent draft modalities text developed in the context of the WTO negotiations on agriculture (WTO 2003) contains a number of useful suggestions to improve the effectiveness of food aid—for example, that it should be fully in grant form and untied.

**Flexibility in Rules and Disciplines** In some ways, flexibility has emerged as the most widespread instrument of special and differential treatment; but the fundamental question of implementation is whether the latitude permitted, in relation to WTO commitments, including tariff bindings or input subsidies, results in policies that are more suitable to development. A more narrow issue is that developing countries' rights to differential treatment in certain instances, including in the URAA, are conditioned on their notification of the existence of certain policies, namely subsidies as of a particular time. While a number of developing countries have availed themselves of these provisions and provided such notifications, there is a general impression that many countries have not fully notified measures that they have been implementing, and therefore, may at some point face challenges to these policies because of their failure to notify them.

In agriculture, there is a serious problem in developing rules that are appropriate to promoting the interests of developing countries because the URAA's overall focus is on improving the policy environment in developed countries, rooted in the legitimate concern that agriculture in some developed countries was protected and supported too much. The rules were, therefore, designed to provide fewer government supports in a more transparent and less trade-distorting way that, if implemented, would have a beneficial impact on developing countries.

In many developing countries, however, agriculture was being penalized, not supported, by government policy. This was certainly even more the case a decade ago, when the Uruguay Round was being negotiated and perhaps most so in the 1980s, the reference years under the URAA for the measurement of supports. Even where agriculture was supported, developing-country capacity to provide such support through budgetary transfers was (and still is) quite limited. In a way, the whole philosophy that drove the URAA was upside down. However, as the framework for the URAA was that of developed-country agriculture, the agreed S&D provisions and even subsequent developing-country proposals to "improve" them have been couched in terms of the same upside-down framework. Thus the URAA provisions in this area call for flexibility by enabling developing countries to reduce their AMS and export subsidies by less, and over a longer period of time, as well as to exempt a larger proportion of the supports they provide from reduction commitments. Since most developing countries do not have positive AMS, these S&D provisions are of limited value.

Flexibility, so far, has been provided for the relatively few—perhaps 15 or so—developing countries, mostly middle- or higher-income that provided significant positive supports to agriculture, and for an even fewer number—10—that had export subsidy commitments. According to the most complete and recent information available, 40 developing countries had notified the WTO on domestic support to agriculture in the period 1995–2000 (ABARE 2002).[7] Probably more countries have used the provisions than have notified the WTO, and notifications for most countries are quite incomplete (FAO 2000). Only eight countries, mostly high-income, notified support that averaged in excess of 10 percent of value added in the agriculture sector. As value added is but a small fraction of gross value, none of these countries came even close to meeting the *de minimis* provisions for exemptions. Indeed the bulk (over 50 percent) of the total amounts notified by such countries as Brazil, the Republic of Korea, Mexico, and Thailand were claimed as exempt and listed under the green box provisions. Few countries claimed support under the *de minimis* provisions, and two of these countries, India and Egypt, accounted for over 85 percent of the total support claimed to be exempt under these provisions. Finally, provisions relating to investment and input subsidies for small and resource-poor farmers have been utilized by a large number (27) of countries but amounted, on average, to a little over 5 percent of total notified support.

The list of 10 countries that notified export subsidies is instructive, in that Indonesia is the only one that is classified as low-income by the World Bank. The others are classified either as middle- or upper-income.[8] Four countries used marketing and transport subsidies for exports (covered by an exemption in URAA Article 9.4); a few countries notified outlays for public stockholding for food security purposes (under footnote 5 to URAA Annex 2, paragraph 3) and domestic food aid to the poor (under footnotes 5 and 6 to Annex 2, paragraph 4); and two countries (the Republic of Korea and the Philippines) notified special treatment provisions in the protection of rice, as a "predominant staple in the traditional diet"(Annex 5, section B) (see WTO 2002a; Youssef 1999).

Over the last several years, developing countries and others have made a number of proposals in the context of the ongoing negotiations on agriculture for rebalancing the URAA to reflect a developmental perspective. Some pertain to changes in the URAA that would improve market access conditions, including, for example, eliminating tariff peaks, not renewing the "Peace Clause" for developed countries, and the like. Others have dealt with issues of assistance to NFIDCs (already discussed), or involve the establishment of new special safeguard measures available only to developing countries (to be discussed below). Still others address the issue of increasing the flexibility in the existing S&D provisions. Some countries have proposed that some or most of these provisions be included in a development box, which would parallel the green box exemptions—which, developing countries believe, tend to focus on measures of primary significance to developed-country agriculture. One submission (WTO 2002b) states:

> Given the fundamental differences in the agriculture production systems and the different role that agriculture plays in developing and developed countries, there is a clear case for devising a development box whose provisions would apply only to developing countries. Agriculture is no doubt multifaceted, but arguments in this regard should not detract focus from the concerns and specific problems of the rural poor of developing countries, which the development box seeks to address.

### *Proposals for Special and Differential Treatment in the Doha Round: What Makes Sense from a Development Perspective?*

The main developing-country proposals for increasing flexibility in the existing S&D provisions call for the following (see WTO 2000a–d; WTO 2001a–b; Green and Priyadarshi 2002.):[9]

- Permanent exemptions in the calculation of the AMS for capital and input subsidies to resource-poor farmers.
- Exemptions from the calculation of the AMS for measures that are targeted on all or some of the following: poverty alleviation, rural development and employment, diversification, food security.
- Raising the *de minimis* level of exempt AMS, either in general or for expenditures related to enhancing food security, the justification being that while in the past developing countries have been unable to spend a lot of resources to promote agriculture or enhance food security, they should not be constrained from doing so in the future.
- Giving credit for negative product-specific support in the form of non-product-specific support in the calculation of permissible AMS, in order to take account of situations in which countries keep food prices artificially low in order to achieve food security objectives for the poor and, therefore, have to compensate farmers by providing them with inputs and other subsidies.
- Exempting from the calculation of the AMS not only capital costs for transport and other marketing infrastructure but also the current transport costs of shipping food from food surplus to food deficit regions within a country.
- Continuation of export subsidies—irrespective of previous commitments.
- Lower rates of reduction of tariffs on agriculture than those agreed for developed countries and possible renegotiation of existing tariff commitments.

In addressing future changes in the S&D provisions of the URAA, consideration needs to be given to the weaknesses in developing-country institutions and in the operations of their markets—key characteristics of developing-country agriculture that distinguish it from agriculture in developed countries. Countries also need to consider, in shaping future public sector involvement in agriculture, what has worked and what has not—that is, experience with "best practice" in government interventions. A recent World Bank paper (WTO 2002) says in this connection:

> Markets and provision of technology are often imperfect because of market failure. . . . The poor are in many cases more affected by market failure than the rich, rural areas more than urban areas, and women more than men. Governments have major roles in enabling the transformation of subsistence oriented rural areas with low incomes and little diversification into areas that are well integrated into markets and with access to modern technology. This requires considerable public investments in infrastructure, agricultural research and human capital. It also requires continuous efforts to

create the appropriate environment for the development of markets and private sector investment.

The recent assessment of country experience undertaken by the World Bank noted above, as well as other literature on rural development, suggests that for developing countries to exploit the advantages of better access to developed-country markets and freer trade in general, they need investments in capacity-building targeting the following:

- The development of necessary infrastructure such as irrigation and improved seeds, as well as better distribution and communication systems.
- Institution building, in the form of research centers that would improve farmers' access to modern production technologies as well as strengthening processing capacity technologies.
- The establishment of effective regulatory and food safety assurance bodies.
- Education and training, particularly in technical areas such as sustainable agriculture, quality control, and packaging.
- Support for the development of local farm organizations, especially for marketing and distribution.
- Programs in support of product diversification, including programs involving government assistance for risk management.
- Support of land reform.

In light of these considerations, what should be the thrust of the revisions in the URAA to make it more development-friendly? Technical, procedural, and substantive changes are needed.

## Special and Differential Treatment

First, on the technical/procedural side, the S&D provisions that exempt the support provided through investment and input subsidies to poor farmers under Article 6.2 are not in the green box list of subsidies that are permanently permitted because they are nondistorting, but are included among the distorting measures of support that are permitted only temporarily. As such, they would have to be reviewed before they can be continued—as if the problems afflicting poor farmers that justify government intervention could be solved in a few years' time.

Article 6.2 subsidies may indeed be actionable under Article 13(b), if they exceed the budgetary limit on subsidies fixed in 1992. This means that if a developing country provided subsidized credit to its poor farmers in excess of that provided in 1992, and was successful in stimulating increases in their production so that it displaced some imports, previous suppliers to its markets could claim "serious prejudice" under the Agreement on Subsidies and Countervailing Duties or "non-violation nullification" under GATT Article XXIII (see Michalopoulos 2001; Diaz-Bonilla and others 2002). It may be unlikely that a developed country that saw its exports decline in these circumstances would complain in the WTO. But this is not the point: the point is that the philosophy and current legal basis of the URAA is not development oriented.

Another technical improvement relates to the way the AMS is calculated, on the basis of the gap between the current administered price and the fixed external reference price from the 1986–88 base period. This base period was inserted in the URAA to help those developed countries that feared that declining world prices would force them to reduce their domestic supports. It did not address the concerns of developing countries, where inflation has typically been high, and where domestic supports that are expressed in nominal prices may prove meaningless in real terms (Tangermann and Josling 1999). Again, the URAA talks in vague terms about "due consideration" to be given to the influence of "excessive rates of inflation" on the ability of countries to honor their AMS commitments. It is clear that the commitments in the AMS, whatever they are, need to be made in real terms.[10]

One of the fundamental changes that developing countries should seek to establish in the present negotiations is that certain policies that may make sense in a development context should always be available to developing countries—or at least to some groups of them. To the extent that the green box does not cover these policies, it should be amended, or a development box should be created, or the URAA should be amended in appropriate ways to provide for such policies (WTO 2000a, 2002b; Green and Priyadarshi 2002).

The selection of policies to go into a development box or the amendments needed would require discussion and negotiation. A starting point would be the existing URAA provisions exempting developing-country subsidies to low-income and resource-poor farmers from reduction commitments, as well as the food security provisions on government stocks and prices.

First, the concept of "low-income or resource-poor producers" to which the measures should apply is difficult to define in practice. A more operationally practical approach might be to exempt from the AMS those programs targeted to all households below a certain poverty line, thus including households that may not "produce" something but which work in agriculture and may be equally or more needy than "resource-poor producers." This approach would include, for example, programs that have an impact on rural labor or other poor consumers.

On the question of targeting, there have been some suggestions for targeting "food security crops" (Ruffer 2002). There are several problems with such targeting. First, the crops that enhance food security may differ from one country to another, which would lead to a complex system of notifications of different crops for different countries. Second, it may well be that there are many poor farmers who do not produce such crops. Should they be excluded from support? It would seem both simpler and more equitable to exempt from restraints all agriculture programs that affect the rural poor, irrespective of the crops they produce. Food security issues are discussed more extensively in chapter 9.

Second, the basic thrust of program support should be in institution-building and improving the way agricultural markets work. On the question of investment subsidies, there is little to add: given the problems affecting agriculture and the poor in most low-income developing countries, government intervention would be necessary to strengthen institutional capacity, improve market operations, and provide support to the urban and rural poor in various ways, including support to expanding the production of individual commodities. Additional support is needed to help build small-farmer organizations, to promote land reform, to strengthen marketing, and to improve financing mechanisms, in addition to the more traditional government services listed in the green box. The programs would need to differ according to whether they focused on subsistence agriculture, smallholders, or commercial farms. None of the subsidies involved should be included in the AMS.

As regards the provision of subsidies to inputs, such as credit, fertilizers, seeds, and so on, past developing-country experience has not been very good. Many such programs have failed in numerous countries. More recent efforts, aimed for example at developing market-based microfinance mechanisms, appear to offer a more viable long-term approach to sustainable rural credit institutions. Similarly, large farmers have to a great extent appropriated the benefits of many traditional fertilizer and seed subsidy programs. New approaches, such as the provision of vouchers to poor farmers, may address the problem better. In general, market-based approaches involving the provision of direct transfers to farmers tend to be superior and better-targeted measures of support than traditional input subsidy interventions as a means of addressing market failure.

Developing countries, however, are often in a quandary. Serious budget constraints do not permit them to provide a safety net for the urban poor through direct income transfers. At the same time, innovative approaches involving microfinance and direct approaches to input delivery to subsistence farmers have not been broadly implemented. In these circumstances, the countries sometimes opt for a "low food price" policy as a second best, which can only be made viable through input subsidies to farmers. Clearly, the best long-term option (which for some developing countries, may be a long time indeed) is a combination of direct transfers with market-based pricing. In the interim, however, it may be unwise to limit the existing flexibility provided by the exclusion of input subsidies to poor farmers from the calculation of the AMS. Similarly, subsidies to internal transport costs to move food to deficit areas may be the most effective way, in the short term, of promoting food security in such regions—but these subsidies should also apply to moving imported food to these areas.

Operations of emergency food stocks should clearly be included in some fashion in the development box. Some clarification of the existing provisions on this score may well need to be considered (for details see Diaz-Bonilla and others 2002). But the stocks may need to be limited in total value, and also not involve discrimination against foreign suppliers.

Finally, programs in support of product diversification for small economies dependent on one or two export crops should be specifically exempted from reductions in the AMS. At present, the exemption to reductions in the AMS on account of support for diversification in Article 6.2 is limited to diversification from "growing illicit narcotic crops"—again, primarily a developed-country priority. On the other hand, small, low-income developing countries—including a number of small island economies which need to diversify their production and export structure in order to reduce their vulnerability to external shocks—do not enjoy an exemption from the AMS for such programs. However, since these programs have to be limited to "minor" crops, they may be difficult to define in practice.

The developing countries should be able to pursue all of these programs as a matter of right. The programs should be included in the URAA, whether in a development box or elsewhere, and should not be considered aberrations or exemptions.

The question of raising the *de minimis* exclusion may no longer be relevant, if a well-defined development box is agreed upon. There is no evidence that the 10 percent exclusion has limited developing countries from providing the support to agriculture they need to provide, and hence it is unclear whether it is necessary to increase the *de minimis* provision from 10 percent to, say, 15 percent. Similarly it is unclear whether the proposal to permit developing countries that have negative support for certain items, as a consequence of consumer food subsidies, to offset these against positive support in the calculation of the AMS would be necessary, if agreement can be reached on truly adequate development-oriented provisions. In this regard, it should also be noted that "low food price" policies tend to have a net negative effect on poor farmers (Ruffer 2002).

The development box should exclude border measures. Tariffs and similar measures raise prices to consumers and have a larger adverse impact on poor consumers, who spend a greater percentage of their incomes on food, while these border measures benefit mostly the bigger agricultural (and food) producers with larger quantities of products to sell. A case could be made for setting a lower pace of tariff reductions by developing countries in the negotiations (see Diaz-Bonilla and others 2002), but this is a matter of the overall negotiating principles to be adopted.

Finally, the issue of export subsidies should be considered separately. These are trade-distorting, perhaps even more so than many forms of domestic support, and most developing countries cannot afford them; so it is in their interest to negotiate tough rules on export subsidies to avoid getting into subsidy contests with developed countries or the more advanced developing-country exporters. The problem here is more political than economic. Economically it may not make much sense for any country to subsidize exports. But because most developed countries have been subsidizing exports in the past and most developing countries have not, reductions in developed-country export subsidies from their present high levels still leaves them with substantially more opportunities for subsidizing exports and thus gaining a commercial advantage against developing countries. An attempt to correct this asymmetry was made in the past by providing developing countries with longer time periods during which to implement reductions in export subsidies. Greater differentiation in future commitments is probably needed in this area, not because export subsidies are a good thing that developing countries should use, but in order to create a more level playing field.[11]

**Country Classification Issues** Targeted programs to help the poor may be of importance to developing countries irrespective of their levels of income or size, and therefore should be available, in principle, for all developing countries to pursue. Perhaps the only exception may be major food-exporting countries. A more restrictive definition could focus S&D provisions to address food security in "food-insecure" countries, which would result in a somewhat narrower list of eligible countries. However, there are several conceptual difficulties in defining "food insecurity" at the country level (see Stevens 2002a, 2002b), and the existing listing of NFIDCs is unsatisfactory, as it includes countries unlikely to be considered "food-insecure." The "product diversification" exception should be limited to small, low-income developing economies that are dependent on one or two crops for the bulk of their export earnings.

Determining any "list" of beneficiary countries involves problems. One is that the longer the list, the more likely the bulk of the benefits would go to the more developed of the countries involved. At the same time, for the list to gain credibility and political acceptance among developing countries, it would have to include the large economies in Asia such as China, India, and Pakistan where the bulk of the world's rural poor are to be found. The inclusion of these countries is likely to increase opposition from developed countries' protectionist interests. The list of countries eligible for S&D benefits should also be consistent with the list of countries that need access to generalized preferences to improve market share. In the end, of course, any list would be the result of political compromise and tend to contain some degree of arbitrariness. But any listing that effectively takes into account the development considerations raised above would probably be an improvement over the situation that prevails today.

**Safeguards** Another important concern of developing countries is the limited capacity of their poor farmers to adjust to a sudden upsurge in agricultural or food imports. This potential danger exists in general, and is exacerbated by the continued use of export subsidies in agricultural trade. This issue is addressed more extensively in chapter 3, but a few observations are in order here.

The problem of import surges is neither new nor limited to agriculture. Most developing countries have a degree of leeway because their bound tariff levels are much higher than their applied rates. For 31 developing countries (excluding Cairns Group members), simple (unweighted) applied tariffs in agriculture averaged 25 percent, compared to 66 percent for bound tariff rates. This suggests that there is considerable scope for them to increase their protection of agriculture, should they wish to do so (Michalopoulos 2001). There are also general provisions for dealing with import surges under the WTO safeguards provisions.

The problem with the existing situation, however, is twofold. First, the margins between applied and bound tariffs are likely to shrink as part of the overall liberalization resulting from the present negotiations. Second, the existing safeguards provisions may be difficult and time-consuming to implement. At the same time, poor farmers in developing countries do not have access to the kind of safety nets available to producers of farm or other products in developed countries. This means that if there is an upsurge of imports, it could have catastrophic effects on poor producers (see FAO 2002a). Of course, the long-term solution to this problem is the establishment of adequate safety nets in these countries, but this will take time to implement. In the meantime, something needs to be put in place to deal with this issue. The answer could be special safeguard provisions for agriculture, available only to developing countries. These provisions could be included in the development box, or could be freestanding. Their key characteristics should be transparency and ease of use, for example, through the determination of price or quantity thresholds; limited duration; and that the developing countries invoking them have not been able to seek compensation under the regular WTO safeguard provisions.[12] The flexibility to use such provisions might be made available only to developing countries that agree to reduce bound tariff rates significantly.

**Transition Periods** Many developing countries, not only the LDCs, have had difficulty in implementing various WTO agreements, including the SPS Agreement. Transition periods under a number of agreements have already expired and many countries say they are experiencing difficulties in establishing the institutions needed for their implementation. Countries facing fiscal constraints often have few resources to direct toward the areas of public administration responsible for overseeing and coordinating the implementation of WTO agreements, which is quite costly. These difficulties were supposed to be overcome through technical assistance and longer transition periods.

The longer transition period of 10 years set by Article 15:2 for the implementation by developing countries of reduction commitments under the URAA has not yet expired. In the case of SPS, it is notable that apparently no country has sought a time-limited exception in whole or in part from obligations under the agreement, although longer timeframes (unspecified) have been explicitly provided for in SPS Articles 10:2 and 10:3. It is actually hard to believe, in light of the frequently voiced concerns of developing countries in this area, that their implementation of the provisions of the SPS Agreement is proceeding entirely on time. It would appear far more likely that countries have just not requested extensions from the WTO, possibly because of their fear of adverse reactions toward their exports.

A very careful look at these transition periods is needed in all areas in which these have been extended on the grounds of institutional weakness, including in SPS. In parallel, efforts are needed by the developing countries themselves, with the support of the international community, to establish the institutions needed for discharging their responsibilities under the SPS Agreement.

**Least-Developed Countries** The international community has made a special effort to address the problems faced by the LDCs. These 49 countries are exempted completely from the AMS reduction commitments and the export subsidy disciplines. Developed countries and some developing countries have also made additional preferential market-access commitments for LDCs.

It was estimated following the UR, that between 80 to 90 percent of the value of LDC merchandise exports overall have duty-free access in their main developed-country markets. Subsequently, the EU announced the EBA initiative, aiming at both duty- and quota-free access to its markets for all LDC exports. At present there is pressure on other developed countries to follow the EU example in the context of the current WTO negotiations. As many of the remaining constraints to LDC exports are in "sensitive" agricultural sectors (and textiles), implementation of the proposal made in 1999 by the Director General of the WTO and supported by the IMF and World Bank to establish duty- and quota-free access for all LDC exports could result in significant further gains in agricultural exports for these countries (in part at the expense of other low-income developing countries), and the LDCs would not have to "offer" any new liberalizing commitments in order to obtain improved market access.

On the other hand, an evaluation of the LDC needs assessments prepared under the Integrated Framework exercise suggests that the main constraints to the expansion of LDC exports derive primarily from weaknesses in institutional capacities as well as other supply side factors, rather than from market access problems (WTO 1998). In particular, these include the following:

a. Infrastructure deficiencies such as erratic power supply, underdeveloped telecommunication networks, and the poor condition of terrestrial, sea, and air transport links.
b. Weaknesses in technological capacity.
c. Underdeveloped financial and banking systems.
d. Shortfalls in a broad range skills and institutional capacity needed to participate in international trade as well as to implement effective trade policies.
e. Deficient regulatory regimes that are unable to cope with weakness in the operations of markets.[13]

The key issues for S&D provisions for the LDCs thus concern how concrete and effective support for trade-related capacity-building measures can be ensured in practically all areas of international trade. In this respect, the LDCs' needs are not qualitatively different from those faced by other low-income countries, and no additional provisions are needed in the URAA or related agreements to deal with their problems. At the same time, it is important that LDCs recognize some of the implications and pitfalls of past developing-country experience with flexibility in the application of WTO rules and disciplines. It could be argued, for example, that existing S&D provisions permit LDCs the most freedom of possible policy choice in areas, such as subsidies, that they can least afford. Tighter WTO disciplines in some policy areas might actually be helpful to LDC governments that wish to introduce and gain domestic consensus for trade policy reform.

## The Ongoing Negotiations on Agriculture

Many of the above suggestions for S&D treatment have been included in the most recent "modalities" draft prepared by the chairman of the negotiating group which suggests approaches for future liberalization commitments in the current WTO negotiations on agriculture (WTO 2003). In particular, the draft includes most of the suggestions for strengthening paragraph 6.2, which concerns the establishment of a special safeguard mechanism available only to developing countries, calculation of AMS in real terms, and other provisions on food aid as noted earlier. For this reason, the draft should be considered a good basis for further negotiations on S&D in agriculture.[14]

At the same time, the draft also contains a large number of provisions permitting developing countries far greater leeway in protecting agriculture through border measures, such as tariffs and tariff quotas, than would be the case for developed countries. Such special and differential treatment could be justified because low-income developing countries do not have the fiscal capacity to support agriculture through less trade-distorting direct income supports. On the other hand, this additional flexibility, over time, could also lead to the same kind of inefficiencies in agriculture that have undermined the competitiveness of many developing-country industries nurtured behind high protective barriers.

## Conclusions and Priorities for the Future

This analysis/assessment of S&D provisions in the WTO agreements that are relevant to agriculture suggests the need for a fundamental reorientation of priorities both by developed- and developing-country members of the WTO.

Two major conclusions arise from the analysis. First, there is increasing recognition that institutions in many developing countries, including those required to implement agricultural trade policies and those that bear the costs of adjustment to globalization, are weak and inadequate to cope with WTO obligations, and that markets in these countries do not work well, requiring government intervention to make them work more efficiently. Second, supply-side constraints create important impediments to the effective integration of many developing countries into international trade, and require assistance, both technical and financial, to overcome them. The most extensive evidence regarding trade-related institutional inadequacies and constraints has been developed in the context of LDCs, but other low-income developing countries suffer from similar inadequacies. This conclusion has major implications about the need to continue and emphasize certain dimensions of S&D.

The overall objective of the international community should be to provide more meaningful S&D treatment, through appropriate instruments, to countries that truly need it. A genuine Development Round of negotiations on agricultural trade must address the legitimate concerns of developing countries—especially those that are low-income and least-developed—about how to develop their food and agriculture sectors. The conceptual underpinning for the reorientation of S&D should be provided by the evolving understanding of the links between agricultural trade and development, and of the constraints faced by different developing countries in integrating effectively into the international trading system. This has been done in the past, in both the GATT and the WTO, and needs to continue in the future. Some of this reorientation involves the general provision of S&D and some of it is specific to agriculture.

The main priorities are as follows:

1. Greater emphasis must be placed on strengthening developing-country institutional capacity. The main differences between developed and developing countries are not in the trade policies they should pursue, but in the capacities of their institutions to pursue them. This requires emphasis on S&D provisions related to technical and financial assistance as well as longer transition periods (which are linked to institutional reform and capacity building). In this context:

   - Transition periods in the WTO agreements linked to developing-country institutional capacity weaknesses need to be reexamined. A number of these transition periods have already expired and need to be urgently addressed. The review of the transition periods should also draw on panels of experts from governments and appropriate international institutions that are knowledgeable about capacity-building efforts and requirements in the areas concerned.
   - Developed countries must increase the coherence between agricultural trade policy and aid to food and agriculture in developing countries. This means, first, avoiding real incoherence, when donors on the one hand provide assistance to increase agriculture or food production in developing countries and on the other undermine their own and the developing countries' efforts by supplying surplus agriculture or food products at subsidized prices into developing-country markets. Second, it means proactive coherence between trade and aid policy, such as would result from a developed-country commitment to support developing-countries in meeting SPS standards in developed countries.

2. Sharper differentiation of developing countries is needed in the provision of S&D. Many problems of institutional capacity that are

common to LDCs and other low-income developing countries with limited participation in international trade are not faced by more advanced developing countries. "Objective" indicators of institutional capacity such as per capita income and share of world trade need to be introduced, which would focus assistance on needy countries and exclude more advanced developing countries. Without a graduation policy that would permit a narrower definition of which countries should be eligible for S&D, developed countries will continue to make commitments to developing countries in general that are not concrete, make concrete commitments only to LDCs that have a very small share of world trade, and rely on their own criteria—which is frequently nontransparent and politically motivated—in determining which countries they will provide with more favorable treatment or market access.

Differentiation and graduation will be difficult for developing countries to accept. Substantial differentiation, however, exists regarding financial flows from all international financial institutions and even from the United Nations Development Programme. In the case of the World Bank, some developing countries get no assistance at all, others are only eligible for loans on hard terms, others for soft loans, and still others for a mix.[15] Why can the principle that has been accepted without serious difficulty on issues of finance not be acceptable regarding trade? It may be difficult to do, but an effort needs to be made.

3. Developing countries should seek improved access to developed-country markets for agricultural products on an MFN basis through reductions of tariff peaks, elimination of remaining quantitative restrictions, and elimination of developed-country export subsidies as soon as practicable, but in any case at a faster rate than that applied to developing countries.
4. Efforts at improving GSP schemes affecting agricultural products should focus on providing deep preferences, such as those currently available or to be made available to LDCs, to other low-income, "food-insecure" or vulnerable countries. Tariff preference margins, including in agriculture where protection is currently very high, can be expected to decline over time as tariffs are liberalized on an MFN basis, and no S&D provisions should inhibit this liberalization. One way to help developing countries that truly need assistance in breaking into foreign markets is to exclude, through graduation, developing countries that do not need it.
5. The agricultural negotiations should result in agreement on measures to enhance food security and stimulate agricultural production of the rural poor in developing countries on a permanent basis. These measures should be articulated as developing-country rights, not as "exceptions" to reductions in the AMS. They should include elements of S&D now included in Article 6:2 of the URAA, expanded as appropriate to provide the following:
   - Direct and indirect investment and input subsidies (including credit) or other supports to households below a poverty line, in order to encourage agricultural and rural development. Such supports could be general, or product-specific, provided they are effectively targeted to the rural poor.
   - Programs that support product diversification in the agriculture of small, low-income developing countries dependent on a very small number of commodities for their exports, including programs involving government assistance for risk management.
   - Foodstuffs at subsidized prices in targeted programs, which do not discriminate against imports, aimed at meeting food requirements of the poor (whether urban or rural) as part of an overall effort to enhance food security.
6. Finally, a new special safeguard provision should be introduced in the URAA which would be available only to developing countries, perhaps only to low-income ones and for others that meet minimal requirements for reducing bound tariff rates. Its purpose should be to provide quick but time-limited protection against import surges that could hurt poor producers.

## CHAPTER ANNEX: SPECIAL AND DIFFERENTIAL PROVISIONS IN AGRICULTURE

*Agreement on Agriculture*

### Provisions Aimed at Increasing Trade Opportunities

***Preamble***

Having agreed that in implementing their commitments on market access, developed country Members would take fully into account the particular needs and conditions of developing country Members by providing for a greater improvement of opportunities and terms of access for agricultural products of particular interest to these Members, including the fullest liberalization of trade in tropical agricultural products as agreed at the Mid-Term Review, and for products of particular importance to the diversification of production from the growing of illicit narcotic crops.

***Flexibility***

**Article 6:2**

(Domestic Support Commitments). In accordance with the Mid-term Review Agreement that government measures of assistance, whether direct or indirect, to encourage agricultural and rural development are an integral part of the development programmes of developing countries, investment subsidies which are generally available to agriculture in developing country Members and agricultural input subsidies generally available to low-income or resource-poor producers in developing country Members shall be exempt from domestic support reduction commitments that would otherwise be applicable to such measures, as shall domestic support to producers in developing country Members to encourage diversification from growing illicit narcotic crops. Domestic support meeting the criteria of this paragraph shall not be required to be included in a Member's calculation of its Current Total AMS.

**Article 6:4 (b)**

(Domestic Support Commitments—calculation of current total AMS). For developing country Members, the *de minimis* percentage under this paragraph shall be 10 per cent.

**Article 9:2(b)(iv)**

(Budgetary outlays for export subsidies)

The Member's budgetary outlays for export subsidies and the quantities benefiting from such subsidies, at the conclusion of the implementation period, are no greater than 64 per cent and 79 per cent of the 1986–1990 base period levels, respectively. For developing country Members these percentages shall be 76 and 86 percent, respectively.

**Article 9:4**

During the implementation period, developing country Members shall not be required to undertake commitments in respect of the export subsidies listed [below], provided that these are not applied in a manner that would circumvent reduction commitments (Art. 9:1[c] and [d]):

- subsidies to reduce the costs of marketing exports of agricultural products,[...] including handling, upgrading and other processing costs, and the costs of international transport and freight; and
- [providing] internal transport charges on export shipments on terms more favourable than those for domestic shipment.

**Article 12:2**

(Disciplines on export prohibitions and restrictions)

The provisions of [Article 12:1] shall not apply to any developing country Member, unless the measure is taken by a developing country Member which is a net food-exporter of the specific foodstuff concerned.

**Article 15.1**

In keeping with the recognition that differential and more favourable treatment for developing country Members is an integral part of the negotiation, special and differential treatment in respect of commitments shall be provided as set out in the relevant provisions of this Agreement and embodied in the Schedules of concessions and commitments.

**Annex 2, para. 3, footnote 5**

(Public stockholding for food security purposes)

For the purposes of paragraph 3 of Annex 2, governmental stockholding programmes for food security purposes in developing countries whose operation is transparent and conducted in accordance with officially published objective criteria or guidelines shall be considered to be in conformity with the provisions of this paragraph, including programmes under which stocks of foodstuffs for food security purposes are acquired and released at administered prices, provided that the difference between the acquisition price and the external reference price is accounted for in the AMS.

**Annex 2, para. 4, footnotes 5 and 6**
(Domestic food aid)
For the purposes of paragraphs 3 and 4 of Annex 2, the provision of foodstuffs at subsidized prices with the objective of meeting food requirements of urban and rural poor in developing countries on a regular basis at reasonable prices shall be considered to be in conformity with the provisions of this paragraph.

***Transition time periods***
**Article 15.2**
Developing country Members shall have the flexibility to implement reduction commitments over a period of up to 10 years. Least-developed country Members shall not be required to undertake reduction commitments.

***Least-Developed Countries***
**Article 16.1**
Developed country Members shall take such action as is provided for within the framework of the Decision on Measures Concerning the Possible Negative Effects of the Reform Programme on Least-Developed and Net Food-Importing Developing Countries.

### *Decision on Measures Concerning the Possible Negative Effects of the Reform Programme on Least-Developed and Net Food-Importing Developing Countries*

***Provisions under Which WTO Members Should Safeguard the Interests of Developing Country Members***
**Paragraph 3(i)**
To review the level of food aid established periodically by the Committee on Food Aid under the Food Aid Convention [1986] and to initiate negotiations in the appropriate forum to establish a level of food aid commitments sufficient to meet the legitimate needs of developing countries during the reform program.

**Paragraph 3(ii)**
To adopt guidelines to ensure that an increasing proportion of basic foodstuffs is provided to least-developed and net food-importing developing countries in fully grant form and/or on appropriate concessional terms in line with Article IV of the Food Aid Convention 1986.

**Paragraph 4**
Ensure that any agreement relating to agricultural export credits makes appropriate provision for differential treatment in favor of least-developed and net food-importing developing countries.

**Paragraph 5**
As a result of the Uruguay Round certain developing countries may experience short-term difficulties in financing normal levels of commercial imports and that these countries may be eligible to draw on the resources of international financial institutions under existing facilities, or such facilities as may be established, in the context of adjustment programmes, in order to address such financing difficulties. In this regard, Ministers take note of paragraph 37 of the report of the Director-General to the CONTRACTING PARTIES to GATT 1947 on his consultations with the Managing Director of the International Monetary Fund and the President of the World Bank (MTN.GNG/NG14/W/35).

**Paragraph 3(iii)**
To give full consideration in the context of their aid programmes to requests for the provision of technical and financial assistance to least-developed and net food-importing developing countries to improve their agricultural productivity and infrastructure.

### *SPS Agreement*

**Article 10:1**
In the preparation and application of sanitary or phytosanitary measures, Members shall take account of the special needs of developing country Members, and in particular of the least-developed country Members.

**Article 10:4**
Members should encourage and facilitate the active participation of developing country Members in the relevant international organizations.

***Transitional time periods***
**Article 10:2**
Where the appropriate level of sanitary or phytosanitary protection allows scope for the phased introduction of new sanitary or phytosanitary measures, longer time-frames for compliance should be accorded on products of interest to developing country Members so as to maintain opportunities for their exports.

**Article 10:3**
With a view to ensuring that developing country Members are able to comply with the provisions of

this Agreement, the Committee is enabled to grant to such countries, upon request, specified, time-limited exception in whole or in part from obligations under this Agreement, taking into account their financial, trade and development needs.

### *Technical Assistance*

**Article 9:1**

Members agree to facilitate the provision of technical assistance to other Members, especially developing country Members, either bilaterally or through the appropriate international organizations. Such assistance may be *inter alia* in the areas of processing technologies, research and infrastructure, including in the establishment of national regulatory bodies, and may take the form of advice, credits, donations and grants, including for the purpose of seeking technical expertise, training and equipment to allow such countries to adjust to, and comply with, sanitary or phytosanitary measures necessary to achieve the appropriate level of sanitary or phytosanitary protection in their export markets.

**Article 9:2**

Where substantial investments are required in order for an exporting developing country Member to fulfill the sanitary or phytosanitary requirements of an importing Member, the latter shall consider providing such technical assistance as will permit the developing country Member to maintain and expand its market access opportunities for the product involved.

## Notes

1. There is extensive literature on these issues. See among others, Das (1998), Diaz-Bonilla and Robinson (2001), and the various submissions and proposals by developing countries in the context of the ongoing negotiations on agriculture (WTO 2000a–d, 2001a–b).

2. For a discussion of the history and conceptual basis for special and differential treatment, see Oyejide (2002).

3. In a few cases, such as antidumping, there are more explicit provisions on how developing countries are supposed to be treated more favorably or in ways that are least damaging to their interests.

4. There is another exception as well: in the Agreement on Subsidies and Countervailing, a special per capita income cutoff has been established.

5. There is extensive literature on this topic. Examples include Karsteny and Laird (1987), Onguglo (1999), UNCTAD (1999), and Topp (2001).

6. As the LDCs would be getting duty-free access, hopefully in all major markets, and the ACP countries, many African and several Latin American countries would be obtaining similar duty-free treatment in various markets, the "binding" of preferences would obviously apply to a much smaller set of countries.

7. Actually ABARE (2002) lists 41 countries, but Mongolia had not been classified as a "developing country" when it acceded to the WTO.

8. The 10 countries are: Brazil, Colombia, Cyprus, Indonesia, Israel, Mexico, Romania, Turkey, Uruguay, and Republica Bolivariana de Venezuela (WTO 2002a).

9. A number of these proposals (by India, the Small Island Economies, the Dominican Republic, Pakistan, and Sri Lanka) were reiterated at the Special Session of the WTO Committee on Agriculture, February 4–8, 2002 (Ruffer 2002).

10. Another issue that developing countries have raised is that because they claimed zero or *de minimis* overall support, they have to keep supports below the 10 percent threshold for each individual product. This again constrains unnecessarily the supports they could offer by comparison with developed countries.

11. There are of course a number of other important issues in the negotiations pertaining to the future rate of AMS reductions by developed countries, limitations on their use of Green Box subsidies, limitations on their use of exports credits, and so on. These are not discussed here as they are not S&D measures in favor of developing countries, but rather involve developing-country proposals to level the playing field by having developed countries accelerate the reductions in their trade-distorting policies.

12. Variants for a safeguard mechanism have been proposed. In one case, some developing countries proposed a safeguard mechanism which would act more like a countervailing action against developed countries that subsidize their exports. There is little reason, however, to differentiate the plight of poor farmers that have been affected by such actions from that of others who have been equally hurt by import surges caused by other factors. The proposal has also been made that the special safeguard be limited to raising tariffs, or to raising them by a certain proportion (Ruffer 2002). It would appear that while these proposals have merit, they would also tend to complicate the use of the mechanism.

13. Based on responses to needs assessment questionnaire, as recorded in WTO (1998).

14. Curiously, an important S&D provision excluded from the draft is the one that would give the right to developing countries to support export diversification. The inclusion of such a provision is especially important for small developing countries dependent on one or two crops for the bulk of their export receipts.

15. The principle has also been accepted in the establishment in 2001of the Advisory Centre on WTO Law, an international institution established in Geneva, Switzerland to assist developing countries pursue cases in the context of the WTO dispute settlement mechanism.

## Select Bibliography

The word *processed* describes informally reproduced works that may not be commonly available through libraries.

ABARE (Australian Bureau of Agricultural and Resource Economics). 2002. "Domestic Support to Agriculture." *Current Issues*, May.

Das, B. L. 1998. *The WTO Agreements: Deficiencies, Imbalances and Required Changes.* Penang: Third World Network.

Diaz-Bonilla, E., and S. Robinson, eds. 2001. "Shaping Globalization for Poverty Alleviation and Food Security." 2020 Focus 8, August 2001. IFPRI, Washington, D.C.

Diaz-Bonilla, E., S. Robinson, M. Thomas, and Y. Yanoma. 2002. "WTO, Agriculture and Developing Countries: A Survey of Issues." Trade and Macroeconomics Paper 81, IFPRI, Washington, D.C.

Diaz-Bonilla, E., M. Thomas, S. Robinson, and A. Cattaneo. 2000. "Food Security and Trade Negotiations in the WTO: A Cluster Analysis of Country Groups." Trade and Macroeconomics Paper 59, IFPRI, Washington, D.C.

FAO (Food and Agriculture Organization). 2000. "Experience with the Implementation of the Uruguay Agreement on Agriculture." CCP 01/11, December. FAO, Rome.

———. 2002a. "A Special Agricultural Safeguard (SAS): Buttressing the Market Access Reforms of Developing Countries." In *Selected Issues Relating to the WTO Negotiations.* Rome: FAO.

———. 2002b. "Towards Improving the Operational Effectiveness of the Marakesh Decision." In *Selected Issues Relating to the WTO Negotiations.* Rome: FAO.

Green, D., and S. Priyadarshi. 2002. "Proposal for a 'Development Box' in the WTO Agreement on Agriculture." Paper presented at FAO Round Table on Special and Differential Treatment in the Context of the WTO Agreement on Agriculture. Geneva, February 1.

Karsteny, G., and S. Laird. 1987. "The Generalized System of Preferences: A Quantitative Assessment of the Direct Trade Effects and of Policy Options." Discussion Paper No.18, UNCTAD, Geneva.

Kessie, E. 2000. "Enforceability of the Legal Provisions Relating to Special and Differential Treatment under the WTO Agreements." Paper presented at WTO Seminar on Special and Differential Treatment of Developing Countries. 7 March, Geneva.

Michalopoulos, C. 2000. "Special and Differential Treatment for Developing Countries in the GATT and the WTO." Policy Research Working Paper 2388, World Bank, Washington, D.C.

———. 2001. *Developing Countries in the WTO.* New York and Hampshire: Palgrave.

Onguglo, B. P. 1999. "Developing Countries and Trade Preferences." In M. R Mendoza, P. Low, and B. Kotschwar, eds., *Trade Rules in The Making.* Washington, D.C.: Brookings.

Otsuki, T., J. S. Wilson, and M. Sewadeh. 2000. "What Price Precaution? European Harmonization of Aflatoxin Regulations and African Food Exports." Processed. World Bank, Washington, D.C.

Oyejide, A. 2002. "Special and Differential Treatment." In B. Hoekman, A. Mattoo, and P. English, eds., *The Trading System and Developing Countries.* Oxford: Oxford University Press for the World Bank.

Ruffer, T., S. Jones, and S. Akroyd. 2002. "Development Box Proposals and Potential Effect on Developing Countries." *Oxford Policy Management,* April.

Stevens, C. 2002a. "Extending Special and Differential Treatment in Agriculture for Developing Countries." Paper presented at FAO Round Table on Special and Differential Treatment in the Context of the WTO Negotiations on Agriculture." Geneva, February 1.

———. 2002b. "The Future of Special and Differential Treatment for Developing Countries in the WTO." Background paper prepared for IDS seminar, May 27–28.

Tangermann, S. 2001. "The Future of Preferential Trade Arrangements for Developing Countries and the Current Round of WTO Negotiations in Agriculture." Processed. April, FAO/ESCP, Rome.

Tangermann, S., and T. Josling. 1999. "The Interests of the Developing Countries in the Next Round of WTO Agricultural Negotiations." UNCTAD, November, Geneva.

Topp, V. 2001. "Trade Preferences: Are They Helpful in Advancing Economic Development in Poor Countries?" ABARE Report, Canberra.

UNCTAD (United Nations Conference on Trade and Development). 1997. "Post-Uruguay Round Tariff Environment for Developing Country Exports." UNCTAD/WTO Joint Study, TD/B/COM.1/14, October. UNCTAD, Geneva.

———. 1999. "Quantifying the Benefits Obtained by Developing Countries from the Generalized System of Preferences." UNCTAD/ITCD/TSB/Misc. 52, October 7. UNCTAD, Geneva.

UNCTAD/WTO. 1997. "Market Access Developments since the Uruguay Round: Implications, Opportunities and Challenges, in Particular for Developing Countries, and Least Developed Countries, in the Context of Globalization and Liberalization." UNCTAD, Geneva.

WTO (World Trade Organization) 1994. "Decision on Measures in Favor of Least-Developed Countries." LT/UR/D-1/3, 15/04/1994. Office of the Secretary General, Geneva.

———. 1998. "Market Access for Exports of Goods and Services from the LDCs: Barriers and Constraints." December, WT/COMT/ LDC/W/11/REV.1. Office of the Secretary General, Geneva.

———. 2000a–b. "Agreement on Agriculture: Special and Differential Treatment and a Development Box." Proposal by Cuba and others. June 23, G/AG/NG/ W/13 and G/AG/NG/ W/14. Office of the Secretary General, Geneva.

———. 2000c. "Special and Differential Treatment of Developing Countries in World Agricultural Trade." Submission by ASEAN. November 10, G/AG/NG/W/55. Office of the Secretary General, Geneva.

———. 2000d. "WTO Negotiations on Agriculture: Proposals by Small Island Developing States." December 29, G/AG/ NG/W/97. Office of the Secretary General, Geneva.

———. 2000e. "Implementation of Special and Differential Treatment Provisions in WTO Agreements and Decisions." WT/COMTD/W/77. Office of the Secretary General, Geneva.

———. 2001a. "WTO Negotiations on Agriculture: Proposals by India." January 15, G/AG/NG/W/102. Office of the Secretary General, Geneva.

———. 2001b. "WTO Negotiations on Agriculture: Comprehensive Proposal by the Arab Republic of Egypt." March 21, G/AG/NG/W/107. Office of the Secretary General, Geneva.

———. 2002a. "Information on the Utilisation of Special and Differential Treatment Provisions." February 7, WT/ COMTD/W/77/Rev.1/Add.4. Office of the Secretary General, Geneva.

———. 2002b. "The Development Box." Non-paper presented by the Dominican Republic, Kenya, Pakistan, and Sri Lanka at the Special Session of the Committee on Agriculture, February 4–8. Office of the Secretary General, Geneva.

———. 2002c. "Report of the Inter-Agency Panel on Short-Term Difficulties on Financing Normal Levels of Commercial Imports of Basic Foodstuffs." June 28, WT/GC/62 and G/AG/13. Office of the Secretary General, Geneva.

———. 2003. "Negotiations on Agriculture, 'First Draft of Modalities for the Further Commitments' (revised)." March 18, TN/AG/W/1.Rev. 1. Office of the Secretary General, Geneva.

Youssef, H. 1999. "Special and Differential Treatment for Developing Countries in the WTO." Working Paper 2, South Centre, Geneva.

15

# SPECIAL TRADE ARRANGEMENTS TO IMPROVE MARKET ACCESS

*Helen Freeman*

## Introduction

The General Agreement on Tariffs and Trade (GATT) and the World Trade Organization (WTO) agreements have provisions that acknowledge a need to improve developing countries' access to world markets. In doing so, GATT and WTO provisions provide for the formation of customs unions or free trade agreements and preferential treatment for developing countries. These are exceptions to the most-favored nation (MFN) treatment principle and most action is taken outside of the GATT/WTO. A major concern about current efforts to negotiate trade agreements is that these are a distraction from multilateral efforts to further liberalize trade. Most developing countries have preferential access to industrial-country markets through tariff preference schemes, but benefits are limited or have been difficult to obtain for their key products (agriculture, textiles, and apparel). The new trade negotiations—the Doha Round—will result in further trade liberalization, including changes to market access and tariffs. These changes will affect the current benefits that developing countries receive under preferential schemes. Developing countries will want to consider the effects of such reform on preferential arrangements but will need to recognize that these arrangements are autonomous trade policy instruments that are not subject to mandates resulting from negotiations in the WTO.

## The Plan of This Chapter

This chapter outlines the GATT/WTO rules relating to trade preferences, provides a brief background of trade preferences, examines the trade preference schemes in the United States (U.S.) and the European Union (EU), examines preferential aspects of several trade agreements, examines the benefits and problems associated with trade preferences, and addresses some options for developing countries on preferential access in the trade negotiations.

## Background

Multilateral, regional, and bilateral trade agreements by their nature provide for preferential access to members' markets—hence the importance of tariffs in any agreement. Both the GATT (negotiated in 1947) and the WTO (its successor since 1995) are based on the MFN obligation of "nondiscriminatory" treatment of all members. This requires that the same trading conditions apply to all members (that is, reciprocity). The MFN obligation precludes special trading arrangements.

From its inception, the GATT allowed member countries to conclude customs unions and free trade agreements under Article XXIV. During the 1947 discussion on the Havana Charter a statement by Lebanon mentioned free trade areas. In 1958

European countries, in the Treaty of Rome, entered into a customs union under GATT Article XXIV. WTO members may establish free trade areas (FTAs) within which the duties and other restrictive regulations on commerce (unless not permitted within the WTO rules) are eliminated on substantially all trade among member countries. FTAs grant more favorable conditions (that is, preferences) on trade with the other partners and are inherently discriminatory in nature, in contrast to WTO agreements. FTAs are permitted under GATT 1994, Article XXIV and WTO GATS Article V (the General Agreement on Trade in Services provision relating to preferential agreements in services). The Understanding on the Interpretation of Article XXIV of GATT 1994, an outcome of 1986–94 Uruguay Round discussions on problems associated the Article, applies to FTAs.

Most WTO Members are now parties to regional trade agreements (RTAs) and FTAs, which differ in membership, scope, and coverage. In 1996, the WTO Committee on Regional Trade Agreements was set up to examine regional groups to assess their consistency with the WTO rules. Countries may join a RTA or FTA for a number of reasons: economic, political, or a combination of both. On the economic side, the expansion of domestic markets after barriers have been removed can create economies of scale. Regional and bilateral FTAs can result in both trade creation and trade diversion, and can raise world welfare if trade creation outweighs trade diversion. Politically, by joining a group, smaller countries may increase their bargaining power either regionally or multilaterally. An RTA/FTA is one whereby tariff structures are lowered among members but members maintain their own separate and varying tariffs toward third countries, such as in the North American Free Trade Agreement (NAFTA). A preferential trade agreement differs from an RTA/FTA in that one country or entity confers nonreciprocal preferences on another group of countries, such as the EU and the Lomé Convention/Cotonou Agreement.

Regional and free trade agreements can take different forms and be regional in scope such as NAFTA (1994) or nonregional such as between the U.S. and Israel (also a bilateral agreement), and the EU agreement with Mexico—or they can be customs unions such as the European Communities (1958), the Southern Common Market (MERCOSUR 1991), and the Caribbean Community (CARICOM 1973). Other examples of bilateral agreements are those between Australia and New Zealand (Australia-New Zealand Closer Economic Relations Trade Agreement—ANZCERTA 1987) and between Canada and Chile (1997)[1] (see box 15.1). In the period 1948–94, the GATT received 124 notifications on RTAs/FTAs and since 1995 over an additional 100 arrangements have been notified to the WTO. The majority fall under GATT Article XXIV, 19 are under the 1979 Enabling Clause (see below), and fewer than 20 are under GATS Article V (WTO Website on Regionalism, 2003).

GATT/WTO rules do provide for exceptions from MFN obligations and since 1979, the Enabling Clause has provided a permanent exception so that developed countries "may accord differential and more favorable treatment to developing countries" through "a system of generalized, nonreciprocal preferences," usually referred to as a Generalized System of Preferences (GSP). These schemes are provided outside of the GATT/WTO structure and rules. Preferential treatment (such as lower tariffs) was the trade policy instrument used by developed countries mainly for manufactures and semimanufactures, to help developing countries overcome their dependence on exports of raw materials with unfavorable long-term price trends and pronounced short-term quantity and price fluctuations. Temperate agricultural products have not been part of preferential treatment under most GSP schemes as they have been excluded or provided only limited access (quotas). Tropical products have MFN tariffs at relatively low levels—or at zero—and such action is a result of the 1979 Tokyo Declaration relating to trade in tropical products.

Twenty-seven industrialized countries provide GSP programs, conceived as autonomous trade policy instruments, providing development-oriented preferences—usually lower tariffs—to developing countries. WTO Members granting GSP preferences under the Enabling Clause include Australia (the first country to introduce a GSP scheme in 1966), Belarus, Canada, the Czech Republic, the EU, Hungary, Japan, New Zealand, Norway, Poland, the Slovak Republic, Switzerland, and the U.S. Under GSP schemes, the beneficiaries, products, and type of preferences granted vary for each donor country.[2]

## BOX 15.1 Trade Agreements: AFTA to SADC

**AFTA (ASEAN Free Trade Area):** Brunei Darussalam, Indonesia, Lao PDR, Malaysia, Myanmar, Philippines, Singapore, Thailand, Vietnam.

**ANZCERTA (Australia–New Zealand Closer Economic Relations Trade Agreement):** Australia and New Zealand.

**APEC (Asia Pacific Economic Co-operation Forum):** Australia, Brunei Darussalam, Canada, Chile, China, Hong Kong (China), Indonesia, Japan, Republic of Korea, Malaysia, Mexico, New Zealand, Papua New Guinea, Peru, Philippines, Russian Federation, Singapore, Taiwan (China), Thailand, United States, Vietnam.

**CARICOM (Caribbean Community):** Antigua and Barbuda, Bahamas, Barbados, Belize, Dominica, Grenada, Guyana, Haiti, Jamaica, St. Kitts and Nevis, St. Lucia, St. Vincent and the Grenadines, Suriname, Trinidad and Tobago. The Bahamas does not participate in the common market and Haiti is not yet a full member.

**CEFTA (Central European Free Trade Agreement):** Bulgaria, Czech Republic, Hungary, Poland, Romania, Slovak Republic, Slovenia.

**COMESA (Common Market for Eastern and Southern Africa):** Angola, Burundi, Comoros, Democratic Republic of Congo, Djibouti, Egypt, Eritrea, Ethiopia, Kenya, Madagascar, Malawi, Mauritius, Namibia, Rwanda, Seychelles, Sudan, Swaziland, Zambia, Zimbabwe.

**EEA (Agreement on the European Economic Area):** Austria, Belgium, Denmark, Finland, France, Germany, Greece, Iceland, Ireland, Italy, Liechtenstein, Luxembourg, the Netherlands, Norway, Portugal, United Kingdom, Spain, Sweden.

**EFTA (European Free Trade Association):** Iceland, Liechtenstein, Norway, Switzerland.

**EU (European Union):** Austria, Belgium, Denmark, Finland, France, Germany, Greece, Ireland, Italy, Luxembourg, the Netherlands, Portugal, United Kingdom, Spain, Sweden.

**Europe Agreements**: The European Union has concluded these with Bulgaria, Czech Republic, Estonia, Hungary, Latvia, Lithuania, Poland, Romania, Slovak Republic, and Slovenia.

**Euro-Med (Euro-Mediterranean Association Agreements) (First-generation):** The European Union has concluded these with Cyprus, Malta, and Turkey.

**Euro-Med (Euro-Mediterranean Association Agreements):** The European Union has concluded these with Tunisia, Israel, Morocco, and the Palestinian Authority.

**Euro-Med (Euro-Mediterranean Co-operation Agreements):** The European Union has concluded these with Algeria, Egypt, Jordan, Lebanon, and Syria.

**FTAA (Free Trade Area of the Americas):** Antigua and Barbuda, Argentina, Bahamas, Barbados, Belize, Bolivia, Brazil, Canada, Chile, Colombia, Costa Rica, Dominica, Dominican Republic, Ecuador, El Salvador, Grenada, Guatemala, Guyana, Haiti, Honduras, Jamaica, Mexico, Nicaragua, Panama, Paraguay, Peru, St. Lucia, St. Kitts and Nevis, St. Vincent and Grenadines, Suriname, Trinidad and Tobago, Uruguay, United States, República Bolivariana de Venezuela.

**Group of Three:** Colombia, Mexico, República Bolivariana de Venezuela.

**MERCOSUR (Mercado Común del Sur/*Southern Common Market* Agreement):** Argentina, Brazil, Paraguay, Uruguay.

**NAFTA (North American Free Trade Agreement):** Canada, Mexico, United States.

**SAARC (South Asian Association for Regional Co-operation):** Bangladesh, Bhutan, India, Maldives, Nepal, Pakistan, Sri Lanka.

**SADC (Southern African Development Community):** Angola, Botswana, Democratic Republic of Congo, Lesotho, Malawi, Mauritius, Mozambique, Namibia, Seychelles, South Africa, Swaziland, Tanzania, Zambia, Zimbabwe.

*Source:* OECD 2002.

In May 2000, the U.S. enacted the African Growth and Opportunity Act (AGOA), and added more products benefiting from lower tariffs to its GSP list for designated sub-Saharan African countries. In September 2000, Canada enlarged its GSP product coverage. In March 2001, the EU granted duty-free access for all least-developed-country (LDC) products, excluding arms, and in April 2001, Japan provided an additional list of LDC industrial products for duty- and quota-free treatment.

The Enabling Clause has also been used by developing countries to enter interregional or global agreements that include the reduction or elimination of tariffs and nontariff barriers (NTBs) on trade among themselves. The 1977 formation of ASEAN and the 1979 Global System of Trade Preferences occurred under the Enabling Clause (see box 15.2). The Enabling Clause also provided that countries identified as LDCs by the United Nations be granted more favorable treatment. These additional concessions for the LDCs allow for discrimination among developing countries of trading preferences based on economic capabilities and needs.[3]

In 1996, WTO members in the Singapore Ministerial Declaration agreed to take measures in favor of LDCs "including provision for taking positive measures, for example, duty-free access on an autonomous basis, aiming at improving their overall capacity to respond to the opportunities offered by the trading system." The 2001 Doha WTO Ministerial Declaration committed members to working toward the objective of quota-free and duty-free access as well as considering additional measures for progressive improvement in market access for LDCs (WTO document WT/MIN(01)/DE/W/1, paragraph 42).

In addition to the GSP and FTA/RTA exceptions, special waivers of MFN or WTO obligations can be granted to members with the approval of three-fourths of WTO members (GATT 1947 Article XXV:5). The U.S., Canada, and the EU have sought waivers—U.S. and Canada in favor of Caribbean countries and the EU in favor of the Africa, Caribbean and Pacific (ACP) countries. Following the signing of the ACP–EU Partnership Agreement (known as the Cotonou Agreement, which replaced the Lomé IV Convention) in February 2002, the parties to the agreement obtained a waiver from WTO members from obligations under Article 1:1 of GATT 1994, once opposition from a number of WTO members was withdrawn in the context of the Doha Round (see WTO Document WT/MIN/DI/IS, November 14, 2001).

Agriculture is of significant importance to many developing countries. It is also a sensitive issue for developed countries, and the strength of the opposition to reform of trade in agriculture resulted in few disciplines in the multilateral context. This situation prevailed until the 1994 Uruguay Round Agreement on Agriculture (URAA), which established more comprehensive rules for agricultural trade. Developed countries' support for their farmers has resulted in major distortions to world agricultural trade. Many tariffs in developed countries for agricultural products are still extremely high, and even higher on "sensitive" products (usually sugar and dairy). Given this situation, preferential arrangements can be potentially valuable. However, the literature on trade preferences and in particular on trade preferences in agriculture is surprisingly limited (Tangermann 2001; Messerlin 2001).

## Preferential Trade: GSP Schemes and Trade Agreements

A 2001 WTO Secretariat Note on "The Generalized System of Preferences. A Preliminary Analysis of

### BOX 15.2 A Brief History of the GSP Schemes

Action on special treatment for developing countries has been undertaken by both the GATT/WTO and UNCTAD. In the 1954–55 Review Session of the GATT Contracting Parties the adoption of Article XXVII bis, dealing with tariff negotiations, contains one of the first indications of differential and nonreciprocal treatment for developing countries. With the Kennedy Round in the 1960s and the increasing number of developing countries becoming GATT Contracting Parties, work on the issue of nonreciprocity led to the 1964 addition to GATT, 1947 of Part IV on Trade and Development. This period and action coincided with the decolonization period especially in Africa and Asia and concerns of former colonial powers about how to provide trade preferences to newly independent developing countries. These trade preferences were seen as instruments of commercial and foreign policy (especially development assistance).

The Generalized System of Preferences was proposed in 1964 by the UNCTAD Secretary General Dr. Prebisch and subsequently adopted at New Delhi at UNCTAD 11(1968)—although developing countries had already raised the issue in the GATT. In 1971 in order to allow the GSP system to become legally operational, the GATT Contracting Parties decided to waive Article 1 for a period of 10 years and then permanently in 1979 through the "Enabling Clause."

the GSP Schemes in the Quad" (in other words, Canada, the EU, Japan, and the U.S.) comments on the lack of data available on the application of GSP schemes. The note provides a brief description of the GSP schemes for the Quad countries, which imported about three-quarters of all LDC exports, with the EU and the U.S. accounting for 63 percent. Western Europe and North America account for 88 percent of LDC exports of manufactured goods but only 45 percent of agricultural exports. Statistics demonstrate that only a few countries have benefited from the GSP programs as a strong concentration of benefits has gone to developing countries with relatively large and diversified economies, including substantial manufacturing sectors. China is the leading beneficiary of schemes in Canada, the EU, and Japan: it is excluded from the U.S. scheme. There are no LDC countries among the top 20 GSP suppliers to Canada. Bangladesh is the only LDC in this category to the EU, and Mauritania the only LDC in this category to Japan (WTO 2001). Given the importance of the U.S. and the EU economies, their preferential schemes are provided in some detail below. The United Nations Conference on Trade and Development (UNCTAD) Web site of the Generalized System of Preferences contains the Handbooks of the countries providing GSP preferences.

## The United States' Generalized System of Preferences

The Office of the U.S. Trade Representative (USTR), the key U.S. government body responsible for trade negotiations, described the GSP as "an important element of U.S. efforts to increase economic development through the expansion of trade opportunities" as all imports of GSP eligible articles are duty-free (see USTR 2002c, 2002e). The U.S. Congress provides the legislative authority for the government to carry out the GSP program. Enacted in 1975, it has been renewed eight times over the past 25 years and it is now extended through December 31, 2008 by the Trade Act of 2002. However, six of those eight renewals occurred during the past eight years of the program's existence. From September 30, 2001 until its August 2002 renewal there was no legislative authority for the program. The stop-and-start nature of the program has produced uncertainty for both developing countries and U.S. businesses, and may be a factor in the program's utilization. The program provides better access to the U.S. market for a range of products imported from over 150 GSP-eligible developing economies (countries, territories, and associations). Least-developed countries are specifically designated in U.S. legislation (see table 15.1).

In 2001 the U.S. imported products were worth approximately US$16 billion under the program. The leading beneficiaries include Angola, Thailand, Brazil, Indonesia, and India, with a concentration of benefits to imports of manufactures and semimanufactured goods (in other words, in accordance with the intent of the program and its emphasis on manufactures). Some agricultural food products and sugar—with an imported value of US$718 million and US$276 million, respectively—benefit from GSP status (see tables 15.2 and 15.3).

Eligibility for GSP status of both countries and goods changes from time to time and this is seen in the U.S. reaction through its GSP program to the economic crisis in Argentina during 2001–02 (see box 15.3). During 2000–01 Belarus and Ukraine were suspended; in 2002 Malta and Slovenia were graduated; and in 2000 Nigeria and Georgia were designated as Beneficiary Developing Countries. The 2001 graduation threshold was US$9,266 (1999 GDP per capita) (see box 15.4).

The original GSP list contained 4,650 articles that are duty-free for all eligible GSP beneficiaries; more than 10,000 products are imported into the U.S. In 1996, a second list added approximately 1,770 duty-free articles for the Least-Developed Beneficiary Developing Countries (LDBDC), defined by the World Bank as those with annual incomes below US$786 (1996 GNP per capita). After the signing of the AGOA in 2000, the law expanded GSP benefits to eligible countries in sub-Saharan Africa by providing GSP status on an additional 1,800 products.

Not all articles are eligible for duty-free access. Prohibited articles include most textiles, watches, footwear, and others. However, GSP eligibility for six categories of textile products applies when the GSP beneficiary signs an agreement with the U.S. certifying that products are handmade. Such agreements have been signed with at least 15 countries including Botswana, Egypt, Malta, Romania, Tunisia, and Thailand. Additional product exclusions include any article that is determined to be import-sensitive (such

**TABLE 15.1 U.S. GSP Beneficiaries, 1999 (Independent Countries[a])**

*The following independent countries are GSP-eligible beneficiaries[b]:*

| Albania | Democratic Republic | Lesotho* | Senegal |
|---|---|---|---|
| Angola* | of Congo* | Lithuania | Seychelles |
| Antigua and Barbuda | Djibouti* | Macedonia, Former | Sierra Leone* |
| Argentina | Dominica | Yugoslav Republic of | Slovak Republic |
| Armenia | Dominican Republic | Madagascar* | Slovenia |
| Bahrain | Ecuador | Malawi* | Solomon Islands |
| Bangladesh* | Egypt | Mali* | Somalia* |
| Barbados | El Salvador | Malta | South Africa |
| Belarus | Equatorial Guinea* | Mauritius | Sri Lanka |
| Belize | Estonia | Moldova | Suriname |
| Benin* | Ethiopia* | Morocco | Swaziland |
| Bhutan* | Fiji | Mozambique* | Tanzania* |
| Bolivia | Gambia, The* | Namibia | Thailand |
| Bosnia and | Ghana | Nepal* | Togo* |
| Herzegovina | Grenada | Niger* | Tonga |
| Brazil | Guatemala | Oman | Trinidad and Tobago |
| Bulgaria | Guinea* | Pakistan | Tunisia |
| Burkina Faso* | Guinea-Bissau* | Panama | Turkey |
| Burundi* | Guyana | Papua New Guinea | Tuvalu* |
| Cambodia* | Haiti* | Paraguay | Uganda* |
| Cameroon | Honduras | Peru | Ukraine |
| Cape Verde* | Hungary | Philippines | Uruguay |
| Central African Republic* | India | Poland | Uzbekistan |
| Chad* | Indonesia | Romania | Vanuatu* |
| Chile | Jamaica | Russia | Venezuela, R.B. de |
| Colombia | Jordan | Rwanda* | Republic of Yemen* |
| Comoros* | Kazakhstan | St. Kitts and Nevis | Zaire |
| Congo | Kenya | St. Lucia | Zambia* |
| Costa Rica | Kiribati* | St. Vincent and | Zimbabwe |
| Cote d'Ivoire | Kyrgyzstan | the Grenadines | |
| Croatia | Latvia | Sao Tome and | |
| Czech Republic | Lebanon | Principe* | |

* Least-Developed Country (LDC).

a. U.S. GSP Beneficiaries also include nonindependent countries and territories and Associations of Countries.

b. Beneficiaries are added or deleted from the list and as of June 2000, Botswana, Gabon, Mongolia, and Western Samoa are now beneficiaries and in January 2002, Malta and Slovenia were graduated.

*Source*: Adapted from USTR, *U.S. Generalized System of Preferences Guidebook*, Office of the United States Trade Representative, Executive Office of the President, Washington, D.C., March 1999 and UNCTAD Web site's GSP Handbook on the Scheme of the United States of America.

as steel, glass, and electronics). When imports exceed the competitive need-limitation (CNL) level they no longer remain eligible for duty-free treatment. This provision enables GSP benefits to apply to less competitive foreign producers by limiting access by the more competitive Beneficiary Developing Countries.

The GSP program's annual review by the U.S. government involves the GSP Subcommittee of the Trade Policy Staff Committee at the Office of USTR. Working to an annual timetable, this subcommittee considers petitions to modify the eligibility of articles and countries for duty-free treatment (see box 15.5).

**TABLE 15.2 Leading Sources of U.S. GSP Imports, 2000**

| Beneficiary Developing Country(BDC) | Total U.S.Imports (US $ millions) | | | Share of U.S.Imports Using GSP (percent) | |
|---|---|---|---|---|---|
| | Duty-Free U.S. | GSP-Eligible | All Products | GSP-Eligible | All Products |
| Angola | 2,844 | 3,010 | 3,343 | 94.5 | 85.1 |
| Thailand | 2,205 | 4,130 | 16,301 | 53.4 | 13.5 |
| Brazil | 2,086 | 4,990 | 13,732 | 41.8 | 15.2 |
| Indonesia | 1,369 | 2,723 | 10,322 | 50.3 | 13.3 |
| India | 1,138 | 2,745 | 10,680 | 41.5 | 10.7 |
| Philippines | 745 | 1,545 | 13,943 | 48.2 | 5.3 |
| Venezuela | 745 | 11,353 | 17,429 | 6.6 | 4.3 |
| South Africa | 583 | 1,105 | 4,204 | 52.8 | 13.9 |
| Russia | 515 | 1,797 | 7,761 | 28.7 | 6.6 |
| Turkey | 435 | 853 | 3,027 | 51.0 | 14.4 |
| Chile | 419 | 1,524 | 3,258 | 27.5 | 12.9 |
| Kazakhstan | 326 | 393 | 431 | 83.0 | 75.6 |
| Hungary | 318 | 1,023 | 2,711 | 31.1 | 11.7 |
| Poland | 317 | 578 | 1,040 | 54.8 | 30.5 |
| Czech Republic | 280 | 470 | 1,069 | 59.6 | 26.2 |
| Argentina | 218 | 2,089 | 3,095 | 10.4 | 7.0 |
| Congo (Kinshasa) | 174 | 178 | 212 | 97.8 | 82.1 |
| Equatorial Guinea | 136 | 144 | 155 | 94.4 | 87.7 |
| Sri Lanka | 122 | 149 | 2,002 | 81.9 | 6.1 |
| Slovenia | 120 | 160 | 314 | 75.0 | 38.2 |
| Total, Top 20 BDCs | 15,095 | 40,959 | 115,029 | 36.9 | 13.1 |
| Total, All BDCs | 16,439 | 60,730 | 172,366 | 27.1 | 9.5 |

*Source:* The Trade Partnership 2001; Derived from U.S. Census data.

**TABLE 15.3 Leading Product Groups Imported by the United States Duty-Free under GSP, 2000**

| Products | Value (US $ millions) | Share of Total GSP Imports (percent) | Value or Duties Saved |
|---|---|---|---|
| Oils and petroleum products | 3,151 | 19.2 | 8.9 |
| Electrical equipment and parts | 1,712 | 10.4 | 56.3 |
| Transportation equipment parts | 1,149 | 7.0 | 29.0 |
| Jewellery and parts | 983 | 6.0 | 56.6 |
| Machinery (including computers), parts | 849 | 5.2 | 28.5 |
| Organic chemicals | 747 | 4.5 | 41.6 |
| Agricultural and food products (excl. sugar) | 718 | 4.4 | 41.8 |
| Plastics and plastic products | 602 | 3.7 | 31.1 |
| Wood and wood products | 533 | 3.2 | 23.0 |
| Iron and steel raw materials | 467 | 2.8 | 13.7 |
| Aluminum mill products | 424 | 2.6 | 14.5 |
| Rubber products | 418 | 2.5 | 14.6 |
| Iron and steel products | 405 | 2.5 | 13.2 |
| Sugar | 276 | 1.7 | 8.2 |
| Leather products | 179 | 1.1 | 5.1 |
| Furniture and parts | 6 | 0.0 | 0.4 |
| Total, Leading Products | 12,617 | 76.8 | 386.5 |
| Total, All GSP Products | 16,439 | 100.0 | 555.3 |

*Source:* The Trade Partnership 2001; Derived from U.S. Census data.

### *The U.S. and the Caribbean Basin Initiative (CBI)*

U.S. trade preferences concerning the Caribbean, authorized by Congress and collectively known as the Caribbean Basin Initiative (CBI), have been used to facilitate the economic development and export diversification of 24 Caribbean Basin and Central American economies. From its 1994 inception, the Caribbean Basin Economic Recovery Act (CBERA) provided certain CBI goods—such as coffee, bananas, and minerals—open access to the U.S. market. These benefits were substantially expanded by the Caribbean Basin Trade Partnership Act of 2000 (CBTPA) with new preference provisions, including expanded benefits for apparel. By 2000, manufactured products (such as apparel and electrical and nonelectrical machinery) amounted to over 50 percent of CBI exports to the U.S. The value of the different schemes under which CBI products entered the U.S. was greatest for CBERA and CBTPA in 2002, with over one-third entering under these programs (see table 15.4).

Benefits are conditioned on compliance with legislated eligibility criteria such as labor rights. Conditionality provisions are used by the U.S. to bring about change on issues with CBTPA beneficiaries. Guatemala provides an example of both the use of criteria and compliance. In mid-2000, the U.S. government conducted an extensive review of each beneficiary country. It suspended its review of Guatemala's labor practices when, in May 2001, the Guatemalan government passed important labor law reforms.

CBTPA (like its predecessor CBERA) applies to many of the same tariff categories covered under the U.S. GSP but it is broader in terms of additional products and more liberal qualifying rules. Its duty-

**BOX 15.3 The U.S. Generalized System of Preferences (GSP) and Argentina's Economic Crisis, 2001–02**

The U.S. government uses its GSP scheme to assist countries undergoing difficult economic circumstances and in 2002 used it to help Argentina. Following an August 2002 presidential proclamation, the eligibility for 57 products (leather goods, nonsensitive agricultural products, industrial chemicals, and others), which accounted for over $126 million in exports in 2001, was restored as products eligible for preferential treatment. Previously they had been covered by the GSP program but were removed, upon reaching a statutorily defined threshold level of the U.S. market share.

The petitioning process for the restoration of product eligibility requires public notification in the Federal Register by the Office of United States Trade Representative (USTR), providing for a comment period and a date for the results of the petitioning. In 2002, Argentina, the Philippines, and Turkey petitioned the USTR to review 17 products and add these to the list of products eligible for GSP treatment.

**TABLE 15.4 U.S. Imports from CBERA Countries, Total and Under-Selected Import Programs, MFN-Free, GSP, and CBERA**

| Import program | 1998 ($1,000) | 1998 (percentage of total) | 2001 YTD ($1,000) | 2002 (percentage of total) |
|---|---|---|---|---|
| CBERA | 3,224,564 | 18.8 | 1,818,366 | 12.8 |
| CBTPA | 0 | 0.0 | 3,469,607 | 24.4 |
| GSP | 195,407 | 1.1 | 150,031 | 1.1 |
| MFN-free | 3,742,325 | 21.9 | 3,753,970 | 26.4 |
| **Subtotal** | **7,162,296** | **41.8** | **7,37,3608** | **64.7** |
| Other | 9,961,985 | 58.2 | 6,870,759 | 35.3 |
| **Total** | **17,124,281** | **100.0** | **14,244,367** | **100.0** |

*Source:* USTR Fourth Report to Congress on the Operation of the Caribbean Basin and Economic Recovery Act, December 31, 2001.

**BOX 15.4 U.S. Generalized System of Preferences (GSP): Criteria and Conditions**

In deciding the eligibility of an import for GSP treatment, the United States considers three main criteria. The article must be:

- from a designated beneficiary country;
- an eligible article as defined for GSP treatment; and
- meet the rules of origin.

In addition, the following factors and conditions are taken into account:

- statement of the requesting country;
- benefits to furthering economic development of a beneficiary country;
- the anticipated impact on comparable U.S. producers;
- the extent of competitiveness of the beneficiary country's eligible products;
- comparable GSP action by other major developed countries;
- market access for U.S. goods and services in the beneficiary country;
- protection of U.S. intellectual property rights;
- reduction of trade-distorting investment practices/policies;
- elimination of trade-distorting export practices; and
- provision for internationally recognized worker rights (of association, of collective bargaining); forced or compulsory labor; minimum age for child employment and acceptable work conditions regarding, for instance, minimum wages, work hours, and occupational and health standards. (Workers rights criteria has been the single most common issue cited in practices filed with the GSP Subcommittee. Of the 224 country practices petitions filed with USTR from 1985 to 2000, 128 concerned workers' rights. Failure to meet this criteria led to temporary or permanent suspension of GSP privileges for Chile, Maldives, Mauritania, Paraguay, Sudan, and Syria and termination for Liberia, Nicaragua, and Romania (Laird and Safadi 2000).

Not all beneficiary countries receive duty-free treatment on the entire list of articles. Exclusion may occur because of the following:

- GSP imports of the article exceed the competitive need-limitation (CNL) (based on dollar value) or exceed more than 50 percent of total U.S. imports of that product;
- the country has been graduated from the program (per capita GNP exceeds the threshold level of the income set for high-income countries by the World Bank) or has been removed because it is deemed no longer to be developing;
- the value-added component in the beneficiary country is insufficient to meet the GSP rule-of-origin requirement (costs of material produced plus processing must equal at least 35 percent of the appraised value of the product); and
- the country fails to supply complete documentation.

The President may waive CNL authority but there are limitations on this waiver. GSP law automatically waives all CNLs for GSP beneficiaries designated as LDBDCs. GSP law requires that all GSP articles be imported directly but GSP status still applies if the indirect shipment of a product takes place through free trade zones or entrepots.

free provisions have declined since 1998 as a proportion of total goods from the region. This corresponded with an increase in the proportion (over 25 percent) of CBI imports entering as MFN duty-free goods, reflecting the liberalization of U.S. tariffs under its Uruguay Round commitments. Apparel, previously excluded from preferential treatment in 2000, accounts for 43 percent of total exports. Other significant exports are cigars, mechanical and electrical equipment, fruits, and coffee.

### *The U.S. and Andean Trade Preferences*

U.S. trade preferences concerning this region have been provided for strategic reasons as evident in the 1991 Andean Trade Preference Act (ATPA) for Colombia, Peru, Ecuador, and Bolivia, reauthorized in 2002 as the Andean Trade Promotion and Drug Eradication Act (ATPDEA). Under the new act, Ecuador was not then eligible for preferences. In return for cooperating with the U.S. in controlling

**BOX 15.5 U.S. Generalized System of Preference: Annual Timetable**

| Action | Target Date |
|---|---|
| Deadline for the acceptance of review petitions | June 1 |
| Announcement for the petitions accepted for review | July 12 |
| Public hearings and submissions of written briefs | September/October |
| U.S. International Trade Commission (USITC) report on the economic impact of petitioned actions | December |
| Public comment on USITC report | December/January |
| Publication of the early warning list showing statistics over a 10-month period of GSP imports that were close to exceeding the CNL | February/March |
| Announcement of results of the reviews | April 1 |
| Effective date of Changes | July 1 |

*Source:* Office of the United States Trade Representative (USTR).

narcotics production and trade, the U.S. offers duty-free and duty-reduced access to the U.S. market for eligible products (numbering 5,600). These countries benefit from both ATPDEA and GSP preferences. In Congress's reauthorizing legislation, existing benefits were extended and expanded and duty-free access was provided for products not covered initially such as apparel, footwear, and tuna. Renewal also resulted in more conditions being imposed, ranging from labor rights and intellectual property rights to resolution of commercial disputes. The U.S. government, following a public comment period, determined that all countries (including Ecuador) were eligible for the expanded benefits.

In 1999, some two-thirds of U.S. imports from the then–ATPA countries were already duty-free, with most entering under provisions other than APTA. APTA beneficiary products include fresh-cut flowers (Colombia accounts for close to half of all U.S. imports), asparagus (Peru is the second-ranking supplier), and processed tuna (not in cans, with Ecuador as a leading provider). In 1999 the portion of exports that qualified exclusively under APTA was less than 10 percent. Of the region's products, coffee (Colombia, Ecuador), shrimps and bananas (Ecuador) are unconditionally free of duty under the general GSP tariff rates (see Kornis 2000).

### *The U.S. and the African Growth and Opportunity Act (AGOA)*

In 2000 Congress established a new framework for U.S. trade, investment, and development policy in sub-Saharan Africa with the African Growth and Opportunity Act (AGOA) for the (then) 34 beneficiaries, by expanding GSP benefits for eligible countries. AGOA increased preferential access of beneficiaries' exports in key areas such as clothing. Beneficiary countries receive duty-free and quota-free access for almost all products for eight years, without the GSP competitive needs limit applying to their exports. An additional 1,800 products, including selected apparel articles subject to special provisions (rules of origin and customs requirements), not available to other GSP countries, have been added to GSP benefits. Substantially all products from sub-Saharan Africa are now eligible to enter the U.S. duty-free. The U.S. imported US$8.2 billion of duty-free goods in 2001 under AGOA, representing about 40 percent of U.S. imports from sub-Saharan Africa. Approximately 17.7 percent of all imports in 2000 were covered under the GSP program. Transportation equipment (over 40 percent), miscellaneous manufactures (nearly 40 percent), and electronic products (37 percent) are the sectors benefiting the most from GSP benefits.

AGOA benefits are conditioned on a number of legislative requirements. In addition to market-based economy provisions such as eliminating trade barriers and efforts to combat corruption, there are requirements relating to U.S. national security, human rights, and international terrorism. The U.S. government conducts reviews of the GSP program and in 2000, Nigeria and Eritrea were added to the list of eligible countries while in 2001, a review of worker rights in Swaziland was terminated because the U.S. had found that Swaziland conformed to these GSP program requirements on worker rights (see table 15.5).

## European Union and Its Preferential Agreements

The EU's GSP and preferential arrangements "form a mosaic of tariffs, quotas and other restrictions on EU agricultural imports" (see Hasha 2002). The EU is the direct source of 40 percent of all preferential trade agreements notified to the WTO and because there is convincing evidence of trade diversion on both import and export sides, future EU policy on these agreements is relevant to the work of the WTO (Messerlin 2001) (see box 15.6).

In 1963 the European Communities and 18 newly independent countries (former colonies of three EC member states) signed the First Yaounde Convention resulting in 18 de facto bilateral, nonreciprocal free trade agreements. Since then, the EU has provided special nonreciprocal tariff reductions for 77 ACP countries under the Lomé Convention. This was renegotiated in 2000 as the Cotonou Agreement. Further unrestricted duty-free access for LDC countries for all products, excluding arms, has been provided under the 2001 "Everything But Arms" Agreement (EBA). (There are 48 LDC countries on the UN list and 39 are ACP countries. The non-ACP LDCs are Yemen, Afghanistan, Bangladesh, Maldives, Nepal, Bhutan, Myanmar, Lao People's Democratic Republic, and Cambodia. For Myanmar all GSP and EBA preferences are suspended). The EBA was initially proposed by the European Communities in 1997 in the preparations for the 1999 WTO Seattle Ministerial Conference. Owing to domestic pressure from agricultural groups, the proposal was amended to provide for longer transition periods with the phasing-out of duty on bananas by 2006 and sugar and rice by 2009. (See Page and Hewitt [2002], which argues that the EBA is trade diverting, discriminatory, and is provided for essentially political—and not development—motives.)

In 1971, the EU introduced its Generalized Scheme of Tariff Preferences. It now applies to most of the 143 independent countries and 36 dependent countries and territories.

Most-favored-nation tariffs on EU agricultural products are high—for example, dairy (ranging from 38.4 to 209.9 percent), cereals (39.2 to 101.1 percent), and sugar (21.4 to 114.4 percent). Imports are highest in the fish and fruits categories with tariffs for the former ranging between 9 and 23 percent and for the latter from 9.0 to 118.1 percent (see table 15.6).

The potential application of very high MFN tariffs enforces minimum import requirements and ensures that imports do not exceed tariff rate quota (TRQ) amounts. Most of the agricultural TRQs are part of preferential trading arrangements. EU concessions on agriculture remain limited (sugar, bananas, beef, and rum) as imports remain restricted to amounts consistent with the Common Agricultural Policy's (CAP) internal price objectives. The unconditional opening of markets to LDCs under the EBA policy was possible because their limited export agricultural potential in temperate products represented little threat to EU interests and domestic pressure groups. EU preferential trading arrangements do not create trade but determine the source of imports.

The EU's current GSP expires in 2004. Product exclusion applies to certain beneficiaries and sectors. The 65 countries benefiting only from GSP preferences are the transition economies and some Asian and Latin American countries, including nine LDCs. Nine countries including Brazil and China have graduated from nine sectors of the EU economy; Brazil, Argentina, Malaysia, and Thailand have lost preferences on specific agricultural commodities; and the Republic of Korea and Taiwan (China) have lost all preferences. Thailand and India lodged complaints in the WTO on the conditions under which the EU grants tariff preferences to developing countries under the GSP scheme (that is, the preferential discrimination). The European Communities settled a related WTO complaint by Brazil (WTO document WI/DS/209) on the form of a tariff-free quota on soluble coffee.

In 2001 the EU revised its GSP scheme to simplify the rules, to harmonize procedures on different arrangements, and to enhance the predictability relating to the eligibility of countries and sectors. Revisions addressed the issue of erosion of tariff preferences by applying "preference modulation" to two categories rather than four under the previous GSP scheme (modulation means that tariff reductions vary by product according to the "sensitivity" of the product for EU producers). Some countries receive incentives (that is, larger tariff reductions) on the condition that they take action on labor, environmental standards, and drugs.

**TABLE 15.5 U.S.–Sub-Saharan Africa Trade: Major U.S. Import Suppliers under the Generalized System of Preferences, and the African Growth and Opportunity Act (YTD Jan.–Jun., AGOA-Eligible Countries Only in US $ millions)**

| Country | AGOA including GSP provisions of the AGOA Act 2001 YTD | AGOA including GSP provisions of the AGOA Act 2002 YTD | GSP 2001 YTD | GSP 2002 YTD | Additional items for AGOA countries 2001 YTD | Additional items for AGOA countries 2002 YTD |
|---|---|---|---|---|---|---|
| Nigeria | 2,335,079 | 2,340,602 | 172 | 75 | 2,334,907 | 2,340,527 |
| Gabon | 448,501 | 608,356 | 18 | 121 | 448,483 | 608,235 |
| South Africa | 395,690 | 556,955 | 260,193 | 233,082 | 135,497 | 323,873 |
| Lesotho | 4,905 | 142,208 | 0 | 169 | 4,905 | 142,039 |
| Madagascar | 13,749 | 61,070 | 3,987 | 3,200 | 9,762 | 57,871 |
| Mauritius | 12,785 | 55,236 | 4,203 | 2,452 | 8,582 | 52,784 |
| Kenya | 17,887 | 48,875 | 1,738 | 2,243 | 16,149 | 46,632 |
| Congo (ROC) | 13,385 | 45,430 | 65 | 2,817 | 13,320 | 42,614 |
| Swaziland | 23 | 28,986 | 17 | 48 | 7 | 28,939 |
| Ghana | 24,784 | 22,904 | 5,839 | 5,856 | 18,945 | 17,048 |
| Cameroon | 16,541 | 22,799 | 293 | 142 | 16,248 | 22,657 |
| Malawi | 16,744 | 21,757 | 16,744 | 1,425 | 0 | 20,332 |
| Cote d'Ivoire | 6,525 | 15,729 | 6,525 | 8,896 | 0 | 6,833 |
| Botswana | 558 | 1,881 | 558 | 440 | 0 | 1,441 |
| Ethiopia | 270 | 1,349 | 270 | 705 | 0 | 643 |
| Tanzania | 206 | 572 | 195 | 286 | 10 | 286 |
| Senegal | 312 | 222 | 312 | 221 | 0 | 0 |
| Namibia | 2 | 136 | 2 | 133 | 0 | 3 |
| Mali | 142 | 90 | 142 | 89 | 0 | 1 |
| Sierra Leone | 191 | 43 | 191 | 43 | 0 | 0 |
| Zambia | 724 | 42 | 714 | 18 | 10 | 24 |
| Guinea | 86 | 28 | 86 | 28 | 0 | 0 |
| Mozambique | 21 | 17 | 21 | 4 | 0 | 13 |
| Mauritania | 0 | 15 | 0 | 15 | 0 | 0 |
| Uganda | 72 | 15 | 72 | 6 | 0 | 9 |
| Rwanda | 33 | 10 | 33 | 10 | 0 | 0 |
| Niger | 42 | 6 | 42 | 6 | 0 | 0 |
| Benin | 0 | 0 | 0 | 0 | 0 | 0 |
| Eritrea | 0 | 0 | 0 | 0 | 0 | 0 |
| Seychelles | 2,233 | 0 | 2,233 | 0 | 0 | 0 |
| Sao Tome & Prin | 0 | 0 | 0 | 0 | 0 | 0 |
| Djibouti | 0 | 0 | 0 | 0 | 0 | 0 |
| Cape Verde | 75 | 0 | 75 | 0 | 0 | 0 |
| Guinea-Bissau | 0 | 0 | 0 | 0 | 0 | 0 |
| Cen African Rep | 0 | 0 | 0 | 0 | 0 | 0 |
| Chad | 0 | 0 | 0 | 0 | 0 | 0 |
| Total | 3,311,565 | 3,975,333 | 304,742 | 262,530 | 3,006,823 | 3,712,804 |

Note: Figures do not add to the totals shown due to rounding.

*Source:* Compiled by the U.S. International Trade Commission 2002.

## BOX 15.6 Parties to Regional Trade or Preferential EU Trade Agreements in Force as of April 2002

**Europe Agreements:** Bulgaria, the Czech Republic, Estonia, Hungary, Latvia, Lithuania, Poland, Romania, Slovak Republic, Slovenia.

**Association Agreements:** Cyprus, Malta, Turkey.

**Stabilization and Association Agreements:** Croatia, Former Yugoslav Republic of Macedonia (FYROM).

**Euro-Mediterranean Association Agreements:** Israel, Morocco, the Palestinian Authority, Tunisia.

**Cooperation Agreements** (Euro-Med Association Agreements concluded, but not in effect, or under negotiation): Algeria, Egypt, Jordan, Lebanon, Syria.

**Other Free-Trade Agreements:** Denmark (Faroe Islands), Iceland, Liechtenstein, Mexico, Norway, South Africa, Switzerland.

**Other Customs Unions:** Andorra, San Marino.

**Association of Overseas Countries and Territories (OCT):** *Anguilla*, Antarctica, Aruba, British Antarctic Territory, British Indian Ocean Territory, British Virgin Islands, Cayman Islands, Falkland Islands, French Polynesia, French Southern and Antarctic Territories, Greenland, *Mayotte*, *Montserrat*, Netherlands Antilles, New Caledonia, Pitcairn, *Saint Helena, Ascension Island, Tristan da Cunha*; South Georgia and the South Sandwich Islands, *St. Pierre and Miquelon*, *Turks and Caicos Islands*, *Wallis and Fortuna Islands*.

**EU-African, Caribbean and Pacific (ACP) Partnership:** *Angola*, Antigua and Barbuda, Bahamas, Barbados, Belize, *Benin*, Botswana, *Burkina Faso*, *Burundi*, Cameroon, *Cap Verde*, *Central African Republic*, *Chad*, *Comoros*, Congo, Cook Islands, *Dem. Rep. of Congo*, Cote d'Ivoire, *Djibouti*, Dominica, Dominican Republic, *Equatorial Guinea*, *Eritrea*, *Ethiopia*, Federated States of Micronesia, Fiji, Gabon, *Gambia*, Ghana, Grenada, *Guinea*, *Guinea-Bissau*, Guyana, *Haiti*, Jamaica, Kenya, *Kiribati*, *Lesotho*, *Liberia*, *Madagascar*, *Malawi*, *Mali*, Marshall Islands, *Mauritania*, Mauritius, *Mozambique*, Namibia, Nauru, *Niger*, Nigeria, Niue Islands, Palau, Papua New Guinea, *Rwanda*, St. Christopher and Nevis, St. Lucia, St. Vincent and the Grenadines, *Samoa*, *Sao Tome and Principe*, *Senegal*, Seychelles, *Sierra Leone*, *Solomon Islands*, *Somalia*, South Africa, *Sudan*, Suriname, Swaziland, *Tanzania*, *Togo*, Tonga, Trinidad and Tobago, *Tuvalu*, *Uganda*, *Vanuatu*, *Zambia*, Zimbabwe.

**Autonomous Trade Measures for the Western Balkans:** Albania, Bosnia-Herzegovina, the Federal Republic of Yugoslavia, Kosovo.

**Generalized System of Preferences (GSP) only:** *Afghanistan*, Argentina, Armenia, Azerbaijan, Bahrain, *Bangladesh*, Belarus, *Bhutan*, Bolivia, Brazil, Brunei Darussalam, *Cambodia*, Chile, China, Colombia, Costa Rica, Cuba, East Timor, Ecuador, El Salvador, Georgia, Guatemala, Honduras, India, Indonesia, Iran, Iraq, Kazakhstan, Kyrgyzstan, Kuwait, *Lao PDR*, Libya, Malaysia, *Maldives*, Moldova, Mongolia, *Myanmar*, *Nepal*, Nicaragua, Oman, Pakistan, Panama, Paraguay, Peru, Philippines, Qatar, Russian Federation, Saudi Arabia, Sri Lanka, Tajikistan, Thailand, Turkmenistan, Ukraine, United Arab Emirates, Uruguay, Uzbekistan, Republica Bolivariana de Venezuela, Vietnam, *Republic of Yemen*; American Samoa, Bermuda, Bouvet Island, Cocos Islands, Cook Islands, Gibraltar, Guam, Heard and McDonald Islands, Macao, Norfolk Island, Northern Mariana Islands, United States Minor Outlying Islands, Tokelau Islands, Virgin Islands (USA).

*Note*: Least-developed countries (LDCs) (or economies) in *italics*.
*Source:* Adapted from WTO Secretariat, based on Developing Country Trade (2001).

### *The EU and Africa, Caribbean, and Pacific Countries: Cotonou Agreement*

Under the Cotonou Agreement, duty- and quota-free access is provided for all industrialized products and 80 percent of agricultural products. Concessions on agriculture have been limited by quotas or only small tariff reductions on most products supported by the EU's CAP. Of particular importance are the ACP protocols for beef and sugar—specifically, EU imports of 52,100 tons of beef from six ACP countries and 1.2 million tons of sugar from 13 other ACP countries and India. Access was further expanded under the EBA initiative for LDCs.

### *The EU's Euro-Mediterranean Partnership*

The EU has provided Mediterranean countries with preferential market access reflecting long-standing trade relationships and important political associations. These countries receive reduced tariffs and

**TABLE 15.6 EU: Applied MFN tariffs by HS Chapters 01–22, 2002 (percent and US$ Billions)**

| HS code | Number of 8-digit HS lines | Description | Simple average (%) | MFN 2002 Min. (%) | MFN 2002 Max. (%) | Standard deviation (%) | Imports 2000 (US$ billion) |
|---|---|---|---|---|---|---|---|
| Total | 10,400 | | 6.4 | 0 | 209.9 | 11.3 | 807.4 |
| | 2,354 | HS Chapters 01–24 | 15.9 | 0 | 209.9 | 20.5 | 56.9 |
| | 8,046 | HS Chapters 25–97 | 3.8 | 0 | 39.8 | 3.7 | 750.5 |
| 1 | 55 | Live animals | 20.6 | 0 | 107.8 | 30.2 | 0.8 |
| 2 | 236 | Meat and edible meat offal | 28.3 | 0 | 192.2 | 31.1 | 2.7 |
| 3 | 324 | Fish & crustacean, mollusk & other aquatic invertebrate | 9.8 | 0 | 23 | 5.7 | 8.6 |
| 4 | 175 | Dairy prod.,birds' eggs, natural honey, edible prod. | 38.4 | 0 | 209.9 | 36.8 | 1.0 |
| 5 | 21 | Products of animal origin, n.e.s or included | 0.2 | 0 | 5.1 | 1.1 | 0.8 |
| 6 | 42 | Live trees & other plant, bulb, root, cut flowers, etc. | 6 | 0 | 10.9 | 3.4 | 1.0 |
| 7 | 108 | Edible vegetables and certain roots and tubers | 12.7 | 0 | 150.1 | 21.3 | 2.4 |
| 8 | 128 | Edible fruit and nuts, peel of citrus fruit or melons | 9 | 0 | 118.1 | 11.5 | 7.3 |
| 9 | 42 | Coffee, tea, mate and spices | 3.1 | 0 | 12.5 | 4.3 | 4.7 |
| 10 | 55 | Cereals | 39.2 | 0 | 101.1 | 27.7 | 1.4 |
| 11 | 83 | Prod. Mill. Indust., malt, starches, inulin, wheat gluten | 22.2 | 1.2 | 84.4 | 16.8 | 0.1 |
| 12 | 79 | Oilseeds, oleaginous, fruit, misc, grain, seed, fruit, etc. | 1.8 | 0 | 52.3 | 6.2 | 4.9 |
| 13 | 18 | Lac, gums, resins & other vegetable saps & extracts | 2.2 | 0 | 19.2 | 5.1 | 0.4 |
| 14 | 8 | Vegetable plaiting materials, vegetable products | 0 | 0 | 0 | 0 | 0.1 |
| 15 | 128 | Animal/vegetable fats & oils & their cleavage products | 8.9 | 0 | 75.8 | 13.2 | 1.7 |
| 16 | 92 | Prep. of meat, fish or crustaceans, mollusks, etc. | 18.5 | 0 | 97.2 | 11.5 | 2.5 |
| 17 | 47 | Sugars and sugar confectionery | 21.4 | 2.1 | 114.4 | 24 | 1.3 |
| 18 | 27 | Cocoa and cocoa preparations | 11.8 | 0 | 68.9 | 13 | 1.6 |
| 19 | 51 | Prep. of cereal, flour, starch/ milk, pastrycooks' products | 16.4 | 7.6 | 49.6 | 10.5 | 0.5 |
| 20 | 321 | Prep. of vegetables, fruit, nuts or other parts of plants | 20.6 | 0 | 146.9 | 13.2 | 2.7 |
| 21 | 42 | Miscellaneous edible preparations | 9.6 | 0 | 21.1 | 5.1 | 1.0 |
| 22 | 175 | Beverages, spirits and vinegar | 5.5 | 0 | 58.6 | 9 | 2.8 |

*Source:* WTO 2002d.

valuable import quotas for fruits and vegetables. The trade objective of the "Euro-Mediterranean Partnership" launched in 1995 is a free trade area by 2010. Euro-Mediterranean association agreements have been concluded between the EU and Tunisia, Israel, Morocco, Egypt, Jordan, and the Palestinian Liberation Organization. These association agreements replace earlier nonreciprocal arrangements and provide for a greater degree of liberalization by the EU's partners than did earlier cooperation agreements and cover concessions on certain agricultural and fishery products and industrial products. They constitute a progressive liberalization of trade through a widening of tariff rate quotas as well. The liberalization timetable varies for the partners—with immediate application for the EU and with a transition period for full implementation by the other partners, except for Israel, whose inclusion is immediate. The transition period is 15 years for Egypt and 12 years for Morocco and Tunisia (see Guth and Chomo 2002, and the EC Web site at http://www.europa.eu.int/comm/external_relations/euromed/index.htm).

### *EU Trade Agreements and the WTO*

EU agreements such as the Cotonou Agreement have been criticized on the grounds of discrimination (that is, non-ACP/Mediterranean countries are excluded) and product coverage. Hence, the challenges in the GATT and more recently in the WTO have been made on the grounds of discrimination and noncompliance with international trade rules. The challenges focused on EU import regimes (for bananas) that favored EU distributors over other distributors and former colonies over other countries—and the general issues of graduation and tariff concessions requiring adherence to conditions on environment, labor, and drugs. Challengers see these provisions as inconsistent with the Enabling Clause's provision of general and nondiscriminatory preferences for all developing countries.

Since 1996 the EU has acted to make its arrangements compatible with WTO rules, by renegotiating and converting current agreements to reciprocal free trade areas. In September 2002, the EU and ACP countries launched negotiations for Economic Partnership Agreements (EPAs) to shift to new trade arrangements (EU Press Release, Brussels July 12, 2002). The basic principles and timeframe for EPA negotiations were set out in the Cotonou Agreement. Seventy-six countries are eligible for EPAs. South Africa and Cuba are also ACP members but EPAs will not be negotiated with them because Cuba as is not a signatory to the Cotonou Agreement and South Africa concluded a Trade, Development, and Cooperation Agreement with the EU in 2000. In addition, the EU has FTAs with Mexico (2001) and various non-EU European countries (see box 15.6). In 2000, the EU began negotiations with MERCOSUR and Chile on separate free trade areas.

WTO provisions for FTAs provide for free trade for substantially all products and no quota restrictions. The EU's FTA agreements include TRQs for sensitive agricultural products that compete with EU products. Its approach has been that these quotas are based on a historical relationship and can be maintained without waivers in FTA agreements. The EU/Mexico agreement covers key trade areas, market access, rules of origin, sanitary and phytosanitary issues, and technical regulations. For agricultural and fisheries products covered by the agreement, the EU is to eliminate tariffs for most products by 2008 and Mexico by 2010. Tariff quotas apply to certain products. The agreement provides for the total liberalization of 95 percent of historical EU imports, but for agriculture, only 62 percent of historical trade will be fully liberalized.

## Other Trade Arrangements: AFTA, NAFTA, and APEC

There are other agreements/arrangements that are of interest because agriculture is a sensitive area and treated accordingly, and because of their contribution to trade liberalization and growth within the region. Countries with FTAs benefit when lower-cost inputs from partner countries displace higher-cost goods manufactured domestically (the trade-creating effect). A possible cost is that trade diversion may occur if the removal of tariff barriers causes high-cost imports from partner countries to replace low-cost imports from the rest of the world. A growing percentage of world trade has been created by regional trade liberalization. After controlling for distance, economic size, and other factors, Frankel finds strong effects for the Association of Southeast Asian Nations (ASEAN) countries with trade increasing an estimated fivefold for its members. The Andean Pact and MERCOSUR are both estimated to increase trade by a factor of 2.5. Intra-EU trade is estimated to be 65 percent larger than prior to the formation of the EU because of the common market among members (see Anderson 2001).

### *AFTA: The ASEAN Free Trade Agreement*

The ASEAN Free Trade Agreement (AFTA), signed in 1992, initially defined "free trade" as the reduction of tariffs to within the range of 0–5 percent but for "highly sensitive" products such as rice and sugar the tariff rate was permitted to remain at higher levels at the end of the implementation period. ASEAN members have promoted economic cooperation through trade with the objectives of creating a single ASEAN market and with helping their members, through greater interregional trade, strengthen their competitive advantage with the rest of the world. To meet the requirements of accession to AFTA, Cambodia and the Lao PDR were required to modernize their trade procedures.

AFTA membership and regional linkages have been a critical factor in growth of manufactures in Asian LDCs. Thailand's economic growth has resulted in it being graduated from both the U.S. and EU GSP programs. The creation of an industrial zone along the border between Thailand and Cambodia provided Thai manufacturers with an opportunity to relocate their production and thereby benefit from low Cambodian labor costs. Cambodia's preferential market access to the EU and U.S. markets under the GSP program demonstrates that such an arrangement represents an opportunity for greater economic growth in both countries.

### *NAFTA: North American Free Trade Agreement*

For the three countries of this agreement—the U.S., Canada, and Mexico—agriculture has been a sensitive subject. NAFTA provides for the retention of TRQs with prohibitive out-of-quota tariffs on a number of products, notably bilateral Canada–U.S. trade in dairy products, U.S. and Mexican exports of poultry and eggs to Canada, Mexican exports of sugar to both U.S. and Canada, and U.S. maize exports to Mexico. Canada's free trade agreement with Chile contains similar exclusions for dairy products, poultry, and eggs. In these agreements there are other examples, again almost exclusively agricultural, in which the period for phasing out trade barriers substantially exceeds the 10-year period set in the Understanding on the Interpretation of Article XXIV of GATT 1994. For most commodities NAFTA's influence has been relatively small, but for a handful of commodities the agreement has had a much larger impact with increased volumes of trade. Among U.S. exports to Canada, wheat products, beef and veal, and cotton have shown the greatest increase while among U.S. exports to Mexico, rice, cotton, fresh apples and pears, cattle and calves, dairy products, and processed potatoes have shown the greatest increase. The greatest increase in agricultural exports from Canada to the U.S. has come from beef and veal and wheat products, and from Mexico to the U.S. the items showing the greatest increase are sugar, peanuts, cattle and calves, tomatoes, and wheat products.

### *APEC: Not a Preferential Trade Agreement But Still Free Trade by 2020*

In the 1994 Bogor Declaration, the Asia Pacific Economic Co-operation Forum's (APEC's) members committed themselves to the establishment of free trade and investment in the Asia-Pacific region, through a process based on "open regionalism." The declaration called for a tariff-free region for developed economies by 2010 and for developing economies by 2020. The focus of APEC's nondiscriminatory approach to regional liberalization is in accordance with its "open regionalism" approach, designed to overcome political considerations among members. "Open regionalism" came to be understood as the gradual reduction of trade barriers on a nondiscriminatory basis; it is explicitly designed to not be a preferential trading arrangement—as APEC has provided, throughout its existence, strong support for the WTO multilateral approach to the liberalization of global trade. A key component of APEC is building capacity for liberalization through the pooling of expertise and the development of shared understandings on the principles of nondiscrimination and "standstill"—that is, a commitment not to raise barriers in the future in 15 action areas, including tariffs (see Scollay 2001).

Within APEC, some members are also parties to preferential trade agreements with different approaches to agriculture. For example, the bilateral Closer Economic Relations agreement (CER) between Australia and New Zealand (ANZCERTA) is the only agreement that meets the GATT 1994 Article XXIV requirement to cover "substantially all" trade.

## Exploring the Benefits of Preferential Treatment

Lower tariffs and quotas provided market access through the various GSP-type programs. This access was expected to enhance the competitive advantage of developing-country exporters and to produce faster growth in their economies. Expected benefits of trade preferences have been described in terms of "hard" economic advantages such as better access to developed-country markets, larger volumes of exports, higher prices earned, improved economic welfare, more jobs, and more rapid economic growth; or "soft" benefits such as a familiarity with markets in developed countries, growing awareness of the need to produce high quality articles and more export-oriented attitudes, and new business alliances (Tangermann 2001).

The critical factor in preference programs is the product coverage benefiting from preferences (lower tariffs and quotas), and the ability of the recipient country to provide those products. For many developing countries, products of greatest interest are agriculture and textile and apparel but these have been excluded or severely restricted as "sensitive" articles. Initially preferential programs were provided for manufactured and semi-manufactured products, with very limited coverage of agricultural products. Successive GATT negotiations have resulted in low MFN tariffs on most industrial products. For agriculture and processed products, even with the URAA, market access is constrained by high MFN tariffs, with much higher tariffs and limited quota access for processed agricultural products. A World Bank study (Hoekman, Ng, and Olarreaga 2003) on the economic impacts of trade preferences on extending the EU EBA initiative (duty- and quota-free market access for tariff peak products) into Quad countries found that LDC exports would increase by 11 percent. A second study by UNCTAD/Commonwealth Secretariat (2002) showed only a 3 percent increase in exports. Both studies ignore (but recognize) the problem of low utilization rates, weak export capacity and supply constraints, and that the benefits are likely to be lower than the simulations (see table 15.7). Economists have tried to quantify the benefits of preferences by examining the utilization rate of those preferences or by examining the value of margin of preference. Economists have also qualified the results of these studies (Tangermann 2001). UNCTAD reported that the utilization rate (that is, the ratio between imports actually receiving the preferences and total imports eligible for preferences) was 77 percent for the U.S., 34 percent for non-ACP LDCs of the EU, 59 percent for Canada, and 73 percent for Japan. Utilization rates vary among LDCs and can be concentrated; for example, Bangladesh was a key LDC exporter to the EU, Norway, Canada, Japan, and Switzerland (Laird, Safadi, and Turrini). The utilization rate can be affected by a number of factors such as capacity to supply (that is, productive capacity), rules of origin requirements relating to imported material and components, social (labor) and environmental requirements, insecurity relating to market access caused by the unilateral nature of GSP programs, and lack of human resources and institutional capability to take advantage of preferential arrangements, such as knowledge of the importing country's tariff structure. Overcoming these constraints requires investment, which is not encouraged by the unpredictability of programs. The high utilization rate associated with Japan's GSP program has been attributed in part to the program's stability—as evident from its expansion in 2001 for 10 years until March 31, 2011. In comparison, the U.S. GSP program, which as noted above has been renewed 6 times in the past 8 years, makes the scheme's continuation difficult to predict and affects both exporters and importers as well as potential investors.

Nontariff barriers (NTBs) such as quotas, technical standards, and sanitary and phytosanitary measures may be a serious impediment to high utilization rates and trading opportunities for LDCs. These apply particularly to agricultural goods and textiles. It has been estimated that 42 percent of LDC exports of agricultural and fishery products face NTBs in Quad countries; for textiles and clothing, the corresponding figure is 66–69 percent (UNCTAD 2002, table 21).

Improved market access is meaningless, however, if developing countries are unable to use such access owing to domestic reasons or the qualified nature of the access. According to UNCTAD, available estimates suggest that in the late 1990s about half of LDC exports to Quad markets, potentially eligible for GSP preferential treatment, did not qualify—because of NTBs. This resulted in unnecessary payment of MFN customs duties, rejected imports, unnecessary testing, spoilage, legal fees, and foregone opportunities in general.

Preference margins and their size is another way of trying to measure the benefits of preferences. The preference margin per unit of product

**TABLE 15.7 Effective Benefits of Quad Countries: Generalized System of Preferences for Least-Developed Countries, Late 1990s**

| | *Imports from LDCs* | | | | | | | |
|---|---|---|---|---|---|---|---|---|
| | Total imports 1 | Dutiable imports 2 | Covered by GSP scheme 3 | Receiving preferential treatment 4 | Total/ dutiable imports (2/1) | GSP-eligible/ dutiable imports (3/2) | Utilization rate (4/3) | Utility rate (4/2) |
| | $ millions | | | | percentage | | | |
| Canada | 256 | 92 | 10 | 6 | 36 | 11 | 59 | 6 |
| EU | 3,562 | 3,101 | 3,075 | 1,035 | 87 | 99 | 34 | 33 |
| Japan | 1,248 | 765 | 314 | 229 | 61 | 41 | 73 | 30 |
| U. S. | 4,975 | 4,247 | 2,282 | 1,747 | 85 | 54 | 77 | 41 |
| U. S., excl. minerals | 2,613 | 2,078 | 113 | 89 | 80 | 5 | 79 | 4 |
| Total | 10,041 | 8,205 | 5,681 | 3,017 | 82 | 69 | 53 | 37 |
| Total, excl. U. S. minerals | 7,679 | 6,036 | 3,512 | 1,359 | 79 | 58 | 39 | 23 |

*Note*: EU excludes Africa, Caribbean, and Pacific LDCs and U.S. excludes Haiti, a beneficiary of the Caribbean Basin Initiative. Canada and U.S. are 1998 data. EU is 1999 data. Japan is 1997 data.

*Source*: UNCTAD 2002, part 2, ch. 3.

exported to a given country is the difference between the MFN tariff and the preferential tariff for that product, both tariffs being expressed as percentages. The identification and measurement of margins is difficult because it requires establishing which benefit was actually caused by trade preferences, that is, the with-and-without comparison. Other factors may affect market access. Tangermann (2001) discusses the work by a number of economists but notes that "their results should be interpreted with much caution. In particular, the actual welfare effects of trade preferences for the recipient countries may deviate significantly from such mechanically calculated preference margins and usually they will be far smaller. For the same reason the actual economic effects of MFN tariff reductions for preference-receiving countries may be considerably smaller than the erosion of preference margins estimated in this mechanical way." With these caveats in mind, 1997 preference-margin data for products into the EU show that for LDCs among African ACP countries (AACP) the aggregate preference margin under GSP would be only 7 percent less than under the Lomé Convention, while the remaining AACP members would lose around 85 percent of the preference margin if GSP rather than the Lomé Convention was applied to their access to the EU (see table 15.8).

A study by Stoeckel and Borrell (2001) examines and discusses the economic effects of preferences on the receiving country, on the granting country, and on third countries. To access the issue of diversion and the importance of preferences, the study uses the GTAP global trade model with trade data and preferences for 1997 under three scenarios: removal of all trade barriers facing non-Cairns Group developing countries, unilateral reform, and multilateral reform. Results are summarized as follows: preferential trade can result in trade diversion; unilateral trade reform by developing countries can be more beneficial than trade preferences; and multilateral nondiscriminatory trade liberalization is the best policy.

## Costs of Trade Preferences

### *Distortion in Developing-Country Economies?*

Preferential access may result in hindering both the economy and the industry by diverting trade opportunities away from preferred, more efficient producers to less competitive suppliers. It also biases resource allocation to industries that are noncompetitive and in the long run takes resources away

**TABLE 15.8 Preference Margins for Selected Groups of Agricultural Products Exported from the AACP to the EU, Lomé Preferences and GSP Preferences Compared, 1999 EU Tariffs (1997 Trade Data)**

| Product group | *Value of preference margin, Least-Developed AACP Countries* | | *Value of preference margin, Other AACP Countries,* | |
|---|---|---|---|---|
| | Lomé preferences (million ECU) | GSP preferences (percentage of Lomé) | Lomé preferences (million ECU) | GSP preferences (percentage of Lomé) |
| Fish | 41.7 | 41.7 (100%) | 115.1 | 14.9 (12.9%) |
| Tobacco | 29.7 | 29.7 (100%) | 38.4 | 10.3 (26.9%) |
| Fresh fruit and vegetables | 3.8 | 3.9 (101%) | 18.8 | 4.0 (21.0%) |
| Processed fruit and vegetables | 0.7 | 0.5 (68.4%) | 19.8 | 2.2 (10.9%) |
| Cereals | 0.0 | 0.0 (0%) | 0.0 | 0 |
| Dairy products | 1.3 | 0.0 (0%) | 0.0 | 0 |
| Beef—general Lomé preferences | 6.0 | 2.0 (33.1%) | 11.1 | 0 |
| Sugar products—general Lomé preferences | 0.5 | 0.0 (0%) | 0.5 | 0 |
| **Total of above products** | **83.7** | **77.8 (93.0%)** | **203.7** | **31.4 (15.4%)** |

*Note:* In this table, 0.0 denotes a positive value less than 0.1, while 0 denotes a zero value.
*Source:* Tangermann 2001.

from more efficient industries and diverts attention from multilateral reform. The sugar and banana industries in some developing countries illustrate these situations.

According to Page and Hewitt (2002) for many of the small Caribbean countries sugar is probably barely viable in the long term without the EU Sugar Protocol (SP). Caribbean countries could live with a gradual decrease in European prices but would not be able to compete with Asian LDCs. St. Kitts and Nevis, Trinidad and Tobago, and Jamaica would be forced out of the sugar business if the EU protocol were to be revoked. Trinidad and Tobago and Barbados would probably benefit from abandoning sugar as this would require them to diversify their economies. For Jamaica, given its costs, it would not be able to compete on the world market and the situation would be difficult. The EU is a very important market for Mauritius with sugar representing 46.6 percent of the value of total agricultural exports to the EU in 1999 (see table 15.9). The value of the preference margin under the Lomé Convention was 4.8 percent while under the SP it is 56.7 percent. As a result, this relationship has locked resources into an industry that, despite subsidies through preferential access to the EU, is struggling—and represented a loss to the economy in 1999. Issues of land allotment, labor laws, and zoning have precluded a rationalization within the sugar industry, and its structure and organizational model have remained unchanged because the industry has been insulated from world markets.

The EBA Agreement provides additional sugar access for LDCs into the EU and given the uncertainty regarding the future of the Sugar Protocol, some sugar producers in SP quota countries such as Mauritius are already investing in sugar industry capacity in LDCs such as Mozambique, so that links to markets can be quickly established (UNCTAD 2002). EU preferences for bananas have induced some African countries to invest in banana production and to try to compete with the low-cost Latin American producers, despite the long-term negative impact of this crop on African land and water

**TABLE 15.9 Preference Margins for Protocol Beef and Sugar Exported from Individual AACP Countries to the European Union under Lomé Provisions, 1999 EU Tariffs (1997 Trade Data)**

| Product and country | Value of preference margin (million ECU) | Percentage of value of total agricultural export to EU of country concerned |
|---|---|---|
| **Protocol beef** | | |
| Botswana | 38.4 | 88.5 |
| Kenya | 0 | 0 |
| Madagascar | 2.3 | 1.2 |
| Namibia | 21.9 | 13.0 |
| Swaziland | 1.1 | 0.8 |
| Zimbabwe | 23.4 | 5.5 |
| **Protocol sugar** | | |
| Congo | 4.1 | 28.0 |
| Kenya | 0 | 0 |
| Madagascar | 5.4 | 2.7 |
| Malawi | 11.0 | 5.3 |
| Mauritius | 168.8 | 46.6 |
| Swaziland | 63.3 | 48.9 |
| Tanzania | 4.0 | 2.9 |
| Uganda | 0 | 0 |

*Source:* Tangermann 2001.

resources (see Stoeckel and Borrell 2001). Developing countries receiving preferential access for sugar (into the EU and the U.S.) and bananas (into the EU) are likely to face difficulties if and when their preferential access erodes significantly or is eliminated.

### *Rules of Origin*

The value of preferences can be eroded by rules of origin (ROO), which are unilateral domestic content requirements. These are seen as a tool of protectionism and are described by Hirsch (2002) as "constituting an indispensable component of any discriminatory arrangement." As there is no uniformity in the various GSP schemes, there is no uniformity of rules. If conditions relating to ROO are complex, preferences often remain unused because meeting these rules is simply too burdensome for many smaller LDCs. In the NAFTA there are over 200 pages devoted to ROO. In developed countries, most rules are formulated in an extremely complex and technical form, requiring special expertise to assess their impact.

Under AGOA margins of preference are substantial for textile and apparel products, other light manufactures, and food products. According to an International Monetary Fund (IMF)/World Bank paper (2002), the administrative requirements involved in documenting eligibility may explain the limited use made of AGOA provisions. By October 2002 only 15 countries had used the AGOA provisions, with most benefits accruing to four countries—Gabon, Lesotho, Nigeria, and South Africa—with fuel accounting for 85 percent of AGOA imports (see also Mattoo, Roy, and Subramanian 2002).

Under each GSP scheme ROO reduces the efficiency of the trade involved and may absorb scarce resources and political capital that might otherwise be used in support of broader-based multilateral and regional initiatives. As tariffs are reduced, the widening use of ROO is increasingly seen as a measure to restrict trade (Hirsch 2002).[5]

The 1994 WTO Agreement on Rules of Origin deals with harmonization at the global level and therefore is not concerned with preferential arrangements. A survey of domestic content rules included in the various trade agreements and non-preferential regulations shows that most local content rates are within the range of 35–62.5 percent, with 62.5 percent applying to certain automobiles under NAFTA and 35 percent provided for in the 1985 Israel–U.S. Free Trade Agreement and in programs such as GSP and CBI.

## BOX 15.7 The Americas: Trade Diversion: Displacement from Markets

Different preferential treatment relating to tuna by the United States in its NAFTA and ATPA agreements had the potential to create a problem for AFTA countries. Until the 2002 extension of ATPA (now the ATPDEA)—which, among other provisions, lowered tariffs on tuna in pouches—ATPA members were concerned that the NAFTA agreement would result in a new competitor in the tuna trade with the United States because under NAFTA, U.S. duty on canned tuna from Mexico will be eliminated by 2008. With tuna from other countries subject to a duty ranging from 6 to 35 percent, the tariff advantage provided an incentive for Mexico to build up its tiny tuna industry. Such a build-up would have created a serious threat to ATPDEA countries as this preferential access to the United States would have made a new competitor out of Mexico and Central America. Legislation creating comparable market access conditions (and lower tariffs) for these beneficiary countries may present a problem for the Philippines, which exports tuna to the U.S. market under less favorable access conditions.

### Multilateral Agreements Versus Free Trade Agreements: Political Economy Costs?

During the 1990s, with the proliferation of trade agreements, there was concern among trade policymakers that such agreements would detract from efforts to obtain multilateral trade liberalization through the WTO. This concern has continued to the extent that WTO Director General Supachai warned members in November 2002 that "by discriminating against third countries and creating a complex network of trade regimes, such agreements pose systemic risk to the global trading system" (quoted in the Financial Times—see de Jonquieres 2002). With their tariff preferences, trade agreements meant that there were winners and losers: in other words, the article or commodity that received the preference and the country that was a member of the agreement was a "winner," while nonmembers were seen as "losers" (see boxes 15.7 and 15.8).

Given such a situation, trade agreements were considered a poor substitute for multilateral trade liberalization. However, fears that these trade agreements represented stumbling blocks and not building blocks for trade liberalization have not eventuated. APEC is not a preferential trade agreement but its ultimate goal is trade liberalization. An examination of APEC's careful policy approach of open regionalism shows that its activities reinforce the multilateral approach. If anything, APEC has acted as a catalyst for negotiations on a range of issues. This was evident in the case of the Information Technology Agreement adopted at the 1996 Singapore WTO Ministerial as a result of a well-structured and coordinated APEC initiative.

Another political economy cost can result when a trade arrangement creates a lack of interest in liberalizing trade in the product where the preferences currently apply. The most often cited examples of this are the access provided on sugar by the U.S. and on sugar and bananas by the EU. Given the value of the preferences some developing countries have little interest in seeing the liberalization of trade for these two commodities. Some reports indicate that the EU has been able to obtain support in the WTO agriculture negotiations for its position on the multifunctional approach to agriculture from some countries that clearly benefit from access to EU markets.

In terms of the budget/development debate in developed countries and the politics of budgetary support for developing countries, trade preferences may be a factor. These are not as visible in budgets as direct aid and therefore may be more easily obtained, provided that domestic industry interest groups do not take political action to counter efforts to provide such preferential access.

### Alternative Options in Trade Negotiations: What Is the Future of Trade Preferences?

As the current round of trade negotiations will seek further reduction in tariffs (especially on processed agricultural products), greater access under TRQs, and simplification of quota administration, there is likely to be some erosion in the value of preferences (in other words, reduced tariffs)

**BOX 15.8 Chile: Strategy for Trade Growth: Access or Diversion?**

Chile currently follows a strategy of negotiating "additive regionalism," that is, bilateral free trade agreements with all of its significant trading partners. In addition to its free trade area with Mercosur, it has agreements with Canada, Mexico, and the European Union and in June 2003 signed one with the United States. One study examining Chile's regional arrangements found that only Chile's agreements with Northern partners (Canada and the European Union and eventually with the United States) provide sufficient market access to overcome trade diversion costs. Owing to preferential market access, however, Chile's strategy is likely to yield gains that are greater than static welfare gains from unilateral free trade. Economic modeling of the results of NAFTA, Mercosur and the additive regionalism approach all point to the usual impetus of improved market access in preferential trading areas. Even for the Chile/Mercosur agreement, if Chile were to lower its external tariff, reducing trade diversion, would be beneficial.

provided to developing countries under current preferential arrangements (see table 15.10; see also Tangermann [2001] for a discussion on the issues of both erosion and compensation for such erosion). These arrangements, whether resulting from GSP-type schemes or from trade agreements, have been established outside of the GATT/WTO system. Developing countries may want to consider whether attention to the issue of preferences detracts from their own domestic liberalization efforts. Ozden and Reinhardt's analysis (2003) of the U.S. GSP program using a dataset of 154 developing countries from 1976 through 2000 finds that countries removed from GSP benefits adopted more liberal trade policies than those remaining eligible. This suggests that developing countries may be better served by fully integrating into a reciprocity-based world trading system rather than continuing with GSP-style special preferences. Of the 154 countries eligible for GSP benefits, 36 have graduated from the program since 1976 (including Singapore, Hong Kong, Taiwan [China], the Republic of Korea, Malaysia, Mexico, and Botswana). The list of major countries remaining eligible include Brazil, India, Indonesia, Turkey, South Africa, and Thailand. In addition to preferential tariff schemes' possible negative effect on the incentive to liberalize, critics have pointed to their underachieving nature, seen in the low utilization rates and especially in the increasingly stringent ROOs. A further shortcoming of these schemes is that developing countries have no way of protecting their "rights" in the various GSP programs, as these arrangements are outside the WTO jurisdiction and subject to the political pressures of the GSP host country.

The European Communities' proposal to the WTO's Special Session of the Committee on Agriculture, December 3–5, 2001, called for an examination of the issues raised by preferential agreements. The EC proposal noted that the maximum value of preferences is limited by the size of the corresponding MFN tariff and that the importance of preferences will decline as MFN rates are reduced; that where preferences exist a sudden removal could cause significant problems; and that the possibility that removal of the preference is in itself a limit on the preference's effectiveness, because this uncertainty limits investment.

Given the discrimination in current preferential trade arrangements under GSP schemes affecting some key developing countries, and the marginal benefit of preferential arrangements to their development, some countries may question whether the preferential approach is of use—or whether negotiating capital should be directed toward greater global liberalization for all, discarding the use of preferences and instead insisting on their WTO rights to achieve greater global market access.

Developing countries will need to decide on whether to make an issue of preferential arrangements and to improve their use through "best endeavors" language, knowing that mandatory language cannot apply to GSP programs. Their decision will depend on the chances of suggesting changes that will provide real benefits compared to the existing preferential treatment. Given the complexity of preferential arrangements (involving beneficiaries, product coverage, and rules administration), however, even "best endeavors" language may be difficult to achieve.

**TABLE 15.10 Preference Margins for Selected Groups of Agricultural Products Exported from the AACP to the European Union Under Lomé Provisions, Hypothetical EU Tariffs after the Next WTO Round (1997 Trade Data)**

| | *Value of preference margin* | | |
|---|---|---|---|
| Product group | (million ECU) | (percentage of value of AACP export to EU of product concerned) | (percentage decrease in preference margin relative to 1999 levels) |
| Fish | 75.0 | 6.3 | 52.1 |
| Tobacco | 24.5 | 5.1 | 64.0 |
| Fresh fruit and vegetables | 8.9 | 2.9 | 60.6 |
| Processed fruit and vegetables | 6.2 | 6.2 | 61.9 |
| Cereals | 0.0 | 0.5 | 10.9 |
| Dairy products | 0.4 | 8.0 | 71.7 |
| **Total of above products** | **115.1** | **5.4** | **56.6** |

*Source:* Tangermann 2001.

Nevertheless, there are some aspects of preferences for which all developing countries may want to take a concerted stand because of their effects on LDCs. These include the following:

- Providing technical assistance for information services and training courses for local producers and exporters using GSP programs.
- Providing predictability and harmonization of rules in preference programs for all developing countries or specifically for LDCs through "best endeavors" language on the issue. It should be noted that increasing the stability and predictability of trade preferences through a set of multilaterally agreed criteria has already been under consideration. The issue of language "binding" members was raised in preparation for the 1999 Seattle WTO Ministerial but the Doha WTO Ministerial only committed members to working toward the objective of quota- and duty-free market access as well as to considering additional measures for the progressive improvement in market access for LDCs (WTO document WT/MIN(01)/DE/W/1, paragraph 42).
- Proposing "best endeavors" language that would result in the adoption of the same approach to tariff cuts and product coverage in preferential schemes.

## Notes

1. See various documents from the WTO, OECD, and UNCTAD on the issue of trade preferences. Examples include "The Generalized System of Preferences: A Preliminary Analysis of the GSP Schemes of the Quad" (WTO); "Mapping of Regional Trade Agreements" (WTO); "Market Access Issues Related to Products of Export Interest Originating from Least Developed Countries" (WTO); "The Relationship between Regional Trade Agreements and Multilateral Trading System" (OECD). See also the UNCTAD Web site of the Generalized System of Preferences (GSP); U.S. *ITC International Economic Reviews* including Andriamananjara (2001) and Anderson (2001) and Laird, Safodi and Turrini.

2. The variability of the schemes means that beneficiaries can change from year to year; as a result, the lists here may already be out of date.

3. For an interesting examination of GATT/WTO provisions on the current trend of "soft law" status for developing countries resulting in their disadvantage inside the WTO legal system, in terms of access to the disputes settlement process, see Olivares (2001).

4. The European Communities (EC) is the signatory to the WTO.

5. For an interesting discussion of Rules of Origin see Hirsch (2002). Hirsch describes the factor of information asymmetry (in other words, the gap between the knowledge of the developed- and developing-country exporters), the widening use of ROOs, and their challenge to the current trading system.

## Select Bibliography

Agama L., and S. Zeleke. 2000. "New Trade and Investment Framework Agreement between the United States and the Common Market for Eastern and Southern Africa." *U.S. ITC International Economic Review* January/February.

Agama, L., 2001. "Assessing the Desirability of a Free-Trade Area in Southern Africa." *U.S. ITC International Economic Review,* July/August.

Anderson, M. M. 2001. "Preferential Trade Agreements: Trade Diversion and Other Worries." *U.S. ITC International Economic Review,* May/June.

Andriamananjara, S. 2001. "Preferential Trade Agreements and the Multilateral Trading System." *U.S. ITC International Economic Review,* January/February.

Barfield, C. 2002. "Preferential Pacts Hurt Trade." *Far Eastern Economic Review,* July 4.

Borrell, B., and D. Pearce. 1999. "Sugar: The Taste Test of Trade Liberalization." Paper prepared for Centre for International Economics, Canberra.

Borrell, B. 1999. "Bananas: Straightening Out Bent Ideas on Trade as Aid." Paper prepared for Centre for International Economics, Canberra.

Bradsher, K. 2002. "Quandary on Trade" (News Analysis), *New York Times,* May 21.

Burki, S. J., E. P. Guillermo, and S. Calvo. 1998. *Trade: Toward Open Regionalism.* Washington, D.C.: World Bank.

Chang, W., and L. A. Winters. 2001. "Preferential Trading Arrangements and Excluded Countries: Ex-Post Estimates of the Effects on Prices." *The World Economy* 24(6): 797–807.

Dean, Judith M. 2002. "Do Preferential Trade Agreements Promote Growth? An Evaluation of the Caribbean Basin Economic Recovery Act." Working Paper, U.S. International Trade Commission, Office of Economics, Washington D.C.

de Jonquieres, G. 2002 "The Challenge for the Multilateral Trading System." FinancialTimes.com.

European Communities. 2001. "Tariff Preferences for Developing Countries." (WTO) Special Session of the Committee on Agriculture, Note. Office of the Secretary General, Geneva.

Guth, J., and V. Chomo. 2002. "The Euro-Mediterranean Partnership." *U.S. ITC International Economic Review,* March/April.

Guth, J. 2000. "European Union and Mexico Conclude Free Trade Agreement." *U.S. ITC International Economic Review,* April/May.

Guth, J. 2000. "New EU Agreements With African Countries Liberalize Two-way Trade." *U.S. ITC International Economic Review,* November/December.

Harrison, G. W., T. Rutherford, and D. Tarr. 2002. "Trade Policy Options for Chile: The Importance of Market Access." *The World Bank Economic Review* 16(1): 49–79.

Hasha, G. 2002. "Trade Among Unequal Partners Changing EU Trade Arrangements With Developing Countries." Agricultural Outlook, USDA Economic Research Service, September. Washington, D.C.

Hensen, F. 2001. "Trade at the Crossroads." Business Credit, June. New York.

Hillberry, R., and C. McDaniel. 2002. "A Decomposition of North American Trade Growth Since NAFTA." *U.S. ITC International Economic Review,* May/June.

Hirsch, M. 2002. "International Trade Law, Political Economy and Rules of Origin." *Journal of World Trade* 36(4): 171–89.

Hoekman, B., F. Ng, and M. Olarreaga. 2003. "Reducing Agricultural Tariffs Versus Domestic Support. What is More Important for Developing Countries." Working Paper 2918, World Bank, Washington, D.C.

International Monetary Fund and the World Bank. 2002. "Market Access for Developing Country Exports." Staff Paper. Washington, D.C.

Jennings, T. F. 2002. "USITC Reports That CBERA Imports Will Likely Increase." *U.S. ITC International Economic Review,* January/February.

Kornis, M. 2000. "U.S. Trade With the Beneficiaries of the Andean Trade Preference Act." *U.S. ITC International Economic Review,* September/October.

Kose, M. A., and R. Riezman. 2002. "Small Countries and Preferential Trade Agreements: How Severe Is the Innocent Bystander Problem?" *Pacific Economic Review* (U.S.) 7(2): 279–304.

Laird, S., R. Safadi, and A. Turrini. 2002. "The WTO and Development." Update of Paper for conference, Tulane University, New Orleans.

Ludema, R. 2002. "Increasing Returns, Multinationals and Geography of Preferential Trade Agreements." *Journal of International Economics* 56(9): 329–58.

Mattoo, A., D. Roy, and A. Subramanian. 2002. "The Africa Growth and Opportunity Act and Its Rules of Origin: Generosity Undermined?" World Bank Policy Research Paper, Washington, D.C.

Messerlin, P. A. 2001. "Measuring the Costs of Protection in Europe: European Commercial Policy in the 2000s." Institute for International Economics, Washington, D.C.

Organisation for Economic Co-operation and Development (OECD). 2002. "The Relationship between Regional Trade Agreements and Multilateral Trading System, Trade Facilitation." TD/TC/WP(2002)17/Final, April 11. Working Party of the Trade Committee, Paris.

Olivares, C. 2001. "The Case for Giving Effectiveness to GATT/WTO Rules on Developing Countries and LDCs." *Journal of World Trade* 34(3): 545–52.

Ozden, C., and E. Reinhardt. 2003. "The Perversity of Preferences: GSP and Developing Country Trade Policies, 1976–2000." Working Paper 2955, World Bank, Washington, D.C.

Page, S., and A. Hewitt. 2002. "The New European Trade Preferences: Does 'Everything But Arms' (EBA) Help the Poor?" *Development Policy Review* 20(1): 91–102.

Peters, G. 2001. "Mexico Leverages Free Trade." *Global Finance,* June, 49–50.

Pollard, W. 2000. "Impact of the Caribbean Basin Economic Recovery Act Declines." *U.S. ITC International Economic Review,* April/May.

Pollard, W. 2001. "Renewal and Expansion of ATPA Could Enhance Effectiveness of the Program." *US ITC International Economic Review,* July/August.

Scollay, R. 2001. "The Changing Outlook for Asia-Pacific Regionalism." *The World Economy* 24(9): 1135–1160.

Stoeckel, A., and B. Borrell. 2001. "Preferential Trade and Developing Countries—Bad Aid, Bad Trade." Prepared for Cairns Group Farm Leaders meeting, Uruguay, Rural Industries Research and Development Cooperation (RIRDC), Canberra.

Tangermann, Stefan. 2001. "The Future of Preferential Trade Arrangements for Developing Countries and the Current Round of Agricultural Trade Negotiations on Agriculture." Paper prepared for FAO, Rome.

Topp, V. 2001. "Trade Preferences: Are They Helpful in Advancing Economic Development in Poor Countries?" Australian Bureau of Agricultural and Resource Economics (ABARE), Canberra.

Trade Partnership. 2001. "The U.S. Generalized System of Preferences Program: An Update." Washington, D.C.

UNCTAD (United Nations Conference on Trade and Development). 2002. "Escaping the Poverty Trap." *The Least Developed Countries Report* 2002, June 18.

U.S. ITC. 2002. "United States-Sub-Saharan Africa Trade Data, Updated Quarterly." U.S. Trade and Investment with Sub-Saharan Africa, July.

USTR United States Trade Representative. 1995. "Comparison of NAFTA, AFTA, CER Trade Agreements." Draft, Washington, D.C.

———. 2002. "New Andean Trade Benefits," Fact Sheet. Office of the USTR, Washington, D.C.

———. 2002a. "Fourth Report to Congress on the Operation of the Caribbean Basin Economic Recovery Act." USTR Web site, Washington, D.C.

———. 2002b. "Comprehensive Report on U.S. Trade and Investment Policy toward Sub-Saharan Africa and Implementation of the African Growth and Opportunity Act." Office of the USTR, Washington, D.C.

———. 2002c. "Generalized System of Preferences (GSP) Guidebook, Part I: Most Frequently Asked Questions." May, Washington, D.C. http://www.ustr.gov/reports/ gsp/faq.html.

———. 2002d. "2002 Trade Policy Agenda and 2001 Annual Report of the President of the United States on the Trade Agreements Program." USTR Web site.

———. 2002e. "USTR Team to Provide Trade Seminars in Argentina and Uruguay." Press release, September 9, Office of the USTR, Washington, D.C.

WTO (World Trade Organization). 2001. "The Generalized System of Preferences: A Preliminary Analysis of the GSP Schemes in the Quad." Committee on Trade and Development, WT/COMTD/ W93. Office of the Secretary General, Geneva.

———. 2002a. "Mapping of Regional Trade Agreements." Note by the Secretariat, Committee on Regional Trade Agreements, WT/REG/W/41, October 11. Office of the Secretary General, Geneva.

———. 2002b. "Market Access Issues Related to Products of Export Interest Originating from Least Developed Countries." Note by Secretariat, Subcommittee on LDC Negotiating Group on Market Access, WT/COMTD/LDC/ W/28, TN/MA/S/7. Office of the Secretary General, Geneva.

———. 2002c. "Material on Regionalism, Scope of RTAs." Office of the Secretary General, Geneva.

———. 2002d. "Trade Policy Review: European Union, Report of the Secretariat." WT/TPR/S/102. Office of the Secretary General, Geneva.

Zahniser S., and J. Link. 2002. "Effects of North American Free Trade Agreement on Agriculture and the Rural Economy." Economic Research Service (ERS) and Trade Report No. WRS0201, July. U.S. Department of Agriculture, Washington, D.C.

# APPENDIX A

# OECD POLICY EVALUATION MATRIX AND TRENDS IN POLICY FOR VARIOUS COMMODITIES

*Cameron Short and Harry de Gorter*

## Introduction

This appendix begins by describing the commodity and policy coverage of the Organisation for Economic Co-operation and Development's (OECD) Policy Evaluation Matrix (PEM) model (see OECD 2001). Trends in protection levels and changes in the policy mix are documented for the grains and oilseeds sector in relation to all other commodities for the OECD as a whole and for the six OECD regions covered in the PEM. The appendix then outlines the basic economic structure of the model.

## Policy Developments in the Grains and Oilseeds Sector

The OECD identifies five categories of support used in the PEM: market price support (MPS) due to border protection (including export subsidies); output price support (OPS) such as deficiency payments; input price subsidies (IPS) such as fertilizer subsidies; area payments such as those in the European Union (EU); and historical entitlements such as those in the United States (U.S.). There are also payments based on overall farm income and miscellaneous payments but these are relatively small.

The PEM has six regions: Canada, the EU, Japan, Mexico, Switzerland, and the U.S. Tables A.1 through A.5 summarize the support for grains and oilseeds in 2001 for both the OECD-6 in the PEM and all OECD countries compared to all other commodities. Tables A.1 and A.2 show that MPS for all commodities represents US$145,269.3 million (63.0 percent) of total support in the OECD, which was US$230,746.0. Area payments are the next largest policy category at 12.6 percent of total OECD support, and these payments equaled US$29,056.7 million.

Table A.3 shows that grains and oilseeds MPS represents 17.0 percent of total OECD MPS, but receive a far higher share of total support in each of the other policy categories of domestic support. The column titled G&O Total in table A.2 shows that grains and oilseeds MPS represents only 38.1 percent of the total grains and oilseed support in the OECD and 30.8 percent for the OECD-6. Support across all policy types is far more uniform in the grains and oilseeds sector for both the OECD and the OECD-6 countries.

Table A.1 shows that the OECD-6 represents most of the support for grains and oilseeds overall in the OECD with the exception of support for oilseeds alone (compare the bottom rows of the OECD and OECD-6 sections). For output support, input support, area payments, and historical entitlements, grains and oilseeds dominate in terms of size

**TABLE A.1 OECD Support for Grains and Oilseeds 2001 (in US$ Millions)**

| | Wheat | Coarse Grains | Rice | Oilseeds | Other Commodities | Total | G&O Total |
|---|---|---|---|---|---|---|---|
| ***OECD*** | | | | | | | |
| Market price support | 1,197.2 | 1,889.0 | 21,266.9 | 321.0 | 120,595.1 | 145,269.3 | 24,674.1 |
| Based on output | 471.3 | 1,935.7 | 1,520.8 | 3,514.4 | 6,761.4 | 14,203.5 | 7,442.2 |
| Based on area planted/ animal numbers | 7,331.3 | 6,695.3 | 164.2 | 1,743.2 | 13,122.7 | 29,056.7 | 15,934.0 |
| Based on historical entitlements | 3,270.2 | 5,661.4 | 175.5 | 117.1 | 3,223.9 | 12,448.0 | 9,224.2 |
| Based on inputs* | 1,919.9 | 2,564.9 | 1,054.8 | 1,227.7 | 19,324.6 | 26,091.9 | 6,767.3 |
| Total** | 14,332.8 | 18,970.1 | 24,339.6 | 7,114.3 | 165,989.2 | 230,746.0 | 64,756.8 |
| ***OECD-6*** | | | | | | | |
| Market price support | 969.5 | 1,851.2 | 14,397.2 | 31.2 | 107,517.2 | 124,766.2 | 17,249.1 |
| Based on output | 354.5 | 1,899.3 | 1,520.8 | 3,514.4 | 5,847.6 | 13,136.7 | 7,289.0 |
| Based on area planted/ animal numbers | 7,232.9 | 6,551.2 | 90.2 | 1,711.0 | 12,505.2 | 28,090.4 | 15,585.3 |
| Based on historical entitlements | 3,264.7 | 5,658.7 | 175.5 | 114.5 | 2,674.0 | 11,887.5 | 9,213.4 |
| Based on inputs* | 1,665.6 | 2,383.1 | 888.8 | 1,177.5 | 17,081.0 | 23,195.9 | 6,115.0 |
| Total** | 13,607.2 | 18,547.5 | 17,082.2 | 6,734.1 | 148,034.8 | 204,005.8 | 55,971.0 |
| ***Canada*** | | | | | | | |
| Market price support | n.a. | n.a. | n.a. | n.a. | 1,856.5 | 1,856.5 | 0.0 |
| Based on output | 17.7 | 93.3 | n.a. | 9.2 | 125.7 | 245.9 | 120.2 |
| Based on area planted/ animal numbers | 129.3 | 71.8 | n.a. | 102.0 | 102.6 | 405.7 | 303.1 |
| Based on historical entitlements | 136.8 | 67.5 | n.a. | 86.5 | 232.2 | 522.9 | 290.8 |
| Based on inputs* | 46.4 | 15.2 | n.a. | 30.4 | 243.2 | 335.2 | 92.0 |
| Total** | 414.6 | 274.5 | n.a. | 289.1 | 2,949.4 | 3,927.7 | 978.2 |
| ***European Union*** | | | | | | | |
| Market price support | 81.1 | 592.2 | 224.3 | 0.0 | 53,392.1 | 54,289.6 | 897.6 |
| Based on output | 39.9 | 30.6 | 1.3 | 10.3 | 3,592.8 | 3,674.8 | 82.1 |
| Based on area planted/ animal numbers | 6,938.5 | 6,071.3 | 77.8 | 1,358.8 | 10,588.2 | 25,034.6 | 14,446.4 |
| Based on historical entitlements | 12.9 | 50.7 | 0.0 | 12.8 | 480.2 | 556.6 | 76.4 |
| Based on inputs* | 1,162.5 | 1,201.4 | 19.1 | 381.9 | 6,455.0 | 9,220.0 | 2,764.9 |
| Total** | 8,206.0 | 7,923.0 | 322.4 | 1,758.0 | 74,873.6 | 93,083.0 | 18,209.4 |
| ***Japan*** | | | | | | | |
| Market price support | 704.6 | 181.1 | 14,164.5 | 0.0 | 27,437.4 | 42,487.7 | 15,050.2 |
| Based on output | 0.0 | 4.9 | 968.9 | 129.2 | 384.4 | 1,487.5 | 1,103.0 |
| Based on area planted/ animal numbers | n.a. | n.a. | n.a. | n.a. | n.a. | n.a. | 0.0 |
| Based on historical entitlements | n.a. | n.a. | n.a. | n.a. | n.a. | n.a. | 0.0 |
| Based on inputs* | 107.8 | 23.0 | 814.9 | 68.3 | 2,253.9 | 3,268.0 | 1,014.0 |
| Total** | 812.5 | 209.1 | 15,948.3 | 197.6 | 30,075.7 | 47,243.2 | 17,167.5 |

**Table A.1 (Continued)**

| | Wheat | Coarse Grains | Rice | Oilseeds | Other Commodities | Total | G&O Total |
|---|---|---|---|---|---|---|---|
| *Mexico* | | | | | | | |
| Market price support | 134.5 | 1,023.2 | 8.5 | 6.1 | 2,871.6 | 4,043.9 | 1,172.3 |
| Based on output | 103.4 | 192.2 | 8.2 | 11.2 | 3.7 | 318.6 | 315.0 |
| Based on area planted/ animal numbers | 0.2 | 1.7 | 0.0 | 0.0 | 70.1 | 72.1 | 1.9 |
| Based on historical entitlements | 69.5 | 928.0 | 9.2 | 8.5 | 242.5 | 1,257.7 | 1,015.2 |
| Based on inputs* | 12.4 | 114.5 | 1.8 | 5.3 | 646.1 | 780.0 | 134.0 |
| Total** | 321.0 | 2,267.2 | 27.8 | 31.1 | 3,889.6 | 6,536.8 | 2,647.1 |
| *Switzerland* | | | | | | | |
| Market price support | 49.2 | 54.7 | n.a. | 25.1 | 2,152.6 | 2,281.6 | 129.0 |
| Based on output | 0.0 | 0.0 | n.a. | 0.0 | 225.6 | 225.6 | 0.0 |
| Based on area planted/ animal numbers | 5.0 | 3.7 | n.a. | 19.9 | 506.1 | 534.6 | 28.6 |
| Based on historical entitlements | 42.3 | 27.0 | n.a. | 6.8 | 681.6 | 757.6 | 76.1 |
| Based on inputs* | 28.3 | 18.1 | n.a. | 4.6 | 245.2 | 296.2 | 51.0 |
| Total** | 131.4 | 107.7 | n.a. | 57.3 | 3,917.8 | 4,214.2 | 296.4 |
| *United States* | | | | | | | |
| Market price support | 0.0 | 0.0 | 0.0 | 0.0 | 19,807.0 | 19,807.0 | 0.0 |
| Based on output | 193.6 | 1,578.2 | 542.5 | 3,354.5 | 1,515.5 | 7,184.3 | 5,668.8 |
| Based on area planted/ animal numbers | 159.9 | 402.8 | 12.3 | 230.3 | 1,238.1 | 2,043.4 | 805.3 |
| Based on historical entitlements | 3,003.3 | 4,585.6 | 166.3 | 0.0 | 1,037.5 | 8,792.7 | 7,755.2 |
| Based on inputs* | 308.0 | 1,010.9 | 53.0 | 687.0 | 7,237.6 | 9,296.5 | 2,058.9 |
| Total** | 3,721.7 | 7,766.0 | 783.7 | 4,400.9 | 32,328.6 | 49,000.9 | 16,672.3 |

* This combines Based upon input use and Based upon input constraints.

** The total includes Based on overall farm income and miscellaneous payments.

relative to other commodities and within the grains and oilseeds sector itself. Table A.3 shows that grains and oilseeds overall received 52.4 percent of total OECD output support, 25.9 percent of input support, 54.8 percent of area payments, and 74.1 percent of historical entitlements in 2001. This means that the various types of direct payments are atypically far more important for wheat, coarse grains, and oilseeds.

The six regions analyzed comprise most of the support for each of the four commodity groups, as shown in table A.5. However, for oilseeds individually, the OECD-6 accounted for only 9.7 percent of total OECD MPS support. OECD-6 total support for rice at 70.2 percent of the OECD total support was also less comparable to these countries' efforts in other categories. By contrast, in coarse grains, the OECD-6 support expenditures comprised 97.8 percent of the total OECD support.

A significant feature of the experiments with area payments and historical entitlements is their concentration in the grains and oilseeds sector in the countries and regions in the PEM as found in the OECD data—especially the U.S., the EU, and Mexico, the first two of which will have a major influence on the Doha Round because of the size of their economies. The grains and oilseeds sector's share of producer support estimate (PSE) is 28.1 percent, almost twice its share of value of production of 17 percent, indicating that it is disproportionately protected. Although MPS is 17.0 percent, most of this (14.6 percent) is for rice. The grains and

**TABLE A.2 Type of Support as a Percentage of Total Support for A Commodity**

| | Wheat | Coarse Grains | Rice | Oilseeds | Other Commodities | Total | G&O Total (%) |
|---|---|---|---|---|---|---|---|
| ***OECD*** | | | | | | | |
| Market price support | 8.4% | 10.0% | 87.4% | 4.5% | 72.7% | 63.0% | 38.1 |
| Based on output | 3.3% | 10.2% | 6.2% | 49.4% | 4.1% | 6.2% | 11.5 |
| Based on area planted/ animal numbers | 51.2% | 35.3% | 0.7% | 24.5% | 7.9% | 12.6% | 24.6 |
| Based on historical entitlements | 22.8% | 29.8% | 0.7% | 1.6% | 1.9% | 5.4% | 14.2 |
| Based on inputs* | 13.4% | 13.5% | 4.3% | 17.3% | 11.6% | 11.3% | 10.5 |
| Total** | 100.0% | 100.0% | 100.0% | 100.0% | 100.0% | 100.0% | 100.0 |
| ***OECD-6*** | | | | | | | |
| Market price support | 7.1% | 10.0% | 84.3% | 0.5% | 72.6% | 61.2% | 30.8 |
| Based on output | 2.6% | 10.2% | 8.9% | 52.2% | 4.0% | 6.4% | 13.0 |
| Based on area planted/ animal numbers | 53.2% | 35.3% | 0.5% | 25.4% | 8.4% | 13.8% | 27.8 |
| Based on historical entitlements | 24.0% | 30.5% | 1.0% | 1.7% | 1.8% | 5.8% | 16.5 |
| Based on inputs* | 12.2% | 12.8% | 5.2% | 17.5% | 11.5% | 11.4% | 10.9 |
| Total** | 100.0% | 100.0% | 100.0% | 100.0% | 100.0% | 100.0% | 100.0 |
| ***Canada*** | | | | | | | |
| Market price support | 0.0% | 0.0% | n.a. | 0.0% | 62.9% | 47.3% | 0.0 |
| Based on output | 4.3% | 34.0% | n.a. | 3.2% | 4.3% | 6.3% | 12.3 |
| Based on area planted/ animal numbers | 31.2% | 26.1% | n.a. | 35.3% | 3.5% | 10.3% | 31.0 |
| Based on historical entitlements | 33.0% | 24.6% | n.a. | 29.9% | 7.9% | 13.3% | 29.7 |
| Based on inputs* | 11.2% | 5.5% | n.a. | 10.5% | 8.2% | 8.5% | 9.4 |
| Total** | 100.0% | 100.0% | n.a. | 100.0% | 100.0% | 100.0% | 100.0 |
| ***European Union*** | | | | | | | |
| Market price support | 1.0% | 7.5% | 69.6% | 0.0% | 71.3% | 58.3% | 4.9 |
| Based on output | 0.5% | 0.4% | 0.4% | 0.6% | 4.8% | 3.9% | 0.5 |
| Based on area planted/ animal numbers | 84.6% | 76.6% | 24.1% | 77.3% | 14.1% | 26.9% | 79.3 |
| Based on historical entitlements | 0.2% | 0.6% | 0.0% | 0.7% | 0.6% | 0.6% | 0.4 |
| Based on inputs* | 14.2% | 15.2% | 5.9% | 21.7% | 8.6% | 9.9% | 15.2 |
| Total** | 100.0% | 100.0% | 100.0% | 100.0% | 100.0% | 100.0% | 100.0 |
| ***Japan*** | | | | | | | |
| Market price support | 86.7% | 86.6% | 88.8% | 0.0% | 91.2% | 89.9% | 87.7 |
| Based on output | 0.0% | 2.4% | 6.1% | 65.4% | 1.3% | 3.1% | 6.4 |
| Based on area planted/ animal numbers | n.a. | n.a. | n.a. | n.a. | n.a. | n.a. | n.a. |
| Based on historical entitlements | n.a. | n.a. | n.a. | n.a. | n.a. | n.a. | n.a. |
| Based on inputs* | 13.3% | 11.0% | 5.1% | 34.6% | 7.5% | 6.9% | 5.9 |
| Total** | 100.0% | 100.0% | 100.0% | 100.0% | 100.0% | 100.0% | 100.0 |

**TABLE A.2 (Continued)**

| | Wheat | Coarse Grains | Rice | Oilseeds | Other Commodities | Total | G&O Total (%) |
|---|---|---|---|---|---|---|---|
| *Mexico* | | | | | | | |
| Market price support | 41.9% | 45.1% | 30.5% | 19.6% | 73.8% | 61.9% | 44.3 |
| Based on output | 32.2% | 8.5% | 29.4% | 35.8% | 0.1% | 4.9% | 11.9 |
| Based on area planted/ animal numbers | 0.1% | 0.1% | 0.1% | 0.0% | 1.8% | 1.1% | 0.1 |
| Based on historical entitlements | 21.6% | 40.9% | 33.2% | 27.3% | 6.2% | 19.2% | 38.3 |
| Based on inputs* | 3.9% | 5.0% | 6.3% | 17.1% | 16.6% | 11.9% | 5.1 |
| Total** | 100.0% | 100.0% | 100.0% | 100.0% | 100.0% | 100.0% | 100.0 |
| *Switzerland* | | | | | | | |
| Market price support | 37.4% | 50.8% | n.a. | 43.7% | 54.9% | 54.1% | 43.5 |
| Based on output | 0.0% | 0.0% | n.a. | 0.0% | 5.8% | 5.4% | 0.0 |
| Based on area planted/ animal numbers | 3.8% | 3.4% | n.a. | 34.6% | 12.9% | 12.7% | 9.6 |
| Based on historical entitlements | 32.2% | 25.1% | n.a. | 11.8% | 17.4% | 18.0% | 25.6 |
| Based on inputs* | 21.6% | 16.8% | n.a. | 8.0% | 6.3% | 7.0% | 17.2 |
| Total** | 100.0% | 100.0% | n.a. | 100.0% | 100.0% | 100.0% | 100.0 |
| *United States* | | | | | | | |
| Market price support | 0.0% | 0.0% | 0.0% | 0.0% | 61.3% | 40.4% | 0.0 |
| Based on output | 5.2% | 20.3% | 69.2% | 76.2% | 4.7% | 14.7% | 34.0 |
| Based on area planted/ animal numbers | 4.3% | 5.2% | 1.6% | 5.2% | 3.8% | 4.2% | 4.8 |
| Based on historical entitlements | 80.7% | 59.0% | 21.2% | 0.0% | 3.2% | 17.9% | 46.5 |
| Based on inputs* | 8.3% | 13.0% | 6.8% | 15.6% | 22.4% | 19.0% | 12.3 |
| Total** | 100.0% | 100.0% | 100.0% | 100.0% | 100.0% | 100.0% | 100.0 |

* This combines Based upon input use and Based upon input constraints.

** The total includes Based on overall farm income and miscellaneous payments.

oilseeds sector accounts for 54.8 percent of the entire area payments and 74.1 percent of historical entitlements in the OECD countries.[1] Deficiency payments are disproportionately used to support oilseed producers.

The significance of grains and oilseeds in terms of agriculture in the OECD countries can be derived from additional computations to the OECD database (grains and oilseeds accounted for 17 percent of the total agricultural production by value). The six regions accounted for 33 percent of world grains and oilseeds production by weight in 2001 but 86 percent of production in OECD countries. The six-region share of world production by weight is higher for coarse grains at 44 percent and significantly lower for rice at only 5 percent. The six regions also accounted for 85 percent of the OECD production of oilseeds, which was 42 percent of world oilseed production. Wheat production in the six regions was 29 percent of world production. The six regions account for 86 percent of both the volume of production and of the PSE for OECD grains and oilseeds. They account for 99 percent of the area payments and historical entitlements and 93 percent of other direct payments (again primarily deficiency payments).

Table A.2 shows that the amounts of protection are very low for Canada in all categories while the EU has significant MPS for rice and high rates of support in area payments and IPS. Japan has very high MPS and significant output support and input support in oilseeds and rice. Mexico uses all policies except area payments while the U.S. relies heavily on output support and historical entitlement

**TABLE A.3 Support to a Specific Commodity as a Percentage of Total Type of Support**

| | Wheat | Coarse Grains | Rice | Oilseeds | Other Commodities | Total | G&O Total (%) |
|---|---|---|---|---|---|---|---|
| ***OECD*** | | | | | | | |
| Market price support | 0.8% | 1.3% | 14.6% | 0.2% | 83.0% | 100.0% | 17.0 |
| Based on output | 3.3% | 13.6% | 10.7% | 24.7% | 47.6% | 100.0% | 52.4 |
| Based on area planted/ animal numbers | 25.2% | 23.0% | 0.6% | 6.0% | 45.2% | 100.0% | 54.8 |
| Based on historical entitlements | 26.3% | 45.5% | 1.4% | 0.9% | 25.9% | 100.0% | 74.1 |
| Based on inputs* | 7.4% | 9.8% | 4.0% | 4.7% | 74.1% | 100.0% | 25.9 |
| Total** | 6.2% | 8.2% | 10.5% | 3.1% | 71.9% | 100.0% | 28.1 |
| ***OECD-6*** | | | | | | | |
| Market price support | 0.8% | 1.5% | 11.5% | 0.0% | 86.2% | 100.0% | 13.8 |
| Based on output | 2.7% | 14.5% | 11.6% | 26.8% | 44.5% | 100.0% | 55.5 |
| Based on area planted/ animal numbers | 25.7% | 23.3% | 0.3% | 6.1% | 44.5% | 100.0% | 55.5 |
| Based on historical entitlements | 27.5% | 47.6% | 1.5% | 1.0% | 22.5% | 100.0% | 77.5 |
| Based on inputs* | 7.2% | 10.3% | 3.8% | 5.1% | 73.6% | 100.0% | 26.4 |
| Total** | 6.7% | 9.1% | 8.4% | 3.3% | 72.6% | 100.0% | 27.4 |
| ***Canada*** | | | | | | | |
| Market price support | 0.0% | 0.0% | n.a. | 0.0% | 100.0% | 100.0% | 0.0 |
| Based on output | 7.2% | 38.0% | n.a. | 3.7% | 51.1% | 100.0% | 48.9 |
| Based on area planted/ animal numbers | 31.9% | 17.7% | n.a. | 25.2% | 25.3% | 100.0% | 74.7 |
| Based on historical entitlements | 26.2% | 12.9% | n.a. | 16.5% | 44.4% | 100.0% | 55.6 |
| Based on inputs* | 13.9% | 4.5% | n.a. | 9.1% | 72.5% | 100.0% | 27.5 |
| Total** | 10.6% | 7.0% | n.a. | 7.4% | 75.1% | 100.0% | 24.9 |
| ***European Union*** | | | | | | | |
| Market price support | 0.1% | 1.1% | 0.4% | 0.0% | 98.3% | 100.0% | 1.7 |
| Based on output | 1.1% | 0.8% | 0.0% | 0.3% | 97.8% | 100.0% | 2.2 |
| Based on area planted/ animal numbers | 27.7% | 24.3% | 0.3% | 5.4% | 42.3% | 100.0% | 57.7 |
| Based on historical entitlements | 2.3% | 9.1% | 0.0% | 2.3% | 86.3% | 100.0% | 13.7 |
| Based on inputs* | 12.6% | 13.0% | 0.2% | 4.1% | 70.0% | 100.0% | 30.0 |
| Total** | 8.8% | 8.5% | 0.3% | 1.9% | 80.4% | 100.0% | 19.6 |
| ***Japan*** | | | | | | | |
| Market price support | 1.7% | 0.4% | 33.3% | 0.0% | 64.6% | 100.0% | 35.4 |
| Based on output | 0.0% | 0.3% | 65.1% | 8.7% | 25.8% | 100.0% | 74.2 |
| Based on area planted/ animal numbers | n.a. | n.a. | n.a. | n.a. | n.a. | n.a. | n.a. |
| Based on historical entitlements | n.a. | n.a. | n.a. | n.a. | n.a. | n.a. | n.a. |
| Based on inputs* | 3.3% | 0.7% | 24.9% | 2.1% | 69.0% | 100.0% | 31.0 |
| Total** | 1.7% | 0.4% | 33.8% | 0.4% | 63.7% | 100.0% | 36.3 |

**TABLE A.3 (Continued)**

| | Wheat | Coarse Grains | Rice | Oilseeds | Other Commodities | Total | G&O Total (%) |
|---|---|---|---|---|---|---|---|
| *Mexico* | | | | | | | |
| Market price support | 3.3% | 25.3% | 0.2% | 0.2% | 71.0% | 100.0% | 29.0 |
| Based on output | 32.4% | 60.3% | 2.6% | 3.5% | 1.2% | 100.0% | 98.8 |
| Based on area planted/ animal numbers | 0.3% | 2.4% | 0.0% | 0.0% | 97.2% | 100.0% | 2.8 |
| Based on historical entitlements | 5.5% | 73.8% | 0.7% | 0.7% | 19.3% | 100.0% | 80.7 |
| Based on inputs* | 1.6% | 14.7% | 0.2% | 0.7% | 82.8% | 100.0% | 17.2 |
| Total** | 4.9% | 34.7% | 0.4% | 0.5% | 59.5% | 100.0% | 40.5 |
| *Switzerland* | | | | | | | |
| Market price support | 2.2% | 2.4% | n.a. | 1.1% | 94.3% | 100.0% | 5.7 |
| Based on output | 0.0% | 0.0% | n.a. | 0.0% | 100.0% | 100.0% | 0.0 |
| Based on area planted/ animal numbers | 0.9% | 0.7% | n.a. | 3.7% | 94.7% | 100.0% | 5.3 |
| Based on historical entitlements | 5.6% | 3.6% | n.a. | 0.9% | 90.0% | 100.0% | 10.0 |
| Based on inputs* | 9.6% | 6.1% | n.a. | 1.5% | 82.8% | 100.0% | 17.2 |
| Total** | 3.1% | 2.6% | n.a. | 1.4% | 93.0% | 100.0% | 7.0 |
| *United States* | | | | | | | |
| Market price support | 0.0% | 0.0% | 0.0% | 0.0% | 100.0% | 100.0% | 0.0 |
| Based on output | 2.7% | 22.0% | 7.6% | 46.7% | 21.1% | 100.0% | 78.9 |
| Based on area planted/ animal numbers | 7.8% | 19.7% | 0.6% | 11.3% | 60.6% | 100.0% | 39.4 |
| Based on historical entitlements | 34.2% | 52.2% | 1.9% | 0.0% | 11.8% | 100.0% | 88.2 |
| Based on inputs* | 3.3% | 10.9% | 0.6% | 7.4% | 77.9% | 100.0% | 22.1 |
| Total** | 7.6% | 15.8% | 1.6% | 9.0% | 66.0% | 100.0% | 34.0 |

* This combines Based upon entitlements input use and Based upon input constraints.
** The total includes Based on overall farm income and miscellaneous payments.

payments. Figure A.1 displays the trends in support for grains and oilseeds over time. The trend downward for MPS is significant and slightly more than that of total support. The overall percentage of protection started at close to 120 percent in 1986 and fell to 50 percent in 1996 but stands at 77 percent in 2001. Average protection is 80 percent for the time period 1986–2001. The move away from MPS and toward the various forms of direct payments, especially area payments and historical entitlements, is also evident. Agricultural support is still dominated by MPS but this is declining and the growing component is made up of area payments and historical entitlements. Purchased input subsidies and output price support have been fairly constant.

All other commodities, however, have a far less pronounced downward trend in protection although the average rate of protection is lower, at about 50 percent (figure A.2). Figure A.3 shows the sharp decline in Canada's protection for grains and oilseeds, unlike for other commodities in this country (figure A.4). There has been no downward trend in U.S. protection for grains and oilseeds, although there is a big shift in policies away from area payments to historical entitlements and OPS (figure A.5). Interestingly, the trend in protection for all other commodities in the U.S. is declining somewhat (figure A.6).

Figure A.7 shows the dramatic drop in MPS for the EU while total support has only a slight downward

**TABLE A.4 Support as a Percentage for Grains and Oilseeds Distributed Among Specific Commodities**

| | Wheat | Coarse Grains | Rice | Oilseeds | Other Commodities | Total | G&O Total (%) |
|---|---|---|---|---|---|---|---|
| ***OECD*** | | | | | | | |
| Market price support | 4.9% | 7.7% | 86.2% | 1.3% | n.a. | n.a. | 100.0 |
| Based on output | 6.3% | 26.0% | 20.4% | 47.2% | n.a. | n.a. | 100.0 |
| Based on area planted/ animal numbers | 46.0% | 42.0% | 1.0% | 10.9% | n.a. | n.a. | 100.0 |
| Based on historical entitlements | 35.5% | 61.4% | 1.9% | 1.3% | n.a. | n.a. | 100.0 |
| Based on inputs* | 28.4% | 37.9% | 15.6% | 18.1% | n.a. | n.a. | 100.0 |
| Total** | 22.1% | 29.3% | 37.6% | 11.0% | n.a. | n.a. | 100.0 |
| ***OECD-6*** | | | | | | | |
| Market price support | 5.6% | 10.7% | 83.5% | 0.2% | n.a. | n.a. | 100.0 |
| Based on output | 4.9% | 26.1% | 20.9% | 48.2% | n.a. | n.a. | 100.0 |
| Based on area planted/ animal numbers | 46.4% | 42.0% | 0.6% | 11.0% | n.a. | n.a. | 100.0 |
| Based on historical entitlements | 35.4% | 61.4% | 1.9% | 1.2% | n.a. | n.a. | 100.0 |
| Based on inputs* | 27.2% | 39.0% | 14.5% | 19.3% | n.a. | n.a. | 100.0 |
| Total** | 24.3% | 33.1% | 30.5% | 12.0% | n.a. | n.a. | 100.0 |
| ***Canada*** | | | | | | | |
| Market price support | n.a. | n.a. | n.a. | n.a. | n.a. | n.a. | n.a. |
| Based on output | 14.7% | 77.6% | 0.0% | 7.6% | n.a. | n.a. | 100.0 |
| Based on area planted/ animal numbers | 42.7% | 23.7% | 0.0% | 33.7% | n.a. | n.a. | 100.0 |
| Based on historical entitlements | 47.0% | 23.2% | 0.0% | 29.7% | n.a. | n.a. | 100.0 |
| Based on inputs* | 50.5% | 16.5% | 0.0% | 33.1% | n.a. | n.a. | 100.0 |
| Total** | 42.4% | 28.1% | 0.0% | 29.6% | n.a. | n.a. | 100.0 |
| ***European Union*** | | | | | | | |
| Market price support | 9.0% | 66.0% | 25.0% | 0.0% | n.a. | n.a. | 100.0 |
| Based on output | 48.6% | 37.3% | 1.5% | 12.6% | n.a. | n.a. | 100.0 |
| Based on area planted/ animal numbers | 48.0% | 42.0% | 0.5% | 9.4% | n.a. | n.a. | 100.0 |
| Based on historical entitlements | 16.9% | 66.4% | 0.0% | 16.8% | n.a. | n.a. | 100.0 |
| Based on inputs* | 42.0% | 43.5% | 0.7% | 13.8% | n.a. | n.a. | 100.0 |
| Total** | 45.1% | 43.5% | 1.8% | 9.7% | n.a. | n.a. | 100.0 |
| ***Japan*** | | | | | | | |
| Market price support | 4.7% | 1.2% | 94.1% | 0.0% | n.a. | n.a. | 100.0 |
| Based on output | 0.0% | 0.4% | 87.8% | 11.7% | n.a. | n.a. | 100.0 |
| Based on area planted/ animal numbers | n.a. | n.a. | n.a. | n.a. | n.a. | n.a. | n.a. |
| Based on historical entitlements | n.a. | n.a. | n.a. | n.a. | n.a. | n.a. | n.a. |
| Based on inputs* | 10.6% | 2.3% | 80.4% | 6.7% | n.a. | n.a. | 100.0 |
| Total** | 4.7% | 1.2% | 92.9% | 1.2% | n.a. | n.a. | 100.0 |

**TABLE A.4 (Continued)**

| | Wheat | Coarse Grains | Rice | Oilseeds | Other Commodities | Total | G&O Total (%) |
|---|---|---|---|---|---|---|---|
| *Mexico* | | | | | | | |
| Market price support | 11.5% | 87.3% | 0.7% | 0.5% | n.a. | n.a. | 100.0 |
| Based on output | 32.8% | 61.0% | 2.6% | 3.5% | n.a. | n.a. | 100.0 |
| Based on area planted/ animal numbers | 11.3% | 86.6% | 1.6% | 0.5% | n.a. | n.a. | 100.0 |
| Based on historical entitlements | 6.8% | 91.4% | 0.9% | 0.8% | n.a. | n.a. | 100.0 |
| Based on inputs* | 9.3% | 85.4% | 1.3% | 4.0% | n.a. | n.a. | 100.0 |
| Total** | 12.1% | 85.6% | 1.1% | 1.2% | n.a. | n.a. | 100.0 |
| *Switzerland* | | | | | | | |
| Market price support | 38.1% | 42.4% | 0.0% | 19.4% | n.a. | n.a. | 100.0 |
| Based on output | n.a. | n.a. | n.a. | n.a. | n.a. | n.a. | n.a. |
| Based on area planted/ animal numbers | 17.5% | 12.9% | 0.0% | 69.6% | n.a. | n.a. | 100.0 |
| Based on historical entitlements | 55.6% | 35.5% | 0.0% | 8.9% | n.a. | n.a. | 100.0 |
| Based on inputs* | 55.6% | 35.5% | 0.0% | 9.0% | n.a. | n.a. | 100.0 |
| Total** | 44.3% | 36.3% | 0.0% | 19.3% | n.a. | n.a. | 100.0 |
| *United States* | | | | | | | |
| Market price support | n.a. | n.a. | n.a. | n.a. | n.a. | n.a. | n.a. |
| Based on output | 3.4% | 27.8% | 9.6% | 59.2% | n.a. | n.a. | 100.0 |
| Based on area planted/ animal numbers | 19.9% | 50.0% | 1.5% | 28.6% | n.a. | n.a. | 100.0 |
| Based on historical entitlements | 38.7% | 59.1% | 2.1% | 0.0% | n.a. | n.a. | 100.0 |
| Based on inputs* | 15.0% | 49.1% | 2.6% | 33.4% | n.a. | n.a. | 100.0 |
| Total** | 22.3% | 46.6% | 4.7% | 26.4% | n.a. | n.a. | 100.0 |

* This combines Based upon input use and Based upon input constraints.

** The total includes Based on overall farm income and miscellaneous payments.

**TABLE A.5 OECD-6 as a Percentage of OECD Total for Selected Commodities and Support Types**

| | Wheat | Coarse Grains | Rice | Oilseeds | Other | Total | G&O Total (%) |
|---|---|---|---|---|---|---|---|
| *OECD-6* | | | | | | | |
| Market price support | 81.0% | 98.0% | 67.7% | 9.7% | 89.2% | 85.9% | 69.9 |
| Payments based on output | 75.2% | 98.1% | 100.0% | 100.0% | 86.5% | 92.5% | 97.9 |
| Payments based on area planted/animal numbers | 98.7% | 97.8% | 54.9% | 98.2% | 95.3% | 96.7% | 97.8 |
| Payments based on historical entitlements | 99.8% | 100.0% | 100.0% | 97.8% | 82.9% | 95.5% | 99.9 |
| Payments based on inputs* | 86.8% | 92.9% | 84.3% | 95.9% | 88.4% | 88.9% | 90.4 |
| Total** | 94.9% | 97.8% | 70.2% | 94.7% | 89.2% | 88.4% | 86.4 |

* This combines Based upon input use and Based upon input constraints.

** The total includes Based on overall farm income and miscellaneous payments.

**FIGURE A.1 OECD—Grains and Oilseeds**

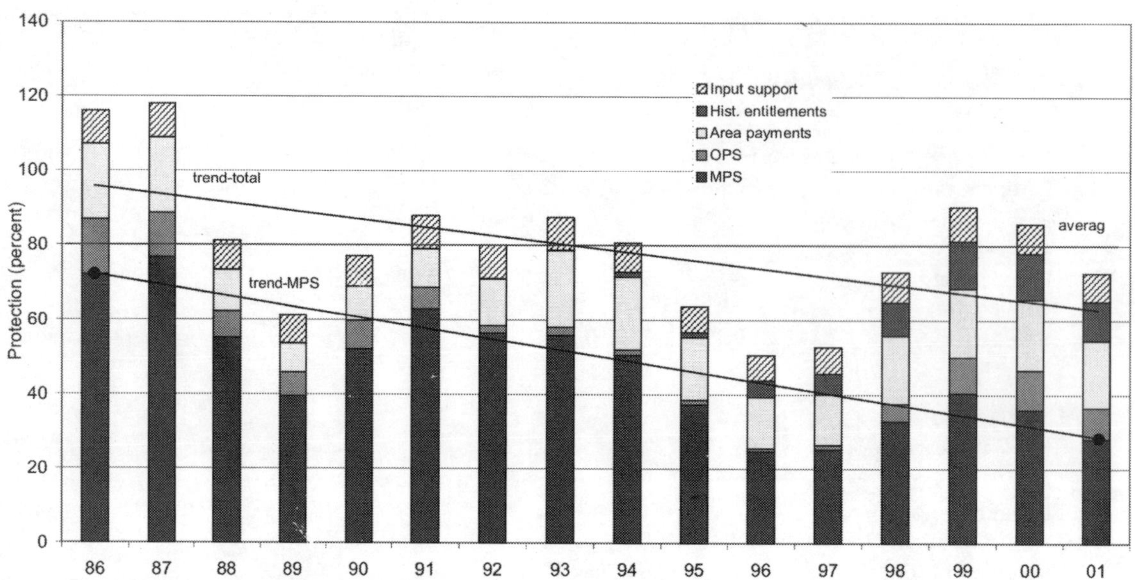


*Note:* "Protection" is the value of support over the value of production at world prices.
*Source:* OECD (2002a).

**FIGURE A.2 OECD—Other Commodities**

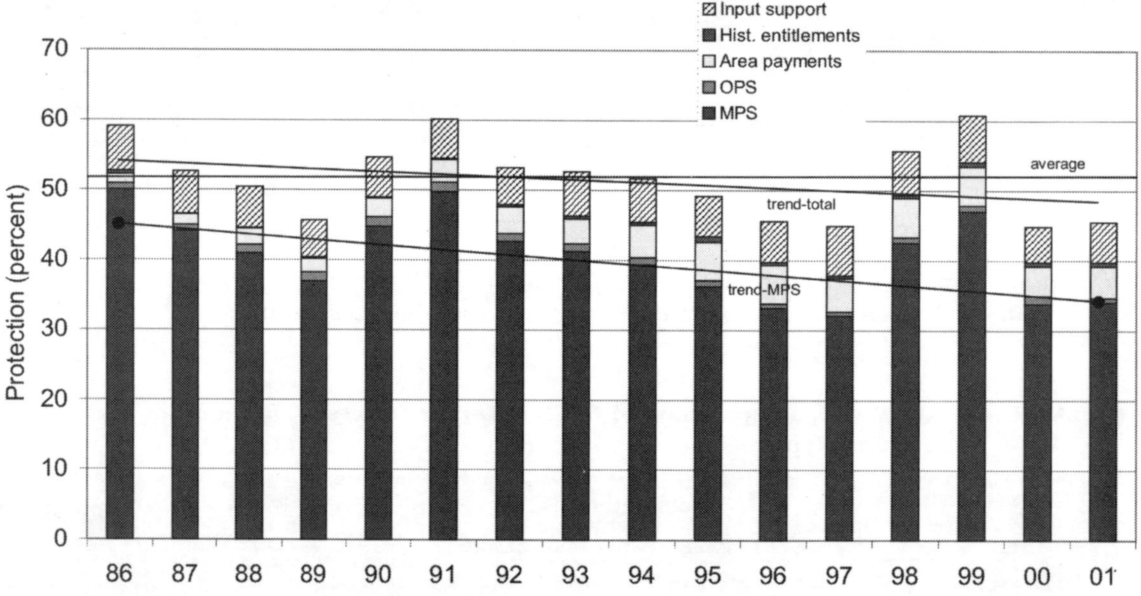


*Note:* "Protection" is the value of support over the value of production at world prices.
*Source:* OECD (2002a).

trend. A large transformation of policy re-instrumentation has therefore occurred away from MPS and IPS to area payments. EU oilseeds have seen a significant reduction in total support (figure A.8) along with rice after 1995 (figure A.9). All other commodities in the EU have an upward trend in protection with a period average protection comparable to that of grains and oilseeds (figure A.10).

Figure A.11 shows that support for grains and oilseeds has increased in Japan since 1986, with very high protection rates of almost 500 percent on average. Support for all other commodities,

**FIGURE A.3 Canada—Grains and Oilseeds**

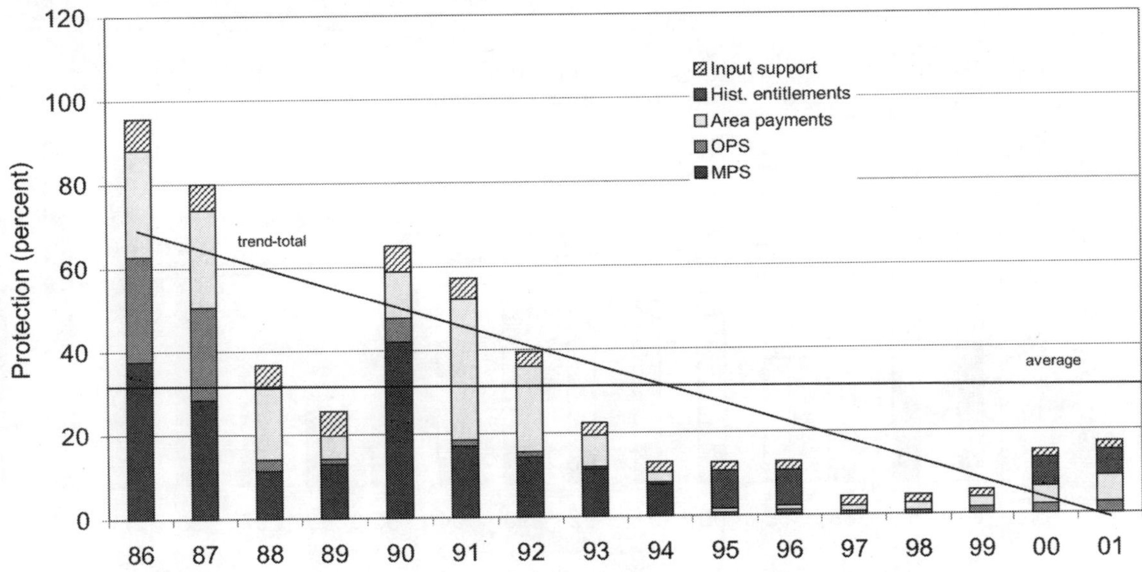


*Note:* "Protection" is the value of support over the value of production at world prices.
*Source:* OECD (2002a).

**FIGURE A.4 Canada—Other Commodities**

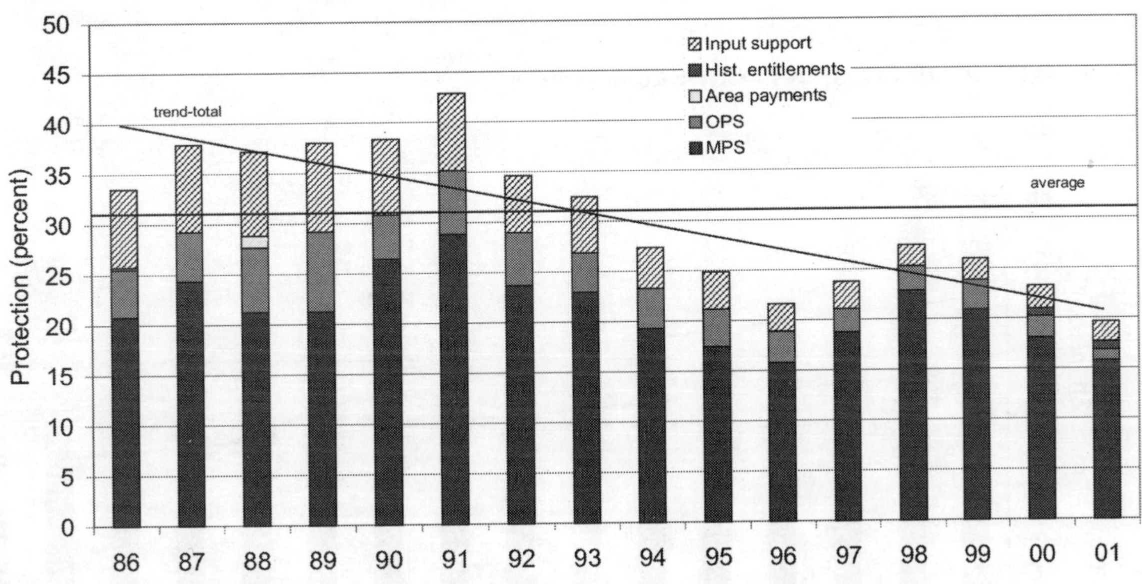


*Note:* "Protection" is the value of support over the value of production at world prices.
*Source:* OECD (2002a).

however, have remained flat and averaged just over 80 percent (figure A.12). MPS in all cases is the bulk of support given to agriculture in Japan.

The trends in support for grains and oilseeds in Switzerland mirrors that of most other countries (other than Japan) with sharp downward trends in total support and a movement toward historical entitlements (figure A.13). However, support was very high in the mid-1980s, reaching a high of almost 450 percent.

For Mexico, the trends in support for grains and oilseeds has varied greatly since 1986 although the trend in total support is positive (figure A.14). The reader should notice, however, the significant

**FIGURE A.5 United States—Grains and Oilseeds**

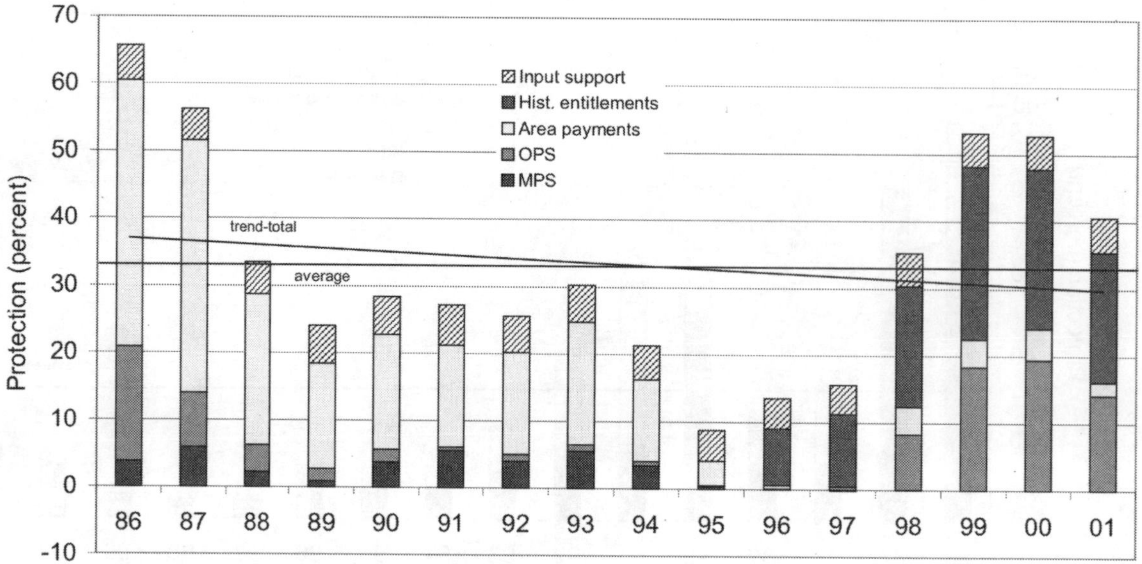


*Note:* "Protection" is the value of support over the value of production at world prices.
*Source:* OECD (2002a).

**FIGURE A.6 United States—Other Commodities**

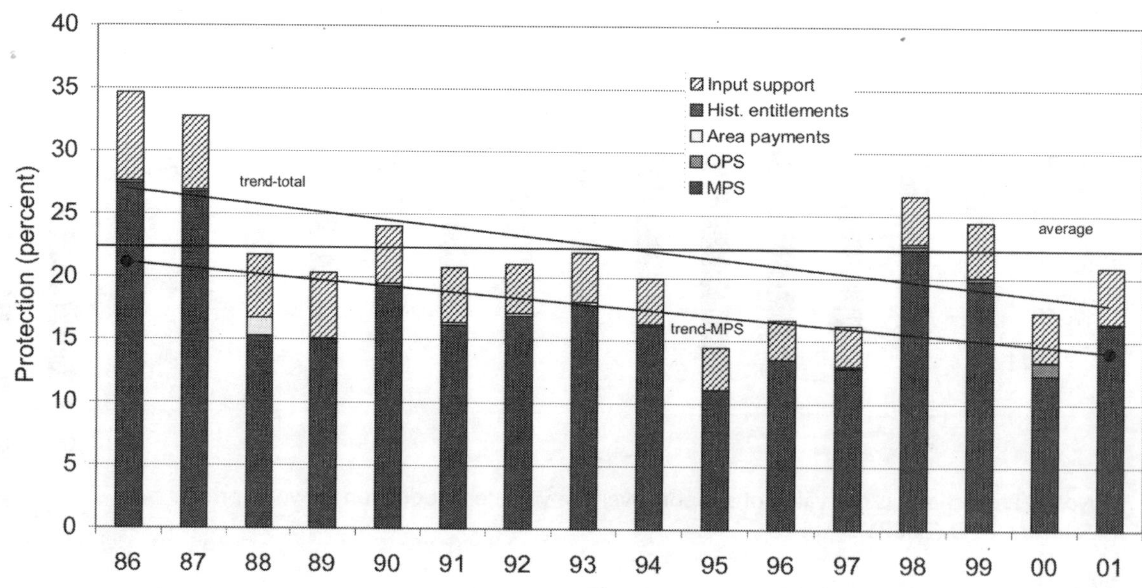


*Note:* "Protection" is the value of support over the value of production at world prices.
*Source:* OECD (2002a).

**FIGURE A.7 European Union—Grains and Oilseeds**

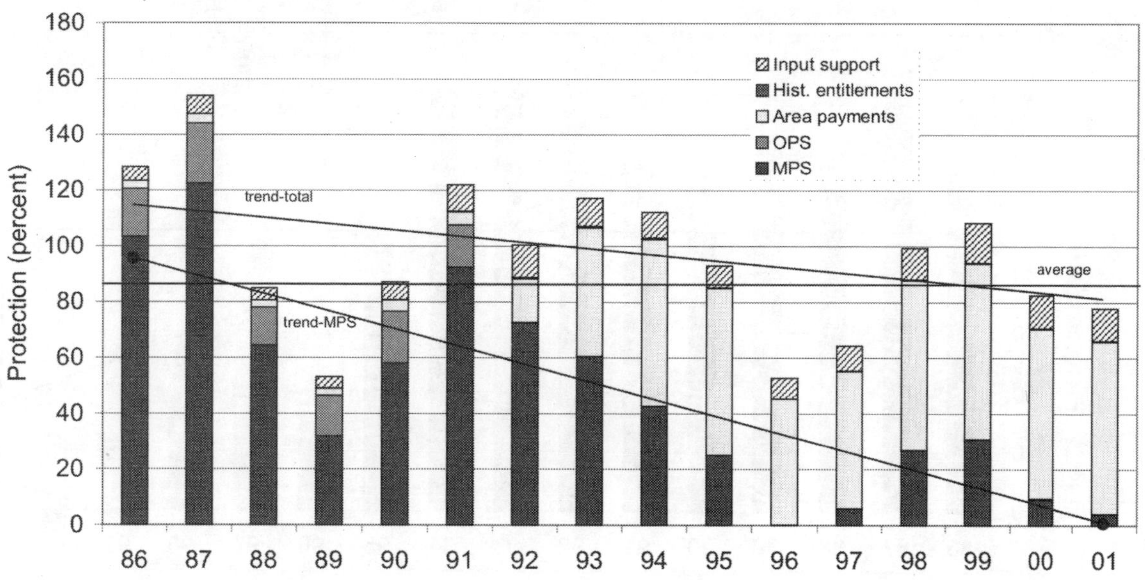


*Note:* "Protection" is the value of support over the value of production at world prices.
*Source:* OECD (2002a).

**FIGURE A.8 European Union—Oilseeds**

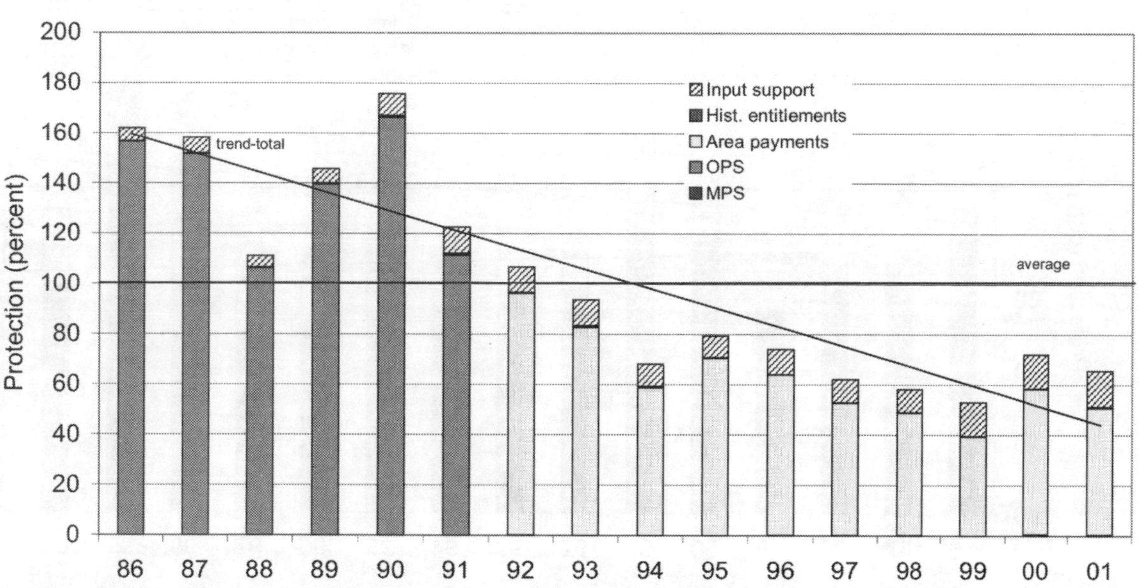


*Note:* "Protection" is the value of support over the value of production at world prices.
*Source:* OECD (2002a).

**FIGURE A.9 European Union—Rice**

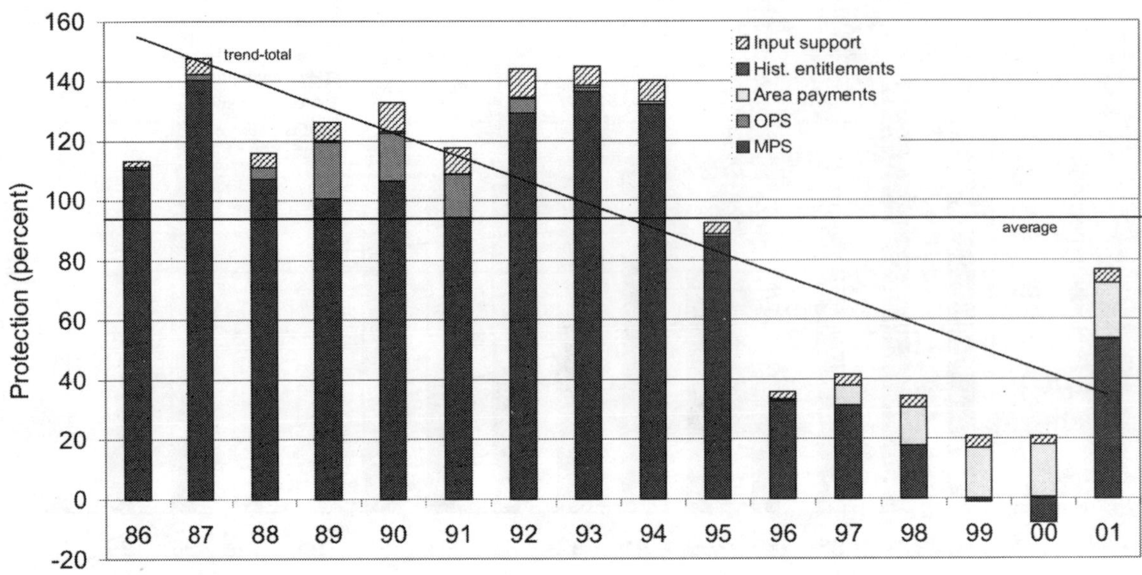


*Note:* "Protection" is the value of support over the value of production at world prices.
*Source:* OECD (2002a).

**FIGURE A.10 European Union—Other Commodities**

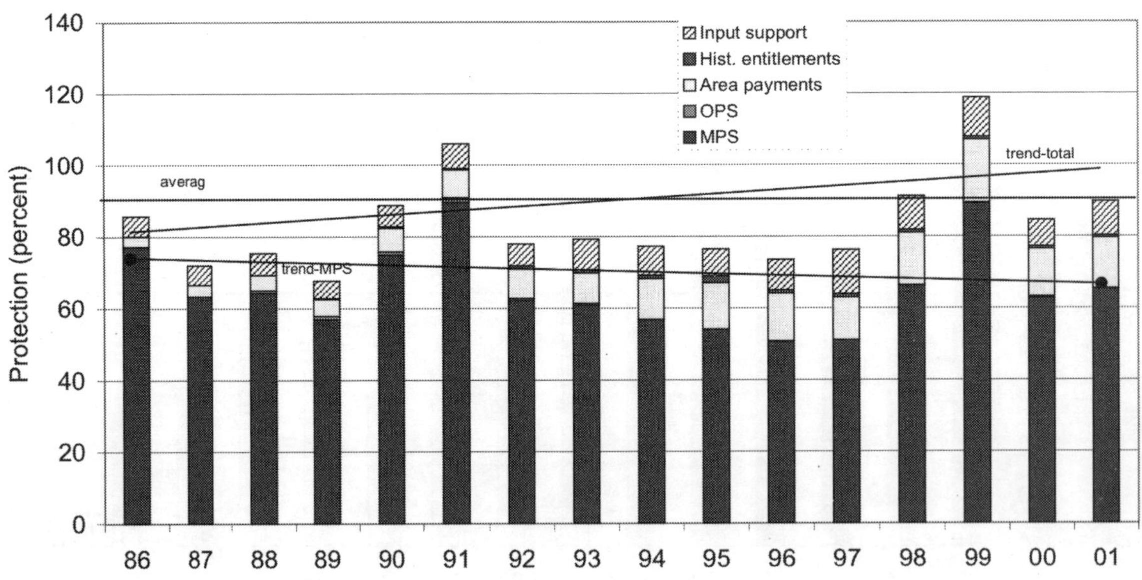


*Note:* "Protection" is the value of support over the value of production at world prices.
*Source:* OECD (2002a).

**FIGURE A.11 Japan—Grains and Oilseeds**

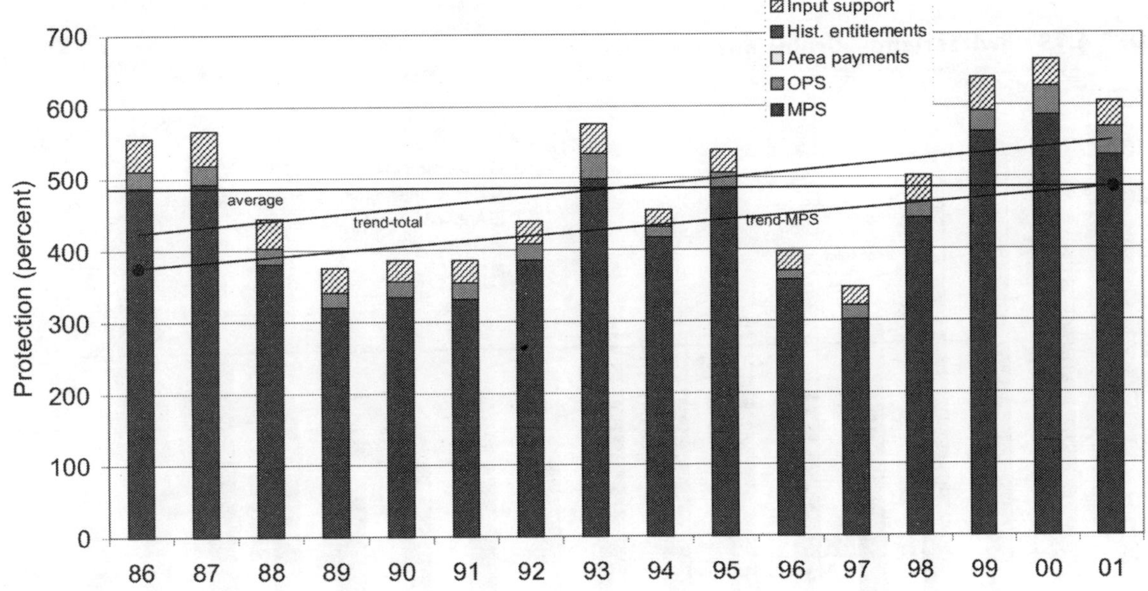


*Note:* "Protection" is the value of support over the value of production at world prices.
*Source:* OECD (2002a).

**FIGURE A.12 Japan—Other Commodities**

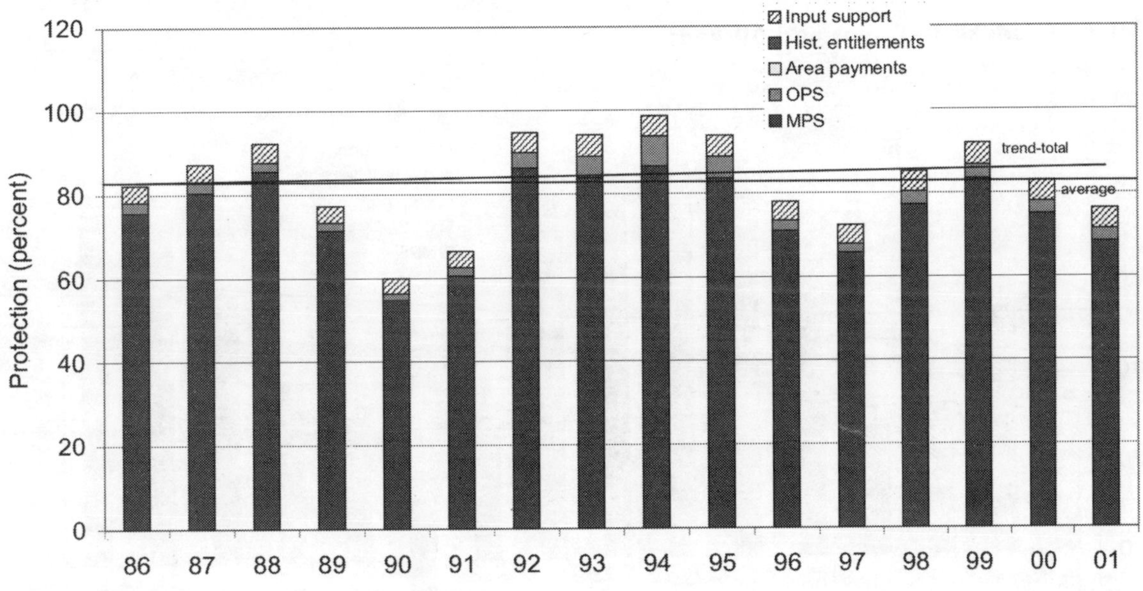


*Note:* "Protection" is the value of support over the value of production at world prices.
*Source:* OECD (2002a).

**FIGURE A.13 Switzerland—Grains and Oilseeds**

*Note:* "Protection" is the value of support over the value of production at world prices.
*Source:* OECD (2002a).

**FIGURE A.14 Mexico—Grains and Oilseeds**

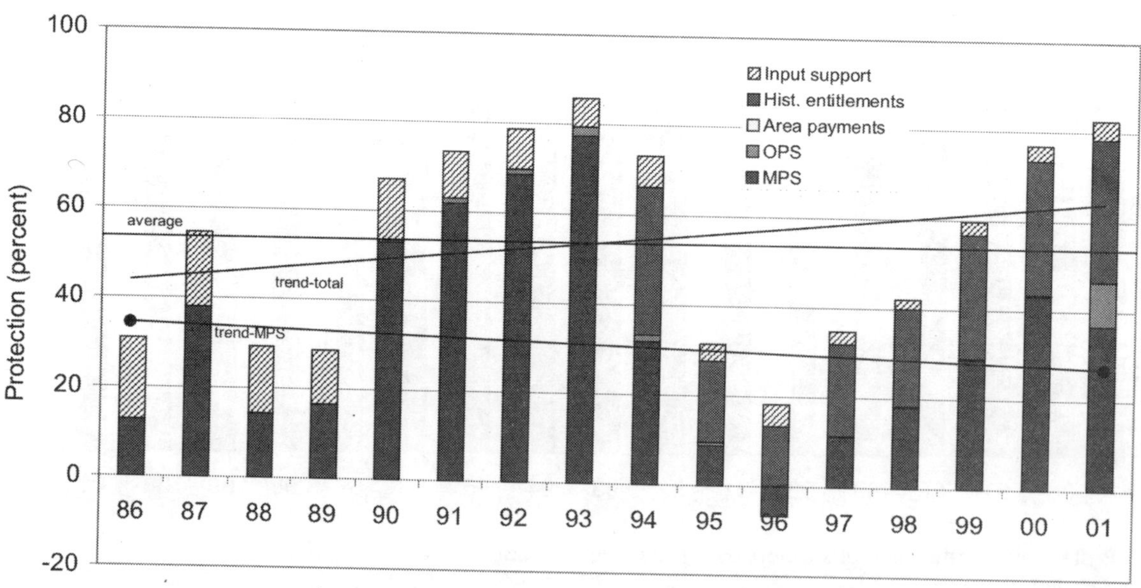


*Note:* "Protection" is the value of support over the value of production at world prices.
*Source:* OECD (2002a).

change in the mix of policies, from MPS and IPS to historical entitlements. (OPS policies were introduced in 2001.) Among the grains and oilseed crops, figure A.15 shows that rice had significant negative protection in the 1980s as did wheat (not shown). Figure A.16 shows that for other commodities, protection follows a similar pattern except more negative support in the 1980s and lower sup-

**FIGURE A.15 Mexico—Rice**

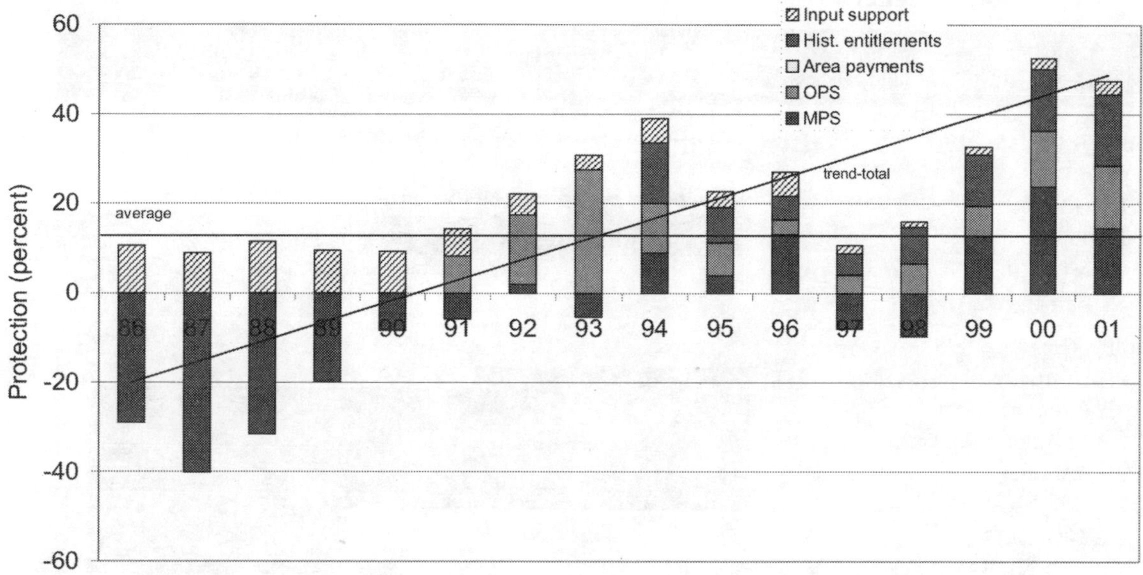


*Note:* "Protection" is the value of support over the value of production at world prices.
*Source:* OECD (2002a).

**FIGURE A.16 Mexico—Other Commodities**

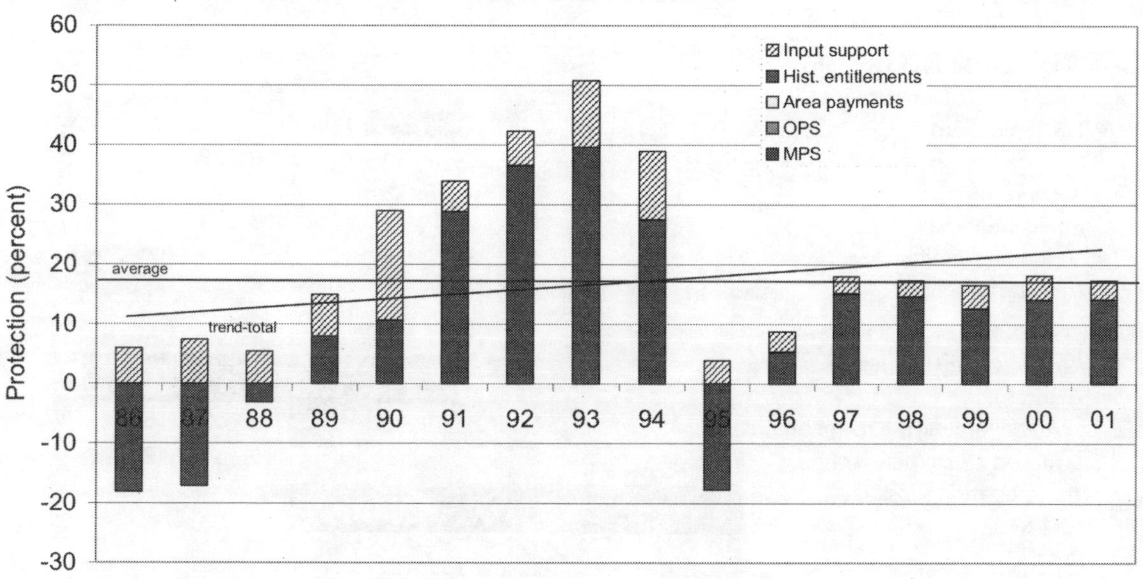


*Note:* "Protection" is the value of support over the value of production at world prices.
*Source:* OECD (2002a).

port in the past decade. A summary of policy developments in Mexico since 1980 is given in table A.6.

One question this appendix seeks to address is whether maintaining the current level of support but changing its composition will make a major difference to developing countries. The alternative policy framework called for by the Cairns Group and more recently by developing countries is the elimination of the special treatment that developed-country agriculture has received in Uruguay Round Agreement on Agriculture (URAA), which is to say, the elimination of support. A strength of

**TABLE A. 6 Policy Instruments for Grains and Oilseeds in Mexico (1980–Present)**

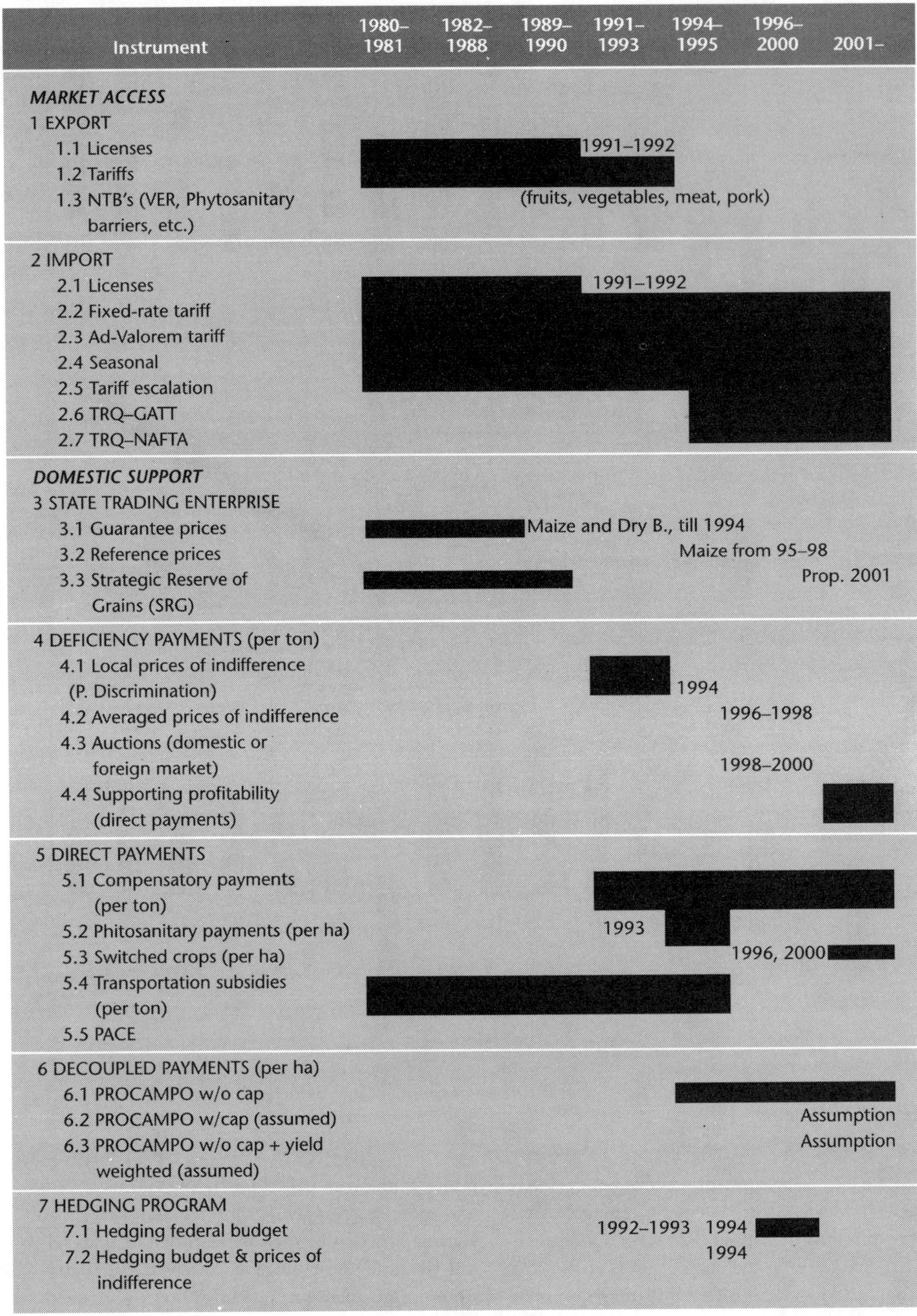

| Instrument | 1980–1981 | 1982–1988 | 1989–1990 | 1991–1993 | 1994–1995 | 1996–2000 | 2001– |
|---|---|---|---|---|---|---|---|
| *MARKET ACCESS* | | | | | | | |
| 1 EXPORT | | | | | | | |
| 1.1 Licenses | | | | 1991–1992 | | | |
| 1.2 Tariffs | | | | | | | |
| 1.3 NTB's (VER, Phytosanitary barriers, etc.) | | | | (fruits, vegetables, meat, pork) | | | |
| 2 IMPORT | | | | | | | |
| 2.1 Licenses | | | | 1991–1992 | | | |
| 2.2 Fixed-rate tariff | | | | | | | |
| 2.3 Ad-Valorem tariff | | | | | | | |
| 2.4 Seasonal | | | | | | | |
| 2.5 Tariff escalation | | | | | | | |
| 2.6 TRQ–GATT | | | | | | | |
| 2.7 TRQ–NAFTA | | | | | | | |
| *DOMESTIC SUPPORT* | | | | | | | |
| 3 STATE TRADING ENTERPRISE | | | | | | | |
| 3.1 Guarantee prices | | | | Maize and Dry B., till 1994 | | | |
| 3.2 Reference prices | | | | | | Maize from 95–98 | |
| 3.3 Strategic Reserve of Grains (SRG) | | | | | | | Prop. 2001 |
| 4 DEFICIENCY PAYMENTS (per ton) | | | | | | | |
| 4.1 Local prices of indifference (P. Discrimination) | | | | | 1994 | | |
| 4.2 Averaged prices of indifference | | | | | | 1996–1998 | |
| 4.3 Auctions (domestic or foreign market) | | | | | | 1998–2000 | |
| 4.4 Supporting profitability (direct payments) | | | | | | | |
| 5 DIRECT PAYMENTS | | | | | | | |
| 5.1 Compensatory payments (per ton) | | | | | | | |
| 5.2 Phitosanitary payments (per ha) | | | | 1993 | | | |
| 5.3 Switched crops (per ha) | | | | | | 1996, 2000 | |
| 5.4 Transportation subsidies (per ton) | | | | | | | |
| 5.5 PACE | | | | | | | |
| 6 DECOUPLED PAYMENTS (per ha) | | | | | | | |
| 6.1 PROCAMPO w/o cap | | | | | | | |
| 6.2 PROCAMPO w/cap (assumed) | | | | | | | Assumption |
| 6.3 PROCAMPO w/o cap + yield weighted (assumed) | | | | | | | Assumption |
| 7 HEDGING PROGRAM | | | | | | | |
| 7.1 Hedging federal budget | | | | 1992–1993 | 1994 | | |
| 7.2 Hedging budget & prices of indifference | | | | | 1994 | | |

**TABLE A.6 (Continued)**

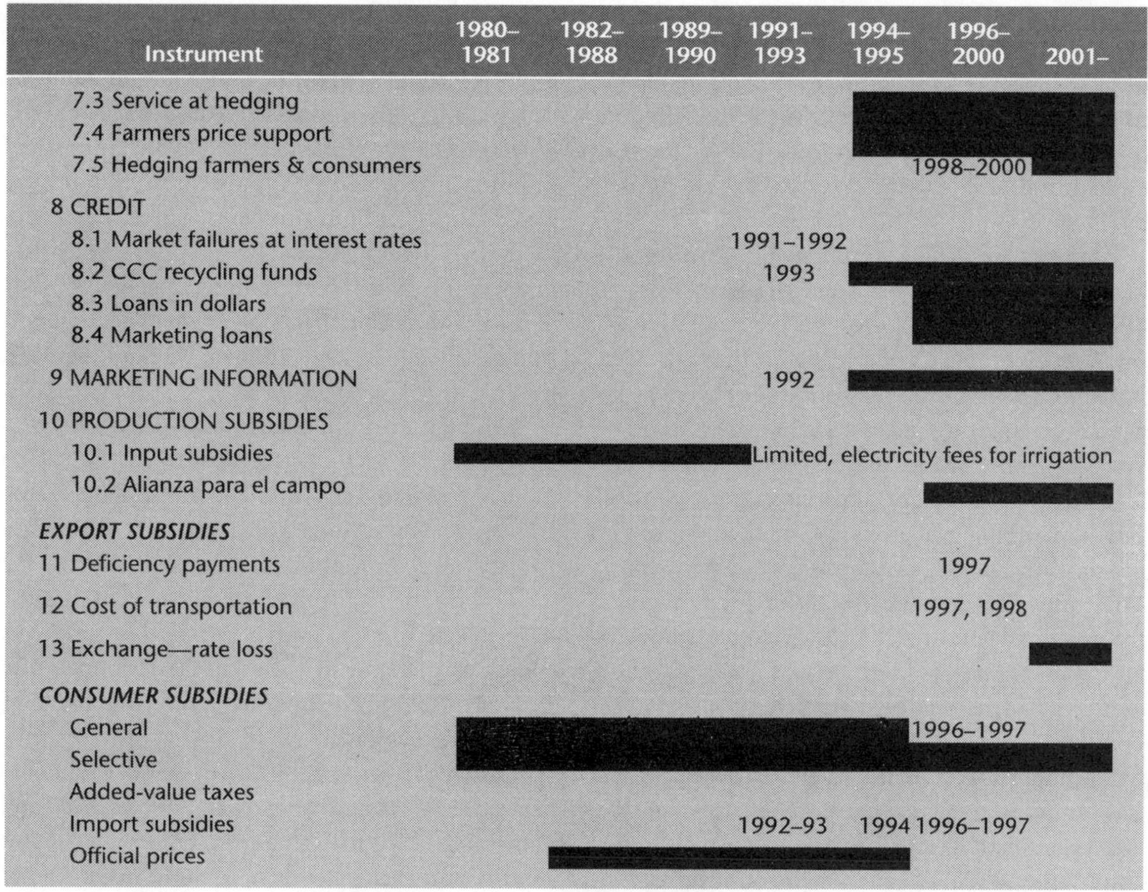

| Instrument | 1980–1981 | 1982–1988 | 1989–1990 | 1991–1993 | 1994–1995 | 1996–2000 | 2001– |
|---|---|---|---|---|---|---|---|
| 7.3 Service at hedging | | | | | | | |
| 7.4 Farmers price support | | | | | | | |
| 7.5 Hedging farmers & consumers | | | | | | 1998–2000 | |
| 8 CREDIT | | | | | | | |
| 8.1 Market failures at interest rates | | | | 1991–1992 | | | |
| 8.2 CCC recycling funds | | | | 1993 | | | |
| 8.3 Loans in dollars | | | | | | | |
| 8.4 Marketing loans | | | | | | | |
| 9 MARKETING INFORMATION | | | | 1992 | | | |
| 10 PRODUCTION SUBSIDIES | | | | | | | |
| 10.1 Input subsidies | | | | Limited, electricity fees for irrigation | | | |
| 10.2 Alianza para el campo | | | | | | | |
| *EXPORT SUBSIDIES* | | | | | | | |
| 11 Deficiency payments | | | | | | 1997 | |
| 12 Cost of transportation | | | | | | 1997, 1998 | |
| 13 Exchange—rate loss | | | | | | | |
| *CONSUMER SUBSIDIES* | | | | | | | |
| General | | | | | | 1996–1997 | |
| Selective | | | | | | | |
| Added-value taxes | | | | | | | |
| Import subsidies | | | | 1992–93 | 1994 | 1996–1997 | |
| Official prices | | | | | | | |

*Source:* Authors.

the PEM is that it has been designed to analyze the differential effects of alternative policies on farmers, landowners, input suppliers, taxpayers, consumers, and the world price and trade.

### *Conceptual Framework*

Chapter 1 of this volume cites several quantitative estimates of the impact that agricultural trade liberalization in rich countries would have on developing countries as a whole. There are other estimates of this from other sources, with broadly consistent conclusions. These tell us little, however, about the impact on income distribution and poverty within individual countries. This topic has been addressed, but for only a few developing countries and usually through a case-study approach, rather than through an integrative multicountry or global model.[2] One reason for the paucity of research on this important topic is that tracing links between trade and poverty requires detailed analysis of policies and institutions that are country-specific (Winters 2001).

Exceptions are the research reported in studies by Levinsohn, Berry, and Friedman (1999); Hertel and others (2002); and Robilliard, Bourguignon, and Robinson (2001). Hertel and others' study, for example, explicitly models the trade policy–poverty connection through factor markets, using the Global Trade Analysis Project general equilibrium framework to model the global linkages, mainly through the effects of liberalization on global price levels. It draws on national household survey data for individual developing countries to estimate expenditures and reliance on different sources of factor income by income strata. This is quite a useful framework, since it allows for modeling in broad terms the effects of all trade policy changes, agricultural and nonagricultural, on all households, agricultural and nonagricultural.

As with all modeling, a computable general equilibrium model (CGE) has some disadvantages—it does not model, for example, the effects of agricultural support policies administered through non-border measures, or the nontrade barriers to agricultural trade. As indicated below, given the idiosyncratic nature of agricultural policies and the differences in the effects of different support policies, careful modeling of these can be quite important in accurately reflecting the impacts of modifying them. This point is underscored by the fact that many of the recent changes in OECD agricultural policies have been in the type of domestic support; this and non-tariff barriers will be major issues for the developing countries in the Doha Round.

This appendix presents an alternative approach to examining the trade–poverty linkages and the effects on income distribution within developing countries of trade reform by rich countries and by the developing countries themselves. The approach uses the OECD's Policy Evaluation Matrix (PEM) model. The strengths of this approach are that (a) this model was specifically developed to capture the differential effects of the many types of agricultural support policies, and (b) it specifies production functions for particular crops (wheat, coarse grains, rice, and oilseeds) that are protected more than other agricultural products on average and in particular are given a disproportionately high level of support through non-border measures such as area payments, historical entitlements, and other direct payments. These crops are also of great interest to a large number of developing countries either as net exporters or importers. Food security concerns in many developing countries focus on the most important staple crop, which is most frequently rice, maize, or wheat.

In some scenarios used in this report, the market structure may be varied to represent the operation of tariff rate quotas (TRQs). In this situation, the link between domestic prices and world prices depends on the regime. A separate domestic market price provides closure in a national commodity market when the quota is binding.

When the TRQ is not binding, the volume of imports is influenced by the tariff rate and domestic demand and production. When the TRQ is binding, however, then it alone determines the volume of imports. Imports affect domestic prices and the world market in both situations. These differences in market structure can have important consequences for policy. For example, raising OPS may have very different effects on trade distortion and transfer efficiency, depending on whether there is a binding quota or not.

Although the PEM analyzes only four commodity groups, it includes linkages with the factor markets, thereby showing the impact on factor earnings from various policy changes. There are two specialized input markets in the PEM, one for land and one for other farmer-owned inputs. A specialized inputs market is one that links one source of demand to each source of supply. The farmer-owned inputs market is modeled like that for purchased inputs.

This approach, combined with household survey data on sources of income and expenditure, allows a detailed mapping from policy instrument to effect on each type of household in its role of producer, consumer, and taxpayer. This information should be useful in examining not only the impacts on the poor in developing countries, but also the question of who gains and who loses in the rich countries. In the context of the Doha Round negotiations, both of these are important considerations in the political economy of reform.

In the PEM, production is represented with constant elasticity of substitution (CES) production functions in producer prices for wheat, coarse grains (including maize), oilseeds, and rice for six major producing regions. The input markets in each region are simulated with demand (first order conditions) derived from the production functions. Factor supply is for the most part simulated with constant elasticity factor supply functions, as in many CGE models, but elasticities are specified taking into consideration the scope of the model and the constraints on resource mobility in agriculture.

In this framework, commodity supply is represented in terms of an aggregate production function and the associated factor demand and factor supply functions (see table A.7 for a summary of

**TABLE A.7 Model Outline**

| Symbol | Definition |
|---|---|
| ***1: Symbols Defined*** | |
| $qs_{ir}, qd_{ir}$ | quantities supplied and demanded of commodity *i* in region *r* |
| $ps_{ir}, pd_{ir}, p_{i0}$ | the supply or demand price of commodity *i* in region *r*; the world price of commodity *i* |
| $xs_{kir}, xs_{kr}, xd_{kir}$ | the quantity of input *k* supplied or demanded for the production of output *i* in region *r*; the index *i* is dropped for aggregate supply |
| $ws_{kir}, ws_{kr}, wd_{kir}$ | the supply or demand price of input *k* for the production of output *i* in region *r*; the index *i* is dropped for aggregate supply price |
| $s_{kir}, \alpha_{kir}$ | the share of input *k* used in the production of output *i* in region *r* and the corresponding share parameter for the production functions |
| $\rho_{ir}, \sigma_{ir}$ | the elasticity parameter for commodity *i* in region *r*, and the corresponding elasticity of substitution for the production functions |
| $\varepsilon s_{ijr}, \varepsilon d_{ijr}$ | the elasticity of supply or demand for commodity *i*, with respect to the price of commodity *j* in region *r* |
| $\beta_{kjir}, \beta_{kir}, \beta_{kr}$ | the input supply elasticity of input *k* for commodity *i* in region *r*, with respect to input price *k*, used for commodity *j*; in region *r*; the input supply elasticity with respect to own price for commodity *i* in region *r*; and the input supply elasticity with respect to own price in region *r* |
| $r_{ir}^{mps}, r_{ir}^{ops}, r_{ir}^{k}, r_{r}^{k}$ | the support rate for commodity *i*, input *k*, in region *r*; the superscript mps and ops are used for market price support and output price support, respectively, while the superscript *k* is shown for policies that affect factor markets |
| $cs_{ir}, cd_{ir}$ | the constants that reflect quality differences (location, season, varieties, and so on) which cause differences between world and regional commodity prices |
| *i, j* | the indexes for the four commodities; $i, j = 1, 2, 3, 4$ for wheat, coarse grains, oilseeds, and rice, respectively |
| *k* | the indexes for the four inputs; $k = 1, 2, 3, 4$ for land, other farmer-owned inputs, hired labor, other purchased inputs, respectively |
| *r* | the index for region; $r = 1, 2, 3, 4, 5, 6, 7$ for Canada, Mexico, the United States, the European Union, Switzerland, Japan, and the rest of the world, respectively; $r = 0$ is used in the equations that feature the world price |

There are three parts to the PEM model:

- commodity demand, commodity supply or production, and equilibrium conditions for the commodity markets;
- the demand, supply, and equilibrium conditions for the factor markets;
- the price relationships; and
- the equilibrium conditions.

***2: Commodity Markets***

Commodity demands are expressed as a function of demand prices and elasticities with a constant elasticity functional form:

[A.1] $$qd_{ir} = qdo_{ir} pd_{1r}^{\varepsilon d_{i1r}} pd_{2r}^{\varepsilon d_{i2r}} pd_{2r}^{\varepsilon d_{i3r}} pd_{2r}^{\varepsilon d_{i4r}} \quad i = 1,2,3,4 \quad r = 1,2,\ldots,7$$

The quantity supply for the rest of the world region has the same form:

[A.2] $$qs_{i7} = qso_{i7} ps_{17}^{\varepsilon s_{i17}} ps_{27}^{\varepsilon s_{i27}} ps_{37}^{\varepsilon s_{i37}} ps_{47}^{\varepsilon s_{i47}} \quad i = 1,2,3,4$$

Supply for the six endogenous regions are based on a constant elasticity of substitution (CES) production function. Production is generally a function of four inputs: land, other farmer-supplied inputs, hired labor, and other purchased inputs, except in the cases of Mexico and Japan where a hired labor input is not specified separately:

[A.3a] $$qs_{ir} = (\alpha_{1ir} xd_{1ir}^{-\rho_{ir}} + \alpha_{2ir} xd_{2ir}^{-\rho_{ir}} + \alpha_{3ir} xd_{3ir}^{-\rho_{ir}} + \alpha_{4ir} xd_{4ir}^{-\rho_{ir}})^{-1/\rho ir} \quad i = 1,2,3,4 \quad r = 1,3,4,5$$

or

[A.3b] $$qs_{ir} = (\alpha_{1ir} xd_{1ir}^{-\rho_{ir}} + \alpha_{2ir} xd_{2ir}^{-\rho_{ir}} + \alpha_{4ir} xd_{4ir}^{-\rho_{ir}})^{-1/\rho ir} \quad i = 1,2,3,4 \quad r = 2,6$$

No rice produced in Canada or Switzerland.

**TABLE A.7 (Continued)**

Market equilibrium requires equating world supply and demand for each of the four commodities:

[A.4] $\sum_{r=1}^{7} qs_{ir} = \sum_{r=1}^{7} qd_{ir} \quad i = 1,2,3,4$

***3: Factor Market Relationships***

The market structure for factors reflects the fact that both land and farmer-owned inputs are relatively specialized and do not freely change use. Even in the case in which farms produce a mix of crops, these will be grown in rotations that restrict the ability to change the output mix. This is especially the case for paddy rice land, which is highly unlikely to be used in the production of other crops in the model, at least within the range of scenarios that the model is suitable for evaluating.

A separate supply functions is specified for land by commodity and region although the supply function for land includes cross-price terms except in the case of rice:

[A.5] $xs_{1ir} = xso_{1ir} ws_{1ir}^{\beta_{11ir}} ws_{2ir}^{\beta_{12ir}} ws_{3ir}^{\beta_{13ir}} \quad i = 1,2,3 \quad r = 1,2,\ldots,6$

The supply functions for land for rice production is:

[A.6] $xs_{14ir} = xso_{14r} ws_{14r}^{\beta_{14r}} \quad r = 2,3,4,5$

A separate supply function is specified for other farmer-owned inputs by commodity and region:

[A.7] $xs_{2ir} = xso_{2ir} ws_{2ir}^{\beta_{2ir}} \quad i = 1,2,3,4 \quad r = 1,2,\ldots,6$

Neither purchased inputs nor hired labor is specialized. A single supply function by region is specified for hired labor and purchased inputs:

[A.8] $xs_{3r} = xso_{3r} ws_{3r}^{\beta_{3r}} \quad r = 1,2,\ldots,6$

and

[A.9] $xs_{4r} = xso_{4r} ws_{4r}^{\beta_{4r}} \quad r = 1,2,\ldots,6$

Factor demand in all cases is represented by the first order condition:

[A.10a] $wd_{kir} = ps_{ir} \frac{fqs_{ir}}{fxs_{kir}} \quad k = 1,2,3,4 \quad i = 1,2,3,4 \quad r = 1,2,\ldots,6$

For the CES production function, the first order condition can be written as:

[A.10b] $xd_{kir} = qs_{ir} \left( \frac{\alpha_{kir} ps_{ir}}{wd_{kir}} \right)^{\sigma_{ir}}$

Market equilibrium equates supply and demand in each input market in each region. For land and other farmer-owned inputs these are:

[A.11] $xs_{kir} = xd_{ir} \quad k = 1,2 \quad i = 1,2,3,4 \quad r = 1,2,\ldots,6$

For hired labor and other purchased inputs, the factor market equilibrium conditions are:

[A.13] $xs_{kr} = \sum_{r=1}^{4} xd_{kir} \quad k = 3,4 \quad r = 1,2,\ldots,6$

***4: Commodity and Factor Price Relationships***

Agricultural policy and other institutional factors create a set of wedges between world prices and demand and supply prices.

[A.14] $pd_{ir} = p_{i0} + r_{ir}^{mps} + cd_{ir} \quad i = 1,2,3,4 \quad r = 1,2,\ldots,6$

[A.15] $ps_{ir} = p_{i0} + r_{ir}^{mps} + r_{ir}^{ops} + cs_{ir} \quad i = 1,2,3,4 \quad r = 1,2,\ldots,6$

[A.16] $wd_{kir} = ws_{kir} - r_{ir}^{k} \quad k = 1,2 \quad i = 1,2,3,4 \quad r = 1,2,\ldots,6$

[A.17] $wd_{kir} = ws_{kr} - r_{r}^{k} \quad k = 3,4 \quad r = 1,2,\ldots,6$

the model structure). This allows one to analyze a change in the value of some exogenous policy parameter, for example an administered price, an area payment, or an input subsidy.

***Cost-Benefit Analysis***

In calculating the costs and benefits of support measures, inputs were classified according to whether they were supplied by or purchased by

**FIGURE A.17 Production and Input Supply Responses to Increased Commodity Price**

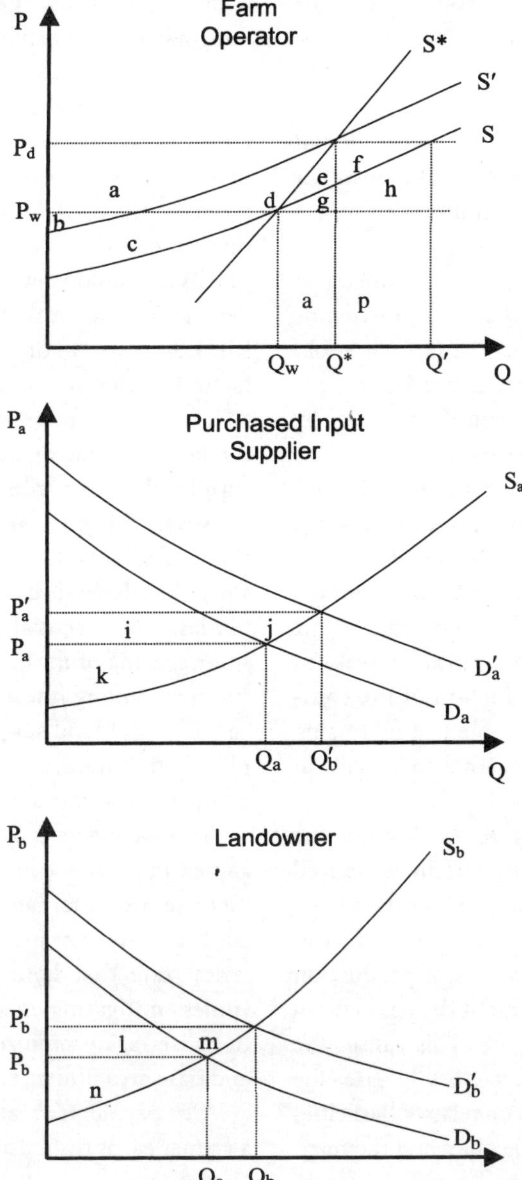


farm households. Inputs supplied by farm households—for instance, land and farm household labor—are called "farm owned." At least three kinds of inputs purchased by farm households were distinguished: fertilizer; hired labor; and a residual aggregate, "other purchased."

An important indicator of the effect of a policy is the "initial incidence" or "which price is affected first." Market price support has its initial incidence in commodity markets while area payments and subsidies to purchased inputs have their initial incidence in the associated factor markets. Regardless of initial incidence, though, the price and quantity links in the model tie the factor and output markets together so that a change in a policy measure that affects any one of the crop or factor markets will end up having some effect on all of them. Figure A.17 contains supply and demand diagrams illustrating the basic components of this representative model. The upper panel shows the commodity supply curve (the demand curve is ignored) and the lower two panels show supply and demand curves for two of the four factors of production (purchased inputs and land, respectively).

Figure A.17 shows how price wedges corresponding to unit market price support or output price support are represented in the PEM crop models. The wedge separates prices paid to domestic producers, $P_d$, from the corresponding price on world markets, $P_w$. The accompanying level of price support is indicated by the area $a + d + e + f + g + h$ and represents the sum of taxpayer and consumer costs (or taxpayer costs only if output price support only).

Consider first the case of no change in input factor prices as production of the crop expands with increased producer prices. The farmer would move along the original supply curve S and produce at Q′. Total revenue would increase by $(P_d–P_w)Q_w + (Q'–Q_w)P_d$. However, farmers' costs increase by area $g + h + o + p$ (albeit with no changes in input prices by assumption) so the net gain in producer profits is area $a + d + e + f$. However, if the supply curve for purchased inputs and land were upward sloping (as depicted in the bottom two panels in figure A.17), the increase in demand for inputs as the production of the commodity increases (owing to the policy of increasing producer prices initially) will generate an increase in input prices.

The bottom panels of figure A.17 show the associated factor market effects. The hypothesized increase in the producer price due to increased market price support translates into outward shifts in demand for both purchased factors of production and land as shown by the new input demand curves labeled $D_a'$ and $D_b'$ in the figure. This causes the quantities and prices of both factors to rise, the degree to which clearly depends on relative elasticities (slopes) of the factor supply schedules and the magnitude in the shift in input demand curves (which, in turn depends on the share of input in production and the relative production elasticities for the inputs).

The increase in input prices will cause the supply curve for output to shift upward to S′ in the top panel of figure A.17. Output will now increase to Q* only and the supply curve with input prices changing is given by S*. S* is the equilibrium adjustment supply curve that plots the production response to the increase in prices received by farmers in the presence of upward-sloping input supply curves (shown for the purchased input and land markets). Farm operators and input suppliers gain area $a$ minus area $c + d + e$. Area $a$ is the increase in farm operator profits due to the increase in price from $P_w$ to $P_d$. Area $c + d + e$ represents the increase in costs due to the higher input prices. The increase in the farm operator's welfare is now smaller than would be the case if input prices were constant, but still greater than zero.

The areas marked $i$ and $j$ in the middle panel of figure A.17 represent the impact of the change in market price support on net incomes of firms supplying purchased inputs. Correspondingly, areas marked $l$ and $m$ in the lower panel show increased profits for landowners. Which of these is the greater depends on the elasticities of factor supply and substitution as well as on the relative importance of the factor bundles in crop production.

The *price* increase will always be the greater for the factor (or factor bundle) exhibiting the lowest supply elasticity, which is land in many cases. However, this does not guarantee that the largest share of total benefits of support go to this factor since that depends on factor shares as well as elasticities. The essential point is that there will be some sharing of the economic benefits of increased support among these two groups of economic agents. But if land supply is very inelastic and supply of other inputs very elastic, then land captures a disproportionate amount of the rents.

Area payments is a category of support that has gained importance in recent years. Such payments increase the rental rate received by a landowner for land used in crop production as compared to the rental rate that land would earn in other uses (unless mitigating effects such as payment limitations, set-aside requirements, voluntary set-aside and base area limitations override it).

Area payments create a wedge between the price a farmer earns from using his land and other owned factors in crop production. Similarly, subsidies to purchased inputs create a difference between the price suppliers receive and the price farmers pay for them.

A payment to land that comes with a requirement to plant induces an increase in the area of land used in crop production. This payment drives a wedge between the effective rental rate received for land used in crop production and the associated rental rate charged (perhaps implicitly) for that land. The equilibrium supply price for land rises, while the equilibrium demand price falls, leading to an increase in the quantity of land and other farm-owned factors demanded and used in crop production, which will be greater or less depending on the elasticity of supply of crop land reflected in the slope of the supply curve for farm-owned factors. In turn, this increased factor use would show up as a rightward shift of the commodity supply schedule that is shown in the top panel of figure A.17 and would cause the associated increases in supply and net trade.

The increased supply results in some drop in world market prices. To the extent that the world market price falls, and that this price fall is transmitted to the domestic market, consumption of the commodity will increase. This is one reason to suspect that increased support made in the form of a payment tied to land would have less of an effect on trade than the same amount of support provided as market price support.

Another reason has to do with the fact that the payment is a subsidy targeted to one factor of production—land—while market price support may be viewed as a subsidy spread more or less evenly across all inputs. The former has less effect on output, based on the assumption that the elasticity of supply of land is less than the elasticity of the supply of nonland factors of production. There is an income gain for farm households and input suppliers as well. Input suppliers gain, in this example, because the increase in commodity production creates additional demand for purchased inputs. This is represented as the rightward shift in the demand curve for purchased factors.

The reader should notice that the extra production constitutes only one of two channels through which suppliers of purchased inputs may be impacted by the area payments. It should be recalled that the model assumes farm-owned factors and purchased inputs are substitutes in production. Insofar as production decisions are concerned, an area payment reduces the cost of land (rental rate) relative to nonland factors of production. If this were the only effect, the demand for purchased inputs would decline. The increased demand shown reflects a "net" substitution effect that is more than offset by the scale effect associated with increased production.

There is again a sharing of the benefits of support among farm households and input suppliers, but this time farm households might be expected to get the lion's share if they are landowners as well. In fact, this result, like the result for commodity trade, also depends heavily on the relative elasticity of supply of land.

Graphical analysis is helpful in illustrating differences in the channels through which support measures produce their effects, and differences in the direction of impacts on selected outcomes. However, the PEM simulations to follow will indicate differences in both the direction and the relative magnitude of effects of small changes in market price support, payments based on output, payments based on input use, and payments based on area planted. Taken together, these findings confirm that the estimated trade and welfare effects of a given amount of support differ depending on the support measure used to provide that support.

The outcome depends on economic efficiency losses and distributive leakages (reallocations) to input suppliers, consumers, taxpayers, and the rest of the world through market price changes. The factors governing the impacts of agricultural policies include the structural characteristics of the agrifood sector (notably the share of inputs supplied from off-farm sources, the share of income coming from off-farm activities, and the extent of competition upstream and downstream from the farm gate); the response of these characteristics to changes in the level of support (production technology, supply elasticities of inputs, demand elasticity of the output, world market conditions, and so on); and the form and distribution through which support is provided (input subsidy versus a tariff, and so forth).

## Structure of PEM

The technique used in the PEM shares many features with general equilibrium modeling but also draws on some of the techniques used in the equilibrium displacement models found in the agricultural economics literature. The latter use multimarket equilibrium elasticities to determine the incidence on all stakeholders of interventions in agricultural input and output markets. These are based on differentiating a system of equations representing production functions, first-order conditions, factor supply, and commodity demand. The results are then calibrated with cost share and elasticity parameters and solved for the multimarket equilibrium parameters.

Multimarket equilibrium models share four characteristics of general equilibrium models:

- The model is calibrated from base period data (consisting of demand, production, and factors of production or production shares) and a set of elasticities.

- Each industry is treated as a representative firm. Consumption is based on a representative consumer.
- The payments to capital are determined residually; in the case of unincorporated businesses these may not be dissociated into the component parts of value added.
- The models simulate normative adjustments to a change in policy or exogenous variables by the representative firms and consumers based on competitive market behavior (usually) rather than the positive behavior built into econometric models.

The behavior assumption used in both types of models means that they are inherently medium- or long-term mapping outcomes from one equilibrium position to another.

## A Disaggregated System of Demand and Production for Mexico

This section of the appendix describes how a disaggregated approach can be used to model both production and demand for Mexico. It can show the impact on the distribution of impact across consumers of different income levels and it does not differentiate impact and supply response between subsistence and commercial farmers. Disaggregated supply and demand sectors are needed to simulate the effects of changes in policy on different types of farm households in Mexico.

The production function for coarse grains is replaced with a household production system for five types of maize-producing farms varying principally by farm size. A single production function continues to be used for wheat, other coarse grains, oilseeds, and rice. The constant elasticity demand function is replaced with a linear expenditure system for each of the five maize-producing farm households and 10 others varying by household income.

### *Expenditure and Consumption Distributions*

The PEM bases demand upon commodities valued at producer prices except for differences between consumer and producer prices caused by subsidies. It follows CGE practice, whereby goods are valued in producer prices with the value added in the marketing chain resulting in a separate demand for transportation, wholesale, and retail services. Goods and services that are genuine inputs are transformed into other products that do generate derived demands for intermediate inputs. When the PEM is changed by including demands for different households these intermediate demands need to be considered.

Finally, many of the expenditure items associated with cereals and oilseeds in household budget surveys reflect a great deal of other value added. Consumers seldom buy wheat but rather flour, bread, wheat tortilla, and a great variety of other similar products. (Flour may be classed as a primary product in CGEs because input-output tables sometimes treat milling as a service industry rather than a manufacturing industry.) Much of the maize and rice purchased is in the form of a grain or flour so there is far less value added. A method is needed, therefore, to reconcile values at the farm gate with intermediate use and values at the consumer level.

One possibility is to go to an input-output table—or shipments data that lie behind input-output tables—to determine quantities used in feed, manufacturing, and final demand. The resulting data can be used to construct simple two-input gross output production functions (in primary input and value added) following Gardner (1975).[3] The easier—if less satisfactory—approach used here is to disaggregate feed use based on the attribution of MPS found in the PSE tables.

Table A.8 shows expenditure by income decile from a 2000 household expenditure survey of about 10,000 Mexican households. Expenditures for wheat, maize, and rice are aggregations by class of the categories listed in table A.9.

To estimate expenditures in 2001, the expenditure pattern found in the household survey (showing greater expenditures than the value of farm production) is "rased" with the farm-level value of consumption from table A.10 and production and total expenditures for each decile in 2001 as control totals. Total expenditures in 2001 is total expenditures in 2000 grossed up by 10.2 percent, which is the growth in private final consumption expenditures (OECD 2002c, p. 3, converted to current U.S. dollars). This procedure essentially assigns the value added in marketing and food manufacturing industries into the other demand. Table A.11 shows the resulting allocation of consumption in 2001 expressed in U.S. dollars per capita. Dividing these by the effective consumer prices calculated from the PSE dataset (using a unit price for "other") gives quantities.

**TABLE A.8 Expenditure by Decile, 2000 in Million Pesos (Per Capita in Parenthesis, US$)**

| Decile | Wheat | Maize | Rice | Other | Total |
|---|---|---|---|---|---|
| 1 | 988 (2.7) | 2,173 (24.4) | 340 (1.6) | 28,380 (351) | 31,881 (379) |
| 2 | 1,456 (3.9) | 3,559 (39.7) | 409 (1.9) | 50,828 (624) | 56,253 (669) |
| 3 | 1,823 (4.8) | 4,035 (44.6) | 353 (1.6) | 68,720 (841) | 74,931 (892) |
| 4 | 2,048 (5.4) | 4,250 (46.8) | 341 (1.6) | 86,132 (1,050) | 92,771 (1,104) |
| 5 | 2,362 (6.2) | 4,070 (44.7) | 372 (1.7) | 108,119 (1,315) | 114,924 (1,368) |
| 6 | 2,636 (6.9) | 4,051 (44.3) | 364 (1.7) | 130,671 (1,586) | 137,721 (1,639) |
| 7 | 3,209 (8.4) | 4,074 (44.5) | 404 (1.8) | 165,809 (2,010) | 173,497 (2,065) |
| 8 | 3,478 (9.0) | 3,988 (43.3) | 331 (1.5) | 212,290 (2,565) | 220,087 (2,619) |
| 9 | 3,575 (9.2) | 3,788 (41.0) | 299 (1.4) | 288,830 (3,477) | 296,492 (3,528) |
| 10 | 4,370 (11.2) | 3,093 (33.2) | 478 (2.1) | 783,026 (9,367) | 790,967 (9,413) |
| Total | 25,946 (6.8) | 37,083 (40.6) | 3,690 (1.7) | 1,922,805 (2,319) | 1,989,524 (2,368) |

*Source:* Private communication, Allesandro Necita (July 2002).

**TABLE A.9 Allocation of Household Survey Expenditure Categories**

| Code | Description | Class |
|---|---|---|
| A001 | Maíz en grano, pozolero, palomero | Coarse grains |
| A002 | Harina de maíz | Coarse grains |
| A003 | Masa de maíz | Coarse grains |
| A004 | Tortilla de maíz | Coarse grains |
| A005 | Fécula de maíz (maicena, polvo para atole) | Coarse grains |
| A006 | Otros productos de maíz: tostadas, hojuelas, pinole, etc. | Coarse grains |
| A007 | Harina de trigo (refinada o integral) | Wheat |
| A008 | Tortilla de harina | Wheat |
| A009 | Galletas saladas | Wheat |
| A010 | Galletas dulces | Wheat |
| A011 | Pan blanco: bolillo, telera, baguette | Wheat |
| A012 | Pan de dulce: en pieza o empaquetado | Wheat |
| A013 | Pan para emparedado, hamburgesa, hot-dog | Wheat |
| A014 | Pasteles y panecillos en pieza o empaquetado | Wheat |
| A015 | Pasta para sopa | Wheat |
| A016 | Otros productos de trigo: pasta para fritura, hojuelas, harina preparada, etc. | Wheat |
| A017 | Arroz en grano | Rice |
| A018 | Otros productos de arroz: harina, tostado, etc. | Rice |
| A019 | Avena | Coarse grains |
| A020 | Otros cereales: centeno, granola, cebada, etc. | Coarse grains |
| A021 | Frituras procesadas de trigo o maíz | Coarse grains |

*Source:* Authors' calculations.

### *Calibration of the Linear Expenditure System (LES)*

In this appendix the three cereals are treated as a single commodity within the linear expenditure system and expenditures are allocated in fixed proportions by income class among the three cereals. An alternative to the fixed proportions would be the constant elasticity of transformation among the three commodities, but this option is not pursued here.

Arc income elasticities were calculated for the change in expenditures between each income decile in table A.8 and smoothed using a three-category

**TABLE A.10 Maize Production Systems**

| | Subsistence Item | Very Small | Small | Medium | Large | Sum or Average |
|---|---|---|---|---|---|---|
| Farm type (size range, Ha) | >2 | 2–5 | 5–10 | 10–18 | <18 | |
| Average size (Ha) | 1.3 | 3.4 | 7.3 | 14 | 37.8 | 11.3 |
| Total land area (Ha) | 108,625 | 549,250 | 1,161,199 | 1,741,706 | 3,439,220 | 7,000,000 |
| Share of households (%) | 13.5% | 26.1% | 25.7% | 20.1% | 14.7% | 100% |
| Number of households | 83,557 | 161,544 | 159,068 | 124,408 | 90,985 | 618,943 |
| Yield (t/Ha) | 1.46 | 1.88 | 2.64 | 2.64 | 2.64 | |
| Adjusted production (t) | 164,618 | 1,071,829 | 3,182,058 | 4,772,832 | 9,424,563 | 18,615,900 |
| Labor (no/Ha) | 1.63 | 0.68 | 0.41 | 0.41 | 0.41 | |
| Total labor | 177,142 | 371,552 | 477,205 | 714,100 | 1,410,080 | 3,150,078 |
| Population | 531,425 | 1,114,655 | 1,431,616 | 2,142,299 | 4,230,240 | 9,450,234 |
| Expenditure per capita (pesos) | 3,415 | 4,353 | 6,418 | 8,913 | 14,261 | |

*Source:* Winters, Davis, and Corral (2001); Authors' calculations; and SARH-DGE 1991 as reported in Heinegg (2001).

**TABLE A.11 Expenditures Per Capita by Decile, 2001 (U.S. dollars)**

| Decile | Wheat | Maize | Rice | Other | Total |
|---|---|---|---|---|---|
| 1 | 2.7 | 24.4 | 1.6 | 351 | 379 |
| 2 | 3.9 | 39.7 | 1.9 | 624 | 669 |
| 3 | 4.8 | 44.6 | 1.6 | 841 | 892 |
| 4 | 5.4 | 46.8 | 1.6 | 1,050 | 1,104 |
| 5 | 6.2 | 44.7 | 1.7 | 1,315 | 1,368 |
| 6 | 6.9 | 44.3 | 1.7 | 1,586 | 1,639 |
| 7 | 8.4 | 44.5 | 1.8 | 2,010 | 2,065 |
| 8 | 9.0 | 43.3 | 1.5 | 2,565 | 2,619 |
| 9 | 9.2 | 41.0 | 1.4 | 3,477 | 3,528 |
| 10 | 11.2 | 33.2 | 2.1 | 9,367 | 9,413 |
| Average | 6.8 | 40.6 | 1.7 | 2,319 | 2,368 |

*Source:* Authors' calculations.

moving average. The resulting income elasticities are shown in table A.12.

One approach to calibrating an LES therefore might be to solve equations for the parameters from base period shares and a set of own price elasticities and income elasticities found in the literature. This approach is sensitive to the values for the income and own price elasticity selected. If those are not consistent with the overall LES assumption and the shares, it is easy to generate contradictory signs on the calibrated parameters and unreasonable elasticities.

The calibration approach used here is to set the value of the minimum consumption bundles as a share income such that it generates satisfactory values overall in terms of price elasticities and the minimum consumption parameters. The individual minimum consumption parameters can then be found simply by inverting the demand functions. Using this procedure will generally result in reasonable values for the minimum consumption parameters consistent with their interpretation. The value for the minimum consumption bundle can be set to give the most reasonable values for all own price elasticities.

To calibrate the minimum consumption parameters, the minimum consumption bundle was set at 75 percent of observed expenditure of the lowest

**TABLE A.12 Expenditure Parameters and Elasticities for the Base Period, 2001**

| Decile | Quantity[a] | Alpha | Gamma[a] | Income Elasticity | Own Price Elasticity |
|---|---|---|---|---|---|
| *Cereals:* | | | | | |
| 1 | 0.219 | 0.069 | 0.169 | 0.632 | −0.283 |
| 2 | 0.348 | 0.051 | 0.199 | 0.526 | −0.458 |
| 3 | 0.392 | 0.025 | 0.275 | 0.303 | −0.316 |
| 4 | 0.412 | 0.015 | 0.318 | 0.210 | −0.240 |
| 5 | 0.402 | 0.014 | 0.289 | 0.230 | −0.290 |
| 6 | 0.403 | 0.011 | 0.292 | 0.211 | −0.285 |
| 7 | 0.416 | 0.006 | 0.340 | 0.126 | −0.187 |
| 8 | 0.410 | 0.000 | 0.401 | 0.013 | −0.021 |
| 9 | 0.392 | 0.000 | 0.383 | 0.013 | −0.022 |
| 10 | 0.350 | 0.000 | 0.341 | 0.013 | −0.026 |
| *Other goods:* | | | | | |
| 1 | 351 | 0.931 | 262 | 1.045 | −0.948 |
| 2 | 624 | 0.949 | 259 | 1.051 | −0.979 |
| 3 | 841 | 0.975 | 249 | 1.063 | −0.993 |
| 4 | 1,050 | 0.985 | 243 | 1.061 | −0.997 |
| 5 | 1,315 | 0.986 | 247 | 1.048 | −0.997 |
| 6 | 1,586 | 0.989 | 246 | 1.043 | −0.998 |
| 7 | 2,010 | 0.994 | 240 | 1.041 | −0.999 |
| 8 | 2,565 | 1.000 | 232 | 1.036 | −1.000 |
| 9 | 3,477 | 1.000 | 234 | 1.026 | −1.000 |
| 10 | 9,367 | 1.000 | 239 | 1.010 | −1.000 |

[a] The units are tonnes for cereals. The quantity of other goods are measured by an index.
*Source:* Authors' calculations.

**TABLE A.13 Maize Production Coefficients**

| *Input:* | Subsistence | Very small | Small | Medium | Large |
|---|---|---|---|---|---|
| Farmer-owned | 0.53 | 0.35 | 0.15 | 0.15 | 0.16 |
| Purchased inputs | 0.00 | 0.28 | 0.59 | 0.59 | 0.57 |

*Source:* Authors' calculations.

income class or US$285 per year. This implies a value of −4 for the flexibility of income for this income decile, which is high in absolute terms but not unreasonably so for the lowest income decile in a developing country.

The minimum consumption levels for cereals range from 169 to 400 kilograms per person per year or 0.5 to 1.1 kilograms per person per day.

Cereals are such a small part of the budget that income elasticities for other goods and services are close to 1.0 and own price elasticities are near –1.0, especially for the high-income deciles. The income elasticity of cereals is about 0.6 for low-income households, declining with increasing income to nearly zero for high-income households. Own price elasticity is −0.283 for lowest-income households but it rises to −0.458 for households in decile 2. This is because of the increase in the size of the gamma parameter. Thereafter the absolute value of own price elasticity declines to nearly zero. The own price demand elasticity for wheat, maize, and rice in the original

PEM are −0.76, −0.15 and −0.24, respectively, so the values calibrated from the LES should give similar overall response to a change in cereals prices—although they would vary considerably in their details.

Demand by farm households is disaggregated from the total demand in table A.12 by solving the appropriate demand functions by decile. Both subsistence and very small farms are in decile 1 while small, medium-size, and large farms are in deciles 2, 3, and 5 respectively. (The farm households are described in the next section.) Both the nonfarm population and this population's income can be found by subtracting out the farm portions. Since the demand systems are linear, total demand is not changed. The resulting demand system then has 15 household types.

### *Disaggregated Maize Production*

The production coefficients in the PEM are based on national costs of production surveys by Mexico's Ministry of Agriculture, SARH-DGE. Unfortunately this report is not yet published so an estimate of costs of production has been made here based on other available sources.[4] The result allows the model to be fully calibrated to illustrate its application.

There has been a major change in the structure of farming in Mexico in the 1990s, perhaps because of the land reform in 1992 and the major changes in the structure of support after Mexico joined the North American Free Trade Agreement (NAFTA) in 1994. Heinegg (2001) shows 2.8 million households producing maize in 1991, 63 percent of which had less than two hectares. Winters, Davis, and Corral 2001 (WDC) have 86.5 percent of their households with more than two hectares. This is a rather critical level, because, according to Heinegg, at about two hectares households switch from being net buyers of maize to net sellers.

The Heinegg distribution of households is inconsistent with expenditure levels in the 1996 and 2000 household expenditure surveys: it generates too many people in the lowest expenditure decile. The structure used in the appendix therefore is based on WDC for the present, but production coefficients are based on Heinegg, with some judgment by the authors.

Following WDC, maize production is represented by five different types of farms varying by size (table A.10). The average farm size of 11.3 hectares can be calculated directly from the distribution of farm types and the average size by farm type. Heinegg reports 6.9 million hectares of land for maize in 1991. Dividing 7 million hectares by the average farm size gives the estimate of 620,000 households and the number of households by each farm type.

Combining Heinegg's yields with the new distribution of land by farm types gives a total estimate of maize production of 17.9 million tons. This was grossed up 4 percent to match with the value for production in the OECD data.

Combining Heinegg's labor per hectare with the new distribution of land by farm types gives a total estimate of labor use of 3.1 million people (for at least part of the year). Assuming two additional family members per worker gives a total population partially dependent on maize production of 9.4 million, which is about 37 percent of the rural population in 2001. It should be possible with better information on the actual share of labor on maize production to refine these estimates and include a labor supply function as part of the LES.

Heinegg also reports household expenditure for maize and other crops. Total income is estimated by applying this ratio to maize expenditure. Results for 1991 are then grossed up to 2001 according to the ratio of rural value added in 2001 to value added in 1999.

Production shares reported in table A.13 are as reliable as the data in table A.10. The land income by farm type was calculated by taking the total returns to labor for maize production in PEM and allocating to each farm type according to its share of land in table A.13. Dividing land income by the value of production gives the land share. The share for other farm-owned input is found analogously using the distribution of labor in table A.10. Purchased inputs were calculated as a residual except for subsistence farms in which the farmer-owned input was the residual and purchased inputs set to zero.

## Notes

1. A large component of the other 39 percent in this category are EU headage payments.

2. Reimer (2002) has a useful survey.

3. See Short (2002) for an application of this method in a PEM context. Both two- and three-input gross output processing sector production functions were calibrated with value added disaggregated in the three-input case.

4. Principally Heinegg (2001), which makes use of 1991 SAH-DGE and Winters, Davis, and Corral (2001), which is based on the de Janvry survey of 951 Ejido households in 1997 for the World Bank.

## Select Bibliography


de Janvry, A., and K. Subbarao. 1986. *Agricultural Price Policy and Income Distribution in India.* Delhi, India: Oxford University Press.

Dewbre, J. H., and C. Short. 2002. "Alternative Policy Instruments for Agriculture Support: Consequences for Trade, Farm Income and Competitiveness." Presented at the Canadian Agricultural Economics Association annual meeting in Calgary, May 30–June 1.

Dewbre, J. H., J. Anton, and W. Thompson. 2001. "The Transfer Efficiency and Trade Effects of Direct Payments." *American Journal of Agricultural Economics* 83:1204–14.

European Commission. 1997. "A Matrix Approach to Evaluating Changes in the EU's Crop Regime." Brussels, Belgium, September.

Gardner, B. L. 1975. "The Farm Retail Price Spread in a Competitive Food Industry." *American Journal of Agricultural Economics* 57:399–409.

Gardner, B. L. 1987. *The Economics of Agricultural Policies.* New York: Macmillan.

Hertel, T., P. Preckel, J. A. L. Cranfield, and M. Ivanic. 2002. "Poverty Impacts of Multilateral Trade Liberalization." GTAP Working Paper 16. Purdue University Center for Global Trade Analysis and Department of Agricultural Economics. West Lafayette, Indiana.

Heinegg, A. 2001. "Effects of NAFTA and PROCAMPO on Mexican Maize Producers: A Farm-Household Microsimulation Model." M.Sc. Thesis, Department of Applied Economics and Management, Cornell University, Ithaca, New York.

Ianchovichina, E., A. Necita, and I. Soloanga. 2001. "Implications of Trade Reform on the Distribution of Income in Mexico." Policy Research Working Paper 2667. The World Bank Development Research Group, August.

Levinsohn, J., S. Berry, and J. Friedman. 1999. "Impacts of the Indonesian Economic Crisis: Price Changes and the Poor." Paper prepared for the Conference on Poverty and the International Economy, organized by the World Bank and Swedish Parliamentary Commission on Global Development, Stockholm, October 20–21, 2000.

Löfgren, H. 1999. "Trade Reform and the Poor in Morocco: A Rural-Urban General Equilibrium Analysis of Reduced Protection." IFPRI TMD Discussion Paper 38.

OECD (Organisation for Economic Co-operation and Development). 2001. "Market Effects of Crop Support Measures." Paris.

———. 2002a. "Agricultural Policies in OECD Countries: Monitoring and Evaluation 2002." Paris.

———. 2002b. "The Transfer Efficiency of Farm Support for Farm Household Income." Paris.

———. 2002c. "Main Economic Indicators." June.

Reimer, J. 2002. "Estimating the Poverty Impacts of Trade Liberalization." GTAP Working Paper 20. Purdue University Center for Global Trade Analysis and Department of Agricultural Economics. West Lafayette, Indiana.

Robilliard, A.-S., F. Bourguignon, and S. Robinson. 2001. "Crisis and Income Distribution: A Micro-Macro Model for Indonesia." Paper prepared for the ESRC Development Economics/International Economics Conference, Nottingham University, U.K., April 5–7, 2001.

Rodrik, D. 2000. "Comments on 'Trade, Growth, and Poverty,' by David Dollar and Aart Kraay." Available at http://ksghome.harvard.edu/~.drodrik.academic.ksg/papers.html.

Sadoulet, E., and A. de Janvry. 1995. *Quantitative Development Policy Analysis.* Baltimore: the Johns Hopkins University Press.

Short, C. 2002. "A Methodology to Evaluate the Impact of Cost Recovery in Canadian Agriculture and Agri-Food Chains." Research and Analysis Directorate, Agriculture and Agri-Food Canada.

Singh, I., L. Squire, and J. Strauss, eds. 1986. *Agricultural Household Models: Extensions, Applications and Policy.* Baltimore: The Johns Hopkins University Press.

Tyers, R., and K. Anderson. 1992. Disarray in World Food Markets: A Quantitative Assessment. Cambridge, U.K.: Cambridge University Press.

Winters, A. 2001. "Trade, Trade Policy and Poverty: What Are the Links?" Centre for Economic Policy Research Policy Paper No. 2382, London.

Winters, P., B. Davis, and L. Corral. 2001. "Assets, Activities and Income Generation in Rural Mexico: Factoring in Social and Public Capital." Working Paper, Agricultural and Resource Economics, University of New England, Australia, June.

# APPENDIX B

# THE AGREEMENT ON AGRICULTURE

***AGREEMENT ON AGRICULTURE as it appears on the WTO Website.***

*Members,*

*Having decided* to establish a basis for initiating a process of reform of trade in agriculture in line with the objectives of the negotiations as set out in the Punta del Este Declaration;

*Recalling* that their long-term objective as agreed at the Mid-Term Review of the Uruguay Round "is to establish a fair and market-oriented agricultural trading system and that a reform process should be initiated through the negotiation of commitments on support and protection and through the establishment of strengthened and more operationally effective GATT rules and disciplines";

*Recalling* further that "the above-mentioned long-term objective is to provide for substantial progressive reductions in agricultural support and protection sustained over an agreed period of time, resulting in correcting and preventing restrictions and distortions in world agricultural markets";

*Committed* to achieving specific binding commitments in each of the following areas: market access; domestic support; export competition; and to reaching an agreement on sanitary and phytosanitary issues;

*Having agreed* that in implementing their commitments on market access, developed country Members would take fully into account the particular needs and conditions of developing country Members by providing for a greater improvement of opportunities and terms of access for agricultural products of particular interest to these Members, including the fullest liberalization of trade in tropical agricultural products as agreed at the Mid-Term Review, and for products of particular importance to the diversification of production from the growing of illicit narcotic crops;

*Noting* that commitments under the reform programme should be made in an equitable way among all Members, having regard to non-trade concerns, including food security and the need to protect the environment; having regard to the agreement that special and differential treatment for developing countries is an integral element of the negotiations, and taking into account the possible negative effects of the implementation of the reform programme on least-developed and net food-importing developing countries;

Hereby *agree* as follows:

## Part I

### *Article 1 Definition of Terms*

In this Agreement, unless the context otherwise requires:

(a) "Aggregate Measurement of Support" and "AMS" mean the annual level of support, expressed in monetary terms, provided for an agricultural product in favour of the producers of the basic agricultural product or non-product-specific support provided in favour of agricultural producers in general, other than support provided under programmes that qualify as exempt from reduction under Annex 2 to this Agreement, which is:
   (i) with respect to support provided during the base period, specified in the relevant tables of supporting material incorporated by reference in Part IV of a Member's Schedule; and
   (ii) with respect to support provided during any year of the implementation period and thereafter, calculated in accordance with the provisions of Annex 3 of this Agreement and taking into account the constituent data and methodology used in the tables of supporting material incorporated by reference in Part IV of the Member's Schedule;

(b) "basic agricultural product" in relation to domestic support commitments is defined as the product as close as practicable to the point of first sale as specified in a Member's Schedule and in the related supporting material;

(c) "budgetary outlays" or "outlays" includes revenue foregone;

(d) "Equivalent Measurement of Support" means the annual level of support, expressed in monetary terms, provided to producers of a basic agricultural product through the application of one or more measures, the calculation of which in accordance with the AMS methodology is impracticable, other than support provided under programmes that qualify as exempt from reduction under Annex 2 to this Agreement, and which is:
   (i) with respect to support provided during the base period, specified in the relevant tables of supporting material incorporated by reference in Part IV of a Member's Schedule; and
   (ii) with respect to support provided during any year of the implementation period and thereafter, calculated in accordance with the provisions of Annex 4 of this Agreement and taking into account the constituent data and methodology used in the tables of supporting material incorporated by reference in Part IV of the Member's Schedule;

(e) "export subsidies" refers to subsidies contingent upon export performance, including the export subsidies listed in Article 9 of this Agreement;

(f) "implementation period" means the six-year period commencing in the year 1995, except that, for the purposes of Article 13, it means the nine-year period commencing in 1995;

(g) "market access concessions" includes all market access commitments undertaken pursuant to this Agreement;

(h) "Total Aggregate Measurement of Support" and "Total AMS" mean the sum of all domestic support provided in favour of agricultural producers, calculated as the sum of all aggregate measurements of support for basic agricultural products, all non-product-specific aggregate measurements of support and all equivalent measurements of support for agricultural products, and which is:
   (i) with respect to support provided during the base period (i.e. the "Base Total AMS") and the maximum support permitted to be provided during any year of the implementation period or thereafter (i.e. the "Annual and Final Bound Commitment Levels"), as specified in Part IV of a Member's Schedule; and
   (ii) with respect to the level of support actually provided during any year of the implementation period and thereafter (i.e. the "Current Total AMS"), calculated in accordance with the provisions of this Agreement, including Article 6, and with the constituent data and methodology used in the tables of supporting material incorporated by reference in Part IV of the Member's Schedule;

(i) "year" in paragraph (f) above and in relation to the specific commitments of a Member refers to the calendar, financial or marketing year specified in the Schedule relating to that Member.

*Article 2 Product Coverage*

This Agreement applies to the products listed in Annex 1 to this Agreement, hereinafter referred to as agricultural products.

## Part II

*Article 3 Incorporation of Concessions and Commitments*

1. The domestic support and export subsidy commitments in Part IV of each Member's Schedule constitute commitments limiting subsidization and are hereby made an integral part of GATT 1994.
2. Subject to the provisions of Article 6, a Member shall not provide support in favour of domestic producers in excess of the commitment levels specified in Section I of Part IV of its Schedule.
3. Subject to the provisions of paragraphs 2(b) and 4 of Article 9, a Member shall not provide export subsidies listed in paragraph 1 of Article 9 in respect of the agricultural products or groups of products specified in Section II of Part IV of its Schedule in excess of the budgetary outlay and quantity commitment levels specified therein and shall not provide such subsidies in respect of any agricultural product not specified in that Section of its Schedule.

## Part III

*Article 4 Market Access*

1. Market access concessions contained in Schedules relate to bindings and reductions of tariffs, and to other market access commitments as specified therein.
2. Members shall not maintain, resort to, or revert to any measures of the kind which have been required to be converted into ordinary customs duties[1], except as otherwise provided for in Article 5 and Annex 5.

*Article 5 Special Safeguard Provisions*

1. Notwithstanding the provisions of paragraph 1(b) of Article II of GATT 1994, any Member may take recourse to the provisions of paragraphs 4 and 5 below in connection with the importation of an agricultural product, in respect of which measures referred to in paragraph 2 of Article 4 of this Agreement have been converted into an ordinary customs duty and which is designated in its Schedule with the symbol "SSG" as being the subject of a concession in respect of which the provisions of this Article may be invoked, if:
   (a) the volume of imports of that product entering the customs territory of the Member granting the concession during any year exceeds a trigger level which relates to the existing market access opportunity as set out in paragraph 4; or, but not concurrently:
   (b) the price at which imports of that product may enter the customs territory of the Member granting the concession, as determined on the basis of the c.i.f. import price of the shipment concerned expressed in terms of its domestic currency, falls below a trigger price equal to the average 1986 to 1988 reference price[2] for the product concerned.
2. Imports under current and minimum access commitments established as part of a concession referred to in paragraph 1 above shall be counted for the purpose of determining the volume of imports required for invoking the provisions of subparagraph 1(a) and paragraph 4, but imports under such commitments shall not be affected by any additional duty imposed under either subparagraph 1(a) and paragraph 4 or subparagraph 1(b) and paragraph 5 below.
3. Any supplies of the product in question which were *en route* on the basis of a contract settled before the additional duty is imposed under subparagraph 1(a) and paragraph 4 shall be exempted from any such additional duty, provided that they may be counted in the volume of imports of the product in question during the following year for the purposes of triggering the provisions of subparagraph 1(a) in that year.

4. Any additional duty imposed under subparagraph 1(a) shall only be maintained until the end of the year in which it has been imposed, and may only be levied at a level which shall not exceed one third of the level of the ordinary customs duty in effect in the year in which the action is taken. The trigger level shall be set according to the following schedule based on market access opportunities defined as imports as a percentage of the corresponding domestic consumption[3] during the three preceding years for which data are available:
   (a) where such market access opportunities for a product are less than or equal to 10 per cent, the base trigger level shall equal 125 per cent;
   (b) where such market access opportunities for a product are greater than 10 per cent but less than or equal to 30 per cent, the base trigger level shall equal 110 per cent;
   (c) where such market access opportunities for a product are greater than 30 per cent, the base trigger level shall equal 105 per cent.

   In all cases the additional duty may be imposed in any year where the absolute volume of imports of the product concerned entering the customs territory of the Member granting the concession exceeds the sum of ($x$) the base trigger level set out above multiplied by the average quantity of imports during the three preceding years for which data are available and ($y$) the absolute volume change in domestic consumption of the product concerned in the most recent year for which data are available compared to the preceding year, provided that the trigger level shall not be less than 105 per cent of the average quantity of imports in ($x$) above.
5. The additional duty imposed under subparagraph 1(b) shall be set according to the following schedule:
   (a) if the difference between the c.i.f. import price of the shipment expressed in terms of the domestic currency (hereinafter referred to as the "import price") and the trigger price as defined under that subparagraph is less than or equal to 10 per cent of the trigger price, no additional duty shall be imposed;
   (b) if the difference between the import price and the trigger price (hereinafter referred to as the "difference") is greater than 10 per cent but less than or equal to 40 per cent of the trigger price, the additional duty shall equal 30 per cent of the amount by which the difference exceeds 10 per cent;
   (c) if the difference is greater than 40 per cent but less than or equal to 60 per cent of the trigger price, the additional duty shall equal 50 per cent of the amount by which the difference exceeds 40 per cent, plus the additional duty allowed under (b);
   (d) if the difference is greater than 60 per cent but less than or equal to 75 per cent, the additional duty shall equal 70 per cent of the amount by which the difference exceeds 60 per cent of the trigger price, plus the additional duties allowed under (b) and (c);
   (e) if the difference is greater than 75 per cent of the trigger price, the additional duty shall equal 90 per cent of the amount by which the difference exceeds 75 per cent, plus the additional duties allowed under (b), (c) and (d).
6. For perishable and seasonal products, the conditions set out above shall be applied in such a manner as to take account of the specific characteristics of such products. In particular, shorter time periods under subparagraph 1(a) and paragraph 4 may be used in reference to the corresponding periods in the base period and different reference prices for different periods may be used under subparagraph 1(b).
7. The operation of the special safeguard shall be carried out in a transparent manner. Any Member taking action under subparagraph 1(a) above shall give notice in writing, including relevant data, to the Committee on Agriculture as far in advance as may be practicable and in any event within 10 days of the implementation of such action. In cases where changes in consumption volumes must be allocated to individual tariff lines subject to action under paragraph 4, relevant data shall include the information and methods used to allocate these changes. A Member taking action under paragraph 4 shall afford any interested Members the

opportunity to consult with it in respect of the conditions of application of such action. Any Member taking action under subparagraph 1(b) above shall give notice in writing, including relevant data, to the Committee on Agriculture within 10 days of the implementation of the first such action or, for perishable and seasonal products, the first action in any period. Members undertake, as far as practicable, not to take recourse to the provisions of subparagraph 1(b) where the volume of imports of the products concerned are declining. In either case a Member taking such action shall afford any interested Members the opportunity to consult with it in respect of the conditions of application of such action.

8. Where measures are taken in conformity with paragraphs 1 through 7 above, Members undertake not to have recourse, in respect of such measures, to the provisions of paragraphs 1(a) and 3 of Article XIX of GATT 1994 or paragraph 2 of Article 8 of the Agreement on Safeguards.
9. The provisions of this Article shall remain in force for the duration of the reform process as determined under Article 20.

## Part IV

### *Article 6 Domestic Support Commitments*

1. The domestic support reduction commitments of each Member contained in Part IV of its Schedule shall apply to all of its domestic support measures in favour of agricultural producers with the exception of domestic measures which are not subject to reduction in terms of the criteria set out in this Article and in Annex 2 to this Agreement. The commitments are expressed in terms of Total Aggregate Measurement of Support and "Annual and Final Bound Commitment Levels".
2. In accordance with the Mid-Term Review Agreement that government measures of assistance, whether direct or indirect, to encourage agricultural and rural development are an integral part of the development programmes of developing countries, investment subsidies which are generally available to agriculture in developing country Members and agricultural input subsidies generally available to low-income or resource-poor producers in developing country Members shall be exempt from domestic support reduction commitments that would otherwise be applicable to such measures, as shall domestic support to producers in developing country Members to encourage diversification from growing illicit narcotic crops. Domestic support meeting the criteria of this paragraph shall not be required to be included in a Member's calculation of its Current Total AMS.
3. A Member shall be considered to be in compliance with its domestic support reduction commitments in any year in which its domestic support in favour of agricultural producers expressed in terms of Current Total AMS does not exceed the corresponding annual or final bound commitment level specified in Part IV of the Member's Schedule.
4. (a) A Member shall not be required to include in the calculation of its Current Total AMS and shall not be required to reduce:
   (i) product-specific domestic support which would otherwise be required to be included in a Member's calculation of its Current AMS where such support does not exceed 5 per cent of that Member's total value of production of a basic agricultural product during the relevant year; and
   (ii) non-product-specific domestic support which would otherwise be required to be included in a Member's calculation of its Current AMS where such support does not exceed 5 per cent of the value of that Member's total agricultural production.

   (b) For developing country Members, the *de minimis* percentage under this paragraph shall be 10 per cent.
5. (a) Direct payments under production-limiting programmes shall not be subject to the commitment to reduce domestic support if:
   (i) such payments are based on fixed area and yields; or
   (ii) such payments are made on 85 per cent or less of the base level of production; or
   (iii) livestock payments are made on a fixed number of head.

(b) The exemption from the reduction commitment for direct payments meeting the above criteria shall be reflected by the exclusion of the value of those direct payments in a Member's calculation of its Current Total AMS.

### *Article 7 General Disciplines on Domestic Support*

1. Each Member shall ensure that any domestic support measures in favour of agricultural producers which are not subject to reduction commitments because they qualify under the criteria set out in Annex 2 to this Agreement are maintained in conformity therewith.
2. (a) Any domestic support measure in favour of agricultural producers, including any modification to such measure, and any measure that is subsequently introduced that cannot be shown to satisfy the criteria in Annex 2 to this Agreement or to be exempt from reduction by reason of any other provision of this Agreement shall be included in the Member's calculation of its Current Total AMS.
   (b) Where no Total AMS commitment exists in Part IV of a Member's Schedule, the Member shall not provide support to agricultural producers in excess of the relevant *de minimis* level set out in paragraph 4 of Article 6.

## Part V

### *Article 8 Export Competition Commitments*

Each Member undertakes not to provide export subsidies otherwise than in conformity with this Agreement and with the commitments as specified in that Member's Schedule.

### *Article 9 Export Subsidy Commitments*

1. The following export subsidies are subject to reduction commitments under this Agreement:
   (a) the provision by governments or their agencies of direct subsidies, including payments-in-kind, to a firm, to an industry, to producers of an agricultural product, to a cooperative or other association of such producers, or to a marketing board, contingent on export performance;
   (b) the sale or disposal for export by governments or their agencies of non-commercial stocks of agricultural products at a price lower than the comparable price charged for the like product to buyers in the domestic market;
   (c) payments on the export of an agricultural product that are financed by virtue of governmental action, whether or not a charge on the public account is involved, including payments that are financed from the proceeds of a levy imposed on the agricultural product concerned or on an agricultural product from which the exported product is derived;
   (d) the provision of subsidies to reduce the costs of marketing exports of agricultural products (other than widely available export promotion and advisory services) including handling, upgrading and other processing costs, and the costs of international transport and freight;
   (e) internal transport and freight charges on export shipments, provided or mandated by governments, on terms more favourable than for domestic shipments;
   (f) subsidies on agricultural products contingent on their incorporation in exported products.
2. (a) Except as provided in subparagraph (b), the export subsidy commitment levels for each year of the implementation period, as specified in a Member's Schedule, represent with respect to the export subsidies listed in paragraph 1 of this Article:
      (i) in the case of budgetary outlay reduction commitments, the maximum level of expenditure for such subsidies that may be allocated or incurred in that year in respect of the agricultural product, or group of products, concerned; and
      (ii) in the case of export quantity reduction commitments, the maximum quantity of an agricultural product, or group of products, in respect of which such export subsidies may be granted in that year.
   (b) In any of the second through fifth years of the implementation period, a Member

may provide export subsidies listed in paragraph 1 above in a given year in excess of the corresponding annual commitment levels in respect of the products or groups of products specified in Part IV of the Member's Schedule, provided that:

(i) the cumulative amounts of budgetary outlays for such subsidies, from the beginning of the implementation period through the year in question, does not exceed the cumulative amounts that would have resulted from full compliance with the relevant annual outlay commitment levels specified in the Member's Schedule by more than 3 per cent of the base period level of such budgetary outlays;

(ii) the cumulative quantities exported with the benefit of such export subsidies, from the beginning of the implementation period through the year in question, does not exceed the cumulative quantities that would have resulted from full compliance with the relevant annual quantity commitment levels specified in the Member's Schedule by more than 1.75 per cent of the base period quantities;

(iii) the total cumulative amounts of budgetary outlays for such export subsidies and the quantities benefiting from such export subsidies over the entire implementation period are no greater than the totals that would have resulted from full compliance with the relevant annual commitment levels specified in the Member's Schedule; and

(iv) the Member's budgetary outlays for export subsidies and the quantities benefiting from such subsidies, at the conclusion of the implementation period, are no greater than 64 per cent and 79 per cent of the 1986-1990 base period levels, respectively. For developing country Members these percentages shall be 76 and 86 per cent, respectively.

3. Commitments relating to limitations on the extension of the scope of export subsidization are as specified in Schedules.

4. During the implementation period, developing country Members shall not be required to undertake commitments in respect of the export subsidies listed in subparagraphs (d) and (e) of paragraph 1 above, provided that these are not applied in a manner that would circumvent reduction commitments.

### *Article 10 Prevention of Circumvention of Export Subsidy Commitments*

1. Export subsidies not listed in paragraph 1 of Article 9 shall not be applied in a manner which results in, or which threatens to lead to, circumvention of export subsidy commitments; nor shall non-commercial transactions be used to circumvent such commitments.
2. Members undertake to work toward the development of internationally agreed disciplines to govern the provision of export credits, export credit guarantees or insurance programmes and, after agreement on such disciplines, to provide export credits, export credit guarantees or insurance programmes only in conformity therewith.
3. Any Member which claims that any quantity exported in excess of a reduction commitment level is not subsidized must establish that no export subsidy, whether listed in Article 9 or not, has been granted in respect of the quantity of exports in question.
4. Members donors of international food aid shall ensure:
   (a) that the provision of international food aid is not tied directly or indirectly to commercial exports of agricultural products to recipient countries;
   (b) that international food aid transactions, including bilateral food aid which is monetized, shall be carried out in accordance with the FAO "Principles of Surplus Disposal and Consultative Obligations", including, where appropriate, the system of Usual Marketing Requirements (UMRs); and
   (c) that such aid shall be provided to the extent possible in fully grant form or on terms no less concessional than those provided for in Article IV of the Food Aid Convention 1986.

### *Article 11 Incorporated Products*

In no case may the per-unit subsidy paid on an incorporated agricultural primary product exceed the per-unit export subsidy that would be payable on exports of the primary product as such.

## Part VI

### *Article 12 Disciplines on Export Prohibitions and Restrictions*

1. Where any Member institutes any new export prohibition or restriction on foodstuffs in accordance with paragraph 2(a) of Article XI of GATT 1994, the Member shall observe the following provisions:
   (a) the Member instituting the export prohibition or restriction shall give due consideration to the effects of such prohibition or restriction on importing Members' food security;
   (b) before any Member institutes an export prohibition or restriction, it shall give notice in writing, as far in advance as practicable, to the Committee on Agriculture comprising such information as the nature and the duration of such measure, and shall consult, upon request, with any other Member having a substantial interest as an importer with respect to any matter related to the measure in question. The Member instituting such export prohibition or restriction shall provide, upon request, such a Member with necessary information.
2. The provisions of this Article shall not apply to any developing country Member, unless the measure is taken by a developing country Member which is a net-food exporter of the specific foodstuff concerned.

## Part VII

### *Article 13 Due Restraint*

During the implementation period, notwithstanding the provisions of GATT 1994 and the Agreement on Subsidies and Countervailing Measures (referred to in this Article as the "Subsidies Agreement"):

(a) domestic support measures that conform fully to the provisions of Annex 2 to this Agreement shall be:
   (i) non-actionable subsidies for purposes of countervailing duties[4];
   (ii) exempt from actions based on Article XVI of GATT 1994 and Part III of the Subsidies Agreement; and
   (iii) exempt from actions based on non-violation nullification or impairment of the benefits of tariff concessions accruing to another Member under Article II of GATT 1994, in the sense of paragraph 1(b) of Article XXIII of GATT 1994;

(b) domestic support measures that conform fully to the provisions of Article 6 of this Agreement including direct payments that conform to the requirements of paragraph 5 thereof, as reflected in each Member's Schedule, as well as domestic support within *de minimis* levels and in conformity with paragraph 2 of Article 6, shall be:
   (i) exempt from the imposition of countervailing duties unless a determination of injury or threat thereof is made in accordance with Article VI of GATT 1994 and Part V of the Subsidies Agreement, and due restraint shall be shown in initiating any countervailing duty investigations;
   (ii) exempt from actions based on paragraph 1 of Article XVI of GATT 1994 or Articles 5 and 6 of the Subsidies Agreement, provided that such measures do not grant support to a specific commodity in excess of that decided during the 1992 marketing year; and
   (iii) exempt from actions based on non-violation nullification or impairment of the benefits of tariff concessions accruing to another Member under Article II of GATT 1994, in the sense of paragraph 1(b) of Article XXIII of GATT 1994, provided that such measures do not grant support to a specific commodity in excess of that decided during the 1992 marketing year;

(c) export subsidies that conform fully to the provisions of Part V of this Agreement, as reflected in each Member's Schedule, shall be:
   (i) subject to countervailing duties only upon a determination of injury or threat thereof based on volume, effect on prices, or consequent impact in accordance with Article VI of GATT 1994 and Part V of the Subsidies Agreement, and due restraint shall be shown in initiating any countervailing duty investigations; and
   (ii) exempt from actions based on Article XVI of GATT 1994 or Articles 3, 5 and 6 of the Subsidies Agreement.

## Part VIII

### *Article 14 Sanitary and Phytosanitary Measures*

Members agree to give effect to the Agreement on the Application of Sanitary and Phytosanitary Measures.

## Part IX

### *Article 15 Special and Differential Treatment*

1. In keeping with the recognition that differential and more favourable treatment for developing country Members is an integral part of the negotiation, special and differential treatment in respect of commitments shall be provided as set out in the relevant provisions of this Agreement and embodied in the Schedules of concessions and commitments.
2. Developing country Members shall have the flexibility to implement reduction commitments over a period of up to 10 years. Least-developed country Members shall not be required to undertake reduction commitments.

## Part X

### *Article 16 Least-Developed and Net Food-Importing Developing Countries*

1. Developed country Members shall take such action as is provided for within the framework of the Decision on Measures Concerning the Possible Negative Effects of the Reform Programme on Least-Developed and Net Food-Importing Developing Countries.
2. The Committee on Agriculture shall monitor, as appropriate, the follow-up to this Decision.

## Part XI

### *Article 17 Committee on Agriculture*

A Committee on Agriculture is hereby established.

### *Article 18 Review of the Implementation of Commitments*

1. Progress in the implementation of commitments negotiated under the Uruguay Round reform programme shall be reviewed by the Committee on Agriculture.
2. The review process shall be undertaken on the basis of notifications submitted by Members in relation to such matters and at such intervals as shall be determined, as well as on the basis of such documentation as the Secretariat may be requested to prepare in order to facilitate the review process.
3. In addition to the notifications to be submitted under paragraph 2, any new domestic support measure, or modification of an existing measure, for which exemption from reduction is claimed shall be notified promptly. This notification shall contain details of the new or modified measure and its conformity with the agreed criteria as set out either in Article 6 or in Annex 2.
4. In the review process Members shall give due consideration to the influence of excessive rates of inflation on the ability of any Member to abide by its domestic support commitments.
5. Members agree to consult annually in the Committee on Agriculture with respect to their participation in the normal growth of world trade in agricultural products within the framework of the commitments on export subsidies under this Agreement.
6. The review process shall provide an opportunity for Members to raise any matter relevant to the implementation of commitments under the reform programme as set out in this Agreement.

7. Any Member may bring to the attention of the Committee on Agriculture any measure which it considers ought to have been notified by another Member.

*Article 19 Consultation and Dispute Settlement*

The provisions of Articles XXII and XXIII of GATT 1994, as elaborated and applied by the Dispute Settlement Understanding, shall apply to consultations and the settlement of disputes under this Agreement.

## Part XII

*Article 20 Continuation of the Reform Process*

Recognizing that the long-term objective of substantial progressive reductions in support and protection resulting in fundamental reform is an ongoing process, Members agree that negotiations for continuing the process will be initiated one year before the end of the implementation period, taking into account:

(a) the experience to that date from implementing the reduction commitments;
(b) the effects of the reduction commitments on world trade in agriculture;
(c) non-trade concerns, special and differential treatment to developing country Members, and the objective to establish a fair and market-oriented agricultural trading system, and the other objectives and concerns mentioned in the preamble to this Agreement; and
(d) what further commitments are necessary to achieve the above mentioned long-term objectives.

## Part XIII

*Article 21 Final Provisions*

1. The provisions of GATT 1994 and of other Multilateral Trade Agreements in Annex 1A to the WTO Agreement shall apply subject to the provisions of this Agreement.
2. The Annexes to this Agreement are hereby made an integral part of this Agreement.

## ANNEX 1 PRODUCT COVERAGE

1. This Agreement shall cover the following products:

| | | | |
|---|---|---|---|
| (i) | HS Chapters 1 to 24 less fish and fish products, plus* | | |
| (ii) | HS Code | 2905.43 | (mannitol) |
| | HS Code | 2905.44 | (sorbitol) |
| | HS Heading | 33.01 | (essential oils) |
| | HS Headings | 35.01 to 35.05 | (albuminoidal substances, modified starches, glues) |
| | HS Code | 8809.10 | (finishing agents) |
| | HS Code | 3823.60 | (sorbitol n.e.p.) |
| | HS Headings | 41.01 to 41.03 | (hides and skins) |
| | HS Heading | 43.01 | (raw furskins) |
| | HS Headings | 50.01 to 50.03 | (raw silk and silk waste) |
| | HS Headings | 51.01 to 51.03 | (wool and animal hair) |
| | HS Headings | 52.01 to 52.03 | (rsw cotton, waste and cotton carded or combed) |
| | HS Heading | 53.01 | (raw flax) |
| | HS Heading | 53.02 | (raw hemp) |

*The product descriptions in round brackets are not necessarily exhaustive.

2. The foregoing shall not limit the product coverage of the Agreement on the Application of Sanitary and Phytosanitary Measures.

## ANNEX 2 DOMESTIC SUPPORT: THE BASIS FOR EXEMPTION FROM THE REDUCTION COMMITMENTS

1. Domestic support measures for which exemption from the reduction commitments is claimed shall meet the fundamental requirement that they have no, or at most minimal, trade-distorting effects or effects on production. Accordingly, all measures for which exemption is claimed shall conform to the following basic criteria:
   (a) the support in question shall be provided through a publicly-funded government programme (including government revenue foregone) not involving transfers from consumers; and,
   (b) the support in question shall not have the effect of providing price support to producers; plus policy-specific criteria and conditions as set out below.

*Government Service Programmes*

2. **General services**

   Policies in this category involve expenditures (or revenue foregone) in relation to programmes which provide services or benefits to agriculture or the rural community. They shall not involve direct payments to producers or processors. Such programmes, which include but are not restricted to the following list, shall meet the general criteria in paragraph 1 above and policy-specific conditions where set out below:
   (a) research, including general research, research in connection with environmental programmes, and research programmes relating to particular products;
   (b) pest and disease control, including general and product-specific pest and disease control measures, such as early-warning systems, quarantine and eradication;
   (c) training services, including both general and specialist training facilities;
   (d) extension and advisory services, including the provision of means to facilitate the transfer of information and the results of research to producers and consumers;
   (e) inspection services, including general inspection services and the inspection of particular products for health, safety, grading or standardization purposes;
   (f) marketing and promotion services, including market information, advice and promotion relating to particular products but excluding expenditure for unspecified purposes that could be used by sellers to reduce their selling price or confer a direct economic benefit to purchasers; and
   (g) infrastructural services, including: electricity reticulation, roads and other means of transport, market and port facilities, water supply facilities, dams and drainage schemes, and infrastructural works associated with environmental programmes. In all cases the expenditure shall be directed to the provision or construction of capital works only, and shall exclude the subsidized provision of on-farm facilities other than for the reticulation of generally available public utilities. It shall not include subsidies to inputs or operating costs, or preferential user charges.
3. **Public stockholding for food security purposes**[5]

   Expenditures (or revenue foregone) in relation to the accumulation and holding of stocks of products which form an integral part of a food security programme identified in national legislation. This may include government aid to private storage of products as part of such a programme.

   The volume and accumulation of such stocks shall correspond to predetermined targets related solely to food security. The process of stock accumulation and disposal shall be financially transparent. Food purchases by the government shall be made at current market prices and sales from food security stocks shall be made at no less than the current domestic market price for the product and quality in question.

4. **Domestic food aid**[6]
   Expenditures (or revenue foregone) in relation to the provision of domestic food aid to sections of the population in need.

   Eligibility to receive the food aid shall be subject to clearly-defined criteria related to nutritional objectives. Such aid shall be in the form of direct provision of food to those concerned or the provision of means to allow eligible recipients to buy food either at market or at subsidized prices. Food purchases by the government shall be made at current market prices and the financing and administration of the aid shall be transparent.
5. **Direct payments to producers**
   Support provided through direct payments (or revenue foregone, including payments in kind) to producers for which exemption from reduction commitments is claimed shall meet the basic criteria set out in paragraph 1 above, plus specific criteria applying to individual types of direct payment as set out in paragraphs 6 through 13 below. Where exemption from reduction is claimed for any existing or new type of direct payment other than those specified in paragraphs 6 through 13, it shall conform to criteria (b) through (e) in paragraph 6, in addition to the general criteria set out in paragraph 1.
6. **Decoupled income support**
   (a) Eligibility for such payments shall be determined by clearly-defined criteria such as income, status as a producer or landowner, factor use or production level in a defined and fixed base period.
   (b) The amount of such payments in any given year shall not be related to, or based on, the type or volume of production (including livestock units) undertaken by the producer in any year after the base period.
   (c) The amount of such payments in any given year shall not be related to, or based on, the prices, domestic or international, applying to any production undertaken in any year after the base period.
   (d) The amount of such payments in any given year shall not be related to, or based on, the factors of production employed in any year after the base period.
   (e) No production shall be required in order to receive such payments.
7. **Government financial participation in income insurance and income safety-net programmes**
   (a) Eligibility for such payments shall be determined by an income loss, taking into account only income derived from agriculture, which exceeds 30 per cent of average gross income or the equivalent in net income terms (excluding any payments from the same or similar schemes) in the preceding three-year period or a three-year average based on the preceding five-year period, excluding the highest and the lowest entry. Any producer meeting this condition shall be eligible to receive the payments.
   (b) The amount of such payments shall compensate for less than 70 per cent of the producer's income loss in the year the producer becomes eligible to receive this assistance.
   (c) The amount of any such payments shall relate solely to income; it shall not relate to the type or volume of production (including livestock units) undertaken by the producer; or to the prices, domestic or international, applying to such production; or to the factors of production employed.
   (d) Where a producer receives in the same year payments under this paragraph and under paragraph 8 (relief from natural disasters), the total of such payments shall be less than 100 per cent of the producer's total loss.
8. **Payments (made either directly or by way of government financial participation in crop insurance schemes) for relief from natural disasters**
   (a) Eligibility for such payments shall arise only following a formal recognition by government authorities that a natural or like disaster (including disease outbreaks, pest infestations, nuclear accidents, and war on the territory of the Member concerned) has occurred or is occurring; and shall be determined by a production loss which exceeds 30 per cent of the average of production in the preceding three-year period or a three-year average based on

the preceding five-year period, excluding the highest and the lowest entry.

(b) Payments made following a disaster shall be applied only in respect of losses of income, livestock (including payments in connection with the veterinary treatment of animals), land or other production factors due to the natural disaster in question.

(c) Payments shall compensate for not more than the total cost of replacing such losses and shall not require or specify the type or quantity of future production.

(d) Payments made during a disaster shall not exceed the level required to prevent or alleviate further loss as defined in criterion (b) above.

(e) Where a producer receives in the same year payments under this paragraph and under paragraph 7 (income insurance and income safety-net programmes), the total of such payments shall be less than 100 per cent of the producer's total loss.

9. **Structural adjustment assistance provided through producer retirement programmes**

(a) Eligibility for such payments shall be determined by reference to clearly defined criteria in programmes designed to facilitate the retirement of persons engaged in marketable agricultural production, or their movement to non-agricultural activities.

(b) Payments shall be conditional upon the total and permanent retirement of the recipients from marketable agricultural production.

10. **Structural adjustment assistance provided through resource retirement programmes**

(a) Eligibility for such payments shall be determined by reference to clearly defined criteria in programmes designed to remove land or other resources, including livestock, from marketable agricultural production.

(b) Payments shall be conditional upon the retirement of land from marketable agricultural production for a minimum of three years, and in the case of livestock on its slaughter or definitive permanent disposal.

(c) Payments shall not require or specify any alternative use for such land or other resources which involves the production of marketable agricultural products.

(d) Payments shall not be related to either the type or quantity of production or to the prices, domestic or international, applying to production undertaken using the land or other resources remaining in production.

11. **Structural adjustment assistance provided through investment aids**

(a) Eligibility for such payments shall be determined by reference to clearly-defined criteria in government programmes designed to assist the financial or physical restructuring of a producer's operations in response to objectively demonstrated structural disadvantages. Eligibility for such programmes may also be based on a clearly-defined government programme for the reprivatization of agricultural land.

(b) The amount of such payments in any given year shall not be related to, or based on, the type or volume of production (including livestock units) undertaken by the producer in any year after the base period other than as provided for under criterion (e) below.

(c) The amount of such payments in any given year shall not be related to, or based on, the prices, domestic or international, applying to any production undertaken in any year after the base period.

(d) The payments shall be given only for the period of time necessary for the realization of the investment in respect of which they are provided.

(e) The payments shall not mandate or in any way designate the agricultural products to be produced by the recipients except to require them not to produce a particular product.

(f) The payments shall be limited to the amount required to compensate for the structural disadvantage.

12. **Payments under environmental programmes**

(a) Eligibility for such payments shall be determined as part of a clearly-defined government environmental or conservation programme and be dependent on the fulfilment of specific conditions under the government programme, including conditions related to production methods or inputs.

(b) The amount of payment shall be limited to the extra costs or loss of income involved in complying with the government programme.

13. **Payments under regional assistance programmes**

(a) Eligibility for such payments shall be limited to producers in disadvantaged regions. Each such region must be a clearly designated contiguous geographical area with a definable economic and administrative identity, considered as disadvantaged on the basis of neutral and objective criteria clearly spelt out in law or regulation and indicating that the region's difficulties arise out of more than temporary circumstances.

(b) The amount of such payments in any given year shall not be related to, or based on, the type or volume of production (including livestock units) undertaken by the producer in any year after the base period other than to reduce that production.

(c) The amount of such payments in any given year shall not be related to, or based on, the prices, domestic or international, applying to any production undertaken in any year after the base period.

(d) Payments shall be available only to producers in eligible regions, but generally available to all producers within such regions.

(e) Where related to production factors, payments shall be made at a degressive rate above a threshold level of the factor concerned.

(f) The payments shall be limited to the extra costs or loss of income involved in undertaking agricultural production in the prescribed area.

## ANNEX 3 DOMESTIC SUPPORT: CALCULATION OF AGGREGATE MEASUREMENT OF SUPPORT

1. Subject to the provisions of Article 6, an Aggregate Measurement of Support (AMS) shall be calculated on a product-specific basis for each basic agricultural product receiving market price support, non-exempt direct payments, or any other subsidy not exempted from the reduction commitment ("other non-exempt policies"). Support which is non-product specific shall be totalled into one non-product-specific AMS in total monetary terms.
2. Subsidies under paragraph 1 shall include both budgetary outlays and revenue foregone by governments or their agents.
3. Support at both the national and sub-national level shall be included.
4. Specific agricultural levies or fees paid by producers shall be deducted from the AMS.
5. The AMS calculated as outlined below for the base period shall constitute the base level for the implementation of the reduction commitment on domestic support.
6. For each basic agricultural product, a specific AMS shall be established, expressed in total monetary value terms.
7. The AMS shall be calculated as close as practicable to the point of first sale of the basic agricultural product concerned. Measures directed at agricultural processors shall be included to the extent that such measures benefit the producers of the basic agricultural products.
8. Market price support: market price support shall be calculated using the gap between a fixed external reference price and the applied administered price multiplied by the quantity of production eligible to receive the applied administered price. Budgetary payments made to maintain this gap, such as buying-in or storage costs, shall not be included in the AMS.
9. The fixed external reference price shall be based on the years 1986 to 1988 and shall generally be the average f.o.b. unit value for the basic agricultural product concerned in a net exporting country and the average c.i.f. unit value for the basic agricultural product concerned in a net importing country in the base period. The fixed reference price may be adjusted for quality differences as necessary.
10. Non-exempt direct payments: non-exempt direct payments which are dependent on a price gap shall be calculated either using the gap between the fixed reference price and the applied administered price multiplied by the quantity of production eligible to receive the administered price, or using budgetary outlays.

11. The fixed reference price shall be based on the years 1986 to 1988 and shall generally be the actual price used for determining payment rates.
12. Non-exempt direct payments which are based on factors other than price shall be measured using budgetary outlays.
13. Other non-exempt measures, including input subsidies and other measures such as marketing-cost reduction measures: the value of such measures shall be measured using government budgetary outlays or, where the use of budgetary outlays does not reflect the full extent of the subsidy concerned, the basis for calculating the subsidy shall be the gap between the price of the subsidized good or service and a representative market price for a similar good or service multiplied by the quantity of the good or service.

## ANNEX 4 DOMESTIC SUPPORT: CALCULATION OF EQUIVALENT MEASUREMENT OF SUPPORT

1. Subject to the provisions of Article 6, equivalent measurements of support shall be calculated in respect of all basic agricultural products where market price support as defined in Annex 3 exists but for which calculation of this component of the AMS is not practicable. For such products the base level for implementation of the domestic support reduction commitments shall consist of a market price support component expressed in terms of equivalent measurements of support under paragraph 2 below, as well as any non-exempt direct payments and other non-exempt support, which shall be evaluated as provided for under paragraph 3 below. Support at both national and sub-national level shall be included.
2. The equivalent measurements of support provided for in paragraph 1 shall be calculated on a product-specific basis for all basic agricultural products as close as practicable to the point of first sale receiving market price support and for which the calculation of the market price support component of the AMS is not practicable. For those basic agricultural products, equivalent measurements of market price support shall be made using the applied administered price and the quantity of production eligible to receive that price or, where this is not practicable, on budgetary outlays used to maintain the producer price.
3. Where basic agricultural products falling under paragraph 1 are the subject of non-exempt direct payments or any other product-specific subsidy not exempted from the reduction commitment, the basis for equivalent measurements of support concerning these measures shall be calculations as for the corresponding AMS components (specified in paragraphs 10 through 13 of Annex 3).
4. Equivalent measurements of support shall be calculated on the amount of subsidy as close as practicable to the point of first sale of the basic agricultural product concerned. Measures directed at agricultural processors shall be included to the extent that such measures benefit the producers of the basic agricultural products. Specific agricultural levies or fees paid by producers shall reduce the equivalent measurements of support by a corresponding amount.

## ANNEX 5 SPECIAL TREATMENT WITH RESPECT TO PARAGRAPH 2 OF ARTICLE 4

*Section A*

1. The provisions of paragraph 2 of Article 4 shall not apply with effect from the entry into force of the WTO Agreement to any primary agricultural product and its worked and/or prepared products ("designated products") in respect of which the following conditions are complied with (hereinafter referred to as "special treatment"):
   (a) imports of the designated products comprised less than 3 per cent of corresponding domestic consumption in the base period 1986-1988 ("the base period");
   (b) no export subsidies have been provided since the beginning of the base period for the designated products;
   (c) effective production-restricting measures are applied to the primary agricultural product;

(d) such products are designated with the symbol "ST-Annex 5" in Section I-B of Part I of a Member's Schedule annexed to the Marrakesh Protocol, as being subject to special treatment reflecting factors of non-trade concerns, such as food security and environmental protection; and

(e) minimum access opportunities in respect of the designated products correspond, as specified in Section I-B of Part I of the Schedule of the Member concerned, to 4 per cent of base period domestic consumption of the designated products from the beginning of the first year of the implementation period and, thereafter, are increased by 0.8 per cent of corresponding domestic consumption in the base period per year for the remainder of the implementation period.

2. At the beginning of any year of the implementation period a Member may cease to apply special treatment in respect of the designated products by complying with the provisions of paragraph 6. In such a case, the Member concerned shall maintain the minimum access opportunities already in effect at such time and increase the minimum access opportunities by 0.4 per cent of corresponding domestic consumption in the base period per year for the remainder of the implementation period. Thereafter, the level of minimum access opportunities resulting from this formula in the final year of the implementation period shall be maintained in the Schedule of the Member concerned.

3. Any negotiation on the question of whether there can be a continuation of the special treatment as set out in paragraph 1 after the end of the implementation period shall be completed within the time-frame of the implementation period itself as a part of the negotiations set out in Article 20 of this Agreement, taking into account the factors of non-trade concerns.

4. If it is agreed as a result of the negotiation referred to in paragraph 3 that a Member may continue to apply the special treatment, such Member shall confer additional and acceptable concessions as determined in that negotiation.

5. Where the special treatment is not to be continued at the end of the implementation period, the Member concerned shall implement the provisions of paragraph 6. In such a case, after the end of the implementation period the minimum access opportunities for the designated products shall be maintained at the level of 8 per cent of corresponding domestic consumption in the base period in the Schedule of the Member concerned.

6. Border measures other than ordinary customs duties maintained in respect of the designated products shall become subject to the provisions of paragraph 2 of Article 4 with effect from the beginning of the year in which the special treatment ceases to apply. Such products shall be subject to ordinary customs duties, which shall be bound in the Schedule of the Member concerned and applied, from the beginning of the year in which special treatment ceases and thereafter, at such rates as would have been applicable had a reduction of at least 15 per cent been implemented over the implementation period in equal annual instalments. These duties shall be established on the basis of tariff equivalents to be calculated in accordance with the guidelines prescribed in the attachment hereto.

### *Section B*

7. The provisions of paragraph 2 of Article 4 shall also not apply with effect from the entry into force of the WTO Agreement to a primary agricultural product that is the predominant staple in the traditional diet of a developing country Member and in respect of which the following conditions, in addition to those specified in paragraph 1(a) through 1(d), as they apply to the products concerned, are complied with:

(a) minimum access opportunities in respect of the products concerned, as specified in Section I-B of Part I of the Schedule of the developing country Member concerned, correspond to 1 per cent of base period domestic consumption of the products concerned from the beginning of the first year of the implementation period and are increased in equal annual instalments to 2 per cent of corresponding domestic consumption in the base period at the beginning of the fifth year of the implementation period. From the beginning of the sixth year of the implementation period, minimum access opportunities in respect of the products concerned correspond to 2 per cent of corresponding domestic consumption in the base period and are increased in equal annual instalments to 4 per cent of corresponding domestic consumption in the base period until the beginning of the 10th year. Thereafter, the level of minimum access opportunities resulting from this formula in the 10th year shall be maintained in the Schedule of the developing country Member concerned;

(b) appropriate market access opportunities have been provided for in other products under this Agreement.

8. Any negotiation on the question of whether there can be a continuation of the special treatment as set out in paragraph 7 after the end of the 10th year following the beginning of the implementation period shall be initiated and completed within the time-frame of the 10th year itself following the beginning of the implementation period.

9. If it is agreed as a result of the negotiation referred to in paragraph 8 that a Member may continue to apply the special treatment, such Member shall confer additional and acceptable concessions as determined in that negotiation.

10. In the event that special treatment under paragraph 7 is not to be continued beyond the 10th year following the beginning of the implementation period, the products concerned shall be subject to ordinary customs duties, established on the basis of a tariff equivalent to be calculated in accordance with the guidelines prescribed in the attachment hereto, which shall be bound in the Schedule of the Member concerned. In other respects, the provisions of paragraph 6 shall apply as modified by the relevant special and differential treatment accorded to developing country Members under this Agreement.

***Attachment to Annex 5***

Guidelines for the Calculation of Tariff Equivalents for the Specific Purpose Specified in Paragraphs 6 and 10 of this Annex

1. The calculation of the tariff equivalents, whether expressed as *ad valorem* or specific rates, shall be made using the actual difference between internal and external prices in a transparent manner. Data used shall be for the years 1986 to 1988. Tariff equivalents:
   (a) shall primarily be established at the four-digit level of the HS;
   (b) shall be established at the six-digit or a more detailed level of the HS wherever appropriate;
   (c) shall generally be established for worked and/or prepared products by multiplying the specific tariff equivalent(s) for the primary agricultural product(s) by the proportion(s) in value terms or in physical terms as appropriate of the primary agricultural product(s) in the worked and/or prepared products, and take account, where necessary, of any additional elements currently providing protection to industry.
2. External prices shall be, in general, actual average c.i.f. unit values for the importing country. Where average c.i.f. unit values are not available or appropriate, external prices shall be either:
   (a) appropriate average c.i.f. unit values of a near country; or
   (b) estimated from average f.o.b. unit values of (an) appropriate major exporter(s) adjusted by adding an estimate of insurance, freight and other relevant costs to the importing country.
3. The external prices shall generally be converted to domestic currencies using the annual average market exchange rate for the same period as the price data.

4. The internal price shall generally be a representative wholesale price ruling in the domestic market or an estimate of that price where adequate data is not available.
5. The initial tariff equivalents may be adjusted, where necessary, to take account of differences in quality or variety using an appropriate coefficient.
6. Where a tariff equivalent resulting from these guidelines is negative or lower than the current bound rate, the initial tariff equivalent may be established at the current bound rate or on the basis of national offers for that product.
7. Where an adjustment is made to the level of a tariff equivalent which would have resulted from the above guidelines, the Member concerned shall afford, on request, full opportunities for consultation with a view to negotiating appropriate solutions.

## Notes

1. These measures include quantitative import restrictions, variable import levies, minimum import prices, discretionary import licensing, non-tariff measures maintained through state-trading enterprises, voluntary export restraints, and similar border measures other than ordinary customs duties, whether or not the measures are maintained under country-specific derogations from the provisions of GATT 1947, but not measures maintained under balance-of-payments provisions or under other general, non-agriculture-specific provisions of GATT 1994 or of the other Multilateral Trade Agreements in Annex 1A to the WTO Agreement.

2. The reference price used to invoke the provisions of this subparagraph shall, in general, be the average c.i.f. unit value of the product concerned, or otherwise shall be an appropriate price in terms of the quality of the product and its stage of processing. It shall, following its initial use, be publicly specified and available to the extent necessary to allow other Members to assess the additional duty that may be levied.

3. Where domestic consumption is not taken into account, the base trigger level under subparagraph 4(a) shall apply.

4. "Countervailing duties" where referred to in this Article are those covered by Article VI of GATT 1994 and Part V of the Agreement on Subsidies and Countervailing Measures.

5. For the purposes of paragraph 3 of this Annex, governmental stockholding programmes for food security purposes in developing countries whose operation is transparent and conducted in accordance with officially published objective criteria or guidelines shall be considered to be in conformity with the provisions of this paragraph, including programmes under which stocks of foodstuffs for food security purposes are acquired and released at administered prices, provided that the difference between the acquisition price and the external reference price is accounted for in the AMS.

5. & 6. For the purposes of paragraphs 3 and 4 of this Annex, the provision of foodstuffs at subsidized prices with the objective of meeting food requirements of urban and rural poor in developing countries on a regular basis at reasonable prices shall be considered to be in conformity with the provisions of this paragraph.

# INDEX

Tables, figures, boxes, and notes are indicated by *t, f, b,* and *n* respectively.